A HISTORY OF THE ENGLISH BIBLE
AS LITERATURE

Revised and condensed from David Norton's acclaimed *History of the Bible as Literature*, this book tells the story of English literary attitudes to the Bible. At first jeered at and mocked as English writing, then denigrated as having 'all the disadvantages of an old prose translation', the King James Bible somehow became 'unsurpassed in the entire range of literature'. How so startling a change happened and how it affected the making of modern translations such as the Revised Version and the New English Bible is at the heart of this exploration of a vast range of religious, literary and cultural ideas. Translators, writers such as Donne, Milton, Bunyan and the Romantics, reactionary Bishops and radical students all help to show the changes in religious ideas and in standards of language and literature that created our sense of the most important book in English.

DAVID NORTON is Reader in English at Victoria University of Wellington, New Zealand, specializing in the Bible and literature, and the English novel. Author of *A History of the Bible as Literature*, 2 vols. (1993), he is a member of the Tyndale Society Advisory Board and serves on the General Advisory Board of *Reformation*.

Volumes published in the series

A HISTORY OF THE BIBLE AS LITERATURE

A History of the Bible as Literature
Volume One: From Antiquity to 1700
by DAVID NORTON
1993: hardback 0 521 33398 9

A History of the Bible as Literature
Volume Two: From 1700 to the Present Day
by DAVID NORTON
1993: hardback 0 521 33399 7

A History of the English Bible as Literature
by DAVID NORTON
2000: hardback 0 521 77140 4
            paperback 0 521 77807 7

A HISTORY
OF THE
ENGLISH BIBLE AS
LITERATURE

DAVID NORTON

Victoria University of Wellington, New Zealand

CAMBRIDGE
UNIVERSITY PRESS

PUBLISHED BY THE PRESS SYNDICATE OF THE UNIVERSITY OF CAMBRIDGE
The Pitt Building, Trumpington Street, Cambridge, United Kingdom

CAMBRIDGE UNIVERSITY PRESS
The Edinburgh Building, Cambridge CB2 2RU, UK   www.cup.cam.ac.uk
40 West 20th Street, New York, NY 10011-4211, USA   www.cup.org
10 Stamford Road, Oakleigh, Melbourne 3166, Australia
Ruiz de Alarcón 13, 28014 Madrid, Spain

First published 2000

Printed in the United Kingdom at the University Press, Cambridge

Typeface Monotype Baskerville 11/12½ pt.   *System* QuarkXPress™ [SE]

A catalogue record for this book is available from the British Library

Library of Congress cataloguing in publication data

Norton, David
A history of the English Bible as literature / David Norton.
p.   cm.
Rev. ed. of: A history of the Bible as literature
Includes bibliographical references.
ISBN 0 521 77140 4 (hardback). – ISBN 0 521 77807 7 (paperback)
1. Bible as literature.   2. Bible – Criticism, interpretation,
etc. – History.   3. Bible. English – Versions – History.   I. Norton.
David. History of the Bible as Literature.   II. Title.
BS585.N67   2000
809'.93522–dc21   99-16897   CIP

ISBN 0 521 77140 4 hardback
ISBN 0 521 77807 7 paperback

Contents

Plates

Preface

My *History of the Bible as Literature* (1993) ran to two volumes and made large demands on the reader's time (and the purchaser's pocket). So the present book cuts down the material to more manageable proportions. It does so mainly by confining the focus to the English Bible, by reducing the number of examples and by omitting the appendices containing sample passages. What has sometimes felt like self-mutilation will be amply rewarded if the reader finds the result pleasing and interesting.

Abbreviations

AV   Authorised Version or King James Bible, 1611
CW   *Collected* or *Complete Works* or *Writings*
DNB   *Dictionary of National Biography*
KJB   King James Bible or Authorised Version, 1611
NEB   The New English Bible, 1970
NT   New Testament
OED   *Oxford English Dictionary*
OT   Old Testament
PB   The Book of Common Prayer
Pollard   *The Holy Bible* (1911 facsimile of 1611 KJB with introduction
            and illustrative documents)
RV   Revised Version, 1885

CHAPTER ONE

Creators of English

THE CHALLENGE TO THE TRANSLATORS

To the early reformers, the Bible was a central part of religion hidden from the people in the occult language of the Church, Latin. For the sake of their souls, the people needed the Bible in their own language. So, in the latter part of the fourteenth century, John Wyclif and his followers, the Lollards, translated the Bible from the Latin Vulgate. Then, from 1525 to 1611 came the great period of English Bible translation. Making a fresh start, William Tyndale and Myles Coverdale translated the whole Bible into English from the original Hebrew and Greek. They, with other lesser-known figures, were the pioneers. A succession of translators developed their work into what became the King James Bible (KJB) of 1611. This Bible slowly became *the* Bible of the English-speaking world; more slowly, it became the Bible acclaimed as literature both for the great original literature which it represented and for the quality of its language.

The translators would have been astonished to find their work acclaimed as literature, and many of them would have been horrified. Wyclif, for instance, condemns priests

who preach tricks and lies [japes and gabbings]; for God's word must always be true if it is properly understood . . . And certainly that priest is to be censured who so freely has the Gospel, and leaves the preaching of it and turns to men's fables . . . And God does not ask for divisions or rhymes of him that should preach, but that he should speak of God's Gospel and words to stir men thereby.[1]

Similarly, Tyndale reviles the popular literature of his time while condemning the Catholic Church's refusal to let the people read the Bible:

[1] 'De Officio Pastorali', ch. 21; F.D. Matthew, ed., *The English Works of Wyclif Hitherto Unprinted* (London, 1880), p. 438. Here and in some of the other quotations in this chapter the English is modernised, with original words given in square brackets. Spelling is modernised throughout. 'Divisions' signifies rhetorical divisions in sermons, or possibly verse divisions, that is, metrical lines.

that this threatening and forbidding the lay people to read the Scripture is not for the love of your souls . . . is evident and clearer than the sun; inasmuch as they permit and suffer you to read Robin Hood, and Bevis of Hampton, Hercules, Hector and Troilus, with a thousand histories and fables of love and wantonness, and of ribaldry, as filthy as heart can think, to corrupt the minds of youth withal, clean contrary to the doctrine of Christ and his apostles.[2]

Fundamentally, literature is a lying alternative to the book of truth.

Whatever we now think of the achievement of the translators must be set against an awareness that the creation of literature was no part of their intention. As the reception of the translators' work is followed, we will see that there was a long period in which the thought that they might have created something worthy of literary admiration would have seemed laughable. The much-repeated modern idea that the KJB is a literary masterpiece represents a reversal of literary opinion as striking as any in the whole history of English literature. One of the prime purposes of this book is to trace and account for this reversal.

Wyclif and his followers and, later, Tyndale and Coverdale were all educated as Catholics and did not necessarily set out to be enemies of the Roman Church, but they found themselves in conflict with it on the inseparable issues of the comprehensibility and the source of truth. In essence the Church was committed to a mystery religion of which it was the infallible guardian and interpreter. In this mystery the Bible was but one source of truth. The Church, directly guided by God, had laboriously developed a theological tradition based on interpretation of the Bible and the wisdom of the Fathers and their successors. The Bible alone was not enough – it was too difficult, too easily misunderstood. The Church, with the Bible and so much more, was the source of truth; moreover, the preservation of its secrets in an occult language to which it alone had access confirmed its power.

Naively, the translators might not see their work as challenging the established theology, but to give the people a basis on which to come at their own sense of the truth was to challenge the Church's power and inevitably to split Christendom. That the Church resisted this was not just a case of an institution protecting its power. Truth, power and the possession of Latin seemed inseparable. If the Church had spent centuries building up an inspired knowledge of the truth, with all the coherence that such knowledge must have, the poor uneducated individual, struggling to teach himself from the Bible alone, could not possibly come

---

[2] *The Obedience of a Christian Man; Doctrinal Treatises*, p. 161.

to know the truth as the Church knew it. For common men Christianity must remain a mystery religion: the salvation of their souls was at issue.

Forces of opposition, worldly and spiritual, gathered round the act of translation. The Church had grown ignorant, corrupt, hungry for power and money. Truth had to be rediscovered to reform or break its power and to bring about the same issue, salvation. If the Church was no longer credible as the voice of God, there was one possible and one sure place to find it, the inspired heart of the individual, and the Bible. Older translators such as Jerome had worked within the Church, facing scholarly and linguistic challenges only, but now language and the possession of the Bible were a major religious battlefront and the translators were in the front line, facing the enormous challenge of rediscovering the truth and creating a new church. The religious responsibility of translating had never been higher.

For the Church, translation and heresy went hand in hand, but the early heretics were still sons of the Church and could not, even if Tyndale wished to, rid themselves of the belief that the Bible was difficult. They had learnt that there were levels of meaning beyond the literal, they had learnt too that every detail of the text was to be pressed for its sacred meaning. This might all seem a heritage of moribund pedantry but it could not be dismissed. The words they chose would not be the whole truth and might perhaps be no more than the beginnings of truth, but they would certainly be examined minutely: if the scholarly did not dismiss them out of hand, they would examine them for their fidelity to the detail of the text (that is, the Vulgate), and if the unscholarly were to use them as the translators wished, it would be with an equal, though sympathetic, attention. Further, the people Tyndale and Coverdale worked for would have the translation alone as the key to truth: such people could not use it as a way to the genuinely sacred text, Latin, Greek or Hebrew, nor could they use it side by side with other translations as an approximation to the truth; they could not even use it with a gloss, since vernacular commentary on the text had yet to be created. The translation had to be, as nearly as possible, perfect in itself.

The challenge to attain accuracy was, from these points of view, enormous. The translators had available to them no sophisticated theory of how accuracy might be achieved, nor did they spend much time developing such a theory. The simple answer was to be, in the first place, literal. Consequent on these overwhelming pressures and this simple answer were other challenges, the first being to make the translation comprehensible to the people.

Roughly, there are four levels of language available to translators, the literal (wherein the vocabulary, idiom and structure of the original language dominate the new language), the common, the literary and the ecclesiastical. All four can be subdivided and each can merge into the other. Ecclesiastical English had yet to be created, and English, in spite of the achievements we now recognise in the late medieval period, and even in the late Elizabethan and early Jacobean times of the KJB translators, had no prestige as a literary language. Given the early translators' hostility to the literary, it is hardly likely they would have used such a register even if it had had some prestige.

Thus the only kind of English acceptable as a first move beyond the literal was common English, and this fitted Tyndale's ideal of making the Bible, at its verbal level, comprehensible to the people. But the common language presents its own challenges. Beyond the fact that it shades into a variety of dialects and may have no established standard, there is the question of its expressive adequacy. When in doubt, older translators had not scrupled to borrow from the original languages, but if the English translators were to do the equivalent and borrow from the Vulgate, they would not only be departing from the common language but also retaining the language of the Roman Church. The linguistic issue was again clouded by the battle of the Reformation. Further, there is the complex matter of prestige. Unless special circumstances such as a reaction against excesses in literary language exist to give prestige to the common language, it is the lowest form of the language. On the other hand the Bible was the highest of books, and there is, usually, a desire to have the prestige of the language match that of the book, that is, a desire to have the feeling evoked by the language match the divine heights of the meaning. Literal translation, with its mysterious dislocations of language and novelties of vocabulary, may perhaps produce some feeling of awe, but a common language version, lacking any such strangeness, demeans. In moving beyond the literal, the early translators had little choice but to abase the Scriptures; if there was a challenge to preserve the prestige of the Bible, it was reserved for their successors.

The early Reformation especially was a time for heroes – heroes on both sides, Sir Thomas More as much as Tyndale. Persecution was inevitable, the martyr's bitter crown likely. Beyond the enormous challenge to definition and accuracy, beyond the challenge to common clarity, there were the challenges of simply finding the courage to work, and then of finding ways of staying alive to prosecute the work and, somehow, to publish it. There were the difficulties of textual scholarship, of discovering the true original texts, of learning Greek and Hebrew with little or no aid from the scholarship of others, there was the sheer size of the undertaking – and so one could go on. The modern scholar, safely salaried in a university, free to pursue his studies with ready access to an enormous accumulated community of learning, can only stand in awe that the work was achieved at all, and he must guess that the early translators must have possessed a certain simplicity not to be daunted into silence by the weight of the task and the pressures of the time. That simplicity, perhaps, mitigated the challenges sketched here: they had to shut their eyes, deafen their ears and work as best they could. Hasty, instinctive answers to enormous problems must often have had to suffice. In short, the reality of getting the work done, the greatest challenge of all, must have rendered manageable all the other challenges.

The later translators, from William Whittingham and his colleagues at Geneva to the scholars assembled under the auspices of King James, were all, more or less, revisers rather than pioneers. Their work was not attended by the same perilous, solitary urgency that had been Tyndale and Coverdale's lot, and the changing nature of their task may readily be imagined. It will be of central interest to see if they believed themselves able to go beyond questions of scholarly accuracy and theological definition to tackle as artists the question of the English of the Bible.

LITERAL TRANSLATION: ROLLE'S PSALTER AND THE WYCLIF BIBLE

The Bible was translated into the English vernaculars in several ways before the time of Wyclif, including verse paraphrases of parts of the Bible such as the poems associated with the seventh-century monk Caedmon, but the main line of English translations starts with the literal, as exemplified by the Psalter of the hermit of Hampole, Richard Rolle (d. 1349). Rolle regarded the Latin Psalms as the 'perfection of divine writing',[3] and clearly loved them as spiritual teaching, perhaps also as literature. In spite of this, in spite also of their obvious poetic aspects, he made no effort to produce a literary translation. Rather, his work is a guide, first to the meaning of the Latin, second, through a commentary, to the meaning of the Psalms. It is not an English equivalent of the Latin, but a literal crib accompanied by a commentary. He describes his intentions thus:

[3] Hope Emily Allen, ed., *English Writings of Richard Rolle* (Oxford University Press, 1931), p. 6.

In this work I seek no strange/strong[4] English, but lightest and commonest and such that is most like unto the Latin, so that they that know not Latin, by the English may come to many Latin words. In the translation I follow the letter as much as I may, and where I find no exact English equivalent, I follow the gist of the text, so that they that shall read it, they need not fear going wrong. (*English Writings*, p. 7)

The first two verses of Psalm 23 show just how closely he 'followed the letter':

Dominus regit me et nihil mihi deerit: in loco pascuae ibi me collocavit. Lord governs me and nothing shall me want: in stead of pasture there he me set.

Super aquam refectionis educavit me: animam meam convertit. On the water of reheting [refreshment] forth he me brought: my soul he turned.[5]

The commentary, which follows each verse, makes up the bulk of the work.

Thus the only real precedent for the translators of the Wyclif Bible, a precedent approved by the Church, was a literal interlinear guide to the Latin. Rolle was treating a limited part of the Bible in a limited way, opening the literal meaning of the words to his audience but not returning the reading of the Psalms to a literal level. The presence of the gloss, which was largely a translation of earlier, orthodox works, ensured this. Rather than presenting an English Psalter to the people, he was presenting them with the Latin Psalter as understood by the Church. Further, it was not the largely illiterate masses to whom Rolle was presenting this work, but a small number of literate people who could afford the substantial cost of a manuscript or were in a position to copy it for themselves. Nor, given the same factors of general illiteracy, and the cost and difficulty of producing manuscripts, could the Wyclif Bible be a work for the masses, no matter how much they themselves might want it.

The precise history of the Wyclif Bible is not known. It is a convenient but inaccurate misnomer to speak of 'the Wyclif Bible', both because John Wyclif himself (c. 1330–80) probably only had a minor hand in the work itself and because there are two distinct translations involved. 'The Wyclif Bible', then, refers to an effort at translation lasting perhaps as long as twenty years from some time in the 1370s. This effort was made by a group of scholars of whom Wyclif was the leading figure if not the chief executant. The two versions of the Wyclif Bible, early and late, represent logical stages in the development of a vernacular Bible.

---

[4] The original has 'strange'; it may have either of these meanings.
[5] *The Psalter or Psalms of David*, ed. H.R. Bramley (Oxford, 1844), p. 83.

There is no firm evidence of literary awareness in the making of the Wyclif Bible. This is what one would expect both from the rigid distinction the Lollards made between literature and religion, that is, between lies and Truth, and from their situation as the first English translators of the whole Bible. The Wyclif translators began with something very like Rolle's work, an extremely literal version that was primarily a guide to the Latin. Then, in the late version, they moved towards a more readable English rendering, one more obviously capable of standing by itself without reference back to the Latin. The difference between the two stages is visible in the opening verses of Psalm 23. In the early version they read, 'the lord governeth me, and no thing to me shall lack; in the place of leswe [pasture] where he me full set. Over water of fulfilling he nursed me; my soul he converted'.[6] Like Rolle's version, this is highly literal, dependent on the Latin for word order and some of its vocabulary. Only the absence of the Latin prevents it from being an interlinear gloss. The late version shows revision of vocabulary though it remains heavily dependent on the Latin; more significantly, there is a cautious movement towards a natural English word order: 'the Lord governeth me, and no thing shall fail to me; in the place of pasture there he hath set me. He nursed me on the water of refreshing; he converted my soul'. In spite of the changes, this is still literal.

The late version has a prologue which, in its fifteenth chapter, discusses problems involved in the making of an English translation and pays particular attention to grammatical equivalence.[7] It begins by arguing the need for vernacular Scriptures and alleges that, 'although covetous clerks . . . despise and stop holy writ as much as they can, yet the common people cry after holy writ to know [kunne] it and keep it with great cost and peril of their life' (*Wycliffite Writings*, p. 67). Thus a desire for the Bible among an educated laity is seen as a desire to understand the basis of the Christian life.

The author describes the purpose of the translation as 'with common charity to save all men in our realm whom God will have saved', and goes on to describe the methods by which the work sought to produce accurate knowledge. Bibles, commentaries and glosses were collected and collated in order to get the best Latin text possible, the text was studied anew, and the older grammarians and divines were consulted on difficult words and sentences to see 'how they might best be understood and

---

[6] Quotations from the Wyclif Bible are taken from the Forshall and Madden edition. The Wyclif Bible numbers this Psalm as 22.

[7] Chapter 15 of the prologue is given in Hudson, *Wycliffite Writings*, pp. 67–72.

translated'. Finally, he tried 'to translate as clearly as he could the meaning, and to have many good and knowledgable [kunnynge] fellows at the correcting of the translation'. Some details of the principles of translation are given: 'the best translating is, out of Latin into English, to translate after the meaning and not only after the words' (p. 68). This closely relates to the difference between the early and the late versions. Hudson comments that 'after the words'

has here a specialised sense: the invariable translation of one Latin word by one English word, neither more nor less, and the adherence in the English version to the exact word order of the Latin original. The debate is not, as a modern critic might suppose, between a close and a free rendering, but between a transposition of Latin into English and a close translation into English word order and vocabulary. (*Wycliffite Writings*, pp. 174–5)

The result of this 'best translating', according to the prologue, is 'that the meaning is as open or opener in English as in Latin, and go not far from the letter; and if the letter may not be followed in the translating, let the meaning ever be whole and open, for the words ought to serve the intention and meaning, or else the words are superfluous or false' (p. 68). The principle that the translation should be as clear as or clearer than the original is at odds with some ideas of faithful translation, for it involves a kind of correction of the original. Nevertheless, the Protestants, or proto-Protestants, preferred to emphasise the comprehensibility of the text and to play down ambiguity and difficulty.

The author's main point, however, is that, providing a truthful and clear rendering of the meaning is not damaged, literal translation is best. Where literalism may damage meaning it may be dispensed with. He develops this by observing that many changes of grammatical constructions are needed for clarity, particularly changes of ablative absolutes, participles and relatives. His guiding principle is that these changes 'will in many places make the meaning open, where to English it after the word would be dark and doubtful'. Not only the words but the grammar must be translated. Fidelity is the key, and the result is a movement away from making English conform to Latin and towards natural English. This enforces on the translator care for the quality of his English: we may say that 'good English' is intended. The author defines 'good' as accurate and clear, but the result may be 'good' in a more literary sense, even though he had no such intentions.

Chapter 15 ends the prologue. The previous fourteen chapters are all aimed at helping the reader's understanding of the Bible by summarising its contents and explaining their significance. Comments on the principles of translation are, then, a last word after the basis for understanding the Bible has been established. Both the general tone and the non-literary sense of the Bible can be seen in the description of the OT as consisting of three parts, which are called 'moral commandments, judicials, and ceremonials': 'moral commandments teach to hold and praise and cherish virtues, and to flee and reprove vices . . . Judicials teach judgements and punishments for horrible sins . . . Ceremonials teach symbols and sacraments of the old law that symbolised Christ and his death, and the mysteries of the Holy Church in the law of grace' (ch. 2; Forshall and Madden edn, I: 3). In short, the Bible is teaching, teaching and more teaching. Even when the prologue treats books known to be poetic, it is resolutely unliterary. The Song of Songs forces on translators the questions of whether they will allow any literary sense of the text and whether they are prepared to allow the text to speak for itself and therefore possibly be read as secular love poetry. This is what the prologue says:

The Song of Songs teaches men to set all their heart in the love of God and of their neighbours, and to do all their business to bring men to charity and salvation, by good example, and true preaching, and willing suffering of pain and death, if need be . . . and this book is so subtle to understand, that Jews ordained that no man should study it unless he were of 30 years and had able mind to understand the spiritual secrets of this book; for some of the book seems to sinful men to speak of unclean love of lechery, where it tells his spiritual love and great secrets of Christ and of his Church. (Ch. 11; I: 40, 41)

The prologue, then, is explicitly afraid of any literal, worldly reading of the text, and the insistence on religious reading is carried over into the presentation of the text. The Early Version ensures spiritual and allegorical understanding by interpolating speakers. The beginning of the Song reads:

The Church, of the coming of Christ, speaketh, saying, Kiss he me with the kiss of his mouth. *The voice of the Father.* For better are thy teats than wine, smelling with best ointments.

The Late Version follows a different route to the same end. Omitting the voice directions, it substitutes lengthy notes. Typical is the gloss on 'thy teats':

that is, the fullness of God's mercy is sweeter to man's soul, than wine most savoury among bodily things is sweet to the taste. In Hebrew it is, *for thy loves are better than wine, etc.*; that is, the love of God is more savoury to a devout soul than any bodily thing to bodily taste.

In these ways the translators make every effort to impose a spiritual reading on the text, and clearly intend that the text should be studied minutely rather than flow as an open piece of literature.

The intentions and implications of the Wyclif Bible are resolutely theological. If, from the perspective of several centuries, a modern critic can see literary value in the relative Englishness and clarity of the Late Version, that is a perspective that has nothing to do either with the translators' intentions or the Lollard readers' attitude to the text.

WILLIAM TYNDALE

Introduction

William Tyndale (?1494–1536) rightly believed himself to be a pioneer. He wrote of his work, 'I had no man to counterfeit [imitate], neither was helped with English of any that had interpreted the same or such like thing in the Scripture beforetime' (1526 NT, p. 15). The Wyclif Bible had been largely suppressed so that he was working almost without English precedent to open the Bible anew to the people. He had to invent his own appropriate English. No subsequent English translators, not even his immediate successor, Myles Coverdale, ever again found themselves in this situation. Tyndale's English became the model for biblical English and he is indeed the father of English biblical translation. From a larger perspective, Sir Thomas More's jibe at the deficiencies of his English vocabulary, that they were such that 'all England list now to go to school with Tyndale to learn English' (*Works*, VIII: 187), has turned out true: more of our English is ultimately learnt from Tyndale than from any other writer of English prose, and many erstwhile illiterates did indeed 'go to school with Tyndale' and his successors.

One such illiterate was William Maldon. His story not only shows the connection between Tyndale's work and reading but movingly illustrates the internecine strength of the conflict over the vernacular Bible. He relates that when he was a young man in the reign of Henry VIII

divers poor men in the town of Chelmsford in the county of Essex where my father dwelt and I born and with him brought up, the said poor men bought the New Testament of Jesus Christ and on Sundays did sit reading in lower end of church, and many would flock about them to hear their reading, then I came among the said readers to hear them reading of that glad and sweet tidings of the gospel, then my father seeing this that I listened unto them every Sunday, then came he and sought me among them, and brought me away from the hearing of them, and would have me to say the Latin matins with him, the which grieved me very much, and thus did fetch me away divers times, then I see I could not be in rest, then thought I, I will learn to read English, and then I will have the New Testament and read thereon myself, and then had I learned of an English primer as far as patris sapientia and then on Sundays I plied my English primer, the Maytide following I and my father's apprentice, Thomas Jeffary laid our money together, and bought the New Testament in English, and hid it in our bedstraw and so exercised it at convenient times. (Pollard, p. 115)

As a consequence of this reading he argued with his mother about worshipping graven images and was beaten by his father. Believing that he was beaten for Christ's sake, he did not weep. This so enraged his father, who thought him past grace, that he attempted to hang him; William was only rescued by the intervention of his mother and his brother. He concludes, 'I think six days after my neck grieved me with the pulling of the halter'.

Tyndale translated more than half the Bible before he was martyred, the NT, the OT to the end of 2 Chronicles, and Jonah.[8] This work put his stamp – his far more than anyone else's – on the language we now know from the KJB. For a long time his achievement went unremarked, and indeed could hardly have been expected to receive much recognition until after its familiar descendant, the language of the KJB, had achieved a solid reputation for excellence. Now few who have read in his translations or controversial works would dissent from C.S. Lewis's judgement that he was 'the best prose writer of his age' ('Literary impact', p. 34).

'His influence,' writes Brooke Foss Westcott, 'decided that our Bible should be popular and not literary, speaking in a simple dialect, and that so by its simplicity it should be endowed with permanence. He felt by a happy instinct the potential affinity between Hebrew and English idioms, and enriched our language and thought for ever with the characteristics of the Semitic mind'.[9] 'Literary' is used here to describe consciously fine writing: thereby the paradox of Tyndale's achievement is well recorded, for it was not literary in that sense and yet it was 'endowed with permanence' and has 'enriched our language and thought'. To be so influential is an outstanding literary achievement, but it does not necessarily follow that Tyndale *deliberately* set out to create English of

---

[8] His version of Joshua to 2 Chronicles appeared in the Matthew Bible, 1537. Coverdale's complete Bible had appeared two years earlier, so in these books the two chief pioneers of English Bible translation each independently produced versions.

[9] *A General View of the History of the English Bible*, 3rd ed., rev. William Aldis Wright (London: Macmillan, 1905), p. 158.

literary quality. The present perception of his achievement, so well demonstrated in David Daniell's *Biography*, has to be set aside for the time being in order to see just what real evidence there is both of his intentions and of his sense of the Bible as literature.

This is not to deny the value of literary appreciation of his translation, but to recognise that a writer may, in spite of himself, achieve something later acclaimed as literature. It is also to restore to something like equivalent value earlier opinions of Tyndale. These different perceptions may well have had as much value in their time as we now feel the modern literary appreciation has. The present study is not a study of achievement but of what people thought they were trying to achieve and of the perception of achievement.

Love for 'the sweet pith within'

To turn to Tyndale's own writings on the Bible and on Bible translation is to see at once that he was a scholar who loved the Bible, and to be confronted with the fact that the language the early English translators use to describe the Bible appears to be full of literary implications. The appearance is usually false. Thomas Bilney (c. 1495–1531), a contemporary of Tyndale's, also a Cambridge man and a martyr, has left an account of his conversion and responses to the Bible which shows the kind of distinction which has so often to be made. His initial response was to the language (this time the language was Erasmus's Latin of 1516): 'but at last I heard speak of Jesus, even then when the New Testament was first set forth by Erasmus; which when I understood to be eloquently done by him, being allured rather by the Latin than by the word of God (for at that time I knew not what it meant), I bought it'. Bilney's original desire to read the Bible, then, was literary: he wished to read it for its style. Literary pleasure was enough so long as he did not know the real meaning of the word of God, but when that real meaning reached him a new pleasure took over: it is described in the same kind of language, but it is clearly not a literary pleasure. Rather, it is a delight in the meaning:

and at the first reading (as I well remember) I chanced upon this sentence of St Paul (O most sweet and comfortable sentence to my soul!) in 1 Tim. 1, 'it is a true saying, and worthy of all men to be embraced, that Christ Jesus came into the world to save sinners, of whom I am the chief and principal.' This one sentence, through God's instruction and inward working, which I did not then perceive, did so exhilarate my heart, being before wounded with the guilt of my sins, and being almost in despair, that even immediately I seemed unto myself inwardly to feel a marvellous comfort and quietness, insomuch that 'my bruised bones leaped for joy.'

After this the Scripture began to be more pleasant unto me than the honey or the honey-comb. (Foxe, *Acts and Monuments*, IV: 635)

The imagery is from the Psalms: 'my bruised bones leaped for joy' is a version of Ps. 51: 8, describing the Psalmist's response to hearing the 'joy and gladness' of God's truth; 'more pleasant unto me than the honey or the honey-comb' is part of the Psalmist's description of 'the statutes of the LORD' (Ps. 19: 10). Traced to their source, the images are not of literary love but of a love for God's truth. Bilney goes on to write that he 'began to taste and savour of this heavenly lesson'. Pleasure in the Scriptures, then, naturally described in terms that seem now to imply literary pleasure, can readily exist as something distinct and much superior, a pleasure in their content or Truth.

Tyndale calls this the pith of the Scriptures, and his love is for the pith. If an identifiable literary love is also present, then it must be searched out with care to avoid confusion with this primary religious love. Of Tyndale's many statements of the true nature of Scripture, the opening of his 'Prologue showing the use of the Scripture' prefixed to Genesis (1530) is the most useful, especially as it anticipates the resounding question in the preface to the KJB, 'is the kingdom of God become words or syllables?' (see below, p. 68):

Though a man had a precious jewel and a rich, yet if he wist not the value thereof nor wherefore it served, he were neither the better nor richer of a straw. Even so though we read the Scripture and babble of it never so much, yet if we know not the use of it, and wherefore it was given, and what is therein to be sought, it profiteth us nothing at all. It is not enough therefore to read and talk of it only, but we must also desire God day and night instantly to open our eyes, and to make us understand and feel wherefore the Scripture was given, that we may apply the medicine of the Scripture, every man to his own sores, unless that we intend to be idle disputers, and brawlers about vain words, ever gnawing upon the bitter bark without and never attaining unto the sweet pith within, and persecuting one another for defending of lewd imaginations and fantasies of our own invention.[10]

---

[10] *Tyndale's OT*, ed. Daniell, p. 7. Though such comment belongs to a different kind of study from the present, this is strong writing, showing Tyndale at his argumentative best. More, Tyndale's arch-critic, recognised a similar strength in another passage, commenting that 'these words walk lo very goodly by the hearer's ear, and they make a man amazed in a manner and somewhat to study and muse' (VIII: 725). This, referring to a passage from Tyndale's *Answer*, p. 49, is the only early example of praise of Tyndale as a writer.

Aptly incorporated in this is an allusion to Paul on the necessity of what we know as 'charity' but which Tyndale, to the disgust of More, translated 'love': 'and though I bestowed all my goods to feed the poor, and though I gave my body even that I burned, and yet had no love, it profiteth me nothing' (1 Cor. 13: 3; Tyndale, 1534). Love is the heart of Tyndale's idea of the Scriptures. They are a precious jewel to those who love them, that is, those who have been given, like Bilney, the gift of understanding and feeling by God. Scripture demands an inner response expressible in the same terms used for literary response, but it is 'the sweet pith within', not 'the bitter bark without' – the divine message, not the words – which is to be felt and loved.

There are two principal aspects to Tyndale's emphasis on the meaning of the Scriptures, feeling and study. He gives definitive priority to feeling, writing repeatedly of the essential purity and brightness of the Scriptures and of how this can only be perceived by those who read or hear them with the true spirit and therefore feel their meaning. This is the simple belief that mitigates the challenges of translation. In his own words, 'if our hearts were taught the appointment made between God and us in Christ's blood when we were baptized, we had the key to open the Scripture and light to see and perceive the true meaning of it, and the Scripture should be easy to understand'.[11]

If this baptismal precondition is met in the heart, then study is also appropriate, but, just as the feeling is not a literary feeling, so too the study is not literary, and is indeed explicitly opposed to the kind of attention popular literature receives. First he insists that Scripture has 'one simple literal sense' (OT, p. 4), a sense which is nevertheless spiritual, for 'God is a spirit, and all his words are spiritual' (*DT*, p. 309). This immediately distinguishes Scripture from literature, for literature is carnal (see above, p. 2), as are readings of the Bible that lack the baptismal feeling. He repeatedly encourages the true reader to 'cleave unto the text and plain story and endeavour thyself to search out the meaning of all that is described therein and the true sense of all manner of speakings of the Scripture' (OT, p. 84). Such searching out pays particular attention to what he calls 'the process, order and meaning of the text'. 'Process' means 'argument' or the larger context of a passage, 'order' the immediate context. He is thus insistent on contextual reading and believes firmly that the light places will illuminate the dark. The need for such careful contextual reading as the key to religious truth is, he claims, his

---

[11] *Expositions*, p. 141 (hereafter *Ex*). See also pp. 5–8, 35, 139, 142, and *Doctrinal Treatises* (hereafter *DT*), pp. 313, 343, 417, 471.

prime motive for translation. After objecting to the Church's traditional methods of exposition, he writes:

Which thing only moved me to translate the New Testament. Because I had perceived by experience how that it was impossible to establish the lay people in any truth, except the Scripture were plainly laid before their eyes in their mother tongue, that they might see the process, order and meaning of the text: for else whatsoever truth is taught them, these enemies of all truth quench it again. (OT, p. 4)

The end result of this love and careful reading of the Scriptures is learning and comfort, or the application of medicine to the soul. He sums up his sense of the Scriptures and their effect thus:

All the Scripture is either the promises and testament of God in Christ, and stories pertaining thereunto, to strength thy faith; either the law, and stories pertaining thereto, to fear thee from evil doing. There is no story nor gest, seem it never so simple or so vile unto the world, but that thou shalt find therein spirit and life and edifying in the literal sense: for it is God's Scripture, written for thy learning and comfort. (*DT*, p. 310)

This enforces a sense of religious purpose: nothing in it would have suggested literary quality to Tyndale's contemporaries. Nevertheless, some literary sense of the Bible may be inferred. It seems that 'the world' denigrated some Bible stories as simple and vile, and he is trying to reform these opinions. Such a reformation could have a literary aspect in addition to the theological purpose, but only a tantalizing glimpse of this possibility emerges, for nowhere does Tyndale develop the idea in a recognisably literary way.

Tyndale's emphasis on reading the Scriptures with the proper feeling for them could have led him to present the text alone. There is some suggestion in his earlier writing that he believed that the meaning of the Bible was open enough for the reader with the right spirit 'that if thou wilt go in and read, thou canst not but understand' (p. 27). This is part of the same feeling that led to the Lollards' desire for their translation to be 'as open or opener' than the Latin (above, p. 8). It is natural that Tyndale should wish for this to be so: it removes the need for the controlling interpretative tradition of the Church at the same time as making the open Bible appear incapable of producing erroneous reading. However, this represents more optimism than real belief. A bare text, by leaving the reader's imagination most room to work, would be most liable to secular literary reading (to say nothing of heresy).[12] In fact,

---

[12] Roger Edgworth, in a sermon of 1541–2, approves of vernacular Scripture 'if we could get it well and truly translated', but doubts who is fit to read it. Everybody believes he understands the Scripture but 'of the hardness of Scripture (in which our new divines find no hardness) riseth all heresies' (*Sermons* (1557), fols. 31b–3a; as given in Mozley, *Coverdale*, pp. 306–7).

the first complete edition of his NT (1526) was such a bare text, but this reflects circumstances beyond his control, not his deliberate intention: in keeping with his insistence on precise contextual reading, and his real recognition that Scripture did offer dark places, he had intended that this edition, like his later translations and editions, should contain explanatory notes. He believed that 'it is not enough to have translated, though it were the whole Scripture into the vulgar and common tongue, except we also brought again the light to understand it by, and expel that dark cloud which the hypocrites have spread over the face of the Scripture to blind the right sense and true meaning thereof' (*Ex*, p. 144). So his aborted first edition (1525) was substantially annotated.

The emphasis on feeling coupled with the emphasis on the pith could also have led Tyndale to conceive of paraphrase as the appropriate way of presenting the Scriptures to the people, but again the concern with studying the meaning led him to reject this option. His objection to 'idle disputers and brawlers about vain words' (above, p. 13) was to the medieval schoolmen who had, he believed, lost all feel for the meaning of Scripture. He maintained the old belief in the detailed significance of the text, and this prevented him from paraphrasing. So, when considering how his work might be improved, he writes:

If I shall perceive either by myself or by information of other that ought be escaped me, or might more plainly be translated, I will shortly after, cause it to be mended. Howbeit in many places me thinketh it better to put a declaration in the margin than to run too far from the text. And in many places, where the text seemeth at the first chop hard to be understood, yet the circumstances before and after, and often reading together, make it plain enough. (NT, 1534, p. 3)

This is his resolution of the problems of translation and presentation of the Truth: to seek for the greatest plainness, to keep close to the original, to gloss where necessary, and to teach his readers how to read the Bible. He is indeed a lover of the Bible, but not of the Bible as literature, and he is ultimately a scholar.

There are perhaps contradictions evident in these attitudes, especially between his insistence on the luminance of the Scriptures for the pure in heart, and his recognition of the difficulties of the Scriptures, between his objection to glossing and his insistence on glossing, and between his objection to non-literal interpretation and his insistence that the literal meaning is spiritual. No more need be made of this than to suggest that it would not be surprising to find a degree of contradictoriness in another area: the conclusion that *his* idea of the Bible is emphatically non-literary may have to co-exist with the recognition that he brought some literary awareness, to say nothing of his literary talent as it is now perceived, to his work. Yet, as one turns to search for evidence of this awareness a single fact stands out: all of Tyndale's own writing apart from his translations is theological, and the evidence for the attitudes so far described abounds. Direct statements of literary awareness and considerations are, relatively, as rare as husks in well-milled corn. Beyond the stylistic decision of major literary consequence that he would translate as simply and clearly as possible, a decision that was of course made for religious reasons, literary questions hardly mattered to him.

Luther and Erasmus

If Tyndale needed influence for the decision to be simple and clear, it came from Erasmus and Luther, both of whom he greatly admired, and later, in a minor way, from More, whom he did not admire. Martin Luther (1483–1546), 'this christian Hercules, this heroic cleanser of the Augean stable of apostasy',[13] is of course the towering figure of the Reformation, and he did as much for the German Bible and language as Tyndale did for the English. He seems to have given more thought to the linguistic reponsibilities of a translator than Tyndale, and the result is not only an influence but an important contrast.

First, he loved the Scriptures, especially the Psalms, and this love had in it a degree of explicit literary appreciation not found in English writers of the time.[14] His 'Preface to the Psalms' is full of literary as well as religious praise, and he even writes of them as having 'more eloquence than that possessed by Cicero or the greatest of the orators'.[15] This is enough to suggest a very different temper from the English in German ideas of the Bible as literature. Nevertheless, he conceived of the language of the Bible, particularly the OT Hebrew, as simple and lowly, so unliterary in fact that it is capable of giving offence. His conclusion is, 'simple and lowly are these swaddling clothes, but dear is the treasure, Christ, who lies in them'.[16]

Luther aimed at clarity and accuracy, but he had a further aim, to write good German. In general this aim led him away from literal

---

[13] Coleridge, essay II of 'The Landing-Place', *Collected Works* 4, *The Friend*, I: 140. This delightful essay contains a fine imaginative rendering of Luther at work as a translator (I: 140–2).

[14] A number of passages from Luther's *Table Talk* suggest literary appreciation. See especially pp. 1–27 (trans. William Hazlitt, new edition (London, 1875)).

[15] *Reformation Writings of Martin Luther*, trans. Bertram Lee Woolf, 2 vols. (London: Lutterworth, 1956), II: 270.   [16] 1523; 1545 revision; *Selected Writings*, IV: 376.

translation, though occasionally in particularly tricky passages he put literalism ahead of naturalness.[17] His idea of good German is the idiomatic German of 'the mother in the home, the children on the street, the common man in the marketplace', for his Bible is for them (IV: 181). In this way his idea of his language fits his idea of the Bible's language, simple and lowly both. Even so, he describes himself as working with the care of an artist like Flaubert or Virgil: 'I have constantly tried,' he writes, 'in translating, to produce a pure and clear German, and it has often happened that for two or three or four weeks we have searched and inquired for a single word and sometimes not found it even then' (IV: 180). This language is to be both clear and vigorous, and he takes an artist's pride in his enemy Emser's admission that his 'German is sweet and good' (IV: 176). Lastly, and very importantly, he sees himself as teaching Germans their own language: he was *deliberately* doing what More had sarcastically but rightly suggested Tyndale was doing.

These ideas are similar to Erasmus's ideas of the Bible language and of vernacular translation, which is hardly surprising since Luther's NT depended on Erasmus's work. In *Enchiridion Militis Christiani*, a work that Tyndale translated, Erasmus describes the language of the Bible as humble. It is imaged as manna, and part of Erasmus's interpretation of it as manna is this: 'in that it is small or little in quantity is signified the humility, lowliness or homeliness of the style, under rude words including great mystery'.[18] He also sees the Scripture as 'somewhat hard and some deal rough and sharp' (pp. 44–5), and later writes that 'the wisdom of God stuttereth and lispeth as it were a diligent mother, fashioneth her words according to our infancy and feebleness . . . She stoopeth down and boweth herself to thy humility and lowness' (p. 50).

Erasmus returned to this idea in his *Paraclesis* which prefaces his 1516 edition of his Greek and Latin NT. It adds one important element to his sense of the nature of the Bible by beginning with a desire for eloquence. This eloquence is to be 'far different than Cicero's' and 'certainly much more efficacious, if less ornate';[19] it is to be modelled on the Bible, and Erasmus believes that the Bible, for all its lowness, is the most moving of writing. If he cannot achieve the eloquence he desires, yet the biblical model will be sufficient:

[17] 'On translating: an open letter', *Selected Writings*, IV: 186. The remaining points are all from this letter.
[18] Anne M. O'Donnell, ed., *Enchiridion Militis Christiani. An English Version* (Oxford University Press for EETS, 1981), p. 44.
[19] Erasmus, *Christian Humanism and the Reformation: Selected Writings*, ed. John C. Olin (New York: Harper, 1965), p. 93.

if there were any power of song which truly could inspire . . . I would desire
that it be at hand for me so that I might convince all of the most wholesome
truth of all. However, it is more desirable that Christ Himself, whose business
we are about, so guide the strings of our lyre that this song might deeply affect
and move the minds of all . . . What we desire is that nothing may stand forth
with greater certainty than the truth itself, whose expression is the more powerful the simpler it is. (p. 94)

This, because it takes biblical eloquence as secondbest, is a backhanded
acclamation of simplicity as eloquence, especially when set against
Luther, but it is significant nonetheless. Whether this or Luther's attitude
and example gave Tyndale a sense of literary possibilities in simplicity is
impossible to tell, but in Erasmus it precedes his wish that there should
be vernacular translations of the Scriptures so that 'even the lowliest
woman' may read them and so that the uneducated may enjoy them:
'would that . . . the farmer sing some portion of them at the plough, the
weaver hum some parts of them to the movement of his shuttle, the
traveller lighten the weariness of the journey with stories of this kind' (p.
97). Literary and religious enjoyment seem inseparable here, and this
passage rang in Tyndale's mind as he formed his resolution to translate
the Bible. Though he never writes of the lowness of the Bible, and never
advocates literary enjoyment, Foxe reports him as saying to a clerical
opponent in the heat of an argument, 'if God spare my life, ere many
years I will cause a boy that driveth the plough shall know more of the
Scripture than thou dost'.[20] The echo is obvious, but the deletion, even
in a spontaneous remark, of suggestions of pleasure, and the use of
'know' in all probability show the final distance between the two men. If
the whole context of Erasmus and Luther's ideas of eloquence and the
Bible lived on in Tyndale's mind, then it was as an undercurrent to the
main tide of his ideas. Nevertheless, these ideas of simple eloquence in
the Bible do anticipate the eventual acclamation of Tyndale's English
for plough-boys as great English.

Tyndale, Thomas More and English

There is one passage in which Tyndale seems to give real evidence of a
conscious literary sense both of his own work and of the originals from
which he worked. It needs to be read in the light of a related passage in
which he uses what sounds to modern ears an exceedingly interesting

---

[20] As given by Mozley, *Tyndale*, p. 34. This is from Foxe's first edition. Later editions such as the one
I have used turn this passage into reported speech (V: 117).

phrase, 'proper English'. In his 'Epistle to the Reader' at the end of his 1526 NT, he reviews ways in which the work might be improved:

In time to come . . . we will give it his full shape: and put out if ought be added superfluously: and add to if ought be overseen through negligence: and will enforce to bring to compendiousness, that which is now translated at the length, and to give light where it is required, and to seek in certain places more proper English, and with a table to expound the words which are not commonly used, and show how the Scripture useth many words, which are otherwise understood of the common people: and to help with a declaration where one tongue taketh not another. And will endeavour ourselves, as it were to seethe it better, and to make it more apt for the weak stomachs. (1526 NT, p. 15)

As a whole this repeats the point that Tyndale is concerned with accuracy and clarity. In detail it defines areas of concern, first to avoid amplification or omission, second with accuracy and clarity of vocabulary, third with different characteristics of different languages. 'Proper English', which at first sight suggests English of good quality, in fact means 'accurate' or 'literal' English. It is one aspect of the problem of 'one tongue taking another'. This use of 'proper English' would already have been apparent had Rolle's passage about translation not been modernised, for the phrase that is given as 'I find no exact English equivalent' reads in the original, 'I fynde na propir Inglys' (above, p. 6). The point is clear in what is effectively Tyndale's first draft of this epistle, the prologue to the unique copy of his 1525 NT. There he beseeches

those that are better seen in the tongues than I, and that have higher gifts of grace to interpret the sense of the Scripture and meaning of the spirit than I . . . if they perceive in any places that I have not attained the very sense of the tongue, or meaning of the Scripture, or have not given the right English word, that they put to their hands to amend it. (Daniell, *Biography*, p. 120)

'Proper English' clearly means 'the right English word', and the only considerations here are sense and meaning.

The key passage must be read in the light of this evidence. It was published two years after the epistle in the preface to *The Obedience of a Christian Man*. Tyndale turns bitterly on those who oppose the vernacular Bible:

Saint Jerome also translated the Bible into his mother tongue: why may not we also? They will say it cannot be translated into our tongue, it is so rude. It is not so rude as they are false liars. For the Greek tongue agreeth more with the English than with the Latin. And the properties of the Hebrew tongue agreeth a thousand times more with the English than with the Latin. The manner of speaking is both one; so that in a thousand places thou needest not but to translate it into the English, word for word; when thou must seek a compass in the Latin, and yet shall have much work to translate it well-favouredly, so that it have the same grace and sweetness, sense and pure understanding with it in the Latin, and as it hath in the Hebrew. A thousand parts better may it be translated into the English than into the Latin. (*DT*, pp. 148–9)

This is a defence against the prevailing view that English cannot properly express the Latin meaning because it lacks the features of Latin grammar, and because it is an aesthetically inferior language. Most of Tyndale's reply is to the first point: he concedes the grammatical differences between English and Latin, and the consequent difficulties of translation, but argues that Greek to some extent and Hebrew to a huge extent are grammatically and syntactically compatible with English. The result is that one may frequently be literal without violating the natural structure of English.[21] His principal point is that English is a good instrument for accurate representation of the originals, especially of the Hebrew. Not only is it a good instrument: on these grounds it is a better instrument than Latin.

Do Tyndale's apparently aesthetic terms, 'well-favouredly', and 'grace and sweetness, sense and pure understanding', go beyond an idea of linguistic correspondence and deliberately invoke a literary sense? What would once have seemed the obvious answer, that they do, now becomes doubtful. 'Grace and sweetness, sense and pure understanding' consists entirely of words that in Tyndale have theological weight. 'Well-favouredly', preceding them, does however give them some aesthetic weight, since he uses 'well-favoured' with connotations of beauty, as in 'Rachel was beautiful and well-favoured' (Gen. 29: 17).

Tyndale does not quite deal with the question of the perceived aesthetic deficiencies of English. Probably he is thinking of translating well-favouredly as translating into good English, that is, English which follows the normal syntax, grammar and vocabulary of English, as far as there is a sense of what is normal. Tyndale does indeed use the phrase 'good English' on one occasion, in response to an aspect of Sir Thomas More's (1478–1535) criticism of his ideas and work, criticism which includes more discussion of the linguistic responsibilities of a translator of the Bible than is to be found in Tyndale. In all probability, More increased Tyndale's awareness of these reponsibilities.

More's chief concern is with heretical tendencies in the translation. Among these is the choice of certain words through which, with some

---

[21] One other translator from roughly this period takes the same view, Ambrose Ussher, see below, p. 95. All other comments from the period take a contrary view of the two languages.

justification, he sees Tyndale as attacking the teaching and practice of the Church. Some of these choices More attacks not only because they have heretical tendencies but because they are poor English, and this leads him to suggest some linguistic principles of translation in the later of his two works against Tyndale, *The Confutation of Tyndale's Answer* (1532).

In the earlier work, *A Dialogue Concerning Heresies* (1529), More instances some false translations of words, refers to the difficulties of translation and responds to the argument against English. Discussing Tyndale's use of 'seniors' for 'priests', 'congregation' for 'Church' and 'love' for 'charity', he observes that 'these names in our English tongue neither express the thing that he meant by them, and also there appeareth . . . that he had a mischievous mind in the change' (*Works*, VI: 286). In particular he comments of 'senior' that in English it 'signifieth nothing at all, but is a French word used in English more than half in mockage', that it misrepresents the Latin and in fact in English signifies an alderman. His primary point is that Tyndale will use any word rather than call a priest a priest. Tyndale accepted the linguistic point only: 'of a truth *senior* is no very good English, though senior and junior be used in the universities; but there came no better in my mind at that time. Howbeit, I spied my fault since, long ere Mr More told it me, and have mended it in all the works which I since made, and call it *an elder*' (*Answer*, p. 16). This is clear evidence not only of the theological pressures on translation but of Tyndale's care for 'good English', that is appropriate English usage, and of More's role in bringing out this awareness.[22]

In *The Confutation* More develops the linguistic point, arguing that 'Tyndale must in his English translation take his English words as they signify in English, rather than as the words signify in the tongue out of which they were taken in to the English' (VIII: 201; see also VIII: 187). Thus in almost playful mood, he writes, 'though I cannot make him by no mean to write true matter, I would have him yet at the least wise write true English' (VIII: 232). He demonstrates his ideas of true English by discussing the appropriate use of certain words, and points of grammar: More has a clear sense of English as a language with its own proprieties. He is ready not only to correct Tyndale's choice of words but also his

[22] 'Elder' seems to modern ears an obvious choice and a real improvement, but this is because it has become a part of standard English through Tyndale's use of it. More did not concede that 'elder' was any improvement in Tyndale's English. He jeers that here Tyndale has 'done a great act, now that he hath at last found out "elder". He hath of likelihood ridden many mile to find out that. For that word "elder" is ye wot well so strange and so little known that it is more than marvel how that ever he could find it out' (*Confutation*, p. 182).

grammar and his style. Although he recognises the dangers of translation and the difficulties of keeping 'the same sentence whole' (VI: 315), he believes Tyndale too often follows the word order of his originals to the detriment of both sense and English style (VIII: 236). As an example he proposes an alternative translation of John 1: 1, remarking, 'I say not this to show that I think that Tyndale meant any evil by this, nor I impugn not in this point his translation so greatly, but it may be borne: but I say the other is in English better and more clear' (p. 237).

More, like Tyndale, respects English as a language. The Messenger in *A Dialogue* comments that opponents of vernacular translation 'say further that it is hard to translate the Scripture out of one tongue into another, and specially they say into ours. Which they call a tongue vulgar and barbarous' (VI: 333). More answers that those who will translate 'well and faithfully' can do so from Latin to English: 'for as for that our tongue is called barbarous is but a fantasy. For so is as every learned man knoweth every strange language to other. And if they would call it barren of words, there is no doubt but it is plenteous enough to express our minds in any thing whereof one man hath used to speak with another' (VI: 337). He concedes there may be a loss in the translation, a loss either of meaning or of aesthetic quality, but this loss is no more on translation into English than it is into any other language. Most important here is the assumption that the translator will naturally strive to give his work some aesthetic quality:

Now as touching the difficulty which a translator findeth in expressing well and lively the sentence of his author, which is hard always to do so surely but that he shall sometime minish either of the sentence or of the grace that it beareth in the former tongue, that point hath lain in their light [been known to them] that have translated the Scripture already either out of Greek into Latin or out of Hebrew into any of them both. (VI: 337)

Tyndale's work, it is worth noting, does not appear to have been attacked by his contemporaries on the ground that he diminished the literary qualities of the Scriptures. The possibility is there in More's arguments but the issue was not perceived as a real one at that time. A closely related charge was more pressing, though it surfaced only once at this time. Bishop Cuthbert Tunstal, whose patronage Tyndale had sought in 1523, attempted in 1526 to suppress the NT. He writes in his prohibition of Lutheran 'children of iniquity' who 'have craftily translated the New Testament into our English tongue . . . attempting by their wicked and perverse interpretations to profane the majesty of Scripture, which hitherto had remained undefiled, and craftily to abuse the most holy word of God and the true sense of the same' (Daniell, *Biography*, p. 190). The charge of falsification was to be the major one, but it is interesting that at this early stage the charge of profaning the majesty of the Scriptures comes first. Essentially it is a complaint that the occult power or holy beauty of the Scriptures has been lost.

This is an important issue in translation. The early translators were necessarily concerned with meaning, but words can be magical as well as meaningful, and their magic may be more important than their meaning, especially when that magic is felt to be their religious essence. An anecdote, normally told to illustrate clerical ignorance, well illustrates this. About the time Tyndale was working, 'a certain boorish English priest' was discovered to be mis-reciting in the Mass, 'quod in ore mumpsimus'. When told that the correct word was 'sumpsimus', 'he replied that he didn't want to change his old "mumpsimus" for some new "sumpsimus"'.[23] Whether or not this proves anything about clerical ignorance, it is true to people's attitudes to the familiar, if incomprehended, sound of their religious formulae. The old priest's adherence to 'mumpsimus' was more than mere conservatism: to have changed 'mumpsimus' to 'sumpsimus' would have been, for him, to undermine the accepted magic of his religious devotion without enlightening him in any real way. A literally-understood religious text, one has to say, is a *sine qua non* neither of religious or moral teaching, nor of religious feeling.

To say this is to make a point not about theology but about the psychology of religion. According to one's theological viewpoint, one may argue that the text interpreted through the accumulated wisdom of the religious consensus is essential to religion, in which case the consensus, as represented by the Church, may well be considered to be the most essential factor. Alternatively one may argue that the directly encountered meaning of the text is fundamental. These opposing ideas are not simply a case of Catholic against Protestant ideas, as all Churches, no matter how important personal reading of the Bible is to them, are based on their own religious consensus, and all have their own interpretations of the text.

At the centre of the charge of profaning the Scripture is the distinction between sacred and profane. In this respect 'majesty' is important. Tunstal, writing in Latin, uses it in the literal Latin sense which became the earliest English sense, 'the greatness and glory of God' (*OED* 1b), or 'the incomprehensible greatness of God' (Wilson, *Christian Dictionary*,

---

[23] Richard Pace, *De Fructu* (1517), p. 80. Ed. and trans. Frank Manley and Richard S. Sylvester (N.Y.: Ungar for the Renaissance Society of America, 1967), p. 103.

1616). The most revealing English use comes in the KJB's rendering of Psalm 29 which calls its reader to 'worship the Lord in the beauty of holiness' (v. 2), and then builds up a description of 'the voice of the Lord', including this: 'the voice of the Lord is powerful; the voice of the Lord is full of majesty' (v. 4). This could be read as a description of the Bible, since the Bible is the voice of the Lord. 'Majesty', it seems from the parallelism, connotes power: it is part of 'the beauty of holiness' (a phrase the KJB uses several times). It is the divine word which comes closest to the secular idea of literary beauty. Yet it was not, in the time of the translators, a literary or secular word. It belonged with 'faith' and 'truth'.

More's insistence on a translator's responsibility to his own language must have moved Tyndale towards a more conscious awareness of his use of English, and Tyndale's *Answer* shows signs of this. Further signs can be seen in some of the revisions he made for his later editions, many of which can be accounted for on no other grounds than a care for the quality of his English.[24] However, this care is essentially for the clarity and naturalness of the language, something that would *now* be recognised as a literary virtue. To take one example, he accepts More's comments on his rendering of John 1: 1, 'in the beginning was that word, and that word was with God and God was that word', that he should have used 'the', not 'that', and that 'God was that word' is not the appropriate word order for English, even though it is the Greek and Latin order. The result is our familiar rendering, 'in the beginning was the word, and the word was with God: and the word was God'.[25]

Tyndale did not reply to *The Confutation*, but it seems More's comments on his language were made to good effect. Whether Tyndale would again claim that he spied his faults ere More told him them matters little since many of his revisions show the two men at one on questions of language where theology is not at issue. This leaves a picture of Tyndale as a devout scholar who never considered the Bible as a work of literature but who nevertheless took great care with his

---

[24] A real issue here is Tyndale's use of a variety of renderings for single words, but it raises problems which cannot be solved definitively: does variety show a care for style or a sense that English vocabulary is unfixed, or merely the difficulties of consistency? Tyndale did not always provide variety where it might be thought possible and desirable, and, as Hammond points out, 'he did take care to recreate the original's repetitiveness where it had either semantic or stylistic importance' (*The Making of the English Bible*, p. 36). Mozley makes the case for seeing the variation as a deliberate literary device, (*Tyndale*, pp. 101–3), and Daniell frequently refers to the variation as evidence of literary sensibility.

[25] Further examples of Tyndale's revisions can be found in Mozley, pp. 287–9, and Daniell, pp. 330–1. The most substantial example of More as a translator of the Bible comes in *The Answer to a Poisoned Book*, where he translates and later paraphrases John 6: 26–71 (11: 21–3, 43–5).

English. His care above all was for accuracy in representing the originals, then for clarity (which might sometimes have to be achieved through glossing since he tried to avoid expanding or contracting the original), lastly for fidelity to his sense of the proprieties of English grammar and vocabulary. There is only one explicit suggestion that he considered matters of style beyond the proprieties, his use of 'well-favouredly': any further sense of his bringing aesthetic considerations to his work must be deduced from literary criticism of his translation carried out with due awareness of the context within which he worked.

No one reading what Tyndale says would be led to a literary sense of the Bible, but as soon as one begins to read him (or, to a lesser extent, More) with an eye and an ear to how he expresses himself, it is obvious that, for all the denigration, English of the early sixteenth century could be a very powerful language. What he says and how he says it, a despised yet powerful language – these are teasing contrasts not to be resolved here. At their heart is the conflict between past and present attitudes. Tyndale was a primary creator of our well-favoured language; moreover, the present century is particularly well-disposed to pithy, rhythmic, unpretentious writing. We see him as a master of common English, but his own time saw him differently. At first his language seemed too far removed from the common, then it seemed too common.

JOHN CHEKE AND THE INKHORN

More desired that Tyndale should 'at the least write true English', and Tyndale was aware that he used 'words which are not commonly used' and 'which are otherwise understood of the common people' (above, p. 20). Sir John Cheke (1514–57), first Regius Professor of Greek at Cambridge, addressed the problem of true common English: 'that, indeed, was Cheke's conceit', writes his biographer, Strype, 'that in writing English none but English words should be used, thinking it a dishonour to our mother tongue to be beholden to other nations for their words and phrases to express our minds. Upon this account, Cheke seemed to dislike the English translation of the Bible, because in it were so many foreign words'.[26] Consequently, he translated Matthew and the beginning of Mark, avoiding words of Latin origin (and attempting also to reform spelling). This incomplete and rough work was not published until 1843.[27] It can hardly have been of influence in its time, but it helps to show both the difficulties of language facing the early translators, and

---

[26] John Strype, *The Life of the Learned John Cheke, Kt* (London, 1705), p. 213.
[27] *The Gospel According to Saint Matthew*, intro. James Goodwin (London and Cambridge, 1843).

the difficulties of comprehension facing those of their readers who lacked Latin and biblical scholarship. Among his choices of words are 'mooned' for 'lunatic', 'tollers' for 'publicans', 'hundreder' for 'centurion', 'bywords' for 'parables', 'orders' for 'traditions', 'freshman' for 'proselyte', and 'crossed' for 'crucified'. For him, rain does not descend but fall: 'and there fell a great shower, and the rivers came down, and the winds blew and beat upon that house, and it fell not for it was ground-wrought on a rock' (p. 40; Matt. 7: 25).

Throughout the century there was a sharp consciousness of the distinction between vocabulary of Anglo-Saxon origin and vocabulary of Latin origin. The significance of Cheke is that he underlines the difficulties there could be at this time even with what seem to be thoroughly ordinary words of Latin origin. Evidence from other comments on the Bible for this point is scarce because of the Protestant need to believe that the Bible was translatable (to say nothing of the wish to believe that it was easy to understand), and because Cheke's is an extreme position. Yet the point, even if treated with scepticism, is not to be dismissed. It is supported by the now familiar words listed as unfamiliar by Gardiner (see below, p. 35), by Martin and his critics (see p. 45), also by Robert Cawdray's (or Cawdrey) *A Table Alphabetical* and by Thomas Wilson's *A Christian Dictionary*. Cawdray's work, published in 1604 but begun much earlier (fol. A2r) was for 'teaching true writing, and understanding of hard usual English words, borrowed from the Hebrew, Greek, Latin or French' (title). 'Hard usual' is the significant collocation. Cawdray thinks of these words as inkhorn terms (fol. A3r), yet almost all of them are now familiar English. As the title goes on it becomes clear that he thinks of this mild inkhornism as a particular difficulty in religious matters: 'whereby [unskilful persons] may the more easily and better understand many hard English words which they shall hear or read in Scriptures, sermons or elsewhere'. A few years later, Wilson writes that

not any, as yet, have set to their hands to interpret in our mother tongue . . . the chief words of our science, which being very hard and darksome, sound in the ears of our weak scholars as Latin or Greek words, as indeed many of them are derived from these languages: and this I have esteemed as no small let to hinder the profiting in knowledge of Holy Scriptures amongst the vulgar: because, when in their reading or hearing Scriptures they meet with such principal words as carry with them the marrow and pith of our holy religion, they stick at them as at an unknown language. (fol. A6r-v)

The English people of the sixteenth century were learning a new English. However simple the language of the Protestant translators may now seem (archaisms apart), it had much in it that the people had to learn before they could understand and appreciate it.

Cheke's objection to words of Latin origin was soon to manifest itself as one side of the conflicting attitudes to what were generally decried as inkhorn terms. George Pettie, writing in 1586, sums up the situation:

For the barbarousness of our tongue, I must likewise say that it is much the worse for them and some such curious fellows as they are, who if one chance to derive any word from the Latin, which is insolent to their ears (as perchance they will take that phrase to be), they forthwith make a jest at it and term it an inkhorn term. And though for my part I use those words as little as any, yet I know no reason why I should not use them, and I find it a fault in myself that I do not use them: for it is indeed the ready way to enrich our tongue and make it copious, and it is the way which all tongues have taken to enrich themselves . . . Wherefore I marvel how our English tongue hath cracked it credit that it may not borrow of the Latin as well as other tongues: and if it have broken, it is but of late, for it is not unknown to all men how many words we have fetched from thence within these few years, which if they should be all counted inkpot terms, I know not how we should speak any thing without blacking our mouths with ink.[28]

By the 1580s English had fetched so many terms from Latin that, for educated readers, Cheke's attitude to the English of Tyndale and Coverdale was thoroughly out of date. Initially, then, it seems that the English of the Bible, in spite of Tyndale's desire to be understood by ploughboys, had a real element of the inkhorn in it. But the pace of borrowing from Latin was so great that the vocabulary of the English Bible quickly came to seem part of a tradition of Anglo-Saxon simplicity, in opposition to the fashionable new English that abounded in Latin neologisms. When Gregory Martin in the Rheims NT deliberately introduced a substantial amount of Latin vocabulary, his work was seen as exhibiting the faults of the inkhorn: all sense of the Protestant Bibles tending that way was lost, even though those Bibles continued to present, as Wilson shows, difficulties of vocabulary to the uneducated.

One early-seventeenth-century writer recognized and commented on this situation. William L'Isle contrasts the Saxon versions of the Scriptures with the Rheims-Douai Bible (a text stuffed 'with such fustian, such inkhorn terms'). The Saxon

hath words for Trinity, Unity, Deity and persons thereof; for Co-equal, Co-eternal, Invisible, Incomprehensible . . . for Catholic and all such foreign words as we are now fain to use, because we have forgot better of our own. I speak not

---

[28] *The Civil Conversation of M. Stephen Guazzo* (London, 1586), unfoliated.

to have them recalled into use, now these are well known, sith I use them and the like myself for the same reason, but to give our tongue her due commendations, to show the wilful and purposed obscurity of those other translators, and to stop the base and beggarly course of borrowing when we need not.[29]

The task of completing and revising Tyndale's work fell to Myles Coverdale (1488–1568), a less scholarly but no less devout man. Not only did he produce the first complete English Bible of the Reformation (1535), but his revisions of his work became the Great Bibles of 1539 etc., and he was involved in the making of the Geneva Bible (1560). His Psalter, as revised for the Great Bible, became the Psalter of the Book of Common Prayer and thus until very recently the familiar version for Anglicans.

This familiar Psalter, like the KJB, has aroused much love and is the basis of Coverdale's reputation for literary achievement, though he also contributed significantly to the English of the prophetic books. For Coverdale, like Tyndale, has his reputation. Lewis expresses it with a memorable image in a paragraph that is particularly interesting as it begins with one of the rare recognitions of the argument being put forward here:

It is not, of course, to be supposed that aesthetic considerations were uppermost in Tyndale's mind when he translated Scripture. The matter was much too serious for that; souls were at stake. The same holds for all translators. Coverdale was probably the one whose choice of a rendering came nearest to being determined by taste. His defects as well as his qualities led to this. Of all the translators he was the least scholarly. Among men like Erasmus, Tyndale, Munster, or the Jesuits at Rheims, he shows like a rowing boat among battleships. This gave him a kind of freedom. Unable to judge between rival interpretations, he may often have been guided, half consciously, to select and combine by taste. Fortunately, his taste was admirable. (pp. 34–5)

Coverdale's defect of scholarship was principally that he knew very little Hebrew, and so, where Tyndale had not pioneered, had to work by choosing among and adapting previous versions, notably in Latin and German. Since he was less able to reproduce the precise verbal detail of the originals and was not tied to the Vulgate, he was arguably freer than Tyndale to adopt what he felt to be the best English way of expressing the meaning, but this freedom may be understood in a different way, as

---

[29] *A Saxon Treatise Concerning the Old and New Testament* (London, 1623), fols. e3r, e3v.

a liberty to pursue the true meaning of the Scriptures, which was his only professed concern in translating them. He writes in the dedicatory epistle in his first Bible 'that I have neither wrested nor altered so much as one word for the maintenance of any manner of sect, but have with a clear conscience purely and faithfully translated this out of five sundry interpreters, having only the manifest truth of the Scripture before mine eyes' (*Remains*, p. 11).

This sets the tone for most of his comments on the Bible and translation: his devotion is to the truth; his zeal is for the people to know the truth. His first Bible also contains a prologue, and to read this with the epistle is to get a sense of a more diplomatic Tyndale, ignoring considerations of literary taste and judgement. Possibly his diffidence prevented him voicing such considerations, for he writes, as Luther never would have written, 'as for the commendation of God's Holy Scripture, I would fain magnify it as it is worthy, but I am far insufficient thereto'. However, the continuation of the paragraph suggests that the praise would have had little of the literary in it:

and therefore I thought it better for me to hold my tongue, than with few words to praise or comment it; exhorting thee, most dear reader, so to love it, so to cleave unto it, and so to follow it in thy daily conversation [conduct], that other men, seeing thy good works and the fruits of the Holy Ghost in thee, may praise the Father of heaven and give his word a good report: for to live after the law of God and to lead a virtuous conversation is the greatest praise that thou canst give unto his doctrine. (p. 15)

Most significant is that he calls the Bible not 'Scripture' or 'writing' but 'doctrine'.

The one linguistic matter he gives consideration to here is variety of vocabulary, an issue he links with the use of a variety of sources because he sees both as relating to truth. In effect, he portrays translation as a hit or miss process: more translations will produce more hits, and a range of synonyms will prevent the truth from being limited by single words. He writes:

sure I am that there cometh more knowledge and understanding of the Scriptures by their sundry translations than by all the glosses of our sophistical doctors. For that one interpreteth something obscurely in one place, the same translateth another, or else he himself, more manifestly by a more plain vocable of the same meaning in another place. Be not thou offended therefore, good reader, though one call a scribe that another calleth a lawyer . . . For if thou be not deceived by men's traditions, thou shalt find no more diversity between these terms than between four pence and a groat. And this manner have I used in my translation, calling it in some place penance that in another place I call repentance, and that not only because the interpreters have done so before me, but that the adversaries of the truth may see how that we abhor not this word penance, as they untruly report of us. (pp. 19–20)

Tyndale considered the matter of varying vocabulary on linguistic grounds, but Coverdale confines himself to the religious motive of 'knowledge and understanding'. Further, he is mindful of More's objections to the tendentiousness of Tyndale's vocabulary, and wants this variety to reflect a spirit of religious compromise with the Roman Catholic Church.[30] Ultimately this is an expression of a translator's diffidence, and it directs the reader, if not exactly away from, certainly beyond the words.

Coverdale's exhortations on the proper use of the Bible are full of religious earnestness. Like Erasmus, he wants the Bible to be everyone's constant occupation, but there is no suggestion of singing or humming or lightening the weary way:

Go to now, most dear reader, and sit thee down at the Lord's feet and read his words, and . . . take them into thine heart, and let thy talking and communication be of them when thou sittest in thine house, or goest by the way, when thou liest down and when thou riseth up . . . in whom [God] if thou put thy trust, and be an unfeigned [sincere] reader or hearer of his word with thy heart, thou shalt find sweetness therein and spy wondrous things to thy understanding, to the avoiding of all seditious sects, to the abhorring of thy old sinful life, and to the establishing of thy godly conversation. (pp. 16–17)

Later in the same vein he writes of bringing children up 'in the nurture and information of the Lord' (p. 21). Coverdale has shorn away the obvious literary implications of Erasmus's ideas even more absolutely than Tyndale did: no one reading the introductory material to his Bible could even suspect the possibility of a rhetorical or worldly pleasure in the Scriptures: sweetness lies in the religious meaning heard by the heart.

In 1538 Coverdale published a version of the NT made from the Vulgate. The prefatory writings to his two editions of this (a third was published in the same year without his concurrence) reflect interestingly his motives in making such a translation and are the only places where he writes about his principles of translation. The translation was designed to counter the charge 'that we intend to pervert the Scripture and to condemn the common translation in Latin which customably is

---

[30] Coverdale's practice is less liberal than his prologue. Mozley (*Coverdale*, p. 106) points out that he followed Tyndale closely in the rendering of contentious ecclesiastical words other than 'penance', and so did not really compromise with More's position.

read in the Church; whereas we purpose the clean contrary' (p. 25). It is thus an attempt at reconciliation, seeking to bring the benefits of the ver- nacular Bible to the orthodox, particularly to those of the clergy who knew little Latin. It is intended, as was Rolle's Psalter, in large part to be a guide to the Latin. Just as Coverdale is not rigorous in his terminology for such things as repentance, so he is not rigorous in his sense of a sole true text of the Bible, and believes that the Holy Ghost is 'the author of his Scripture as well in the Hebrew, Greek, French, Dutch and in English, as in Latin' (p. 26).

This was a parallel Latin-English Bible and Coverdale describes himself as 'very scrupulous to go from the vocable of the text' (p. 29); that is, he sought to be as literal as possible. He recognised limitations to this literalness because of the differing natures of the languages, so he writes of using 'the honest and just liberty of a grammarian' (p. 28), which means respecting, as Luther, More and Tyndale had done, what he calls 'the phrase of our language' (p. 33). His motive is solely the reader's 'better understanding' (p. 28), and for this reason he writes with a 'tempered' pen: 'because I am loath to swerve from the text, I so temper my pen, that, if thou wilt, thou mayest make plain construction of [the Latin] by the English that standeth on the other side. This is done now for thee that art not exactly learned in the Latin tongue and would- est fain understand it' (p. 28). His care for 'the pure and very original text' (p. 29) of the version he is translating is such that, if he finds it nec- essary to expand it for the sake of clarity, he puts the expansions in square brackets, so that the text is 'neither wrested nor perverted' (p. 28). Later the same kind of care was taken with the Great Bible, though the intended annotations were not, in the end, printed.[31]

Whether this brief description of his linguistic principles is applicable to his other translations is uncertain: the nature of this NT perhaps demanded a greater literalness than he felt appropriate for them, and the statement that he tempered his pen does suggest that his inclination was to be less literal. Further, this was his one biblical translation where the conditions which Lewis described do not pertain and he was con- trolled by a single text in a language he knew well.

This NT, then, gives some suggestion of a linguistic freedom in his other Bibles. If it is set beside his one deliberate attempt at a literary translation of some parts of the Bible, then it appears that he would have translated very differently in all his Bibles had he untempered his pen.

---

[31] This care is described in a letter by Coverdale and others to Cromwell in 1538 (*Writings*, pp. 493–4).

This attempt was his *Ghostly Psalms and Spiritual Songs*, made sometime prior to 1539 when it appears in a list of proscribed books. It is an attempt to redirect secular literary pleasure to what Coverdale regards as the only proper object of pleasure, religion. He quotes on the title page Jas. 5: 13, 'if any of you be merry, let him sing Psalms'. He would have it 'that when we are merry, our pastime and pleasure, our joy, mirth and gladness is all of [God]' (pp. 537–8). In his prefatory address he echoes Erasmus:

would God that our minstrels had none other thing to play upon, neither our carters and ploughmen other thing to whistle upon, save Psalms, hymns and such godly songs as David is occupied withal! And if women, sitting at their rocks [distaffs] or spinning at the wheels, had none other songs to pass their time withal than such as Moses' sister, Glehana's wife, Debora, and Mary the mother of Christ have sung before them, they should be better occupied than with 'hey nony nony, hey troly loly' and such like fantasies. (p. 537)

Thus this book is founded on a sharp distinction between the secular and the religious and does not involve approval of secular literature. He presents 'such songs as edify and corrupt not men's conversation' (p. 538). The right use of singing these is

to comfort a man's heart in God, to make him thankful and to exercise him in his word, to encourage him in the way of godliness and to provoke other men unto the same. By this thou mayest perceive what spiritual edifying cometh of godly Psalms and songs of God's word, and what inconvenience followeth the corrupt ballads of this vain world. (p. 539)

Coverdale seems to have loved such songs. He writes in his preface to the Apocrypha in his first Bible of 'the prayer of Azarias, and the sweet song that he and his two fellows sung in the fire', and notes that he has included such songs in part 'for their sakes also that love such sweet songs of thanksgiving' (Mozley, *Coverdale*, p. 96). Clearly the love is religious in essence.

The contents do nothing to deny the earnest tone of the preface and little to create a merry alternative to secular songs. The Psalms especially are significant because of the reputation of Coverdale's prose Psalms. Here is the opening stanza of Psalm 137:

> At the rivers of Babylon
> There sat we down right heavily;
> Even when we thought upon Sion,
> We wept together sorrowfully.
> For we were in such heaviness,
> That we forgot all our merriness,

And left off all our sport and play:
On the willow trees that were thereby
We hanged up our harps truly,
And mourned sore both night and day. (p. 571)

This is a terrible struggle with rhyme and metre, expanding Coverdale's own rhythmical prose versions to banality. To go back to his first Bible (which he later slightly improved) makes blatant the contrast: 'by the waters of Babylon we sat down and wept, when we remembered Sion. As for our harps, we hanged them up upon the trees, that are therein'. This amounts to more than just the observation that Coverdale was a far better prose translator than poet: his prose translation did not meet his ideas of literary form but is far better writing. The paradox is that if Coverdale had tried to translate the Psalms in his Bibles in what he felt to be a literary manner, he would not have created versions capable of arousing any kind of literary affection. If, as we legitimately may, we find literary quality in his work, it is in spite of himself, for not only is there no explicit evidence of literary intentions in it, but there is evidence that he had no respect for literature and was not trying to be, by his own standards, literary.

CHAPTER TWO

From the Great Bible to the Rheims-Douai Bible: arguments about language

OFFICIAL BIBLES

The Bible in English was part of the larger battle, political as much as theological, for the English Reformation. The clergy's political allegiance might be relatively easily diverted from Rome to London, but beliefs were not so readily changed. By no means all the clergy were enthusiasts for the vernacular Bible: if they could not suppress it they could at least attempt to make it more acceptable to themselves, that is, more like the Vulgate. An attempt to do this was made in 1542. Though it came to nothing, it remains of interest because it gives further evidence of just how much the question of English vocabulary was tied up with larger issues. In parliament the archbishop 'asked members individually whether without scandal, error and manifest offence of Christ's faithful they voted to retain the Great Bible in the English speech. The majority resolved that the said Bible could not be retained until first duly purged and examined side by side with the [Latin] Bible commonly read in the English Church'. The work went into committee, and the last one hears of it is a list of Latin words which Stephen Gardiner, Bishop of Winchester, 'desired for their germane and native meaning and for the majesty of their matter might be retained as far as possible in their own nature or be turned into English speech as closely as possible' (Pollard, p. 117). Clearly Gardiner would have preferred these meaningful and majestic words to remain untouched. As one surveys the list, two things become apparent: many of the words are theologically important, and many are now familiar parts of English vocabulary. Here are some of Gardiner's words in the form he gives them:

Ecclesia, Poenitentia, Contritus, Justitia, Justificare, Idiota, Elementa, Baptizare, Martyr, Adorare, Simplex, Sapientia, Pietas, Presbyter, Sacrificium, Sacramentum, Gloria, Ceremonia, Mysterium, Religio, Communio, Perseverare, Hospitalitas, Charitas, Benedictio, Humilitas, Synagoga, Ejicere,

Distribueretur, Senior, Apocalypsis, Satisfactio, Contentio, Conscientia, Idolum, Prudentia, Apostolus, Societas, Idololatria, Confessio, Imitator, Innumerabilis, Infidelis, Paganus, Virtutes. (Pollard, p. 117)

The limitations of the vocabulary available to Tyndale and Coverdale are strikingly illustrated. Moreover, any time they ventured towards such words they were in danger not only of identifying their work with the Church they opposed, but also of maintaining a religion based on the preservation of divine mystery, hidden from the people and interpreted by the Church. The manner of English translation was a fundamental issue of the Reformation.

Though this attempt to make the English Bible latinate, ecclesiastical and majestic failed, anxiety about the proper use of the Bible persisted. Henry VIII's proclamation of 1541 warns lay readers that they should not 'presume to take upon them any common disputation, argument or exposition of the mysteries therein contained, but that every such lay man should humbly, meekly and reverently read the same for his own instruction, edification and amendment of his life' (Pollard, p. 113). The Great Bibles to which the proclamation applied were the first authorised English Bibles, and they declared themselves 'the Bible appointed to the use of the Churches'. Coverdale's prologues and dedications were replaced by a 'prologue or preface' by Cranmer (1489–1556), 'the most reverend father in God, Thomas Archbishop of Canterbury, Metropolitan and Primate of England'. This exhorts readers, if in a somewhat gentler tone, to exactly that kind of reading demanded in the King's proclamation:

How shouldest thou understand if thou wilt not read nor look upon it: take the books into thine hands, read the whole story, and that thou understandest keep it well in memory; that thou understandest not, read it again and again; if thou can neither so come by it, counsel with some other that is better learned. Go to thy curate and preacher, show thyself to be desirous to know and learn. And I doubt not but God seeing thy diligence and readiness, if no man else teach thee, will himself vouchsafe with his Holy Spirit to illuminate thee and to open unto thee that which was locked from thee.

The next major Bible was the Geneva Bible, but the direct successor of the Great Bibles was the Bishops' Bible of 1568. This, the Bible on which the KJB translators were instructed to base their work, was presented to the public as a revision for accuracy of the Great Bible.[1] The

---

[1] The best study of the text is Gerald Hammond's, and his verdict is unfavourable: 'for the most part the Bishops' Bible is either a lazy and ill-informed collation of what had gone before, or, in its original parts, the work of third-rate scholars and second-rate writers' (*The Making of the English Bible*, p. 143).

translators were instructed to revise where 'it varieth manifestly from the Hebrew or Greek original'. Only in one respect were they to consider English for its own sake: they were to find 'more convenient terms and phrases' for 'all such words as soundeth in the old translation to any offence of lightness or obscenity' (Pollard, p. 126). Given the later evidence of obscene reading of the Bible (see below, pp. 109 ff.), it seems likely that they were to remove possible *doubles entendres*. I doubt if bowdlerisation was contemplated as that would have been inconsistent with literalness. The translators worked separately rather than in committee, and so probably had to interpret the instruction as they saw fit. One of the translators, Richard Cox, Bishop of Ely, wrote that 'I would wish that such usual words as we English people be acquainted with might still remain in their form and sound, so far forth as the Hebrew will well bear; inkhorn terms to be avoided' (Pollard, p. 123). If this is a response to the instruction we may infer that some of the Bishops, like those who had tried for a revision in 1542, wished to Latinise the English, producing thereby some of the traditional grandeur and mystery of biblical language. Many of the Bishops were still close to Roman Catholicism in spirit, but any tendencies they had towards a re-Latinising of the English Bible were to be overshadowed by the Roman Catholic translation.

Cranmer's preface is retained, but preceding it is a preface by the organiser of the work, Archbishop Matthew Parker (1504–75), which shows some subtle changes in attitude to the proper use of the Bible. It takes Christ's words, 'scrutamini scripturas', 'search ye the Scriptures',[2] for text, and exhorts the private reader to study the Bible: 'let not the volume of this book, by God's own warrant, depart from thee, but occupy thyself therein in the whole journey of this thy worldly pilgrimage to understand thy way how to walk rightly before him all the days of thy life'. This implies both private readers and private ownership, which is probably a testimony to the popular domestic impact of the Geneva Bible. Like Tyndale and Cranmer, Parker believes that 'the only surety to our faith and conscience is to stick to the Scriptures'. However, though he also believes that 'no man, woman, or child, is excluded from this salvation', he is less optimistic about Scripture being rightly understood than his predecessors:

For not so lieth it in charge to the worldly artificer to search, or to any other private man so exquisitely to study, as it lieth to the charge of the public teacher to search in the Scriptures, to be the more able to walk in the house of God

---

[2] John 5: 39. Parker habitually quotes the Vulgate and then translates it without reference to the text in the Bishops' Bible itself.

(which is the Church of the living God, the pillar and ground of truth) to the establishing of the true doctrine of the same and to the impugning of the false.

The official Bibles, then, encourage a studiously devout reading of the Bible without hinting at pleasure of any sort. Cranmer is relatively liberal in his belief in the Bible's comprehensibility and so more encouraging towards private study than Parker, who prefers the Bible to be for the clergy, allowing them to teach the people better. Cranmer's readers, it seems, should pore over the very detail of the text, while Parker's lay readers should look to the Church in preference to the Bible.

Parker develops Tyndale's wish to have his work corrected and Coverdale's advocation of a variety of translations into a new point in the address preceding the Psalms:

Now let the gentle reader have this Christian consideration within himself that, though he findeth the psalms of this translation following not so to sound agreeably to his ears in his wonted words and phrases as he is accustomed with: yet let him not be too much offended with the work, which was wrought for his own commodity and comfort. And if he be learned, let him correct the word or sentence (which may dislike him) with the better, and whether his note riseth either of good will and charity, either of envy and contention not purely, yet his reprehension, if it may turn to the finding out of the truth, shall not be repelled with grief but applauded to in gladness, that Christ may ever have the praise.

The acknowledgement of a customary linguistic form is important, but of special interest is the invitation to think of the English text as unfixed, and the encouragement to the learned reader to adjust it as he thinks fit for 'the finding out of the truth'. This is an effort to destabilise the translation in the search for truth. Most scholarly users of the Bible until, roughly, the middle of the seventeenth century did indeed treat the English text as unfixed and were not much concerned to cite a particular version accurately. For them biblical truth did not lie in any particular form of English words. Unless the scholars were translators or were critics of theological and ecclesiastical tendencies that they disliked, they had little interest in the precise language of the English Bible. Such an attitude has implications for the literary fortunes of the English of the Bible: as long as there is a weak sense of the English of the Bible, it can only be a linguistic influence in the vaguest way and can hardly be appreciated. On the other hand, unscholarly people were becoming closely familiar with the English of the Bible: for them it could be an imitable, admirable standard.

OPPOSING CAMPS

The Geneva Bible

The Bible and Holy Scriptures contained in the Old and New Testament. Translated according to the Hebrew and Greek, and conferred with the best translations in divers languages. With most profitable annotations upon all the hard places, and other things of great importance as may appear in the Epistle to the Reader. Such is the full title of the Geneva Version of the Bible (1560), prepared, probably under the leadership of William Whittingham (c. 1524–79), by the Protestants living there in exile. The title shows the two aims, to provide as good a translation of the Hebrew and Greek texts as possible, and to make clear any difficulties. The frank acknowledgement of 'hard places' contrasts strikingly with Tyndale's idea of 'one simple literal sense': there is a clear movement through these Bibles towards recognition of difficulties and attempts at explication.

Although the Geneva Bible did not have the sanction of the Church of England, it became the most popular of the translations which preceded the KJB and was the only Protestant Bible to rival it for a long time after its appearance. One simple reason for this is that Bibles, especially those in private ownership, have a long life. The Roman Catholic Thomas Ward (1652–1708), writing in 1688, attacks the Protestant Bibles using, as well as the KJB, 'such English translations as are common and well-known in England even to this day, as being yet in many men's hands: to wit, those Bibles printed in the years 1562, 1577 and 1579'.[3] Even the much less popular Bishops' Bible continued to be used in some churches, according to Bishop William Beveridge, 'to our days' (1710). He says that the KJB is so little altered from the Bishops' Bible that people perceived no difference between the two versions.[4] But there were more particular reasons for the Geneva Bible's success: it was produced at a price that allowed for private ownership, and there were its

---

[3] *Errata of the Protestant Bible* (1688; Dublin, 1810), p. 19. He is not exaggerating. Sixteenth-century Geneva Bibles with eighteenth-century inscriptions are quite common. More extraordinary is a 1585 Geneva Bible in the Victoria University of Wellington library that belonged to a Norfolk village family; it contains signatures, comments and records that date from 1696 to 1877. Evidently it was still a valued family possession at the time of emigration to New Zealand. Such Bibles are ample evidence of the longevity of Bibles as books.

Plate 7 shows some handwritten annotations in a 1551 Tyndale NT, and plate 8 is typical of the kind of inscriptions to be found at the beginnings or endings of Bibles, or at some of the major breaks such as the beginning of the NT. These inscriptions, in two different hands, show that this NT continued to be used long after it had been superseded.

[4] *A Defence of the Book of Psalms*, pp. 13–14.

'profitable annotations'. These were so popular that there were at least eight editions of the KJB between 1642 and 1715 which used them, and they continued in some form in other Bibles. The Geneva Bible as a whole was sufficiently popular to be published steadily until 1644. The popularity of the Geneva Bible is also suggested by the extent to which it is quoted in preference to other English versions until, roughly, the 1630s (see below, pp. 103 ff.). Shakespeare, for instance, used it, the KJB translators cite it rather than their own version in their preface, and it was used in the Cromwellian *Soldiers' Pocket Bible* (1643).

Only one contemporary account that could possibly refer to its literary merits survives, as far as I can discover. The poet and would-be Lord Chancellor of Ireland and Archbishop of Dublin, Sir John Harington (1560–1612), calls it 'the best translation read in our Church',[5] but does not indicate in what way it is best. The comment precedes a quotation about the duties of bishops in which Harington makes one alteration of Geneva's English, so it is difficult to presume that anything other than accuracy is meant.

The only preliminary material is a dedication 'to the Most Virtuous and Noble Queen Elizabeth' and the epistle to the reader, which contains this about translating into English: 'the which thing, albeit that divers heretofore have endeavoured to achieve, yet considering the infancy of those times and imperfect knowledge of the tongues, in respect of this ripe age and clear light which God hath now revealed, the translations required greatly to be perused and reformed'. As usual, the emphasis is on textual accuracy, but, unlike the prefaces to the Great and Bishops' Bibles, this preface discusses the translators' practice. The following is its most interesting passage, particularly as it relates to literal translation and Tyndale's observation of the congruity between Hebrew and English (see above, p. 20):

For God is our witness that we have by all means endeavoured to set forth the purity of the word and right sense of the Holy Ghost for the edifying of the brethren in faith and charity.

Now as we have chiefly observed the sense, and laboured always to restore it to all integrity, so have we most reverently kept the propriety of the words, considering that the apostles who spake and wrote to the Gentiles in the Greek tongue rather constrained them to the lively phrase of the Hebrew than enterprised far by mollifying their language to speak as the Gentiles did. And for this and other causes we have in many places reserved the Hebrew phrases, notwith-

---

[5] *A Short View of the State of Ireland* (written 1605), ed. W. Dunn Macray (Oxford and London, 1879), p. 14.

standing that they may seem somewhat hard in their ears that are not well practised and also delight in the sweet sounding phrases of the Holy Scriptures. Yet
lest either the simple should be discouraged, or the malicious have any occasion
of just cavillation, seeing some translations read after one sort and some after
another, whereas all may serve to good purpose and edification, we have in the
margin noted that diversity of speech or reading which may also seem agreeable to the mind of the Holy Ghost and proper for our language.

This contrasts with Tyndale's comments about the possibility of translating Hebrew phrases literally in that it supposes that such literalism will
sound harshly in English ears.

It is one of the most striking passages so far from the translators
because it seems to be aware that their language could be made to fit to
contemporary standards, but rejects this possibility. The passage is not
sufficiently explicit for one to know what kind of 'delight in the sweet
sounding phrases' the writer has in mind, but the recognition of some
such delight is one of the few pieces of evidence there is for the generally assumed point of view that such considerations played a real part in
the forming of the language of our Bible translations. It might be argued
that this must have had some positive effect on the translation, but such
an argument would have to ignore the translators' statement that they
did not try to conform their language to normal or good or well-sound-
ing English but rather sought to represent the alien qualities of the
Hebrew.[6]

The Rheims-Douai Bible

The Roman Catholic reluctance to have the Bible in English persisted
into the seventeenth century, but the need to counteract the heresies of
the Protestant Bibles, and the desire to exercise a proper control over
Bible reading led eventually to the Rheims-Douai Bible. The NT was
published in 1582 but the OT, for financial reasons, did not appear until
1609 (Genesis to Job) and 1610 (Psalms to Esdras IV). The NT is doubly
interesting. Not only did it have a real influence on the KJB (the OT was
published too late to be significant), but it was the primary element in
the most important debate of this, the key period of English translation,
on the way the Bible should be translated.

---

[6] Although they talk of 'the lively phrase of the Hebrew' it is unlikely that they considered the
qualities of the Hebrew as having literary merit. 'Lively' at this time was a synonym for 'living',
as in the Injunctions of 1538 on the provision and reading of Bibles which describe the Bible as
'the very lively word of God' (Pollard, p. 112, n. 1).

Although the controversy between the Catholics and the Protestants was a bitter, if not a desperate one (not just souls but institutions were at stake), from the present point of view there are important respects in which there is no real difference between the two sides. Chief among these is the insistence on the true understanding of the text. That the two sides differed bitterly on the nature of that true understanding is, for this history though not for them, a minor matter. Because both sides insisted on true understanding, the charge of corruption for literary reasons was one each side brought against the other but strenuously sought to avoid. The result was a re-emphasis on the need for literal translation that, ironically, helped to produce the particular literary qualities of the KJB.

The title page of the NT makes the point of understanding not once but three times. The arguments, annotations 'and other necessary helps' are 'for the better understanding of the text, and specially for the discovery of the CORRUPTIONS of divers late translations, and for clearing the CONTROVERSIES in religion of these days'. Ps. 119 [118]: 34 is quoted, 'give me understanding, and I will search thy law, and will keep it with my whole heart', as is a passage from St Augustine arguing that Scripture is to be read 'to our instruction and salvation' (and adding a special commendation of texts 'which make most against heretics'). A further text from Augustine also emphasising understanding appears on the next page.

The whole translation was largely the work of Gregory Martin (d. 1582), an Oxford Hebraist and Roman Catholic who was part of the college of exiles at Douai and later at Rheims from 1570 onwards. The preface to the NT is the central document. It gives more attention to literary issues than is to be found anywhere else at this time. Martin clearly recognises literary possibilities in translation and he explicitly rejects them. Yet his rejection allows for effects not too far different from literary effects. Three issues occupy him, translation into the vernacular, the use of the Vulgate as the basic text, and the manner of translating. He by no means concedes that vernacular translation is necessary. He stands at the opposite extreme from Tyndale's optimistic view of the openness of the text's meaning, and yet the two men probably would not have disagreed on this matter if it did not involve the whole status of the Church's teaching, and if the matter of allegory were not so contentious to Tyndale. Martin expresses Tyndale's belief exactly at one point: 'none can understand the meaning of God in the

Scriptures except Christ open their sense',[7] and like Tyndale he uses the image of the shell and the kernel. However, he believes that the shell is much harder than Tyndale would have it be (fol. B1r), and he makes much of the difficulties and mysteries of the text. So, where Tyndale believes that the spirit of Jesus operating from within is the key to truth, Martin, the orthodox Roman Catholic, believes that this spirit is transmitted through the Church, which is therefore the guardian of understanding and so of greater importance than the text alone of the Scriptures.

Some of Martin's objections to the practice of Protestant translators lead to the formulation of his own principles of translation. He complains of the Protestants 'most shamefully in all their versions, Latin, English and other tongues, corrupting both the letter and the sense by false translation, adding, detracting, altering, transposing, pointing and all other guileful means' (fol. B1v). Such complaints inevitably force him towards greater literalness than they had practised. He complains further of what he sees as culpable license in changing accustomed names, and adds that they 'frame and fine the phrases of Holy Scriptures after the form of profane writers, sticking not for the same to supply, add, alter or diminish as freely as if they translated Livy, Virgil or Terence'. 'Fine' here is used in the sense of 'refine', and implies 'beautify'. He is moving towards a point from the creator of the Vulgate, Jerome, which he quotes on the next page, that, though other writings may be translated sense for sense, Scripture must be translated word for word.[8] But before he reaches Jerome he elaborates the point, demonstrating again how close he can be in principle to the Protestants.

He charges the Protestants with a 'meretricious manner of writing', but then adds:

of which sort Calvin himself and his pew-fellows[9] so much complain that they profess Satan to have gained more by these new interpreters, their number, levity of spirit, and audacity increasing daily, than he did before by keeping the word from the people. And for a pattern of this mischief, they give Castalion,[10]

---

[7] Preface to the NT, fol. A4v. The source for this belief is the story of Jesus on the road to Emmaus (Luke 24). Martin refers to this in a note.

[8] 'I myself not only admit but freely claim that when I translate the Greeks, except for the Holy Scriptures, where even the order of the words is a mystery, I do so not word for word but sense for sense' (*Selected Letters of St Jerome*, trans. F.A. Wright (London: Heinemann; N.Y., Putnam's, 1933), letter 57: 5).   [9] He spells this 'pue-fellowes': is one to see a derogatory pun here?

[10] Sebastian Castellio, Castalio or Chateillon, a Protestant opposed to Calvin. In 1551 he published a Ciceronian Latin Bible which became a byword as an unsuccessful attempt at literary translation.

adjuring all their Churches and scholars to beware of his translation, as one that hath made a very sport and mockery of God's holy word. (fol. B2r)

His conclusion is that Calvin and Beza are 'as bad or worse' (this is the marginal summary). Both sides, then, agree that anything like literary treatment of the text is inadmissible, and this agreement is reinforced by the example of Castellio.

Martin turns from this and other objections to describing his own practice. First, exactly as did Tyndale, he seeks pardon for any errors he may have committed, and he promises to correct them if he sees them himself or if they are pointed out to him, assuring his reader 'it is truth that we seek for, and God's honour'. He then immediately tackles the question of his language, claiming to have used

no more license than is sufferable in translating of Holy Scriptures: continually keeping ourselves as near as is possible to our text and to the very words and phrases which by long use are made venerable, though to some profane or delicate ears they may seem more hard or barbarous, as the whole style of Scripture doth lightly to such at the beginning. (fol. B2r)

This acknowledges that both the originals and his translation are unliterary from a profane point of view; nevertheless, it is a feature of the sacred writing which one should not be shocked by and which the translator has a duty to preserve.

Martin makes a virtue of this barbarousness in several ways. It differentiates the Bible from secular literature and connects with Jerome's advocation of literal translation. He continues:

We must, saith St Augustine, speak according to a set rule, lest license of words breed some wicked opinion concerning the things contained under the words . . . Whereof our holy forefathers and ancient doctors had such a religious care that they would not change the very barbarisms or incongruities of speech which by long use had prevailed in the old readings or recitings of Scriptures . . . And St Augustine, who is most religious in all these phrases, counteth it a special pride and infirmity in those that have a little learning in tongues and none in things, that they easily take offence of the simple speeches or solecisms in the Scriptures. (fol. B2v)

This echoes the Geneva preface (see above, p. 40) and leads to one of Martin's reasons for using the Vulgate rather than the Greek as his base text for the NT: 'it is so exact and precise according to the Greek, both the phrase and the word, that delicate heretics therefore reprehend it of rudeness' (fol. B3v). Such explicit recognition of difference from literary standards, even ordinary standards, of propriety is only matched by the

Geneva preface. Its emergence at this time may reflect the growing sense that a prestigious form of English was being created elsewhere.

At the end of the preface Martin returns to his principles of translation. He repeats that his frequent literalism 'may seem to the vulgar reader and to common English ears not yet acquainted therewith, rudeness or ignorance', but appeals to the future: 'all sorts of Catholic readers will in short time think that familiar, which at the first may seem strange, and will esteem it more when they shall otherwise be taught to understand it than if it were the common known English' (fol. C3r). This reflects More's jibe that 'all England list now to go to school with Tyndale to learn English' (see above, p. 10).[11] English words and phrases were of course being formed by the language of the translators.

Just as Tyndale had appended tables 'expounding certain words' to the books of the Pentateuch, so Martin here draws his reader's attention to a table at the end of his book for 'the explication of certain words in this translation, not familiar to the vulgar reader, which might not conveniently be uttered otherwise'. By comparison with Bishop Gardiner's list, Martin's is a little disappointing. There are several reasons for this in addition to its shortness – it contains fifty-five words. The Rheims NT is a major source of vocabulary,[12] but only as it supplied words for the KJB, and of the six words on the list which are also found in the KJB, three are technical terms of religion found in earlier English Bibles. The other three are 'allegory' (which goes back to Wyclif), 'anathema' (which goes back to Tyndale in combination with 'maranatha' in 1 Cor. 16: 22, the only place it is used in the KJB; Martin is the first to use it elsewhere), and 'eunuchs' (Martin is the first to use this in the NT, but the *OED* has several older examples).

At least twenty of the remaining forty-eight words are now familiar in the sense in which Martin uses them, but here the other reasons for the disappointing nature of the list appear. Only four of these appear to be original. They are 'abstracted', 'adulterating', 'co-operate' and 'neophyte', of which the *OED* notes that it did not come into general use before the nineteenth century. Also on the list is 'victim': it might well be added to these four since, although it finds an earlier example, the *OED* observes that 'the Rhemish translators of the Bible were the first to make

---

[11] 'Seniors', which More objected to in Tyndale, is used by Martin. In the annotation to 1 Pet. 5: 1, Martin writes, 'because we follow the vulgar Latin translation, we say *Seniors* or *Senior*: whereas otherwise we might and should say according to the Greek, *The Priests*'. This conveniently reflects how far Martin's literalism takes him.

[12] One thinks only of the latinate terms which the KJB took over, but occasionally Martin is the source of lively colloquialisms such as 'to blaze abroad' (Mark 1: 45).

free use of the word as English, and its general currency dates only from the latter part of the seventeenth century'. Many others such as 'mere-tricious' could have been added. However, of none of these can one say with confidence that they owe their existence to Martin. All his now-familiar words are of Latin or Greek origin, three-quarters of them ante-date his work, and two of his inventions seem not to owe their currency to his work: all this reflects the general tendency to borrow from these languages. The Rheims NT was not, on this partial evidence,[13] the nec-essary source of some of our present English vocabulary. Nevertheless, Martin emerges as a sensitive and informative figure, even as a man before his time, in matters of language. He was right: a good proportion of his strangeness has become familiar, but little of this is due to his work.

Important reasons lie behind Martin's use of strange words, reasons which distinguish him as a theoretician of Bible translation not only from Tyndale but also from More. First, he does not share their confidence in the expressive resources of English. So he uses words such as 'exinanited' and 'exhaust' (the first a notorious failure, the second familiar but not original) 'because we cannot possibly attain to express these words fully in English' (fol. C3v), and because they do not hinder but rather help his intention that the reader should study minutely the meaning of the text. So he continues, 'we think much better that the reader staying at the difficulty of them, should take an occasion to look in the table following or otherwise to ask the full meaning of them, than by putting some usual English words that express them not, so to deceive the reader' (fol. C3v). Readability is sacrificed not only to accuracy but to understanding.

Though this has, to profane ears, an anti-literary effect, it helps to pre-serve the professional vocabulary of theology, and it may have the effect of creating a distinct form of English capable of arousing religious awe. Language has other purposes besides meaning, and if Latin had lost all its meaning for the people, that is no reason for dismissing those other purposes in restoring meaning. Martin's attitude to the ploughman is not that of Erasmus or Tyndale. In his vision of the ideal days of the past,

---

[13] Fuller evidence is to be found in J.G. Carleton, *The Part of Rheims in the Making of the English Bible* (Oxford University Press, 1902). Several other writers from the period give lists of strange words in the Rheims NT. Among these words are 'penance', 'precursor', 'propitiate' (Marten, fol. Aiiir), 'abstracted', 'acquisition', 'advent', 'adulterating', 'co-operate', 'prescience' (Fulke NT), 'resus-citate' (Marten and Fulke) 'evangelize' (Wither of Colchester, fol. A3r, Marten and Fulke), 'prepuce' (Wither, Marten, Fulke and KJB preface, p. 11) 'avarices' (Edward Legh, *Critica Sacra* (London, 1639), fol. A5r), 'prevaricated' (Fulke and Legh), and 'tunic' (KJB preface). The KJB uses 'propitiation' and 'evangelist', but nothing else that comes close to the words given here.

he writes that 'the poor ploughman could then in labouring the ground sing the hymns and psalms either in known or unknown languages, as they heard them in the holy Church, though they could neither read nor know the sense, meaning and mysteries of the same' (fol. A3r-v). Consequently he links his retention of Latin terms with solemnity, that is, with an effect of religious mystery rather than meaning: 'we say, "the advent of our Lord", and, "imposing of hands", because one is a solemn time, the other a solemn action in the Catholic Church: to signify to the people that these and suchlike names come out of the very Latin text of the Scripture' (fol. C3v). This goes beyond More's and Gardiner's arguments for the retention of the old ecclesiastical terms: it shows a desire to create language of the appropriate religious quality. If this is a religious rather than a literary desire, still the difference is not very great: words are used to create feeling. An extremity of literalness is used to ends that are almost literary.

Martin could do this in part because of his demand for close study. For him the meaning did not have to be defined and clear within the text. The resources of annotation were available, bringing in the developed understanding of the Church. He was presenting not just the text but the text *and* the Church: the margin is the primary reading.

Whereas the Wycliffites had wanted their version to be 'as open or opener' than their original (see above, p. 8), Martin's presentation of text and Church produces a different idea of faithfulness to the original: 'we presume not in hard places to mollify the speeches and phrases, but religiously keep them word for word and point for point, for fear of missing or restraining the sense of the Holy Ghost to our fantasy'.[14] Thus ambiguity is preserved, even if it is present in the Greek but resolved in the Latin (see fol. C4r). The same is done with alien idioms (again the theory of the Geneva translators is reflected). This is not through a sense of compatibility of languages such as Tyndale observed between Hebrew and English, but through a sense of the religious possibilities in incompatibility. He observes that sometimes he follows Hebrew phrases which the Greek and Latin have also followed because 'there is a certain majesty and more signification in these speeches, and therefore both Greek and Latin keep them, although it is no more the Greek or Latin phrase than it is the English' (fol. C4r).

---

[14] Fol. C3v. Anthony Marten sums up Protestant reactions to the English Martin produced as a result of this practice: 'and therefore have you left such unperfect sentences, and have given such absurd terms, as every good man doth pity and lament your great fruitless labour' (fol. Aiiv). See also Wither, fol. A3r.

Martin uses 'majesty' here as Tunstal had used it (above, p. 24). His literalism, then, tends to preserve the vocabulary, form and ambiguity of the original. Though this runs directly counter to the Protestant ideal of revealing the truth within the text through native English clarity, Martin sees it not only as a better preservation of the truth but sometimes as a linguistic virtue. Here he departs from the Geneva translators. In his view such a method retains some of the true feeling of the text. The occult quality of biblical language is preserved. The purpose is religious but the effect is, in a sense, literary: genuine aspects of the literary nature of the originals – ambiguity and structure of language – are preserved.

Martin, it should be noted, is not consistent in his attitude to vocabulary. On the one hand he makes a virtue of strangeness, on the other he argues that his strangeness will become familiar. Though he himself does not resolve the contradiction it may be that the resolution lies in the idea of truth: the strange vocabulary is necessary because English does not always give the true sense of the original, but it will become familiar as the true sense is understood. This true sense is religious, not secular. Though the vocabulary becomes familiar, it need not become a part of the common, profane language.

Martin was working fifty years later than Tyndale. The distinction between a pure native English and Latin English was being eroded: not only were Ciceronian standards of writing reasserting themselves as the Renaissance gained strength, but there was, as we have seen mildly expressed by Pettie (above, p. 28), a real feeling of creative revelry in the possibilities writers were discovering in the use of Latin vocabulary in English. Martin was well aware of this situation, and he found in it a justification for his own new words, adding at the end of the argument we have been following this question: 'and why should we be squeamish at new words or phrases in the Scripture, which are necessary, when we do easily admit and follow new words coined in court and in courtly and other secular writings?' (fol. C4r). Though there is no real approval of the secular trend here, its precedent was clearly significant.

As with the Protestant translators, there can be no doubting the sincerity of Martin's work. Whatever each side in its bitterness might say about the other, each sought the clearest and most accurate presentation of the truth. Each sought the greatest practicable literalism, each was decidedly anti-literary. Could they have set aside their mutual hostility, they would have found themselves with a larger measure of agreement than disagreement. Martin differs from the Protestants most significantly in his attitude to the related questions of the expressive ability of English, the clarity of the bare text and the need to preserve some sense of religious quality in the language. He differs also, but much less significantly from a literary point of view, in his choice of basic text, though this choice is so hedged with qualifications that the difference is far from absolute. Lastly, and very importantly, he differs in the degree of attention he gives to literary questions in arguing about principles of translation. Though he is far more prepared to draw out unliterary qualities both in his own work and in the originals, he makes the problems of literariness and religious English into pressing issues. Consequently the KJB translators could not work as most of their Protestant predecessors had done, blithely ignoring these major issues.

The Martin–Fulke controversy

Prefaces to translations bring out the best in translators, especially the best in Martin, but the controversy between the Roman Catholics and the Protestants which surrounded the Rheims NT reflects little real credit on either side. It is an unseemly brawl, with no occasion lost to abuse and discredit the other side, and no concession given to any sincerity on the other side. Nevertheless, it is a brawl which adds to the understanding of the issues just summarised in useful ways, again ways that the KJB translators could not ignore.

On the one side is Martin's *A Discovery of the Manifold Corruptions of the Holy Scriptures by the Heretics of our Days, specially the English Sectaries, and of their foul dealing herein, by partial and false translations to the advantage of their heresies, in their English Bibles used and authorised since the time of schism* (1582). On the other the main work is William Fulke's *A Defence of the Sincere and True Translations of the Holy Scriptures into the English Tongue against the manifold cavils, frivolous quarrels and impudent slanders of GREGORY MARTIN.*[15] Fulke (1538–89) was associated at college with Thomas Cartwright (1535–1603), a leading Puritan who also wrote a refutation of Martin's work. Again the title is indicative: *A Confutation of the Rhemists' Translation, Glosses and Annotations on the New Testament, so far as they contain manifest impieties, heresies, idolatries, superstitions, profaneness, treasons, slanders, absurdities, falsehoods and other evils. By occasions whereof the true sense, scope and doctrine of the Scriptures, and human authors, by them abused, is now given.* This work was begun in 1583, and part of 'a letter written by sundry learned men [including Fulke] unto Mr Cartwright, to provoke and encourage him

---

[15] London, 1583. References in the following are to Hartshorne's edition, which contains both works.

to the answering of the Rhemists', given at the beginning of the volume, helps to spell out the feeling of the time:

[the Papists] have of late enterprised a new course whereby they might persuade unskilful men that the divine Scriptures and heavenly oracles stand on their side. For what else do they project by the translation of the New Testament and their adjoined unsavoury silly annotations (where like runnagate jugglers they cast mists on most clear things) than that a conceit might stick in men's minds that the Holy Scriptures are foully by us stained and that whatsoever is in them truly and soundly expressed, the same most firmly strengtheneth their opinions and utterly teareth up ours.

However, this voluminous work (it runs to some 760 pages) was not published until 1618, so Fulke remains the influential spokesman of the time. Unlike Cartwright, he became a pillar of the Church of England, and his work had a currency throughout the time of the making of the KJB. New editions of the *Defence* were published in 1617 and 1633, and Fulke repeated his arguments in his parallel NT which set the Rheims NT against the Bishops' Bible NT and confuted all the Roman Catholic arguments, glosses and annotations. This was published in 1589 and went through three subsequent editions. One important point about these works is that they reprinted Martin's work in full, in the confidence that the impartial reader that Martin was so fond of would agree with their views. Thus Martin's work also remained current, but within the context of confutation.

One target of Fulke's attack is Martin's language. He adheres to More and Tyndale's principles of English, that translation 'must observe the English phrase' (p. 347), and that it must be current English (see, e.g., pp. 179, 219–20). However, he does not believe, as Martin does, in the translator's ability to mould speech:

We are not lords of the common speech of men; for if we were, we would teach them to use their terms more properly: but seeing we cannot change the use of speech, we follow Aristotle's counsel, which is to speak and use words as the common people useth, but to understand and conceive of things according to the nature and true property of them.[16]

Further, he advocates common speech despite his admission of Martin's point that English is 'not so fruitful of words' (p. 588), that is, is more restricted in vocabulary, than Latin. This too is a real change from More and Tyndale. It reflects not only the changing sense of English but also the pressure that Martin's strange vocabulary placed on attitudes to

[16] Pp. 267–8. Though he writes as if he is a spokesman for the translators, this is license on his part. As he admits, he never had dealings with any of the English translators (p. 89).

English. Fulke is not in disagreement with Martin's attitude to English but with its consequence, and so he is forced back to disputing the translators' ability to mould language. On this point time has proved Martin right and Fulke wrong.

These views provide the basis for the attack. In the 'epistle dedicatory', Fulke describes the Rheims text as 'obscured without any necessary or just cause with such a multitude of so strange and unusual terms as to the ignorant are no less difficult to understand than the Latin or Greek itself'.[17] Martin too disliked strange and unusual terms, though his idea of them was different: he objected, as had More, to the Protestant's avoidance of vocabulary associated with Roman Catholic doctrines. Unlike Fulke's, his dislike generally did not extend to the question of style, though he did object to 'new strange words' that are 'rather Hebrew to [the people] than English' (p. 588). However, this objection relates only to the presentation of Hebrew names. He observes that Castellio used profane terms 'for foolish affectation of fineness and style', but that the English Calvinists did so 'for furthering their heresies' (p. 256).

When Martin summed up his attack on the English translator's faults of vocabulary he made the mistake of concluding by quoting Demosthenes, 'what are these? words or wonders?' (p. 569). Fulke returns the charge with interest, placing Martin with the inkhorn writers Martin himself scorned:

As for the 'wonders of words' that Demosthenes spake of, I know not where more properly they shall be found than in your affected novelties of terms such as neither English nor Christian ears ever heard in the English tongue: *scandal, prepuce, neophyte, depositum, gratis, parasceve, paraclete, exinanite, repropitiate* and a hundred such like inkhorn terms. (p. 569)

Fulke goes on to charge him with inconsistency in this practice, but what is of most interest is that he recognises and reproves the desire to maintain religious language or, in Fulke's own words, 'the ecclesiastical use of terms' (p. 495). He charges Martin with seeking 'holiness . . . in vain sound of words' (p. 493), and adds later, punning on 'sound': 'but it is the sound of an unknown word that you had rather play upon in the ears of the ignorant, than by any sound argument out of the Scripture to bring them to the knowledge of the truth' (p. 494). Thus a choice is clearly set before the KJB translators: ecclesiastical sound or sound argument.

[17] P. 5. Cartwright was later to comment that the language remains 'partly for the sottish superstition of keeping of words rather than sense, and partly for the unnecessary new-fangledness of foreign speech, as it were untranslated' (*Answer*, p. 189).

An interesting squabble about rhetoric and eloquence erupts over Fulke having, in a previous work, labelled what Martin takes to be a solecism a 'soloecophanes'. This rare term from classical rhetoric means something which appears to be a solecism but is not. Martin begins the quarrel:

And as for the word 'soloecophanes', we understand him that he meaneth a plain solecism and fault in grammar . . . but Mr Fulke saith that he meaneth no such thing, but that it is an elegancy and figurative speech, used of most eloquent authors; and it is a world to see, and a Grecian must needs smile at his devices, striving to make St Luke's speech here [Luke 22: 20], as he construeth the words, an elegancy in the Greek tongue. (p. 132)

Fulke hesitates to claim elegancy for the Greek. He produces his original passage where he had described 'soloecophanes' as 'a figure used of the most eloquent writers that ever took pen in hand' (p. 135), and then, even if in context it looks like quibbling, makes a very important point: 'where find you that I affirm St Luke's speech here to be an elegancy in the Greek tongue? yea, or "soloecophanes" to be nothing else but an elegancy and figurative speech? A figure indeed I say that it is; but are all figures elegancies, or all figurative speeches elegancies of speech?' (p. 136). It is impossible to tell if he takes this position because he cannot prove the Greek to be eloquent or because he does not want to. However, the general point that not all figures are elegancies qualifies the impression given by books of rhetoric based on the Bible that because it contains identifiable examples of the varieties of figurative speech the Bible is therefore eloquent. This will need to be kept in mind when the KJB translators are seen discussing figures in the text. Of course this whole period was a time when the study of rhetoric was a basic part of education. All the translators were trained in rhetoric. Tyndale's first translation, designed to show he was qualified to translate the Bible, was of the rhetorician Isocrates. But it is clearly wrong to make the simple jump from knowledge of rhetoric and awareness of figures in the Bible to the conclusion that the Bible was regarded as a literary work. This is by no means always so.

The debate between Fulke and Martin ranges far more widely than I have indicated, but the rest of it is mostly concerned with theological detail. What is of real importance is that the areas of debate surveyed here developed and focussed the main linguistic and literary issues involved in translation and kept them current during the time of the making of the KJB.

DOES THE VERBAL FORM MATTER?

In spite of all the discussions of the language of the Rheims NT, the Protestants were most concerned with its margin, and the bulk of their criticisms (represented particularly by Fulke's NT and Cartwright's *Confutation*) is directed against the arguments, glosses and annotations. If it was in these that the real issue lay – for they rather than the text represented the Roman Catholic understanding – then did the particular translation have any real importance in the end? One aspect of Protestant thinking held that it did not. This aspect first appears in English with Coverdale's advocation of a variety of translations (above, p. 30), and is later touched on by the Bishops' Bible (above, p. 38). The existence of differing English translations, coupled with the need to discredit the Roman Catholics, brings it out again.

Anthony Marten (1583) refutes the Roman Catholic objection to the Protestant variety in this way: 'we grant indeed that our translations differ in words, but very seldom in sense: if at any time in sense, yet never in matter of great importance . . . the difference of our translations is rather in sound of words than in sense or meaning' (fol. Aiir). Having thus emphasised the distinction between form and content at the expense of form, he boldly challenges the Rhemists:

But what do ye of the seminary of Rheims think if we should receive into our Church the translation which ye yourselves lately made (simply I mean, and nakedly without any of your corrupt notes and blasphemous glosses), would not the very same confirm all our opinions in the chiefest matters, as much in a manner as our own translations? For it is not your fantastical and new-devised terms that can make Christ's true religion contrary to itself, that can alter the sense and meaning of the Holy Ghost, that can either enfeeble our true and grounded positions, or strengthen your false and forged objections. (fol Aiiv)

Explicitly, it is not the language that can alter the Bible's meaning. Cartwright makes the same argument – 'if you had given your people your translation alone, we doubt not but they should . . . have found relief in it against extreme famine which your unfaithfulness hath thrust them unto' (*Answer*, p. 88) – and backs it with a declaration that the original Scriptures are incorruptible through verbal alteration (p. 93).

George Wither, Archdeacon of Colchester (1540–1605), in his *View of the Marginal Notes of the Popish Testament*, was content to work by quoting the Rhemish text and notes, and then giving his answer, because 'it will well appear that when out of their most partial translation, which they of purpose have framed for their best advantage, the things which they

gather will not follow nor be confirmed, that they are utterly destitute of
all help of the Scriptures, howsoever they labour to wring them to their
purpose' (fol. A4v). This argument could be two-edged, and the Roman
Catholic John Heigham (fl. 1639) was to claim that the KJB in fact supported Roman Catholic, not Protestant views,[18] and so he worked to
refute the 'errors of our time . . . by express texts of their own approved
English Bible' (from the title). He in turn was confuted by Richard
Bernard (1568–1641), who claimed that the Rhemists had been disowned
by their superiors because their work 'laid open to the people the naked-
ness and deformity of their Romish doctrines'. He goes on: 'and therefore have I the more willingly produced the same against themselves; the
power and lustre of God's word, though clouded and disguised by their
purposed obscurity and improprieties, yet competently shining forth for
their conviction by this unwilling wounding of Rome by the outworks of
Rheims'.[19]

Bernard's fuller views on this issue are expressed in a book he wrote
as a guide for ministers, and they sum up the complexities involved. He
counsels ministers to read the Bible

> in the translation to vulgar people, and in that which is most commonly received
> and best approved, and even as it is there set down, without addition, detrac-
> tion or change of any thing therein. It is not fit that everyone be a public con-
> troller of a public received translation. As it may argue some presumption and
> pride in the corrector, so it may breed contention and leave a great scruple and
> cast doubts into the hearers' minds what reckoning to make of a translation;
> and it gives great advantage to the Papists, who thereby labour to forestall many
> that they smally account of our translations; which we see can never be so well
> done and generally approved of, but some particular persons will be censuring
> the same, and that not only in private (a thing happily tolerable if the censure
> be true and wisely proceeded in) but also they must needs show their skill in
> pulpits . . . It is very necessary that the translation be most sound.[20]

However, Bernard does not want the ministers to stick to one translation
for themselves. He further advises, 'for translations, bring them to the
original text, and by that try them, and see the emphasis of the words,
the manner of speaking and the grammatical constructions' (p. 27).
'Theologus', he argues, 'must be philologus' (p. 35), and he gives a long
list of texts of the Bible, concordances, annotations, commentaries, etc.,
that a minister should have and study (pp. 38–42).

---

[18] *The Gag of the Reformed Gospel*, 2nd edn (1623), pp. 4–5.
[19] *Rheims Against Rome* (London, 1626), fol. A2 r-v.
[20] *The Faithful Shepherd* (London, 1607), p. 16.

In effect there is to be a fixed text for the people but not for the clergy. The willingness among the scholarly to discount the particular verbal form in their belief in the essential unchangeable truth of the text is inseparable from the general tendency of the time not to quote accurately from any particular translation of the Bible (see below, pp. 103 ff.). In a different way, it is also at one with the practice in the controversies of quoting one's opponent in full, so that his work is effectively republished in the confidence that all true believers will see its folly. The real consequence for literary attitudes to the Bible is that the form of words, that is, the literary form of the text, ceases to matter. Although this works, as already observed (p. 38), against literary appreciation of the translations, it may also accidentally work towards their appreciation: if the literary nature of the text, like the spiritual nature, is conceived of as belonging to the pith, not the husk, then that nature is appreciable even when the husk is an unappreciated English translation. This tendency of thought will be seen in the work of Thomas Becon (below, pp. 140 ff.).

CHAPTER THREE

The King James Bible

Other issues of importance were raised by one of the most eminent
English Hebrew scholars of the time, the dogmatic and contentious
Hugh Broughton (1549–1612). Although he was not included among the
King James translators, he gave them the benefit of his advice; his argu-
ments about translation were as familiar to the KJB translators as
anyone's.

He believed in the divinely inspired infallibility and perfection of both
Testaments (but not of the Apocrypha).[1] So, writing in connection with
the work then being done on the KJB, he declares, 'the Old Testament
is all written in the Jew's tongue, and God's style passing all man's wit,
and maketh up one body, having not one word idle or wanting'.[2] This
premise, coupled with a refusal to admit any possibility of textual corruption,[3] leads to his entire scholarly effort, which is to 'clear' the
Scriptures, that is, open their true meaning so that the consistency, the
'one body, having not one word idle or wanting', is revealed. Much of
this involves reconciliation of apparent conflicts (there can be no *real*
conflicts in a divinely inspired text) of chronology and genealogy.
Broughton's first work, *A Consent of Scripture* (1588), tried to harmonise
Scripture chronology, and he continued to hold forth on this subject to
the end of his life. Literary questions are necessarily involved, and he is
frequently at pains to distinguish literal and figurative language in the
text. For instance, he propounds as a principle of interpretation that 'the
first penner of the matter and all writers of it must use all certain and

---

[1] 'All who hold the Apocrypha part of the Holy Bible make God the author of lying fables and
vain speech, whereby wisdom would they should not come side by side with the holy books, nor
under the same roof' (*Works*, III: 664; though this was published as one volume, it is made up of
four 'tomes' with erratic pagination, so the tome is given before the page reference).

[2] III: 696. For a similar statement on the NT, see III: 703.

[3] He writes that the Papists would triumph 'if we Protestants confess the [Hebrew] text to be corrupted: that I will never do, while breath standeth in my breast' (*Epistle*, p. 9).

sure plainness, until all doubts be removed'. He has in mind the problems of reconciliation between Kings and Chronicles: the story in Kings 'is most exact', but in Ezra's version in Chronicles, 'the abridger's grace standeth in short speech, with close helps to call unto the larger declaration' (*Epistle*, p. 22). So Ezra can use 'terms in rare elegancy, and hard' because he and the people knew the true facts of the story as given in Kings, and because the people 'knew well that Ezra could not have from God any authority to check God's former authority'. 'Matters of plain story' are for him 'the ground of all' (pp. 18, 19, 20). He follows the Jewish saying 'that to miss in one letter is a corruption of the whole world'.[4] Here he is at his most characteristic, reconciling 2 Chron. 22: 2 with 2 Kgs 8: 26, using 'proper' to mean literal:

scholars little thought that one syllable, 'Ben', being unproper in the two and forty years, but supposed proper, and contrariwise proper in Joas but supposed in our cursed table unproper, should disturb all the Bible. Yet, as the little spark of the tongue enflameth the whole wheel of creation, so one syllable being mistaken hath kindled a flame through all our Bible that must be quenched. (p. 25)

Faith depends on the infallible perfection of the Bible, and this perfection is only revealed through the most careful attention to the way the language is used.

Such an attitude, like the Fulke–Martin controversy, was for the KJB translators a pressure away from any kind of liberty for the sake of the quality of their English. Further, without necessarily implying literary quality, it involves consideration of stylistic questions and particularly of figurative language. But Broughton's premises, that the Scriptures are divinely inspired and perfect, and that they contain what we would call literary elements, lead him to the view that the Bible is the best literature. The title of one of his translations is indicative: 'the Lamentations of Jeremy, translated with great care of his Hebrew elegancy and oratorious speeches; wherein his six-fold alphabet stirreth all to attention of God's ordered providence, in kingdoms' confusion'. The last part of this is all one with his concern to harmonise the Bible: the alphabetical ordering is to him one more example of 'God's ordered providence'. Even so, unless 'elegancy and oratorious speeches' refers to no more than this alphabetical ordering, the title gives a rhetorical view of Lamentations. At the beginning of the preface he goes further: 'Jeremy's Lamentation I have set over into our tongue with care to set forth, so near as our speech could, the oratorious bravery of his words. But all

---

[4] 'A request to the *Arch.* of *Cant.*', *Epistle*, p. 57.

men, yea all Greeks, though their learning and eloquence were poured
into one head, would come nothing near his heavenly gayness' (*Works*,
II: 314). 'Gayness' appears an odd term for Lamentations, but
Broughton uses it because of the pleasure he takes in the writing which
brings 'more joy for learned style than sadness by speech of the nation's
fall' (II: 315).

This pleasure comes back to admiration of harmony in technical
matters:

And Jeremy at the kingdom's ruin penneth his Lamentations with a watchful
eye, very much for phrase, using from Moses, David, Solomon, Isaiah and all
former, terms uttered of the destruction which he saw and felt. But his alphabet is more wonderful, to show in man's confusion God's distinction . . .[5] The
chap. 3 hath thrice every letter in order, that by three witnesses God's looking
to his letters might be seen. These being matters of elegancy more than bare
necessity, show that no less watchfulness was over the words of sentences.
(*Epistle*, p. 5)

Characteristically, he adds: 'which thing should move us to hold the text
uncorrupt'. The effect of this kind of point is to emphasise that the
Hebrew of the OT and the Greek of the NT are more than expressions
of meaning: they are artful language, and translation must recognise
this. As he writes in the preface to his translation of Daniel, 'also the
oratory for the members of the sentences, wherein the prophets are very
sweet, must in all languages be tendered' (*Works*, I: 167).

The airing Broughton gives to his ideas of the sweet oratoriousness of
the Scriptures must have served to remind the KJB translators that there
was more to translation than meaning. But he never advocates a rhetorical or poetical translation, and is absolutely clear that the duty of translators is to be as faithful to the meaning of the original as possible.

All he says of English style in the *Epistle*, which was published in 1597,
is that a translation 'should have a mild style, to win all to a good work'
(p. 43), which is exasperatingly vague. After the publication of the KJB
he writes: 'I blame not this, that they keep the usual style of the former
translations in the Church, that the people should not be amazed. For
the learned, the Geneva might be made exact, for which pains whole
thirty years I have been called upon, and spent much time to my great
loss, by wicked hindrance' (*Works*, III: 663). English style is hardly even
a minor matter for Broughton: the usual style will do because it is familiar, and he returns us squarely to the issue of exactness. He judges a

---

[5] The marginal summary reads, 'Jeremy's distinct art, of a confused state, in a sixfold alphabet'.

translator's duty to be 'to show the right meaning of old hid doings, which by mistaking blame the holy letters' (*Epistle*, p. 17).

Some indication of how this duty was to be fulfilled comes from a letter of 1593. Broughton was to work on the Geneva Bible with five other scholars, making only necessary changes; 'the principle of harmonising the Scripture was to prevail, and there were to be short notes'.[6] In the *Epistle* he sets out principles for fulfilling this duty. The text is not to be amended but 'honored, as found, holy, pure', ambiguous prophecies must be cleared by study 'and staid safety of ancient warrant', and clever circumlocutions in the text must be studied to avoid 'foolish and ridiculous senses' (p. 3). Repetitions must be translated identically (the KJB translators specifically excused themselves from doing this, but it became a principle of the RV), the old Greek translation, the Septuagint, as used in the NT, should be given in the margin of the OT, and nothing in the translation should 'disannul the text', since 'that fault is exceeding great, for a man to take upon him to be wiser than God' (p. 4). Lastly, in some places strict literalness is too harsh and a degree of paraphrase is permitted (pp. 50–1). Only here is any freedom left for consideration of the demands of the English language. Otherwise Broughton could not be more insistent on literal accuracy.

Broughton addressed to the translators an 'advertisement how to examine the translation now in hand, that the first edition be only for a trial, and that all learned may have their censure'. It was perhaps his last attempt to influence the KJB, if only by opening the way for post-publication criticism. It contains some new, if not very serious suggestions, such as that seventy-two translators should do the work in memory of the Septuagint, and that gardeners should help 'for all the boughs and branches of Ezekiel's tree to match the variety of the Hebrew terms', for there are sixteen kinds of thorns in the Hebrew. 'We should', he continues, 'by common consent, for near tongues, express this variety, that the holy eloquence should not be transformed into barbarousness. By right dealing herein, great light and delight would be increased. The Hebrew would be in honour among all men when the inimitable style should be known how it expressed Adam's wit' (*Works*, III: 702). At the back of this lies an equation between literal translation and eloquence in translation: the translation would be eloquent not as English but as Hebrew and Greek in English. Though he and Gregory Martin would have been horrified to be bracketed together, Broughton's argument here is

---

[6] The letter is not in *Works*. This is *DNB*'s summary.

essentially the same as Martin's on the desirability of preserving the occult quality of biblical language (see above, p. 48). Neither thought that such fidelity to the original would produce English eloquence, yet their attitude, by encouraging un-English translation, helped to change English language and literature.

Much of Broughton's work was ignored. But however little the KJB translators responded to its detail, it contributed significantly to the intellectual atmosphere of the time by encouraging a reverence for the eloquence of the original without arguing for an equivalent eloquence in English, but above all by demanding the whole truth and arguing that it could only be revealed through the closest attention to the words and syllables of the perfect originals.

RULES TO MEET THE CHALLENGE

The challenge to the translators of the King James Bible or Authorised Version of 1611[7] was substantially different to that faced by Wyclif, Tyndale and Coverdale. They were not pioneers but revisers. They had as bases for their work not only a variety of translations but also explicit and detailed discussion of the issues they faced. They inherited a very substantial continuity of practice: their predecessors all aimed at the most accurate possible presentation of the truth, and all except Martin used simple native English as far as possible. None aimed at literary effect, all agreed in deploring any such aim. But Martin had introduced the possibility of ecclesiastical effect and had developed latinate English as a source of vocabulary. The sense that the Bible was not a literary work and did not stand up to the tests of literary and linguistic correctness had become much more explicit in the later translators. The advocation of literalness had grown stricter, and there had been an increasing recognition of the hardness of Scripture, even a recognition that Scripture was in many places ambiguous. Coupled with these recognitions was a greater emphasis on the importance of the margin as the location for the real meaning or meanings of the text.

The request for a new translation began with the puritan John

---

[7] These titles are sometimes run together, but neither is the proper title of *The Holy Bible, containing the Old Testament and the New: newly translated out of the original tongues: and with the former translations diligently compared and revised by his Majesty's special commandment. Appointed to be read in Churches.* An abbreviated title has been a historical necessity, the Americans preferring 'The King James Bible' and the English 'The Authorised Version'. Since the version was never officially authorised but is the Bible whose creation is associated with James I of England, I prefer 'The King James Bible'.

Reynolds. At the conference at Hampton Court in January 1604 he moved 'his Majesty, that there might be a new translation of the Bible, because those which were allowed in the reigns of Henry the eighth and Edward the sixth were corrupt and not answerable to the truth of the original'.[8] It is an odd petition. This was not one of the topics that Reynolds had said he would raise, and so appears almost as a casual interjection. Moreover, the argument for it appears to have been brief and weak: Reynolds instances three Great Bible readings, apparently ignoring the existence of the Bishops' Bible, which had corrected the sense in two of the readings. It may be that Reynolds' intention was to push the conference into accepting the Geneva Bible as the official Bible of the Church, for it corrects where he demands correction, and the two revisions he suggests are exactly those of the Geneva Bible.[9] Understandably, there was a scornful response: 'to which motion, there was at the present no gainsaying, the objections being trivial and old, and already, in print, often answered; only, my Lord of London [Bishop Bancroft] well added, that if every man's humour should be followed, there would be no end of translating' (pp. 45–6). James's response may have surprised Reynolds. If the suggestion was a covert attempt to promote Geneva, it failed instantly: James thought that the worst of the translations because of the anti-monarchist tendencies of some of the Geneva notes.[10] Yet he took up the idea, hoping for a uniform translation, by which he meant one the whole Church would be bound to. His other particular interest, following his dislike of Geneva, was 'that no marginal notes should be added' (pp. 46–7). Textual accuracy, theological neutrality and political acceptability were the qualities desired, and the aim a single, generally acceptable text. There follows an ambiguous passage which appears to suggest that the kind of objections instanced by Reynolds were minor matters. James comments, 'rather a Church with some faults than an *innovation*', and adds, 'if these be the greatest matters you be grieved with, I need not have been troubled with such importunities and complaints' (p. 47). Does one sense here a general

---

[8] William Barlow, *The Sum and Substance of the Conference . . . at Hampton Court January 14 1603* (London, 1604; facsimile, intro. by William T. Costello and Charles Keenan, Gainesville: Scholars' Facsimiles & Reprints, 1965), p. 45.

[9] 'Bordereth' (Tyndale, Great Bible and Bishops' Bible) is objected to in Gal. 4: 25; Ps. 105: 28, 'they were not obedient' (Coverdale, Great Bible), should be 'they were not disobedient' (Geneva), and Ps. 106: 30, 'then stood up Phineas and prayed' (Great), should be 'executed judgement' (Geneva, followed by 1611; Coverdale and Bishops' have 'executed justice').

[10] James instanced Exod. 1: 19, where the Hebrew women's disobedience is said to be lawful, and 2 Chron. 15: 16, where Asa is criticised for deposing his mother: 'he lacked zeal: for she ought to have died'.

satisfaction with the overall accuracy of the earlier Bibles, perhaps irrespective of particular versions?

Nevertheless, the task was the same that their predecessors had set themselves, to make their translation as answerable to the truth of the original as possible. To achieve this, the largest group of translators for any of the Bibles since the legendary seventy-two of the Septuagint was selected. They were clear in their recognition of the task and its purpose. The preface, commonly held to have been written by Myles Smith (d. 1612), speaks for them:

Truly, good Christian reader, we never thought from the beginning that we should need to make a new translation, nor yet to make of a bad one a good one . . . but to make a good one better, or out of many good ones, one principal good one, not justly to be excepted against; that hath been our endeavour, that our mark.[11]

Thus the task, next the means and the ultimate purpose, truth: 'to that purpose there were many chosen, that were greater in other men's eyes than in their own, and that sought truth rather than their own praise'.

Instructions for their work were drawn up. Some make interesting reading in the light of what has gone before. First, a basic text is specified, the Bishops' Bible. This is to be 'as little altered as the truth of the original will permit' (Pollard, p. 29). Crucially, this sets a limit: it specifies revision only where fidelity to the meaning of the originals is an issue. No more is said on general principles. The next three instructions show the influence of the Fulke-Martin controversy. First, following Martin's objection, names are to be given in their traditional form. Next, following More and Martin, 'the old ecclesiastical words [are] to be kept, *viz.* the word "Church" not to be translated "Congregation" etc.'. Also, 'when a word hath divers significations, that to be kept which hath been most commonly used by the most of the ancient Fathers, being agreeable to the propriety of the place and the analogy of the Faith'.

Chapter divisions are to be left unchanged if possible and Scriptural cross-references may be given in the margin, but, importantly, marginal notes are forbidden, except 'for the explanation of the Hebrew or Greek words which cannot without some circumlocution so briefly and fitly be expressed in the text' (p. 29). Principally this is to avoid schismatic tendentiousness. As with the earlier instructions, there is an element of moderation here: the aim of making a version 'not justly to be excepted

---

[11] P. 9. The foliation of the original preface is difficult to use (only one page has a foliation mark), so for convenience I have numbered the pages, beginning at 1, which is fol. A3v.

against' is well visible. But it is the potential for literary effect that is most interesting here. Attention is taken away from the margin and restored to the text, which is to have a word-for-word accuracy if at all possible. Modification of the text through considerations for English is, in effect, forbidden, and Broughton's principle of preserving the alien qualities of the originals is enforced.

The remaining instructions concern the method of conducting the work, and are designed to ensure that the greatest care possible is taken at every stage. It is interesting, then, to note how little the instructions on principles deal with fundamentals. Certainly the controversies and the now substantial history of translation had thrown the emphasis onto even the smallest details, but what they had also done was to establish such agreement on fundamentals that it went without saying that the only method was to be as literal as possible and to make the language as clear as possible. The omissions from the instructions are as revealing as the inclusions.

THE PREFACE

The preface, entitled 'The translators to the reader', is of interest first for the manner in which it is written. Its vocabulary shows a much greater reliance on latinate words than the translation itself, often creating effects of alliteration, sonority and grandeur, and the structure of the writing is more rhetorical, especially in the early part, than anything from the earlier English translators or controversialists. The main characteristics are repetition and elaboration, but not in the simple manner of biblical parallelism. Sentence structures are generally elaborate, and every effort is made to give them variety. This looks like a deliberate attempt at fine writing, and is certainly in a higher style than that of the translation itself. It seems that revision and translation have forced on the translators something lower, possibly much lower, than their idea of good writing.

To begin with, here is a passage characteristic both of the attitudes and style of the preface. It follows the theme of Parker's preface to the Bishops' Bible:

But now what piety without truth? what truth, what saving truth, without the word of God? what word of God whereof we may be sure without the Scripture? The Scriptures we are commanded to search. John 5: 39. Isa. 8: 20. They are commended that searched and studied them. Acts 17: 11 and 8: 28–29. They are reproved that were unskilful in them or slow to believe them. Matt.

22: 29, Luke 24: 25. They can make us wise unto salvation. 2 Tim. 3: 15. If we
be ignorant, they will instruct us; if out of the way, they will bring us home; if
out of order, they will reform us, if in heaviness, comfort us; if dull, quicken us;
if cold, inflame us. 'Tolle, lege; tolle, lege', take up and read, take up and read
the Scriptures, for unto them was the direction, it was said unto St Augustine
by a supernatural voice. 'Whatsoever is in the Scriptures, believe me,' saith the
same St Augustine, 'is high and divine; there is verily truth and a doctrine most
fit for the refreshing and renewing of men's minds, and truly so tempered that
every one may draw from thence that which is sufficient for him, if he come to
draw with a devout and pious mind as true religion requireth'. (pp. 2–3)

The attitude to Scripture is thoroughly familiar: it is truth to be searched
and studied. As for the language, it shows a real care for words and structure. There is for instance the play on 'command' and 'commend': 'the
Scriptures we are commanded to search. They are commended that
searched and studied them'. Such word play brings out strikingly the
manner in which the prose moves forward by the repetition of an
element coupled with a new element.

What I have quoted so far is but a quarter of the paragraph. It builds
inexorably to a massive sentence detailing the totally religious, unliterary effects of the Scriptures. In this last sentence, it is as if, to adapt a
famous phrase from later in the preface, the writer has not used one word
or phrase precisely when he could use another no less fit as commodiously. The Bible has just been described as 'a fountain of most pure
water springing up unto everlasting life':

And what marvel? The original thereof being from heaven, not from earth; the
author being God, not man; the enditer, the Holy Spirit, not the wit of the apostles or prophets; the pen-men such as were sanctified from the womb and
endowed with a principal portion of God's spirit; the matter, verity, piety, purity,
uprightness; the form, God's word, God's testimony, God's oracles, the word of
truth, the word of salvation, etc., the effects, light of understanding, stableness
of persuasion, repentance from dead works, newness of life, holiness, peace, joy
in the Holy Ghost; lastly, the end and reward of the study thereof, fellowship
with the saints, participation of the heavenly nature, fruition of an inheritance
immortal, undefiled, and that never shall fade away: happy is the man that
delighteth in Scripture, and thrice happy that meditateth in it day and night. (p.
3)

Though this may not be prose one would unreservedly admire, it
bespeaks an author highly aware of language, and suggests more than
the major point, that the prose the translators used for the translation
was not what they would have considered good prose: Myles Smith, for
one, had sufficient sense of language, including a sense of something like

parallelism (though the term was not then known), not only to translate in a literary manner if he so chose, but also to be aware of structural qualities in the Hebrew. Is it possible to add to the conclusion that the translators did not translate in a manner they would have considered literary, the suggestion that they had some awareness of what is now regarded as the central element in Hebrew poetic structure? Can one go as far as Gustavus S. Paine does when he asks who gave the KJB its literary polish? After referring to the literary output of the translators, he writes:

the difficulty is that, to a modern reader, the thought occurs that nothing in all their many volumes of sermons and other writings seems to march with the Bible cadence quite as does the prefatory address . . . On this similarity (which does not extend to his sermons), must rest any case for saying that Smith brought to the final editing its real inspiration. (*The Men*, p. 133)

This is a product of the natural but unnecessary desire to find a creative genius behind what one takes to be a great creation. Many arguments work against it: so much of the quality of the KJB depends on an established tradition of literal translation of the originals, and so much depends on translations already made, that, even if there was strong evidence that the KJB translators (or even just Myles Smith) intended to make the language of the translation literary, they had little scope for doing so. Further, Smith's style in the preface, though it has elements vaguely in common with biblical parallelism, owes much more to the complexities of Latin sentence structures. Parallelism, also, is by no means exclusively a Hebrew device. Lastly, to be aware of characteristics is not necessarily to appreciate them. Smith's preface reminds us of what was abundantly clear in Tyndale, that the translators could be very able users of language. Unless one can demonstrate that its cumulative and repetitive structure was influenced by the language of the Bible, the style of the preface is not evidence of literary appreciation of the Bible.

The author is God, the enditer the Holy Spirit, Smith claims, but he does not go so far as claiming for the Septuagint, as some have done not only for that version but for the KJB, that the translators were inspired. This idea is glanced at and rejected. Jerome's view is adopted: the seventy were interpreters, not prophets. Smith's reasons for this begin to reveal ideals of translation: 'they did many things well, as learned men; but yet as men they stumbled and fell, one while through oversight, another while through ignorance, yea, sometimes they may be noted to add to the original, and sometimes to take away from it' (p. 4). The ideal is simple and familiar: to make the most accurate and scholarly translation possible. Paraphrase is precluded. Further concepts of translation appear as developments from the idea of the Bible as the word of God:

> we do not deny, nay we affirm and avow, that the very meanest translation of the Bible in English, set forth by men of our profession . . . containeth the word of God, nay, is the word of God. As the King's speech which he uttered in Parliament, being translated into French, Dutch, Italian and Latin, is still the King's speech, though it be not interpreted by every translator with the like grace, nor peradventure so fitly for phrase, nor so expressly for sense, everywhere. (p. 7)

This argument depends on the familiar distinction between content and form; implicitly, style is a mere extra, a decoration.[12] In this the translators differ most particularly from those who maintain that the Bible or the KJB is the word of God, but who blur the distinction between content and form, and so argue that the word of God, because it has literary form and the best author, must be the greatest literature.[13] The translators are not arguing that they themselves are the instruments whereby God speaks in English; rather, they are the means whereby God's meaning is rendered into English.

The example of the King's speech indicates three aspects to translation, grace, fitness of phrase and accuracy of sense. 'Grace' clearly refers to qualities of style, and this is one of the few clear indications of awareness of a literary dimension in the work of translation.[14] Fitness of phrase seems ambiguous. The modern reader would see in it a literary dimension, but this would be incorrect. 'Fitly' is used in the sixth of the instructions to the translators to mean 'accurately': 'words which cannot, without some circumlocution, so briefly and fitly be expressed in the text'. 'Fit' is used unambiguously elsewhere in the preface to mean 'appropriate', as in the observation that at one time the Greek language 'was fittest to contain the Scriptures' because of its widespread use (p. 4; 'contain' again shows the division between content and form). Similarly, 'fit' and its variations are used in the KJB without literary connotations.

---

[12] Many images in the preface confirm this, for instance: 'translation it is that openeth the window to let in the light, that breaketh the shell that we may eat the kernel' (p. 3). This last image was used by Tyndale (above, p. 13).

[13] This argument is anticipated in the preface: 'we cannot follow a better pattern for elocution than God himself' (p. 11). 'Elocution' here refers to choice of words, and particularly to the use of a variety of words for single things. It does not have the full sense of fine writing that later ages might read into it.

[14] The sixteenth of Wilson's definitions of 'grace' in the second edition of his *Christian Dictionary* seems appropriate here: 'elegance of speech, which made Christ gracious and amiable to all. Ps. 45: 3. *Full of grace are thy lips*. Luke 4: 22. *Words full of grace*'.

The closest to a literary use is in 'a word fitly spoken is like apples of gold in pictures of silver' (Prov. 25: 11). 'So fitly for phrase, so expressly for sense' must therefore be read as consisting of two roughly synonymous phrases.

A similar trio occurs later in the same paragraph. Smith observes that the Septuagint does not come near the original 'for perspicuity, gravity, majesty' (p. 7). The *OED*, taking its use here as an example, defines 'perspicuity' as 'clearness of statement or exposition; freedom from obscurity or ambiguity; lucidity'. This would now be an aesthetic term, but for the translators it described a quality of meaning. 'Gravity' and 'majesty', however, are moving towards their present aesthetic overtones, particularly as differences in quality between the original and the Septuagint are being noted.[15]

It is clear, then, that the translators had some literary sense of the work of translation, but a careful reading of the rest of the preface leaves the reader with an overwhelming awareness of their quest for truth and clarity. This is summed up as the 'desire that the Scripture may speak like itself, as in the language of Canaan, that it may be understood even of the very vulgar' (p. 11), which is exactly the desire of Tyndale. Earlier their work is described as 'the opening and clearing[16] of the word of God' (p. 2). Two aspects of this opening and clearing are given special attention: inconsistent translation and the use of the margin. Here is how the issue of the use of the margin is dealt with:

Some peradventure would have no variety of senses to be set in the margin lest the authority of the Scriptures for deciding of controversies by that show of uncertainty should somewhat be shaken. But we hold their judgement not to be so sound in this point. For though 'whatsoever things are necessary are manifest', as St Chrysostom saith, and as St Augustine, 'in those things that are plainly set down in the Scriptures all such matters are found that concern faith, hope, and charity'. Yet for all that it cannot be dissembled that, partly to exercise and whet our wits, partly to wean the curious from loathing of them for their everywhere plainness . . . it hath pleased God in his divine providence here and there to scatter words and sentences of that difficulty and doubtfulness, not in doctrinal points that concern salvation (for in that it hath been vouched that the Scriptures are plain), but in matters of less moment, that fearfulness would better beseem us than confidence . . . Therefore, as St Augustine saith, that variety of translations is profitable for the finding out of the sense of the Scriptures: so diversity of signification and sense in the margin, where the text

---

[15] For 'majesty', see also pp. 24 above, and 72 below.
[16] 'Clearing' is used partially as a synonym of 'opening'. It also has a sense of the removal of difficulties or apparent inconsistencies, perhaps of rectifying the text. Broughton (see below, p. 75) uses it in this sense when he writes, 'I cleared our Lord's family'.

is not so clear, must needs do good, yea, is necessary, as we are persuaded. (p. 10)

The square emphasis on sense here works against a literary reading of the text; it again implies that the meaning is to be found between or behind the words, and it demands that the reader attend to a choice of words.

Much less is made here than in Geneva or Rheims of literary deficiencies in the Scriptures, but clearly the KJB translators were aware of such deficiencies. 'Plainness' is not necessarily a pejorative term, but the translators see it as arousing loathing among the curious.

Inconsistency has two main aspects: the same word, phrase or even passage in the original may be translated differently in different places, or different words may be represented by the same English word. The preface concentrates on the translators' use of various words for a single original word, and they may well be replying to Broughton:

An other thing we think good to admonish thee of, gentle reader, that we have not tied ourselves to an uniformity of phrasing or to an identity of words, as some peradventure would wish that we had done . . . But that we should express the same notion in the same particular word, as for example, if we translate the Hebrew or Greek word once by 'purpose', never to call it 'intent', if one where 'journeying', never 'travelling' . . . we thought to savour more of curiosity than wisdom, and that rather it would breed scorn in the atheist than bring profit to the godly reader. For is the kingdom of God become words or syllables? why should we be in bondage to them, if we may be free? use one precisely when we may use another no less fit as commodiously? . . . niceness in words was always counted the next step to trifling. (p. 11)

In this the translators were following the example of their predecessors and also reflecting a certain looseness in the spirit of the age. Variety of translation is at one with the tendency to inconsistent phrasing of quotations from the Bible evident in the preface itself and in a number of seventeenth-century writers (see below, pp. 103 ff.). However, a large number of scholars came to think, with Broughton, that inconsistency was a mistake. The preface to the RV NT calls it 'one of the blemishes' in the KJB, and the RV followed the opposite policy.

Such an even-handed attitude to English vocabulary is responsible for some of the quality of the language of the KJB. An example will help to demonstrate this. One of the KJB's most famous lines, 'consider the lilies of the field, how they grow: they toil not, neither do they spin' (Matt. 6: 28), is also rendered, 'consider the lilies how they grow: they toil not, they spin not' (Luke 12: 27). The second version is little known and inferior as English. As translations, they render different Greek verbs with the same English word, 'consider'. The first variation ('lilies of the field', 'lilies') exactly reflects a difference in the Greek: the resonant phrase exists because of literal translation. The last part of the sentence is identical in the Greek of both gospels, οὐ κοπιᾷ, οὐδὲ νήθει, but the KJB in one instance produces the memorable cadence of 'they toil not, neither do they spin' and in the other more accurately reflects the structure of the Greek in the staccato pair of parallel phrases, 'they toil not, they spin not'. Thus three aspects of the KJB translators' work can be seen in this one example: failure to distinguish between different words in the original, literal translation happily producing a phrase of memorable quality, and varying translations in one case producing another such phrase. There is no way of knowing if the last variations were produced for literary reasons, or even, if they were, which version the translators actually considered the better: they could have argued for the parallelism of Luke's version.

The fact that the translators deliberately adopted this policy of inconsistency (even if only because of precedent) is the only evidence that shows a sense of reponsibility towards the English language. However, the passage from the preface does not show genuinely literary motives, even if it lays open the way for choice of vocabulary on literary grounds. The concern is still with precision. 'Fit', as has been shown, does not carry aesthetic connotations, and 'commodiously' is used in the sense of usefully or beneficially for conveying sense.[17] A similar point is made by Ward Allen about the final phrase quoted: 'by niceness Dr Smith means the domination of thought by words rather than the domination of words by thought, or exactness' (*Translating for King James*, p. 12).

The point has now been touched on several times that the preface, like writings of the other translators, shows less concern for literary questions than would appear from a casual reading. The vocabulary is potentially but not actually aesthetic. Since the point is important, several other phrases must be glanced at. Imagery of richness and perfection is frequent, beginning with the phrase, 'not only . . . the riches, but also . . . the perfection of the Scripture' (p. 3). Coming after a statement that 'whatsoever is to be believed or practised or hoped for is contained in' the Scripture, it clearly applies to the Bible's quality as truth. The same is true of another phrase that seems to denote aesthetic quality, 'a treasury

[17] Wilson paraphrases a use of 'commodious' as 'convenient and fit for their purpose'. He writes of a particular reading of the NT Greek 'bearing a more commodious sense by far' (*Christian Dictionary*, 8th ed., p. 77).

of most costly jewels'. Here it is in alliterative, sonorous context: Scripture is 'a physician's shop . . . of preservatives against poisoned heresies; a pandect of profitable laws against rebellious spirits; a treasury of most costly jewels against beggarly rudiments' (p. 3). And here is a similar image used in relation to the translators' job of revision: 'whatsoever is sound already (and all is sound for substance in one or other of our editions . . .), the same will shine as gold more brightly being rubbed and polished; also if any thing be halting or superfluous or not so agreeable to the original, the same may be corrected and the truth set in place' (p. 7). Rubbing and polishing would appear to imply revision of literary quality, but, in the light of the other examples, the tendency to repetition of ideas and the context, again, of 'truth', it must be read as only potentially aesthetic. Finally, the same applies to the statement, 'neither did we disdain to revise that which we had done, and to bring back to the anvil that which we had hammered' (p. 10). Throughout, the translators have in mind the truth of their work.

Their contemporaries would have understood them to have had this in mind. It is only when the connotations of vocabulary have shifted sufficiently from the religious to the aesthetic that the translators could have been understood to be writing of literary qualities in their work.

BOIS'S NOTES

So far the evidence has been of the same sort as is available for the earlier translations. But in the case of the KJB direct evidence exists of the way the work was carried out. There is a copy of the Bishops' Bible with interlinear revisions by the translators, and there is a manuscript draft of the Epistles from the second Westminster company which seems to have been prepared to enable further scholarly opinion on the revision to be sought, probably in obedience to instruction nine.[18] Neither gives any explanations for the changes, so one can do no more than infer the reasons for them, and such inferences are dangerous. They should not be made until a sound sense of the translators' purposes and preoccupations is established. A third source of evidence, still subject to varying interpretation, does record discussion. It is the notes made by one of the

---

[18] The Bishops' Bible is in the Bodleian Library, Bib. Eng. 1602; Allen and Edward C. Jacobs, *The Coming of the King James Gospels* (Fayetteville: University of Arkansas Press, 1995) gives the NT annotations. The draft of the Epistles is in Lambeth Palace Library, MS 98, published in Ward Allen, ed., *Translating the New Testament Epistles 1604–1611: A Manuscript from the King James's Westminster Company* (Ann Arbor: University Microfilms International for Vanderbilt University Press), 1977.

translators, John Bois, during the final revision of the Epistles and Revelation. They show the Greek text being criticised and analysed, both for the exact meaning of words and phrases, and the figures of speech and grammatical constructions used; they show word-for-word translations being made and set alongside more English renderings, synonyms being listed, alternative translations being compared, and, finally, they show signs of literary sensitivity in considering both the Greek and possible English renderings. Almost all the notes concern the truth of the text, as in the following, which includes the idea of truth. I give it first as it appears in Bois's notes, then in Allen's translation, which will be used for the subsequent notes. It concerns Col. 2: 2, which reads in the KJB, 'that their hearts might be comforted, being knit together in love, and unto all riches of the full assurance of understanding'. Bois writes:

being knit together in love, [and instructed] in all riches etc. τό συμβιβάζω utrumque significat, et compingo, et instruo, sive doceo: non abhorret itaque a vero, apostolum utriusque significationis rationem habuisse.

being knit together in love, [and instructed] in all riches etc. The word συμβιβάζω [knit together, compare] signifies both at once, join together, and instruct, or teach: it is not inconsistent with the truth therefore, that the apostle took account of both meanings.[19]

This is characteristic. The care for the truth of the writing involves a careful examination of possible meanings to the extent of supposing a deliberate play on the meaning of a word. Scholarly examination of the text here necessitates a literary awareness. As is usually the case in these notes, the translation eventually adopted is not given.

Of the nearly 500 notes, only three give a clear sense of literary awareness in the choice of English (another four are at best ambiguous evidence). That there are so few shows that almost all of the translators' attention was devoted to scholarship, but the work was not absolutely bereft of literary considerations.

The note to Rom. 11: 31 is the first to have a clear literary aspect:

Theophylact places a comma after ἠπείθησαν [not believed] although commonly the comma is placed after ἐλέει [mercy]. A.D. thinks that the common punctuation ought to be retained, because otherwise the transposition will be extremely harsh, and that other punctuation rests upon the authority of no transcripts. (p. 41)

---

[19] *Translating for King James*, pp. 62–3. Where Bois uses English, Allen italicises. Allen adds literal translations of the Greek words discussed in square brackets.

'A.D.' is Andrew Downes, one of the translators. He appears to be reinforcing the conclusions of textual scholarship with appeal to the possible consquences on the literary quality of the English.

The next note concerns 2 Tim. 1: 3 and is one of the clearest examples of care for the sound of the English:

ὡς ἀδιάλειπτον ἔχω] [without ceasing I have] i.e. ἔχων ἀδιάλειπτον etc. [without ceasing having] . . . For if the words are accepted as they sound at first hearing, it will make an ill-joint for this clause with the preceding. I therefore thus soften the harshness of the speech, *I give God thanks whom I serve from mine Ancestors with a pure conscience*, then the following words all the way to the beginning of verse five I enclose in parenthetical marks. (p. 71)

Though this makes plain a care for English, it is perhaps no more than a care for clarity. But what is of equal interest is that this criticism and suggestion was not accepted. The phrase objected to survives unaltered from the Bishops' Bible.

Lastly, here is the one note which contains literary considerations only; it concerns Hebr. 13: 8:

yesterday, and to day the same, and for ever] A.D. If the words be arranged in this manner, ὁ λόγος [the statement] will be σεπνότερος [more majestic]. A.D. (p. 87)

It is significant, however, that this too was not the version adopted, which was 'Jesus Christ the same yesterday, and today, and for ever'. Since Downes follows the word order of the Greek, and the eventual version differs from preceding versions, one can only guess that it was adopted as being the most accurate interpretation of the Greek. The final version is arguably less majestic than Downes's suggestion. Thus even when there is clear evidence of the existence of care for English, there is further evidence that this was not allowed to affect the translation.

CONCLUSION

The combined evidence of the preface and Bois's notes makes the conclusion inescapable that while the translators had a literary sense of their work, it was totally subordinated to their quest for accuracy of scholarship and translation. Whatever one considers the positive literary qualities of the KJB to be, they do not exist through a deliberate attempt on the part of either the KJB translators or their predecessors to write good English.

It is reasonable to assume that had it been a major intention of the

KJB translators to produce a fine English version of the Scriptures, the result would have been quite unlike the KJB; it would have lost its scholarly merit and very likely have had little esteem among the people. Much of the quality of the KJB as English exists because the translators and their predecessors strove for something other than writing stylish English. Their fidelity to the originals transmitted some, perhaps much, of their alien but real literary quality into English. The search for clarity and the ideal of simple comprehensibility inherited from Tyndale, though much older than him, were better ultimate criteria for literary quality than any the translators might have adopted as a deliberate literary principle.

EPILOGUE: BROUGHTON'S LAST WORD

The translators anticipated a hostile reception for their work:

Zeal to promote the common good, whether it be by devising any thing ourselves or revising that which hath been laboured by others, deserveth certainly much respect and esteem, but yet findeth but cold entertainment in the world. It is welcomed with suspicion instead of love, and with emulation [disparagement] instead of thanks; and if there be any hole left for cavil to enter (and cavil, if it do not find a hole, will make one), it is sure to be misconstrued and in danger to be condemned. This will easily be granted by as many as know story or have any experience. For, was there ever anything projected, that savoured any way of newness or renewing, but the same endured many a storm of gainsaying or opposition? . . . For he that meddleth with men's religion in any part, meddleth with their custom, nay, with their freehold; and though they find no content in that which they have, yet they cannot abide to hear of altering. (Preface, pp. 1, 2)

However, if there was a general storm such as they anticipated, almost all direct evidence of it has disappeared. While the work was going on, as the translators report, 'many men's mouths have been open a good while (and yet are not stopped) with speeches about the translation, so long in hand, or rather, perusals of translations made before' (p. 6). Presumably these mouths remained open – and not with wonder – yet, had not Hugh Broughton carried out his determination to censure the new translation, it might seem that the KJB fell into a vacuum.

The truth is probably this: for all the significance 1611 now has in the history of the English Bible, the publication of the KJB was not an event. Publication then was not the kind of occasion it is usually made into now. Moreover, there was no mechanism for the critical reception of new work. What discussion there was was verbal (though if the work was controversial it drew forth replies in the form of pamphlets or books). But there are more particular reasons why the publication of the KJB, if an event at all, was not much of one. First, it was left to make its way in competition with existing Bibles, especially the Geneva, which continued to be highly popular. Second, and perhaps more important, most people were not concerned with the precise verbal form of their Bible: one translation was as good as another. This, of course, presents a paradox: it appears to go against the abundance of evidence that the KJB translators were pressured to be, and indeed tried to be, as literally accurate as reasonably possible. But, as has been seen (above, pp. 53 ff.), the separation of pith and husk led to a downplaying of the husk, and the evidence of the way the Bible was quoted at this time shows a paraphrastic disregard for the literal word of whatever translation was being used. If translation was but a guide to the truth of the original for those unable to read the original, it is perhaps not surprising that the same kind of scholars who demanded accuracy in a translation for the people should be unconcerned with fidelity to a mere translation themselves. Lastly, the KJB did not appear intially in a popular form but as a large and expensive folio. This too muted the impact of its publication.

A consequence of this lack of reception for the KJB is that the year 1611 is hardly a truer historical dividing point than, say, the turn of a century. The same Bibles continued to be read. The Roman Catholic Bible and attitude to Bible translation continued to be a matter of controversy. The Psalms and other poetic parts of the original Scriptures continued to rise in reputation, and they continued to be translated. Nobody was interested in the merits of the new Bible as a piece of English writing.

It is therefore better to close the story of the literary and linguistic attitudes of the Bible translators with the only extant comment on the qualities of the new Bible, for Broughton's reaction, though perhaps owing much to his own disappointments, still reflects much of the spirit of the time. It also in significant ways begins the movement towards the RV, some of the early critics of which were mocked as Broughtons. His response, 'a censure of the late translation for our Churches, sent unto a right worshipful knight, attendant upon the King', was written in either 1611 or 1612 (when he died), and begins: 'the late Bible, right worshipful, was sent me to censure, which bred in me a sadness that will grieve me while I breathe. It is so ill done. Tell his Majesty that I had rather be rent in pieces with wild horses than any such translation by my consent should be urged upon poor Churches' (*Works*, III: 661). Broughton's objections, of which he lists ten, show, as one would expect, that the KJB did indeed receive the minute cavilling attention that Myles Smith had feared. The most colourful is the second objection, which is to Jesus being called the son of God in Luke 3: the translators, he writes,

in fifteen verses bring fifteen score idle words for accompts in the day of judgement, and bring Joseph to be the son of all men there, where thus Saint Luke meant: Jesus was called of the Father My Son, being son of Joseph, as men thought . . . A Jew of Amsterdam objected the Bishop's error to deny the New Testament, that omitted how Christ should come of David. Thereupon I cleared our Lord's family. Bancroft raved. I gave the anathema. Christ judged his own cause.[20]

The argument is entirely about accuracy of translation and the removal of inconsistencies in matters such as chronology. Broughton has nothing to say of the English qualities of the translation. To judge from his remarks, such considerations are irrelevant.

---

[20] III: 661. 'The Bishops' are the translators of the Bishops' Bible. Bishop Bancroft was one of the KJB translators.

CHAPTER FOUR

Literary implications of Bible presentation

PRESENTATIONS OF THE TEXT, 1525–1625

At all times there are probably more hearers than readers of the Bible. Sometimes they hear the incomprehensible sounds of a foreign language. Sometimes they hear brief extracts, often no more than a fragment of a verse, used as the basis of sermons, or as authorities in arguments or even as decorations for discourses. Sometimes they hear sustained readings, a chapter or more at a time, perhaps forming part of a methodical progress through the Bible. Sometimes also they hear parodies. The heard Bible, one may suggest, was best known as a fragmentary, interpreted thing, presented within some religious context. Further, it is likely that for many people in the period of the translators, rather as in the present century, the words of any particular text could vary from one hearing to the next. Not only were there alternative versions in print, but the educated, at least, were constantly producing their own translations or paraphrases of a verse as they cited it (see below, pp. 103 ff.). The people probably did not become familiar with a fixed form of words for any of the parts of the Bible. This would have been true even of that most popular part of the Bible, the Psalms. Though the Sternhold and Hopkins Psalter held sway, it gives many of the Psalms in two or three versions, and they might also be heard in the PB version and the differing versions of the Bible translations. Since the Bible, the PB and the singing Psalter were often bound together, it would not be uncommon to have within the covers of one volume as many as five different versions of a Psalm, two prose and three verse. For at least a century following Tyndale's NT the people would have had a sense that the English form of the Bible was unfixed. It is difficult to do more than speculate what effects the heard text had in this time. That they were various is certain, that they produced much sense of the Bible as a literary entity is doubtful.

If, however, one turns to the printed text as a shaper of reading, one can go further. This was the time when the text was given to the literate population as a reading text; by 1625 it was available in something like the variety of presentations we have now. The only main presentation missing was the kind that was introduced at the end of the nineteenth century for appreciation as literature.

To read the Bible to oneself is an essentially private experience. If the reader is reading the text by itself, he is as likely to be having a literary experience of some sort as he is to be having a religious experience. The more that text is presented without doctrinal interference, the more it has the potential to be a genuinely literary text. If, further, prose and poetry are distinguished in the presentation, then a rudimentary sense of different literary forms is conveyed. Conversely, the more interpretive or ordering material is included, the more the reader's attention is taken away from the text alone and the less the text exists as a literary entity. Not only does such editorial material control and limit the text's imaginative possibilities in a ruthlessly doctrinal way (not until the eighteenth century does one find Bibles with annotations that point to literary matters), but it breaks up the singleness of the reader's engagement with the text.

Now, some Bibles, by their size or their cost, were not suited to private reading. It is of course a limitation of the possibilities of literary experience to confine them to private reading, and the presentation of the text in lectern Bibles may well have influenced the way that it was read aloud and therefore the way that it was experienced aurally. But what can be examined most profitably here is the relationship between private reading and visual presentation, and in this, size is a crucial factor. The large folio Bibles were rarely read privately. Not only was this an economic matter – few people could afford such Bibles – it was also a matter of manageability. Anything larger than the quarto Geneva Bible was likely to rule itself out as a private literary text. Consequently there is an element of unreality in considering, say, the Great Bible: the effects of its size dominate. But this does not make such folio Bibles irrelevant. In the early days of the printed English Bible they were the only form in which the whole text was available. Though they were not often privately owned, they were studied – as indeed their makers hoped they would be.

Tyndale, as has already been seen (above, p. 15), intended to publish his first NT with annotations, and a sample of these can be seen in plate 1. However, the first complete printing (Herbert 2)[1] lacks annotations and, unintentionally, is as literary a presentation of the text as there has

---

[1] All the Bibles mentioned in this chapter are identified by their number in A.S. Herbert's *Historical Catalogue* for ease of identification.

ever been. The only extra-textual material is Tyndale's address to the reader. The text is neatly printed in black letter as prose; it has clear and frequent paragraph divisions which keep the narrative or argument moving in easy steps, but not so easy that the context and continuity are destroyed. If a care for paragraphing bespeaks a care for the flow of the text and for the reader's ease of comprehension, then Tyndale is a most solicitous, not to say literary, punctuator. There is no significant history to be traced here, however: Coverdale and the Great Bible generally follow Tyndale, though without preserving all his breaks, and then the whole question becomes a minor, almost invisible issue as verse division takes over. Indeed, the Bishops' Bible does not bother with paragraphs at all, and it is a historical curiosity that the KJB ceases to mark paragraph divisions after Acts 20.

Tyndale's first NT has decorative capitals at the beginnings of books, but nothing else bar the quality of the typography to convey a visual impression that the volume is special or grand (the typography is obviously superior to that of the NTs shown in plates 3 and 7). Titles in individual books are given at the top of each pair of pages, and the chapters are divided from each other by a simple heading giving the chapter number. Two variations only are made to the presentation: the genealogies are given as lists, and, much more importantly, the songs at the beginning of Luke are clearly presented as poetry (plate 2). Thus both visually and in terms of the lack of interference with the text, this book is a literary presentation of the NT. Its appearance is exactly that of a secular prose work. The text alone engages the reader's mind and imagination, and the printing preserves, in the few instances where it is appropriate, a sense of literary forms.

In terms of size also it resembles a novel to modern eyes, though a long one, being just over 700 pages. Physically, it is thoroughly well-adapted to private ownership and reading.

There are gradual but significant changes visible through the later editions. Not all of them preserve the verse form of the Luke songs. The 1536 folio (Herbert 27) reduces them to paragraphs, marking their verse form only by using different capitals from normal. There appears, however, to have been a growing interest in pleasing the eye of the reader: illustrations appear in Revelation, and initial capitals become more elaborate, being at their best in the 1536 quarto (Herbert 19). There is a certain sense of grandeur conveyed by these illustrations, and this fits with the move to larger formats. The results feel less private and more awe-inspiring.

What is most significant about all the later editions is the inclusion of extra-textual material. Tyndale's new preface moves to the front of the book (which is where his original prologue had been in 1525), detailed tables of contents appear, and there is some other prefatory material. It all reminds the reader that he is opening the book of truth. References and notes make their appearance in the margin, but they do so in most of the editions without impinging on the text: it still remains in the middle of each page as a pure entity for the reader, but if the reader's eye strays to the margin he is at once reminded that the book is to be studied as truth. If the reader pays real attention to the margin then the continuity of the text as a piece of writing is lost. At least two editions (Antwerp, 1534, and London, 1536; Herbert 13 and 27) go further by having marks, usually asterisks, within the text to draw the reader's attention to the margin. This happens only rarely in the 1534 edition, and the practical difference for a reader coming to it from the earlier editions is minimal. But in historical terms the change is major: extra-textual material is intruding into the text and beginning to break down its continuity and completeness.

Coverdale's NTs belong here. Setting aside his version from the Vulgate, they show no significant changes from the asterisked Tyndales just noted. Still the text is in paragraphs, with a poetic form used for the songs in Luke. Apart from one very small edition (Antwerp: G. Montanus, 1538; Herbert 43) produced for the cheap end of the market, there is an increase in the number of illustrations, especially in the Matthew Crom octavo (Antwerp, 1538; Herbert 40), and there are some annotations at the ends of chapters (plate 3). Even so, the bare text can still be read with no more difficulty than in the London Tyndale of 1536.

All these texts represent personal or perhaps family, rather than public, Bibles. What is most significant about them is that they are directed towards study of the text. It is of course a historical accident that they begin with a bare text. Tyndale's intention was to create a study text. The possibilities of continuous reading as if of a literary text result from the remnants of the feeling that the Bible is easy to understand, but more from the fact that this was a pioneering publication: it takes time to develop a set of annotations. These NTs lead directly to the heavily-annotated Geneva texts.

The first of the complete Bibles, Coverdale, 1535 (Herbert 18), is more of a literary Bible than the last of the NTs just described. As with the early Tyndales, this is readily accounted for on pioneering grounds. Only rarely does it intrude on the text with an asterisk. Though it gives a list of contents before each book, it has almost no prefatory material or annotations, and does no more than place some cross-references at the foot of the page. It too distinguishes the songs in Luke as poetry, and does the same with OT songs, including Lamentations, but not, significantly, Psalms, Job or the Song of Songs, thus stopping short of a consistent recognition in the printed form of differences between prose and poetry. Illustrations are confined to title pages and the beginnings of books. The most striking visual difference, the division of the page into two columns, may seem to be of no real significance for a reader, for this is still essentially a paragraph Bible, presenting an uninterrupted reading text; nevertheless, it marks the beginning in English Bibles of distinctive biblical form.[2] The Bible was beginning to look like itself (plate 4).

Unlike the NTs, this Bible adopts an old practice of placing letters in the margin at regular intervals to help the reader locate passages within chapters. Here, like the first appearance of asterisks, it is quite unobtrusive, but it too is of major historical importance for the printed English Bible: it anticipates verse division, one of the most significant of all obtrusions.

The Matthew Bible of 1537 (Herbert 34) presents some important changes. It is more awe-inspiring, not merely in being a larger folio, but in the amount of red ink it uses in the substantial prefatory material and, particularly, in the quality and quantity of its engravings. It is a Bible for public show. Nevertheless, it was also intended as a study Bible: it is annotated, often at such length that the bottoms of columns have to be used and the page is blackened. A series of hieroglyphics intrudes into the text to draw the reader to the annotations. Though all this militates very strongly against literary reading, the use of poetic form now includes the Psalms, thus extending the reader's consciousness of literary forms. Finally, the presentation of the Song of Songs is interesting. Coverdale's text is followed, but statements of who is speaking are added in red print (plate 5). This forces the religious allegory onto the text and makes it difficult for the reader to perceive the text literally. So despite the changed presentation of some of the poetry, the Matthew Bible is a strong move away from the literary towards the religious and the ecclesiastical.

The main Bibles of the time, the Great Bibles, do not reach the standards of Matthew. Illustrations are few and small, and the whole appear-

---

[2] Two-column printing goes back to the Gutenburg Bibles, and they imitated manuscript practice.

ance is less likely to produce awe, though by no means poor (plate 6). Prose and poetry are not distinguished, and, though there are few annotations, the text is often interrupted with signs. All in all, they are thoroughly adequate for their job of providing Churches with impressive volumes of the largest size, but there is a half-heartedness to them in their double role. They are a somewhat mystifying text for any reader because the hieroglyphics within the text hint at special significance without explaining what that might be. There are summaries at the beginnings of chapters, but it is rare for these to have any doctrinal content such as is contained in the summary at the beginning of the Song of Songs: 'a mystical song of the spiritual and Godly love between Christ the spouse and the Church or congregation his spousess'. This is the only gloss given to that book. It is as if the makers of the Great Bibles, though obviously working to produce a public text, had in mind some studious private reading but have stopped short of providing a proper apparatus for this. Their text is part way between a plain reading and an annotated study text.

There were several attempts to produce cheaper Bibles for private ownership, notably those revised by Edmund Becke in the middle of the century. One of these was in five parts (1549–51; Herbert 81 etc.); the OT has chapter summaries and some annotations, with intrusive marks in the text, but they are not so frequent as to interfere seriously with continuous reading. However, the edition of Tyndale's NT published in the same size by the same printers in 1551 (Herbert 96) is more heavily annotated, and 'the printer to the reader', which may be by Becke, makes clear the expectation of close study rather than continuous reading. The annotations are 'for the better understanding of the text', and the writer adds that he has increased their number and set them at the ends of chapters, with numbers in the text to draw the reader's attention to them. Thus the presentation of the text is broken up, and literary reading effectively discouraged. Moreover, a specific kind of religious reading is encouraged, fragmentary study. The reader is being directed to texts rather than to the text (plate 7).

The Geneva Bible, and also the Rheims-Douai Bible, place the emphasis very strongly on private ownership, close study and doctrinal correctness. They are personal teaching Bibles. Everything in them works against a continuous reading of the text alone. Whittingham, in his preface to the Geneva NT of 1557 (Herbert 106), discusses the presentation and its purpose. The book is aimed at 'the simple lambs, which partly are already in the fold of Christ, and so hear willingly their

Shepherd's voice, and partly wandering astray by ignorance, tarry the time till the Shepherd find them and bring them unto his flock' (fol. **iir). The first thing Whittingham has done to profit this kind of reader is to divide 'the text into verses and sections, according to the best editions in other languages' (fol. **iiv). This is the first English Bible to have verse divisions (chapter divisions are much older), and is a very significant move away from a literary Bible, for it carries the visual interruption of the text to an extreme. In the Geneva Bibles each verse begins on a new line, as if it is a new paragraph. The effect is not only to destroy the literary (and theological) continuity that presentation in prose paragraphs gave, but also to say strongly to the reader that the Bible can and perhaps should be read in minute fragments. Implicitly, Tyndale's insistence on the 'process, order and meaning' of the text is destroyed. Though this is the most serious consequence of verse division as practised by the makers of the Geneva Bible, there is also the consequence that any visual distinction between prose and poetry is destroyed. The Bible in this form is neither prose nor poetry (plate 9). Just as poetry is printed with a capital letter at the beginning of each line, so each verse begins with a capital letter even if it is not the beginning of a sentence. The whole text is in the form that the Day and Seres 1551 Tyndale used for the Benedictus (plate 7). Moreover, this develops the implications of the double columns. From now on the Bible had its own distinctive visual forms that were an instant statement to any reader that it was not a secular text and that it should be read with an attitude appropriate to the book of truth.

Whittingham's next innovation is to distinguish typographically any words added to the text for the sake of clarity. This is a visual reminder that the text is not the true one but a translation. Again attention is directed away from the continuity and purity of the English version as a self-contained literary structure. His intention as an annotator is not merely to supply the reader with an NT, but also to supply the equivalent of commentaries, either for those who cannot afford them or for those who have not opportunity or time to read them.

Yet not all is loss from the literary point of view, especially in the NT as against the whole Bible. The change from black letter to Roman type[3] represents an enormous gain in clarity and so reduces the effort of attention needed to follow the text. It is also a move away from adornment to utility: black letter, imitative of script, was becoming a visual statement

---

[3] Roman type had been used for Exodus, Leviticus and Deuteronomy in Tyndale's 1530 Pentateuch.

of antique majesty. Black letter against Roman type is, in small degree, the equivalent of the Vulgate against vernacular translation.

The Geneva Bible as a whole became available in a range of formats which present different effects. Three from the same printer, the King's printer Robert Barker, show this: his octavo of 1608, his quarto of 1610 and his folio of 1612 (Herbert 296, 303, 312). Both the quarto and the folio show a substantial increase in the number and length of annotations.[4] Indeed, there is so much annotation that it frequently intrudes into the main columns of the text. The folio accommodates this relatively easily, and the text itself remains clear enough and distinct from the annotations. If one can ignore the marks within the text and the staccato effect of the verse division, then the text may be read without too much interference from the annotations. In the quarto the pressures of space have caused a reduction in the print size for the text and in the border around the annotations, so that many pages, especially in the NT, are black with print (plate 11). The marks within the text are nearer to the size of the text itself, so pulling the reader more strongly towards the notes than does the folio. Both books are blatantly study Bibles, but the folio, because of the space available on the page, retains a greater readability.

Space again affects the octavo: it necessitates a marked reduction in annotation and an elimination of the illustrations. A characteristic page from this presents the text in two columns of print so small that it has to be peered at; there are summaries at the beginnings of chapters and at the tops of pages, and a margin strewn with cross-references. It is hardly a pleasing Bible to use, but the possibility is again present of reading the text uninterruptedly.

At the time of the publication of the KJB, then, Geneva Bibles were available for all levels of the market, and it was possible for the purchaser to choose to a limited extent how far he wanted to have a text that was readable without interruption.

The Geneva Bible of 1560 (Herbert 107) and many but by no means all of the subsequent editions contain a small number of illustrations. At first sight this seems to be a continuation of the love of decoration so evident in the Matthew Bible, but the address to the reader shows that this is not so. After repeating Whittingham's description of the aids for understanding, the address continues:

---

[4] Lawrence Tomson's notes on the NT were added in 1576, and, in 1599, Franciscus Junius's notes on Revelation.

Furthermore whereas certain places in the books of Moses, of the Kings and Ezekiel seemed so dark that by no description they could be made easy to the simple reader, we have so set them forth with figures and notes for the full declaration thereof that they . . . by the perspective and as it were by the eye may sufficiently know the true meaning of all such places. Whereunto also we have added certain maps of cosmography which necessarily serve for the perfect understanding and memory of divers places and countries, partly described, and partly by occasion touched, both in the Old and New Testament.

Second sight bears this out. The illustrations are for the most part diagrams or maps. Often they are of considerable complexity, as in 'the vision of Ezekiel' (plate 10). Where there is something more like a picture, as in the illustration for 'the garments of the high priest' (Exodus 28), the priest is not put in a scene, and, paralleling what was happening in the texts, there are letters within the picture which relate to the notes below. This is very different from, say, the Matthew Bible. The pleasure in pictorial narrative that its Low German illustrations show is drastically diminished. The change from picture to diagram is the pictorial equivalent of the movement away from literary presentation of the text; that it is done in the name of understanding is exactly consistent with the history of attitudes to translation.

In visual terms the Geneva Bible was the century's most influential version, but in some respects the Rheims NT (Herbert 177), less pleasing though it is, presented better solutions to the problems of combining a reading text with verse division and annotation. The bulk of the annotations is placed at the ends of chapters, is clearly marked off by lines, and is distinguished further by the use of a smaller typeface. The reader wanting a continuous text can jump over these lumps in a twinkling. But what is most effective is the removal of verse numbering to the margins. This allows the prose paragraphing to appear with proper clarity, and removes the need for capital letters within sentences that flow over the verse divisions. The verse form of the songs stands out, especially as it is emphasised through the use of italics (plate 12). The Rheims NT is as resolutely doctrinal a Bible as the Geneva Bible, but it shows that the demands of doctrine and reference need not break up the continuity of the reading text or destroy the awareness of literary form. It is a pity that the KJB did not follow this example.

The folio Bishops' Bibles are essentially a piece of grand church architecture, very impressive but hardly suited to the private reader. Yet they have tables, a diagram (plate 14), maps and various editorial addresses to the 'gentle reader' that make it clear that Parker was trying to create something like a study Bible as well as a church Bible. This desire is also visible in the kind of marginal annotation shown in the plate and in the arguments given at the beginnings of chapters. By comparison with Geneva, the annotations are light and uncontroversial (many pages have none, but a few have their margins filled). The desire and, one presumes, the demand for instruction were inescapable at this time. Even in this ecclesiastical version it competes with the desire for majesty.

Not all Bishops' Bibles were folios. There are black-letter octavos such as Jugge's of 1569 and 1573 (Herbert 126, 135), produced for the private market, and some copies have been used like Geneva Bibles: there are underlinings, comments, names and dates.[5] As one might expect from the example and popularity of Geneva, these octavos are more heavily annotated than the folios. Thus the anti-literary tendencies evident of the Geneva Bible and the Douai OT become quite marked in official Bibles as soon as they are printed for private ownership.

The KJB as printed by Robert Barker in 1611 (Herbert 309) is an even grander piece of Church architecture than the Bishops' Bible in terms of its size and the impressiveness of its prefatory material (plates 14 and 15). The engraved titlepage is superior to that of any of the earlier English Bibles. Though the KJB lacks illustrations except in the prefatory material, its presentation of the text is similar to that of the Bishops' Bible, the verses being given as individual numbered paragraphs in the same size of black-letter type. Instead of the chapter summaries also being in black letter, they are clarified by being in Roman type. One of Geneva's annoying practices is adopted, the use of small Roman type for words not in the original. The margin is free from the kind of annotations that dominate Geneva and Rheims-Douai: all it has are cross-references and notes on literal or alternative readings. The main typographical change from the Bishops' Bible is the enclosure of the columns, headings and margins in boxes such as can often be seen hand-ruled in older Bibles. As in the first two-column Bibles, nothing but the heading goes across both columns. There is no knowing whether the KJB was presented in this way to give an appearance of puritanical rigidity as well as neatness, but that is the effect. Visually, it is the text in corsets (plate 16).

The obvious use of such a volume is ecclesiastical, the obvious effect awe-inspiring earnestness. Could one imagine it as a privately-read

---

[5] The Bible Society's copy of the 1569 edition is inscribed, shakily, 'Thomas Johnson his Booke 1666' opposite the NT titlepage, and, on the same page, there are various calculations of the age of the book, the latest being made in 1848.

Bible, it would present a striking retreat from the doctrinal studiousness of Geneva and Rheims-Douai, and something of a retreat from the Bishops' Bible's compromises with the desire to instruct. Very rarely it tries to impose a doctrinal reading, as in the Song of Songs where the allegorical interpretation is present both in the summaries at the beginnings of the chapters and at the top of the pages. Even so, the text is far from the kind of literary form that Tyndale's first NT showed. No sense at all is conveyed of either poetry or prose, or of any distinction between the two. It is further interrupted by hieroglyphics and the use of Roman type. If size did not debar it, therefore, the KJB in its first form would represent a minor move back towards literary form.

The most interesting editions of the KJB from a literary point of view are not the folios but the smaller editions suitable for private ownership. These began to appear in 1612 and are indeed a move back towards a literary presentation of the text such as the great first volume suggested could happen. If we take three more Barker Bibles representing the smaller formats of the KJB in its early years, his 1612 quarto, 1615 octavo and 1620 duodecimo (Herbert 313, 343, 377), two significant facts emerge. First, Roman type is used: the grandeur of black letter is replaced by clarity for the private reader. Second, although the quarto and octavo retain the headings and the marginal material of the folio, the duodecimo is a bare text with only the page headings retained. Though these headings very occasionally point to an interpretation, the text is largely returned to the response of the private reader.

The duodecimo is the barest text since Tyndale's first NT, but it still differs in significant respects, all connected with verse division. Each verse is a separate numbered paragraph. Paragraph marks only hint at the breaks and continuities of prose. Because of the demand verses make on space, and because of the sheer length of the Bible, the text is still in two columns. The text thus does not look like any literary works the reader might be familiar with, nor does it give any sense of literary form. The literary gain of a nearly uninterrupted pure text is balanced against the fact that the text is presented not in the form of a work of literature but unmistakably in the form of a Bible.

Viewed as a whole, the changing presentations have important literary consequences, but none of them, except perhaps the movement away from presenting poetry as poetry, represents a deliberate reaction against literary presentation, for none of the presentations were conceived of as literary. In terms of the printing history of the time, they represent efforts to develop appropriate theological or ecclesiastical presentations, or a combination of both, modified as necessary by economic factors. Only in one respect can this movement be considered theologically retrograde: Tyndale's sense of the continuity of the text and the importance of context is progressively destroyed by the development of annotation and verse division.

From 1617 onwards the English people had an almost complete range of choice of the kind of Bible they could use. One of the choices they could make was between a bare and an annotated text. A reading text was available if anyone wanted just that. The fact that the Geneva annotations were so popular and later found their way into some versions of the KJB suggests that few people really wanted the bare text: they wanted the theological text. Popular demand in this way matched the dominant tendency in Bible publishing for private ownership, the tendency away from literary to theological presentation.

JOHN LOCKE'S CRITICISM OF THE PRESENTATION OF THE TEXT

Critical attention to the implications of chapter and verse division was rare. The philosopher John Locke (1632–1704) made the most important points, and his ideas were occasionally repeated. He identifies a major difficulty in understanding Paul's sense in his Epistles as

the dividing of them into chapters and verses . . . whereby they are so chopped and minced, and, as they are now printed, stand so broken and divided that not only the common people take the verses usually for distinct aphorisms, but even men of more advanced knowledge in reading them lose very much of the strength and force of the coherence and the light that depends on it. Our minds are so weak and narrow that they have need of all the helps and assistances [that] can be procured to lay before them undisturbedly the thread and coherence of any discourse, by which alone they are truly improved and led into the genuine sense of the author. When the eye is constantly disturbed with loose sentences that by their standing and separation appear as so many distinct fragments, the mind will have much ado to take in and carry on in its memory an uniform discourse of dependent reasonings, especially having from the cradle been used to wrong impressions concerning them, and constantly accustomed to hear them quoted as distinct sentences, without any limitation or explication of their precise meaning from the place they stand in and the relation they bear to what goes before or follows. These divisions also have given occasion to the reading these Epistles by parcels and in scraps, which has further confirmed the evil arising from such partitions. (*Epistles of St Paul*, p. vii)

Now, Locke's concern is the old, old theological concern with understanding the true meaning. Yet the kind of reading he wants to promote by eliminating the misleading divisions is only to be distinguished from a literary reading by its purpose. His description of how he had to read the Epistles to understand them properly would have won approval from the author of *Practical Criticism*, I.A. Richards:

I concluded it necessary, for the understanding of any one of St Paul's Epistles, to read it all through at one sitting and to observe as well as I could the drift and design of his writing it. If the first reading gave me some light, the second gave me more; and so I persisted on reading constantly the whole Epistle over at once till I came to have a good general view of the apostle's main purpose in writing the Epistle, the chief branches of his discourse wherein he prosecuted it, the arguments he used and the disposition of the whole.

This, I confess, is not to be obtained by one or two hasty readings: it must be repeated again and again, with a close attention to the tenor of the discourse and a perfect neglect of the divisions into chapters and verses. (p. xv)

The tiny shift needed to make reading both theological and literary is accomplished by putting the point in the context of a care for 'pleasure and advantage', as Anthony Blackwall was to do. Blackwall is as concerned with 'the beauty and strength of the period' as with 'the conclusiveness of the reasoning and the connection and dependence of the context' (*Sacred Classics*, II: 124–5; this immediately precedes his plagiarising the first passage quoted from Locke).

The kind of presentation Locke and Blackwall want (save that neither would eliminate commentary) is that which Tyndale had given his NT, continuous prose ordered only by paragraph breaks and occasional larger divisions, and poetry distinguished visually. In a very important way, the pure religious text and the pure literary text are identical. It is the *practical* religious text that is so different from the literary text. Tynedale's insistence on 'the process, order and meaning of the text' is exactly Locke's insistence on reading Paul whole. Yet it was historical accident rather than choice that led Tyndale to present the pure text. The utility of verse division for study and reference outweighed its disadvantages. Hardly anybody before Locke was aware that there were disadvantages, and all the cogency of Locke's argument was insufficient to persuade the world that the disadvantages outweighed the utility. Most KJBs and other versions have retained it, though some ways have been found to minimise its interference with the text.

CHAPTER FIVE

The struggle for acceptance

THE DEFEAT OF THE GENEVA BIBLE

Sir Arthur Quiller-Couch, lecturing at Cambridge during the First World War, asked his audience to assent with him 'that the Authorised Version of the Holy Bible is, as a literary achievement, one of the greatest in our language; nay, with the possible exception of the complete works of Shakespeare, the very greatest'. He was confident of agreement – 'you will certainly not deny this' – for he was enunciating a generally-held belief.[1] The English Bible, embodiment of the world's greatest collection of literature, matched the originals for quality of language, even if it did not convey their truth with the utmost accuracy; it was the creation of masters of the English language whose work was perfected through the artistry of the King James translators; such was its quality of language that it was instantly acclaimed and given due supremacy over all other versions.

A present-day reader might well assent to the literary judgement, but the historical aspect is a myth. However fine the English of the translators from Tyndale on now seems, no one in their time appreciated it. It was all too obviously poor, if it was worth considering at all. And that was the way it continued to appear to most people until well into the eighteenth century. Must one therefore conclude that the English Bible was the proverbial pearl cast before swine? And that the swine at some point in the eighteenth century received an illumination, that they were suddenly dazzled by the pearl? Or is the truth that the English Bible was less of a pearl and the English people of the sixteenth and seventeenth centuries much less swine-like than they might seem?

It would be foolish to treat perhaps ten generations of English readers and listeners from the time of Tyndale to the mid-eighteenth century as swine, and foolish not to question the real nature of the pearl. What if

---

[1] *On the Art of Reading* (Cambridge University Press, 1920), p. 155.

those ten generations were as right about the English Bible as the succeeding ten generations with their opposite view? The enjoyment of
good writing is no modern invention, the formation of unsound judgements does not just belong to the past.

Just how little the English translators worked as literary artists I have
already shown. If there was instant acclaim for the KJB, all evidence of
it has been lost, whereas evidence of dissatisfaction has survived. In
short, there has been a reversal in the KJB's literary fortunes, from
vilification to the highest praise, that must be recognised and accounted
for. What did the Victorians see in the KJB that the Jacobeans did not?
Where are the historical lines to be drawn between these attitudes? Are
our present views, like Quiller-Couch's, still one with those of the
Victorians? These are the basic questions. To answer them will not be to
prove one attitude right and another wrong. If literary adulation has led
to myth not history, so the rediscovery of history does not, in itself, mean
literary revaluation: at most it may suggest a need for revaluation.
Appreciation and, as a secondary matter, estimation of quality, depend
upon reading the text, not on a study of how that text has been read and
valued.

It is one thing to be the Bible of the official Church, another to be the
Bible of the people. In 1611 the people had their Bible, the Geneva, and
the KJB was simply the Church's third attempt to produce its own Bible.
To become the Bible of the people it had to dominate the field of Bible
production and to be the form of words habitually used when a text is
quoted, for that is the hallmark of acceptance and the key to specific literary appreciation. If 'the Bible' becomes synonymous with a particular version, then all the generalised ideas of perfection, with their
consequent literary admiration, will apply to that version.

The last regular edition of the Geneva Bible was published in 1644.
Thereafter, to buy a Bible meant to buy a King James Bible. Other versions continued in circulation, but gradually the commercial identity of
'English Bible' and 'King James Bible' became also a popular identity:
with only one major version available this was inevitable. In spite of the
later perception of the KJB's superiority, this publishing triumph owed
nothing to its merits (or Geneva's demerits) as a scholarly or literary rendering of the originals: economics and politics were the key factors. It
was in the very substantial commercial interest of the King's Printer,
who had a monopoly on the text, and the Cambridge University Press,
which also claimed the right to print the text, that the KJB should
succeed. In the trial of the man principally responsible for suppressing

the Geneva Bible, Archbishop Laud (1573–1645), there is a report that because the KJB, described as 'the new translation without notes', was 'most vendible', the King's Printer forbore to print Geneva Bibles for 'private lucre, not by virtue of any public restraint, [and so] they were usually imported from beyond the seas'.[2] 'Most vendible' probably means most profitable to the King's Printer, since Robert Barker had invested substantially in the KJB. The Geneva Bible appeared more marketable, and its continued importation was not just for sectarian reasons but because there was a popular demand. Indeed, Laud gives the Geneva Bible's commercial success as one of his reasons for its suppression:

by the numerous coming over of [Geneva] Bibles . . . from Amsterdam, there was a great and a just fear conceived that by little and little printing would quite be carried out of the kingdom. For the books which came thence were better print, better bound, better paper, and for all the charges of bringing, sold better cheap. And would any man buy a worse Bible dearer, that might have a better more cheap? And to preserve printing here at home . . . was the cause of stricter looking to those Bibles.[3]

The puritan Michael Sparke, a London bookseller and importer of Bibles in defiance of the monopoly, publisher too of Laud's opponent William Prynne, gives an identical picture in his attack on printing monopolies, *Scintilla* (1641; reprinted in Herbert, pp. 183–7). He documents price rises, notes how much cheaper the imported Bibles are, and charges the King's Printer with commercial exploitation of his monopoly. Like Laud, he writes in several places of the 'better paper and print' of the imports. Ironically, then, the KJB's triumph over its rival came about in part because it was an inferior production: in fair competition it would probably have lost, but its supporters had foul means at their disposal.

Perhaps more important than the commercial question was the same political matter that had figured at the inception of the KJB, the anti-monarchic tendency of some of the Geneva notes. Laud cites James I's objection to this tendency and observes 'that now of late these notes

---

[2] William Prynne, *Canterbury's Doom*, p. 515.

[3] *Works*, IV: 263. An opposite, somewhat obscure account of imported Bibles is given by Thomas Fuller. He describes Bibles imported from Amsterdam and Edinburgh about 1640 'as being of bad paper, worse print, little margin', and having 'many most abominable errata'. These, he says, were complained about 'as giving great advantage to the papists' (*Church History of Britain* (1655) 3 vols. (London, 1868), book XI, section 3, 29; III: 462–3). Fuller lived through this time, so the reader may choose betwen his account and that of two adversaries immediately concerned with the issue. Judgement of the Bibles of this time, in terms of their printing qualities, would be a complex matter, and Laud, Sparke and Fuller's arguments are all shaped by other interests.

were more commonly used to ill purposes than formerly, and that that
was the cause why the High Commission was more careful and strict
against them than before' (*Works*, IV: 262). With Charles I shortly to lose
his head, there can be no doubting the genuineness of this motive.
Prynne, for his part, was sure that the annotations were a sticking-point,
though he attributes a different motive, a fear that they 'should over-
much instruct the people in the knowledge of the Scriptures' (*Canterbury's
Doom*, p. 181).

No other grounds for the suppression are suggested, though it is reasonable to suppose that the desire for religious uniformity influenced
Laud as it had James I, and that he had a real sense of the Geneva Bible
as the Bible of his Puritan opponents. Even allowing full weight to these
suppositions, there is nothing in them to suggest that the triumph of the
KJB owed anything to its relative merits as a translation. The question
seems not to have occurred to either side, and it is significant that Sparke,
Prynne and Laud all talk of the Bible with or without notes, as if the
notes rather than the text were the chief identifying characteristics of the
two versions. In the same way, size could be the identifying factor, for
churches still needed, as specified in the proclamation of 1541, Bibles 'of
the largest and greatest volume' (Pollard, p. 112). This need could only
be fulfilled by, successively, the Great Bible, the Bishops' Bible and the
KJB, all printed in the largest size and appointed to be read in churches.
Between 1612 and 1641 the phrasing of requests for such Bibles – which
could now only mean the KJB – seems to have been evenly divided
between 'a Bible of the latest edition' or 'last translation', and 'a Bible of
the largest volume'. In 1634 Laud himself specified 'the whole Bible
of the largest volume', whereas Archbishop Abbott, who in 1616 had
used the same words, in 1619 specified 'the Bible of the new translation'.[4]
It may have gone without saying that Bibles 'of the largest volume' and
Bibles without notes meant the KJB, but such phrases do suggest that
people found it difficult to distinguish the KJB from the Geneva Bible as
a version, but relatively easy to distinguish it as an artefact.

The general popularity of annotated Bibles needs no comment, but
in the contest between Geneva and the KJB there is evidence not just
that notes were popular but that they were, in the eyes of many, more
important than differences of version. It was not the Geneva *text* that the
Puritans fought for in the face of the Laudian opposition (the Puritan
Westminster Confession is, perhaps tactfully, silent on what English

[4] R.T. Davidson, 'The authorisation of the English Bible', *Macmillan's Magazine*, Oct. 1881, cited
    in Pollard, p. 34.

version should be used): rather, they kept the annotations available by incorporating them in new editions of the KJB. At least nine of these hybrids were published from 1642 until 1715; all but one came, it seems, from Amsterdam, as the later Geneva Bibles had done. This adds to the irony of the KJB surviving because it was inferior as a book: the text which had had so much effort expended on it to ensure its superior accuracy, the same text which came to be revered for its particular verbal felicity, also survived because people were relatively indifferent to precise verbal form: they did not judge between the Geneva and the KJB *as translations*. This indifference is attributable not only to the belief that the translations did not fully express the original, but to the difficulties of understanding the plain text, whether because its English in either version was still found to be hard, or because the words were comprehensible but the meaning hard. Anthony Johnson, less than a century later, comments that the KJB's lack of annotation roused complaints from some 'that they could not see into the sense of the Scriptures' (*Historical Account*, p. 98).

Some significance may attach to the fact that the KJB was not insisted on by the authorities as the only Bible of the land. Pollard notes of the words on the title page, 'appointed to be read in Churches', that they 'are purely affirmative, not exclusive (unlike, for instance, the "these to be observed for holy days, and none other" of this very volume)' (pp. 33–4): neither churches nor people were compelled to use the KJB.[5] Older versions remained in use, the Bishops' Bible NT continued to be printed until 1617, and annotated revisions of parts of the OT (1616–23) by Henry Ainsworth (1571–1622/3), minister of a separatist congregation in Amsterdam, continued to be printed in London as well as Amsterdam until 1639, apparently without official hindrance. If the authorities before Laud were wholeheartedly engaged in establishing the KJB as the Bible of the land, so apparently benign an attitude seems extraordinary. Laud himself did not insist on the KJB but was content with opposing the Geneva Bible. The Church and the State were not so much for the KJB, or even for a uniform Bible, as they were against the Geneva Bible. They may also have been aware of the practical difficulties of insisting on the KJB. Duncan Anderson plausibly suggests that had an attempt made in 1636 to insist on the KJB as the official Scottish Bible been

---

[5] Though scholars agree that the KJB was never officially authorised, it is described as 'the authorised Bible' (Ambrose Ussher) as early as 1620. The comment that the KJB is 'allowed as authentic, by special order of King James' (see below, p. 98) may reflect opinion in the 1630s or 40s that the KJB was authorised.

followed through, the people would have rejected it.[6] Strangulation of the Geneva Bible in the press was the most diplomatic and effective long-term policy for the establishment of the KJB in England, Scotland and the American colonies that could have been hit on.

THE FAILURE OF REVISION

Ambrose Ussher

More than the defeat of Geneva was needed to assure the success of the KJB. The most serious threat came from attempts at revision during Commonwealth times, but about 1620 there was an attempt of some interest because it includes the earliest extant comments on the KJB after Broughton's, and because it advocates, if only in general terms, a more stylish approach to translation. The author was Ambrose Ussher (1582–1629), brother of James Ussher, Bishop of Armagh, whose calculations provided the basis for the dates commonly included in the KJB from 1701 on.[7] He translated most of the Bible (omitting the major prophets and the gospels, and leaving three books partly in Latin), and went as far as writing a dedicatory epistle to James I, though presumably this was never sent: the work remains in manuscript in Trinity College, Dublin. Ussher writes of 'exacting and perfecting' a translation, and sees the KJB as hasty work: 'the cook', he writes, hath 'hasted you out a reasonable sudden meal', whereas his work is 'leisurely and seasonably dressed', in other words, more carefully and delightfully made. 'A reformed version', he argues, must have 'two parts, one, new change of matter, the other change of choicer words'. For the first part he offers a large number of new interpretations not to be found in any other translations, and for the second he implies that he is offering a more elegant translation. Unlike the translators so far discussed, he suggests that elegance of style is to be found in the originals and preserved in the translation. He accepts what was becoming a commonplace (see below, pp. 147 ff.), that divine inspiration necessarily results in perfect oratory – 'the prophets, having received from God a mouth, [are] most perfect orators

---

[6] *The Bible in Seventeenth-Century Scottish Life and Literature* (London: Allenson, 1936), chapter 1.

[7] See his *The Annals of the World* (London, 1658), which translates his earlier Latin work. The famous calculations that the world was created 'upon the entrance of the night preceding the twenty-third day of October', 4004 BC, and that man was created on the 28th, 'which is our Friday', are on the first page. John Lightfoot had earlier fixed the time for man's creation 'about the third hour of the day, or nine o'clock in the morning' (*A Few and New Observations upon the Book of Genesis*, London, 1632; *Works* (2 vols., London, 1684), I: 692; see also I: 1020–1 and II: 1322–4).

and the very prime' – and argues that a translator should therefore search and inquire after words 'that like as in water face answereth to face, as Solomon speaketh [Prov. 27: 19], so they answer in appearance form to form'. He is ambiguous as to how this aesthetic aspect of translation should be achieved but, interestingly, sees it as having been part of the aim and practice of the KJB translators and their predecessors. 'This drift', he says, 'is intimated in the preface of our new translators', but just what part of the preface he has in mind is anybody's guess. Nevertheless, he distinguishes his and their practice from that of some unspecified other translators who 'strangely keep the very original specialties and properties, and so clap them into the text'; one may say with Dr Johnson, who wrote of another use of 'property', 'I know not which is the sense in [these] lines'. The nearest Ussher comes to explaining what he means is to write approvingly of preserving the Hebrew word order where possible. He echoes Tyndale's sense of the similarity between Hebrew and English (above, p. 20):

The Hebrew tongue, as wanting cases, doth resemble our common languages and seldom doth admit any more dislocation than do they. Wherefore, where in the Hebrew we find . . . an elegant displacing of words, and which addeth a force and a strength to the sentence, or a grace, if it falleth altogether as conveniently into the English, that is noted; which observance also is by our English interpreters in most places religiously entertained.

We need not disentangle just what principles of translation Ussher had in mind – he is neither a representative nor an influential figure, simply by far the earliest to suggest that the English Bible should be as stylish as the Hebrew, and that the KJB to some extent has this literary virtue.

Commonwealth attempts at revision

In Commonwealth times the Puritans might have tried to reintroduce Geneva but apparently did not. They might also have tried to promote annotated Bibles, but only in the first year of the Commonwealth was a KJB with Geneva notes published in London. The evidence of the continuing popularity of Geneva makes explanation for these two failures desirable, and the explanation no doubt remains a commercial one. The office of King's Printer had lapsed with the King, but the monopoly on the KJB text remained. Cromwell conferred it on Henry Hills and John Field in 1656, and at that time Field also became printer to Cambridge University. Having a monopoly on the KJB text, he had no interest in reviving the Geneva Bible. What did happen was attempted – and again abortive – revision of the KJB. Had the results been published, they would have delayed the establishment of the KJB as *the* English Bible and might themselves have taken the KJB's place as the object of modern veneration.

The precise history is obscure, but we know why revision was attempted and what the revisers wished to achieve. The earliest sign of an official move came from John Lightfoot (1602–75). At the tail-end of a sermon to the House of Commons in 1645, he recommended 'a review and survey of the translation of the Bible', adding these comments:

> It was the course of Nehemiah when he was reforming that he caused not the law only to be read and the sense given, but also caused the people 'to under-stand the reading', Neh. 8: 8. And certainly it would not be the least advantage that you might do to the three nations, if not the greatest, if they by your care and means might come to understand the proper and genuine reading of the Scripture by an exact, vigorous, and lively translation.[8]

Nothing has changed since the time of the translators: understanding and accuracy are still the priorities. 'Vigorous and lively' suggests that Lightfoot, like Broughton, whose works he edited, would have taken sty-listic matters into consideration, and that he had no special admiration for the style of the KJB. It is impossible to tell whether he had in mind that the English should be vigorous and lively by native standards or that it should represent the Hebrew as literally as possible in order to bring its alien vigour and life into English.

Controversy about the accuracy of the KJB and other Bibles contin-ued in the 1650s, as John Webster, in an eccentric attack on the educa-tion system, implies by writing of 'the errors and mistakes that still remain and are daily discovered in all translations' of the Bible.[9] Some of these came from corruption of the KJB text through careless print-ing, and the desire to correct such errors was commonly associated with the desire for a revised translation. In January 1657 an official revision was initiated. At Parliament, as Bulstrode Whitelocke reports, the Grand Committee for Religion 'ordered that it be referred to a sub-com-mittee to send for and advise with Dr [Bryan] Walton . . . and such others as they shall think fit, and to consider of the translations and impressions of the Bible, and to offer their opinions therein to the committee'.[10] Webster referred to translations: while he is hardly a reliable witness, the recurrence of the plural here suggests that in the 1650s the Geneva Bible

---

[8] *A Sermon Preached before the Honourable House of Commons at Margaret's, Westminster, upon the 26th day of August, 1645* (London, 1645), p. 30.   [9] *Academiarum Examen* (London, 1654), p. 7.
[10] *Memorials of the English Affairs* (London, 1682), p. 645.

(among others, perhaps) was very much alive. 'Impressions', on the other hand, refers to the difficulties caused by badly printed editions. Anthony Johnson's account of this episode suggests that one of the motives behind this attempted revision was a continuing preference for the Geneva Bible. He writes that 'some of the Presbyterians were not well pleased with this translation [KJB], suspecting it would abate the repute of that of Geneva' (*Historical Account*, p. 98).

The opinions offered to the sub-committee, insofar as they concerned translations, not impressions, could have been on questions of English style, but the continuation of Whitelocke's passage suggests that none such were made. Once again accuracy was all:

This committee often met at Whitelocke's house and had the most learned men in the oriental tongues to consult with in this great business, and divers excellent and learned observations of some mistakes in the translations of the Bible in English; which yet was agreed to be the best of any translation in the world; great pains were taken in it, but it became fruitless by the Parliament's dissolution.

Presumably the agreement that the KJB was 'the best of any translation in the world' was an agreement that it was the least inaccurate, but what is of most importance is that such a critical – if not literary-critical – judgement should have been reached. Out of context it could well become a literary opinion. There is no knowing if it was a judgement that reflected the general opinion of late Commonwealth times, but it came from the leaders of scholarship and was sure to help mould opinion.

Bishop Bryan Walton (1600–61), the first named of the sub-committee, was editor of the highly respected Polyglot Bible; he was to write that 'the last English translation made by divers learned men at the command of King James . . . may justly contend with any now extant in any other language in Europe'.[11] Such was the considered result of the attempt at revision: affirmation in the most general terms of the KJB's quality. Yet there is no evidence to suggest why this conclusion was reached. It is likely that, with the collapse of the Commonwealth and the political demise of the Puritans, the political will to revise the KJB also collapsed. The weight of the particular objections to the KJB's renderings was insufficient to sustain the work of revision, and the objections themselves may simply have appeared finicky.

---

[11] *The Considerator Considered* (London, 1659), p. 5. This translates part of the preface to the Polyglot Bible; 'may justly contend' weakens the force of 'eminet' in the original.

This, of course, is speculation. The full story is irrecoverable. What does survive is discussion of how the KJB should be revised, and this includes consideration of linguistic matters. Precisely how what follows fits with the discussions at Whitelocke's house is, again, unknowable, but the most active promoter of revision, the Baptist divine, Henry Jessey (or Jacie, 1601–63), eventually became one of a group of revisers appointed in the latter days of the Long Parliament (1652 or 1653 – the authorities vary), and presumably the two sets of discussions followed similar lines. Jessey's biographer, E.W. (probably Whiston), gives an account of the principles of revision without keeping clear whether he is expressing his own or Jessey's ideas. Jessey's knowledge of the originals was, Whiston relates, such that he was called 'a living concordance' (*Life of Jessey*, p. 62). He believed 'that our language is not copious and significant enough to bear the true import of every word, the sacred languages being so full'. As a consequence of this – and of annotations and explanations to the unlearned that the original reads in such a way – there is 'a diversity of rendering the texts [which] hath been a stumbling to many, and an occasion of reproach to others'. Therefore Jessey conceived it 'our duty to endeavour to have the whole Bible rendered as exactly agreeing with the original as we can attain'. This duty should be carried out under the supervision of 'godly and able men' appointed by public authority to ensure the soundness of the work since he feared it might otherwise be a dangerous precedent tending 'at the last to bring in other Scriptures, or another gospel, instead of the oracles of God and the gospel of our Lord Jesus Christ'. He recruited many for this work, writing to them of 'a strange desire in many that love the truth to have a more pure, proper [literally accurate] translation of the originals than hitherto'. This work 'was almost completed, and stayed for nothing but the appointment of commissioners to examine it and warrant its publication' (pp. 45–7). No specimen of the work survives, nor any account of why so much labour came to nothing.

Whiston reports that the only objection to 'so worthy and noble a design' was that it might be supposed needless since the KJB 'is most correct and allowed as authentic by special order of King James' (p. 48). If this reflects opinion current when the work was begun, say in the 1640s but possibly in the 1630s (Whiston gives no dates), it is the earliest extant favourable opinion of the KJB's merits as a translation to reach publication. Significantly, it only involves 'correctness'. Whiston quotes Jessey's somewhat ungrammatical response to such opinion: 'by way of confession that the last is the best translation, and is in most material things exact and true. And the translators were learned, sincere and diligent;

and therefore [Jessey] encourages all Christians to prize and value it' (p. 48). Whiston qualifies the picture by observing that 'the Church of England doth not exempt the aforesaid translation from all deficiency, and do show in their pulpits continually how the text may be better translated' (p. 50). From his point of view of 'fifty years and more since that translation was finished', 'the knowledge of the Hebrew and Greek hath been improved even to admiration since that time, and so consequently a translation might be undertaken and made to be more perfectly agreeable with the original' (pp. 48–9). Advancement of scholarship was constantly to be alleged as a chief reason for revision through to and beyond the making of the RV.[12]

Much of the rest of Whiston's account makes detailed criticism of the KJB and then lays down principles of revision. It is not always clear that he is reporting Jessey, and he includes the principles of John Row, Hebrew professor at Aberdeen, another leading light in the push for revision and a man whom Jessey often consulted. Since there is no visible disagreement between these three men, their views may be taken together.[13] The KJB is accused of being made to speak 'the prelatical language' in using words like 'bishopric' and 'hell' instead of 'charge' and 'grave' (p. 49),[14] and there are objections to its inclusion of the Apocrypha, of 'scandalous and Popish pictures' (p. 57),[15] and its

---

[12] Just how common the argument was at this time is difficult to tell: Robert Boyle reports it and associates it with Archbishop Ussher (see below, p. 110), but I have not come across it elsewhere.

[13] See Whiston, *Life of Jessey*, pp. 50–60. Another version of Row's principles, different in wording and order, is given in Mombert, *English Versions*, pp. 444–5.

[14] While the Puritans thought it too prelatical, others such as Robert Gell found it too Calvinist. Theological tendentiousness was unavoidable.

[15] Not everyone wanted the Apocrypha excluded, as is clear from the following contemporaneous example of obscene mockery of Puritans and the book (the Puritan in this case seems to have been an early fundamentalist):

> It was a puritanical lad
> That was called Mathias,
> And he would go to Amsterdam
> To speak with Ananias.
> He had not gone past half a mile,
> But he met his holy sister;
> He laid his Bible under her breech,
> And merrily he kissed her.
>
> 'Alas! what would they wicked say?'
> Quoth she, 'if they had seen it!
> My buttocks they lie too low: I wisht
> Apocrypha were in it!'

'Of a Puritan', *Merry Songs and Ballads*, ed. John S. Farmer, 5 vols. (New York: Cooper Square, 1964), I: 73.

inappropriate canonising of men such as Matthew but not Job
(Mombert, *English Versions*, p. 444). 'Evil divisions of chapters, verses or
sentences' need rectifying, 'which will not wrong but illustrate the texts'
(pp. 59, 56). Questions of accuracy begin with the observation that

Many places which are not falsely may be yet better rendered, or more consonant to the text, as the salutation of the apostle Paul in almost all his epistles
translated, 'grace be unto you, and peace from God our Father, and from the
Lord Jesus Christ', might be as well, if not better rendered, 'grace be unto you,
and peace from God the Father of us and the Father of the Lord Jesus Christ'.
(pp. 50–1)

Quibbling and hesitant as this is, it concerns the true meaning of the
original and its clear expression in English, not felicity of expression.
The examples conclude with the observation, 'how often doth the
margin amend the line' (p. 51). Jessey argued that until a new authorised
translation appeared, readers should supply its lack by, among other
things, diligently observing the margin, 'which in above eight hundred
places is righter than the line' (pp. 59–60). Omissions from and additions
to the original are noted, but some additions are allowed for the sake of
'true English' (p. 52), provided the principle of italicising the additions is
extended. Inaccuracies are noted, especially in grammatical correspondence such as superlatives translated as positives, actives as passives and
plurals as singulars.

Though the translation should be in 'true English', 'good English',
which is perhaps a degree better, is in itself not enough. The inclusion
of the name of God in phrases such as 'God forbid', where the reading
should be 'let it not be' (e.g. Luke 20: 16), is objected to although 'these
above cited phrases be good English', for they set a bad precedent to the
youth of the nation by emboldening them 'to swear idly by that holy
name when they are playing or fighting' (pp. 53–4). Accuracy and
profane linguistic consequences demand a change from 'good English'.
This is, in passing, the earliest extant comment on the English Bible
influencing, for better or worse, the English language. Jessey's next point
is that 'some harsh expressions may be made more gentle and soft', but
his concern is not with eloquence, rather with passages where the kindness of God is not sufficiently revealed. So 'where it is said, "Go thou"
. . . etc., they translate, "Get thee out", etc., which manner of speech
doth not hold forth that kindness the Lord intended' (p. 54). Certainly
this reveals a sensitivity to language, but it is a sensitivity to theological
implications, not to language as language.

Consistency of vocabulary does not trouble Jessey – he never suggests, as Broughton had done, that the same word in the original should be rendered always with the same English word – but clarity does. His principle is simple, that 'obscure words should be made more plain for mean people to understand' (p. 55). No attention is to be paid to reproducing the vocabulary of the original, so more, including proper names, should be in English words and less in Hebrew, Greek or Latin; he even suggests that English words not understood in Scotland should be made idiomatic (p. 58; Mombert, p. 445). Such changes would not have made the English Bible appear any more admirable to literary men of the time, and they might also have lowered its ecclesiastical tone. Unlike some of his predecessors, Jessey gives no examples of inkhorn difficulties, but he produces the first example of difficulty with archaism in the KJB, 'this one old word "occupy", which hath various significations' (p. 55). Regrettably, though he claims 'many instances might be made' besides 'occupy', he gives no others, and one must wait a century for detailed commentary on archaisms in the KJB.

So far nothing suggests that the English of the Bible should be other than accurate and comprehensible and, as lesser issues, contemporary and immune to profanity. But with the question of style a theologically based aesthetic comes in that is, eventually, as much a basis for appreciation of the KJB as it is a principle for revising it. Jessey believed Hebrew to be the perfect language:

it was his particular judgement that in the latter days, when the promises of the Gentiles' fullness and the Jews' conversion shall be accomplished, one effect of pouring out of the spirit will be a pure language (Zeph. 3: 8–9), both as to the manner of speech and form of sound words, as also in respect of the tongue itself which shall then be spoken, which he judged would be the Hebrew; and he was not alone in this his opinion. (p. 62)[16]

It is appropriate, therefore, to learn Hebrew not only as a key to the Bible but as a preparation for the latter days. Here a telling ambiguity enters: Whiston's account slides without distinction between Hebrew itself and biblical English. Jessey's knowledge of Hebrew is related, and next his 'faithful fixed memory of all texts', as if this is part of his knowledge of Hebrew. Then comes this, preceding the passage just quoted, part of the same paragraph, yet referring to Jessey's use of English:

---

[16] I doubt whether this idea of the language of the last days was widespread among Christians. Lightfoot ascribes it to the Jews (I: 1012). David Maclagan notes that 'some Kabbalists hold that the Hebrew alphabet was the one used by God as a medium for the creation of the world' (*Creation Myths*, London: Thames and Hudson, 1977, p. 30).

His tongue also was so familiarised to [the Bible's] language that in his ordinary conversation it flowed from him so free, sweet and proper, as if it were his mother phrase, to the great admiration and instruction of the hearers: which way of speaking he exhorted all Christians unto . . . as being most savoury and seasoned with salt and grace (Col. 4: 6), and best beseeming Christians of the new Jerusalem.

Through his reverence for the originals, especially the Hebrew, he has modelled a new English speech on that of the KJB. Such language modifies current English towards an idea of perfection, and such a chain of thought leads towards the conclusion that style modelled on the idioms and figures of the Hebrew is the best form of English. He encouraged others 'to speak and write in Scripture style' – though what he had particularly in mind was the restoration of the Jewish calendar as a means towards reviving Hebrew (p. 63).

Jessey studied the characteristics of biblical language, particularly 'the tropes, improper and borrowed phrases . . ., the metaphors, ellipses, metatheses and other figures, and foreign elegancies throughout the Bible' (p. 61), and he looked to have these reproduced in the English. The NT gave him precedent: 'Hebraisms, being so much honoured as to be kept frequently up in the New Testament, should be carefully observed in translations where they do not destroy sense or doctrine' (p. 55). Style is important to him, but not English style. Rather, the style of the Hebrew should be matched as literally as possible, giving, for instance, 'redeeming thou shalt redeem' instead of the KJB's 'shalt thou surely redeem' (Num. 18: 15). This he calls translating 'exactly, *verbum verbo*' (p. 56). Inconsistently, he allows this principle to be broken on one other ground besides sense or doctrine, the pleasingness of the English: if the Hebrew form of oath in Ps. 95: 11 were rendered literally, there 'would be unpleasing aposiopesis [a sudden halting as if unable to go on]' (p. 56).

Jessey and his colleagues had evidently given minute attention to the KJB. Their chief motives for revision are truth to the original and doctrinal purity, but more explicit awareness of language for its own sake enters their considerations than had entered into the considerations of any earlier English translators. They have a sense of what constitutes good English and that the KJB may be admired in places for its English, but this is largely subordinated to a reverence for the peculiar eloquence of the Hebrew (the Greek is not commented on) and a desire to reflect that eloquence literally in English. The potential for literary admiration of the KJB's literal renderings is high, and there is a clear sense that a biblical English is now separately identifiable. It may be taken as a model for the improvement of English, not because it is good or bad as English, but because, until it is revised, it is nearest to the pure language, Hebrew. This sense of biblical English perhaps ran deeper than the detailed objections to the KJB, and it helps to account for the failure of the revision. As the best available version, the KJB must necessarily be admired.

But criticism had not quite finished. The century's most substantial attack on the KJB's accuracy appeared in 1659, Robert Gell's *An Essay toward the Amendment of the Last English Translation of the Bible. Or, a* proof, *by many instances, that the last translation of the Bible may be* improved. This seems to have fallen on deaf ears, for it was also the century's last attack: there were no further published discussions or attempts at revision. Its real interest lies in the concession that the KJB is generally thought to be 'so exact . . . that it needs no essay towards the amendment of it': Gell himself thinks it 'good, yea, far better than that new one of the Low Dutch so highly extolled' (preface). The size of this work, over 800 densely printed pages, and the fact that it was published so late in Gell's life (1595–1665) make it likely that it was conceived and begun long before 1659: it represents the last blast of early dissatisfaction with the KJB rather than the prevailing opinion of 1659. By the Restoration in 1660, we may conclude, initial dissatisfaction had had its day: the KJB was now established as the English Bible and was generally regarded as an accurate rendering of the originals.

QUOTING THE GOOD BOOK

The gradual acceptance of the ideas that there is a reliable text of the Bible in English and that that Bible is the KJB is reflected in the way the Bible is quoted. The prefaces to the various versions generally do not quote their own version. This may in part be due to the difficulties of book production since there would probably have been only one manuscript of the final version and it may have been in the hands of the printer rather than the writer of the preface. Nevertheless, the prefaces are characteristic of sixteenth- and seventeenth-century quotation in their careless attitude to the English text. Parker and Martin prefer to quote in Latin and add their own independent English version. Smith twice coincides with the KJB, more often with the Geneva Bible, and he frequently gives an independent version apparently made as he is writing. The following is typical:

the reproof of Moses taketh hold of most ages: 'you are risen up in your fathers' stead, an increase of sinful men' [Num. 32: 14]. 'What is that that hath been done? that which shall be done: and there is no new thing under the sun' [Eccles. 1: 9], saith the wise man: and St Stephen, 'as your fathers did, so do you' [Acts 7: 51]. (p. 2)

The first quotation is not quite exactly from the KJB, which reads 'ye' rather than 'you', the second is independent and the third coincides with Geneva. Though Smith does not quote the originals, it is probable that he thought of the Bible as the Hebrew and Greek (or perhaps Latin) Bible, and worked from this, sometimes remembering English versions as he wrote.

Moving away from the translators, Archbishop Laud is a revealing figure because of his role in securing the dominance of the KJB. His work reflects the currency of the Geneva Bible rather than the Bishops' Bible before 1611, for he continued to use Geneva into the late 1620s. In the early 1620s he gives the texts of his sermons from Geneva, but by the middle of the decade he uses the KJB but gives Geneva's alternative renderings. Sermon IV, June 1625, takes as its text Ps. 75: 2–3, giving it thus: 'when I shall receive the congregation, *or, when I shall take a convenient time*, I will judge according unto right. The earth is dissolved, *or, melted*, and all the inhabitants thereof; I bear up the pillars of it' (*Works*, I: 93; italics Laud's). The first verse is from the KJB, with Geneva's readings as the alternative, but in the second verse Laud varies the KJB, and the alternative, 'melted', is his own suggestion. So, fourteen years after the publication of the KJB, Laud is using it as his main source, but he is neither contented with its readings nor willing to make a final choice between it and Geneva.

Laud did eventually choose the KJB – his last clear use of Geneva is his 1629 adaption of 2 Sam. 15: 4 (I: 158) – but there is still no sign that he was contented with its readings. Against this, he seems not to have wanted a revision: rather, he, like Parker, Martin and Smith, treats the English versions as guides to the word of God in the originals rather than as the word of God in English. The versions are no more than versions, and can be treated freely. So he had available to him as he worked not only the Vulgate and the Greek NT (there is no proof in his quotations that he used the Hebrew), but several English versions, including the PB, his preferred choice for Psalms, and 'our old English translation',[17] which he cites once as giving a 'happy' rendering (I: 207), but he had no

---

[17] His editor identifies this as PB, but it is not.

consistent principle of choice among them. When he gives a Greek phrase from 2 Pet. 2: 17, he does not look up the English versions, which almost unanimously give 'with a tempest', but translates 'by a whirlwind' (I: 101). Moreover, he seems occasionally to have worked from the Latin, so, presumably by accident, coinciding with Rheims. He paraphrases Matt. 11: 28, writing, 'he calls oft upon them that "are weary and heavy laden to refresh them"': 'refresh' seems to come straight from 'reficiam' (I: 188). This suggests that his looseness with the Bible text goes beyond his cavalier approach to the English versions: his use of versions in the ancient languages can be just as free.

John Donne (1572–1631) is of special interest quite apart from his claims as a major writer, because he had the highest opinion of the eloquence of the Bible and makes constant use of a range of English Bibles. But it was not the English Bible whose eloquence he revered, and the primary characteristics of the way he uses it are those already seen. One of his Whit Sunday sermons touches on looseness and gives a small but representative sample of his treatment of the text. He notes that Peter, preaching to the centurion Cornelius, takes his text inaccurately from the OT (Acts 10: 34, quoting Deut. 10: 17), and comments 'that neither Christ in his preaching nor the Holy Ghost in penning the Scriptures of the New Testament were so curious as our times in citing chapters and verses, or such distinctions, no, nor in citing the very, very words of the places' (*The Sermons*, V: 44). If this is a fair description of his time's attitude to accuracy of quotation – and it is certainly true of curiosity in giving references – then it refers to quotation from the Hebrew and the Greek (the Latin only to a lesser extent), not the English. He does not develop the point but gives an example, Isa. 6: 10, which 'is cited six several times in the New Testament' (e.g. Matt. 13: 15, Acts 28: 27), and shows that the writers of the NT 'stood not upon such exact quotations and citing of the very words'. The point fits with his English and, sometimes, his Latin quotations. Donne himself misquotes the passage, apparently giving the KJB from memory: instead of 'make their ears heavy, and shut their eyes', he gives 'make their eyes heavy and shut them'. In the same paragraph he is inaccurate in quoting Acts 10: 43 from the very chapter which gives the text of his sermon and which one might therefore suppose he had open in front of him. Still more revealingly, he quotes Peter's text twice in the paragraph, first giving the KJB's 'no respecter of persons' (Acts 10: 34), a phrase that has become part of the KJB's legacy to the English language, then, moving closer to Geneva and Rheims (both have 'accepter of persons'), 'no such accepter of persons'. 'Such' is part of his habitual adaption of quotations to his context, but the main variation appears either because he is as free with the English text as the apostle was with the OT, or because, like Laud in 1625, he is deliberately invoking both current English versions. The first possibility is the more likely: in repeating the text of his own sermon, which is given verbatim from the KJB at the beginning, he makes minor variations which are neither demanded by context nor prompted by other English renderings. This suggests more than freedom with the text: it invokes an age in which grammar and spelling – language in general – were unfixed. The times as well as the precedent of the Bible, the variety of the English versions as well as Donne's own temperament, all worked against accuracy of quotation.

Contrasting with this predominating freedom, Donne occasionally shows the beginnings of a scholarly interest in comparing English versions with each other and with the originals. The most notable instance comes in his third Prebend sermon, 1626, where he gives the Hebrew reading of Ps. 64: 10 and various English readings going back to Wyclif, noting that Wyclif follows Jerome and is grammatically true to the Hebrew (VII: 248). His purpose is no more than to establish the correct reading, and the reference is occasioned only because Wyclif gives the reading he considers correct. No wider view of the relative merits of the translations is taken, and indeed there is little cause for expecting any stylistic comparison from one who believed that translations 'could not maintain the majesty nor preserve the elegancies of the original' (VI: 56). Such comparisons of versions are so rare that they do nothing to qualify Don Cameron Allen's considered verdict that 'when we study Donne's method in a sermon, or in all the sermons of a definite year, or in all his quotations from a given book of the Bible, we find that he selects his texts as he pleases, that he is governed by no particular preferences, and that he does not seem to make the slightest attempt to secure the best reading'.[18]

Though the Geneva Bible continued to be used at least into the 1640s, Laud's movement towards the KJB is representative. By the 1630s some writers such as the period's foremost writer of divine lyric poetry, George Herbert, were using the KJB and the PB Psalms as a matter of course, and after the Restoration there is no evidence of the continuing use of Geneva by the learned: by this time the KJB had effectively won its battle for acceptance. But acceptance as what? As Smith, Donne and Laud all demonstrate, there was another issue besides that of which version, the issue of how any version was used. It was one thing for the KJB to defeat

---

[18] Dean Donne sets his text', *ELH* 10 (1953), 208–229, p. 228.

Geneva, another for it to be *the* Bible. As long as people continued to show a real carelessness with its wording it was neither accepted theologically as the definitive form of the word of God in English, nor was it linguistically established.

There is no need to examine further writers here; rather, it will be enough to observe individuals' use of the text in passing. Besides the demise of Geneva, a tendency to quote the KJB with increased accuracy will be evident from the Restoration onwards. If we take accuracy of quotation as an indicator of acceptance as the Bible (in other words, as an alternative to the originals that was good enough to allow one to work without reference to them), then the KJB was well on the way to being *the* Bible for the English by 1660. Nevertheless, there is a particularly marked difference between popular knowledge of the KJB's words and the attitude of the learned to them, and both popular affection and the approval of the educated were needed for the KJB to become thought of as *the* Bible and as a work of English literature.

THE LITERARY RECEPTION

John Selden and dirty ears

Slight as is the evidence for the scholarly reception of the KJB, the evidence for its literary reception is still slighter. This is hardly surprising, for it was almost inconceivable that a prose translation for accuracy should meet English literary standards. There is no record of favourable reaction beyond the obscurity of Ussher's epistle and the compliment of imitation paid by more extreme Protestants such as Jessey, but unfavourable reactions, growing out of mockery of the Bible (see below, pp. 165 ff.), made themselves felt. The best-known report of these comes in the mid-century 'table talk' of a man with many claims to fame, not least his enormous knowledge of Hebrew and the translations, John Selden (1584–1654). It is supported by a man best known for his contributions to science, Robert Boyle.

Selden begins by praising the English Bibles' accuracy in terms that resemble Walton's: 'the English translation of the Bible', he says, explicitly referring to both the KJB and the Bishops' Bible, 'is the best translation in the world and renders the sense of the original best'.[19] But when he turns to style the other side of the coin of accuracy shows:

---

[19] *Table Talk* (1689); Frederick Pollock, ed., *Table Talk of John Selden* (London: Quaritch, 1927), p. 10.

There is no book so translated as the Bible. For the purpose, if I translate a
French book into English, I turn it into English phrase and not into French
English. 'Il fait froid': I say it is cold, not it makes cold; but the Bible is translated into English words rather than into English phrase: the Hebraisms are
kept and the phrase of that language is kept. As for example, 'he uncovered her
shame', which is well enough so long as scholars have to do with it, but when it
comes among the common people, Lord what gear [mockery] do they make of
it. (p. 11)

This is directly opposite to Tyndale's view of the natural affinity between
Hebrew and English. The literalness of the KJB is recognised and
accepted only as being appropriate in a crib for scholars or as something
scholars will understand, but Selden clearly thinks this is a bad principle
of translation and would prefer an idiom-for-idiom version.

A similar view seems to have been held by the satirist Samuel
'Hudibras' Butler (1612–80), who describes a hypocritical non-conformist as using 'the old phrases of the English translation of the Bible
from the Jewish idiom as if they contained in them more sanctity and
holiness than other words that more properly signify the same thing'.[20]
Whatever the non-conformist thought of the KJB, Butler clearly saw it
as a translation so literally made that it often failed to express meaning
with the accuracy that might have been achieved.

As so often, the contrary view can be found. Thomas Fuller (1608–61),
best known for his *Church History of Britain*, thought highly of the purity
of his native Northamptonshire dialect. He writes that 'we speak, I
believe, as good English [as] any shire in England because . . . the last
translation of the Bible, which no doubt was done by those learned men
in the best English, agreeth perfectly with the common speech of our
country'.[21] This is a unique comment from a seventeenth-century pen,
so it is difficult to know how much weight to give it, especially as Fuller
himself, in spite of the opportunities the *Church History* gave him, writes
nothing else of the sort. At least once, we may say, someone in the
century cared to think of the KJB translators as deliberately choosing
the best English. It is also unusual for a country dialect to be thought of
as a standard for the language by an educated man. But Fuller's remark
is neither entirely idiosyncratic nor just an example of local brag. Only
a few of the century's comments on the Bible represent popular rather
than educated views, and it is likely that the KJB's language seemed

[20] *Characters*, ed. Charles W. Dawes (Cleveland and London: Press of Case Western Reserve
University, 1970), p. 54.
[21] *Worthies*, Northamptonshire, p. 278. As given in John Eglington Bailey, *The Life of Thomas Fuller*
(London, 1874), p. 63.

normal, and therefore good, to some country people. Whether that was because, as he thinks, it was essentially in their language, or because the sequence of English Bibles had by this time moulded some dialects towards their English must remain an open question. Whatever the answer, Selden's report is not invalidated, for it is supported by other pejorative comments on the literalism and is at one with the prevailing scorn of older English and with the tendency towards archaism in the KJB.

Selden's example of the unnaturalness of the language is intriguing. First, it refers to a Geneva rather than a KJB rendering, 'he hath uncovered his sister's shame' (Lev. 20: 17). For him there is no real linguistic distinction between the two versions (or between them and the Bishops' Bible); he could as readily have made the point from the KJB which uses 'shame' in this sense elsewhere. Second, this is an example of the same sort as Jessey's 'occupy'. These, the only two words singled out by early commentators on the language of the KJB, are both examples of words that were picked on by the prurient mockers of the time. As Shakespeare had Falstaff observe, 'occupy' 'was an excellent good word before it was ill sorted' (*Henry IV, Part II*, II: iv: 145). It had come to mean 'to deal with or have to do with sexually' (*OED* sense 8). *OED* notes that it almost disappeared from use in the seventeenth and most of the eighteenth centuries, and remarks that 'this avoidance appears to have been due to its vulgar employment'. The KJB, generally going back to Coverdale, was not only somewhat archaic (Jessey's ostensible point) but insensitive in retaining 'occupy', which sounded lewd to dirty ears. A century later the biographer Thomas Birch was to write that the wits of this time employed 'a great deal of impudence in perverting inspired expressions to a bad purpose as if they contained obscene thoughts'.[22]

Milton pointed out that the Bible would have to be included in any list of books to be proscribed for obscenity since it 'oftimes relates blasphemy not nicely' (*Areopagitica*, II: 517; also see below, p. 176). George Wither (the poet), writing only a few years after the publication of the KJB, gives further evidence. In his version of the Song of Songs, he had rendered the KJB's 'the joints of thy thighs' (7: 1) as 'the knitting of the thighs'. His traducers found this obscene (*Scholar's Purgatory*, p. 51). Wither defends himself vigorously. He asks, 'what obscenity is in that more than in the Holy Ghost's own words?', and then goes on to show that this reaction to his phrase is part of the general impudence that

---

[22] *The Life of the Honourable Robert Boyle* (London, 1744), p. 160.

Birch described. The Song of Songs was commonly treated as obscene 'by those presumptuous libertines and scoffing atheists who make application of them according to their own humours [and] . . . wilfully pervert them to wicked purposes' (p. 58). He adds that he knows 'it ordinary among such as those to cavil at our most approved translations' (p. 59), and that 'the story of the incest of that Lot [Gen. 19: 30–38], of Tamar [2 Sam. 13], and divers other passages in Holy Scripture are more subject to abuse than the Canticles' (p. 57). So the KJB was jeered at for obscenity, but this jeering was not a particular response to the KJB; rather, it was a general one at this time (and earlier) to some of the language and content of the English Bibles. Selden's comments on mockery of literal translation, like Jessey's on archaism, are more than they appear: they reflect also the horror of the pious at the age's prevailing prurience.

Robert Boyle against the wits

Robert Boyle (1627–91), for all his scientific work a diligent student of theology and an energetic supporter of Bible translations for missionary work, wrote the century's most substantial English work on the Bible's general qualities of language, structure and coherence, *Some Considerations Touching the Style of the Holy Scriptures*. Begun in 1652 but not published until 1661, this is a youthful work of no great quality, now chiefly of interest for the way it confirms some of the observations already made and combines them with ideas of the qualities of the originals that had become widespread at this time. Boyle had been, by his own admission, 'one of the greatest despisers of verbal learning', but Archbishop Ussher helped him 'to turn grammarian' by encouraging him to distrust translations and study the original languages.[23] So he early learnt, as he relates in the same letter, to think of 'our last translation' in much the same way as Walton and his fellow committee-members, as 'much more correct than our former was, and preferable to most I have met with in other languages', but also as one which might be framed 'in many places more correct': many texts 'may be rendered more fully, or more warily, or more coherently to the context, or more congruously to the analogy of faith, or that of reason'. There is no sign here of concern with the style of the translation. All that matters is correctness, and from this point of view the KJB is *relatively* good.

---

[23] Letter to Lord Broghill, as given in Louis Trenchard More, *The Life and Works of the Honourable Robert Boyle* (New York: Oxford University Press, 1944), pp. 69–70.

If the learned Archbishop Ussher had turned the budding scientist into a fairly typical student of the Bible, contemporary mockery of the Bible's language helped turn him from student to writer: his avowed purpose in *Some Considerations* is to defend the original Scriptures against the scorn of

divers witty men who freely acknowledge the authority of the Scripture [but] take exceptions at its style, and by those and their own reputation divert many from studying, or so much as perusing, those sacred writings, thereby at once giving men injurious and irreverent thoughts of it, and diverting them from allowing the Scripture the best way of justifying itself and disabusing them. (pp. 1–2)

Boyle's quarrel with these wits is based on a single, familiar premise, that the whole verbal form as well as the content of the originals was divinely inspired. He believes God's words should command the same reverence as his deeds, whereas the wits, who are now less reverent than he had initially allowed them to be, 'impiously presume to quarrel as well with his revelations as his providence and express no more reverence to what he hath dictated than to what he doth' (pp. 3–4).

Though 'there are', Boyle writes, 'I know not how many faults found with the style of the Scripture', much of the book is taken up with countering the following objections (objections which show he uses 'style' to include matters such as literary structure and historical consistency):

some of [the wits] are pleased to say that book is too obscure, others, that 'tis immethodical, others that it is contradictory to itself, others, that the neighbouring parts of it are incoherent, others, that 'tis unadorned, others, that it is flat and unaffecting, others, that it abounds with things that are either trivial or impertinent, and also with useless repetitions. (p. 4)

Boyle's counter-arguments do not entirely dismiss these faults. Only the originals are perfect: no criticism of them can be justified. Translations, however, are man-made, so criticism may be admitted, and it seems at times as if he is defending the originals at the expense of the translations, including the Vulgate. His report of the English translators' language and the people's reaction to it is remarkably close to Selden's, though almost certainly totally independent, given the delayed publication of both works:

the style of the Scripture is much more disadvantaged than that of other books by being judged of by translations. For the religious and just veneration that the interpreters of the Bible have had for that sacred book has made them in most places render the Hebrew and Greek passages so scrupulously word for word, that for fear of not keeping close enough to the sense they usually care not how much they lose of the eloquence of the passages they translate . . . in translating the Old Testament, interpreters have not put Hebrew phrases into Latin or English phrases, but only into Latin or English words, and have too often besides, by not sufficiently understanding, or at least considering, the various significations of words, particles and tenses in the holy tongue, made many things to appear less coherent and less rational, or less considerable, which by a more free and skilful rendering of the original would not be blemished by any appearance of such imperfection. (pp. 7–9; see also pp. 153–4)

This sums up the whole tradition of translation: the English translators (among others) were preoccupied with literal translation, and did not consciously attempt to produce English that they themselves would have considered good; moreover, it confirms that the early readers of their work understood them to have been literal not stylish.

Boyle seems to feel no need to defend the KJB; if, as he later suggests, the people were beginning to regard it with 'affectionate veneration', the intelligentsia were not. Besides, there were, whether or not he realised them, practical advantages to conceding the KJB to their attack: the wits could bring their own standards to bear on the English, but few if any of them could substantiate their arguments from the Hebrew. Even if they could, their standards might not be appropriate for a true appreciation of it. So he argues that ''tis probable that many of those texts whose expressions, as they are rendered in our translations, seem flat or improper or incoherent with the context, would appear much otherwise if we were acquainted with all the significations of words and phrases that were known in the times when the Hebrew language flourished and the sacred books were written' (pp. 12–13). This is blatantly hypothetical. He is not really arguing at all, rather suggesting ways of squaring the appearance of Scripture with the incontestable position, based on the premise of divine inspiration, that the Scripture is perfectly written.

Boyle develops his ideas of the literary quality of the Bible in countering the objection suggested in the passage just quoted, 'that the Scripture is so unadorned with flowers of rhetoric, and so destitute of eloquence, that it is flat, and proves commonly inefficacious upon intelligent readers. Insomuch that divers great wits and great persons, especially statesmen, do either despise it, or neglect to study it' (p. 147). These are his heads of argument:

First, that as to divers parts of the Scripture, it was not requisite that they should be adorned with rhetorical embellishments.

Next, that the Bible seems to have much less eloquence than indeed it has to those that read it only in translations, especially the vulgar Latin Version.

Thirdly, that by reason of the differing notions several sorts of men, especially of distant nations and climates, have of eloquence, many passages that are thought uneloquent by us may appear excellently expressed to another part of mankind.

Fourthly, that there are in the Scripture a multitude of those texts wherein the author thought fit to employ the ornaments of language, conspicuously adorned with such as agree even with our notions of eloquence.

And lastly, that it is very far from being consonant to experience that the style of the Scripture does make it unoperative upon the generality of its readers, if they be not faultily indisposed to receive impressions from it. (pp. 150–1)

The first four neatly summarise his main arguments – the Bible is and is not eloquent; it has its own standards of eloquence which we cannot appreciate, and we fail to appreciate that it meets our standards – but the last, incidental as it is within the context of the work, is of real historical importance. He recurs to it at the end of the book, claiming that 'there is scarce any sort of men on which the Scripture has not had a notable influence, as to the reforming and improving many particular persons, belonging to it, and to the giving them an affectionate veneration for the book whereunto they owed their instruction' (p. 223). The two key elements are the recognition of the changeability of standards of eloquence and the appeal to the experience of a different kind of reader from the witty men, the generality of readers. Now, the primary purpose of eloquence is to make writing influential: if the Bible in translation is so influential, its style can hardly in truth be faulty. Influence on the lives of the people, familiarity and, in Boyle's key phrase, 'affectionate veneration' were to be major factors in the escalating reputation of the KJB as eloquence, and eventually (to preserve for once a sometimes pedantic distinction) as literature.

Yet they did not necessarily lead to literary conclusions, and it is worth emphasising that affectionate veneration, even when felt by poets, is not necessarily a literary feeling. The religious poet Henry Vaughan (?1621–95) was given a Bible, presumably the KJB, as his first book and learnt to read from it. He tells us in 'To the Holy Bible' that as he grew up he neglected it for other books, 'and never thought / My first cheap book had all I sought'. Eventually the Bible wooed him back 'with meek dumb looks', which suggests that he shared the prevailing view of the simplicity and lowness of the Bible as writing. It is the Bible's spiritual effect on him that he loves, the way it sends rays into his soul that refine him, the way it overcomes his sinful strength and leads him to the secret favours of the Holy Ghost and to exalted pleasures; he concludes,

> Living, though wert my soul's sure ease,
> And dying mak'st me go in peace:
> Thy next *effects* no tongue can tell;
> Farewell, O book of God! farewell![24]

This shows affectionate veneration at its most eloquent without taking one to a particular version or even to something that one thinks of as literature at all. It is a hymn to the Holy Spirit in the book.

To return to Boyle: his work as a whole confirms the low opinion of the literary qualities of the translations while suggesting a growing sense of the originals as literature – or, rather, it suggests a growing *desire* to respect the originals as literary achievements, since, even though Boyle worked hard at the languages and at one stage in his life hired a man to read him a weekly chapter of Genesis in the original, his argument is almost always theoretical. What is most striking is the sense that some of the literary effect of the originals may be being felt in the KJB despite the prejudice against it as a conveyor of literary effect. Only in this does his work provide something new.

Boyle and Selden, one has to admit, provide precious little evidence for generalisations about the literary reception of the KJB. There may well be more evidence to be found, but there is unlikely to be much. One cannot believe that the KJB was commented on as English writing to such a small extent before the middle of the century, but, given the evidence of the translators, of their adversaries in controversy, and of these few surviving comments on their work, it is just as impossible to believe that there was favourable discussion of its language. When later critics, in the thoroughness of their literary reverence, put forward the idea that the KJB had *always* been greatly admired, they did so without evidence. The seventeenth century did admire the Bible as literature, but one has to be precise: it admired either the actual or the imagined originals, not the translations. The growth and expression of this admiration is a much larger subject in this period than the fortunes of the KJB.

---

[24] *Henry Vaughan, Poetry and Selected Prose*, ed. L.C. Martin (London: Oxford University Press, 1963), p. 378.

CHAPTER SIX

The Psalter in verse and poetry

'FIDELITY RATHER THAN POETRY'

Thomas Becon, so often a repeater of traditional ideas, declared the book of Psalms to be 'the treasure house of the Holy Scripture' because 'it containeth whatsoever is necessary for a Christian man to know. There is nothing in the law, nothing in the prophets, nothing in the preaching of Christ and his apostles, that this noble minstrel, king and prophet [David] doth not decantate and sing with most goodly and manifest words' (*Works*, III: 144v). As both essential teaching and as poetry, the Psalms were central to early English literary ideas of the Bible in ways that the prose Bible could not be.

Though the division is crude and in some cases inappropriate, the verse Psalters may be divided into two groups, versifications and poetifications, according to whether the teaching or the poetry is paramount. Another way of describing the division is between versions for the people and versions for the literati. The versifications for the people fit interestingly with the prose translations, for, despite being in a blatantly literary form, there is a strong anti-literary or anti-aesthetic element to them, and they were generally scorned by the literati.

Not only were the Psalms believed to be central expressions of biblical truth, but there was also a long tradition of their popular use, and, being relatively brief, they could more easily be published in a form suited to the private individual than a whole Bible or even the NT. Almost all the Psalters were published in cheap formats that were easy and convenient to own. Anthony Gilbie reflects the spirit inherent in these formats in the preface to his translation of Beza's paraphrase of the Psalms, writing that 'now even the simplest poor man for a small piece of money may, by diligently reading in this book of that rare man Theodore Beza, attain to a better understanding of these holy Psalms of David'.[1] Such books are closer to the heart of popular

---

[1] Theodore Beza, *The Psalms of David*, trans. Anthony Gilbie (London, 1581), fol. A5r.

knowledge of the Bible from the mid-sixteenth century than the complete Bibles.

The very fact of being in verse may also have helped to make them more of the people's Bible than the prose translations. There was a real prejudice against prose in this century, and at least one translator, Christopher Featherstone, notes this and uses it as an extra justification for adding a metrical translation of *The Lamentations of Jeremy* to his annotated prose version made 'for the profit of all those to whom God hath given an insight into spiritual things' (from the title; 1587). He writes of his version 'being gathered into proper and pithy metre, which for the most part holdeth those fast tied to those things which they would scarce afford one look if they were written in prose' (Epistle).

The pre-eminent verse Psalter of this and the next century was the much maligned but immensely popular Sternhold and Hopkins, more than 600 editions of which were published through to 1828. It grew out of the selection of nineteen Psalms (expanded to thirty-seven in the second edition) translated by Thomas Sternhold (d. 1549), who had been one of Edward VI's grooms. Sternhold addresses the King thus in his preface, nicely contrasting 'verity' and 'vanity', and asking to be judged by the original:

Seeing further that your tender and godly zeal doth more delight in the holy songs of verity than in any feigned rhymes of vanity, I am encouraged to travail further in the said Book of Psalms, trusting that as your grace taketh pleasure to hear them sung sometimes of me, so ye will also delight not only to see and read them yourself, but also to command them to be sung to you of others, that as ye have the Psalm itself in your mind, so ye may judge mine endeavour by your ear.[2]

He seems to be reporting and anticipating a normal private aesthetic pleasure here, though a pleasure that is clearly linked to study in the reference to having the Psalm itself in mind.

Sternhold's Psalms were added to until they formed part of a complete Psalter, sometimes with two or even three versions of individual Psalms. Its character is suggested by the full title:

The Whole Book of Psalms: collected into English metre by Thomas Sternhold, John Hopkins and others, conferred with the Hebrew, with apt notes to sing them withal. Set forth and allowed to be sung in all churches of all the people together, before and after morning and evening prayer; and also before and after sermons, and moreover in private houses, for their godly solace and

---

[2] *All Such Psalms of David as Thomas Sternhold . . . did in his life draw into English metre* (London, 1549), fol. Aiiir.

comfort, laying apart all ungodly songs and ballads, which tend only to the nourishing of vice and corrupting of youth.

To large numbers of people it gave a pleasure not unlike that of the 'ungodly songs and ballads'. Literary men, by contrast, largely despised it for its lack of variety, the general banality of the versification, and the tendency to expand and explain the text. Sometimes the explaining leads to a kind of de-poeticising through removal of the imagery, so the Lord is not my shepherd but 'is only my support' in Psalm 23 as translated by William Whittingham.

Here is a typical Sternhold Psalm:

> Domine Deus noster. Psal. viii. T.S.

The prophet, considering the excellent liberalities and fatherly providence of God towards man whom he made as it were a God over all his works, giveth thanks, and is astonied with the admiration of the same.

Sing this as the 3. Psalm.

> O God our Lord, how wonderful,
>   are thy works everywhere?
> Whose fame surmounts in dignity,
>   above the heavens clear.
> 2 Even by the mouths of sucking babes,
>   thou wilt confound thy foes;
> For in these babes thy might is seen,
>   thy graces they disclose.
>
> 3 And when I see the heavens high,
>   the works of thine own hand:
> The sun, the moon, and all the stars,
>   in order as they stand.
> 4 What thing is man, Lord, think I then,
>   that thou dost him remember?
> Or what is man's posterity,
>   that thou dost him consider?
>
> 5 For thou hast made him little less,
>   than Angels in degree:
> And thou hast crowned him also
>   with glory and dignity.
> 6 Thou hast preferred him to be Lord,
>   of all thy works of wonder:
> And at his feet hath set all things,
>   that he should keep them under.

7 As sheep and neat, and all beasts else,   [cattle
   that in the fields do feed:
8 Fouls of the air, fish in the sea,
   and all that therein breed.
9 Therefore must I say once again,
   O God thou art our Lord:
How famous and how wonderful,
   are thy works though the world.

Even without the argument at the beginning (which is not Sternhold's), this is a thoroughly clear exposition of the meaning, and the verse is simple and regular: if not memorable, it is easily learnt by heart. For memorable phrases such as 'babes and sucklings' one has to turn to Coverdale, or, later, to the KJB for 'thou hast made him a little lower than the Angels'. The rounded echo of sound that most versions have between the last and first verse is lost in an echo only of meaning, and some of the lines sustain the charge of banality, even of metrical ineptitude, as in 'therefore must I say once again'. The tendency to explain shows up in the rendering of verse two, which in Coverdale (presumably the Great Bible was Sternhold's main source) reads, 'out of the mouth of the very babes and sucklings hast thou ordained praise, because of thine enemies, that thou mightest destroy the enemy and the avenger'. Sternhold has done his best to explain a difficult compression of thought. If this is not quite translation of imagery, the turning of Coverdale's 'whatsoever walketh through the paths of the sea' into 'all that therein breed' certainly is.

Though most of the content of the English prose versions survives, the overall effect is of simplification: the text is quietly adapted to the desire for easy understanding and simple form. There are obvious grounds, then, for this version's popular appeal, and just as obvious grounds for scorn by poets and critics. Such versification represents the quest for truth at the expense of literary or linguistic quality, and it fits with an anti-aestheticism found particularly among the Puritans.

The quest for truth is familiar enough from the prose translators, but its importance to the versifiers needs to be recognised. Most explicit is Thomas Drant (d. ?1578). His *A Medicinable Moral* (1566) contains a verse translation of two books of Horace's *Satires*, which the title proclaims are 'Englished according to the prescription of St Jerome', and 'the wailings of the prophet Jeremiah, done into English verse'. Horace has been 'changed and much altered', but not Lamentations, because 'the Hebrew poets write an infallible truth: the Greek and Latin poets write forgeries and lyings'. Consequently his approach is totally different, even though he is still writing verse:

That thou mightest have this rueful parcel of Scripture pure and sincere, not swerved or altered, I laid it to the touchstone, the native tongue [i.e. Hebrew]. I weighed it with the Chaldee Targum and the Septuagint. I desired to jump so nigh with the Hebrew that it doth erewhile deform the vein of the English, the proprieties of that language, and ours being in some speeches so much dissemblable. (Preface)

So a poetic translator, no less than the Geneva translators or Gregory Martin, is willing to sacrifice literary qualities for accuracy. This is from a translator who otherwise is thoroughly willing to treat his original loosely.

In the following year the same Matthew Parker who wrote the preface to the Bishops' Bible begins his Psalter (?1567) with a verse epistle to the reader which is entirely about how the verse is to be read for its sound. But then, in a long poem 'Of the virtue of the Psalms', he lists his priorities as a translator:

> Verse clear to frame: was first pretence,
>   I followed Hierome next:
> Third Chaldee glose: fourth seventy sense,
>   rhythm, time, were fifth and sext.[3]

Clarity is first, accuracy second, third and fourth, technique last. Ornamentation is not mentioned. The order is the more striking in the context of the apparently literary insistence on reading the verse aright for its sound. Parker's priorities are only different from those of the later translators in his placing clarity before accuracy, and his final prayer might be that of all the translators so far considered: 'God grant these Psalms: might edify, / that is the chiefest thing' (fol. Biiiv).

The insistence on truth to the original and the anti-aesthetic streak became stronger in the seventeenth-century. Most of the versifiers took the approach of the American Puritans who made *The Bay Psalm Book* (1640; famous as the first book printed in America), and Francis Rous (the elder, 1579–1658). John Cotton's preface to *The Bay Psalm Book* argues the legitimacy of translating the Psalms into English metre; further, because 'the Lord hath hid from us the Hebrew tunes . . . [and] the course and frame . . . of their Hebrew poetry', translators do not have to try to imitate them but may use 'the graver sort of tunes of their

---

[3] *The Whole Psalter*, fol. Biiv. Since Parker insists on his sound being observed, I have preserved his punctuation – the colon marks the caesura – and much of his spelling.

own country songs [and] the graver sort of verses' (fol. **2r). However, this is to be done without taking any 'liberty or poetical license to depart from the true and proper sense of David's word'. So they 'have respected rather a plain translation, than to smooth our verses with the sweetness of any paraphrase, and so have attended conscience rather than elegance, fidelity rather than poetry' (fol. **3v). 'Fidelity rather than poetry', this was the prevailing choice. Like many of their fellow Psalmists, they criticise Sternhold and Hopkins, but not surprisingly their complaint is quite different from that of the literati: it is 'that they have rather presented a paraphrase than the words of David translated according to the rule' (fol. **2v). The rule they have in mind is Hezekiah's command that praises should be sung unto the Lord 'with the words of David and of Asaph the seer' (2 Chron. 29: 30). The verses that result from these principles are, as they admit, 'not always so smooth and elegant as some may desire or expect' – witness 'The Lord to me a shepherd is, / Want therefore shall not I' – but they remind readers who desire elegance 'that God's altar needs not our polishings' (fol. **3v).

Francis Rous's ideal was very similar, 'that the Holy Ghost might speak his own sense and as near as may be in his own words'.[4] If ever there is a conflict between sense and 'fit cadence', then 'sense, which is of more importance' (fol. A4r), wins. Further, 'poetical painting hath been mainly avoided, as casting lightness upon the divine gravity of those spiritual songs, whose virtue communicates itself most not by enticing words of men's wisdom but by demonstration of the spirit' (fol. A3v). Similarly, he has omitted 'some elegant and more refined words . . . in favour to the common capacities' (fol. A3v), since general comprehensibility matters more than the pleasure of a few.

Rous and *The Bay Psalm Book* have one other important element in common. Both, it goes without saying, are based on the originals, but as a second source they follow, in Cotton's words, 'our English Bibles'. *The Bay Psalm Book* does this by using 'the idioms of our own tongue instead of Hebraisms, lest they might seem English barbarisms' (fol. **3r), and Rous explicitly uses the KJB, from which, he says, 'few places have been altered, except where some very probable cause hath appeared' (fol. A3v); moreover, he gives the KJB in parallel. Both versions thus endorsed the accuracy and general style of the KJB, so giving early evidence of its advancing status as *the* English version, and helping, perhaps, to secure this status.

[4] *The Psalms of King David in English Metre* (London, 1646), fol. A3v.

Rous's version was carefully examined and corrected under the auspices of the General Assembly of the Church of Scotland, and became the official Scottish Psalter, enjoying a high reputation for accuracy but a mixed one for poetic quality. Thus England, Scotland and America each came to have as their main verse renderings Psalters which placed fidelity ahead of felicity and which reflected the prevailing religious hostility to art. However much the literary reputation of the originals was rising during the century, it had little impact on the people's Psalters. The separation between religion and poetry remained powerful.

'A GREAT PREJUDICE TO THE NEW'

One might well wonder why this explicitly unpoetic method of translating poetry should have been so successful. The answer lies principally with the people. The people of England had come to know the Sternhold and Hopkins Psalter by heart: participation, familiarity, pleasure and a reluctance to change were inseparable. By the end of the seventeenth century it was their treasured possession in the worship of the Church, and it was under threat. It was at last losing its battle against rival versions, particularly in the face of competition from Tate and Brady's Psalter (1696). This sparked some debate that anticipates arguments about the KJB and at times involves it. The Sternhold and Hopkins Psalter was more obviously antiquated than the KJB, thoroughly open to aesthetic objection, but much more loved.

Bishop William Beveridge (1637–1708) spells out the arguments with engaging intransigence in his posthumous defence of Sternhold and Hopkins against Tate and Brady. It is his dogmatic view – by no means indefensible though never so bluntly expressed – that 'it is a great prejudice to the new that it is new, wholly new; for whatsoever is new in religion at the best is unnecessary' (*A Defence*, p. 3). In other days he would have been a great defender of the Vulgate, and it is instructive to see the same kind of conservatism that opposed vernacular translation manifesting itself in relation to those very translations: so many ideas broadly connected with the language of the Scriptures repeat themselves. His paternalistic reason is this:

when a thing hath once been settled, either by law or custom, so as to be generally received and used by [the people] for a long time together, it cannot be afterwards put down and a new thing set up in its stead without giving them great offence and disturbance, putting them out of their road and perplexing

their minds with fears and doubts which way to take, and inclining them also to
have an ill opinion of the Church they live in. (p. 4)

The line of defence for the Sternhold and Hopkins Psalms is obvious,
simply that they are old. But besides this, they belong to a time that,
though less artful and learned, surpassed the present in 'wisdom, piety
and devotion' (p. 16). The people love them and 'ye never hear them . . .
complain that . . . [they] are too plain, too low or too heavy for them';
rather, 'the plainer they are, the sooner they understand them, the lower
their style is, the better it is suited to their capacities, and the heavier they
go, the more easily they can keep pace with them' (pp. 42–3). Beveridge
builds on this a very important claim for both Sternhold and Hopkins
and the KJB, that they have established an individual style that is ecclesiastical, unliterary English:

the style of the Scripture, of which the Psalms are part, is all such. There are
no enticing words of man's wisdom there, no flights of wit, no fanciful expressions, no rhetorical, much less poetical, flourishes. But everything necessary for
mankind to believe and do is delivered there in such a plain and familiar style
that all sorts of people may understand it. When Almighty God Himself speaks
of Himself, He condescends so low as to use such words and expressions as we
commonly use among ourselves. And seeing the whole Scripture is written in
such a style, all translations of it must be so too, or else they cannot be true translations. And, therefore, this is so far from being a fault that it is one of the greatest excellencies of this old translation of the Psalms that it doth not only keep
to the sense of the text but to the same manner of expressing it which is there
used. (pp. 43–4)

It would be untrue to Beveridge to insist that he is describing the originals or that he is prescribing a method of translation rather than a style.
The paragraph started as it finishes, with the translations as its subject.
God, it seems, did not so much speak vulgar Hebrew or Greek as the
same language 'as we commonly use among ourselves'. Indeed, the
translations, Sternhold and Hopkins as well as the KJB, are inspired.
Only when a translation disagrees with the original is it 'not of divine
inspiration but human invention'.

Zeal to defend Sternhold and Hopkins leads Beveridge into a flat
contradiction of his Augustan contemporaries' admiration for French
and Latin. As he understands it, the main objection to Sternhold and
Hopkins is 'that there are many old words in it which are now grown
obsolete and out of use' (p. 49). He concedes there may be a few, but
the people 'still use those words, or, at least, understand them as well as
any that are in common use among them'. This may be dubious, but

he adds pertinently that 'it is, we know, among the common people that the language of every nation is best preserved' (p. 50). So he challenges the Augustans: 'what exception, then, can be taken against those old words? Are they not all true English words? And is it any fault that they are not Latin or French? It must come to that at last, for ye can scarce find any better English' (p. 51). This is not just rhetoric. He discusses a number of examples, of which none is more interesting than 'the word that most stumble at . . . at the very threshold in the first verse of the first Psalm', for this is an example where not only does he admit misunderstanding but he documents it from the alteration made in some editions:

> The man is blest that hath not bent
>   To wicked rede his ear,
> Nor led his life as sinners do,
>   Nor sate in scorner's chair.

That which they find fault with here is the word 'rede', which they say is now grown out of use, so that many do not know the meaning of it. But must the word be blamed for the people's ignorance? This is not only the best but the only English word I know of in all our tongue that signifies that which we otherwise call 'advice' or 'counsel'. For these two words, the one is taken from the French, the other from the Latin, but 'rede' is truly and originally an English-Saxon word, commonly used to this day in Germany, from whence our language came . . . And therefore 'rede', as it is written in the translation of the Psalms (not 'read', as in some later editions) is properly a true English word, and was always used in the same signification as we now use 'counsel' and 'advice', words plainly of foreign extraction. And, therefore, I can see no reason why it should give place to them. It is very hard that a native of our own country should be cast out only to make way for a foreigner, and that too for no other reason but because he is old. (pp. 74–5)

'Counsel' goes back to middle English, and 'advice' has a long history; Tyndale used the former, while the KJB has both. This and the last comment betray Beveridge's bigotry, but still the argument is of real importance: adulation of the vernacular translations keeps natural company with a highly un-Augustan reverence for the Teutonic roots of the language such as we have previously seen from Cheke (above, pp. 26 ff.). In a sense, the battle between the inkhorn and the native strain is being fought again.

Several anecdotes confirm the accuracy of Beveridge's portrait of popular attitudes. From the other side of the fence, Nahum Tate himself (1652–1715) tells this story:

[Simon Patrick,] the late Bishop of Ely, upon his first using of his brother Dr Patrick's new version [of the Psalms] in his family devotion, observed, as I heard himself relate the passage, that a servant-maid of a musical voice was silent for several days together. He asked her the reason, whether she were not well or had a cold? adding that he was much delighted to hear her because she sang sweetly and kept the rest in tune. 'I am well enough in health', answered she, 'and have no cold; but, if you must needs know the plain truth of the matter, as long as you sung Jesus Christ's Psalms, I sung along with ye; but now you sing Psalms of your own invention, you may sing by yourselves.' (*Promoting Psalmody*, pp. 20–1)

Here is a new mumpsimus (see above, p. 24). The degree of the ignorance may be exceptional,[5] but it is a salutary reminder that affection and knowledge can be as separate as the two trees in the Garden of Eden. One wonders if the good Bishop did anything for the maid's soul by turning to the title page and showing her the translators' names. The tale also shows how easily the people could do as Beveridge did, attribute divine authorship to a translation.

Tate gives another vivid illustration of the popularity, and the religious and cultural efficacy, of Sternhold and Hopkins. He quotes the outstanding churchman of the time, principal founder of the Society for Promoting Christian Knowledge (SPCK) and the Society for the Propagation of the Gospel in foreign parts (SPG), the saintly Thomas Bray, who writes 'that through the fondness of people for Psalm-singing many have recovered their reading, which they had almost forgot, and many have learned to read for the sake of singing Psalms where it has been practised to some advantage in the performance'. Tate adds:

'Tis likewise certain that in his own country parish the young men that used to loiter in the churchyard, or saunter about the neighbouring grounds and not come into the church till the divine service was over, upon his ordering a Psalm to be sung before prayers began, they came flocking into the church, where, by this means, he had 'em present both at the prayers and preaching. (pp. 6–7)

Bray, the great spreader of Christian culture, could turn into reality the theory that literary appreciation (of a sort) would make people more religious. There is a precedent here that many familiar with the use of soul and pop music in modern congregations will recognise, though in his time the lure of a contemporary idiom was unnecessary. Sternhold and Hopkins was a kind of classical pop music to thousands upon thousands.

[5] But not unique: perhaps about the beginning of the present century, a young curate declared to his congregation, 'if the King James Version was good enough for St Paul, it is good enough for me' (as given in Newton, *The Greatest Book*, p. 53).

AN ASIDE: VERSE EPITOMES OF THE BIBLE

A by-product of the relationship between versification and the Bible was the creation over a long period of verse epitomes of the Bible. The most notable in this century are the 'Thumb Bible' (1614) of John Taylor, 'the water poet' (1580–1653), and John Lloyd's *A Good Help for Weak Memories* (1671). They underline an important point about the use of verse. Lloyd informs his reader that 'meeting long since with a little Latin book called *Gemma Fabri*, being alphabetical distichs upon the Bible, I was strongly persuaded that something of that nature in English would be very profitable towards the remembering, repeating and finding out of places of Scriptures', but he adds a warning that 'if thou expectest a poetical flash, thou wilt be disappointed; neither is it possible, where a person is tied to matter, laconic brevity and initiating letters' (fol. A2r). This is thoroughly in keeping with the literal approach to versifying the Psalms, and emphasises that verse, quite legitimately, could be nothing more than an *aide-mémoire*. Nevertheless, the results have a certain curiosity value that warrants a brief description, especially as Taylor's work was popular enough to be reprinted until early in the present century and would have been many children's introduction to the Bible.

This popularity had more to do with size than poetic quality, for the 'Thumb Bible' was among the smallest books ever printed, the pages originally measuring 32 x 29 mm., and containing only two lines of verse each. Typical of its uninspired but easily remembered couplets is this summary of Proverbs:

> The wisest man that ever man begot
> In heav'nly Proverbs shows what's good, what's not.

Lloyd was more ambitious, though no more poetic. Every chapter of the Bible is reduced to a couplet beginning in sequence with the letters of the alphabet so that, as he explains, if you are

desirous to have a boy or girl of ten years or upwards to tell you in what chapter any historical passage is, let him read one chapter every day in order, and learn the distich (or two lines) which are the contents thereof. When he hath learned twenty distichs or more, examine him of particular passages in the chapters he hath passed, as, in what chapter is set forth Sarah's barrenness; he presently calls to mind this distich:

> Quell'd's Sarah's hope of seed; Hagar doth scorn
> Her mistress, flies; returns: Ishmael's born.

He considereth that Q is the first letter in the distich, which is the sixteenth in the Christ-cross-row; thence he concludes it must be in the sixteenth or thirty-sixth chapter of Genesis.

I have known two children who by this easy task, in half a year's time, would hardly miss any historical passage from the first of Genesis to the end of Ruth. (fols. A2r–A3v)

He adduces other advantages such as that the work may act as a kind of concordance and as a summary of moral instruction, and includes verses for remembering such things as the numbers of chapters in the Bible or the names of the apostles. As a sample, this is what he does with the first four chapters of Genesis, producing a kind of telegram verse:

1. All's made in six days, heav'n, earth, light, seas vast:
   Sun, moon, stars, fish, fowls, beasts, and man at last.
2. Blest is the Sabbath, woman formed, man
   In Eden placed; wedlock there began.
3. Craft of the serpent, man's fall wrought, all cursed.
   A Saviour promised. Man from Eden thrust.
4. Driv'n by pale envy, Cain doth Abel kill,
   Is cursed. His seed the land of Nod doth fill. (p. 1)

Doubtless this was a noble undertaking, but hardly likely to lead its poor victims, whatever it might do for their 'weak memories', to a love either for verse or for the Bible. It is at the furthest possible remove from *Paradise Lost*, and makes abundantly clear how little an ostensibly literary medium, verse, might have to do with a literary sense of the Bible.

IDEAS OF BIBLICAL POETRY

Developing in tension with the versifications is the history of ideas of biblical poetry and of artistic translation of that poetry. Patristic ideas of biblical poetry were being revived, both to encourage appreciation of it and to rescue poetry from its general denigration as profane lying. So Barnabe Googe (1504–94) reports Jerome's opinion that 'the divine and notable prophecies of Isaiah, the Lamentations of Jeremy, the songs and ballads of Solomon, the Psalter of David and the book of Job were written by the first authors in perfect and pleasant hexameter verses'.[6] He builds on this to convince his reader of the high regard the ancient fathers, holy prophets and Holy Ghost (which even spoke through Virgil) had for verse.

Hereafter testimonies from the Fathers to the poetic nature of the

---

[6] Marcellus Palingenius, trans. Googe, *The Zodiac of Life* (1560); intro. Rosamond Tuve (New York: Scholars' Facsimiles & Reprints, 1947), unpaginated preface.

originals become relatively common. The following comes from a French work that so impressed Sir Philip Sidney (1554–86) that he began a translation of it:

What shall we say then to the poetries, specially of David, considering that he was afore all the poetries of the heathen, but that those poetries are not an imitation but a simple affection: if we seek there for songs of victory, we have of them, but they concern the God of Hosts; if for bridesongs, they be not wanting, but if they be of God and of them that fear him; if for burning loves, there be songs of the very love itself, howbeit kindled of God himself: if for shepherd's songs, it is full of them, but they concern the Everlasting for the shepherd and Israel for the flock. The art of them is so excellent that it is an excellence even to translate them.[7]

The commendation of translation may well have encouraged Sidney to make his own translation of the Psalms, and the praise of the originals may similarly have encouraged him to pen an important passage in his *An Apology for Poetry* (written 1580). He writes tentatively, as if the idea is a daring new one. Not only is this because the idea had not yet taken hold; it is also because Sidney was well aware of the real estrangement between poetry and religion:

And may I not presume a little farther, to show the reasonableness of this word 'vates', and say that the holy David's Psalms are a divine poem? If I do, I shall not do it without the testimony of great learned men, both ancient and modern. But even the name Psalms will speak for me, which, being interpreted, is nothing but songs; then, that it is fully written in metre, as all learned Hebricians agree, although the rules be not yet fully found; lastly and principally, his handling his prophecy, which is merely poetical. For what else is the awaking his musical instruments, the often and free changing of persons, his notable *prosopopeias*, when he maketh you, as it were, see God coming in his majesty; his telling of the beasts' joyfulness and hills' leaping but a heavenly poesy wherein almost he showeth himself a passionate lover of that unspeakable and everlasting beauty to be seen by the eyes of the mind, only cleared by faith? But truly, now having named him, I fear me I seem to profane that holy name, applying it to poetry, which is among us thrown down to so ridiculous an estimation: but they that with quiet judgements will look a little deeper into it, shall find the end and working of it such as, being rightly applied, deserveth not to be scourged out of the Church of God. (pp. 5–6)

There is a mixture here of dependence on authority[8] and what might well be genuine appreciation.

---

[7] Philip of Mornay, trans. Philip Sidney and Arthur Golding, *A Work Concerning the Trueness of the Christian Religion* (1587), p. 425.

[8] Israel Baroway has traced possible non-English sources for this passage, principally the preface to the poetic books in Tremellius's Latin OT (1575–9) in 'Tremellius, Sydney, and biblical verse', *Modern Language Notes* 49 (1934), 146–7, and 'The accentual theory of Hebrew prosody', *English Literary History* 17 (1950), 115–35, pp. 118–22.

Sir John Harington (1561–1612), also in an 'apology of poetry', repeats Sidney's report of the state of Hebrew scholarship and uses biblical poetry to help defend poetry from the association with lies:

some part of the Scripture was written in verse, as the Psalms of David and certain other songs of Deborah, of Solomon and others, which the learnedest divines do affirm to be verse and find that they are in metre, though the rule of the Hebrew verse they agree not on. Sufficeth it me only to prove that by the authority of sacred Scriptures both parts of poesy, invention or imitation and verse, are allowable, and consequently that great objection of lying is quite taken away and refuted.[9]

There is nothing disinterested in this praise. If to promote a literary idea of the Bible will defend poetry, then by all means argue that the Bible has poetic parts. Revealingly, Harington later reversed his position, remarking in his lives of the Bishops:

I am grown an unfit praiser of poetry, having taken such a surfeit of it in my youth that I think now a grey head and a verse do not agree together, and much less a grave matter and a verse. For the reputation of poetry is so altered by the iniquity of the times that whereas it was wont to make simple folk believe some things that were false, now it makes our great wise men to doubt of things that be true.[10]

He instances a versification of the creed that had two lines of dubious soundness, and so, in his mature devotion, comes close to a total reversal of his earlier views: 'wherefore, though I grant the Psalms and hymns may and perhaps ought to be in verse, as good linguists affirm Moses and David's Psalms to be originally, yet I am almost of opinion that one ought to abjure all poetry when he comes to divinity' (II: 202). None so virtuous as a reformed sinner, perhaps, yet this *volte face* underlines the way attitudes to the Bible typically differed according to whether it was religion or literature that mattered most to the individual.

THE SIDNEY PSALMS

Sometimes coexisting with, sometimes replacing the anti-aestheticism is the desire already seen in the first of the verse translations, Coverdale's (above, p. 33), to compete with secular literature. This goes beyond the straightforward preference for 'the holy songs of verity' reported by Sternhold. Again Parker is representative:

---

[9] G. Gregory Smith, ed., *Elizabethan Critical Essays*, 2 vols. (Oxford University Press, 1904), II: 207.
[10] *Nugae Antiquae*, newly arranged by Thomas Park, 2 vols. (London, 1804), II: 201.

Depart ye songs: lascivious,
   from lute, from harp depart:
Give place to Psalms: most virtuous,
   and solace there your heart. (*The Whole Psalter*, fol. Biir)

Another to make this point was Michael Drayton (1563–1631). He versified many biblical passages 'to the advancing of God's glory and the beautifying of his Church'. He doubts not that his reader will 'take as great delight in these as in any poetical fiction', for 'I speak not of Mars . . . nor of Venus . . . but of the Lord of Hosts that made heaven and earth; not of toys in Mount Ida, but of triumphs in Mount Sion; not of vanity but of verity, not of tales but of truths'.[11] There was a continuing battle to convert readers and listeners to an appreciation of the poetic parts of the Bible.

The most extreme example in this century of the wish to foster through translation an appreciation of the Psalms as poetry is the version begun by Sir Philip Sidney and completed by his sister, the Countess of Pembroke (1561–1621) after his death. It had no public success beyond being known to a few writers, for it was not published until 1828. But this is not negligible, for among the few were Donne, Jonson, Herbert, Daniel, Greville and Harington. The admiration of such writers helped to foster a much more ambitious artistic approach to the Psalms in the seventeenth century.

Donne praised the Sidney Psalms in a poem 'Upon the translation of the Psalms . . .', showing not only how they were admired but particularly how intelligent literary men disliked Sternhold and Hopkins: the Psalms, he writes, are

   So well attired abroad, so ill at home,
   So well in chambers, in thy Church so ill,
   As I can scarce call that reformed until
   This be reformed . . .
   And shall our Church, unto our Spouse and King
   More hoarse, more harsh than any other sing?

To take one of these versions for 'chambers' is to reveal some significant contrasts, even though Psalm 8, translated by Sidney, does not show the collection at its best:

   O Lord that rul'st our mortal line,
     How through the world thy name doth shine:

---

[11] *The Harmony of the Church* (1591); *The Works of Michael Drayton*, ed. J. William Hebel, 5 vols. (Oxford: Shakespeare Head Press, 1961), I: 2, 3.

That hast of thine unmatched glory
Upon the heav'ns engrav'n the story.

From sucklings hath thy honour sprung,
Thy force hath flowed from babies' tongue,
Whereby thou stopp'st thine en'mies prating
Bent to revenge and ever-hating.

When I upon the heav'ns do look,
Which all from thee their essence took;
When moon and stars my thoughts beholdeth,
Whose life no life but of thee holdeth:

Then think I: Ah, what is this man
Whom that great God remember can?
And what the race, of him descended,
It should be ought of God attended?

For though in less than angels' state
Thou planted hast this earthly mate;
Yet hast thou made ev'n him an owner
Of glorious crown, and crowning honour.

Thou placest him upon all lands
To rule the works of thine own hands:
And so thou hast all things ordained,
That ev'n his feet have on them reigned.

Thou under his dominion placed
Both sheep and oxen wholly hast;
And all the beasts for ever breeding,
Which in the fertile fields be feeding.

The bird, free-burgess of the air;
The fish, of sea the native heir;
And what things else of waters traceth
The unworn paths, his rule embraceth.
    O Lord that rul'st our mortal line,
    How through the world thy name doth shine!

The most striking difference from Sternhold's version is the difficulty of
the syntax, a difficulty evident throughout the collection. The reader's
ease is not consulted, and this is hardly likely to appeal to the unsophis-
ticated. Whether or not one takes this complexity as a deliberate artful-
ness, there are many appreciable signs of art: the careful repetition of
the opening lines as a coda to the last verse is particularly effective, and
the use of the break between verses three and four produces a good sense
of progression and climax, though spoilt by the awkwardness of 'whom

that great God remember can'. Sternhold and Sidney's versions are of about the same length, but Sidney gives much more attention to the animal kingdom at the end: rather than just naming the animals, he evokes them, and he adds 'fertile' to the fields, which both fills out the metre and produces alliteration and description. Differences of this sort make it unsurprising that the Sidney Psalter should have remained unpublished while Sternhold and Hopkins went from strength to strength. Complex in sense and form, unadapted to the traditional tunes and unaccompanied by music, the Sidney Psalter could not appeal to the religious populace.

GEORGE WITHER AND THE PSALTER

The most notable exponent of a poetic approach to the Psalms was George Wither (1588–1667), a minor and indefatigable poet; to him belongs the very real credit of writing the first book in English on literary aspects of the Bible, *A Preparation to the Psalter* (1619). This is a discussion of the nature of the Psalms and of principles of translation. It is also a defence of poetry. Wither records something of the development of his appreciation of the Psalms. He describes himself as one who had almost adopted the prevailing literary enthusiasm for the classics, an enthusiasm which scorned the Psalms as 'simple and foolish', 'homely writings' (pp. 68–9). But he began to read the book, 'although it seemed not over-pleasing when I first began to taste thereof' (p. 69), and, through much study, came to believe them the best poetry. This belief brought with it a sense that he had previously read the Psalms without understanding (p. 21). Consequently,

having upon some occasion taken more notice of the excellency of the Book of Psalms than I had formerly done, and withal observing what poor esteem those incomparable hymns have amongst the common sort of men in respect of that which the elegancy of profane poems hath obtained, being trimmed up in those their natural ornaments of poesy, which the Psalms have been in some sort deprived of, I grew somewhat jealously desirous to see the majesty of those writings, if it were possible, in some measure restored, either by the public appointment of the Church or by him on whose private endeavours God should be pleased to give a blessing to that purpose. (p. 3)

Fundamental, then, to his undertaking of a translation were his dissatisfaction with the literary qualities of available translations and his continuing high regard for poetry. The translations he was dissatisfied with were primarily Sternhold and Hopkins, and the prose translations of the KJB and the PB. What is more problematic is to determine what version or versions of the Psalms he was reading during his conversion to them. He appears to have known a little Hebrew, enough at least to risk transliterating a few lines, but not much. His own ambiguous statement is that he had had a glimpse of the Hebrew and its poetry (p. 61). This at its best could not have been a sufficient basis for appreciating the originals. He read all the scholarly commentaries and discussions he could find: they were essential to his understanding, but they do not constitute a text. If his English reading was tied to a particular text, it was that of the PB,[12] and perhaps, therefore, he learnt to love the Psalms through this, and so appreciated it without acknowledging the fact. Yet he based his own version on the KJB, and his comments on translations show dislike, especially of the prose. The truth is likely to be this: he read translations, including the PB, the KJB and paraphrases, but the version he learnt to appreciate was an imagined, not a real one, which he identified in his own mind with the Hebrew. It was all the easier for him to do this because he could not read the Hebrew properly. Thus he writes as if he is discussing the originals but, except where he is illustrating his idea of the form of Hebrew poetry, he gives examples from his own translations, which is the nearest he can get to realising the imagined version he has come to love.

Wither is far from the only writer for whom one has to posit a nonexistent text. Many commentators pretend to write about the originals even though they are incapable of reading it. Further, those who could read Hebrew read into its poetry a non-existent form. They too in a sense were reading an imagined text. If one responds that the text exists only as it lives in the reader's imagination, and therefore is just as unreal, there is still a real difference, for here we are talking of an idea of a text which cannot be read, a text which the critic believes to be different in qualitative ways from the version of the text he has actually read, rather than of an idea of a text which has been read, an idea that is believed to be identical with the read text.

Wither's supreme opinion of the Psalms comes from the combination of his religious assent to them and his belief in poetry as the highest form of writing. He is one of the few critics to deal with the question of assent; he writes that the Psalms have to be read in the belief that they are 'the truth of God, inspired by the Holy Spirit, without falsehood or contradiction'. But, he perceptively argues, if the reader

---

[12] One paragraph in Wither's *Scholar's Purgatory* (pp. 87–8) assembles verses from the Psalms that are applicable to his own situation. Where a specific source is identifiable, it is the PB.

come rather with the same indifference wherewith he undertakes the study of other writings, they shall appear to be so strange a medley of passions and such distracted pieces of poesy to his carnal ear that they will not be esteemed unnecessary alone but perhaps ridiculous, and instead of making him a better Christian, carry him with the atheist into a contemptible opinion both of them and their author the Holy Ghost. (*Preparation*, p. 90)

Though his arguments are based mostly on faith, they also come from his genuine personal response to the Psalms. He recognises that others respond differently, and he accounts for this by fairly identifying the basis of his high literary opinion as faith. He couples this point with the idea that all the ornaments of rhetoric are to be found in the Bible, though crucially they operate in a different way from profane rhetoric:

Moreover, the rhetoric of these poems is rather framed to win attention from souls than to delight the ears of the body. Yea, they are expressions of spiritual passions, and therefore it is impossible they should please or move carnal men. They have as many elegancies – as proper expressions, as fit epithets, as rare metaphors, as lofty hyperboles, and every way as many ornaments of speech – as the most renowned authors. And wherefore then are they not so esteemed of? Even because we love not the matter, or by reason of that antipathy which is between our natures and goodness. (p. 69; see also pp. 75, 77)

An interesting change is evident here. Elsewhere we have seen the question, 'wherefore are they not so esteemed?', replied to on the ground that translations lose the literary qualities of the originals; now the answer depends on religious assent and on the opposition between sacred and profane. Wither appears to be casting around for any convenient defences against the poor reputation.

His sense of divine inspiration is similar to Broughton's (see above, pp. 56 ff.). He writes, keeping clear the basis in his personal faith, 'for my part I believe their authority who have affirmed that these Psalms and holy mysteries were first delivered by the Holy Ghost in verse. And as I persuade myself, they were then such as best fitted those times and the elegancy of that tongue, so I am also out of doubt that they are yet uncorrupted' (p. 63). However, he goes beyond Broughton in bringing out some of the literary consequences: 'the Holy Ghost hath not in vain written this part of his word originally in numbers [verse]; and therefore I think that even the form of these poems ought to be considered with that reverend heed as if some sacred mystery were included therein' (p. 65). This provides a basis for arguing that generally literal translations like the KJB in fact give the best poetic rendering of the original, providing one accepts that the basis of the poetic form is parallelism. But

Wither argues differently. Partly on the authority of the Fathers, partly on the opinion of modern commentators, he describes the form of Hebrew poetry as consisting 'of divers numbers [metres] intermixed, sometimes equally, sometimes unequally, and oftentimes with rhymes in the periods of sentences; not much unlike some of our English numbers, which admit not very naturally of such kinds of verse as are usual with the Latins' (p. 59). But he is not content, as most of his predecessors had been, to leave the matter to authority: he goes on to demonstrate the similarities of Hebrew and English verse by printing and transliterating some lines of Hebrew. This at the least has the merit of looking persuasive, though he is honest enough to point out difficulties of transliteration, apparent irregularities of lines and visual imperfections in the rhymes. He suggests such deficiencies were covered in the speaking or singing.

Wither's veneration of poetry leads to a striking point about the nature of the Psalms. Referring to Augustine and his contemporary, the grammarian Priscian, he argues that 'God who is the lover of all concord is doubtless best pleased in those things which come nearest to the imitation of himself' (p. 63). So poetry is more apt for God than prose: because of its order and regularity, it gives 'a greater gravity, a higher and more majestic style to that which is delivered than those words can which are ordinarily tumbled together in prose without respect to place or quantity' (pp. 63–4). Here he has stepped well away from the dominant emphasis on the meaning of the text and posited that its very form is meaningful not only because it was dictated by the Holy Ghost, but because it has a harmony analogous to the essential nature of God. This is a striking movement, for in it is the potential to break down the decorative theory of literature. If the literary form helps to express the religious significance of the writing, then form is no longer a matter of surface but of essence, and the divorce between religion and literature cannot be sustained.

Wither's theory of translation is tied in with these ideas. He believes that 'in every language verse hath more elegancies than prose can have' (p. 7). There is an 'extraordinary majesty and pleasingness . . . in numbers' which makes it 'the most fitting language to express sacred things'. Significant here is the way 'majesty' catches both a religious and a literary meaning. Their coming together here shows, in spite of Wither being confined to the language of the ornamental theory, how literature and religion necessarily become inseparable to a man who thinks as Wither does.

At this point he has to face one of the basic objections to verse translation, that it is 'impossible for the translator so to keep himself to the original (in a matter where every letter and syllable is of such moment) but that either for the measure or the rhyme he shall be sometime forced to let go much of the true meaning of the words' (p. 7). He does not try to get round this by arguing the validity of paraphrase. Rather, he accepts the premise that the Bible should be translated as closely as possible and rejects paraphrase. He reports that, 'reserving only the proprieties of our language, I have chosen rather to confine myself wholly to the text . . . lest I should seem to distrust the force of God's own words and teach his Holy Spirit how to speak' (p. 16). This is not an advocation of literal translation, as the phrase, 'reserving only the proprieties of our language', shows. But equally it is not an advocation of ornamental translation. He rejects paraphrase because, although 'the pains would be much less and peradventure the verse would be more pleasing also to some readers', he finds 'no such want of ornament in our prophet's expressions that I need to borrow from elsewhere, nor is often his way of delivery so difficult as that it must require many circumstances to illustrate his meaning' (p. 16). Though there is no want of ornament, he admits the writing could be improved if he would allow himself to do so. What he is really advocating, and it is a radical new step, is dynamic equivalent translation.

This is inevitable given the attitudes already seen: Wither wishes to be as accurate and literal as possible but recognises that the meaning and effect of the text is more than the literal meaning of the words. This becomes explicit when he confronts the view that had prevailed in the prose translations, that he should 'keep every Hebraism unaltered' (p. 16). His reply is emphatic and novel:

for that is ever best translated and with most ease understood which we express in words and phrases suitable to our own tongue. And they who think out of a reverend respect of the Hebrew to preserve always in their versions her own natural speech, instead of the right which they imagine to give that sacred tongue, do much injure it: because the same phrases which have an extraordinary emphasis in their own language, being verbatim reduced into another, are many times of no force . . . And therefore my opinion is that every translator of the Holy Scriptures ought so to convert those Hebraisms or Graecisms as, if it were possible, they might have the same power. (p. 17)

The novelty is that this theory of translation takes regard not only of meaning but of effect — 'emphasis', 'force', 'power'.

When Wither describes his own practice, he modifies his theories somewhat in concession to 'our English translation because I would give the less cause of offence to the captious reader' (p. 22). Whether he is referring to the KJB or the PB is unclear, but he adds, clearly referring to the KJB, that 'I have joined with my comment [his accompanying commentary] the prose of the last English translation, dividing it according to the parts of the Psalm' (p. 24). Had he done this (his *Psalms of David* did not include the KJB), he would have anticipated the first instance of an English prose translation being presented in a kind of poetic form by over a hundred years.

He elaborates his views in the preface to *The Psalms of David*:

For, the Hebraisms being in some places obscure . . . I do use expressions best agreeable with our English dialect and the vulgar capacity.

Moreover, when the repetition of the same word or clause, or when two or three synonyms together in one sentence, as 'hear', 'give ear', 'attend', or, where either a periphrasis or a transposition of some words seems not so graceful in English as in the Hebrew, nor so powerfully to express the meaning of the Holy Ghost by the same idioms of speech, I have not superstitiously tied myself to the Hebrew phrase, nor to any strict order or number of words (except some mystery seemed thereby touched upon), but, using rather brevity where circumlocution appeared needless, and affecting the dialect most proper to our own tongue, I laboured to deliver the meaning of the original text as powerfully, as plainly and as briefly as I could.

One may well argue that what in effect he is describing is paraphrase, but the most striking thing about this passage is that it shows that he was aware of some of the elements of parallelism and yet did not appreciate them. He sees no more than synonymous repetition and alters it because it is not as graceful and powerful in English as in Hebrew. This leaves the door open for appreciation of the parallelism, but only as a Hebrew elegancy. What he offers his reader as a consequence is the Psalms done to early-seventeenth-century literary standards rather than a translation which, by ignoring the literary question, preserves some real measure of the Hebrew art.

Wither is the nearest contemporary of the KJB translators to complete a respectable poetic version of the Psalter, so it is worthwhile to show the kind of results he achieved. Here is his version of Psalm 23:

> The Lord my pastor deigns to be,
>   I nothing, now, shall need:
> To drink sweet springs he bringeth me
>   And on green meads to feed.
> For his name-sake, my heart he glads,
>   He makes my ways upright:

> And, I, the vale of death's black shades,
>   Can pass without affright.
> 2 Thy staff, thy presence, and thy rod
>   My joyful comforts are,
> And thou before my foes (O God)
>   My table shalt prepare,
> Oil on my head poured out thou hast,
>   My cup doth overflow,
> And thou, on me, whilst life doth last,
>   Thy favours wilt bestow,
> 3 Yea, Lord, thy goodness and thy grace
>   Shall always follow me:
> And, in thy house my dwelling place
>   For evermore shall be.

If one could consider this version without remembering others, then the impression is by no means unfavourable, and Wither's claim of power, plainness and brevity can be tested. Neither the rhymes nor the rhythm appear forced, even if some of the rhymes are not true rhymes, and there is a simple mellifluence. Particularly in the last four lines there is a conclusive clarity of statement: the parallelism of 'shall always follow me' and 'for evermore shall be' is emphasised by the closeness of the rhythm and sealed by the rhyme. Wither is by no means an incompetent translator.

Comparison with either the KJB or the PB substantiates the claim of plainness, for Wither's vocabulary is as simple as theirs. On the one hand, 'deigns', 'glads' and 'meads' may smack of poetic elaboration and diction, but 'he makes my ways upright' simplifies 'he leadeth me in the paths of righteousness' (KJB). The claim of preferring brevity to circumlocution is borne out. While there are some elaborations, Wither's version is often more concise, especially in the last four lines. Such gains and losses, often corresponding to gains or losses in quality, are generally dictated by the form he has chosen. Moreover, his version confirms how little he appreciated the original's parellelism and repetition, for, except in the last four lines, he has generally damaged these as they are represented in the more literal versions. This is most obvious in the last four lines of the first verse and the first two of the second. There is no clear connection between 'my heart he glads' and 'he makes my ways upright', whereas in the KJB (but not the PB) a powerful elaborative effect is obtained, so that 'he leadeth me in the paths of righteousness' creates an understanding of the otherwise obscure words it follows, 'he restoreth my soul'. So, in gaining English poetic form, Wither has destroyed, perhaps unknowingly, real qualities of the Hebrew verse that the more literal prose of the KJB and PB, again perhaps unknowingly, preserve.

This is a key point. Wither provides an example of a contemporary of the King James translators applying alternative criteria for translation to a part of the Bible that was known to be poetic. These criteria put recognition of literary quality ahead of literal accuracy, and they conform to contemporary ideas of literary quality. Wither's own idea of English literary quality is a restrained and sober one, and he appears as a competent practitioner of his own views. Here in the KJB and the PB literal translation is at its peak for the period, and, in the metrical version, dynamic equivalence is respectably demonstrated. Neither party appreciated the formal qualities of the Hebrew as poetry. The paradox is that literal translation, scorned from a literary point of view, preserves more of the literary quality of the original than the deliberately literary translation.

One other difference reinforces this point. Wither's version contains only one phrase capable of ringing in the ear by itself, 'my cup doth overflow'. This is surely as resonant as the KJB's famous words, 'my cup runneth over'. By contrast, the KJB and PB have several phrases that are now classical. In the KJB there is the striking opening, 'the Lord is my shepherd; I shall not want'. Wither arguably brings out the continuation of the pastoral image more clearly in his non-literal interpretation, 'to feed' in the fourth line, but this is insufficient compensation. Both the KJB and the PB have, 'yea, though I walk through the valley of the shadow of death', which is again classical, but impossible in the contemporary poetic form. Wither's equivalent lacks not only the vivid phrase, but also the sense of development from what has gone before and the sense of the extremity of the image.

So one might continue. Contemporary ideas of literature clearly hindered awareness of actual literary quality, and what was perceived to be literary form diminished that quality. The PB and the KJB had the intrinsic qualities necessary to *become* felt as literature.

Wither's overall place in the history of literary ideas of the Bible is ambiguous: he is both an original and a representative figure. The interest he now seems to deserve was not accorded to him in his time and no notice was taken of him by later translators or commentators. He is representative in his piety, in his belief in accurate translation, in his sense that the Bible contained poetry and in his belief in the high value of poetry, but no one had combined these beliefs as he did. Further, nobody writing in English at this time explored their beliefs with his persistence. Among the English poets who preceded Wither, Sidney was perhaps closest, but he did not share Wither's belief, so representative of the prose translators, in accurate translation. Wither, then, is unique in holding this combination of beliefs, all of them to be found separately or in some limited combination among his contemporaries. The consequence is that the inherent tensions between the religious and the literary beliefs produce what is, for this period in English, a novel theory of biblical translation that in outline anticipates modern theories of dynamic equivalent translation. It also produces a combination of literary and religious thought that significantly alters both, pointing to the demise of the decorative theory of literature and to the integration of form and meaning that was to become so important to later thinkers.

CHAPTER SEVEN

'The eloquentest books in the world'

THE ELOQUENT BIBLE

Thomas Becon and 'the glorious triumph of God's most blessed word'

Another facet of the Bible as literature needs to be followed through the sixteenth and seventeenth centuries, the development of ideas of the eloquence of the Scriptures (the Scriptures rather than the English Bible). These ideas also have a history that goes far back into antiquity; moreover, they developed in England with considerable influence from Europe. So to begin with the popular and voluminous Thomas Becon (?1512–67) is to start in the middle of a ride with blinkers on.

Becon describes himself as one of little talent who has therefore 'not attempted matters of high knowledge' but rather sought to teach the people.[1] Like so many Protestants, he had a dual sense of God's word (though it might be better to think of it as triple, since Christ is so often called the word, as in the second of the Thirty-nine Articles of the Church of England (1562)). As well as the Bible, the word is 'the law of the spirit written in the heart of the faithful' (III: fol. 392r). This definition comes in a short piece, 'The diversity between God's word and man's invention', which well illustrates the character of his work. It consists of 41 absolute contrasts, some of which seem to describe 'the law of the spirit' and others the Bible. Similarly, 'man's invention' refers primarily, as the preface makes clear, to the traditions and doctrines of the Catholics, and yet also to secular literature including 'the writings of the heathen philosophers' (III: fol. 389r). Becon likes to work in large, resounding generalities. 'God's word is the truth . . . Man's invention is a lie' (fol. 392r), that is the essence of all his statements.

The implications of this doctrinal simplism are picked up in one of

---

[1] *Works*, ed. John Ayre, 3 vols. (Cambridge, 1843–4), I: 27. Other references are to the first edition (see bibliography).

the most interesting pieces about the Bible from this century, 'The glorious triumph of God's most blessed Word',[2] which is presented in the form of a monologue spoken in English by 'God's word'. This is the 'word' in both senses. So it says, 'I am the word of God having my being before all worlds . . . For as God is from everlasting, so am I. And as God hath no beginning neither shall have any end, so likewise am I without both beginning and end' (III: 472r). Yet it is also embodied as the Bible, and most of the monologue has 'God's word' speaking in its character as the Bible. This ambiguity is matched by another of greater importance for us. It is not clear whether Becon means the originals, some translation, or any version, original or translation, indifferently. The last possibility is probably the right one: the Bible is speaking in English without any sense of impropriety in so doing. Moreover, when Becon eagerly refutes the standard Roman Catholic charge against vernacular Bibles, that they are heresy, he ignores the question of translation:

How can I be heresy that am the pure word of God? If I were the word of a fleshly man, which is without the spirit of God, it were no marvel though I were heresy. For that is born of flesh, is flesh. But seeing I am the word of God, which is the alone verity, which cannot lie, which is faithful in all his words, whose truth abideth for evermore, how is it possible for me to be heresy, or to teach any pernicious doctrine? (fol. 497v)

The overt premise is simple, that the Bible is truth, but there is a hidden premise, that the Bible remains absolute truth in any version.

Becon appears to be blithely unaware of the attitude he is taking to questions of text and translation. What he illustrates is the Protestant desire, possibly the Protestant need, to slide over distinctions and to make whatever vernacular text is being used as divine as the original. Other aspects of this attitude have already been seen in the suggestions that if the glosses were removed from the Roman Catholic Bible no essential differences would be found, and, to some extent, in the indifference to the precise wording of the English text (above, pp. 53 ff.).

The consequence is statements such as this from the preface: 'now as touching the excellency and dignity of God's word, who knoweth not that it doth so far excel all other kinds of doctrine that no comparison may be made between them . . . The word of God is in all points perfect, sufficient, constant, comfortable, lively etc.' (fol. 469v). This not only describes both spirit and book, it indifferently describes the originals and

---

[2] First published in *Works*; preface dated 1563.

translations. In his vagueness Becon comes very close to claiming a kind of literary perfection for both the originals and the English versions.

The word of God counters the familiar observation that 'others despise me as barbarous and rude doctrine, unworthy to be read of them that delight to have eloquence and ornate erudition' (fol. 471v), with the time-honoured point that all the best philosophers, poets, orators and historians of the ancient world 'borrowed of me all that ever they have in their works, being either good or Godly' (fol. 475v). Yet Becon accepts that the Bible has not the eloquence of such writers, and so dismisses eloquence:

Wherefore I cannot marvel enough at the madness of some men, which, for a little vain eloquence and painted manner speaking, forsake me the alone fountain of all wisdom and the treasure-house of all Godly and necessary knowledge, as a thing that is rude, barbarous and unpleasant to the ear, and run with hands and feet unto profane and ungodly authors, which as they teach a little vain and trifling eloquence, so do they bring forth to the readers or hearers many wicked and pernicious opinions. (fol. 475v)

But then comes a change. He is not prepared to allow even this insignificant superiority to the profane authors. Having dismissed eloquence, he now follows the old argument that Scripture has its own perfect eloquence; it is no accident that the last part of this sounds exactly like Broughton on the harmonic perfection of the Scriptures:

But they object that I am rude, gross, barbarous, impolite, untrimmed, unpleasant, uneloquent, etc. I answer, if this be the true eloquence, as all truly learned men do define, to express a matter with apt, open and evident words, and even with such terms as be most fit to make the thing whereof it is entreated plain and manifest to them that either read or hear it, I dare boldly affirm then that the true and pure eloquence is only found in me, which express my matter with so apt and convenient words that none can be found more fit for the purpose, as I may pass over, that there is nothing superfluous, nothing wanting, nothing out of order in all my letters, but all thing reposed and set in such comely degree as no man can justly wish it to be otherwise. (fols. 475v-6r)

All that prevents this from being a comment on the English Bibles is that one cannot believe either that Becon intended it as such, or that it would have been read as such. Yet if this is coupled either with a belief in the immutability of the Bible even through translation, or, more interestingly, with a belief that a translation is accurate, with 'nothing superfluous, nothing wanting, nothing out of order' (three most advocated and sought-after qualities in translation), it becomes a belief in the perfect eloquence of the translation. The KJB and its predecessors, as we have seen, did not aim for eloquence such as the world knew it, but they did aim for precisely the kind of accuracy needed to pick up this idea of eloquence.

The consequence in Becon is as resounding a claim of the literary quality of the Bible as any in this century:[3]

Have they a desire to read poetry? Who among all the ethnic poets is able to compare with our poet, musician, prophet and king David, whose verses do far excel theirs, not only in truth but also in all other things, lying except, whether ye will consider the pleasantness or the honest sweetness or the learned handling of things or the pithy and quick sentences? Yea, our poet's verses do far excel the other, seeing there is contained in them no filthiness, no scurrility, no jesting, no foolish talk, nor yet any thing that may defile and corrupt good manners. Let Simonides, Pindarus, Orpheus, Alcaeus, Flaccus, Catullus, Tibullus, Propertius, Gallus, Serenus, with all the other rabble of poets, be read and searched, and yet shall they never be able to compare with our David.

Have they a desire to read oratory? Who are able to compare with my orators? As I may let pass the other, may not Isaiah and Jeremy be worthily compared both for gravity and all virtue of speech to the most excellent orators of the gentiles, whether it be Cicero, Pericles, Demosthenes, Isocrates, or any other? (fol. 476r-v)

Like many others, Becon fails to join demonstration to assertion. He should not be blamed for this. A sure faith did not need argument. Besides, argument from authority was, and had long been, a most respectable way of arguing. It was fundamental to the Roman Catholic Church. Scientific methods of thought, which, in their insistence on first-hand observation, have more in common with the Protestant insistence on searching the Scriptures, had yet to promote a recognition of the need for evidence. There is, however, one work in which he comes nearer to giving a critical account of the text and his response to it, his relatively early exposition of Psalm 115 (116). There can at least be no doubting the genuineness of his response:

in my judgement and opinion this Psalm . . . far excelleth and challengeth the pre-eminence, as I may so speak. For verily so oft as I read it me think I am in a joyful and delectable paradise, where all kind of pleasures do abound, and so oft as I taste of it, it seemeth unto me like a golden flood, which floweth forth with most goodly and pleasant streams; to conclude, this Psalm, so oft as I hear the words of it, beateth and replenisheth mine ears with such sweet and delectable harmony as none may justly be compared unto it, so that neither

---

[3] The claim is particularly interesting from a modern literary point of view because it closely anticipates another passage where the voice of God defends the literary quality of the Bible, Jesus' reply to Satan's advocation of the Greek classics in Milton's *Paradise Regained* (IV: 331–64; see below, p. 177).

Mercurius, Apollo, nor his son Orpheus, nor yet any other . . . are able to compare with this our minstrel David. (*David's Harp*, 1542; I: 143v)

Passages such as this do something to reinforce one's sense that at the back of the non-textual arguments to literary conclusions, arguments which may well be uncritical, even facile, there is a genuineness of feeling that is in some way literary. Real admiration of the KJB could be founded on these arguments.

Manuals of rhetoric

Another foundation for literary appreciation of the Bible in general and eventually the KJB in particular was formed by a strengthening in the relationship between rhetoric and the Bible during the latter half of the sixteenth century. Perhaps the first Englishman of this century to make the basic point about figures and tropes and the Bible was Richard Sherry (c. 1506–55). He argues that 'not only profane authors without them may not be well understood, but also that they greatly profit us in the reading of Holy Scripture, where if you be ignorant in the figurative speeches and tropes, you are like in many great doubts to make but a slender solution'.[4] His concern, of course, is to reach a sound understanding. This was to remain primary in Christian treatments of rhetoric, which include manuals of rhetoric, instruction books for priests and compilations of religious images. Representative of the manuals of rhetoric, *The Garden of Eloquence* (1577) by Henry Peacham (the elder, 1546–1634), is essentially a dictionary of terms with examples, many of which are biblical. Peacham writes in the preface of 'the goodly and beautiful flowers of elocution . . . whose utility is so great that I cannot sufficiently praise them, and the knowledge of them so necessary that no man can read profitably or understand perfectly either poets, orators, or the Holy Scriptures without them' (fols. Aiiv–Aiiir). Poets and orators are healthy company if the Bible is to be appreciated as literature. Peacham's many biblical examples usually follow the Great Bible, sometimes the Geneva or the Bishops', and they are not necessarily accurate. As a result, *The Garden of Eloquence* shows that the English Bible can be read for its rhetoric (and indeed cannot be read accurately without an awareness of rhetoric), but it does not imply a particular text or suggest that the precise English wording is of literary importance. It is up to the reader to infer that his particular Bible is eloquent. When this implica-

---

[4] *A Treatise of Schemes and Tropes* (London, 1550), fol. A7v.

tion is coupled with the text of the KJB, as it is, somewhat inaccurately, in the rhetorics by John Smith (1656) and John Prideaux (1659), the further implication is that the KJB is eloquent.

Elsewhere the implication was occasionally spelt out. A commender of Wilson's dictionary, Roger Fenton, writes: 'though it be a dictionary interpreting words and phrases, yet it is a divine dictionary, teaching the language of the Holy Ghost in our own native tongue; which if a man could once attain to speak naturally and kindly he would be more powerfully eloquent than if he spake with the tongues of men and angels' (Wilson, 1612, unfoliated). This can be taken as suggesting that the English of the Bible is a perfect divine language, and it encourages true Christians to model their language thereon. Popular familiarity with the KJB was to be the main foundation for love of its English, and by the time of its publication a theoretical basis for this love is visible.

Eloquence and divine inspiration

The most interesting of the other works to promote the idea of biblical eloquence is by Robert Cawdray, already noted as compiler of the first English dictionary. Though the prime purpose of his massive *A Treasury or Storehouse of Similes* (1600) is instructional, it also tends towards literary praise of the Bible as in the following passage:

And although in every other kind of learning, human discipline and philosophy, there may be singular ornaments and peculiar garnishments effectually to delight the mind and to draw it by example and imitation to virtue and honesty, yet for the true and perfect attaining and fuller bringing to pass of these things, there be none of greater nor yet of like force and efficacy to those that are used by the holy prophets in their divine writings and prophecies: so that to him that is any whit reasonably seen, either in the works of nature or in heavenly contemplations, it may easily appear how that their writings and prophecies are not barren, rude, ignorant and unartificial, but profitable, learned and eloquent. For the Holy Scripture, being given by inspiration from God, fully and sufficiently instructeth the mind and furnisheth the conscience and soul with most sweet food and wholesome nourishment. (fol. A3r)

The final sentence is the key. Cawdray recognises an aspect of literary form in the Bible. Because he does not separate the form and the spiritual quality he also sees the form as supreme, for it too is 'given by inspiration from God'. This is no more than an extension of the division between sacred and profane, for the reader 'cannot choose but perceive by how many degrees divine learning and sacred studies do

incomparably surmount all profane skill and human knowledge, and
how far things heavenly and eternal do excel things earthly and transitory' (fol. A3v).

In making explicit the equation between divine inspiration and literary supremacy, Cawdray is of real importance. He points us forward to
a large number of seventeenth-century figures, but he is not original.
Besides the parallels with Becon, there are signs of this idea in English
at least as early as 1533: Lord John Berners remarks that 'except the
divine letters, there is nothing so well written but that there may be found
necessity of correction'.[5] Its longer descent is from Augustine's *On
Christian Doctrine*; earlier still the Christian apologist, Lactantius, had
pointed to this way of thinking by asking, 'is God, the contriver both of
the mind, and of the voice, unable to speak eloquently?',[6] and before
that, there is the same idea in the Bible itself when Moses protests his
lack of eloquence, and the Lord responds, 'who hath made man's
mouth. . . ? have not I the Lord. Now therefore go, and I will be with thy
mouth' (Exod. 4: 11–12). Rather, Cawdray is making clearer than anyone
else so far a basic way of thinking that leads to the claim that the Bible
is the greatest literature. The literary conclusion is not founded on real
literary criteria but on a single theological criterion, and it requires no
literary demonstration to support it. It is an article of faith.

Rather than build an alternative rhetoric on the Bible, Cawdray sees
the eloquence of the Bible as supreme by accepted standards of eloquence. Thus the holy prophets

learnedly beautify their matter and, as it were, bravely garnish and deck out
their terms, words and sentences with tropes and figurative phrases, metaphors,
translations, parables, comparisons, collations, examples, schemes and other
ornaments of speech, giving thereby unto their matter a certain kind of lively
gesture, and so consequently attiring it with light, perspicuity, easiness, estimation and dignity. (fol. A3v)

In brief, the prophets are masters of the classical art of rhetoric. Yet the
vast body of the book does nothing to support these great claims. The
first two entries for 'anger' are typical:

1. As continual shogging [shaking] doth much bruise and shake the body: so
   daily *anger* doth wound and mar the mind. Prov. 16: 32.
2. As a child for want of experience, seeking with a sword to annoy others,
   woundeth himself: so *anger* that intendeth to endamage others is most hurtful
   to itself. (pp. 24–5)

[5] *The Golden Book of Marcus Aurelius, ante* 1533, prologue; as given in *OED*, 'Letter', II: 3.b.
[6] William Fletcher, trans., *The Works of Lactantius*, 2 vols. (Edinburgh, 1871), I: 409–10.

The lack even of a biblical reference for the second of these worthy precepts is characteristic. Even where there are references, as in the first entry, they usually do not supply the image. Prov. 16: 32 reads, 'he that is slow to anger is better than the mighty; and he that ruleth his spirit than he that taketh a city' (KJB). For the most part Cawdray has supplemented his own collection of similes with biblical references to verses that deal with the same topic. Thus, while his introduction provides a theoretical basis for appreciation of the Bible's eloquence in any version, his book itself demonstrates how wide the gap could be between theoretical admiration and practical appreciation.

DIVINE INSPIRATION

In the seventeenth century, whether believed in or not, divine inspiration became the central issue in literary attitudes to the originals. William Chillingworth (1602–44), a controversialist mostly on the Protestant side, makes the necessary initial point in flatly asserting the primacy of faith over human reason where the Bible is concerned: 'propose me anything out of [the Bible]', he declares, 'and require whether I believe it or no, and seem it never so incomprehensible to human reason, I will subscribe it with hand and heart, as knowing no demonstration can be stronger than this, God hath said so, therefore it is true. In other things I will take no man's liberty of judgement from him, neither shall any man take mine from me.'[7] Faith and reason were two separate elements in the seventeenth century's idea of the mind of man: divine inspiration and the consequent literary ideas belonged with faith.

Chillingworth's remark exhibits the dogmatic simplification that characterises most (but not all) of the century's religious ideas. The Westminster Confession of Faith (1647) takes us further. It became the basic statement of Presbyterianism and is widely representative of the century in its attitude to its first subject, the Holy Scriptures. In the original Hebrew and Greek these are 'immediately inspired by God, and by His singular care and providence kept pure in all ages, [and] are therefore authentical'.[8] Directly associated with this inspiration are 'the heavenliness of the matter, the efficacy of the doctrine, the majesty of the style, the consent of all the parts, the scope of the whole (which is to give all glory to God), [and] the full discovery it makes of the only way of

[7] *The Religion of Protestants a Safe Way to Salvation* (Oxford, 1638), p. 376.
[8] Philip Schaff, ed., *The Creeds of the Evangelical Protestant Churches* (London, 1877), pp. 598–673; p. 604.

man's salvation' (p. 603). These are 'incomparable excellencies'. Implicitly the style is not only 'majestic' (that standard adjective) but perfect. The authors appear to regard these qualities as self-evident, for they present them as 'arguments whereby [the Scripture] doth abundantly evidence itself to be the Word of God'. Inspiration and perfection were indissoluble in most seventeenth-century minds, so the circularity of arguing from inspiration to perfection and then back again seemed unexceptionable.

The Presbyterian Richard Baxter (1615–91) develops this, for he characterises many of the century's attitudes to inspiration in answering his own questions, 'who be they that give too little to the Scriptures, and who too much; and what is the danger of each extreme?' Some people who give too little to the Scripture 'think it is culpably defective in method', and others 'think it culpably defective in phrase, aptness or elegancy of style'. No significant imperfection should be admitted in the art of the Scriptures. Baxter develops the point in describing what he sees as excessively enthusiastic views. Some people 'say that the Scriptures are so divine, not only in matter but in method and style, as that there is nothing of human . . . imperfection or weakness in them'.[9] Earlier he had explained that while every word in the Bible is infallibly true, 'yet in the manner and method and style' the Bible partakes 'of the various abilities of the writers and consequently of their human imperfections'. This is a possibility allowed for but not developed in the Westminster Confession. Set against most of the opinions to be looked at here, it is moderate indeed, and there is a cause: the argument from divine inspiration to literary perfection was being turned on its head by 'infidels', as he calls them, to denigrate the Bible. If the Bible can be shown to be 'less logical than Aristotle, and less oratorical and grammatical and exact in words than Demosthenes or Cicero', then its divinity is disproved because God would not write something that was imperfect. The truth of the Bible is, of course, far more important to Baxter than its style and 'method'. If praise of these makes the Bible's divinity questionable, then the praise may be jettisoned. So he allows that, even if it were true that the Bible was inferior to the classics, 'it would be no disparagement to the certain truth of all that is in it'.[10]

Among the other positions of excessive reverence which Baxter enumerates, the following are of some interest here. Some men 'feign [the Bible] to be instead of all grammars, logic, philosophy and all other arts

[9] *A Christian Directory* (1673); *Works* I: 710–11.
[10] *The Reasons of the Christian Religion* (1667); *Works* II: 144.

and sciences, and to be a perfect particular rule for every ruler, lawyer, physician, mariner, architect, husbandman and tradesman to do his work by' (*Works*, I: 710–11). In other words, they view the Bible as a divinely given compendium of all knowledge. Some believe that 'men may not translate the Scripture, turn the Psalms into metre, tune them, divide the Scripture into chapters and verses, etc., as being derogatory alterations of the perfect word', and some 'that God hath so preserved the Scripture as that there are no various readings and doubtful texts thereupon, and that no written or printed copies have been corrupted, when Dr Heylyn tells us that the King's Printer printed the seventh commandment, "thou shalt commit adultery"'.[11] The last of these attitudes was a real temptation because it meets the need to believe of those not educated enough to compare versions or consult other languages: it allows translation to be divinely inspired and so could be an absolute basis for literary admiration of 'the Bible God uses and Satan hates' (as a sticker which became current in the mid-1980s describes the KJB).

Just as divine inspiration led many to believe in the perfection of the Scriptures, so it led some to believe another position that the Westminster Confession might be taken as implying, that biblical Hebrew and Greek – often just the Hebrew – were perfect languages. We have already seen Jessey express such an attitude to the Hebrew (above, p. 101), and the erudite John Lightfoot spells it out. He thinks it needless to praise Hebrew, because nobody dispraises it, and adds, 'other commendations of this tongue needeth none than what it hath of itself, namely, for sanctity it was the tongue of God, and for antiquity it was the tongue of Adam: God the first founder, and Adam the first speaker of it'. In effect, it was the unfallen language. At the tower of Babel it fell and, though later restored, it was 'far from former perfection'. In relation to other languages, it is 'a lender to all, and a borrower of none. All tongues are in debt to this, and this to none'. He concludes wittily (or obscurely), 'to speak of the grace and sweetness and fulness of the Hebrew tongue is to no purpose to relate, for even those that cannot read this tongue have read thus much of it'. New Testament Greek is given a similar eulogy, but here the effect is more striking because it works against the classical sense of the language. 'This glorious tongue', which he thinks is probably 'maternal from Babel' and so implicitly lineal from Hebrew, is, he proclaims, 'made most glorious by the writing of the New Testament in this language'; it is 'the Greek of Greek'. 'Homer watered

---

[11] I: 711. The reference is to Heylyn's account of the 'Wicked Bible' of 1631 (Herbert 444).

the tongue, and in succeeding ages it flourished till it grew ripe in the New Testament'. Lightfoot believes God 'honoured all the [Greek] letters by naming himself after the first and the last', and that He deliberately spread the language through the world in preparation for the coming of Jesus 'that we might hear Christ speak in his own language'.[12] In short, both languages are perfect as used by God and because used by God. There could be no stronger demonstration of the power of faith in divine inspiration to produce convictions of linguistic or literary perfection.

JOHN DONNE

John Donne was one of the foremost proponents of the supreme literary quality of the originals, and if his scholarship and intellect take him beyond the hypothesising of most of the commentators, he is nevertheless typical of the century in the broad outline of his views. In his sermons he was 'ever willing to assist that observation, that the books of Scripture are the eloquentest books in the world, that every word in them hath his weight and value, his taste and verdure [savour]' (*The Sermons*, IX: 226). His most striking assistance of this observation comes as an aside to a discussion of the particular sense of two words in Ps. 6: 10, 'which in the original are "Iashabu" and "Ieboshu"'. These, he says, 'have a musical and harmonious sound, and agnomination [word-play] in them', which leads him to note 'that the Holy Ghost in penning the Scriptures delights himself not only with a propriety but with a delicacy and harmony and melody of language, with height of metaphors and other figures, which may work greater impressions upon the readers, and not with barbarous or trivial or market or homely language' (VI: 55).[13] Not only is there an explicit sense of delight in style, but the point is made from observation of the Hebrew: in both respects Donne goes beyond his predecessors, for they depended on authority and their own beliefs, and stopped short of such aestheticism. Lastly, there is the apparently general rejection of any idea of low style in the Scriptures, a rejection which modern scholars, as well as Donne's contemporaries and the Fathers, would find difficult to sustain, especially for much of the NT. Donne knew that he was running counter to ancient opinion, so he goes on to explain it away, making a particular point of the present 'perfect

---

[12] *Erubhin or Miscellanies*, chapters 30 and 33; *The Works*, 2 vols. (London, 1684), I: 1012–3, 1015.

[13] In similar vein he notes elsewhere that 'the Holy Ghost seems to have delighted in the metaphor of building' (VII: 302).

knowledge' of the original languages, and, a point already noted, of the deficiencies of translations:

it is true that when the Grecians and the Romans and St Augustine himself undervalued and despised the Scriptures because of the poor and beggarly phrase that they seemed to be written in, the Christians could say little against it but turned still upon the other safer way, 'we consider the matter and not the phrase', because for the most part they had read the Scriptures only in translations, which could not maintain the majesty nor preserve the elegancies of the original . . . howsoever the Christians at first were fain to sink a little under that imputation that their Scriptures have no majesty, no eloquence,[14] because these embellishments could not appear in translations, nor they then read originals, yet now that a perfect knowledge of those languages hath brought us to see the beauty and glory of those books, we are able to reply to them that there are not in all the world so eloquent books as the Scriptures, and that nothing is more demonstrable than that if we would take all those figures and tropes which are collected out of secular poets and orators, we may give higher and livelier examples of every one of those figures out of the Scriptures than out of all the Greek and Latin poets and orators; and they mistake it much that think that the Holy Ghost hath rather chosen a low and barbarous and homely style than an eloquent and powerful manner of expressing himself. (VI: 55–6)

Since Donne includes the Greeks among the scorners of Scripture and hinges his argument on the use of translations, he would seem to be referring only to the Hebrew, but elsewhere he includes parts of the NT as eloquent. One cannot therefore take this as a thoroughly thought-out argument: in spite of the demonstration with which it begins, it probably speaks more of what he wishes to believe than of sustained appreciation. His concluding point is a matter of faith, that the Holy Ghost would not have chosen a low style. Even so, what he wishes to believe is striking, that the 'phrase' of the Scripture is so majestic and eloquent that one need not argue from its 'matter' to demonstrate its excellence.

The passage suggests two reasons why he did not appreciate the English translations. First, simply, they are translations; second, they may well have struck him as being in 'homely language'. He neither admired such language nor found in it any representation of the qualities of the original. Such attitudes connected with his sense of appropriate style for sermons, and it is no surprise to find him bringing in the eloquence of the Scriptures when he discusses this. He believed that 'God shall send his people preachers furnished with all these abilities to be "tubae", trumpets to awaken them, and then to be "carmen

---

[14] Here the distinction between 'majesty' and 'eloquence' has all but disappeared. 'Majesty' is becoming an aesthetic term.

musicum", to sing God's mercies in their ears in reverent, but yet in a
diligent and thereby a delightful manner, and so to be music in their
preaching and music in their example' (II: 167). 'Religion is a serious
thing', he argues,

> but not a sullen; religious preaching is a grave exercise, but not a sordid, not a
> barbarous, not a negligent. There are not so eloquent books in the world as the
> Scriptures . . . .: whatsoever hath justly delighted any man in any man's writing
> is exceeded in the Scriptures. The style of the Scriptures is a diligent and an
> artificial [artful, artistic] style, and a great part thereof in a musical, in a metri-
> cal, in a measured composition, in verse. (II: 170–1)

He instances two of the commonly accepted poetic parts, Habakkuk 3
and the Song of Songs (elsewhere he gives examples from both
Testaments (IV: 179–80)). Just as the style of Scripture is supremely
delightful, so sermons should aim to delight by their style: it is a call to
the serious use of all the poetic resources of the language in preaching.
Bible language is to be a model, but he is not recommending imitation of
the style of the English Bibles. Nor indeed is he recommending wit and
eloquence for their own sake, for he says in another sermon that 'it is not
many words, long sermons, nor good words, witty and eloquent sermons
that induce the Holy Ghost, for all these are words of men' (V: 36–7).

There are only a few such passages in Donne's sermons – the eloquence of the Bible was not, in the end, a primary matter for the great
poet turned Dean – but his careful listeners and, later, readers would
have been impressed not only with a conviction of the eloquence of the
originals but also with a sense that religion and delight in language were,
to put it at its lowest, compatible. An aesthetic sense of biblical language,
based on faith but sometimes supported by demonstration, had never
before been so strongly expressed in English, nor the conviction that this
same delight could be aimed at in the diligent composition of sermons.
What these readers and hearers would not have gained was any conviction that delight could be taken in the English translation or that they
should think of any particular English text as *the* Bible: Donne, as we
have seen (above, p. 105), gave too much emphasis to the Vulgate and the
originals, and was too loose and eclectic with the English versions for
such convictions to be generated.

CONQUERING THE CLASSICS

In spite of his demonstration from the Hebrew and his insistence on
delight, Donne is more typical than original in the broad outline of his

ideas. His listeners and readers might well have come across them else-where. One last passage from his sermons shows the continuity with what was fast becoming a commonplace:

But St Paul is a more powerful orator than Cicero, and he says, 'the invisible things of God are seen by things which are made, and thereby man is made inexcusable' [Rom. 1: 20]; Moses is an ancienter philosopher than Trismegistus, and his picture of God is the creation of the world. David is a better poet than Virgil, and with David, 'coeli enarrant, the heavens declare the glory of God' [Ps. 19: 1]; the power of oratory, in the force of persuasion, the strength of con-clusions, in the pressing of philosophy, the harmony of poetry, in the sweetness of composition, never met in any man so fully as in the prophet Isaiah, nor in the prophet Isaiah more than where he says, 'levate oculos, lift up your eyes on high, and behold who hath created these things' [Isa. 40: 26]. (IV: 167)

An earlier English example of this has already been seen in Becon (above, p. 140), and there were continental, Jewish and patristic antece-dents.

In similar vein, the Puritan divine, Henry Lukin (1628–1719), expanded the range of genres compared to include narrative, explicitly working from continental authorities:

For delightful stories of strange remarkable providences of God, of noble and daring achievements of men, the various fortunes which many have tried, and the strange disasters and difficulties which many have passed and at length arrived at the height of honour and greatness, or some good issue of all their adventures and dangers, there is no book can furnish us with more eminent instances than the Scriptures. What history can parallel the stories of Joseph, Moses, the Children of Israel, dwelling in Egypt, going out thence, entering into the land of Canaan? of Samson, David and his worthies? Solomon, Elijah, Elisha, Esther, Job, Daniel, the three Hebrew children, Nebuchadnezzar and many others? For rhetoric the whole Scripture abounds with tropes and figures; and although there is nothing pedantic in it, there is such a mixture of loftiness and gravity as becomes the Author and matter of it: so, as we may boldly affirm with Mirandulanus and Mornay (the glory of the Italian and French nobility), that the flower and masterpiece of Grecian oratory is not to be compared with the eloquence of the prophet Isaiah.[15]

Still more substantial are the Baptists Thomas De Laune (d. 1685) and Benjamin Keach (1640–1704). Their *Tropologia: A Key to Open Scripture-Metaphors* (1682) is in some respects the culmination of the line of Bible-based rhetorics. In the address to the reader they tread a careful line between human and divine eloquence: the Bible, they argue, is 'unadorned with the plausible paint of human eloquence', its 'mode of

---

[15] *An Introduction to the Holy Scripture* (London, 1669), pp. 8–9.

speech . . . is plain and savours of no human blandishment or artificial beauty' (fol. A2r). On the other hand, 'it wants not a grave, genuine and majestical dignity of elocution suitable to those sacred mysteries it twofolds'. They appeal to the effect of the Scriptures, for 'the best witness of [this] is the taste and experience of that sweetness which many have found in it', and support their whole argument by referring to 1 Cor. 2: 1, 4, where Paul 'disowns his human eloquence but not that divine elocution in which he excels'. They understand that he uses 'words truly spiritual which could powerfully and effectually move their hearts', not 'those plausible affectations and artifice of words which the orators of his time made use of, who fed their auditors with the vain glory of words, in the contemplation and delight of which they went away without any other improvement than what bare rhetoric could afford'. This traditional distinction fits with, say, Jessey's attitude to biblical language but has little in common with Donne's belief in the artistry of the Hebrew. It is part of the Puritan antipathy to art, and it goes along with the recognition Donne refused to make, that there is a 'humility' and a '(seeming) rudeness' in the Bible, and that it is 'written in the common language' (fol. A2v).

Nevertheless, the idea of the supreme eloquence of the Bible is so strong that they are soon elaborating it with as much insistence as Donne, save only for the repeated reservation that they mean 'not a jingling affectation of words or sentences' (which could be said to be exactly what Donne had found), 'but the use of tropes and figures which nervate sense and move the affections of the hearer or peruser' (fol. A4r). This elaboration depends largely on authorities, and has as an integral element the argument from divine inspiration, for 'it may be safely asserted that, considering the method and style that was thought most convenient by the Sovereign Dictator of this blessed writing, the argument of which it treats, and the manner of expression there, no other writing can parallel it' (fol. A2v). There is, therefore, 'in Scripture a peculiar and admirable elegance, so that I may boldly say that Cicero's smooth and elaborate blandishments are but exercises of puerility in comparison of the grave, lively and venerable majesty of the prophet Isaiah's style'. They proceed to authorities. For instance, 'Beza, that great philologist, says that Paul's writings, when he treats of the mysteries of the Divinity, far exceeds the grandiloquence of Plato, the flourishes of Demosthenes, and the exact method of Aristotle and Galen' (fol. A3r). Many of these authorities note and reject the apparent barbarousness of the language, and Keach and De Laune repeatedly give the twin responses that the Scriptures are supremely effective and that 'their eloquence, an inseparable companion of divine wisdom, is to be esteemed the best and most elegant by the faithful, unless we suppose that God who immediately dictated them to his amanuensis spoke nonsense and is inferior to his creatures in that qualification, which is downright blasphemy, and any asserting that deserves not only derision but the severest castigation' (fols. A3v–A4r). The supreme eloquence of the Scripture is now to be an article of faith.

Although Keach and De Laune's ideas of biblical eloquence apply to the originals, their English examples come from the KJB alone, and accuracy is the rule rather than the exception: the variations are usually minor. The implication, not explicitly realised in any of these works, is that the original's eloquence may be seen in the KJB. Keach and De Laune call this 'our excellent English translation', but this is not the praise it seems to be. It is part of their explanation for the first part of their work using the original Hebrew and Greek: 'there are many tropes, peculiar to those sacred languages, which our excellent English translation rather expounds than renders verbatim' (fol. A4r). The other parts use the KJB, and the preface shows the kind of effect this could have. They quote Bibliander's preference for the style of the Bible and follow it with his example, Isa. 25: 6, 'to prove the native grace and beauty of the Hebrew, the elegancy of which no man can be ignorant of that understands the Hebrew' (fol. A3r). They give the verse first in Hebrew characters, then transliterated, then in the words of the KJB. No further comment is made, but the careful English reader who knew no Hebrew would see in the English a playing on the alliterative 'feast' and 'fat' as well as the development from 'wine on the lees' to 'wines on the lees well refined': 'a feast of fat things, a feast of wine on the lees, of fat things full of marrow, of wines on the lees well refined'. The only inaccuracy is that 'wine' should be plural both times. Then such a reader might spell through the transliteration and see there an apparent punning such as Donne had observed, 'misthe schemaniim, misthe schemariim schemaniim memychaiim, schemariim mesykkakiim'. He would have reason to conclude that the English was elegant but that the unknown Hebrew was far more so because of the much greater identity of sounds. In this way the authors' explicit purpose is sustained, but the ground is being prepared for the conviction of the original's eloquence to become an idea of the translation's eloquence.

CONFLICT OVER THE BIBLE AS A MODEL FOR STYLE

De Laune and Keach have gone much further than usual in distinguishing between the originals and the KJB, and in giving, however hollowly,
explicit praise to the KJB. In most of the commentators there is an
ambiguous looseness towards the text: at heart they mean the originals,
but increasingly they use the KJB for illustration, so preparing a ground
for it to be admired. They merit the censure that the rambling Quaker,
Samuel Fisher (1605–65) applied to the eminent Puritan theologian,
John Owen (1616–83):

> What thou meanest, I say, or which of all these three sorts of writing, whether
> the first manuscripts only, or the transcripts and translations also, or the first two
> only and not the last, or all three, which are all three commonly called . . . the
> Holy Scriptures, when thou predicatest these glorious things of the Scripture,
> thou dost not very distinctly declare, but goest on in generals . . .; so that he had
> need to be wise that very easily discerns thy mind and what thou meanest.[16]

Owen was a specially apt target for Fisher because he represented the
opposite extreme to Quakerism which Fisher characterised as owning
'not the said alterable and much altered outward text and letter, or
Scripture, but the holy truth and inward light and spirit . . . to be . . . the
word of God' (preface; fols. A4v-B1r). Owen had proclaimed, in a
passage Fisher quotes (II: 124),

> that as the Scriptures of the Old and New Testament were immediately and
> entirely given out by God himself, his mind in them represented unto us without
> the least interveniency of such mediums and ways as were capable of giving
> change or alteration to the least iota or syllable, so by his good and merciful
> providential dispensation, in his love to his word and Church, his whole word
> as first given out by him is preserved unto us entire in the original languages,
> where, shining in its own beauty and lustre, as also in all translations so far, as
> they faithfully represent the originals, it manifests and evidences unto the con-
> sciences of men, without other foreign help or assistance, its divine original and
> authority.[17]

Such thinking shows how the century's typical praise of the Bible,
vaguely meaning the originals, could become admiration of the KJB:
the key is that it should be accepted as a faithful rendering of the original, and the perception of it as a literal translation could easily be taken
as fulfilling this condition.

[16] *Rusticus ad Academicos* (London, 1660), exercitation II: 4.
[17] *Of the Divine Original, Authority, Self-Evidencing Light and Power of the Scriptures* and *A Vindication of the Purity and Integrity of the Hebrew and Greek Texts* . . . (Oxford, 1659), p. 153. The passage is from *A Vindication*.

Ideas of the Bible's divinely inspired superiority of eloquence led, from about the middle of the century, to increasing discussion and debate about the Bible as a model for human eloquence. This was not necessarily debate about whether the Bible should be a model, for to proclaim as Jeremy Taylor does in *Holy Living* (1650) that 'the Holy Ghost is certainly the best preacher in the world, and the words of Scripture the best sermons',[18] is not in itself to define a style: that definition would come from one's idea of the Holy Ghost's style, and on this there was radical disagreement which continued an older debate as to whether or not sermons should be ornate.

In 1654 the Presbyterian Thomas Hall (1610–65) argued that biblical eloquence could be taken as a model. This was tantamount to offering the KJB as a model for style, since, in spite of his sense of the inferiority of translations to the original, he used the KJB for examples. Noting Paul's disclaimer of eloquence, the 'wisdom of words' (1 Cor. 1: 17), he comments:

> that which he condemns is vain, affected strains of eloquence, and pompous words, whereby the simplicity of the Gospel was corrupted and souls kept thereby from Christ: now this is the abuse and not the right use of learning which Paul condemns. The Scripture itself is full of divine eloquence and rhetoric, and it may lawfully be used by a minister of the Gospel, not for ostentation but edification, for, being sanctified, it is a furtherance and not a hindrance to the hearers.[19]

It is not a flourishing but a subdued eloquence that he is recommending to preachers for imitation. This is something quite contrary to the spirit of John Donne, and yet we are still within the context of writers who proclaim the artistic supremacy of the Scriptures. Donne's discovery of a wit not unlike his own in the Bible is as far removed from this sense of eloquent plainness as his own exuberant sermon style is from that of so many preachers in the second half of the century. In a sense the Bible could be all things to all men, since it ranged from poetry full of figures to the most prosaic simplicity: a general agreement to admire it could conceal fundamentally different attitudes to language.

The major Reformation preacher Robert South (1634–1716) developed both the comparison with the classics and the plain ideal of style for sermons in his sermon 'The scribe instructed', preached at Oxford in July 1660, and his Ascension Day sermon, 1668, also preached at

---

[18] *The Whole Works of . . . Jeremy Taylor*, 10 vols. (London, 1859–62), III: 165. Taylor himself emphasises the plainness of the Scriptures, and characteristically rephrases the KJB.

[19] *Vindiciae Literarum, The Schools Guarded* (London, 1654), p. 43.

Oxford, on Luke 21: 15, 'for I will give you a mouth and wisdom'. He combines religious argument and literary criticism in presenting Christ as the supreme orator, arguing typically in 'The scribe instructed' that he 'was undoubtedly furnished with a strain of heavenly oratory far above the heights of all human rhetoric whatsoever' because he was 'the word', but adding that his sermons are 'of that grace and ornament, that, as the world generally goes, they might have prevailed even without truth, and yet pregnant with such irresistible truth, that the ornament might have been spared; and indeed it still seems to have been used rather to gratify than persuade the hearer' (*Sermons*, III: 3–4). In this view eloquence is a pleasing addition to truth, and South argues that preachers are justified in using it to give something of the same pleasingness to their sermons. Some people, he recognises, would call this 'a blending of man's wisdom with the word, an offering of strange fire', and would even see it as 'the next door to the being profane', but he justifies it from the Bible, for, and this is his cardinal point, 'in God's word we have not only a body of religion but also a system of the best rhetoric'. Apparently carried away by enthusiasm, he adds, 'and as the highest things require the highest expressions, so we shall find nothing in Scripture so sublime in itself but it is reached and sometimes overtopped by the sublimity of the expression' (III: 21). That the art of the Bible should sometimes be even higher than its truth is an unprecedented claim – not one, as it turned out, that he or any other devout person cared to repeat.

South supports his idea of biblical eloquence with as resounding a catalogue of its excellencies as any so far seen (III: 21–2), but he is at his most interesting in the later sermon. There he cites three passages as examples of how 'a due fervour gives [a discourse] life and authority, and sends it home to the inmost powers of the soul with an easy insinuation and a deep impression' (IV: 154), and does with the first as George Orwell was to do with Eccles. 9: 11,[20] showing how it might appear in a bad version:

Thus when Christ accosted Jerusalem with that melting exprobration in Matt. 23: 37–8, 'O Jerusalem, Jerusalem, thou that killest the prophets and stonest them that are sent unto thee, how often would I have gathered thy children together, even as a hen gathereth her chickens under her wings, and ye would not! Behold, your house is left unto you desolate'. Now what a relenting strain of tenderness was there in this reproof from the great doctor as well as saviour of souls, and how infinitely more moving than if he had said only, 'O ye inhab-

---

[20] 'Politics and the English Language'; *The Collected Essays, Journalism and Letters of George Orwell*, 4 vols. (Harmondsworth: Penguin, 1970), IV: 162–3.

itants of Jerusalem, how wicked and barbarous is it in you thus to persecute and stone God's prophets! And how can you but expect some severe judgement from God upon you for it?' Who, I say, sees not the vast difference in these two ways of address as to the vigour and winning compassion of the one and the low dispirited flatness of the other in comparison. (IV: 154–5)

The point is impressive because his version adequately represents most of the meaning of the verses, but it is not a point specifically about the KJB: it would retain its validity in any language or version that gives a close translation of the original. While this example neatly demonstrates the effectiveness of the imagery, the remaining two examples praise an eloquence not of language or of figure but of meaning. So he cites Paul's 'true and tender passion' in 2 Cor. 11: 29 ('who is weak, and I am not weak? who is offended, and I burn not?'), and the arguments Paul uses in his farewell address to the elders of Ephesus (Acts 20: 18–35), especially verse 31, which he gives, amending the opening words, as 'remember how that for the space of three years I ceased not to warn every one night and day with tears'. South calls these tears 'arguments in comparison of which he knew that the most flowing rhetoric of words would be but a poor and faint persuasive' (IV: 155). His point is that rhetoric is not used for its own sake but that the best way to persuade is always taken.

Detailed comments such as these give South's views an authority not often seen in the seventeenth century. There is a scientific element in his literary method: he does not merely assert, nor does he rely on authorities, rather, he supports his argument with analysed evidence. Moreover, he almost exhibits and persuades to a literary pleasure for its own sake in the Bible. One has to say 'almost' because in the end his idea of biblical eloquence has a religious purpose: it is a model for eloquence and a justification for its use in preaching to persuade people to religious belief. Lastly, when he comes to particulars of the kind of eloquence he is recommending to preachers, it emerges as something much more like modern prose than, say, the prose of Donne's sermons. Indeed, he is in reaction against the virtuosity and verbosity that had been characteristic of sermons, good and bad, but which was now being rejected in favour of a logical, ordered, clear and simple method.

Just as, given the limits of a sermon, South is thorough in showing the Bible's eloquence, so he is thorough in describing 'flaunting affected eloquence', and in defining what wit should be. One kind of false eloquence is 'a puerile and indecent sort of levity' which detracts 'from the excellency of things sacred by a comical lightness of expression', and seems to play 'with truth and immortality' as if the preacher neither believed

what he said nor wanted to be believed. It is full of 'vain, luxuriant alle-
gories, rhyming cadences of similary words', 'shreds of Latin or Greek
. . . a "Deus dixit", and a "Deus benedixit"', also 'the "egress, regress"
and "progress", and other such stuff, much like the style of a lease' (III:
32–3). A second kind of false eloquence is practised by 'those who cry up
their mean, heavy, careless and insipid way of handling things sacred as
the only spiritual and evangelical way of preaching, while they charge
all their crude incoherences, saucy familiarities with God, and nauseous
tautologies upon the spirit prompting such things to them, and that as
the most elevated and seraphic heights of religion'; such preachers are
full of 'the whimsical cant of "issues, products, tendencies, breathings,
indwellings, rollings, recumbencies", and Scriptures misapplied' (III:
34–5). In the later sermon South notes that the 'fustian bombast' of all
this false eloquence is most admired by those who understand it least,
particularly 'the grossest, the most ignorant and illiterate country
people' (IV: 151).

Though South is arguing for an eloquence based on the Bible, the
usually non-conformist practisers of both these kinds of eloquence that
he (and many others) derided equally believed that their language was
Bible-based. Most outspoken was a skilled religious controversialist who
carried much weight among the dissenters, the extraordinary Robert
Ferguson (c. 1638–1714), nicknamed 'the plotter' for his involvement with
two attempts to kill James II in 1692. His general view of biblical eloquence is the same as South's: it is divinely inspired and cannot be criticised 'without offering reproach to God, who as well guided the sacred
amanuenses in the words and expressions they revealed things in, as in
the things themselves they did reveal' (*Interest of Reason*, p. 281). Nor do
they differ on the purpose of eloquence, for he believes that 'the Holy
Ghost in giving forth the Scripture hath usurped no words, tropes,
phrases, figures, or modes of speech, but what are proportioned to his
end, namely the instructing us in faith and obedience' (p. 280). So
Scripture is not 'only the rule of what we are to believe and practise, but
also the measure of our expressions about sacred things' (p. 292). But he
identifies the qualities he finds in this eloquence as the very ones South
was attacking: 'the Bible', he argues (and even here South and most
other theologians of the time would have had to agree), 'is replenished
and adorned with all sort of figurative expressions. There are hardly any
tropes or figures in rhetoric of which numerous examples do not occur
in the Holy Writ' (p. 281). But then Ferguson parts company, for, in his
view, 'many of the expressions quarrelled with in sermons and practical

tracts are nothing else but the very terms and phrases which the Holy Ghost condescendeth to express sacred things by'; they cannot be objected to in the writing of men 'without reflections on the wisdom of God who useth them in the like cases and to the same purposes' (p. 292). These expressions, 'merely upon the account of their being rhetorical tropes, have been traduced as "fulsome metaphors"' (p. 282), or as '"luscious and rampant metaphors"' (p. 279).

While Ferguson underlines the extent to which the general outline of South's attitude to biblical eloquence was widely held, the contrast between the two men when they come to specifics shows that South's views were both part of the ongoing quarrel about sermon style (now a quarrel between the Church of England and the dissenters) and a manifestation in relation to the Bible of a general change in literary taste.

The heart of South's idea of eloquence comes in his description of what the style and method of sermons should be, a description that his own sermons competently model. 'Wit in divinity', he declares, 'is nothing else but sacred truths suitably expressed', and he characterises true wit as 'a severe and a manly thing' (*Sermons*, III: 33). It consists in 'strength of argument, clearness of consequence, exactness of method and propriety of speech' (III: 35): organisation and logic are its primary characteristics, and South is meticulous about the organisation and attendance to logical consequences in his own sermons. The language should not tickle the ear but sink into the heart (IV: 153). For this it needs three things, 'great clearness and perspicuity, an unaffected plainness and simplicity, and a suitable and becoming zeal and fervour' (IV: 149). The apostles' preaching succeeded because it was 'plain, natural and familiar, and by no means above the capacity of their hearers' (IV: 153). Plainness is made the cardinal virtue.

South's position is exactly that of the scientists as reported by Thomas Sprat in *The History of the Royal Society* (1667). Just as strongly in reaction against 'this vicious abundance of phrase, this trick of metaphors, this volubility of tongue which makes so great a noise in the world' (p. 112), and associating it like South with 'the artifice, the humours and passions of sects' (p. 62), he describes the Royal Society's remedy:

to return back to the primitive purity and shortness when man delivered so many *things* almost in an equal number of words. They have exacted from all their members a close, naked, natural way of speaking, positive expressions, clear senses, a native easiness, bringing all things as near the mathematical plainness as they can, and preferring the language of artisans, countrymen and merchants before that of wits or scholars. (p. 113)

'Unaffected plainness and simplicity', 'the language of artisans, country-men and merchants': what is so striking about these ideals is not just that they are consonant with so many descriptions of the Bible's language, but that they accord with the essentially popular nature of the language of much of the originals and of translations such as Tyndale's, written in an English for ploughboys. The Restoration change in taste had in it the potential to become a real admiration of the native English elements in the KJB. Given that it was now standard practice to use the KJB, if not with absolute fidelity, to illustrate points about the style of the Bible, given also that the language of the KJB was now thoroughly familiar to the people, it might seem surprising that the admiration that placed the originals ahead of the classics did not become literary admiration for the KJB. The ground seems to have been thoroughly prepared, people were ready to admire the eloquence of the Bible, and the excellence of the KJB could so easily have been inferred from a South or a Ferguson. Surely with the Restoration the KJB's time should have come? Yet if people did actually feel that the KJB was a fine piece of English, no one was prepared to say so.

Sprat gives an important clue: the latter part of the seventeenth century looked forward to the perfection of English and the previous century's reservations about the language's potential still lingered. He writes:

The truth is, [English] has been hitherto a little too carelessly handled and, I think, has had less labour spent about its polishing than it deserves. Till the time of King Henry the Eighth there was scarce any man regarded it but Chaucer, and nothing was written in it which one would be willing to read twice but some of his poetry. But then it began to raise itself a little and to sound tolerably well. From that age down to the beginning of our late Civil Wars it was still fashioning and beautifying itself. (pp. 41–2)

The Wars brought both good and bad, and left the language capable of rapid perfection. Sprat believes 'that our speech would quickly arrive at as much plenty as it is capable to receive, and at the greatest smoothness which its derivation from the rough German will allow it' (p. 42). Late Elizabethan and early Jacobean English was yet to be thought of as a high point of the language, and English was still not considered capable of the same perfection as was achieved at the height of the Greek and Roman civilisations – for these civilisations were still the yardstick for most educated men in spite of the gathering assertion of Hebraic superiority and the developing controversy about the roles of English and the classical languages in education. The inescapably Teutonic origins of much of the English language did not supply the kind of plainness the orthodox Restoration men were looking for and they long remained a ground of reproach to the language. Consequently, while the Restoration approached a position from which the KJB could be admired as an English achievement, its attitude to the Bible, in spite of some practical demonstrations of superiority from the KJB, had too much of the theoretical in it to overcome traditional attitudes that still rested on classical culture.

A related clue comes from a friend of Sprat and member of the Royal Society, the paraphraser of the Psalms Samuel Woodford (1636–1700). An authentic member of the seventeenth century's Bible-supreme club, he is nevertheless not quite at one with Sprat in his view of English, believing

that if the English dialect, not only as it is spoken at this day but as it was in use the last age, were seriously and impartially examined, it will appear not only as copious and significant for prose but as comprehensive of the sublimest notions of verse as any modern language in Europe, and to equal, if not in some qualities exceed, those of old Rome and Athens. (*A Paraphrase*, fols. b2v–b3r)

So English is supreme, even in 'the last age', and this could include the English of the KJB, for Woodford writes of 'excellent prose' as the basis of so many bad literal versifications of the Psalms (fol. aA3v).

Moreover, Woodford observes that the KJB's language is beginning to seem good because of its familiarity (he is writing of the language he has adopted in his version of the Psalms):

Besides I have been forced to make use, though as sparingly as I could, of several terms and manners of speaking not to be found in our late exact writers, nor so well fitted for the numerosity of verse as might be wished, which yet by reason of our translation of the Holy Bible and by frequent use seem not altogether so rough as else they would: rather choosing to confine myself to expressions and phrases generally known and allowed of in the Church than appear guilty of any innovation. (fols. b3v–b4r)

This undercuts the implication that he thought the KJB excellent prose, but what is most relevant here is that he suggests this roughness was not just a matter of the time the KJB was made but of characteristics of the Hebrew poetry such as 'insensible connections' (by which he means imperceptible connections), 'and frequent change and shifting of persons'. These, he writes, are 'discernible enough by our own versions', and the consequence is that the English find the Psalms 'so difficult and harsh to our ears, even in prose' (fol. b4r). The KJB, then, still sounded bad in a time that was becoming accustomed to it, not just because it was in an English believed to be inferior to the English of the present and the imagined ideal of English to come, but because it represented a literature that did not conform to the Restoration ideals of exactness, smoothness and clarity. So Woodford wants to go beyond South's silent 'improvement' of the KJB's prose and, in effect, 'correct' the poetry of the original. The result is, as he confesses, prolixity (fol. b4v): the opening five words of Psalm 23 expand to six lines in his version.

The differences between South and Ferguson, Church of England man and fervent non-conformist, and between South and Woodford, preacher and would-be poet, find expression in their tastes in the Bible. South in the end emphasises the NT, especially the words of Jesus and Paul, while Ferguson and Woodford emphasise OT poetry. Others recognised and recorded this contrast. The latitudinarian Bishop Simon Patrick (1625–1707), in the course of *A Friendly Debate* (London, 1669) between a conformist and a non-conformist, argues in detail against the non-conformist's use of language. He notes simply that the 'Psalms are pieces of divine poetry in which passions are wont to be expressed much otherwise than they ought to be in plain and familiar speech' (pp. 85–6), effectively denying that the Psalms are an appropriate model for religious speech, especially when the non-conformists not only use their figures of speech but 'go beyond them'. Similarly, William Sherlock (1641–1707), Dean of St Paul's and the principal target of Ferguson's work, retorts to Ferguson that

there is a vast difference between poetical descriptions such as the book of Canticles is, and practical discourse for the government of our lives: the first requires more garnish and ornament and justifies the most mysterious flights of fancy, the second requires a plain and simple dress which may convey the notions with ease and perspicuity to the mind. And therefore that which is not only justifiable but commendable in a divine song, which ought to have something great and mysterious, and to describe everything with pomp and ceremony, is not only a ridiculous affectation but a very hurtful vanity in a preacher, whose business is to instruct the rude and ignorant, not to amaze and astonish his hearers with poetic raptures.[21]

This too suggests a reason for the age's failure to admire the KJB: the non-conformists were giving its more poetic aspects a bad name by overusing and abusing them. In short, the orthodox were moving towards prose: their acclaim for Hebrew poetry as superior to classical poetry was

[21] *A Defence and Continuation of the Discourse Concerning the Knowledge of Jesus Christ* (London, 1675), p. 168.

hedged with practical qualifications because their opponents had taken the poetry as their own.

THE BIBLE 'DISPUTED, RHYMED, SUNG AND JANGLED'

Almost all the evidence so far has come from devout sources and involves reverent attitudes. Where reverence could lead to belief in literary perfection, irreverence, reversing the logic, could lead to the opposite belief. It is time to follow some of the scattered evidence of irreverent attitudes from the time of the early translators on, which contains further suggestions of literary responses. Thomas More describes Jerome as greatly complaining of and rebuking the 'lewd homely manner that the common lay people, men and women, were in his days so bold in the meddling, disputing and expounding of Holy Scripture' (*Complete Works*, VI: 334). He fears the same thing will happen as a consequence of the Bible in English, that it will be treated 'presumptuously and unreverently at meat and at meal'. Neatly and pertinently, he adds, 'and there when the wine were in and the wit out, would they take upon them with foolish words and blasphemy to handle Holy Scripture in more homely manner than a song of Robin Hood. And the same would, as I said, solemnly take upon them like as they were ordinary readers to interpret the text at their pleasure' (VI: 335). Interpreting the text at pleasure, as if it were an ordinary text, was indeed to have fearful results in atheism and deism; it was also to produce a movement More – or Tyndale, to look no further – would have reprehended, 'the Bible as literature'. But in the shorter term wine and wit did fulfil Sir Thomas's fears.

In his last speech to parliament (1545), Henry VIII complained that the 'most precious jewel, the Word of God, is disputed, rhymed, sung and jangled in every alehouse and tavern'.[22] This indicates the popular interest in the new phenomenon of an available and permitted English Bible. The Bible in English was, if one may put it that way, *the* cultural event of the sixteenth century. Everybody, whether devout or not, was engaged with it, and this engagement inevitably led to familiarity with its content and, in a vaguer way, with its language. It suffered the usual fate of a work known to most of the people, dissection, adaptation, parody and satire. 'Rhymed, sung and jangled' implies, I think, not so much engagement with the language of the translation as with the content. This would be in keeping with the various downplayings of the

---

[22] As given in A.G. Dickens, *The English Reformation* (1964; Glasgow: Fontana/Collins, 1967), p. 264.

importance of the language of particular versions. The Bible's stories were being constantly rehashed, and, one may infer, generally debased in the process. 'Disputed' suggests something rather different: now that the Bible was an open Bible, people were able to test it independently by their own reason.

Most of this disputation was reverent (if not decorous) study of the text, such as at the meetings of the Puritans at Wisbech about 1588 described by the Roman Catholic priest William Weston:

Each of them had his own Bible, and sedulously turned the pages and looked up the texts cited by the preachers, discussing the passages among themselves to see whether they had quoted them to the point and accurately and in harmony with their tenets. Also they would start arguing among themselves about the meanings of passages from the Scriptures – men, women, boys, girls, rustics, labourers and idiots – and more often than not . . . it ended in violence and fisticuffs.[23]

There is no suggestion of literary considerations in this kind of report, but if one follows such textual disputation into the particular context suggested by Henry VIII, the ale-house –

> For many great Scriptureans may be found
> That cite Saint Paul at every bench and board,
> And have God's word, but have not God the word[24]

– literary consequences do become apparent. In the middle of the fifteenth century the Lollards are described by Bishop Reginald Pecock as knowing 'by heart the texts of Holy Scripture' and pouring 'them out thick at feasts and at ale-drinking and upon their high benches sitting'.[25] Foxe shows the alehouse context continuing; he relates that some of the young men at Cambridge used to meet at the White Horse Inn to discuss new religious ideas at about the time that Tyndale may have been in Cambridge (*Acts and Monuments*, V: 415). However, the alehouse context was, not surprisingly, a dangerous one. Henry Knighton complained in the early fifteenth century that a consequence of the Wyclif translation was that 'the pearl of the gospel is scattered abroad and trodden underfoot of swine, and what is wont to be the treasure both of clerks and laymen is now become the jest of both'.[26] In the draft for a royal proclamation dated about 1540, the reader of the Bible is warned that if he

[23] *The Autobiography of an Elizabethan*, trans. Philip Caraman (London: Longmans, 1955), pp. 164–5.

[24] Harington, 'Of Reading Scriptures', *The Letters and Epigrams of Sir John Harington*, ed. Norman Egbert McClure (NY: Octagon, 1977), p. 281.

[25] *The Repressor*, I: 129; quoted in Deanesly, *The Lollard Bible*, p. 362.

[26] *Chronicon Henrici Knighton*, II: 151–2; quoted in Deanesly, p. 239.

has any doubts about a particular part he should not have 'thereof any open reasoning in your open taverns or alehouses' (Pollard, p. 114); the proclamation goes on to make it clear that 'contentions and disputations' were going on 'in such alehouses and other places unmeet for such conferences'.

Later in the sixteenth century, Gregory Martin, concerned that the Bible in the vernacular leads not only to private interpretation but to irreverence, paints a vivid picture:

yet we must not imagine that in the primitive Church, either every one that understood the learned tongues wherein the Scriptures were written, or other languages into which they were translated, might without reprehension read, reason, dispute, turn and toss the Scriptures; or that our forefathers suffered every schoolmaster, scholar or grammarian that had a little Greek or Latin straight to take in hand the Holy Testament; or that the translated Bibles into the vulgar tongues were in the hands of every husbandman, artificer, prentice, boys, girls, mistress, maid, man; that they were sung, played, alleged of every tinker, taverner, rhymer, minstrel; that they were for table talk, for alebenches, for boats and barges, and for every profane person and company. (Rheims NT, fol. A3r)

Though this is the Roman Catholic Church defending its territory, it seems too probable and is too consistent with other evidence not to have a substantial degree of truth to it, and it is one of the few points that Fulke and Cartwright[27] do not dispute, even though, as defenders of the open Bible, it would be greatly to their advantage to be able to refute it. Martin goes on to repeat Henry VIII's point: 'look whether the most chaste and sacred sentences of God's holy word be not turned of many into mirth, mockery, amorous ballets and detestable letters of love and lewdness, their delicate rhymes, tunes and translations much increasing the same' (fol. Biv).

WIT, ATHEISM AND THE SAD CASE OF THOMAS AIKENHEAD

Something worse than irreverence was abroad in these times too. There were atheists, and they too, as Wither observed (above, p. 110), could reach literary conclusions from non-literary premises. One of them was the playwright Christopher Marlowe (1564–93). In a 1593 Privy Council paper one Richard Baines specifies blasphemies which he claims to have heard Marlowe utter. This is second-hand, but even if it were dismissed

---

[27] See Cartwright's *Answer*, pp. 52–9, esp. p. 58, and *The Text of the New Testament of Jesus Christ . . . with a confutation . . . by W. Fulke* (London, 1589), point 9.

as a worthless account of Marlowe it would still be valuable as evidence of 'blasphemies' that had some currency at the time among secular wits.[28] For instance, if Adam lived 6,000 years ago he could not have been the first man since 'the Indians and many authors of antiquity have assuredly written of above 16 thousand years agone'. The supernatural is rejected, with consequences such as Moses being an Egyptian-trained juggler, and 'that Christ was a bastard and his mother dishonest'; this makes 'the Angel Gabriel . . . bawd to the Holy Ghost'.

Baines reports that Marlowe 'saith likewise that he hath quoted a number of contrarieties out of the Scripture', and 'that if he were put to write a new religion, he would undertake both a more excellent and admirable method, and that all the New Testament is filthily written'. It is a pity the report is not more specific, but Marlowe is clearly at the opposite extreme from, say, Cawdray: his premise is that the Bible is a merely mortal production, and so he reaches negative literary conclusions. If these conclusions depend on nothing more than the atheistic premise, then they are as little respectable as Cawdray's.

A century later infidelity and denigration of the Bible as the least eloquent of all books proved to be a fatal collocation, as the extraordinary case of the unfortunate Edinburgh eighteen-year-old, Thomas Aikenhead, shows.[29] The trial took place in 1696. For a year Aikenhead, usually in company with some students from the university who turned from drinking and thinking companions to witnesses against him, gave vent to daringly atheistic, or, as some thought of them, deistic, opinions. Some of these concerned, in the almost identical words of three of the witnesses and the prosecutor, 'divinity or the doctrine of theology', which he affirmed 'was a rhapsody of feigned and ill-invented nonsense'; he mocked the incarnation or 'theantropos', for instance, as 'as great a contradiction as Hircus Cervus', 'that is a goat and ane hart in one animal', and maintained the deistic view 'that God, the world and nature are but one thing, and that the world was from eternity'. Most of his remarks concerned the 'poetical fictions and extravagant chimeras' of the Bible, a book 'so stuffed with madness, nonsense and contradictions that [he] admired the stupidity of the world in being so long deluded by [it]'. Indeed, the Bible was 'worse than the fictions of the

---

[28] Baines's testimony is reprinted in Paul H. Kocher, 'Marlowe's atheist lecture', in Clifford Leech, ed., *Marlowe: a collection of critical essays* (Englewood Cliffs, NJ: Prentice Hall, 1964), pp. 159–66. The testimony is pp. 159–61.

[29] Transcriptions from the trial and some supplementary material are to be found in Thomas Bayley Howell's *Complete Collection of State Trials*, 21 vols. (London, 1816), XIII: 917–40, from which I quote *passim*.

poets, for they had some connection, but [it] had none'. He scoffed at the OT as 'Ezra's fables, by a profane allusion to Aesop's fables', and at the NT as 'the history of the imposter Christ' who learned magic in Egypt and played pranks on the imaginations of the 'silly witless fishermen', his disciples. Yet Jesus was inferior to that other Egypt-trained magician, Moses, who 'was both the better artist and better politician'. Other witnesses report that the comparison was between Jesus and Mahomet, whom Aikenhead preferred.

If this is all an obvious intellectual reaction against the pious excesses of mysterious Christianity, it is also, perhaps, as unreasonable as what it attacks. A glance here at Sir Thomas Browne (1606–82) will help to make this point. In his *Religio Medici* ([1642] 1643), he relates how his reason almost took him to a position like Aikenhead's, and he claims he 'could show a catalogue of doubts [about the Bible] never yet imagined or questioned',[30] and goes on to give examples which a studious atheist could well have made use of. Reason also suggested literary opinions to him, and he confesses that 'there are in Scripture stories that do exceed the fables of poets, and to a captious reader sound like Gargantua or Bevis: search all the legends of time past, and the fabulous conceits of these present, and 'twill be hard to find one that deserves to carry the buckler unto Samson' (p. 21). If this sounds like the scurril Aikenhead refined, it also marks the point of division, for Browne, who has already divided the soul into a triumvirate of faith, reason and passion, switches the ground from reason to faith, and carries on with only a comma for pause, 'yet is all this of an easy possibility if we conceive a divine concourse or an influence but from the little finger of the Almighty'. Now Browne and Aikenhead, the one working from belief, the other from unbelief, are on opposite paths. Browne sums up his position with a reference to divine inspiration, a claim for the literary supremacy of the Bible and a contrast with the Koran:

These are but the conclusions and fallible discourses of man upon the word of God, for such I do believe the Holy Scriptures; yet were it of man, I could not choose but say it was the singularest and superlative piece that hath been extant since the creation . . . The Alcoran of the Turks (I speak without prejudice) is an ill-composed piece, containing in it vain and ridiculous errors in philosophy, impossibilities, fictions and vanities beyond laughter, maintained by evident and open sophisms, the policy of ignorance, deposition of universities and banishment of learning. (p. 24)

---

[30] *Religio Medici and Other Works*, ed. L.C. Martin (Oxford: Clarendon, 1964), pp. 21–2.

Surely, a modern reader must think, Browne is being ironic here, condemning the Koran for, among other things, the very kind of faults he would have found in the Bible had he let himself. Yet faith can make the one supreme and the other so ill-composed. On the other hand, Aikenhead, with his strong desire not to believe, can find Mahomet a better artist than Jesus. Browne, like Chillingworth (see above, p. 147), is open in his rejection of reason where it conflicts with faith, but Aikenhead, though elevating reason, shows himself equally biassed.

Aikenhead of course recanted and repented, sending a 'petition and retraction' to the court before the trial, and leaving behind a last speech probably intended for the scaffold. Both give accounts of how he had gone astray, quite different accounts which may nevertheless both be parts of the whole truth. His first explanation is that the opinions expressed were not his 'own private sentiments and opinions, but were repeated by me as sentiments and opinions of some atheistical writers . . . being exceedingly imposed upon to give an account of the abominable and atheistical principles contained and asserted in them'. If this transparently reveals a delight in playing with fire, the second explanation shows a more *sympathique* Aikenhead who from the age of ten had been 'searching good and sufficient grounds whereon I might safely build my faith'. He writes:

it is a principle innate and co-natural to every man to have an insatiable inclination to truth, and to seek for it as for hid treasure, which indeed had its effect upon me, and my reason therein so mastered me that I was forced of necessity to reject the authorities and testimonies both of my parents and others instilled into me. So that I went further and examined the point more reasonably, that I might build my faith upon incontrovertible grounds, and so I proceeded until that the more I thought thereon the further I was from finding the verity I desired; so that after much ponderings I found my education altogether wrong, not only because it was impossible for me or any that I conversed with to produce any grounds really sufficient to confirm the same; but with the greatest facility sufficient ground could be produced for the contrary. And this I profess and declare was the only cause that made me assert the things that I asserted and deny the things that I denied.

What is so striking besides the about-face from the earlier explanation is the denigration of reason, seen as an allegorical force like one of the deadly sins in a morality play. The dilemma here is just that which Browne solved by the abandonment of reason. But Aikenhead was too late with his solution. Whatever he was personally, laudable seeker of truth in an ignorant age, satanic blasphemer of revealed religion, rebellious youth or intellectual martyr, he was also a young man fatally caught between the spirits of two ages, tried by an essentially medieval spirit of blind faith for the essentially modern 'crime' of trusting his reason. He was found guilty of blasphemy and sentenced to hang on January 8th, 1697. There was real feeling against the sentence, but the ministers of the Church were, as a member of the Privy Council described them, 'of a narrow set of thoughts and confined principles, and not able to bear things of this nature'. Aikenhead, an emblem of the dangers of a reasoned approach to the literature of the Bible in a century wherein divine inspiration was a cornerstone of faith, was duly hanged, 'holding all the time the Holy Bible in his hand'.[31]

Richard Head's popular *The English Rogue* (1665), an apparently autobiographical narration of knavery and lechery helps make important points here. One anecdote about stealing a hogshead of wine by substituting one of water ends with the narrator leaving this epigram on one of the hogsheads:

> What Moses did in the Creator's name
> By art Egyptian magic did the same.
> Since I have read of water turned to wine,
> This miracle is opposite to mine.
> For I (though never yet a Rhenish hater)
> Have by my art converted wine to water. (p. 137)

The narrator claims to have heard this repeated to him, with variations on the anecdote, 'as a very good jest', and doubtless it was at least as good without the story. The very jestingness is significant: the tone of many of the surviving atheistic criticisms of the Bible is like that of Aikenhead's second explanation, thoroughly earnest, as if they are products of the search for truth, yet the apparent atheism must often have been no more than the desire to find laughter in the deadly serious. This particular epigram's references to Moses and magic have obvious affinities with reason's explaining away of an element that the faithful took as a proof of Christianity, the performance of miracles, yet it is not a denial of Christianity. Rather, it helps to show that the kind of ideas that led to Aikenhead's execution were part of the intellectual currency of the time.

Head's next episode, the only other one of the whole work to refer to such ideas, confirms their currency. He gives 'some hints' of one of his companion's 'desperate, irreligious and atheistical tenets' (heading of ch. 29, p. 138). The companion does not deny God's existence but queries

---

[31] Robert Chambers, *Domestic Annals of Scotland*, 3 vols. (Edinburgh and London, 1861), III: 166.

his justice and refuses to accept arguments from the Scriptures 'since they are full of contradictions and contain many things incredible'. This is the familiar general observation of the unfaithful. Specifically, the companion, a condemned thief, says:

'Neither do I know, since we are forbidden murder, why Abraham should kill his son Isaac, and the same person commit adultery with his maid Hagar (which is largely described), and yet we are commanded the contrary. If we borrow or steal, we are enjoined to make restitution, notwithstanding, the Israelites were permitted to borrow the Egyptians' earrings without giving satisfaction. In this manner I could cavil ad infinitum, and yet this Book is the basis of Christianity. Let me tell you plainly. Religion at first was only the quaint legerdemain of some strong pated statesman who, to overawe the capriciousness of a giddy multitude, did forge the opinion of a punisher of all human evil actions.' (p. 139)

Just as Browne 'could show a catalogue of doubts', so the deistically inclined thief 'could cavil ad infinitum', and to dismiss religion as 'quaint legerdemain' is at one with Aikenhead scoffing at Christ or Moses as a magician. It is no surprise to find Mahomet in the next sentence, even if the companion's point is simply that he was a religious imposter.

The English Rogue was originally printed secretly and sold in places like alehouses. Yet if we pass from this sordid context to the houses of the nobility, the same kind of ideas are to be found. John Donne in his commemoration service for Lady Danvers (George Herbert's mother, d. 1627) writes

that she lived in a time wherein this prophecy of St Peter [2 Pet. 3: 3] . . . was over-abundantly performed, that there should be scoffers, jesters in divine things and matters appertaining to God and his religion. For now, in these our days, excellency of wit lies in profaneness: he is the good spirit that dares abuse God, and he good company that makes his company the worse or keeps them from goodness. (*Sermons*, VIII: 86)

Later in the century the most notorious wit of them all, the licentious courtier, John Wilmot, Earl of Rochester (1648–80), indulged in such profanity. Gilbert Burnet, D.D., published a very popular and earnest pamphlet, *Some Passages of the Life and Death of the Right Honourable John Earl of Rochester* (London, 1680), sketching the life and detailing how the dying man, through his urging, came to hold proper views. Rochester declared to him that 'they were happy that believed, for it was not in every man's power' (p. 71), and this led them to discuss revealed religion. Rochester 'said, he did not understand that business of inspiration: he believed the pen-men of the Scriptures had heats and honesty, and so writ, but could not comprehend how God should reveal his secrets to mankind' (p. 72).

Burnet gives the following summary of the doubts about the content and style of the Scriptures that this rational incomprehension led to:

God's communicating his mind to one man was the putting it in his power to cheat the world; for prophecies and miracles, the world had been always full of strange stories, for the boldness and cunning of contrivers meeting with the simplicity and credulity of the people, things were easily received, and being once received passed down without contradiction. The incoherences of style in the Scriptures, the odd transitions, the seeming contradictions chiefly about the order of time, the cruelties enjoined the Israelites in destroying the Canaanites, circumcision and many other rites of the Jewish worship, seemed to him unsuitable to the Divine nature; and the first three chapters of Genesis he thought could not be true unless they were parables. (pp. 72–3)

Like most atheists and deists, he evidently knew the Bible quite well, and his views might not have seemed irreligious, either to himself or others, in more modern times. But in this time to deny inspiration was to destroy faith. To start from cavils, as Burnet insists, was 'to prepossess one's mind against the whole' (p. 99), and so Rochester cried down the Scriptures much as Aikenhead did. Burnet records,

I told him I saw the ill use he made of his wit, by which he slurred the gravest things with a slight dash of his fancy; and the pleasure he found in such wanton expressions as calling the doing of miracles 'the showing of a trick' did really keep him from examining them with that care which such things required. (p. 87)

This is as much detail as could be expected from one zealous to promote proper faith, yet it underlines the continuity and general uniformity of the views reached by allowing irreverent reason full play. Whether or not Rochester's views were the conclusions of his own unaided wit, they show how the period imposed a kind of uniformity upon the unfaithful as well as the faithful, and, with the evidence from *The English Rogue*, reveal Aikenhead as a victim of his age.

CHAPTER EIGHT

Writers and the Bible 1: Milton and Bunyan

'THE BEST MATERIALS IN THE WORLD FOR POESY'

Passages proclaiming the literary superiority of the Scriptures to all literature were given a new turn by the poet Abraham Cowley (1618–67) in his 'Preface to poems' (1656). He describes the current situation of poetry as one in which with grief and indignation he sees 'that divine science employing all her inexhaustible riches of wit and eloquence either in the wicked and beggarly flattery of great persons, or the unmanly idolising of foolish women, or the wretched affectation of scurril laughter, or at best on the confused antiquated dreams of senseless fables and metamorphoses' (p. 12). Reform of poetry's subject matter rather than of the art itself is needed:

Amongst all holy and consecrated things which the devil ever stole [and] alienated from the service of the Deity, as altars, temples, sacrifices, prayers and the like, there is none that he so universally and so long usurped as poetry. It is time to recover it out of the tyrant's hands and to restore it to the Kingdom of God, who is the father of it. It is time to baptize it in Jordan, for it will never become clean by bathing in the water of Damascus. There wants, methinks, but the conversion of that and the Jews for the accomplishment of the kingdom of Christ. (pp. 12–13)

The reform is of two kinds: it is not merely that poetry will be reformed, but, so high is his conception of poetry, men will be reformed and, given the conversion of the Jews, the kingdom of God established by the reunification of poetry and religion. Religion is necessary to poetry, but poetry itself is holy and necessary to religion. He is thus one of the earliest proponents of the idea that literary pleasure will lead to religious improvement. Moreover, he does not believe that poetry will be damaged by confining itself to religious subjects. Rather, 'it will meet with wonderful variety of new, more beautiful and more delightful objects; neither will it want room by being confined to Heaven' (p. 13).

Here it is that his major claim comes, that 'all the books of the Bible are either already most admirable and exalted pieces of poesy, or are the best materials in the world for it' (p. 14). This claim is what gives the new twist to his catalogue of the literary excellences of the Bible:

What can we imagine more proper for the ornaments of wit or learning in the story of Deucalion than in that of Noah? why will not the actions of Samson afford as plentiful matter as the labours of Hercules? why is not Jephthah's daughter as good a woman as Iphigenia? and the friendship of David and Jonathan more worthy celebration than that of Theseus and Perithous? Does not the passage of Moses and the Israelites into the Holy Land yield incomparably more poetical variety than the voyages of Ulysses and Aeneas? Are the obsolete threadbare tales of Thebes and Troy half so stored with great, heroical and supernatural actions (since verse will needs find or make such) as the wars of Joshua, of the Judges, of David and divers others? Can all the transformations of the gods give such copious hints to flourish and expatiate on as the true miracles of Christ or of his prophets and apostles? (pp. 13–14)

In short, for Cowley the Bible was the best material for a practising poet to elaborate on using all the skills at his command. No one did this better than John Milton (1608–74).

JOHN MILTON

Milton's third wife, Elizabeth Minshull, recalled that Cowley was one of the three English poets Milton most approved of,[1] but this does not mean that Cowley was a necessary influence on his progress to the creation of the greatest English biblical poem: Milton was travelling towards *Paradise Lost* (1667), and also *Paradise Regained* (1671) and *Samson Agonistes* (1671), well before Cowley's work appeared, and it perhaps was no more to him than fraternal encouragement to his own travail. He, like Cowley, is essentially a classicising poet who chooses the Bible as his quarry, and his work is testimony to the literary potential a great poet could find in the Scriptures. His work had enormous influence on both literary taste and religious ideas,[2] and was written with intimate and, at times, open

---

[1] *The Life Records of John Milton*, ed. J. Milton French, 5 vols. (New Brunswick, NJ: Rutgers University Press., 1949 etc.), V: 122, 322–3.

[2] Defoe's Robinson Crusoe 'entered into a long discourse with [Friday] about the devil, the original of him, his rebellion against God, his enmity to man, the reason of it, his setting himself up the dark parts of the world to be worshipped instead of God'. Coleridge commented jovially on this, 'I presume that Milton's *Paradise Lost* must have been bound up with one of Crusoe's Bibles; or I should be puzzled to know where he found all this history of the Old Gentleman. Not a word of it in the Bible, I am quite sure' (*Robinson Crusoe*, ed. Angus Ross (Harmondsworth: Penguin, 1965), p. 219; *Marginalia, Collected Works* 12, II: 164).

familiarity with the KJB. Moreover, Milton proclaimed the literary supremacy of the Bible. Yet, for all this, his literary attitude to the Bible had its contradictions, and his real effects on others' attitudes were perhaps similarly contradictory.

Milton, it almost goes without saying, was a faithful and a formidable scholar of the Bible in Hebrew, Greek, Latin and English, but, though he used the Latin of the Junius-Tremellius Latin Bible and and the English of the KJB whenever convenient for his quotations, his fidelity was primarily to the originals. His knowledge of these began in his boyhood when, as he recalls, he devoted himself 'to an earnest study of the Old and New Testaments in their original languages', and listed 'under general headings all passages from the Scriptures which suggested themselves for quotation, so that [he] might have them ready at hand when necessary'.[3]

Nowhere in his works does he discuss the merits of the KJB (or any other English version), nor Junius-Tremellius, but the quotations in his prose works show that, before his blindness, he used them freely, varying from them as often as not. They were, for him, convenient rather than authoritative: real authority lay with the originals, and many of his variations are corrections to conform with their readings. Other variations come about through adaptation to context, condensation and paraphrasing; sometimes, perhaps often, he worked from memory. One might expect him to have trusted much more to his memory after he had lost his sight, but he did not; rather, he took special care to surmount the difficulties of blindness, with the result that he jumps from making just under half his quotations agree with the Latin or the English to making four-fifths of them agree.

Now, Milton had owned from childhood, perhaps from his fourth birthday, a small quarto KJB (Barker, 1612) which shows abundant signs of use,[4] and he was obviously thoroughly familiar with its text. It would be easy to conclude, as does one of his biographers, that 'its diction, its imagery, its rhythms early became a part of him',[5] but very little in his quotations or in his prose or poetic styles suggests that he adopted any particular attitude to its diction and rhythms. He seems, like so many of his contemporaries, not to have considered it as English but to have regarded it as the most accurate but yet improvable rendering of the original. The Hebrew and the Greek he did regard as dictated by God, as his very few comments on the language as language show. Divine

---

[3] *Christian Doctrine*, 'Epistle'; *Prose Works*, VI: 119.   [4] See *Works* XVIII, 274–5 and 559–61.
[5] William Riley Parker, *Milton: a Biography*, 2 vols. (Oxford: Clarendon, 1968), I: 10.

inspiration, for example, justifies the un-Attic character of NT Greek, for he attributes the abundance of Hebraisms and Syriacisms to deliberate intent on God's part: it 'was the majesty of God, not filing the tongue of Scripture to a Gentilish idiom, but in a princely manner offering to them as to Gentiles and foreigners grace and mercy, though not in foreign words, yet in a foreign style that might induce them to the fountains' (*Tetrachordon, Prose Works*, II: 671).

Milton's reverence for the originals and their language extends naturally to a reverence for their literary quality. The sentence just quoted finishes with a reference to the Greeks as being 'high and happy' in their literature, yet still having 'to acknowledge God's ancient people their betters', and to Hebrew as 'the metropolitan language'. As this suggests, he inherits the twin patristic ideas of priority and supremacy. A year earlier, in *The Reason of Church Government*, he had argued that the OT songs were superior to the best hymns and odes in the classics 'not in their divine argument alone, but in the very critical art of composition', and that they 'may be easily made appear over all the kinds of lyric poesy to be incomparable' (*Prose Works*, I: 816). He returned to the argument in an emphatic comparison of the Scriptures with the classics in *Paradise Regained*. Satan advises Jesus to study the literature and thought of Greece, to which he gives the highest and, indeed, most orthodox praise; this is Jesus' counter-argument:

> if I would delight my private hours
> With music or with poem, where so soon
> As in our native language can I find
> That solace? All our law and story strewed
> With hymns, our Psalms with artful terms inscribed,
> Our Hebrew songs and harps in Babylon,
> That pleased so well our victor's ear, declare
> That rather Greece from us these arts derived,
> Ill imitated, while they loudest sing
> The vices of their deities, and their own,
> In fable, hymn or song, so personating
> Their gods ridiculous, and themselves past shame.
> Remove their swelling epithets thick laid
> As varnish on a harlot's cheek, the rest,
> Thin sown with aught of profit or delight,
> Will far be found unworthy to compare
> With Sion's songs, to all true tastes excelling,
> Where God is praised aright, and Godlike men,
> The Holiest of Holies, and his saints;
> Such are from God inspired, not such from thee;

Unless where moral virtue is expressed
By light of nature not in all quite lost.
Their orators thou then extoll'st, as those
The top of eloquence, statists indeed,
And lovers of their country, as may seem;
But herein to our prophets far beneath,
As men divinely taught, and better teaching
The solid rules of civil government
In their majestic unaffected style
Than all the oratory of Greece and Rome:
In them is plainest taught, and easiest learnt,
What makes a nation happy, and keeps it so,
What ruins kingdoms, and lays cities flat;
These only with our law best form a King.

(IV: 331–64)

OT poetry and oratory are superior to those of the Greeks not just in
subject matter and teaching but in style. Greek literature is no more than
a degenerate imitation of Hebrew, though some scornful concession is
given to Greek eloquence in the references to 'swelling epithets thick laid
/ As varnish on a harlot's cheek', and 'the top of eloquence'. But this is
only a seeming superiority: Sion's songs 'are from God inspired', the
prophets are 'men divinely taught', plainly writing in 'majestic
unaffected style'. This recalls his earlier description of the style of the
entire Bible as 'sober, plain, and unaffected' (*Of Reformation, Prose Works*,
I: 568). The speech leaves Satan 'quite at a loss', and is clearly meant to
be definitive. In intent, then, it stands as an invitation to admire the Bible
not merely as divine truth but as the best writing; it is an outstanding
example of the century's swell of praise for the originals.

Satan's temptation to classical culture has no foundation in the biblical story, yet Milton places it very emphatically within the poem as the
last of the substantial temptations, to be followed only by the storm and
the briefly narrated temptation at the temple. Satan has accepted that
he cannot tempt Jesus 'to a worldly crown', and insinuates that he is
'addicted more / To contemplation and profound dispute' (IV: 213–4), a
point that passes without contradiction. Thus, by position and by nature,
this temptation, invented by Milton, is implicitly the most difficult of all,
and we may perhaps read as much significance into this as into the resolution of Jesus' answer. The tension between classicism and biblicism
is fundamental to Milton as Christian artist, and the styles and methods
of his great biblical works suggest that, in important ways, it remained
unresolved. While the context of the temptation within the structure of

the poem suggests its importance, the context of a poem (and, indeed, of works) with so many classical elements gives a dramatic sense that Jesus' answer is thesis rather than synthesis. The passage, persuasive as it probably was to those who wished to be persuaded, fails to be properly convincing as a literary judgement, and so exists as one more testimony to the power of faith to subvert some writers' genuine literary opinions. By allowing Satan to be silenced by this argument, Milton is reducing the dynamic of the argument to something similar to the countless tracts of the period where a Mr Wiseman educates a Mr Attentive.

From the beginnings of his career, Milton found it difficult though not impossible to accept biblical literature, in the original or in translation, as it was. Some of the complexities of his attitudes are reflected in his English versions of the Psalms. His paraphrases of Psalms 114 and 136, composed when he was fifteen, show a strong desire to rewrite the originals, and they point to the man who was to expand the confused brevity of the opening of Genesis to the controlled grandeur of *Paradise Lost*. So, in Psalm 114, apparently working with both the KJB and the PB in front of him, the terseness of the PB's 'the sea saw that, and fled: Jordan was driven back' is indulgently expanded to four lines:

> That saw the troubl'd sea, and shivering fled,
> And sought to hide his froth-becurl'd head
> Low in the earth, Jordan's clear streams recoil,
> As a faint host that hath receiv'd the foil.

This is a coat of many colours over a bare body, showing Milton a successor to poets such as Sidney. Yet Milton's two later sets of Psalms, 80–88, composed in 1648, and 1–8, composed in 1653 after his blindness, show an increasing fidelity both to the originals and to the KJB, and have much in common with the literal versifications that so dominated English psalmody. The 1648 Psalms may well reflect the controversy over Rous's version, for they attempt to meet the twin desires of suitability to the established tunes and the presentation of a literal translation of the Hebrew. Milton uses a fully rhymed common metre and advises his reader that, except for the parts in italics, he has given 'the very words of the text, translated from the original'. The appearance of fidelity, which is often also a fidelity to the KJB, is bolstered by his inclusion of notes supplying the Hebrew or a literal translation of it. However, the sheer amount of italics – which does not represent the full extent of the paraphrasing – suggests a continued difficulty with the bareness of the text.

The later Psalms, though they do not attempt to conform to the demand for Psalters such as Rous's, are closer still to the KJB, frequently using its words and succumbing less to the temptation to elaborate. Some striking lines appear almost unchanged, as in the first line here, 'Out of the mouths of babes and sucklings thou / Hast founded strength because of all thy foes' (Ps. 8: 2). He also preserves less memorable language. The first verse of Psalm 1, 'blessed is the man that walketh not in the counsel of the ungodly, nor standeth in the way of sinners, nor sitteth in the seat of the scornful', appears minimally changed:

> Bless'd is the man who hath not walked astray
> In counsel of the wicked, and i' th' way
> Of sinners hath not stood, and in the seat
> Of scorners hath not sat.

He obviously wants to be faithful to the KJB's words – arguably he is responding to the power of some of its phrases – and seems to be experimenting to see how nearly they can be read as English poetry. However, none of either of these groups of Psalms is a notable success, and it is no surprise to find that his last Psalm paraphrase, Adam and Eve's dawn hymn (*Paradise Lost*, book V: 153–208), is so loosely based on Psalm 148 and the song of the three children in Daniel as hardly to be a paraphrase at all. The looseness is far greater than adaptation to the narrative context would require: it is principally the result of Milton's need to create with all due eloquence a fitting example of prelapsarian hymnody. Here the received art of the Bible is, in effect, rejected for Milton's own conception of appropriate art.

Milton's seemingly inevitable decision to write an epic on the fall of man allowed him to combine his artistic allegiance to the classics with his Christian beliefs, and this combination is likely to produce in the reader a mixed attitude to the Bible as literature. It naturally enforces an admiration for classical form at the expense of the Bible's narrative method, expanding as it does a few spare pages into twelve books; moreover, it is full of classical devices, references and language, and it adds to the biblical story episodes to rival similar episodes in Homer and Virgil. Milton may, for instance, claim at the beginning of book IX to be neither 'skilled nor studious', nor 'sedulous by nature to indite / Wars, hitherto the only argument / Heroic deemed', yet he has already taken this epic high ground to himself in telling so vividly of the war in heaven. The subject matter of the old epics in effect contributes to his poem, indeed, classical subject matter pervades *Paradise Lost* as much as does biblical.

One small example must suffice, since the enforcement the poem gives to classical culture is at once obvious and less interesting here than the positive encouragement given to appreciation of the Bible; after describing the bridge built by Sin and Death between earth and hell, he introduces a classical comparison with a Virgilian formula:

> So, if great things to small may be compared,
> Xerxes, the liberty of Greece to yoke,
> From Susa his Memnonian palace high
> Came to the sea, and over Hellespont
> Bridging his way, Europe with Asia joined,
> And scourged with many a stroke th' indignant waves.
>   (X: 306–11)

The witty allusion to Virgil's 'sic parvis componere magna solebam' (Eclogue I: 23) aggrandises the Miltonic incident by deflating a major achievement of the classical world, but at the same time the source for the effect is classical; moreover, the classical achievement is invoked in a sentence of latinate complexity that revels in the exotic sound of classical names and invokes, as a further diminishing element, the original Latin sense of 'indignant'. The tug of the passage, then, in method, matter and language, is to the classics, but the point is of course the superiority of the Christian subject, which the poem shows over and over to be 'higher argument' (IX: 42).

Yet Milton's language does not look only towards Latin and Greek, for language was much more of a problem to him than narrative method and matter. It was an enormous challenge, one he comments on several times in the poem, to find an 'answerable style' (IX: 20), especially for the inhabitants of heaven and for unfallen man. Somehow it must merit the praise for eloquence that Raphael and Adam bestow on each other in book VIII; Milton must be seen to be following the 'voice divine' of his holy muse and so soaring 'above th'Olympian hill' (VII: 2–3), for he is writing

> adventurous song,
> That with no middle flight intends to soar
> Above th'Aonian mount, while it pursues
> Things unattempted yet in prose or rhyme. (I: 13–16)

He has to find the highest possible style. Given his attitude to the divine inspiration of the very words of the originals, given also his attempt in some of his Psalms to use the language of the KJB, one might expect him to adopt a style like that of the originals and therefore similar to that of the KJB. Yet there were reasons against this beyond his predilection for the classical. First, much of the poem has no biblical source, second, his general sense of biblical style as 'sober, plain, and unaffected', standard as it is, hardly fitted his aspiration, and third, he may have recognised the dangers of falling into biblical pastiche, for he remarks in *Eikonoclastes* that 'it is not hard for any man who hath a Bible in his hands to borrow good words and holy sayings in abundance; but to make them his own is a work of grace only from above' (*Prose Works*, III: 553). Strictly speaking, this does not concern style, but he had of course to make the Bible's language his own, and if the result is generally far from sober plainness, there is an obvious but understandable inconsistency not just in the two styles but in his ideas. He may, though, have thought of himself as writing under a new inspiration from the same source that inspired Moses, in which case the inconsistency in his ideas diminishes.

The predominant grandeur of the style is convincingly apt for his purposes and so tends to persuade the reader that it, rather than the language of the KJB, is the appropriate language for biblical material as literature, but another key element in the style is its flexibility. The sentence structures may never be brief and simple, and so never correspond to those of the KJB, but the vocabulary may be, and there is, for instance, a surprisingly large number of lines made entirely of monosyllables. So the reader, convinced of the greatness of the style, is occasionally startled by the ease and strength with which it can use the exact words of the KJB. The best instance is Adam's confession to God that he has eaten of the tree:

> This woman whom thou mad'st to be my help,
> And gav'st me as thy perfect gift, so good,
> So fit, so acceptable, so divine,
> That from her hand I could suspect no ill,
> And what she did, whatever in itself,
> Her doing seemed to justify the deed;
> She gave me of the tree, and I did eat. (X: 137–43)

The instant recognisability of the last line, unaltered from Gen. 3: 12, makes the conclusion to this simple sentence incandesce. Not only is Milton anchoring his poem at one of its most moving moments to the very text of the Bible, he is also demonstrating, and demonstrating magnificently, the poetic, even metrical power that can be found in the KJB. So, while the whole poem is inescapably a vindication of the supremacy of Christian subject matter and classical method, it is not a complete denial of the KJB. Its readers are occasionally encouraged to admire literary achievement in their own English Bibles, and to accept that Milton's few pronouncements on the superiority of biblical literature have a validity that can go beyond content to language.

JOHN BUNYAN

After the cathedral splendours of Milton, John Bunyan (1628–88) is like a dissenting meeting-house. Yet the two belong together as the greatest Christian writers in English, and *The Pilgrim's Progress* (1678) overtopped *Paradise Lost* to become the most popular English religious work of the imagination. Like *Paradise Lost*, it has been both a central part of the religious education of generations and a creator of attitudes to the Bible. Indeed, though it lacks a narrative base in the Bible such as Milton's poems had, *The Pilgrim's Progress* is close enough to the Bible in some of its subject matter, language and imagery to be thought of by some critics as written in the style of the KJB. So the nineteenth-century historian, John Richard Green, could proclaim that in no book

do we see more clearly the new imaginative force which had been given to the common life of Englishmen by their study of the Bible. Its English . . . is the English of the Bible. . . . so completely has the Bible become Bunyan's life that one feels its phrases as the natural expression of his thoughts. He has lived in the Bible till its words have become his own.[6]

Green, writing in the full flush of late-Victorian literary reverence for the KJB, also attributed Milton's 'loftiness of phrase' to the Bible (p. 602), which, given the disparity between the two writers, speaks much of the kind of thoughtlessness that could enter into such claims. Nothing could be further from the super-Olympian ambition of Milton's invocations than the modest but moving words of the preface to Bunyan's autobiographical *Grace Abounding to the Chief of Sinners* (1666):

I could also have stepped into a style much higher than this in which I have here discoursed, and could have adorned all things more than here I have seemed to do: but I dare not: God did not play in convincing of me; the devil did not play in tempting of me; neither did I play when I sunk as into a bottomless pit, when the pangs of hell caught hold upon me: wherefore I may not play in my relating of them, but be plain and simple, and lay down the thing as it was. (pp. 5–6)

In general terms he is describing the prevailing perception of biblical style. Indeed, he invites comparison between an aspect of his writing and the Bible in arguing essentially the same point in 'The author's apology

---

[6] *A Short History of the English People* (1874); new edition (London: Macmillan, 1888), p. 627.

for his book' prefaced to *The Pilgrim's Progress*. He is particularly concerned to defend his use of allegory by appeal to the example of the
Bible, but the point extends to include the question of how far religious
writing needs to be artful. He takes it as axiomatic that 'Solidity indeed
becomes the pen / Of him that writeth things divine to men', and argues
specifically about his use of allegory:

> But must I needs want solidness, because
> By metaphors I speak; was not God's laws,
> His gospel-laws in older time held forth
> By types, shadows and metaphors? Yet loth
> Will any sober man be to find fault
> With them, lest he be found for to assault
> The highest wisdom.   (p. 142)

So he takes the Bible as a faultless *literary* model because it comes from
God, 'the highest wisdom'. His sense of 'solidness' is that it is 'as a dark
ground or foil' to set off the beauty of God's truth: although the Bible
'for its style and phrase puts down all wit' (p. 142), that is, is superior to
all rhetoric and poetry, this is not because it possesses wit, rather because,
as he puts it in a fine image, 'dark clouds bring waters, when the bright
bring none' (p. 140). So *The Pilgrim's Progress*, 'my little book', is empty of
rhetoric, 'void of all those paintings that may make / It with this or the
other man to take'. Yet it is superior to superficially fine work because of
its religious truth: it 'Is not without those things that do excel / What do
in brave but empty notions dwell' (p. 141).

The closeness that there can be between Bunyan's and the KJB's styles
– a closeness which seems to justify an identification between the two –
is visible when Christian and Hopeful wade into the river of death:

They then addressed themselves to the water; and entering, Christian began to
sink, and crying out to his good friend Hopeful, he said, 'I sink in deep waters,
the billows go over my head, all his waves go over me, Selah.'

Then said the other, 'Be of good cheer, my brother, I feel the bottom and it
is good.' Then said Christian, 'Ah my friend, the sorrows of death have compassed me about, I shall not see the land that flows with milk and honey.' And
with that a great darkness and horror fell upon Christian so that he could not
see before him; also here he in great measure lost his senses so that he could
neither remember nor orderly talk of any of those sweet refreshments that he
had met with in the way of his pilgrimage. (p. 266)

Christian's two sentences are a mixture of quotation, allusion and imitation, clearly intended to invoke the Psalms without ever becoming an
exact quotation. His first sentence could easily be mistaken for a quota-

tion, especially as it uses the characteristic refrain, 'Selah', but it is an adaptation of Ps. 42: 7, 'all thy waves and thy billows are gone over me', and Ps. 69: 2, 'I sink in deep mire, where there is no standing: I am come into deep waters, where the floods overflow me'. Most striking is the way Bunyan has adopted biblical parallelism. 'The sorrows of death have compassed me about' is almost a quotation from Ps. 18: 4, and it balances the next phrase as if the whole of the sentence, not just the biblical cliché, 'land that flows with milk and honey', were a single quotation. This is a deliberate effect: Bunyan knew the KJB far too well to accidentally misquote. If *The Pilgrim's Progress* were full of such writing then what Green thought was true, that the KJB's words have become Bunyan's own, would be undeniable. But he does not often write in this way. His characteristic style with its very different sound shows in the rest of the passage. The KJB rarely uses participial phrases such as 'crying out to his good friend Hopeful', but they are a standard unit of structure for Bunyan. Rather than subordinating 'crying' to 'he said', the KJB would co-ordinate to give 'crying and saying'. The last sentence, 'and with that' etc., shows the characteristic pace of Bunyan's prose. Moreover, while its opening statement is an allusion (Gen. 15: 12), none of the remaining expressions have anything of the KJB in them.

George Eliot describes her heroine Dorothea Brooke at the beginning of *Middlemarch* as having 'the impressiveness of a fine quotation from the Bible . . . in a paragraph of today's newspaper'. Bunyan's prose may not be that of 'today's newspaper', but the description shows one of the effects of his use of biblical quotations and allusions. Fine as his prose so often is, it generally serves to highlight the quotations through its contrast with them, underlining their religious value and perhaps also implying that they have the quality George Eliot sees in Dorothea, 'that kind of beauty which seems to be thrown into relief by poor dress'. Not everyone would take the inference, but those of Bunyan's many, many readers who read him less for his teaching than for his ability to tell a story and create character in simple but energetic language, might well have found themselves relishing the language and image as well as the truth of the KJB. If so, *The Pilgrim's Progress*, more commonly read by generations than any book but the KJB, helped to form a love for the language of the KJB itself, as represented in isolated quotations, and also to form a respect for it as a source for imaginative literature and the imagery therein.

It is difficult to believe that Bunyan did not contribute to a literary as well as a religious sense of the KJB, and that he did not help show later writers ways they might use it, but just how this contribution worked, and over what period, anyone may guess. In the end these facts remain, that the first and greatest writer to found his work closely on the KJB neither adopted its style nor showed any more sense of it as a literary work than, say, the English Psalm translators had done. He did not think of adorning his work with biblical quotations but of using the Bible as the final source for, as he puts it, citing Isa. 38: 19, 'the truth of God' he always aims at (preface to *Grace Abounding*, p. 4). This is most blatant in *The Life and Death of Mr Badman* where discussion of Mr Badman's sins constantly leads Attentive to ask Wiseman what the Bible says of the particular sin, a request Wiseman always responds to copiously.

Grace Abounding shows Bunyan's response to the Bible – which in his case is always the KJB, known with an intimacy few have ever approached – to have had a pathological intensity. Having heard a man talk well of the Bible, he recalls that he 'began to take great pleasure in reading, but especially with the historical part thereof' (section 29, p. 14). This pleasure in narrative seems to have been matched by a pleasure in language, so one reads in this part of the book of him hearing four women talk 'as if joy did make them speak; they spake with such pleasantness of Scripture language' (38, p. 17), and then of how Paul's epistles in particular 'were sweet and pleasant to me' (46, p. 19). But if indeed his recollection of pleasure in narrative was a literary one, already he has made the familiar movement from appearing to describe an aesthetic response to describing a religious one. In the same paragraph he continues, 'I was then never out of the Bible, either by reading or meditation, still crying out to God that I might know the truth'. When he comes to examples he leaves no doubt as to the purely religious nature of his pleasure; quoting from Luke 14: 23, 22, he comments, 'these words, but especially them, "And yet there is room", were sweet words to me; for, truly, I thought that by them I saw there was place enough in heaven for me' (68, p. 25). This is the essence of his sense of Scripture: he loves it as he sees in it promise of his salvation, fears it as it seems to prove his damnation. Just as the Scriptures can be sweet, they can be 'most fearful and terrible' (222, p. 72).

This is where Bunyan's peculiar intensity comes in. It is as if he is not reading words at all, but encountering and wrestling with a nightmare world of physical things. The whole Bible seems to live inside his head, not only obsessing him, but sallying forth with individual texts over whose selection he has no control, to wrestle, assault and torture him, sometimes also to salve him. As if he himself is on a pilgrimage, he meets with Scriptures or is followed by them; they come suddenly upon him, tearing and rending his soul, fastening on it like fetters of brass, even striking him down as dead; sometimes every sentence of the Bible seems to be against him, 'more I say than an army of forty thousand men that might have come against me' (246, p. 79). As suddenly, different Scriptures come on him, releasing him, spangling in his eyes and sweetly visiting his soul. Ultimately this tells us about Bunyan rather than about the Bible. 'I have sometimes', he writes, 'seen more in a line of the Bible than I could well tell how to stand under, and yet at another time the whole Bible hath been to me as dry as a stick; or rather, my heart hath been so dead and dry unto it that I could not conceive the least dram of refreshment, though I have looked it all over' (conclusion, p. 104). He is the most intense and subjective of readers.

His work could only produce a similar response to the KJB in those who shared his rare temperament. For the majority of his vast numbers of readers it would be an emphatic encouragement to revere the truth of the KJB and also, though less emphatically, to appreciate both fineness in biblical quotations and, to an extent greater than in Milton, the possibility of incorporating the KJB's language into creative work. It might also mislead readers into taking what is in fact Bunyan as authentic KJB.

CHAPTER NINE

The early eighteenth century and the King James Bible

'ALL THE DISADVANTAGES OF AN OLD PROSE TRANSLATION'

The superior language

Yet how beautiful do the holy writings appear, under all the disadvantages of an old prose translation? So beautiful that, with a charming and elegant simplicity, they ravish and transport the learned reader, so intelligible that the most unlearned are capable of understanding the greater part of them. (*A Miscellany of Poems*, p. 30)

So exclaims in 1731 the very minor poet and critic, John Husbands (1706–32). He seems to be saying that the KJB, in spite of being rather bad by his standards, is, after all, very good. This curious combination of praise and dispraise is one of a line of such remarks that reflects conflicting forces among the literati of Augustan England. Before exhibiting these remarks, some of the forces need to be sketched.

The phrase 'an old prose translation' suggests the three main negative elements. The disadvantage of being a translation needs no comment – everybody believed that translation must necessarily be inferior to the original, especially if that original was divinely inspired – but we are accustomed to admiring prose and do not think of the language of a hundred years ago or less as particularly old. In contrast, the eighteenth century was vividly aware that the English it used for literature (to look no further) was very different from – and, most thought, far better than – that of pre-Restoration literature: 'the language of the present times is so clean and chaste, and so very different from our ancestors, that should they return hither they would want an interpreter to converse with us'.[1] Rewritings of the best old authors such as Chaucer and Shakespeare abounded. Dryden, prefacing his adaptation of *Troilus and Cressida* (1679), had this to say of Shakespeare's language:

---

[1] Blackmore, *Essays upon Several Subjects* (London, 1716), p. 99.

it must be allowed to the present age that the tongue in general is so much refined since Shakespeare's time that many of his words and more of his phrases are scarce intelligible. And of those which we understand, some are ungrammatical, others coarse, and his whole style is so pestered with figurative expressions that it is as affected as it is obscure.[2]

This is criticism as much of the time as of its greatest author. Comments such as this are not, so far, to be found on the KJB's language, but they represent what must have been in people's minds when they dismissed it as old.

Dryden wanted 'a perfect grammar' of the language as the foundation for 'an exact standard of writing and of speaking' (p. 225). The eighteenth century did its best. Dictionaries helped standardise meaning, spelling and, consequently, pronunciation; grammars, modelled on Latin grammar, not on observation of English in use, fixed themselves on the tongue like marriage, for better or worse. What is more, the century believed it was doing well. Leonard Welsted (1688–1742) illustrates this with all the enthusiasm so characteristic of minor critics. Though others might disagree, he believes that 'the English language does at this day [1724] possess all the advantages and excellencies, which are very many, that its nature will admit of, whether they consist in softness and majesty of sound, or in the force and choice of words, or in variety and beauty of construction'.[3] Sound, vocabulary and grammar, if that is what the last phrase means, are all as perfect as can be. Further, the language has only recently reached this aesthetic excellence: 'it is not, unless I mistake, much more than a century since England first recovered out of something like barbarism with respect to its state of letters and politeness . . . we have laid aside all our harsh antique words and retained only those of good sound and energy; the most beautiful polish is at length given to our tongue, and its Teutonic rust quite worn away' (pp. 321–2).[4] The prejudice against the native element in the language is rampant. The very term 'Augustan' expresses both the prejudice against the past and the contentment with the present. Initially it was used for the writers of Charles II's reign (1660–85), but Welsted and others used it as it is still used, for their own time, the time of Pope and Addison, with extension back to Dryden. It

---

[2] *The Works of John Dryden*, 20 vols., ed. Alan Roper and Vinton A. Dearing (Berkeley, Los Angeles and London: University of California Press, 1961 etc.), XIII: 225.

[3] 'A Dissertation Concerning the Perfection of the English Language, the State of Poetry, etc.' (1724); in Elledge, *Eighteenth-Century Essays*, I: 320–48; p. 324.

[4] 'Politeness' was much used in this century; as an adjective it corresponds to our 'cultivated', and is often used interchangeably with 'polished'.

suggests a selfsatisfied comparison with the time of Virgil, Horace and Ovid. In such a situation, the KJB was doubly disadvantaged. Not only was it old, but its linguistic roots were largely Teutonic in vocabulary and often Hebraic in form.

The nearest we can get to detail of how this sense of the Augustan perfection of English affected reading of the KJB comes from a Roman Catholic source. An Irish priest, Cornelius Nary (1660–1738), made a new translation of the NT from the Vulgate, 'diligently compared' with the Greek and other translations (Dublin, 1719). He claims in the title that he is working 'for the better understanding of the literal sense', yet his preface points to revision not of Gregory Martin's scholarship but of his language, which 'is so old, the words in many places so obsolete, the orthography so bad, and the translation so very literal, that in a number of places it is unintelligible, and all over so grating to the ears of such as are accustomed to speak, in a manner, another language, that most people will not be at the pains of reading [it]' (fol. A2v). Except that people did read it, much of this could apply to the KJB, and the comment is notable for combining aesthetic and practical objections, as well as looking to a standard in the objection to the spelling.

The disadvantage of prose reflects the fact that interest in literary aspects of the Bible at this time concentrated on the poetic parts. Wither had already argued that prose was a poor substitute for verse translation (see above, p. 133), and now the much-pilloried John Dennis thought along similar lines, arguing this way in his most representative work, *The Grounds of Criticism in Poetry* (1704):

it is ridiculous to imagine that there can be a more proper way to express some parts and duties of a religion which we believe to be divinely inspired than the very way in which they were at first delivered. Now the most important part of the Old Testament [the prophecies] was delivered not only in a poetical style, but in poetical numbers . . . because they who wrote them believed that the figurative passionate style and the poetical numbers . . . were requisite to enforce them upon the minds of men. (pp. 139, 140)

The divine precedent demands that a proper (here probably meaning 'appropriate' rather than 'accurate') translation be in verse. Consequently, when Dennis cites a biblical passage for its literary quality he uses his own verse paraphrase, but when he cites the Bible for its meaning alone he uses the KJB. 'Poetry', he argues, 'is the natural language of religion, and . . . religion at first produced it as a cause produces its effect' (p. 131). Prose is a later and lesser invention, 'by no means proper' for religion (p. 132). Referring to the ancient Greeks, he explains that 'the wonders of religion naturally threw them upon great passions, and great passions naturally threw them upon harmony and figurative language, as they must of necessity do any poet' (p. 132). Turning to Christianity, he elaborates: 'because if the ideas which these subjects afford are expressed with passion equal to their greatness, that which expresses them is poetry; for that which makes poetry to be what it is is only because it has more passion than any other way of writing' (p. 139). The quality of poetry lies in its power to move the passions, and the passions are most moved by religious subjects given appropriate poetic expression.

Longinus and Boileau

One line of thought that began to break down prejudice against an old prose translation came from Longinus' treatise, *Peri Hupsous*. This was translated into English as *Of the height of eloquence* (John Hall, 1652), *Of the loftiness or elegancy of speech* (J. Pulteney, 1680), *An essay upon sublime* (anonymous, 1698), and *On the sublime* (William Smith, 1739). These changes encapsulate an important shift in literary attitudes. In a general way, 'eloquence' and 'sublime' evoke the same thing, a sense of what is best in writing, but they have a basic difference. 'Eloquence' points towards all the rhetorical devices of a piece of writing and indicates a technical judgement of literature: its main purpose is persuasion, and there had of course been many arguments mounted that the Bible fulfilled this purpose in spite of its apparent lack of eloquence, arguments that tried to shift the basis for judgement from technical qualities to effectiveness. With the advent of 'sublime' as a key word for literary quality this shift in basis became widely accepted. Not only did effectiveness become a primary criterion for quality, but a new kind of effectiveness came to be admired, not the power to *persuade* but the power to *move*, particularly to move to heights of emotion.

Longinus defines sublimity as a quality which pleases, rather than persuades, all men at all times. It uplifts souls, filling them 'with a proud exaltation and a sense of vaunting joy' (ch. 7, p. 107), or, in Hall's phrase, 'a transport of joy and wonder' (p. xi).[5] This is the aspect of his work that meant so much to the eighteenth century, even if it was at odds with Augustan ideas of a polished, regulated, neoclassical perfection. If sublimity of effect was a criterion for aesthetic quality, then any writing –

---

[5] For ease of reference I have used T.S. Dorsch's 1965 translation, *On the Sublime*, and then selected among Hall, Pulteney and Smith, whose version predominated after 1739.

indeed, any object – which produced this effect could be admired whether or not its style appeared admirable. This was of great importance for literary estimation of the Bible in translation, if not always as a cause of that estimation, then certainly helping to legitimise it and to make it fashionable.

There is a second crucial element for biblical appreciation in Longinus's idea of the sublime, its religious dimension. He identifies the two prime sources of the sublime as 'the ability to form grand conceptions' and 'the stimulus of powerful and inspired emotion' (ch. 8, p. 108); the latter Hall calls 'fierce and transporting passion' (p. xii), while both Pulteney and Smith understand this as the pathetic, 'by which is meant that enthusiasm and natural vehemency which touches and affects us' (Pulteney, p. 24). Longinus pushes both these sources towards divinity. Sublimity is not just 'the echo of a noble mind' (ch. 9, p. 109), it 'carries one up to where one is close to the majestic mind of God' (ch. 36, p. 147). Pulteney puts this most interestingly: it has in it 'something supernatural and divine, two qualities which almost equal us to the gods themselves' (pp. 134–5). In his dedication, Hall writes that the sublime 'must therefore have somewhat I cannot tell how divine in it' (fol. B3 v.), and, now translating, he proclaims that 'there is nothing nearer divine inspiration' (p. xiv; ch. 8, p. 109). Sublimity bespeaks divinity. So too does the Bible. It was difficult, following Longinus, not to think of the Bible as sublime, especially as he himself, in a famous passage, had taken one of his examples of sublimity from the Bible.[6] After a Homeric example of passages 'which represent the divine nature as it really is, pure, majestic and undefiled', Longinus observes: 'so too the lawgiver of the Jews, no ordinary person, having formed a high conception of the power of the Divine Being, gave expression to it when at the very beginning of his laws he wrote: "God said" – what? "Let there be light, and there was light; let there be land, and there was land"' (ch. 9, p. 111). If an honoured pagan could find sublimity in the Scripture, how much more might the Christian find? Longinus' most important translator, one of the founding fathers of French literary criticism, Nicolas Boileau-Despréaux (1636–1711), spelt the point out: 'Longinus himself, in the midst of the shades of paganism, did not fail to recognise the divinity that there is in these words of Scripture' (*Oeuvres Complètes*, III: 443). For

---

[6] Since it is so rare for a Greek author to cite the Bible, the authenticity of this passage is often questioned. However, it was accepted as genuine by most people in the eighteenth century (Smith, who takes the passage as an occasion for a discourse on biblical simplicity and sublimity, reports some dispute (pp. 128 ff.)).

a facile repetition wherein the single instance of Longinus has become an all-embracing plural, there is this by the controversialist Charles Leslie (1650–1722) – it is of added interest as it is also an example of the phrase we will be following: 'the heathen orators have admired the sublime of the style of the Scriptures. No writing in the world comes near it, even with all the disadvantage of our translation, which, being obliged to be literal, must lose much of the beauty of it.'[7]

Boileau seized on Longinus' remark. Misrepresenting what Longinus says but true to the underlying tendency of his work, Boileau argues that Longinus does not mean by 'sublime' what orators call the sublime style, but the extraordinary and marvellous which elevates and ravishes:

The sublime style always seeks great language, but the sublime can be found in a single thought, in a single figure, in a single turn of phrase. A thing can be in the sublime style and yet not be sublime, that is, may have nothing extraordinary or astonishing in it. For example, 'the sovereign disposer of nature in one word created light': that is in the sublime style, yet it is not sublime because there is nothing particularly marvellous in it . . . But, 'God said, Let there be light, and there was light': this extraordinary turn of expression which marks so well creation's obedience to the creator is truly sublime and has something divine in it. (III: 442)

Opposition to these claims led Boileau to elaborate them in his posthumous tenth reflection on some passages of Longinus (1713). He insists that there is no opposition between simplicity and sublimity (III: 409): simple language can create, can even enhance, sublimity. So 'God said, Let there be light, and there was light' 'is not only sublime, but all the more sublime because, the words being very simple and taken from ordinary language, they make us understand wonderfully, and better than all the finest words, that it is no more difficult for God to make light, heaven and earth than for a master to say to a servant, "bring me my cloak"' (III: 412). The point is well made. If the Bible is all the more sublime for not trying to match the grandeur of its content with grandeur of style, then the language of ploughboys may be the very means for conveying its sublimity, that is, its power to elevate the soul. But, just as few English critics were able to match Boileau's nice perception of the relationship between expression and meaning, so none of them, except in the most general terms, was able to bring out the potential for appreciation of the Tyndalian tradition of translation.

---

[7] *The Truth of Christianity Demonstrated* (London, 1711), p. 153.

The growth of a commonplace

The tension between Longinian or pseudo-Longinian ideas and the time's hostility to the old, the prosaic and the translated helped to produce observations such as that by Husbands. By the time he wrote, it had become a commonplace to appreciate the KJB with reservations. Mostly what was praised could be found in any version; the reservations applied particularly to the form of the KJB, but only because that was now the generally used version. This note was first sounded by the much-admired essayist, defender of the ancients against the moderns and patron of Swift, Sir William Temple (1628–99). It follows a discussion in his essay 'Of poetry' (1690) that develops the tussle between Longinian ideas and the age's sense of decorum. It is affecting power rather than technical ability that distinguishes a true poet:

Whoever does not affect and move the same present passions in you that he represents in others, and at other times raise images about you, as a conjurer is said to do spirits, transport you to the places and to the persons he describes, cannot be judged to be a poet, though his measures are never so just, his feet never so smooth, or his sounds never so sweet.[8]

This is not to dismiss technical merit but to put it in its proper place.

Having turned his back on giving rules for poetry, Temple gives a history of it, dealing first with its antiquity. Biblical poetry merits discussion not as being superior to the classics but as an example of how poetry is older than prose in many nations. Job is discussed as the most ancient book of the Bible and allowed to be an 'admirable and truly inspired poem'. But its origin is not Jewish, so he turns to the most ancient Hebrew poem, Deborah's song (Judges 5). Here he launches the commonplace, remarking that he never read this 'without observing in it as true and noble strains of poetry and picture as in any other language whatsoever, in spite of all disadvantages from translations into so different tongues and common prose' (p. 185). An obviously genuine Longinian response to literary power is tempered by dislike of the translations. Implicitly, some poetic quality is independent of poetic form. Temple does not develop this; rather, it lies in his work like a grain of mustard seed accidentally sown.

The next occurrence of this kind of remark comes ten years later from the much-maligned minor poet, Queen Anne's physician, Sir Richard

---

[8] Samuel Holt Monk, ed., *Five Miscellaneous Essays by Sir William Temple* (Ann Arbor: University of Michigan Press, 1963), p. 183.

Blackmore (?1658–1729), in the preface to his *Paraphrase on the Book of Job* (1700). Though the following paragraph makes the point twice, it is worth giving in full because it suggests several important connections:

The language in which this book is written is Hebrew, and considering the obscurity of the style or manner of expression in the eastern parts of the world, their eloquence as well as their customs and habits being very different from ours, 'tis very strange that a literal translation of this book, as it is now found in the Bible, especially considering how long since it was written, how little the language is at present known, and how much the idiom of it is lost, should not be found more harsh, and be less capable of being understood than it is. I am confident that if several of the Greek poets should be verbally translated, they would appear more obscure, if not altogether unintelligible. As if in a literal translation the book of Job written in an eastern language does so much affect us and raises in our minds such an admiration of its beauty and majesty, what a wonderful and inimitable kind of eloquence must be supposed in the original when we cannot translate verbatim a good poet from one modern language into another, though it be that of our nearest neighbours, without a great diminution of its excellence. (pp. xlii–xliii)

To begin with, it is typical that the remark should accompany praise of the originals. This is hardly surprising, but the way the effectiveness of the translation is used to bolster a sense of their perfection is. That the Bible seems to survive translation, even in a poor old medium, better than any other writings is used as a new argument for the old point that the Bible is superior to the classics. Now, one of the most important literary debates of this time concerned the relative merits of classical and contemporary literature – the ancients versus the moderns. One might well expect the opinion of the Bible's literary superiority, with this new and commonly repeated argument supporting it, to have widened that debate into a three-sided contest, but it did not. Opinion on the relative merits of the Bible and the classics, rather than being a part of 'the battle of the books', was a counter-current to it. The majority of those who voiced an opinion gave the palm to the Scriptures, but, as in the past, this was usually for religious rather than literary reasons. The Bible was edging its way into literary discussions, but only in a few works did it claim the spotlight.

Blackmore's passage points to a second new way of thinking in his recognition of different standards of eloquence. He recurs to this in explaining why he has 'not attempted a close translation of this sacred book [Job], but a paraphrase' (p. lxxiv). The original does not meet modern European standards of literary method; rather, it is repetitious and irregular; it has broken and obscure connections, and it neglects transitions (pp. lxxv–lxxvi). Such candid recognition of 'faults' is rare in an advocate of biblical literature who believes in the divine inspiration of the Bible,[9] but Blackmore prevents his observations from being a reproach to the style of the Bible by using the idea of different tastes:

I would not peremptorily condemn their taste, for the opinion of beauty and ornament seems not to be capable of being determined by any fixed and unalterable rule . . . What we censure as careless, wild and extravagant, strikes them with more admiration, and gives them greater pleasure than all our elaborate and orderly contrivances. All that can be said is that our tastes are different, and if they are barbarous to us, we are so to them . . .

We in this part of the world are all so full of Homer and Virgil, and so bigoted to the Greek and Latin sects, that we are ready to account all authors heretical that are without the pale of the classics. (pp. lxxvi–lxxvii)

Admiration for the Bible has pushed him to a sharp piece of criticism. As we shall see when it is echoed by Husbands (below, p. 204), this is capable of making any age look at its own standards.

Two better-remembered figures, Edward Young (1683–1765), author of *Night Thoughts on Life, Death and Immortality*, and James Thomson (1700–48), author of *The Seasons*, are, compared with Blackmore, mere echoers, showing that what Temple and Blackmore were initiating was indeed becoming a general idea. Young compares Job's description of the horse (Job 39: 19–25, given from the KJB with two minor variations) with a description in Virgil:

Now follows that in the book of Job, which under all the disadvantages of having been written in a language little understood, of being expressed in phrases peculiar to a part of the world whose manner of thinking and speaking seems to us very uncouth, and, above all, of appearing in a prose translation, is nevertheless so transcendently above the heathen descriptions that hereby we may perceive how faint and languid the images are which are formed by mortal authors when compared with that which is figured, as 'twere, just as it appears in the eye of the creator.[10]

Thomson, taking Temple's view of the relative merits of the Bible and the classics, supplies an interesting new adjective for the KJB. Discussing the best poets' happiness in singing the works of nature, he drops in this aside before going on to praise Virgil: 'the book of Job, that noble and ancient poem, which, even, strikes so forcibly through a mangling translation, is crowned with a description of the grand works of nature, and

---

9 Blackmore explicitly connects divine inspiration with 'eloquence and the right art of persuasion' in the preface to *Essays upon Several Subjects* (London, 1716), pp. xxxiii–xxxiv.

10 *The Guardian* 86 (Friday, June 19, 1713); in *The Guardian*, p. 313. This essay is sometimes attributed to Sir Richard Steele.

that too from the mouth of their almighty author'.[11] Comments such as these point to a growing use of the KJB, the beginning of a Longinian willingness to judge it by its effect, and yet a persistent prejudice against it over a period of some forty years (1690–1731).[12]

Even less remembered than Blackmore is the critic Henry Felton, D.D. (1679–1740), yet his *A Dissertation on Reading the Classics* (1713) was popular enough to reach a fifth edition in 1753. After another example of the commonplace, he goes on to something extraordinary:

> For, let me only make this remark, that the most literal translation of the Scriptures, in the most natural signification of the words, is generally the best; and the same punctualness which debaseth other writings preserveth the spirit and majesty of the sacred text: it can suffer no improvement from human wit, and we may observe that those who have presumed to heighten the expressions by a poetical translation or paraphrase have sunk in the attempt, and all the decorations of their verse, whether Greek or Latin, have not been able to reach the dignity, the majesty and solemnity of our prose, so that the prose of Scripture cannot be improved by verse, and even the divine poetry is most like itself in prose. (pp. 129–31)

This has suddenly moved far from prejudice, and we might seize on it as evidence that the English of the KJB, 102 years after its publication, has taken its place as literature. But Felton is contradicting most of his contemporaries, and he does not take the simple, apparently unavoidable next step of giving the KJB itself explicit praise. He is a harbinger, well in advance of the main company. He has jumped to a point the age was not ready for, arriving there because he is arguing less from the experience of reading the KJB against verse translations than from a peculiar application of the common idea that God's poetry can receive no improvement from human wit. This had never before been taken as proving that a literal prose translation is best ('punctualness' means literal precision of translation). Moreover, it must have helped his many readers towards an esteem for both the originals and the translation to read these assertions under the dogmatic running headings, 'The Scripture only sublime', and 'Above all improvement'.

More outspokenly than any of his contemporaries, Felton is taking the

---

[11] Preface to the second edition of *Winter* (1726).

[12] Though most expressions of the idea concentrate in this time, there are at least two later examples, the preface to *Choheleth*, ascribed to J. Dennis Furley (London, 1765), pp. xxii–xxiii, and, 95 years later, Le Roy J. Halsey's declaration that 'there is no stronger proof of the indestructible character of the poetry of the Bible, and of its inherent sublimity and beauty, than this fact, that through all the disadvantages and disguises of a literal prose translation, many passages of the poetical books, and nearly all the Psalms, still retain the spirit and rhythm and very music of the bard' (*Literary Attractions*, p. 74).

Scriptures as 'a very masterpiece of writing', and 'as absolutely perfect in the purity and justness either of style or composition'. These phrases were first published two years before Felton's work, but they are the more significant because they are part of an objection to such ideas by the Earl of Shaftesbury.[13] That such ideas could provoke moderating comment suggests how strong they were becoming.

Though Felton's resounding claims could not be further removed from Dennis's ideas on biblical poetry and translation, his starting-point is Dennisian: 'the thoughts which are natural to every sacred theme are so far exalted above the heathen poetry or philosophy that the meanest Christian, however he may fail in diction, is able to surpass the noblest wits of antiquity in the truth and greatness of his sentiments' (pp. 165–6). This underlines just how much his conclusions are theoretic rather than experiential, and so in essence belong with the arguments from divine inspiration. Others managed to bring to their comments a greater sense of authentic response, and tried to take up the challenge Blackmore had recognised and rejected, of adapting their tastes and critical ideas to the Hebraic. The most interesting of these is another follower of Dennis, Charles Gildon (1665–1724), as he presents himself in *The Laws of Poetry Explained and Illustrated* (1721). He too echoes the commonplace in his observation that the reader will find in 'some of the songs or odes of the Hebrew poets . . . that heat, that divine enthusiasm, that true sublime, which is nowhere else to be met with, at least in that perfection which even our vulgar translations give us' (p. 115). Yet he also shows the prejudice against the KJB dwindling towards insignificance. As a substitute for Pindar he invites his reader to admire the true sublime of the Hebrew odes. He gives three examples, Moses' song (Exod. 15: 1–18), and Psalms 18 and 127, and refers to others, confident that they need no commentary to produce 'the highest transport and pleasure' in readers with 'any soul or genius for poetry' (p. 116). Moses' song is given from the KJB, Psalm 127 from the PB, and this leads him to a passage as fascinating as Felton's:

I have chosen to give two of these songs . . . in the diction of our translators of the Bible, because it is more strong and close than any of those paraphrastic efforts in rhyme . . . The public translators had only in their view the rendering the Hebrew text as fully and close as they possibly could, without endeavouring at the smooth and polished expression that should give their words a numerousness and an agreeable sound to the ear. By this means they have retained a much

---

[13] *Characteristics of of Men, Manners, Opinions, Times, etc.* (1711); ed. John M. Robertson, 2 vols. (1900; Gloucester, Mass.: Peter Smith, 1963), II: 302.

more valuable quality, that is, the sense, the spirit, the elevation and the divine force of the original; whereas those gentlemen, who have attempted any part of the Old Testament in rhyme, have . . . lost the force and energy of the divine song in the weak ornaments of modern poetry: at least, this I can say for myself, that I never found my soul touched by the best of these performances . . . though it has been scarce able to support the violent emotions and excessive transports raised by the common translation. (p. 120)

At last the moving power of the poetry as given in the KJB and the PB is allowed full weight. It touches Gildon's soul with violent emotions. The possibilities in Longinus as presented by Boileau have become quite explicit. The KJB and PB are being read as superb literature, and men of taste are invited to admire them. But still there are limitations. The two translations are not appreciated as achievements in their own right, nor is the Hebrew poetry presented as necessarily the best poetry. Rather, the KJB and the PB are the most affecting translations of any ancient poetry, classical or biblical, in instances where a Milton or a Dennis has not given a superior version. Psalm 18 is given for preference in 'that sublime diction with which Mr Dennis has clothed it' (p. 117). As in Felton, the quality most admired in the KJB and PB is their literal fidelity to the originals. The frequent emphasis on literalness at this time suggests that the alien nature of their English was more obvious to the Augustans than to later readers.

In a sense Gildon is doing no more than repeat Felton's argument 'that the prose of Scripture cannot be improved by verse, and even the divine poetry is most like itself in prose', and adding to it testimony to the experience of reading the prose translations. But the effect of his arguments is of a quiet correction of Felton's excesses. The Scripture is not the 'only sublime'; it is perhaps not even the pinnacle of sublimity, the translation is not 'above all improvement'. If Gildon is an outspoken enemy of rhyme, still he is an admirer of Augustan diction, so elevated in Dennis's versions, and Augustan 'numerousness', that is, command of poetic harmony. He encourages literary admiration of the Bible *through* the KJB, but, however close it may seem, this is not the same as encouraging admiration *of* the KJB. Only when the writing is as abstract and theoretical as Felton's does it *seem* that the KJB itself is to be admired.

Longinus' gift of the word 'sublime' to critical vocabulary opened up a major new way of thinking about poetry, but the Augustan critic still lacked that crucial word, 'literature'. In his earlier *The Complete Art of Poetry*, this leads Gildon into severe difficulties which he only half realises, for he is trying to write a complete art of literature rather than of poetry. Though he attempts to give 'poetry' the wider force of 'literature' by distinguishing it from 'verse', the attempt is largely a failure, in part because it contradicts his real tastes, in part because the idea of sublimity has not broken down the over-rigid form/content duality of the rhetorical idea of literature. Gildon often writes as if a critic has to choose between form and content, and so should make the choice Tyndale made of the pith over the husk. The first dialogue, 'Of the nature, use, excellence, rise and progress of poetry', concludes with this Sidneian point: 'though number and harmony have been allowed likewise one of the causes of poetry, yet imitation is the most valuable part, for there may be just imitations, that is, true poems, without that most known kind of number and harmony which we call verse'.[14] He never moves on from this to suggest that there are other verbal qualities that a critic might admire in prose; the kind of argument Boileau had made for the sublime power of simple prose appropriately used is totally lost on him.

To leave Gildon for a moment: only one critic was able to make this kind of move, the nonconformist clergyman Samuel Say (1676–1743) in his posthumous 'An essay on the harmony, variety and power of numbers, whether in prose or verse' (1745).[15] The title alone is sufficiently striking in its willingness to consider prose not only as a literary medium, but as one capable of 'numbers'. Say's method is not prescriptive but deductive and relativistic ('the genius of one language [is not] to be measured by another' (p. 467)). Like many later critics, he believes that the sound must reflect the sense, and he analyses passages to show wherein their quality lies. At one point he turns to the Bible for examples. He argues that there exist what he calls expletive particles and also expletive sentences which 'are necessary to the ear where they are not necessary to the sense' (p. 467). Thus he observes that 'do' is present in Luke 10: 11 ('even the very dust of your city . . . we do wipe off against you') to prevent the disagreeable grouping of sounds, 'we wipe' (p. 468). This attributes taste and artistry to the translators. As examples of expletive sentences, that is, sentences 'that are not necessary to the sense . . . and yet may be necessary to the hearer, that he may receive with delight and retain forever the truths so artfully and strongly impressed upon his mind', he gives the beginnings of Psalm 78 and Isaiah, quoting the KJB exactly bar one omission in the Isaiah. The Psalm he gives thus:

> 1. Give ear, O my people, to my law:
>   Incline your ears to the words of my mouth.

---

[14] I: 88; see Sidney, pp. 10–11.   [15] In Elledge, ed., *Eighteenth-Century Essays*, I: 456–83.

> 2. I will open my mouth in a parable:
> I will utter dark sayings of old. (p. 467)

What he seems to have in mind is the synonymous parallelism, which he notes 'appears to be the perpetual practice of heavenly wisdom in the Psalms and in the Prophets'. It is a matter for regret that he did not develop the point. More startling, though, is his presentation of the quotations as free verse. The Psalm is exactly as the RV was to set these words 140 years later. He makes no comment on this procedure, and it is such a fleeting instance that we cannot grant it any historical importance. Yet, if we interpret his action favourably (there seems no reason not to), we may say that one eighteenth-century critic was able to read the KJB's prose as verse; his is a truly exceptional mind, jumping from the muddled quarrel with the technical implications of 'poetry' to what, on a minuscule scale, looks like a modern perception. Moreover, he shows the unrealised potential in lesser, more industrious critics like Gildon.

A different but important theoretical consequence of Gildon's separation of form and content is that what he takes to be the essence of poetry – its content, including its images – is translatable and 'may be in all languages' (I: 77). Though this falls well short of Felton's idea of the translatability of biblical poetry, it helps to show how some Augustans, reacting against their age's polish, were moving, in one sense, towards a non-textual idea of the Bible, and, in another, towards appreciation of biblical poetry translated into prose. The first sense remains undeveloped, and the furthest Gildon can go with the latter in *The Complete Art* is to comment on Jesus's use of fiction in his parables (I: 56), and to reproduce, sometimes verbatim, Sidney's discussion of Nathan's parable to David (2 Sam. 12: 1–4; Sidney, p. 25): his purpose is Sidney's, to prove that 'the feigned images of poetry' are more efficacious than 'the regular instruction of philosophy' (I: 56), and so to defend fiction. Again it is striking that he has to call these parables 'poetry'. He seems not to have known 'fiction' in its modern sense, though, unlike 'literature', it was beginning to be used at this time. Richard Daniel, dedicating his version of the Psalms to the king, contrasts the Odyssey and the Aeneid with the story of David, and remarks that 'the adventures of that brave prince, without the beauties of fiction to support them, are much more entertaining than anything we can meet with in the heathen story'.[16] However, it is revealing that Johnson did not record this sense of 'fiction'

---

[16] *A Paraphrase on Some Select Psalms* (London, 1722), fol. A4 r.

in his dictionary. The limitation of vocabulary is, in Gildon, a limitation of thought. However much he may stretch 'poetry' as his word for literature, he is still locked in to a way of thinking that does not recognise prose as a worthy medium. The 'collection of the most beautiful descriptions, similes, allusions, etc., from Spenser and our best English poets, as well ancient as modern' which makes up volume two contains no prose and only one brief, forgettable biblical paraphrase (''Tis Zion then, 'tis Zion we deplore'). This is another statement of Gildon's taste and a fair reflection of the real taste of so many Augustans: in spite of their theoretical gropings away from the formal connotations of poetry and towards new ideas that were eventually to help recognition of the KJB as literature, they still did not appreciate literal prose as found in the KJB. The commonplace we have been following is the natural expression of this situation.

JOHN HUSBANDS

John Husbands, who began this chapter, would be quite unknown did not his only work, *A Miscellany of Poems by Several Hands* (1731), contain Samuel Johnson's earliest publication, a Latin translation of Pope's 'Messiah'. He begins by presenting Hebrew poetry as one kind of primitive poetry; like several of his predecessors he wants the English to develop divine poetry, and he offers this 'natural poetry' as the model:

To praise Him however in the worthiest manner, we must copy after those representations we have of Him in the Holy Scriptures, where He has been pleased to descend in some measure to human eyes, and is become more familiar to mankind. There the inspired authors have left us the noblest examples of this divine kind of writing. We have not only a religion but a language from heaven. There poetry is the handmaid to piety, and eloquence sits beside the throne of truth. What innumerable beauties might our poetry be furnished with from those sacred repositories? What a pleasing variety of Godlike sentiments, what noble images, what lofty descriptions might from thence be transplanted into our tongue? These are the writings which far surpass all human compositions. No other books, however useful or excellent, can stand in competition with them. (pp. 9–10)[17]

What is so curious here is that he offers up this supreme poetry for imitation as if no one had yet transplanted it into English – as if not only the prose translations but all the verse translations and even Milton were

---

[17] Because Husbands's preface is unpaginated, I have used the printer's letters as a guide, counting the first page as one; so, b=7, c=15, d=23, etc.

failures – and his own ordinary collection of verse paraphrases were a first step to this new poetry. Husbands' conceit of novelty is enormous, yet it should not blind us to the typicality of what he says: even the neatness of his use of the idea of divine inspiration, 'we have not only a religion but a language from heaven', looks like plagiarism of Joseph Spence: 'we are not only blessed with instructions but favoured too with a language from heaven'.[18]

Sadly, Husbands makes only limited progress in describing this natural poetry. He admires it – to the point of adoration – along with all the other primitive poetry he knows of, but his description of it shows, like Gildon's remarks, the limits of this un-Augustan movement of the Augustans:

For the strength and energy of the figures and the true sublimity of style are a natural effect of the passions. No wonder therefore that their diction is something more flourished and ornamental, more vigorous and elevated, more proper to paint and set things before our eyes than plain and ordinary recitals. This sort of poetry is more simple, and at the same time worthy of the majesty of God, than that which is regular and confined, which must with difficulty express the dictates of the Holy Spirit, and would be apt to give some alloy to the sublimity of the sense. (p. 19)

Felton could move from this to advocation of literal translation. Husbands, however, turns to a review of opinion on the form of the poetry. Accepting that the Hebrews 'were very inaccurate in the art of numbers' (p. 24), indeed, that their numbers 'are no more than Aristotle thinks requisite in a good oration', he suddenly adds, 'in other respects the style of their poetry, to speak a little paradoxically, seems to have been prose' (p. 27). So often the history of criticism seems to be a tale of lost opportunities. This suggests so much for an understanding of the originals, of the relationship between form and content, and for an appreciation of the KJB's prose as the appropriate form of translation, but Husbands can go no further. His practical notion of appropriate translation is exactly the 'regular and confined' method he argues is inappropriate. So, critically, he resorts to the limitations of translation and an appeal to adopt new critical standards and read not as a neoclassicist but as the Hebraic standards themselves dictate.

The first of these ideas, the limitations of translation, leads him to an explicit statement of the perennial sense that the Scriptures are so much better as poetry than they appear: 'a modern reader of the Holy

---

[18] *An Essay on Pope's Odyssey* (Oxford, 1726), p. 57.

Scriptures ought to make great allowances since many beauties must be lost to him' (p. 29). To this he adds Blackmore and Gildon's argument that 'a strictly literal version' of even so 'regular' an author as Virgil would be unreadable, and the commonplace observation of the ravishing beauty of 'an old prose translation' follows immediately.

The appeal for different critical standards is worth careful attention even if much of it is very like Blackmore (see above, p. 196):

It may be considered farther that the eastern people differ something from us in their notions of eloquence. We condemn them for being too pompous, swelling and bombast; perhaps they despise us for being languid, spiritless and insipid. People are apt to form their notions of excellence from their own perfections, and their notions of things from objects with which they are most conversant. Our art of criticism is drawn from the writers of Rome and Athens, whom we make the standard of perfection. But why have not the Jews as much right to prescribe to them as they have to prescribe to the Jews? Yet to this test we endeavour to bring the Sacred Books, not considering that the genius and customs of the Israelites were in many things very different from those of the Greeks or Romans. (p. 32)

To place 'pompous, swelling and bombast' against 'languid, spiritless and insipid' is an instructive caricature, on the one hand rough, sublime intensity, on the other refined restraint such as most of the Augustans practised with their polished numerousness and admired through their criticism by rules. But what is most significant is that Husbands' argument does not apply just to his time. The effort from Josephus to the Renaissance to understand Hebrew poetics in terms of classical metre, and now the effort to transform the poetry into Miltonic blank verse or Augustan heroic couplets – all are attempts to make it conform to 'notions of excellence' drawn from each time's 'own perfections'. The effort still continues, even if it seems to us that our poetic forms in particular can be very close to the Hebrew. The insistence in most modern versions, especially those made with a deliberately literary attitude to the originals, on presenting all the acknowledged poetic parts in some kind of free verse is often nothing more than a visual statement that we should regard the writing as verse rather than prose. We are no more capable than the Augustans of distinguishing the technical form, verse, from the vague notion of certain qualities designated 'poetry'. 'Prose' and 'poetry' are still antithetical, as if there is more difference between the two than the merely formal. Given the flexibility of our literary appreciativeness, this usually matters little, but it may be that the presentation of the supposed poetic parts in truncated lines of print that at least look like verse is a masquerade of the same sort, if not to the same degree, as presenting them in heroic couplets or Sternholdian common metre. It is easy to be literal and give the appearance of verse; moreover, that appearance draws out the only obvious formal quality, parallelism, without necessarily imposing what might be a falsifying metre or an even more falsifying rhyme, but it still implies a kind of poetic form such as we are familiar with is everywhere to be found in the poetry. Too often the parallelism does not accommodate itself in the literal translations to our notion of the right sort of visual length for a line of poetry, with the result that line endings either impose a new structure or become meaningless. Too often, also, there is no evident parallelism, and then the line endings are, again, a masquerade. Our notions of poetic form could hardly be further removed from those of the Augustans, yet the way Husbands puts Blackmore's argument should make us question ourselves and wonder whether Felton's claim that the poetry is most like itself in literal prose does not retain a truth that our Bible makers have forgotten.

Where Husbands is at his best as a critic of the text is not with the poetry but with the prose. Ideas of poetry do not interfere, and he develops Longinus and Boileau's perception of sublimity in simplicity to good effect, eliciting much that is powerful in the KJB – which, for this part of his discussion, he uses regularly. The following is typical of his ability to find original and persuasive examples, and of the way he discusses them:

How concisely, how emphatically is Jacob's love for Rachel comprised in one verse? 'And Jacob served seven years for Rachel, and they seemed unto him but a few days, for the love he had unto her' [Gen 29: 20]. There is more of nature, of expressiveness, of affection in that simple passage than in all the motley descriptions of a French or Italian romance. The whole passion of love is crowded into a few words. The beauty of such passages as these, where the affections are to be described and made, as it were, visible to us, does not consist in a flourish of words or pomp of diction, not in the *ambitiosa ornamenta* of rhetoric, but in a natural and easy display of tender sentiments, and in opening those softnesses which are supposed to arise in the bosoms of the persons introduced. For this purpose nothing is more effectual than a decent simplicity of language. 'Tis this simplicity which in such instances constitutes the just, proper and sublime more than all the glittering descriptions and little prettinesses which a modern author might probably use on such occasions. (pp. 59–60)

The example is better than the discussion; he is more interested in criticising current literary practice than in locating the power of the verse, which indeed 'does not consist in a flourish of words', but in the briefest possible presentation of facts. It is an example of what, following

Blackwall (see below, p. 210), we may call the translatable sublime, for the mind and imagination dwell on these facts, realising just how powerful a love must be to make a man serve seven years and think them but a few days. The facts are as eloquent as the language is inconspicuous. It is not the particular diction of the KJB that creates the sublimity, for it is to be found in any unelaborated translation: in such examples a distinction between form and content *is* helpful. Not all the sublimities Husbands identifies are as independent of the language but none of them depend on qualities peculiar to the KJB. The power is *in* rather than *of* the KJB.

The section Husbands most particularly evokes admiration for is Joseph's story. If, like many of his contemporaries, he works too much by exclamation, nevertheless there is enough of example and discussion to sustain his opinion that 'never was any story, from the beginning to the end, contrived more artfully, never was any plot for the stage worked up more justly, never any unfolded itself more naturally than this of Joseph' (p. 66). Here he has escaped the preoccupation with poetry and found power where few of his contemporaries thought to find it. Lukin in the previous century (above, p. 153) and Blackwall (*Sacred Classics*, I: 3) thought to mention this story, while Pope in a note to book XVI of his translation of *The Odyssey* remarked the superiority of Joseph's discovery of himself to his brothers (Gen. 45: 1–15) to Ulysses' discovery to Telemachus, and went on to a few general comments on the power of the story.[19] Steele devoted one issue of *The Tatler* to it partly to prove 'that the greatest pleasures the imagination can be entertained with are to be found there, and that even the style of the Scripture is more than human'.[20] However, he does not go beyond plot summary and exclamation at a few beauties. Such remarks furnished Husbands with the hint, if he needed one, for discussion; what is new is the length and quality of the discussion. By following Boileau's perception of the relationship between sublimity and simplicity, and by reading the Bible for himself, Husbands has come to a modern perception – and something like a modern demonstration – of literary qualities in a biblical narrative.

Though what Husbands finds to admire in the stories of Genesis has little to do with the unique qualities of the KJB, he elsewhere suggests a critical awareness of them. His taste for literal Hebraisms perhaps owes

[19] *Poems*, X: 131. He also refers his reader to Longinus' comment on Genesis and concludes that Job, 'with regard both to sublimity of thought and morality, exceeds beyond all comparison the most noble parts of Homer'.

[20] No. 233, 5 Oct., 1710; *The Tatler*, ed. Donald F. Bond, 3 vols. (Oxford: Clarendon, 1987), III: 204.

something to Addison's briefly expressed enthusiasm for them – certainly Addison's comparison between Hebrew energy and the 'elegant and polite forms of speech which are natural to our tongue' in *The Spectator* 405 anticipates Husbands. There Addison gave his opinion that 'our language has received innumerable elegancies and improvements from that infusion of Hebraisms which are derived to it out of the poetical passages in Holy Writ'.[21] Husbands gives examples of these admirable Hebraisms such as dawn being expressed as 'the eyelids of the morning' (p. 39; Job 41: 18). He also shows himself willing, as no one before him had been, to comment on both literary success and failure in the KJB. He finds 'an uncommon grandeur and solemnity of phrase in the English version' of Deborah's song (Judges 5; p. 43), but by contrast the KJB shares in the general failure to render Job adequately: 'that unaffected majesty, that comprehensive brevity, that lovely simplicity in which consists its beauty never have been preserved in the version. In the version generally the thoughts are wire-drawn or . . . distilled and quite drawn off till the spirit evaporates and nothing remains but a *caput mortuum*' (p. 75). In these fleeting remarks and in his exposition of the quality of Genesis, Husbands shows himself something better than a representative and synthesising figure, worthy to be remembered for more than his connection with Johnson, his pioneering enthusiasm for primitive poetry or his version of the age's most frequent comment on the KJB. Had his work been better known, or, perhaps, had he lived to develop the perceptions, he might have hastened on literary appreciation not only of the Scriptures but of their English representatives.

ANTHONY BLACKWALL

The classical scholar Anthony Blackwall (1674–1730) also deserves separate recognition, largely but not only because of the size of his work: he devotes the whole of volume one and some of volume two of *The Sacred Classics Defended and Illustrated* (1725, 1731) to praise of the Bible as literature, having already given the public a substantial foretaste of his views in *An Introduction to the Classics* (pp. 81–124). There he places the Scriptures ahead of the classics, though the latter are his subject. He argues 'that the Bible is the most excellent and useful book in the world, and to understand its meaning and discover its beauties 'tis necessary to be conversant in the Greek and Latin classics' (p. 82). To prove the point

[21] Ed. Donald F. Bond, 5 vols. (Oxford: Clarendon, 1965), III: 514.

he gives some thirty pages of parallel passages where the classics are indebted to both Testaments.

Many critics lamented both the general profanity of the age and its neglect of the Scriptures. Blackwall's intention in *The Sacred Classics* is to remedy the neglect (if not the profanity) by demonstrating the purity of the Greek of the NT and imbuing a love for its perfections. A major cause of the neglect is that young scholars such as he addresses take 'the charge of solecisms, blemishes and barbarisms' in the NT Greek for granted and so either neglect it or read it 'with careless indifference and want of taste' (I: 13). Like a latter-day Broughton, he will admit no blemish in the Scripture. He argues, as so many in the previous century had, from divine inspiration:

Now for this reason that the holy writers were under the influence and direction of the spirit of infinite wisdom, who does all his wondrous works in proportion, harmony and beauty, I am fully persuaded he would not suffer
improprieties and violations of the true and natural reason and analogy of
grammar to be in writings dictated by himself, and designed for the instruction
and pleasure of mankind to the end of the world. If we consider God, says an
excellent person, as the creator of our souls, and so likeliest to know the frame
and springs and nature of his own workmanship, we shall make but little
difficulty to believe that in the book written for and addressed to men he hath
employed proper language and genuine natural eloquence, the most powerful
and appropriated mean to work upon them. But solecism and absurd language
give an offence and disgust to all people of judgement and good sense, and are
not appropriate means to work and prevail upon human minds. (I: 160–1)

This is not just a familiar argument rolled out with striking candour and simplicity: the idea of the divine purpose has undergone a subtle shift. Where previously perfect, or at least appropriate, eloquence had been a characteristic of the inspired writing, now God is imagined as deliberately writing literature: it is 'designed for the instruction and pleasure of mankind'.

Blackwall could not be at a further remove from the developing idea of the OT poetry as primitive and artless, and one might instantly dismiss him as archaic and uncritical. Yet his emphasis on the NT as lit-
erature is novel for this time, and, within limits, he does give his ideas critical demonstration. He begins by agreeing with the deprecators of NT Greek that it contains Hebraisms, but defends them on two grounds, that they invigorate the Greek and conform to Greek grammar. Few critics were persuaded by the latter argument, but the former connects with Addison and Husbands' brief observations and must have helped his readers to appreciate English Hebraisms. His first example is typical:

To do things acceptable to God is common language. To do things acceptable before, or in the presence of God is a Hebraism; but does it not enlarge the thought, and enliven and invigorate the expression? And is it any breach of the rationale of grammar, or does it any ways trespass upon concord or government? It places every serious reader under the inspection and all-seeing eye of the most highest, and therefore is apt to inspire him with a religious awe for that immense and adorable presence. (I: 6–7)

The last sentence could give the reader of the KJB a sharpened appreciation of 1 Tim. 2: 3 and 5: 4, but, more often than Husbands', Blackwall's discussion of his examples is limited to the exclamatory, as in the two rhetorical questions here. It is not persuasive to read that 'St Luke is indeed admirable for the natural eloquence and easiness of his language. And don't the rest write with a wonderful perspicuity and a very beautiful and instructive plainness?' (I: 43), unless one already agrees, and then persuasion is hardly necessary. For the reader who thinks only of the English NT, the book is a kind of guided tour, Blackwall a Cicerone who says no more than 'look!' By the end he appears to have invited his young acolyte to admire everything in the NT indiscriminately but, given his belief in the inspired perfection of the writing, he could hardly have encouraged discrimination.

'I must desire the friends of this sacred book,' he writes at the end of the volume, 'to read it carefully and study it in the original, and to esteem it as an immense treasure of learning that requires all their abilities and all their reading' (I: 367). His method makes it inevitable that he should think he is writing for the Bible's friends – it is preaching for the converted – and the volume of praise from other writers in the years preceding his work makes it likely he found a substantial audience even if he made few converts. They would have been encouraged as never before to join appreciation of the NT as literature to their growing taste for Hebrew poetry. An account survives of one of these converts' reactions, but, alas, the convert exists only in fiction: it is the villainous Lovelace's somewhat less villainous correspondent, Robert Belford, in Samuel Richardson's *Clarissa* (1747–8). Immediately after finding the first of Clarissa's four meditations from the Bible, Belford comes across *The Sacred Classics*:

I took it home with me, and had not read a dozen pages when I was convinced that I ought to be ashamed of myself to think how greatly I have admired less noble and less natural beauties in pagan authors, while I have known nothing of this all-excelling collection of beauties, the Bible! By my faith, Lovelace, I shall for the future have a better opinion of the good sense and taste of half a score parsons whom I have fallen in with in my time and despised for *magnifying*, as I thought they did, the language and the sentiments to be found in it in preference to all the ancient poets and philosophers. And this is now a convincing proof to me, and shames as much an infidel's presumption as his ignorance, that those who know least are the greatest scoffers. A pretty pack of would-be wits of us, who censure without knowledge, laugh without reason, and are most noisy and loud against things we know least of![22]

Richardson himself needed no converting, and the passage is not dramatically persuasive; it has the character of a reference to authority and suggested further reading, since it follows Belford's surprised comments on the power and quality of the Bible. Lovelace confirms that Belford is right to admire the 'beauty and noble simplicity' of the Bible, and reproves him for having been ignorant of it.[23]

Whether Lovelace, or Richardson-through-Lovelace, means the KJB is uncertain – probably, like so many casual commentators, he means the originals as they happen to be represented by the KJB – but Blackwall constantly directs his readers' talent for sublime admiration to the Greek, even though, echoing ideas of the Bible's translatability, he claims that 'the true sublime will bear translation into all languages, and will be great and surprising in all languages, and to all persons of understanding and judgement' (I: 277). In *An Introduction* Blackwall gave his examples from the KJB, but here he rarely uses it: Greek examples predominate, and the English is usually his own. Thus the cause of the Bible as literature is given a solid nudge towards the NT and towards the idea of uniform excellency, but the cause of the KJB is only advanced in so far as his Greekless readers can see the excellence of the originals in it.

'A KIND OF STANDARD FOR LANGUAGE TO THE COMMON PEOPLE'

A standard

If the age was not in love with the KJB, it was becoming thoroughly accustomed to it. Locke observes that 'Paul's Epistles, as they stand translated in our English Bibles, are now by long and constant use become a part of the English language, and common phraseology, espe-

---

[22] Ed. Angus Ross (Harmondsworth: Penguin, 1985), p. 1126.

[23] P. 1146. Clarissa's meditations consist of biblical extracts, unlike the pastiche her predecessor, Pamela, indulges in (*Pamela* (1740); 2 vols. (London: Dent, 1914 etc.), I: 284–7). Richardson later added to Clarissa's meditations and published them separately, one of his aims being to raise 'in the minds of the contemners of religion a due estimation of the Sacred Books' (*Meditations Collected from the Sacred Books* (London, 1750), p. ii).

cially in matters of religion'. The poet Alexander Pope (1688–1744) refers to 'those general phrases and manners of expression which have attained a veneration even in our language from being used in the Old Testament'.[24] Though this is a variation on the commonplace discussed earlier, the jump from familiarity to 'veneration' is striking. Yet it is veneration for Hebraisms in English rather than a general veneration for the KJB's English. Another of the age's great writers, Jonathan Swift (1667–1745) uses the observation in a strikingly original way. It comes as part of an argument for that great eighteenth-century goal of 'ascertaining and fixing our language for ever' for fear that it will 'at length infallibly change for the worse'.[25] In his view it is better to fix the language in an imperfect state than not to fix it at all. There are many qualities of classical and romance languages that he could wish English possessed, but, showing abundant scorn for his contemporaries, he is more afraid that the language will be changed for the worse. Indeed, thoroughly uncharacteristically for an Augustan, though few moderns would disagree, he sees English as having received most improvement between 1558, the accession of Elizabeth I, and the rebellion of 1642 (IV: 9). He builds on what he presents as the Earl of Oxford's 'observation, that if it were not for the Bible and Common Prayer Book in the vulgar tongue, we should hardly be able to understand anything that was written among us an hundred years ago':

which is certainly true: for those books, being perpetually read in churches, have proved a kind of standard for language, especially to the common people. And I doubt whether the alterations since introduced have added much to the beauty or strength of the English tongue, although they have taken off a great deal from that simplicity which is one of the greatest perfections in any language . . . no translation our country ever yet produced hath come up to that of the Old and New Testament . . . I am persuaded that the translators of the Bible were masters of an English style much fitter for that work than any we see in our present writings, which I take to be owing to the simplicity that runs through the whole. Then, as to the greatest part of our liturgy, compiled long before the translation of the Bible now in use, and little altered since, there seem to be in it as great strains of true sublime eloquence as are anywhere to be found in our language; which every man of good taste will observe in the Communion Service, that of Burial, and other parts. (pp. 14–15)

The claim that the KJB and the PB are the best of English translations is probably an echo of the argument made by Felton, Gildon and others

---

[24] Locke, *A Paraphrase and Notes*, p. xi; Pope, preface to *The Iliad*, *Poems*, VII: 18.
[25] 'A proposal for correcting, improving and ascertaining the English tongue' (1712); in Herbert Davis (ed.), *The Prose Works of Jonathan Swift*, 14 vols. (Oxford: Blackwell, 1957), IV: 14.

that they are the best English translations from any source, but the idea that they are stylish in their own right is new. Even so, one cannot be sure whether Swift, if pressed, would have claimed the KJB as a great work of English literature. He holds that the translators were artists of a sort, 'masters of an English style', and he qualifies by adding, 'much fitter for that work'. Explicit praise, redolent of Longinus and Boileau, is reserved for the liturgy – here Swift achieves an honourable critical first. Some dozen years later the freethinking deist Anthony Collins (1676–1729) refers sarcastically to the English being charmed with 'the beauty of holiness in our Common Prayer Book',[26] so it seems likely that Swift was articulating a view that was beginning to be generally held. Certainly the biblical 'beauty of holiness' had been used in connection with biblical sublimity as early as 1713. Steele, writing in *The Guardian*, uses it to sum up 'the effect which the sacred writings will have upon the soul of an intelligent reader' (no. 21, pp. 103–4). He had just praised, though without reference to the KJB, the story of Jesus on the road to Emmaeus (Luke 24). The only praise of the PB I have found which antedates Swift comes from the arch-defender of Sternhold and Hopkins, and of anything old in religion, Bishop Beveridge. He admires the language but goes no further than this: 'considering the plainness and perspicuity, the soundness and propriety of speech which is used in it, the least that can be said of the Common Prayer is that all things in it are so worded as is most for the edifying of all those that use it'.[27]

Swift is a useful witness, a stimulating and original figure, but hardly an influence on his time in his desire to elevate the KJB and the PB as standards for the language. That they went on operating as standards owes nothing to his argument – he was arguing to a select group of political and literary leaders – and everything to their continued intensive use by the people. This intensive, and, for the most part, exclusive use was leading the people to a feeling that the KJB was verbally inspired. Beveridge credibly reports that 'most people reading the Scripture no otherwise than it is translated into their own language . . . look upon everything which they find in such a translation as the word of God, especially if it be publicly owned and commonly used as such among them' (*A Defence*, p. 34).

[26] *A Discourse of the Grounds and Reasons of the Christian Religion* (London, 1724), p. 2.
[27] Beveridge, 'The excellency and usefulness of the Common Prayer', sermon preached 27 November, 1681; *The Theological Works of William Beveridge*, 12 vols. (Oxford, 1844–8), VI: 377.

PHOTOGRAPHIC ACKNOWLEDGEMENTS

The plates in this volume are reproduced by permission of the Bible Society and the
Syndics of the Cambridge University Library

1. Tyndale's first, fragmentary New Testament, 1525 (Herbert 1). This is the first page of Bible text printed in English and the only illustrated page that survives from this edition. The typeface approximates to script, and, as was common practice, 'n's are

The gospell of S. Mathew.
The fyrst Chapter.

Hys ys the boke of the generacio of Iesus Christ the sonne of David/The sonne also of Abra=

¶Abraham begatt Isaac:
Isaac begatt Iacob:
Iacob begatt Iudas and hys bre= (thren)
Iudasbegat Phares: and Zaram of thamar:
Phares egatt Esrom:
Esrom begatt Aram:
Aram begatt Aminadab:
Aminadab begatt naassan:
Naasson begatt Salmon:
Salmon begatt boos of rahab:
Boos begatt obed of ruth:
Obed begatt Iesse:
Iesse begatt david the kynge:
¶David the kynge begatt Solomon, of her that was the (wyfe of vry:
Solomon begat reboam:
Roboam begatt Abia:
Abia begatt asa:
Asa begatt iosaphat:
Iosaphat begatt Ieram:
Ioram begatt Osias:
Osias begatt Ioatham:
Ioatham begatt Achas:
Achas begatt Ezechias:
Ezechias begatt Manasses:
Manasses begatt Amon:
Amen begatt Iosias:
Iosias begatt Iechonias and his brethren about the tyme of the captivite of babilen.
¶After they were led captive to babilen/ Iechonias begatt

Margin notes:

* Abraham and David are fyrst re= hearsed/ because that christe was chefly promysed vnto them.

Saynct mathew leveth out certe= yne generacions/ z describeth Ch= ristes linage from solomõ/after the lawe of Moses/ but Lucas descri= beth it accordyng to nature/frõ na= than solomõs br= other. For the la= we calleth them a mannes childrē which his broder begatt of his wy= fe lefte behynde hym after his dẽ the.deu.xxv.c.

often omitted, and a nearly horizontal line placed over the preceding vowel instead. The antiquated use of a slash as a punctuation mark, so prominent here, is last visible in plate 4.

shall come apon the / and the power off the hyest
shall over shaddowe the. Therfore also that holy thynge which shalbe borne / shalbe called the
sonne of god. And marke / thy cosen Elizabeth /
hath also conceaved a sonne i her olde age.. And
this is the. vj. moneth to her / which was called.
barren / for with god shall nothinge be vnpossi-
ble. Mary sayd : beholde the hondemayden off
the lorde / be it vnto me even as thou hast sayde.
And the angell departed from her.

    Mary arose in thoose dayes / and went into
the mountayns with hast into a cite off iewry /
ād entred in to the bousse off Zacary / ād saluted
Elizabeth. And it fortuned / as Elizabeth herde
the salutacion of Mary / the babe sprongein her
belly. And Elizabeth was filled with the holy
goost / and cryed with a loude voyce / and sayde:
Blessed arte thou among wemen / and blessed is
the frute off thy wombe. And whens hapeneth
this to me / that the mother off my lorde shulde
come to me? Loo / as sone as the voyce of thy salutacion sownded in myne eares / the babe lepte
in my belly for ioye. And blessed arte thou that
belevedst / For thoose thingf shalbe performed
which were tolde the from the lorde.

And Mary sayde.

My soule magnifieth the lorde.
And my sprete reioyseth in god my savioure /
For he hath loked on the povre degre off his hō-
demaydē. Beholde nowe from hens forth shall
    all generacions call me blessed.
    For he that is myghty hath done to me greate
                                                    R ij

2. Tyndale's first complete New Testament, 1526 (Herbert 2). The distinction between
paragraphed prose and the apparently free verse form of the Magnificat is clearly
marked. Giving 'And Mary said' centred and enlarged is particularly effective, but such

thingſ/ and bleſſed ys his name:
And hys mercy is always on thē that feare him
thorow oute all generacions.
Hē hath ſhewed ſtrengthe with his arme/ he
hath ſcattered them that are prowde in the ym
maginacion of their hertſ.
He hath putt Doune the myghty from theirſe aſ
tſ/ and hath exalted them of lowe degre.
He hath filled the hōgry with goode thigſ: And
hath ſent awaye the ryche empty.
He hath remembred mercy: and hath holpē his
ſervaunt Iſrahel.
Even as he promiſed to oure fathers/ Abrahā
and to his ſeede for ever.
And mary aboode with her iij. monethes/ And
retourned home agayne.

Elizabethſ tyme was come that ſhe ſhulde be
delyvered/ And ſhe brought forth a ſonne. And
her neghbourſ and her coſins herde tell howe/
the lorde had magnified hys mercy vppon her/
and they reioyſed with her.

And hit fortuned the eyght daye: they cā to cir
cūciſe the childe: ād called his name Zacari after
the name of his father/ ād his mother āſwered/
ād ſayd: not ſoo/ but he ſhalbe called Jhō. And
they ſayd vnto her: There ys none of thy kyne/
that is named with thys name. And they made
ſignes to hys father/ howe he wolde have hym
called. And he axed for wrytynge tables and
wroote ſaying: hys name is Jhō. And they mer
velled all. And hys mought was opened imme
diatly/ and hys tonge/ and he ſpake lawdynge
god. And feare cam om all them that dwelt nye

imaginative typography is rare. Chapter headings – 'The second Chapter', etc. – are
given in the same form.

come home / Iesus preuented hym / & sayde : What thynkest
thou Symon? Of whome do the kynges of the earth take toll
or tribute? Of theyr chlozen / or of straungers? Then sayde
Peter to hym. Of straungers. Iesus sayde vnto hym: Then
are the chyldzen fre. ✳ Neuerthelesse lest we offende them /
go thy waye to the see / and cast thyne angle / and take the
fysshe that fyrst commeth vp / & when thou hast opened hys
mouth thou shalt fynde a pece of twenty pens / take that / &
geue it them for me and the. ⊦

Mat.22.c

❡ He teacheth hys dyscyples to be humble / and har-
meles / to auoyde occasyons of euell / & one to forgeue
anothers offence.

The .xviii. Chapter. ✠

AT the same tyme came the dyscyples vnto Iesus / and
sayd: Who is the greatest in the kyngdome of heauē?
And Iesus called a chylde vnto hym / and set hym in
the myddest amonge them / and sayde: Verely I saye
vnto you: Except ye turne and become ✳ as chlozē / ye shall
not entre in to the kyngdome of heauen. Whoso euer therfore hūbleth hym selfe as thys chylde / the same is the greatest in the kyngdome of heauen. And who so receaueth soch a
chylde in my name / receaueth me. ✳ But who so offendeth
one of these lytle ones whych beleue in me / it were better
for hym / that a mylstone were hanged aboute hys necke / &
he drowened in the depth of the see. Wo vnto the worlde because of sklaunders. ✳ Yee ther muste sklaunders come: but
wo vnto that man / by whome sklaunder commeth . ⊦ But
yf thy hāde or thy foote offende the / cut hym of: and cast hym
from

Marc.9.d.
Luck.9.e.

1.Pet.2.a.

Marc.9.e.
Luck.17.a

1.Cor.11.d
Luck.17.a
⊦Mat.5.d
Mar. 9.e.

3. A characteristic early New Testament, showing some typical illustrations, the
beginning of the intrusion of annotation into the text, and the beginning of

from the. It is better for the to entre in vnto lyfe / lame or
crepell/ then that thou shuldest haue i two handes or two fete
and be cast in to euerlastynge fyre. And yf thyne eye offence
the/ plucke it out/ and cast it from the. Better it is for the to
entre in vnto lyfe wyth one eye / then to haue two eyes/ ꝧ
to be cast in to hell fyre. Take hede/ that ye despyse not one
of these lytle ones. For I saye vnto you: theyr angels do al-
waye beholde the face of my father whyche is in heauē: ¶
For the sonne of man is come to saue that whych is lost.
How thynke yer: ꝧ yf a man haue an hundreth shepe/ and one
of them be gone astraye/ dothe not he leaue the nyntye and
nyne in the mountaynes/ ꝧ goeth/ ꝧ seketh: that one whych
is gone astraye? And yf it happen that he fynde it / verely I
saye vnto you: he reioyceth more ouer it/ then ouer the nynty
ꝧ nyne whych wente not astraye. Euen so is it not the wyll
before your father in heauen / that one of these lytle ones
shulde perysh.

Luck.15. a

✠ ✳ Yf thy brother trespasse agaynst the/ go and tell
hym hys faute betwene the and hym alone. Yf he heare the
thou hast wonne thy brother. But yf he heare the not/ then
take yet wyth the one or two / ✳ that in the mouth of two
or thre wytnesses / euery matter maye be stablyshe d. Yf he
heare not them / tell it vnto the congregacyon. Yf he heare
not the congregacyon/ holde hym as an heythen and pub-
lycan. Verely I saye vnto you: ✚ ı What so euer ye shall
bynde vpō earth/ shalbe bounde also in heauē: ꝧ whatso euer
ye lowse vpō earth/ shalbe lowsed also in heauē. Agayne I
saye vnto you: yf twoo of you shall agre vpō earth (for what
thynge so euer it be that they wolde desyre) they shall haue
it as

Leut. 19. d
Eccl.17. b.
Luck.17. a

Num. 35. ı
Deu. 17. b
and. 19. c.
2. Cor. 13 a
✠ Mar. 16 c

commentary at the end of chapter 17. The one paragraph break has become difficult
to spot. This is from Coverdale's 1538 New Testament (Herbert 40).

The gospell of S. Marke.

The first Chapter.

Mal.3.a
Mat.11.b
Luc.7.c

Esa.40.a
Mat.3.a
Luc.3.a
Iohã.1.b

Iohã.3.d

Mat.3.a

Mat.3.b
Luc.3.c
Iohã.1.c

Mat.3.b
Luc.3.c
Iohã.1.d

Some
reade:
In who
I am ba-
ptised.

Mat.4.a
Luc.4.a

This is the begynnynge of the gospell of Iesus Christ the sonne of God, as it is wrytté in the prophetes. Beholde, J sende my messaúger before thy face, which shal prepare thy waye before the. The voyce of a cryer is in the wyldernes: prepare the waye of the LORDE, make his pathes straight.

Ihon was in the wyldernes, and baptysed, and preached the baptyme of amendment, for the remyssion of synnes. And there wente out vnto him the whole londe of Iewry, and they of Ierusalem, and were all baptysed of him in Iordan, and knowleged their synnes.

Ihon was clothed with Camels heer, and with a lethron gerdell aboute his loynes, and ate locustes and wylde hony, and preached, and sayde: There commeth one after me, which is stronger then J: before whom J am not worthy to stoupe downe, and to lowse vp the lachet of his shue. J baptyse you with water, but he shal baptyse you with the holy goost.

And it happened at the same tyme, that Iesus came out of Galile from Nazareth, and was baptysed of Ihon in Iordan. And as soone as he was come out of the water, he sawe that the heauens opened, and the goost as a doue cõmynge downe vpon him. And there came a voyce from heaué: Thou art my deare sonne, in whom J delyte.

And immediatly the sprete droue him in to the wyldernes: and he was in the wyldernes fourtye dayes, and was tempted of Sa-

than, and was with the wylde beestes. And the angels mynistred vnto him.

Mat.4.b
Luc.4.b

But after that Ihon was taken, Iesus came in to Galile, and preached the gospell of the kyngdome of God, and sayde: the tyme is fulfylled, and the kyngdome of God is at hande: Amende youre selues, and beleue the gospell.

Mat.4.c
Luc.5.a

So as he walked by the see of Galile, he sawe Symon and Andrew his brother, castinge their nettes in the see, for they were fyßhers. And Iesus sayde vnto thê: folowe me, and J wil make you fyßhers of mé. And immediatly they left their nettes, and folowed him.

Iere.16.c
Eze.47.b

And when he was gone a lytle further from thence, he sawe James the sonne of Zebede, and Ihon his brother, as they were in the shyppe mendynge their nettes. And anone he called them. And they left their father Zebede in the shyppe with the hyred seruauntes, and folowed him.

Luc.4.d
Iohã.2.b

And they wente in to Capernaum, and immediatly vpon the Sabbathes, he entred in to the synagoge, and taught. And they were astonnyed at his doctryne: for he taught them as one hauynge power, and not as the Scrybes.

Mat.7.c

And in their synagoge there was a man possessed with a foule sprete, which cried and sayde: Oh what haue we to do with the, thou Iesus of Nazareth. Art thou come to destroye vs? J knowe that thou art euen ye holy one of God. And Iesus reproued him, and sayde: holde thy tonge, and departe out of him. And the foule sprete tare him, and cried with a loude voyce, and departed out of him. And they were all astonnyed, in so moch that they axed one another amonge thê selues, and sayde: What is this? What new lernynge is this? for he cõmaundeth the foule spretes with power, and they are obedient vnto him. And immediatly the fame of him was noysed rounde aboute in the coastes and borders of Galile.

Luc.4.d

And forth with they wente out of the synagoge, and came in to the house of Symõ and Andrew, ẁ James and Ihon. And Symons mother in lawe laye, ⁊ had the feuers, and anone they tolde him of her. And he came to her, and set her vp, and toke her by ye hande, and the feuer left her immediatly. And she mynistred vnto them.

Mat.8.b
Luc.4.d

At euen whan the Sonne was gone downe, they brought vnto him all that were sick and possessed, and the whole cite was gathered together at the dore, and

Mat.8.b
Luc.4.c

CC iiij

---

4. Coverdale's 1535 Bible (Herbert 18), the first complete Bible printed in English. The key feature is the introduction of columns. Apart from the running heading, no attempt is made to break them up.

¶ The Ballet of

Balettes of Salomon: called in Latyne Canticũ Canticorum.

¶ A mysticall deuyce of the spirituall and godly loue betwene Christ the spouse/and the churche or congregacyon his spousesse. Salomon made this Balade or songe by hym selfe & his wyfe the daughter of Pharao/vnder the shadow of hym selfe fygurynge Christ and vnder the person of his wyfe the Churche.

a* That is/the cheafe & most excellẽt Balet/ as the saynct of saynctes/ the kynge of kynges which was moche to saye after the maner of speakyg of the hebrues/ as the cheafe saynct/the cheff kyng. Wherfore it is to be supposed/that amõge the W. and fyue other songẽ (of whiche. iij. Reg. iiij d)this hath bene estemed & iudged the cheafe & principall.

¶ The fyrst Chapter.
¶ The voyce of the churche.

That thy mouth wold geue me a kysse/for thy brestẽ are more pleasaũt then wine/ & that because of the good & pleasaũt sauour. Thy name is a swete smellyng oyntmẽt/ therfore do the maydens loue the: pree that same moueth me also to runne after the.

¶ The spousesse to her companyons.

The kyng hath brought me in to his preuy chambre. We wyll be glad and reioyce in the/we thynke more of thy brestes then of wyne:well is them that loue the.

¶ The voyce of the church in persecucyon.

B I am black(O ye daughters of Jerusalem)lyke as the tentes of the Cedarenes / & as the hangynges of Salomon:but yet am I fayre & welfauoured withall. Maruell not at me that I am so black: & why? the sunne hath shyned vpon me.

¶ The voyce of the Synagoge.

For when my mothers chyldren had euell wyll at me/they made me þ keper of the vyneyarde. Thus was I fayne to kepe a vyneyarde/which was not myne awne.

¶ The voyce of the churche to Christ.

Tell me(O thou whom my soule loueth) where thou fedest/where thou restest at the noone daye:lest I go wronge/and come vnto the flockes of thy companyons.

¶ Christ to the Churche.

C If thou knowe not thy selfe (O thou fayrest amonge wemen(then go thy waye forth after the fotesteppes of the shepe/as though thou woldest fede thy goates besyde þ shepe herdes tentes. There wyll I tary for the (my loue)with myne host and with my charettes/ which shalbe no fewer then Pharaos. Then shall thy chekes & thy neck be made fayre/& hanged with spãges & goodly iewels:a neck bande of golde wyll we make the with syluer botons.

¶ The voyce of the churche.

When the kynge syteth at the table / he shall smell my Nard*:for a bondell of Myrre (O my beloued)lyeth betwixte my brestes. O I cluster of grapes of Cypers / or of the vyneyardes of Engaddi art thou vnto me / O my beloued.

¶ Christ to the Churche.

O how fayre art thou(my loue)how fayre art thou:thou hast doues eyes.

¶ The Churche to Christ.

O how fayre art thou (my beloued) how well fauored art thou? Oure bed is decte with floures/the sylyng of oure house are of Cedre tree/& oure balkes of Cypresse.

¶ The. ij. Chapter.
¶ The voyce of Christ.

I Am the floure of the felde/ & lylye of the valleys: as the rose amonge the thornes/so is my loue amonge the daughters.

¶ The voyce of the churche.

Lyke as the apple tree amõge the trees of the wod/so is my beloued amõge the sonnes. My delyte is to syt vnder hys shadowe / for hys frute is swete vnto my throte. He bryngeth me in to his wyne seller/and loueth me specyally well. Refresh me wyth grappes/ comforte me with apples / for I am syck of loue. His left hand lyeth vnder my heade/and his ryght hande embraceth me.

¶ The voyce of Christ.

I charge you(O ye daughters of Jerusalem)by the Roes & hyndes of the felde/ that ye wake not vp my loue nor touche her/ tyll she be content her selfe.

¶ The voyce of the Churche.

Me thynke I heare the voyce of my beloued:lo/there cometh he hoppynge vpõ the moũtaynes/& leapyng ouer the lytle hilles. My beloued is lyke a Rooo; a yonge hart. Beholde/he standeth behynde oure wall / he loketh in at the wyndowe / and peyeth thorow the grate. My beloued answered and sayde vnto me.

¶ The voyce of Christ.

O stande vp my loue/ my doue/ my beutyfull/& come:for lo/þ wynter is now past/ & the rayne is awaye & gone. The floures are come/vp in the felde / the twystynge tyme is come/the voyce of the turtle doue is hearde in oure lande. The fygge tree bryngeth forth her fygges/the vynes beare blossoms/& haue a good

a wyfe of y̆ daughters of Ben Jamin. And whan theyr fathers or brethren come vnto vs to complayne, we wyll saye vnto them: haue pytie on vs for their sakes, because we reserued not to eche man his wyfe in tyme of warre, y̆ Neither haue ye geuen vnto thē, that ye shuld synne at this tyme.

And the chyldren of Ben Jamin dyd euē so: and toke them wyues accordyng to the nombre of them that daunced whom they caught. And they went, and returned vnto their enheritaunce, and repayred the cyties, and dwelt in them.

And the children of Israel departed thēce at that tyme, y̆ went euery man to his trybe, and to his kynred, and went out from thence every man to hys enheritaunce. ✱ In those dayes there was no kyng in Israel: but eue- rye man dyd that which semed ryght in his owne eyes.

Jud.rbll.b. and.rbij.a.

¶ The ende of the boke of Jud- ges, called in the Hebrue Sophtim.

¶ The boke of Ruth.

¶ The fyrst Chapter.

¶ Elimelec goeth with hys wyfe and chyldren into the lande of Moab.

IT fortuned, that ✱ (in the dayes of a certayne iudge) when the Jud- ges iudged, there fell a darth in the lande, and a certen man of Bethlehē Juda wēt for to soiourne in y̆ cōtreye of Moab.he and hys wyfe, and his two sonnes. The na- me of the man was Elimelec, and the name of hys wyfe, Naomi: and the names of his two sonnes were, Mahlon and Chilion, ād they were Ephraites, out of Bethlehē Ju- da. And when they came into the lande of Moab, they contynued there. And Elimelec Naomies husband dyed, and she remayned with her two sonnes, which toke thē wyues of the nacyons of the Moabites : the ones name was Orpha, y̆ the others Ruth. And

they dwelled there aboute a ten yere. And Mahlon and Chilion dyed also euen both of them, and the woman was lefte desolate of her two sonnes and of her husbande. Then she stode vp with her daughters in lawe, ād returned from the contrey of Moab: for she had heard saye in the countrey of Moab, how that the Lord had vysyted hys people, and geuē them bred. Wherfore she departed out of the place where she was, and her two daughters with her. And they went on their waye to returne vnto y̆ lande of Juda.And Naomi sayde vnto her two daughters in lawe: go and returne eche of you vnto your mothers house: and the Lord deale as kynd- lye with you, as ye haue dealt with y̆ deed, and with me. And the Lord geue you, that you maye fynde rest, ether of you in y̆ house of her husbande: And whan she kyssed them, they lift vp their voyce, and wepte, y̆ sayde vnto her: we wyll go with y̆ vnto thy folke. And Naomi sayd: turne agayne my daugh- ters: for what cause will you go wyth me? Are ther any mo chyldren in my wombe ,to be yo husbādes? Turne agayne my daugh- ters, ād go: for I am to olde to haue an hus- band. And yf I sayd, I haue hope, yf I toke a man also this nyght: yee and though I had all readye borne sonnes, wolde ye tarye af- ter them, tyll they were of age? or wolde ye for them so lōg refrayne frō takyng of hus- bandes? Not so my daughters: for it greueth me moche for youre sakes, that the hande of the Lorde is gone out agaynst me.

B

C

And they lift vp their voyces, ād wepte agayne, y̆ Orpha kissed her mother in lawe, but Ruth aboade styll by her. And Naomi sayde : se, thy syster in law is gone backe a- gayne vnto her people ād vnto her goddes: returne thou after her. And Ruth answered: entreate me not to leaue the , and to returne frō after the: for whether thou goest, I wyll go also.y̆ where thou dwellest, there I wyll dwell : thy people shalbe my people, and thy God my God, where thou dyest, there wyll I dye, y̆ there will I be buried. The Lord do so and so to me , yf ought then death onlye departe the and me alonbre.

When she saw y̆ she was stedfastly myn- ded to go wyth her , she lefte speakyng vnto her.And so they went both, vntyll they ca- me to Bethlehem. And when they were co- me to Bethlehem, it was noysed of thē tho- row all the cytie, and the wemē sayd: is not this Naomi? And she answered thē: call me not Naomi✱(that is to saye, beutifull)but call me, Mara,✱ (that is to saye, bitter,)for y̆ Allmightye hath made me verye bitter. I went out full: and y̆ Lorde hath brought me home agayne emptie. Why then call ye me Naomi: seing y̆ Lorde hath humbled me, and the allmightie hath brought me vnto aduersyte? And so Naomi

D

✱

✱

---

6. The first Great Bible, Cranmer, 1539 (Herbert 46). The form of the text is typical, the illustration characteristic of the Old Testament illustrations (a different style is used for the New Testament), and the initial capital is one of a standard set used throughout. Not even the break between books disturbs the columnar presentation.

and from the power of al that hate vs.

Ier.xxi.c
Gene.ii.c
Hebr.vi.r.

Co fulfyl the mercye promiled to our fathers, and to remember his holy couenaunt.

And to perfourme the othe whyche he sware to our father Abraham,for to giue vs.

That we deliuered out of the power of our enemyes,myghte serue hym wythoute feare all the daies of our lyfe,in such holines and rightuousnes as are accept before hym:

And thou chylde shalt be called the Prophet of the hyest,for thou shalt go before the face of the Lorde to prepare hys wayes.

Mal.iiii.a
zach.iii.d
Chrift is p
day spring
thatgeueth
light tothe
that sit in
darknes of
the igno-
raunce of
God.
To turne
the hertes.
When he
loked.x.c
Hayle full
of grace.xc
Hys arme

And to giue knowledge of Caluacion vnto hys people for the remiffion of synnes.

Through the tender mercy of our God, wherby the ✷day spring from on hye hath bisited vs.

To gyue lyghte to them that sate in darknes and in shadow of death,and to guyde our fete into the waye of peace.

And the chyld grew and wexed strong in spirit and was in wildernes tyl the day came when he shoulde shewe hym selfe vnto the Israelytes.

☞The Notes.

.1. To make the children haue suche an hert to god as Abraham and the fathers had.

.2.That is,whe he shewed fauour or grace to mt.

3.Full of grace,is as muche to saye,as to whome God hath shewed aboundannt fauour.

4.The arme of God is Christe by whom he worketh great and myghty thynges.

Afficted,

.5.God vysiteth hys people, when accordynge to hys promise he sheweth them some greate benifite and agayne,when by punishme nte and aduersite he calleth them to repentaunce.

¶ The.ii.Chapter.

¶ The byrthe and circumsition of Christ Howe he was receyued into the temple. How Simion and Inna prophesied of hym

---

7. Day and Seres edition of Tyndale's New Testament, 1551 (Herbert 96). The Benedictus is given in the form that was to be so commonly used for verse division but is here quite distinct from prose. The manuscript annotations are copies of words from the text and an imitation of the hand for a note. The attention with which the page

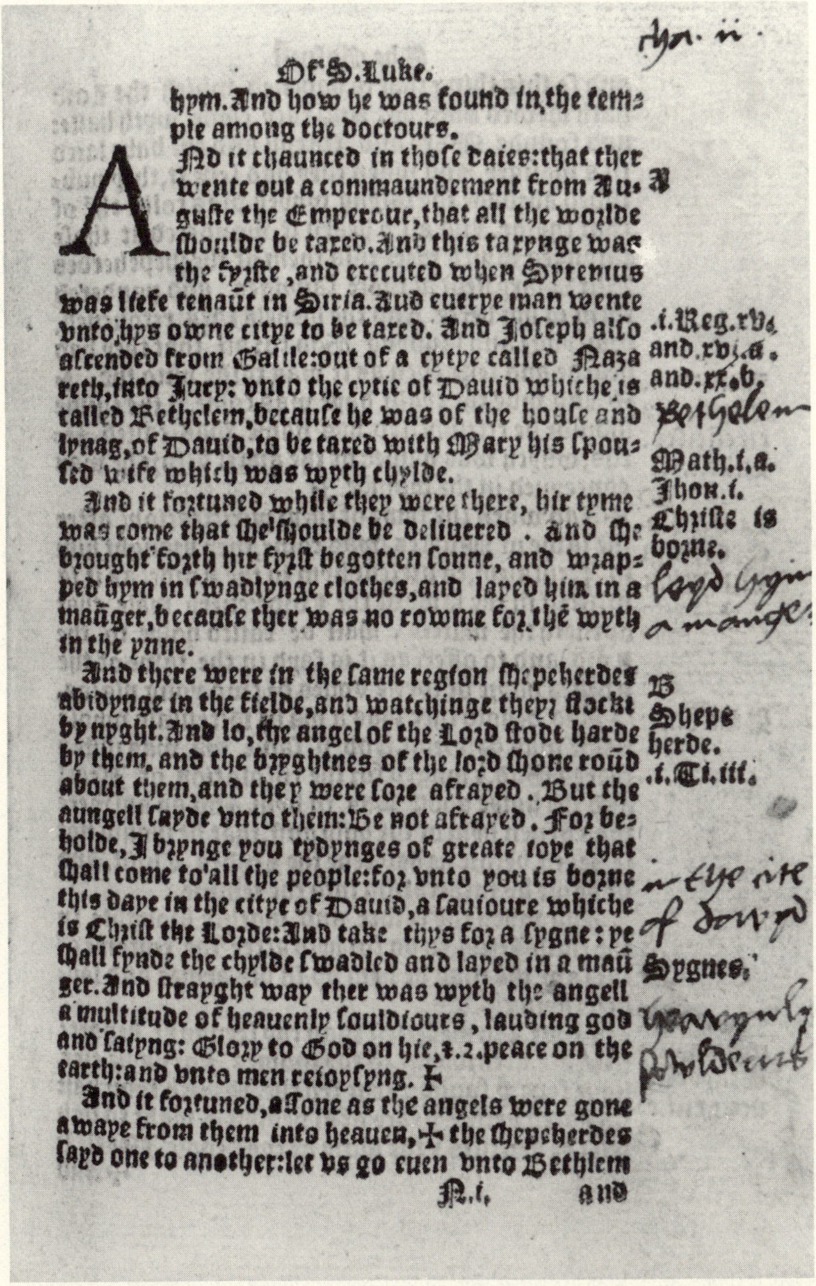

hym. And how he was found in the tem=
ple among the doctours.

ND it chaunced in those daies: that ther
wente out a commaundement from Au=
guste the Emperour, that all the worlde
shoulde be taxed. And this taxynge was
the fyrste, and executed when Syrenius
was lefe tenaūt in Siria. And euerye man wente
vnto hys owne citye to be taxed. And Joseph also
ascended from Galile: out of a cytye called Naza
reth, into Jury: vnto the cytie of Dauid whiche is
called Bethlem, because he was of the house and
lynag, of Dauid, to be taxed with Mary his spou=
sed wife which was wyth chylde.

And it fortuned while they were there, hir tyme
was come that she shoulde be deliuered . And she
brought forth hir fyrst begotten sonne, and wrap=
ped hym in swadlynge clothes, and layed him in a
maūger, because ther was no rowme for them wyth
in the ynne.

And there were in the same regfon shepeherdes
abidynge in the fielde, and watchinge they flockt
by nyght. And lo, the angel of the Lord stode harde
by them, and the bryghtnes of the lord shone roūd
about them, and they were sore afrayed . But the
aungell sayde vnto them: Be not afrayed . For be=
holde, I brynge you tydynges of greate ioye that
shall come to all the people: for vnto you is borne
this daye in the citye of Dauid, a sauioure whiche
is Christ the Lorde: And take thys for a sygne: ye
shall fynde the chylde swadled and layed in a maū
ger. And strayght way ther was wyth the angell
a multitude of heauenly souldioures , lauding god
and sayng: Glory to God on hie, &.2.peace on the
earth: and vnto men reioysyng. †

And it fortuned, asone as the angels were gone
awaye from them into heauen, † the shepeherdes
sayd one to another: let vs go euen vnto Bethlem

N.i.   and

Marginal notes (handwritten and printed):
Luc. ii.
A
i.Reg.xv.
and.xvi.a.
and.xx.b.
Bethlem
Math.i.a.
Jhon.i.
Christe is
borne.
layd hym
a mange.
B
Shepe
herde.
i.Ti.iii.
in the cite
of dowd
Sygnes.

has been scrutinised is evident from the correction of the accidental omission of the
chapter number in the top right corner.

8. From the same New Testament as plate 7, an example of the kind of inscription often to be found in Bibles. Such inscriptions give us a glimpse of the people who owned Bibles. If, as appears likely, the handwriting belongs to the seventeenth century, the inscription is evidence of the longevity of Bibles (the hand is not the same as that in plate 7). The alphabets at the top of the page, with their hesitations and repetitions, suggest the connection between the Bible and literacy. As far as they can be made out, the inscriptions read:

Mary Shaylor is my name
and with my pen I rot [wrote] the same
but if my pen it had beene

W William Tin
dale vnto the christian reader.

Ere haste thou (most deare reader) the newe Testament or couenaunt made with vs of God
in Christes bloude. Whyche I
haue loked ouer agayn (now at
the laste) with all diligence, and
compared it vnto the Greke, and
haue weded out of it many faultes, whiche lacke
of helpe at ye beginnyng and ouersyght, dyd sow
therin. If oughte seme chaunged, or not altogether agreynge wyth the Greke, let the fynder of
the faulte compter the Hebrue phrase, or maner of
speach left in the Greke wordes: Whose preter-
perfectence and presentence is of bothe one, and
the futurcence is the optatiue mode also, and the
futurtence is oft the imperatiue mode in the ac-
tiue voyce, and in the passiue euer. Likewise per
son for person, nombre for nombre, and interro-
gation for a conditional, and suche lyke is wyth
the Hebrues a commen vsage.

¶ I haue also in manye places set lyght in the
margent to vnderstande the text by. If any man
fynd faultes either wyth the translatio or ought
beside (which is easier for many to dooe, then so
well to haue translated it theym selues of theyr
owne preguaunt wittes at the beginnyng with-
oute an example) to the same it shall be lawe-
ful to translate it them selues and to putte what
they lust therto, If I shall perceiue either by my
selfe or by the information of other, that oughte
be escaped me, or myght be more playnly transla
ced: I wil shortlye after cause it to bee amended.
Howbeit, in many places, me thynketh it better

B.i.   to

beter i should have mended
every leter

This is my hand this is
my deed and he is a knaue
that doth it reade

I loue thee I loue thee so
peurly I doe loue thee

I will loue thee I will loue thee
euer more amen and amen

60 And his mother answered, and sayd, Not so, but he shalbe called Iohn.

61 And they said vnto her, There is none of thy kynne, that is named with this name.

62 And they made signes to his father, how he would haue him called.

63 Then he asked for wryting tables, and wrote, saying, His name is Iohn. and they merueyled all.

64 And his mouth was opened immediatly, and his tōgue also, and he ᵐspake in praising God.

65 Then feare came on all thē that dwelt nye vnto them. and all these sayinges were noysed abrode throughout all the hyl countrey of Iurie.

66 And all they that heard them, layd *them* vp in their harts, saying, What maner childe shal this be? And theⁿ hand of the Lord was wyth him.

67 And his father Zacharie was filled with the holy Gost, and prophecied saying,

68 *Blessed be the Lord God of Israel: for that he hathⁿ visited and redemed his people.

69 *And hath raysed vp the ᵒ horn of saluation, vnto vs, in the house of his seruāt Dauid.

70 *Euen as he promised by the mouth of his holy Prophetes, which were synce the world began, *saying,*

71 That he would saue *vs* from our enemies, and from the hands of all that hate vs.

72 That he would shewe mercie towards

our

Marginal notes (left):

m Not onely for his benefite in par donig his faut: but also to shewe that he was iustely ponished for his incredulitie.

n In declaring himself myndeful of his people, &therfore is come from heauen to visit and redeme them.

o When the promesses of God seemed to haue failed, & the state of Israel to haue perished, thē sent he his Christe who by his inuincible strength, as with a stronge horn ouer threwe his ennemies.

Marginal notes (right):

'The mightie power of God.

G Chap.2.d. matth.1.d. exo.3.c. The song of Zacharie. Gen.50.d. psal.132.c. iere 23.a. & 30.b. Amos 9.

9. Whittingham's Geneva, 1557 New Testament (Herbert 106). Because of the introduction of verse division the distinction between verse and prose has been obliterated. As in poetry, the beginning of a new verse is given a capital letter even when it is not the beginning of a sentence. However, the distinction between the text

our fathers, and remembre his holy couenant.

Gen.22.e.
iere.31.f.
heb.6.c.

73 *And ŷ othe which he sware to our fa-*
ther Abraham:

74 *VVhichwas,*that he would graunte vnto vs, ŷ we deliuered out of the hands of
our ennemies, should serue hym wythout
feare

x.Pet.1.c.
'To whome
no hypocrisie
can be acce-
ptable.

75 All the dayes of our lyfe, in *holynes
and righteousnes"before hym.

76 And thou babe shalt be called ŷ Pro-
phete of the hyest : for thou shalt go before the face of the Lord , to prepare his
wayes:

77 *And* to geue knowledge of saluation
vnto his people, by the remission of their
synnes.

Mala.4.a.
zach.3.b,
& 4.c.
"Or, branche
of a tree, mea-
ning the Mes-
sias.

78 Through the tender mercie of our
God, wherby*the"day spring from an hye
hath visited vs.

79 To geue lyght to them that sit in
darcknes, and in the shadowe of death, &
to gyde our feete into the way of peace.

80 And ŷ chylde grewe & waxed strong
in spirite , and was in ᴾ wildernes, tyl the
day came, when he should shew hym self
vnto Israel.

p He meaneth
that part of Iurie
which was left in-
habited, wher also
the grosse & rude
people dwelled.

THE II. CHAPTER.

The byrth and circumcision of Christe . he
was receaued into the temple. Simeon and An
na prophecie of him . He was found among the
doctours. His obedience to father and mother.
And maries wisdome.

'So much as
was subiect to
the Romains.

A
ANd it chanced in those dayes , that
there came a comandement from August the Emperour , that all the "world

m.iii.

---

and the supplementary material is well made, and the use of Roman type represents a
great advance in clarity over the difficulties presented by the same passage in plate 7.

10. The first Geneva Bible, 1560 (Herbert 107). The full variety of the original textual aids is visible. At the top is about half of the 'argument'. The diagram betrays its foreign provenance in the use of 'aquilon' and 'midi'. Only the initial capital is purely decorative. The willingness to run titles, arguments and illustrations across the full width of the page represents, with the new typeface, a considerable advance in sophistication of printing.

THE REVELATION OF SAINT
IOHN THE APOSTLE AND EVAN-
geliſt, with the Annotations of
Franc. Iunius.

CHAP. I.

1 *He declareth what kind of doctrine is here handled,* 8 *euen his theſis, the beginning and ending:* 12 *Then the myſtery of the ſeuen candleſticks and ſtarres* 20 *is expounded.*

He ⸱ Reuelation of ᵇ Ieſus Chriſt, which God gaue vnto him, to ſhewe vnto his ſeruants things which muſt ſhortly bee done: which he ſent, and ſhewed by his Angel vnto his ſeruant Iohn.

2 Who bare record of the word of God, and of the teſtimonie of Ieſus Chriſt and of all things that he ſaw.

3 Bleſſed *is* he that readeth, and they that heare the words of this propheſie, and keepe thoſe things which are written therein: for the time is at hand.

4 ² Iohn to the ſeuen ᶜ Churches which are in Aſia. Grace be with you, and peace ⸱ from him, ᵉ Which ⸱ is, and Which was, and which is to come, and from ⸱ the ᵉ ſeuen Spirits which are before his Throne,

5 And from Ieſus Chriſt ⸱ which is that ⸱ faithfull witneſſe, *and* ⸱ that firſt begotten of the dead, and that Prince of the kings of the earth, vnto him that loued vs, & waſhed vs from our ſinnes in his ⸱ blood,

6 And made vs ⸱ Kings and Prieſts vnto God euen his Father, to him I ſay, be glory, and dominion for euermore, Amen.

7 Behold, hee commeth with ⸱ clouds, and euery ⸱ eye ſhall ſee him: yea, euen they which

pearced him thorow: and all kinreds of the earth ſhall waile before him. Euen ſo, Amen.

8 ⁶ I ⸱ am ᶠ Alpha & Omega, the beginning and ſ ending, ſaith the Lord, Which is, & Which was, and which is to come, *euen* the Almightie.

9 ⁷ I Iohn, euen your brother and companion in tribulation, and in the kingdome and patience of Ieſus Chriſt, was in the ᵍ Ile called Patmos, for the word of God, and for the witneſſing of Ieſus Chriſt.

10 And I was *raviſhed* in ʰ ſpirit on the ⸱ Lords day, and heard behind me a great voyce, as it had bene of a trumpet,

11 Saying, I am Alpha and Omega, that firſt and that Laſt: and that which thou ſeeſt write in a booke, & ſend it vnto the ſeuen Churches which are in Aſia, vnto Epheſus, & vnto Smyrna, & vnto Pergamus, and vnto Thyatira, and vnto Sardis, and vnto Philadelphia, and vnto Laodicea.

12 ⁸ Then I turned backe to ᵏ ſee the voyce that ſpake with me: 9 and when I was turned, I ſawe ſeuen golden candleſticks,

13 And in the mids of the ſeuen candleſticks, one like vnto the ſonne of man, clothed with a garment downe to the feete, and girded about the paps with a golden girdle.

14 His head and haires were white as white wool, and as ſnow, & his eies were as a flame of fire,

15 And his feete like fine braſſe burning as in a furnace: and his voyce as the ſound of many waters.

16 And he had in his right hand ſeuen ſtarres: and out ⸱ of his mouth went a ſharpe two edged ſword, and his face *ſhone* as the ſunne ſhineth in his ſtrength.

17 ¹⁰ And when I ſaw him, I fell at his feete as dead: ¹¹ then he laid his right hand vpon mee, ſaying vnto mee, Feare not: ¹² I am that ⸱ firſt

11. Barker's 1610 Geneva quarto (Herbert 303), showing the extent to which annotation can dominate the page even in a relatively large format.

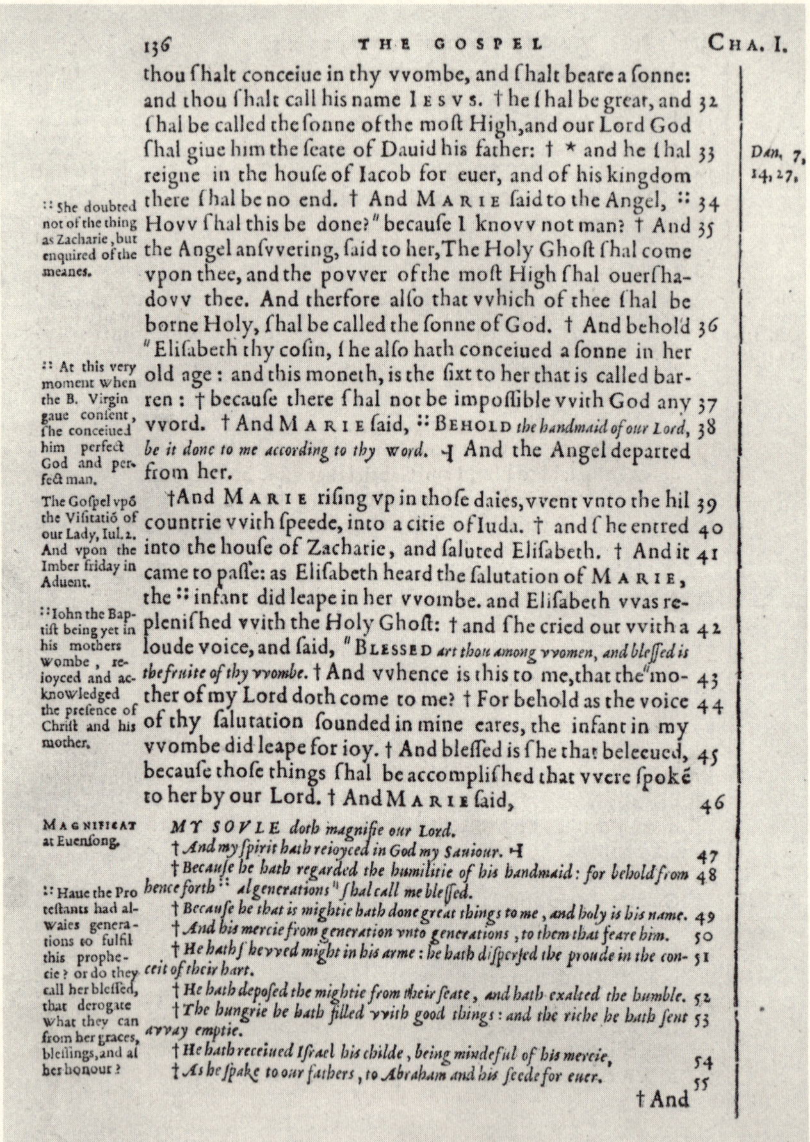

thou fhalt conceiue in thy vvombe, and fhalt beare a fonne:
and thou fhalt call his name IESVS. † he fhal be great, and 32
fhal be called the fonne of the moft High, and our Lord God
fhal giue him the feate of Dauid his father: † * and he fhal 33
reigne in the houfe of Iacob for euer, and of his kingdom
there fhal be no end. † And MARIE faid to the Angel, ∷ 34
Hovv fhal this be done?" becaufe I knovv not man? † And 35
the Angel anfvvering, faid to her, The Holy Ghoft fhal come
vpon thee, and the povver of the moft High fhal ouerfha-
dovv thee. And therfore alfo that vvhich of thee fhal be
borne Holy, fhal be called the fonne of God. † And behold 36
"Elifabeth thy cofin, fhe alfo hath conceiued a fonne in her
old age : and this moneth, is the fixt to her that is called barren : † becaufe there fhal not be impoffible vvith God any 37
vvord. † And MARIE faid, ∷ BEHOLD *the handmaid of our Lord,* 38
be it done to me according to thy word. ⸿ And the Angel departed
from her.

†And MARIE rifing vp in thofe daies, vvent vnto the hil 39
countrie vvith fpeede, into a citie of Iuda. † and fhe entred 40
into the houfe of Zacharie, and faluted Elifabeth. † And it 41
came to paffe: as Elifabeth heard the falutation of MARIE,
the ∷ infant did leape in her vvombe. and Elifabeth vvas replenifhed vvith the Holy Ghoft: † and fhe cried out vvith a 42
loude voice, and faid, "BLESSED *art thou among vvomen, and bleffed is*
the fruite of thy vvombe. † And vvhence is this to me, that the mo- 43
ther of my Lord doth come to me? † For behold as the voice 44
of thy falutation founded in mine eares, the infant in my
vvombe did leape for ioy. † And bleffed is fhe that beleeued, 45
becaufe thofe things fhal be accomplifhed that vvere fpoké
to her by our Lord. † And MARIE faid, 46

MY SOVLE doth magnifie our Lord.
† *And my fpirit hath reioyced in God my Sauiour.* ⸿ 47
† *Becaufe he hath regarded the humilitie of his handmaid : for behold from* 48
hence forth ∷ *al generations* " *fhal call me bleffed.*
† *Becaufe he that is mightie hath done great things to me , and holy is his name.* 49
† *And his mercie from generation vnto generations , to them that feare him.* 50
† *He hath f hevved might in his arme : he hath difperfed the proude in the con-* 51
ceit of their hart.
† *He hath depofed the mightie from their feate , and hath exalted the humble.* 52
† *The hungrie he hath filled vvith good things : and the riche he hath fent* 53
avvay emptie.
† *He hath receiued Ifrael his childe , being mindeful of his mercie,* 54
† *As he fpake to our fathers , to Abraham and his feede for euer.* 55

† And

Marginal notes (left column):

∷ She doubted not of the thing as Zacharie , but enquired of the meanes.

∷ At this very moment when the B. Virgin gaue confent, fhe conceiued him perfect God and perfect man.

The Gofpel vpõ the Vifitatiõ of our Lady, Iul. 2. And vpon the Imber friday in Aduent.

∷ Iohn the Baptift being yet in his mothers vvombe , reioyced and acknowledged the prefence of Chrift and his mother.

MAGNIFICAT at Euenfong.

∷ Haue the Proteftants had alvvaies genera-tions to fulfil this prophe-cie? or do they call her bleffed, that derogate vvhat they can from her graces, bleffings, and al her honour?

Right margin:
Dan. 7,
14, 27.

12. Rheims New Testament, 1582 (Herbert 177). The Magnificat and the Benedictus
are clearly distinguished as poetry, and the paragraphing of the prose has been kept
clear by removing verse numbers to the margin. Verse beginnings no longer

56   †And MARIE taried vvith her about three moneths:
and fhe returned into her houfe.

57   † And Elifabeths ful time vvas come to be deliuered: and The Gofpel vpō the Natiuitie of S. Iohn Baptift Iun. 24. called Midſōmer day.
58 fhe bare a fonne. † And her neighbours and kinſfolke heard
that our Lord did magnifie his mercie vvith her, and they did
59 congratulate her.   † And it came to paffe: on the eight day
they came to circuncife the childe, and they called him by
60 his fathers name, Zacharie. † And his mother anfvvering,
61 faid, Not fo, but he fhal be called Iohn. † And they faid to
her, That there is none in thy kinred that is called by this
62 name. † And they made fignes to his father, vvhat he vvould
63 haue him called. † And demaunding a vvriting table, he
Lu.1,13.   vvrote, faying, "⋆ Iohn is his name. And they al marueled.
64 † And forthvvith his mouth vvas opened, and his tonge, and
65 he fpake bleffing God. † And feare came vpon al their neighbours: and al thefe things vvere bruited ouer al the hil-coun-
66 trie of Ievvrie: † and all that had heard, laid them vp in their
hart, faying, What an one, trovv ye, fhal this childe be? For the
67 hand of our Lord vvas vvith him.   † And Zacharie his father
vvas replenifhed vvith the Holy Ghoft : and he prophecied,
faying,

68   †BLESSED BE OVR LORD *God of Ifrael: becaufe he hath vifited and* BENEDICTVS at Laudes.
vvrought the redemption of his people : ⊣
69   † *And hath erected the horne of faluation to vs, in the houfe of Dauid his*
feruant.
70   † *As he fpake by the mouth of his holy Prophets, that are from the beginning.*
71   † *Saluation from our enemies, and from the hand of al that hate vs :*
72   † *To vvorke mercie vvith our fathers : and to remember his holy teftament,*
Gen. 22, 73   †⋆ *The othe vvhich he fvvare to Abraham our father, † that he vvould giue*
6.   74 *to vs,*
That vvithout feare being deliuered from the hand of our enemies, vve may
ferue him.
75   † *In holines and" iuftice before him, al our daies.*
76   † *And thou childe, fhalt be called the Prophet of the Higheft : for ⋆ thou fhalt*
Mal.3,1.   *goe before the face of our Lord to prepare his vvaies.*
77   † *Te giue knovvledge of faluation to his people, vnto remiffion of their finnes,*
78   † *Through the bovvels of the mercie of our God, in vvhich" the ⋆Orient, from*
Zac.3.9.   *on high, hath vifited vs,*
6, 12.   79   † *To illuminate them that fit in darkenes, and in the fhadovv of death : to di-*
Mal. 4,   *rect our feete into the vvay of peace.*
2.
80   † And the childe grew, and vvas ftrengthened in fpirit, and
vvas ꝛꝛin the deferts vntil the day of his manifeftatiō to Iſrael. ꝛꝛMarke that he was a volunta-
rie Eremite, and chofe to be fo-
litarie from a childe, til he was to preach to the people. in fo much that antiquitie counted him the firft Eremite. *Hiero. in vit. Pauli.*

S   ANNOT.

---

automatically get a capital letter. Following the chapter there is a page and a half of
annotations. This format makes for an effective combination of reading text and
annotation.

27:9 And thou shalt make the court of the tabernacle on the south side, euen full south: the curtaines for the court shalbe of whyte twined silke of an hundreth cubites long for one side.

10 And twentie pillers therof, with their twentie sockets of brasse: but the knops of the pillers and their whopes shalbe siluer.

11 In likewise on the north syde there shalbe curtaynes of an hundred cubites long, and twentie pillers, with their twentie sockets of brasse, and the knops and the whopes of siluer.

12 And the breadth of the court whiche is westwarde, shall haue curtaynes of fiftie cubites, and the pillers of them shalbe ten, and the sockets of them ten.

13 Fiftie cubites shalbe in the court eastwarde, euen full east.

14 The curtaynes of one syde shalbe of fifteene cubites, the pillers of them three, and the sockets three.

15 And likewise on the other side shalbe curtaines of fifteene cubites, with their three pillers and three sockets.

16 And in the gate of the court shalbe a vayle of twentie cubites of blewe silke, purple, and scarlet, and white twyned silke wrought with needle worke, and foure pillers with their foure sockets.

17 All the pillers rounde about the court shalbe whoped with siluer, and their knoppes shalbe of siluer, and their sockets of brasse.

18 The length of the court shalbe an hundred cubites, and the breadth fiftie on euery side, and the heyght of the curtaynes shalbe fiue cubites of whyte twyned silke, and their sockettes of brasse.

19 All the vessels of the tabernacle in all maner of seruice, and the pinnes therof, yea and all the pinnes also of the court, shalbe of brasse.

20 And thou shalt commaunde the chyldren of Israel that they geue thee pure oyle oliue beaten for the light, that they may make the lampes to borne allwayes.

21 In the tabernacle (a) of the congregation without the vayle whiche is before the witnesse, shall Aaron & his sonnes dresse the lampes both euening and morning before the Lorde: and it shalbe a statute for euer vnto the generations of the chyldren of Israel.

¶ The

In fiftie.

(a) In the tabernacle of the congregation so called, because that Israel resorted and was gathered together there at a certayne and an appointed tyme, or because that god resorted thyther to speake with Moyses and his successors, as before, chap.c.3 and 9 I wyll assemble with thee thyther, & speake with thee: and Numb.17.a. before the witnesse, where I wyll assemble you. Some do translate, in ÿ tabernacle of conuenant: but the olde interpreter, in the tabernacle of witnesse.

13. Bishops' Bible 1568 folio (Herbert 125). These facing pages from Exodus 27 show the standard style of illustration and the one contrasting attempt at a diagram in the fashion of the Geneva Bible. A count of the number of pillars shows that the diagram is not quite accurate, while the picture is very inaccurate. What look like inverted

A B. The length of the court, a hundred cubites on the south side, in which there are 10 pillers of 5 cubites hye, with their sockettes and heades, and curtaines of twined linnen.
C D. The like length on the north side.
B C. The south side 10 cubites long, in which there are 10 pillers of 5 cubites high, with their sockettes and heades, and curtaines of twined linnen.
A D. The east side is also 50 cubites long.
F. The curtaines of twined linnen of 50 cubites long, and 3 pillers of 5 cubites high, with their heades and sockettes.
Y. The curtaines on the side over against it.
G. Curtaine of 20 cubites long, beyng at the entry of the court embroidered with 4 pillers.
H. The stakes or pinnes to which the cordes of the tentes are fastened.

commas in the margin are a peculiarity of the Bishops' Bible. Parker calls them semicircles and uses them to mark parts that 'may be left unread in the public reading to the people, that thereby other chapters and places of the Scripture making more to their edification and capacity may come in their rooms' (fol. *i).

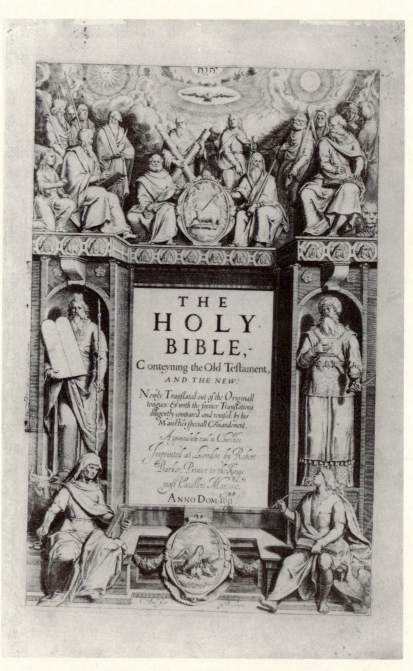

14. King James Bible, 1611 (Herbert 309). Title page.

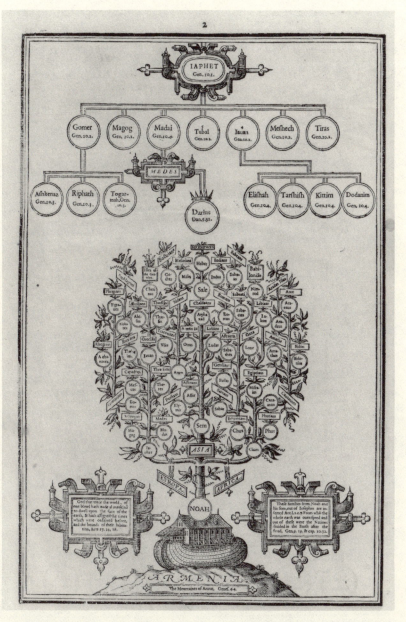

15. King James Bible, 1611. The second of 34 pages giving 'the genealogies of Holy Scriptures'. These are part of the prefatory material. They begin with God and end with Christ. Only here and in the title page does the KJB give in to the decorative urge.

from henceforth all generations shall call me blessed.

49 For he that is mighty hath done to mee great things, and holy is his Name.

50 And his mercy is on them that feare him, from generation to generation.

51 *Hee hath shewed strength with his arme, *he hath scattered the proud, in the imagination of their hearts.

52 *He hath put downe the mighty from their seates, and exalted them of low degree.

53 *Hee hath filled the hungry with good things, and the rich hee hath sent emptie away.

54 Hee hath holpen his seruant Israel, *in remembrance of his mercy,

55 *As he spake to our fathers, to Abraham, and to his seed for euer.

56 And Mary abode with her about three moneths, and returned to her owne house.

57 Now Elizabeths full time came, that shee should be deliuered, and shee brought foorth a sonne.

58 And her neighbours and her cousins heard how the Lord had shewed great mercy vpon her, and they reioyced with her.

59 And it came to passe that on the eight day they came to circumcise the childe, and they called him Zacharias, after the name of his father.

60 And his mother answered, and said Not so, but he shalbe called Iohn.

61 And they said vnto her, There is none of thy kinred that is called by this name.

62 And they made signes to his father, how he would haue him called.

63 And he asked for a writing table, and wrote, saying, His name is Iohn: and they marueiled all.

64 And his mouth was opened immediatly, and his tongue loosed, and hee spake, and praised God.

65 And feare came on all that dwelt round about them, and all these || sayings were noised abroad thorowout all the hill countrey of Iudea.

66 And all they that had heard them, layde them vp in their hearts, saying, What maner of childe shal this be: And the hand of the Lord was with him.

67 And his father Zacharias was filled with the holy Ghost, and prophesied, saying,

68 Blessed bee the Lord God of Israel, for hee hath visited and redeemed his people,

69 *And hath raised vp an horne of saluation for vs, in the house of his seruant Dauid,

70 *As he spake by the mouth of his holy Prophets, which haue bene since the world began:

71 That wee should be saued from our enemies, and from the hand of all that hate vs,

72 To performe the mercy promised to our fathers, and to remember his holy Couenant,

73 *The oath which he sware to our father Abraham,

74 That hee would grant vnto vs, that hee beeing deliuered out of the hands of our enemies, might serue him without feare,

75 In holinesse and righteousnesse before him, all the dayes of our life.

76 And thou childe shalt bee called the Prophet of the Highest: for thou shalt goe before the face of the Lord to prepare his wayes,

77 To giue knowledge of saluation vnto his people, || by the remission of their sinnes,

78 Through the || tender mercy of our God, whereby the || day-spring from on high hath visited vs,

79 To giue light to them that sit in darknes, and in the shadow of death, to guide our feet into the way of peace.

80 And the childe grew, and waxed strong in spirit, and was in the deserts, till the day of his shewing vnto Israel.

CHAP. II.

1 Augustus taxeth all the Romane Empire: 6 The natiuitie of Christ: 8 one Angel relateth it to the shepherds: 13 many sing praises to God for it. 21 Christ is circumcised. 22 Mary purified: 28 Simeon and Anna prophecie of Christ: 40 who increaseth in wisdome, 46 questioneth in the Temple with the doctours, 51 and is obedient to his parents.

AND it came to passe in those dayes, that there went out a decree from Cesar Augustus, that all the world should be || taxed.

2 (And this taxing was first made whē Cyrenius was gouernor of Syria)

3 And all went to bee taxed, euery one into his owne citie.

4 And Ioseph also went vp frō Galilee, out

Marginal notes

*Esay 51.9.
*Psal. 33. 10.

*2. Sam. 2. 6.

*Psal. 34. 10.

*Iere. 31. 3, 20.
*Psal. 132. 10. gen. 17. 19.

|| Or, things.

*Psal. 132. 18.

*Iere. 23 5. and 30. 9.

*Gene. 22. 16.

|| Or, for.

|| Or, bowels of the mercy.
|| Or, Sunne-rising, or branch, Zac. 3.8. esay 11. 1. malach. 4. 2. numb. 24. 17.

|| Or, inrolled.

---

16. King James Bible, 1611. This is the standard format for the text. No distinction is made between prose and the songs. Though not visible here, paragraphs are indicated by a mark following a verse number. The formality of the boxed presentation of the text is new in printed Bibles, but it is not uncommon to find older Bibles with such lines ruled in by hand. The Geneva and Bishops' Bibles' willingness to break up the insularity of the columns has disappeared.

The common people

The coming of the vernacular Bible made readers of many such as William Maldon (see above, p. 10), and the association between the Bible and learning to read is both ancient and continuing. What Maldon did by choice generations of children have done of necessity, having not only religious material but the text of the KJB as a central element in their growth to literacy and piety. This, coupled with the hearing of the text in the family, in school and in church, gave the KJB, once it was the established version, a unique place in their literary and linguistic consciousness. It was nursery story, primer, adolescent and adult reading, present from the alpha to the omega of verbal consciousness. In a fragmentary way its language, imagery, story and poetry, to say nothing of its faith, was the highest common factor in the mental environment of millions over many generations. Home is not always loved, but, as anyone who has ever been homesick knows, there is a close link between the familiar and love, and, as anybody, astonished that other people can love a place that seems so awful, knows, that love has little to do with objective merit. Such love created a new basis for literary opinion of the Bible, the basis of sentiment. It was independent of scholarly ideas of inspiration and of fashionable literary standards, hitherto the prime forces in moulding opinion, and it begins to give its own stamp to opinion of the KJB by the middle of the eighteenth century. This sentiment is similar to the love for the Sternhold and Hopkins Psalter but more slowly gained the kind of intensity that characterised that love in the seventeenth century. In part this was because the KJB was not the popular music of the people, in part because it was not yet under pressure from rival versions.

The development of Bible primers, and family and school Bibles, at first reflected and then promoted the educational use of the Bible. The Reformation brought the Bible into the family before it came into the church. Doubtless whole households read the Lollard Bible together. In the early 1540s a draft proclamation seems to envisage family reading, exhorting that every man 'use this most high benefit quietly and charitably every of you to the edifying of himself, his wife and family' (Pollard, p. 114). Benjamin Franklin tells a tale of such reading from a few years later:

This obscure family of ours was early in the Reformation, and continued Protestants through the reign of Queen Mary, when they were sometimes in danger of trouble on account of their zeal against popery. They had got an

English Bible, and to conceal and secure it, it was fastened open with tapes under and within the frame of a joint stool. When my great great grandfather read in it to his family, he turned up the joint stool upon his knees, turning over the leaves then under the tapes. One of the children stood at the door to give notice if he saw the apparitor coming, who was an officer of the spiritual court. In that case the stool was turned down again upon its feet, when the Bible remained concealed under it as before.[28]

Persecution was a great encourager of home religion.

From the beginning of the seventeenth century Thumb Bibles and other verse presentations of biblical material were published for children, but family Bible reading differs in that it presents the child with the text as well as the content. Publishers began deliberately to present children with the text later in the century, the first notable example being *The King's Psalter* (London, 1670). The title continues: 'containing Psalms and hymns, with easy and delightful directions to all learners, whether children, youths or others, for their better reading of the English tongue'; the work is dedicated 'to the instructors of youth'. It is a religious miscellany, complete with illustrations, ranging from a rhymed alphabet through a version of Herbert's 'The altar' and Psalms from the PB to passages from the KJB, 'all which', the title concludes, 'are profitable, plain and pleasant'. If this is not just a cliché or a pious wish, the coming together of learning to read, the KJB and delight ('delightful directions') nicely suggests how such early reading led some to a love that might be literary.

School (rather than family) Bibles began to appear in 1737 with an NT published in Glasgow, and in eighteenth-century Scotland 'children were generally taught to read in country schools, by first using the Shorter Catechism, then the Proverbs, afterwards the New Testament, and lastly the Bible'.[29] One curious anecdote from Defoe affords a glimpse of the use of the KJB text in schools early in the eighteenth century. With good reason,[30] he shows no surprise at it being so used, but what happens to the text intrigues him. Going into a school in Somerset, he writes,

I observed one of the lowest scholars was reading his lesson to the usher, which lesson it seems was a chapter in the Bible, so I sat down by the master till the

---

[28] Leonard W. Labaree et al., eds, *The Autobiography of Benjamin Franklin* (New Haven and London: Yale University Press, 1964), p. 50.

[29] J. Lee, *Memorial of the Bible Societies in Scotland* (Edinburgh, 1826), p. 195n. Quoted by Herbert in his entry for the 1737 NT (Herbert 1037).

[30] By this time the Bible was long established in schools. Foster Watson gives samples from school statutes that specify Bible reading as long ago as 1552 (*The English Grammar Schools to 1660* (1908; London: Cass, 1968), pp. 57–62).

boy had read out his chapter. I observed the boy read a little oddly in the tone of the country, which made me the more attentive because on enquiry I found that the words were the same and the orthography the same as in all our Bibles. I observed also the boy read it out with his eyes still on the book and his head like a mere boy, moving from side to side as the lines reached cross the columns of the book; his lesson was in the Cant. 5: 3, of which the words are these, 'I have put off my coat, how shall I put it on, I have washed my feet, how shall I defile them?'

The boy read thus, with his eyes, as I say, full on the text. 'Chav a doffed my cooat, how shall I don't, chav a washed my veet, how shall I moil 'em?'

How the dexterous dunce could form his mouth to express so readily the words (which stood right printed in the book) in his country jargon, I could not but admire.[31]

The modern reader might also admire. Was 'the dexterous dunce' translating the KJB's English into his English as he read (Defoe believes he was), or was the text sufficiently familiar, and his literacy sufficiently weak, that this was how he knew the KJB? Is this another mumpsimus? The anecdote is unique, but it does suggest a real familiarity with the text, if not a fidelity to it (if the learned could misquote why should not a dunce misread?): the boy had made it his own.

The Geneva Bible, containing not only the text but the understanding of the text given in prefaces, notes and diagrams, was the first great English Bible for home religion. However, the first Bible to *describe* itself as a family Bible was S. Smith's *The Complete History of the Old and New Testament: or, a Family Bible* (London, 1735; NT 1737). In the spirit of *The King's Psalter*, Smith writes in the preface, 'how laudable it is for a parent, and what a fine amusement for a child, to hear the holy writ read? It confirms the former in his religion, and at the same time initiates the other into the sacred mysteries'. His title continues, 'with critical and explanatory annotations, extracted from the writings of the most celebrated authors, ancient and modern. Together with maps, cuts, etc., curiously designed and engraved in copper.' This gives a fair sense of his and later family Bibles. They are usually large volumes well suited to reading out loud or to sitting impressively on a table in the centre of the living room of a middle-class or would-be middle-class family: in this respect they are the ancestors of coffee-table books. They are copiously illustrated and full of information, sometimes theological, sometimes not. In Smith's case, for instance, the Geneva arguments are used along with the headings from the KJB and annotations from many sources.

---

[31] *A Tour Through Great Britain* (1724–6), 2 vols. (London: Dent, 1928), I: 219.

The desire to provide information beyond mere commentary went so far that Thomas Bankes's family Bible of ?1790 even recorded that there are 3,566,480 letters in the two Testaments (nowadays this is mere useless information, but such facts were useful to the Masoretes checking the accuracy of their handwritten copies of the text).[32]

The first NT for children published in England seems to have been Joseph Brown's 1766 *The Family Testament, and Scholar's Assistant: calculated not only to promote the reading of the Holy Scriptures in families and schools, but also to remove that great uneasiness observable in children upon the appearance of hard words in their lessons, by a method entirely new* (London). This contains 'an introduction to spelling and reading in general . . . and directions for reading with elegance and propriety'. Other attempts to present parts of the Bible in a form attractive to children followed. One of the most notable was *A Curious Hieroglyphic Bible; or, select passages from the Old and New Testaments, represented with emblematical figures, for the amusement of youth: designed chiefly to familiarize tender age, in a pleasing and diverting manner, with early ideas of the Holy Scriptures* (London, 1784; Dublin, 1789). The 'emblematical figures' are engravings representing particular words, and this popular little book is dedicated 'to the parents, guardians, and governesses, of Great Britain and Ireland'.[33]

Not everybody was happy with the general use of the Bible to teach

---

[32] Here is more such useless information from Bankes:

	OT	(Apoc)	NT	Total
Books	39		27	66
Chapters	929	(183)	260	1189
Verses	23,214	(6,081)	7,959	31,173
Words	592,439	(152,185)	181,253	773,692
Letters	2,728,100		838,380	3,566,480

'And' occurs 35,543 times in the OT, 10,684 in the NT, while 'Jehovah' occurs 6,855 times. The middle and shortest chapter of the Bible is Psalm 117, the middle verse Ps. 118: 8, and the middle time 2 Chron. 4: 16. Ezra 7: 21 has all the letters of the alphabet (in old editions it begins 'And J, euen J'). In awe of the labour of older and more diligent scholars, I have not checked this information. But the figure for 'Jehovah' does not easily stand up to examination . . .

[33] Hieroglyphic Bibles go back to 1687 in Germany, while the use of hieroglyphics for teaching reading is a little older. The *Orbis Pictus* of J.A. Comenius (Nuremburg, 1657), using illustrations reminiscent of the diagrams of the Geneva Bible, was adapted into English by Charles Hoole in 1658. Such works were of course associated with religion, so the *Nolens Volens: or, you shall make Latin whether you will or no* of Elisha Coles (London, 1658) was published with *The Youth's Visible Bible*. Hieroglyphic Bibles were available in England and America from about 1780 (see W.A. Clouston, *Hieroglyphic Bibles: their origin and history* (Glasgow, 1894), also Virginia Haviland and Margaret N. Coughlan, *Yankee Doodle's Literary Sampler of Prose, Poetry and Pictures* (New York: Crowell, 1974), pp. 18–19).

reading. Sarah Trimmer (1741–1810), known as 'Good Mrs Trimmer', argued in the preface to the third edition of her *Sacred History* (1796) that 'every part of early instruction ought to be held in subordination to the study of religion'.[34] The Bible should not be used without this end in mind. So she declares:

The opposite customs which have, of late years, prevailed in many schools and families, of either suffering the Scriptures to be read by children in a promiscuous manner, or totally neglected, may be justly regarded as principal causes of the profaneness and libertinism of the age . . . it is presumptuous to suppose we can educate youth properly without them; and it may justly be considered as an irreverent act to make use of God's Holy Word with no further end in view than to the improvement of pupils in the art of reading. (I: vii)

Needless to say, this lengthy work supplements its selections from the KJB 'with annotations and reflections, particularly calculated to facilitate the study of the Holy Scriptures in schools and families' (subtitle).

The successors to these books are still published, and reading programmes based on the Bible continue to be created, but the story does not need pursuing here; the inescapable familiarity with the KJB (and then with more recent versions) that the whole story both reflects and promotes is the crucial point. What Augustine wrote of the Bible of his time is now true of the KJB: 'as the child grows this book grows with him'.[35] The KJB in relation to Augustan literary standards had 'all the disadvantages of an old prose translation', but it was becoming a standard of language capable of challenging the much less stable literary standard of the Augustans.

[34] *Sacred History* (1782 etc.); 3rd ed., 6 vols. (London: 1796), I: viii.
[35] *Confessions* III: 5; trans. R.S. Pine-Coffin (Harmondsworth: Penguin, 1961), p. 60.

CHAPTER TEN

Mid-century

ROBERT LOWTH'S *DE SACRA POESI HEBRAEORUM*

Several French critics were moving towards understanding of the form of Hebrew poetry from observation of its characteristics but without reference to known standards. The Cistercian Abbot Claude Fleury observes that the poetry 'abounds with repetitions, and the same thoughts are expressed twice over in different terms . . . these repetitions are the most obvious and common mark of the poetic style'. The Benedictine Dom Augustin Calmet, believing 'that the art of versifying alone no more makes the poet than the numbers and measures make the poetry', builds a little on this. In terms that could fit the KJB, he argues that

this natural poetry . . . consisted altogether in the style and not at all in the measure of the syllables. The whole was nothing else but figurative, sublime and sententious expressions, wherein they generally affected a kind of repetition of the same thing in different terms in the two parts of the same sentence, and sometimes we find a sort of rhyme and cadence which are so obvious and remarkable that we need not be at much pains to discover them.[1]

Just what he means by 'a sort of rhyme and cadence' is left unspecified: the very vagueness opens a possibility that was developed later, that there could be a kind of rhyming of sense rather than sound.

Neither man goes further than what has been quoted: the point is not stressed but the seed is sown. Several Englishmen at this time took note of the repetitions. Luke Milbourne, one of the many would-be reformers of Sternhold and Hopkins, remarks that 'the repetitions in the Hebrew are so charming that I could not but think they would be very beautiful in English, as particularly in the 118th Psalm',[2] but the remark

---

[1] Quotations from both authors are from *Antiquities Sacred and Profane*, translated from the French by W. Tindal (London, 1724–7), pp. 5, 29 and 30–1.
[2] *The Psalms of David in English Metre* (London, 1698), preface (unpaginated).

is unique and undeveloped, and it does not occur to him that these repetitions might already be found in the English of the KJB. Blackmore's contrary view is probably more representative. He 'avoided the immediate repetition of the same thought in words little different from the first, which is so very common' in Hebrew poetry, because it is contrary to present ideas of eloquence (*A Paraphrase*, p. lxxv). Wither had earlier adopted the same attitude (see above, p. 136). Repetition was all too easy to see in the poetry, even if the full extent of the parallelism was not, and, with the occasional exception of a man like Milbourne, it was not admired. This is probably why it is so little commented upon. As long as it was possible to believe that the form of the poetry was metrical and, perhaps, rhymed, there was no need to attend to formal characteristics that were distasteful.

The kind of cultural relativity already seen in Blackmore (above, p. 195) – they have one standard of eloquence, we another – was only just beginning to be developed in England. One English writer noted something like this idea, and gave it the kind of turn that was being developed in France, observing that 'no book can be so plain but that it is requisite for the perfect understanding of it that men should be acquainted with the idioms and proprieties of the original language and the customs and notions which were generally received at the time when it was written'.[3] Rather than encouraging one to appreciate what one can without being put off by the rest, this encourages one to read Hebrew poetry as a Hebrew would have. The significance lies less in the intrinsic interest of the idea – it is no more than a brief generalisation – than in its author, William Lowth: his son Robert, the most substantial and significant figure in the history of the Bible as literature in the eighteenth century, developed this passing hint, Felton's notion of the appropriateness of literal translation for Hebrew poetry, the French ideas noted here, and the preoccupation with the sublime into the century's most famous English work on Hebrew poetry.

Robert Lowth (1710–87), was for nine years Oxford Professor of Poetry; later his eminence in the Church was such that he was offered the Archbishopric of Canterbury. From our point of view his work divides into two parts which span the most crucial period in the development of the KJB's literary reputation, the first and most substantial part being his greatest achievement, *De Sacra Poesi Hebraeorum Praelectiones.*

---

[3] *Directions for the Profitable Reading of the Holy Scripture* (1708). As given in Thomas R. Preston, 'Biblical criticism, literature, and the eighteenth-century reader', Isabel Rivers, ed., *Books and their Readers in Eighteenth-Century England* (Leicester University Press, 1982), pp. 97–126; p. 100.

Though this belongs with the many discussions of the originals as literature, it has significant consequences for attitudes to the KJB. The less substantial part, his work on the English language and his opinions on the KJB, will need consideration later.

De Sacra Poesi Hebraeorum consists of thirty-four Latin lectures given in his capacity as Oxford Professor of Poetry between 1741 and, at the latest, 1750. They were published in 1753, and the extensively annotated English translation by George Gregory, *Lectures on the Sacred Poetry of the Hebrews* (1787), continued to be published until 1847. Moreover, the chief arguments were repeated and, in some instances, developed, in his highly respected *Isaiah* (1778). The greatest immediate importance of the lectures lay in their choice and valuation of their subject. Lowth's exhortation at the very end of the lectures to the Oxford students to pursue Hebraic studies makes the crucial point:

consider it as a work worthy of your utmost exertions to illustrate and cultivate this department of literature. You will find it no less elegant and agreeable than useful and instructive, abounding in information no less curious for its extent and variety than for its great importance and venerable sanctity, deserving the attention of every liberal mind, essential to all who would be proficients in theology. (II: 434)

Thirty-four lectures composed with a scholarship and elegance that must have appealed to all who heard or read them constituted a discovery of 'a few of the more delightful retreats of this paradise' (II: 435), and an argument for the supremacy of the Hebraic poetry of unparalleled thoroughness. They are a milestone in the long history of preference for the Bible over the classics. What had been the shakily-founded opinion of a minority became a demonstrated truth for many. Moreover, the demonstration that large parts of the OT were of great literary quality and susceptible to rational literary criticism set a seal on the growing literary sense of the Bible. Lowth finished the work of critics such as Blackwall, making it all but impossible for the unprejudiced not to think of the Bible as a literary as well as a religious work. None of the translators and few of the annotators in the latter part of the century could work without recognising that they were dealing with literary as well as sacred texts, and some of them this recognition was paramount.

Even to make these two points about Lowth is to show at once that there is continuity as well as originality in *De Sacra Poesi Hebraeorum*. Many of his attitudes and points are old. To begin with, he seems to reinforce the old prejudice that only poetry is worth consideration as literature, and the opening lecture is a standard Augustan exposition of the nature of poetry: its object is utility, its means pleasure (I: 6–7). But, if pleasure is subservient to moral purpose, it is the pleasure that most interests Lowth:

For what is a poet destitute of harmony, of grace and of all that conduces to allurement and delight? or how should we derive advantage or improvement from an author whom no man of taste can endure to read? The reason, therefore, why poetry is so studious to embellish her precepts with a certain inviting sweetness . . . is plainly by such seasoning to conciliate favour to her doctrines . . . (I: 10)

This is the old ornamental theory of poetry, and at once he speaks of 'all the decorations of elegance' (I: 11). One might expect Lowth to be about to continue the sixteenth- and seventeenth-century search for classical figures in the scriptures, but his description of criticism suggests something different. It is 'a particular department of science' (I: 4): the suggestion of scientific method is apt, for one of the characteristics of the lectures is the 'cautious reserve' (II: 311) with which Lowth examines his evidence. He declares that, 'as in all other branches of science, so in poetry art or theory consists in a certain knowledge derived from the careful observation of nature', and he insists that rules come from art, not art from rules. Moreover, if we are to understand the power of art 'in exciting the human affections . . . we must consider what those affections are and by what means they are to be excited' (I: 45). His scientific criticism, then, is not only to be deductive but to have a foundation in psychology.

To return to the first lecture: Lowth's idea of poetry seems to be based on the classics and is high to the point of absurdity – the dominion of the Caesars would have been ended once for all if the killers of Caesar had spoken poetry of quality to the people after the Ides of March (I: 26). Now however, perhaps with a glance at the Puritan distrust of literature, he makes a turn reminiscent of Dennis: 'but after all we shall think more humbly of poetry than it deserves unless we direct our attention to that quarter where its importance is most eminently conspicuous, unless we contemplate it as employed on sacred subjects and in subservience to religion' (I: 36). Here he seems to be one of those who argue from content to quality. He is at once an aesthete and a religious moralist, an open-minded investigator and a representative of the old positions. The period he spans is one of important development in ideas of the originals as literature and fundamental change in ideas of the KJB. The seemingly contradictory attributes he displays place him as the perfect representative of this time.

Lowth repeats the familiar views that the original purpose of poetry was religious and that only when serving this purpose does it appear 'to shine forth with all its natural splendour, or rather to be animated by that inspiration which on other occasions is spoken of without being felt' (I: 36). As is evident elsewhere, he does not distinguish between divine and poetic inspiration,[4] though he does allow individuality to the sacred authors and always treats the writings as if they are human productions (I: 347). He holds two other old views, that oldest is best and that biblical poetry is superior to classical poetry; these come out as he claims that his observations on poetry and religion

are remarkably exemplified in the Hebrew Poetry, than which the human mind can conceive nothing more elevated, more beautiful or more elegant; in which the almost ineffable sublimity of the subject is fully equalled by the energy of the language and the dignity of the style. And it is worthy observation that as some of these writings exceed in antiquity the fabulous ages of Greece, in sublimity they are superior to the most finished productions of that polished people. (I: 37)

Here is yet another familiar notion, sublimity: it is a key to how Lowth will transform his compendious baggage of received ideas. He remarks in a footnote to lecture 14 concerning Burke's distinction between the beautiful and the sublime that 'after all that has been said, our feelings must be the only criterion' (I: 302), and this, out of context, summarises how his idea of sublimity operates: he works from the intensity of his feelings. Though we have often seen the ideas in the passage just given issue from theory rather than feeling, in Lowth they issue from the deepest conviction: he loves the sacred poetry with a passion second to none, and everywhere the lectures tell of this love.

In such ways Lowth begins to build for his lectures a framework redolent of Augustanism and received ideas, yet containing promise of something new even in its repetition of the old: he will develop old ideas so methodically, fully and intelligently that some of them become new. What is most striking about this opening is that, more than any other work we have yet seen, it enforces an aesthetic approach: if harmony and grace and all that conduces to allurement and delight are essential to poetry, then biblical poetry, being the best, must show them at their best. The lectures are indeed to be a 'subtle research after beauty and taste'.

Lowth's taste is principally for the sublime. He never tackles the relationship between sublimity and his sense of the utility of poetry as phi-

---

[4] One of the proofs he offers for the connection between prophecy and poetry is that 'they had one common name, one common origin, one common author, the Holy Spirit' (II: 18).

losophy in pleasing dress. Indeed, as soon as he starts to consider the origin of poetry ideas of utility disappear into the background:

The origin and first use of poetical language are undoubtedly to be traced into the vehement affections of the mind. For what is meant by that singular frenzy of poets which the Greeks, ascribing to divine inspiration, distinguished by the appellation of 'enthusiasm', but a style and expression directly prompted by nature itself and exhibiting the true and express image of a mind violently agitated? when, as it were, the secret avenues, the interior recesses of the soul are thrown open, when the inmost conceptions are displayed, rushing together in one turbid stream, without order or connection. (I: 79)

'The inmost conceptions' this poetry displays were religious conceptions. The attitude here is thoroughly Longinian, and Lowth acknowledges Longinus when he turns explicitly to the sublime. Sublimity is 'that force of composition, whatever it be, which strikes and overpowers the mind, which excites the passions and which expresses ideas at once with perspicuity and elevation, not solicitous whether the language be plain or ornamented, refined or familiar' (I: 307). Passion and poetry belong together and sublimity is the essence of poetry. It comes from and works on the passions. He draws this distinction, echoing what we have already read:

The language of reason is cool, temperate, rather humble than elevated, well arranged and perspicuous, with an evident care and anxiety lest any thing should escape which might appear perplexed or obscure. The language of the passions is totally different: the conceptions burst out in a turbid stream, expressive in a manner of the internal conflict; the more vehement break out in hasty confusion, they catch, without search or study, whatever is impetuous, vivid or energetic. In a word, reason speaks literally, the passions poetically. (I: 309)

Though the way the point is made sounds thoroughly mid-eighteenth-century, the idea itself looks so far forward that we can find D.H. Lawrence expressing it in 1918 as if it is new:

free verse is . . . direct utterance from the instant, whole man. It is the soul and the mind and body surging at once, nothing left out. They speak all together. There is some confusion, some discord. But the confusion and the discord only belong to the reality as noise belongs to the plunge of water . . . in free verse we look for the insurgent naked throb of the instant moment.[5]

The image of a turbid stream or the plunge of water is the same, as is the fascination with the passions of the moment and the acceptance of confusion in the form of the utterance. Lowth and Lawrence have in

[5] 'Poetry of the present' (1918); in Vivian de Sola Pinto and Warren Roberts (eds.), *The Complete Poems of D.H. Lawrence* (London: Heinemann, 1964), pp. 184–5.

common a high sense of the value of revealing the true feelings of a moment and an awareness that the appropriate form of expression differs from accepted poetic standards. The latter point must be returned to; for now it is enough to see the fundamental tendency of Lowth's idea of the sublime, and how fine the dividing line is in his work between the derivative, the typically Augustan, and something very modern.

One of the most striking aspects of the *Lectures* is that they drastically widen the sense of poetry in the OT. Until now the poetic parts had been reckoned to be the Psalms, the Song of Songs, the bulk of Job, the various interposed poems from Moses' song (Exodus 15) on, including a few passages from the Prophets such as Habakkuk 3, and, sometimes, Proverbs. Lowth extended poetry to include the Prophets, and devoted lecture 18 to arguing that 'the writings of the Prophets [are] in general poetical'. Indeed, he gives 'the first rank' (II: 4) among the kinds of Hebrew poetry to the prophetic, and in many places declares that Isaiah is 'the first of all poets for sublimity and eloquence' (I: 166; see particularly II: 847).

Another important general argument connects closely with Lowth's positive idea of confusion as an aspect of poetic sublimity. By insisting as his father had that 'we must see all things with their eyes, estimate all things by their opinions; we must endeavour as much as possible to read Hebrew as the Hebrews would have read it' (I: 113), Lowth was not only establishing a major point about the need for a historical imagination but setting the foundation for the new standards that we have just observed. Several times he warns his audience against the error 'of accounting vulgar, mean or obscure passages which were probably accounted among the most perspicuous and sublime by the people to whom they were addressed' (I: 167), so cajoling his audience to accept his idea of Hebraic literary taste. Augustan standards are neither the only ones nor the best ones, he is telling the next generation of youth 'addicted to the politer sciences and studious of the elegancies of composition' (I: 51). There is of course an element of faith in this move – the Hebrews must have felt this way and, implicitly, their judgement must have been the best – but it is essentially healthy and sane.

The emphasis on historical imagination is highly important, but even more important for the development of taste and for changing attitudes to the KJB is the way Lowth uses what was pejorative language. He has just juxtaposed the kind of language often used for the KJB's English – 'vulgar, mean' – with key Augustan words for literary excellence. His frequent acknowledgement of passages in the Bible which 'appear to us harsh and unusual, I had almost said unnatural and barbarous' (I: 321) turns such terms into something like praise.

In part this transformation is due to the way he uses such terms. In one of the best pieces of close demonstration Lowth has to offer, Job 3: 3 is compared with Jer. 20: 14–15. Just to write that 'the meaning is the same, nor is there any very great difference in the phraseology, but Jeremiah fills up the ellipses, smoothes and harmonises the rough and uncouth language of Job' (I: 315), in the context of a preference for the Job passage – 'the Hebrew literature itself contains nothing more poetical' (I: 313) – is to give 'rough and uncouth' a new meaning.

The *Lectures* are best remembered for their exposition of parallelism. Though Lowth does not develop this until quite late, it grows out of the first subject he treats in detail, not the metre of Hebrew poetry but the fact that the poetry is metrical. The distinction is typical of his caution. His opening observation, 'that scarcely any real knowledge of the Hebrew versification is now to be obtained' (I: 52), is not a prelude to yet another attempt on the secret of Hebrew verse, but exactly what it appears, a statement of limitations he will stay within. He has the highest opinion of the importance of metre, so it is important to him to show that the Hebrew poetry was metrical even if he cannot recover the secret. Here he argues from theory to literature rather than the other way round:

But since it appears essential to every species of poetry that it be confined to numbers and consist of some kind of verse (for indeed, wanting this, it would not only want its most agreeable attributes but would scarcely deserve the name of poetry), in treating of the poetry of the Hebrews it appears absolutely necessary to demonstrate that those parts at least of the Hebrew writings which we term poetic are in metrical form. (I: 56)

Once he has satisfied himself of this he has, of course, established one area in which the originals are necessarily more beautiful than can now be appreciated. This idea, again a familiar one, is frequently apparent in the lectures. So, having shown parts of the Song of Songs than which 'nothing can . . . be imagined more truly elegant and poetical', he adds that 'the discovery of these excellencies . . . only serves to increase our regret for the many beauties which we have lost, the perhaps superior graces which extreme antiquity seems to have overcast with an impenetrable shade' (II: 340). This is not his typical method, but it does permit him and his audience to assume that whatever can be demonstrated scientifically is yet less than what was originally there. The poetry was

indeed metrical but 'he who attempts to restore the true and genuine
Hebrew versification erects an edifice without a foundation' (I: 67). And
what can be demonstrated is the form of the sentences. Here is how he
embarks on what he is later to call parallelism:

as the poems divide themselves in a manner spontaneously into periods, for the
most part equal, so the periods themselves are divided into verses, most commonly couplets, though frequently of greater length. This is chiefly observable
in those passages which frequently occur in the Hebrew poetry in which they
treat one subject in many different ways, and dwell upon the same sentiment;
when they express the same thing in different words, or different things in a
similar form of words; when equals refer to equals, and opposites to opposites:
and since this artifice of composition seldom fails to produce even in prose an
agreeable and measured cadence, we can scarcely doubt that it must have
imparted to their poetry, were we masters of the versification, an exquisite
degree of beauty and grace. (I: 68–9)

Lowth does not develop the discussion here; rather, he adds a
comment on the translatability of the poetry that appears, in Gregory's
translation, to refer to the KJB:

a poem translated literally from the Hebrew into the prose of any other language, whilst the same forms of the sentences remain, will still retain, even as
far as relates to versification, much of its native dignity, and a faint appearance
of versification. This is evident in our common version of the Scriptures, where
frequently
       'The order chang'd, and verse from verse disjoin'd,
       'Yet still the poet's scattered limbs we find.'   (I: 71)

The original Latin for 'in our common version of the Scriptures' is
simply, 'in vernacula' (p. 32). The idea has major implications for appreciation of the KJB as a representation of the original poetry.

The primary exposition of parallelism comes in lecture 19:

The poetical conformation of the sentences, which has been so often alluded to
as characteristic of Hebrew poetry, consists chiefly in a certain equality, resemblance, or parallelism between the members of each period; so that in two lines
(or members of the same period) things for the most part shall answer to things,
and words to words, as if fitted to each other by a kind of rule or measure. This
parallelism has much variety and many gradations; it is sometimes more accurate and manifest, sometimes more vague and obscure. (II: 34)

Three kinds are distinguished: synonymous, the commonest, in which
'the same sentiment is repeated in different but equivalent terms' (II: 35);
antithetic, in which 'a thing is illustrated by its contrary being opposed
to it' (II: 45); and 'synthetic or constructive parallelism', 'in which the

sentences answer to each other not by the iteration of the same image or sentiment, or the opposition of their contraries, but merely by the form of construction' (II: 489); this last is confessedly a catch-all category, covering anything that does not fit into the first two. There is nothing rigid in all this; as he makes explicit in *Isaiah*, 'sometimes the parallelism is more, sometimes less exact, sometimes hardly at all apparent' (p. xx). This raises a major point often forgotten in restatements and revisions of Lowth. It must be painfully apparent to anyone who has tried to read the poetic parts of the KJB using parallelism as a guide to the true form that it is often no help. But to try to read this way is to apply Lowth's ideas simplistically, as if what he had really said was that 'the unvarying element in the Hebrew poetry is the constant balance of lines of about equal length' (Gardiner, *The Bible*, p. 109). He not only admits that there are places where parallelism is hardly apparent, but suggests that parallelism may work over larger structures than simple pairs, and these larger structures may involve unparallelled lines. There may be triplet parallelisms in which 'the second line is generally synonymous with the first, whilst the third either begins the period or concludes it, and frequently refers to both the preceding' (II: 42). Next he observes that 'in stanzas (if I may so call them) of five lines, the nature of which is nearly similar, the line that is not parallel is generally placed between the two distichs'. He gives Isa. 31: 4 as an example:

> Like as the lion growleth,
> Even the young lion over his prey;
> Though the whole company of shepherds be called
> together against him:
> At their voice he will not be terrified,
> Nor at their tumult will he be humbled.   (II: 423)

Lowth does not explore the implications of this pattern (and so perhaps contributes to the simplification of his ideas). Nevertheless, if there are unparallelled lines, and parts of the poetry where parallelism is not apparent, it would seem that parallelism is not to be found everywhere in the poetry: consequently parallelism cannot be taken as the general system it is often thought of as being.

The idea of stanzas suggests larger units of form. Lowth points out one other stanza-like pattern, groups of four lines with alternate parallelisms, like a quatrain rhyming ABAB, and then once more leaves things tantalisingly in the air. How often, one might ask, does what could be called couplet parallelism simply break down, and how often, and in what ways, is it developed into more sophisticated structures? The questions go to the heart of the sense of formal artistry in Hebrew poetry. As such, they are likely to be answered according to the critic's willingness or unwillingness to discover such artistry. At least two critics, John Jebb in the mid-nineteenth century and Richard Moulton at the end of that century, were willing, and their conclusions will be seen later. No one has taken the opposite line: Lowth's ideas of parallelism have proved to be so generally helpful for appreciation of the poetry that, however much his analysis of the kinds of parallelism may have been questioned, the fundamental observation has not been. The seed of doubt sown by the suggestion of unparallelled lines and of parts where parallelism is hardly apparent has fallen on stony ground.

Unlike previous attempts on the secret of Hebrew verse, Lowth's description of parallelism is sufficiently cautious to be applicable to most of the poetry (and to some of the prose, though he does not proceed so far). Now something of the formal artistry of the poetry was open to all. Moreover, it was artistry that could be perceived to some extent in literal translation, and this opened the door to new appreciation of such translations. It also provided a basis for a new idea of translation: the Hebrew poetry might be most literally translated by combining fidelity to its words with fidelity to the one aspect of its poetic form that remained apparent.[6] It could appear as poetry without adopting the alien ornaments of neo-classical verse. Where Say had hinted at the possibility of seeing the prose of the KJB as free verse, Lowth, in his version of Isaiah, introduced free verse into English. As we shall see, a number of translators followed his example in the short term, and the many modern versions that give the poetry the appearance of poetic form owe something to Lowth. What is more, in one narrow area of poetry, Lowth broke the mould of English verse and anticipated the verse of Whitman and Lawrence. And he did this not by being an avant-garde radical but by pursuing the implications of his cautious scholarship.

In lecture 27 Lowth links parallelism, sublimity and translations. 'Brevity of diction', he argues, is 'conducive to sublimity of style' (II: 250), and this brevity is everywhere evident in the poetry. Yet it goes with a copiousness and fullness. Part of the effect of parallelism is that the Hebrew poets 'amplify by diversifying, by repeating, and sometimes by adding to the subject; therefore it happens that it is frequently, on the whole, treated rather diffusely, but still every sentence is concise and

---

[6] 'But this strict attention to the form and fashion of the composition . . . is . . . useful and even necessary in the translator who is ambitious of preserving in his copy the force and spirit and elegance of the original' (*Isaiah*, p. xxx).

nervous in itself. Thus it happens in general that neither copiousness nor vigour is wanting'. He adds that 'the most literal versions therefore commonly fail in this respect, and consequently still less is to be expected from any poetical translations or imitations whatever' (II: 251). This is sharp. The *Lectures* constantly suggest the need for translation that responds to the literary character of the texts and so, on the surface, are close to the desires of all the translators who attempted to match their notions of the original beauties with contemporary beauties, invariably expanding and regularising the originals. Such translators of course applied their own standards of elegance. Lowth is suggesting that the true way to achieve the end of an appropriately effective literary translation is to match the parallelistic brevity of the originals. Prose translations such as the KJB might match the brevity and retain, as he had noted earlier, 'a faint appearance of versification' (I: 71), but his ideal of translation is to couple the literal brevity with a clear appearance of versification that reveals the parallelism. He was to give the world an example with *Isaiah* in 1778. In the meantime his ideas filtered slowly through to translators. The chief of them was the conviction that the Bible could not be translated without a sense that it was literature as well as truth.

UNCOUTH, HARSH AND OBSOLETE

Anthony Purver and archaic words

In the latter half of the eighteenth century, battles similar to those that had been fought over the Psalter were fought over the much more vital territory of the whole English Bible. Central figures were the makers of new versions: they had to attack the KJB to justify their efforts. The KJB's increasing age was its greatest weakness. Study of the Greek and Hebrew texts had advanced. Scholars believed they had a better understanding of the texts and that they had improved on the texts available to the KJB translators. Moreover, much of their scholarship now involved the explicit literary awareness of the texts that Lowth did so much to foster. The question was not just whether the KJB had translated the truest texts but whether it was accurate in the sense of being an appropriate rendering of the literary characteristics of the originals. Yet advances in scholarship were as nothing compared to the continuation of the Augustans' sense of improvements in the English language. The arguments about the KJB's language had been foreshadowed on one side by the attacks on Sternhold and Hopkins, by Nary's complaints about Gregory Martin's language, and by a number of complaints of the uncouthness, harshness and incomprehensibility of the KJB, and, on the other side, by Pope and Swift suggesting that the language was not only venerated but becoming 'a kind of standard' (see above, p. 211). But such foreshadowings give little idea of the detail and interest of the criticism that was to come, especially in the 1760s: that decade produced the most fascinating criticism of the language of the KJB ever to appear.

The first in this period to publish a list of uncouth and obsolete expressions in the KJB, also the first to publish a work devoted to the need for a new translation, was the Cambridge-educated divine, Matthew Pilkington (1705–65), in his *Remarks upon Several Passages of Scripture: rectifying some errors in the printed Hebrew text; pointing out several mistakes in the versions; and showing the benefit and expediency of a more correct and intelligible translation of the Bible* (1759):

> The uncouth and obsolete words and expressions that are met with in our English version of the Bible are generally intelligible and convey the ideas the writers had in view; but as our language is very much improved in politeness and correctness since that version was made, it may properly be wished that the Scriptures might receive every advantage which the improvement of our language can give them, especially as the delicacy of some people's ears is pretended to be disgusted with every uncouth sound. (p. 114)

In its attitude to the English language, this is Welsted's view. It is no accident that it makes us look back. Pilkington formed his ideas on language while Augustan attitudes were at their strongest.

In support of his argument Pilkington gives the earliest example of the unhistorical idea that the KJB was a literary rather than a scholarly revision. He alleges that improvement of the language was one of the main motives which led King James to order a new translation, for the earlier translators 'appeared so well to have understood the Scriptures that little more than the language of it was altered by the translators in King James's time' (p. 114). He seems to be attributing his own ideas to the translators, for he goes on to argue for the same kind of revision, that is, literary revision. He believed that the KJB might be improved in 'those expressions which, though delivered in words of common use, may be called uncouth from their being in some measure unintelligible' (p. 115). Here are two of his examples and his conclusion:

> Isa. 27: 8. 'In measure, when it shooteth forth, thou wilt debate with it: He stayeth his rough wind, in the day of the east wind.' Here are words, intelligible, and in common use; but when they are thus connected the sentence is no more

intelligible than it was in the former version . . . Nahum 2: 7. 'Her maids shall lead her as with the voice of doves, taboring upon their breasts.' The sentiment is evidently, as the Latin, Greek and Chaldee versions give it, that the maids of her that was led away captive should mourn as doves and beat upon their breasts, as persons in the utmost distress; and 'taboring' was certainly very injudiciously put for 'smiting', which was the word in our former version. – These instances are here mentioned farther to show the benefit and expediency of a more correct and intelligible translation of the Bible than we have at present, and that a translator should not too strictly adhere to any of the former versions. (pp. 117–18)

The point is well made, and it is curious that few other critics in any period have ventured to give examples of incomprehensibility in the KJB.

The most interesting part of the argument is his list (p. 115) of 'some of those words and expressions, which would certainly be altered by persons of such learning and judgement as would, undoubtedly, be appointed to undertake a new translation' (pp. 114–15). Here are over two-thirds of his entries, chosen because they are also listed by the most important of the mid-century critics, Anthony Purver:

Advisement	Afore	Albeit	Aliant
Ambushment	Anon	Ate	Bestead
Bettered	Bewray	Blains	Chaws
Daysman	Discomfiture	Fet	Fray
Haply	Holpen	Hosen	Kerchiefs
Lade	Laden	Leasing	Leese
Listed	Listeth	Magnifical	Marishes
Mete	Meted	Munition	Nurture
Poll	Polled	Purtenance	Seethe
Seething	Servitor	Silverlings	Sith
Sod	Sodden	Tablets	Trow
Unwittingly	Wastness	Wench	Wert
Wist	Wotteth		

Hough and houghed their horses and chariots
We do you to wit

What is particularly interesting is that although there are many words here which a present-day reader would readily agree are obsolete, there are also some which would not be assented to, such as 'albeit', 'ate', 'discomfiture', 'laden', 'nurture', and 'unwittingly'. Yet the coincidence of two independent writers citing the same words gives a real likelihood that these words were obsolete at that time. The greater detail of Purver's work will allow us to take this observation further.

Anthony Purver (1702–77) is one of only two men who made complete independent English versions of the Bible in this century.[7] Prefaced to his work is a discussion of principles of translation that includes both detailed criticism of the KJB's English and substantial lists of faulty words and phrases. Like Bunyan, Purver was an artisan. While apprenticed as a shoemaker in Hampshire, he read Fisher's *Rusticus ad Academicos* and found himself called and commanded by the divine spirit to translate the Scriptures. He became a Quaker and an occasional teacher; he studied Hebrew, Chaldee, Syriac, Greek, Latin and, probably, other languages, and he read as widely as anyone in biblical translations and in scholarly (including rabbinic) and literary commentary on the Bible. From about 1733 he laboured at his translation, finishing it in 1763. A year later it was published in two volumes as *A New and Literal Translation of all the Books of the Old and New Testament*, but it became known as the Quakers' Bible.

Purver's work was received unkindly. John Symonds, for instance, wrote that

it might well be expected that so desperate a critic should be perfectly skilled in his native tongue, but the following specimens of his taste will show that he boldly usurped a province for which he was totally unqualified. Matt. 5: 22: 'blockhead'. Mark 8: 11: 'began *to query* with him'. 12: 4: 'And him they stoned, *nay, broke his head*' . . .

Such are the flowers with which Purver has so liberally adorned his boasted translation. From a vicious affectation of what is natural and easy he sometimes falls into very gross indecencies. (*Observations*, pp. 91–2)

---

[7] The other, who signs himself J.M. Ray but seems to have been one David Macrae (1750–1816), licentiate preacher of the Church of Scotland (Herbert, p. 320), deserves only a footnote, in spite of all his eccentric labours. The full title gives some sense of the work: *Revised Translation and Interpretation of the Sacred Scriptures, after the eastern manner, from concurrent authorities of the critics, interpreters and commentators, copies and versions; showing that the inspired writings contain the seeds of the valuable sciences, being the source whence the ancient philosophers derived them; also the most ancient histories and greatest antiquities: with a philosophical and medical commentary; the use of the commentary is not to give the sense of the text, as that is done in the interpretation, but to describe the works of nature, showing the connection of natural science with revealed religion.* In the preface to the second edition (Glasgow, 1815), dated 1802, Ray tells – quite unconvincingly, given the appalling obscurity with which he writes – of his 'great delicacy of expression' which is intended to remove the aversion to the Bible of youths of unprincipled minds (p. iv). He also makes a number of remarks on the superiority of the Scriptures as literature to all other writing in both the preface and the notes: the reader who struggles sufficiently with the preface will find, for instance, that 'there is no book or history, real or romantic, so entertaining and instructive as the Bible, or that has so great a variety' (p. iv).

One might say that Purver's sin was that he attempted, in places, an English for cobblers, and then wonder whether the greatest of self-taught translators, writing an English for ploughboys, might not have suffered similarly at the hands of critics who demanded a stylish as well as a scholarly translation. But that is a false track. New Bibles are rarely acclaimed, and what matters here is not Purver's translation but his criticism of the KJB.

Like Pilkington's, Purver's attitude to language is full of Augustan pride, echoing ideas that prevailed when he was a young man:

Language was anciently rude and unpolished, and it was proper even for the inspired writings to be delivered in that of the times: hence nouns are frequently repeated in the original where they may much better be rendered by pronouns, according to the improvements of grammar and manner of speech now, especially in this part of the world, without any diminution or alteration of the sense at all. In such a case certainly our language is to be like it self, and not made uncouth to no manner of purpose. (I: viii)

He maintains this view about developments in the English language. Addison 'is justly esteemed the best writer of our language' (I: xii), and Purver asks his reader to compare the preface to the KJB with Addison's writings, 'and see what difference of language there is in a hundred years' (I: v). He is careful not to let this appear a merely personal opinion. Though he takes a just pride in thinking for himself, he also knows where he is in relation to scholarship and opinion (see, for example, I: xvi), and here, as in many places, he cites authorities who express the same view. This helps to identify him, where English is concerned, as a man who applied the standards of the age he grew up in to the KJB.

Four pages of the 'introductory remarks' are given to the axiom that 'a translation ought to be true to the original', eleven to the axiom that 'a translation should be well or grammatically expressed in the language it is made in', and fourteen to an appendix giving lists of various faults in the KJB. There are further remarks and lists prefaced to the NT. The emphasis thus falls squarely on what is most interesting to us, issues of language. On the one hand, Purver believed that a translation should be literal, on the other, as already noted, that 'our language is to be like it self'. Though he also believed the language 'ought to be plain and suited to common capacities' (I: vi), this represents a major difference from Tyndale's desire to present the Bible in simple contemporary prose that everyone could understand. The desire is, within limits, to show the language at its best, and he frequently writes of ways the translation may be given an elegant turn. Moreover, he works with a literary awareness.

To quote his own version of Eccles. 12: 10, 'he endeavoured to find agreeable words; however, what is written is right, the words of truth'. His note to this reads: 'by Sandys, worthy to be transcribed for the poetry, "He found out matter to delight the mind; / And every word he writ, by truth was signed"'. This attitude reflects both the growing literary awareness of the Bible and the Augustan sense of the perfection of English.

The long discussion of principles equally reflects the general eighteenth-century desire to set down rules for this perfection. Yet, in attacking the KJB from this point of view he provides strong evidence of the hold the KJB was gaining on the popular mind, as well as of the sense that there is an appropriate Biblical English that is different from current English:

Yet the obsolete words and uncouth ungrammatical expressions in the sacred text pass more unheeded as being oftener read and heard, especially when the mind is filled with an imagination, that a translation of the Scriptures must be so expressed . . .

There ought to be the greatest exactness even in spelling the Scripture because our children learn to read by it. (I: v, vi)

He is in fact testifying to important factors which will make the KJB seem less obsolete, uncouth and ungrammatical than it appears to him, and the obvious difference from Selden's picture of the common people (see above, p. 107) shows such a change already taking place.

Purver then gives some examples of obsolete English; it is, as with Pilkington's list, the presence of a number of words in this paragraph that are now standard English which is of particular interest:

The following preterperfect tenses and participles are become old, viz. baken (baked) bitten (bit) folden (folded) holden (held) holpen (helped) laden (loaded) lien (pret. lay, part. lain) mowen (mowed) ridden (rid) slidden (slid) spitted (spit) stricken (struck) unwashen (not washed) wakened (awaked) waxen (become) withholden (withheld) upholden (upheld), but some of *en* in termination sprinkled about, especially when passive, may give an agreeable relish of age, as broken, begotten, forgotten; and other such continue, i.e. done, given, gone, known, seen, slain, taken, chosen, spoken, thrown, written, smitten, fallen, born, torn, sworn, stolen, shewn, hewn, driven, drawn, lain, risen, forsaken, striven, sown, shaken, etc., and for a participle rotten; *a* is also obsolete where *o* is used now, in the preterimperfects bare, brake, drave, forgat, gat, spake, sware, ware, ate, laded, slang, spat, strake; but swore and begot sound too vulgar to be used of God. (I: vi–vii)

In the last two examples, one should note in passing that, despite his principles, Purver has some sense of a special religious English that differs from the English he advocates. He too has some 'imagination that a translation of the Scriptures must be so expressed'.

Purver's three categories, which one may call the archaic, the familiarly archaic and the familiar, are useful, but the words now need redistributing. Only 'smitten' and 'lain' need moving from the familiar to the familiarly archaic. 'Stricken' is now familiarly archaic rather than archaic (the main KJB use is 'stricken in age' or 'years', which Johnson finds antiquated and the *OED* archaic, yet 'stricken' survives in other uses such as 'the stricken ship'; 'stricken in years', though it would not be used, is well known). 'Bitten', 'laden', 'mowen' (mown), 'ridden' (of horses) and, of course, 'ate' are all familiar, not archaic. Familiar also are two of his three familiarly archaic words, 'broken' and 'forgotten'.

The bulk of Purver's evidence comes in the lists appended to the 'introductory remarks' and to the 'additional remarks' that preface the NT. Many of the words would not now be regarded as obsolete. Among them is 'unwittingly' (which Pilkington also gives). Purver's alternative for this is 'unawares'. The *OED* states clearly, 'in very frequent use c 1380–c 1630, and from c 1815', and refers to 'unwitting', which it says was 'rare after c 1600 until revived (perhaps after UNWEETING . . .) c 1800'. By the time of the RV (1885), it had once again become thoroughly acceptable. The RV once changes 'unwittingly' to 'unawares' (Josh. 20: 5), once reverses the two words, and thirteen times uses 'unwittingly' where the KJB has 'ignorance' or 'unawares'. 'Unwittingly', then, shows that a word could be archaic in the eighteenth century yet current in the nineteenth. It also shows that Purver and Pilkington's evidence is sound enough to bring this to light.

I have given 'unwittingly' first because of the clarity of the *OED*'s evidence. The remaining examples are a few particularly interesting words which seem to have become obsolete and then been revived primarily through their use in the KJB. The first two are words which probably owe much to famous contexts in the KJB, 'ponder' and 'heritage'.

'Ponder', for which Purver gives 'consider', may have survived or revived through one famous verse: 'but Mary kept all these things and pondered them in her heart' (Luke 2: 19; the translation is Tyndale's). The *OED* has among many examples only one from the eighteenth century, from Cowper, 1791. The revival was probably helped by a mid-nineteenth-century hymn, 'Ponder anew / What the Almighty can do' (*Hymns Ancient and Modern*, 382).

'Heritage' is only used twice by Shakespeare but comes thirty times in the KJB. Alexander Geddes, a translator and critic we will meet several times, classes it among 'words and phrases which, though obsolete in common use, are still intelligible to one acquainted with the scripture style'.[8] The *OED*'s only example between 1639 and 1810 is from John Wesley's translation of the Psalms (1738) and is clearly biblical. Yet the word was familiar enough in the nineteenth century. One verse makes clear how dominant the KJB could be both as a source and a preserver of language: 'lo, children are an heritage of the Lord: and the fruit of the womb is his reward' (Ps. 127: 3). The sentiment and the wording, especially the Hebraism 'fruit of the womb', have made this ring in the English language.

'Eschewed' is a curious variation on this type of example. Purver gives 'refrained from'. The KJB gives it, in various forms, only four times, Shakespeare uses it only once in one of his obscurer plays (*Merry Wives* 5: 5: 237), and Johnson calls it 'a word almost obsolete'. The *OED* quotes this from Johnson but adds, 'it is now not uncommon in literary usage'. George Campbell, another to give examples of peculiarities of vocabulary in the KJB, lists 'eschew' among 'words totally unsupported by present use . . . Terms such as some of these, like old vessels, are, I may say, so buried in rust as to render it difficult to discover their use.'[9] In this case it is Coverdale's use of it in the PB Psalter that seems to be crucial: 'eschew evil and do good' (Ps. 34: 14). The KJB echoes this in its usages (especially 1 Pet. 3: 11), yet it alters the words I have just quoted to 'Depart from evil . . .'. This suggests that 'eschew' was of dubious currency by 1611. Nevertheless, this is a clear case of a word rescued from obsolescence, but probably, this time, by the PB.

It may be that sometimes this kind of evidence exists without showing that the KJB was a cause of revival. 'Warfare', for which Purver has 'war', appears from the *OED* to have been extensively used in the fifteenth and sixteenth centuries and then to have revived in the mid-nineteenth.[10] Shakespeare, though war figures so much in his plays, does not use it. The KJB has it five times, once only going back to Tyndale and once to Coverdale; twice it sounds modern without going back to

---

[8] *A Letter to the Right Reverend the Lord Bishop of London [Robert Lowth] containing queries, doubts and difficulties relative to a vernacular version of the Holy Scriptures* (London, 1787), p. 2. The other words he gives are worth noting as being mostly words we would not consider obsolete: 'ambushment', 'meet', 'wroth', 'banquet', 'banner', 'bereave', 'bewail', 'portray', 'discomfit', 'marvel', 'obeisance' and 'progenitors'. Some of his contemporaries thought he went too far: *The Monthly Review*, for instance, objected that 'banquet', 'banner', 'bewail', 'portray' and 'progenitors' 'are still in very frequent use' (new series, 1 [Jan. 1790], 56).

[9] *The Four Gospels*, 2 vols. (London, 1789), I: 579.

[10] Symonds includes this in a brief list of words that Purver should not have objected to (*Observations*, p. 100).

either of them: 'the Philistines gathered their armies together for warfare' (1 Sam. 28: 1), and 'cry unto [Jerusalem] that her warfare is accomplished' (Isa. 40: 2). Are these strong enough contexts to preserve the word? Johnson's evidence suggests that 'warfare' was preserved within the general context of religion as four of his five examples are religious. Is the KJB here merely *reflecting* the survival of a now-common word in a religious context?

'Changes' or 'change', which Purver would alter to 'suits' in phrases such as 'changes of raiment' (Gen. 45: 22 etc.), suggests another possibility. 'Change' in this sense the *OED* records first from Greene in 1592. It then gives two Biblical examples before jumping to 1815, and it records 'a change of clothes' first in 1876. Johnson seems barely familiar with this meaning, his closest definition being 'that which makes a variety; that which may be used for another of the same kind', and he quotes 'thirty change of garments' from Judg. 14: 12, 13, which is modern in meaning. Shakespeare four times uses 'change' with a word for clothing, but each time as a verb. Does 'change' in this Biblical sense enter the language as a Hebraism (the phrase in fact goes back past Greene to Tyndale), or has the Bible just by chance picked up a stray usage from its period and happened to anticipate modern usage?

Lastly, 'avenge' is one of the words which Purver would argue lacked 'the currency requisite' even in 1611, since the only examples Johnson has are Biblical. Purver would amend it to 'revenge'. Johnson suggests that 'avenger' was a little more widely used. The *OED* has nothing between Milton and Sheridan (1799) bar the phrase 'the avenger of so many treasons' in the controversial divine, Conyers Middleton (1741), but shows a clear history back to Langland and Wyclif. In the immediate history of the KJB, 'avenge' goes back to Tyndale, and it is only the linguistically independent Rheims-Douai version that uses 'revenge' ('avenger' is perhaps less old, since Tyndale does not use it; biblically, it originates with Coverdale). Now, especially in the form 'avenger', the word is quite familiar. The KJB uses 'avenge' and variants 46 times, 'revenge' only 18. With Shakespeare the position is drastically reversed: he uses 'avenge' and its variants six times, 'revenge' 237 times. 'Avenge' therefore does seem to have faded even before 1611, but the KJB has kept it alive not only by the frequency of its use but also by its use in memorable verses: 'out of the mouth of babes and sucklings hast thou ordained strength because of thine enemies, that thou mightest still the enemy and the avenger' (Ps. 8: 2), and 'how long, O Lord . . . dost thou not judge and avenge our blood?' (Rev. 6: 10).

These few examples can only suggest the case that some words and phrases faded from use about the beginning of the seventeenth century, and then reappeared early in the nineteenth, and that the KJB caused some of these reappearances, acting as a kind of uncrowded Noah's ark for vocabulary for perhaps two hundred years. Beyond this specific case about the history of vocabulary, Purver and his fellow critics show that in their time the language of the KJB appeared more objectionable than it has since. Their standards did not accommodate the standards of the KJB.

Revision gets a bad name

Purver is most interesting in revealing the objections to the KJB: other translators give a better sense of what these late-Augustans thought might be appropriate language for the English Bible as a rendering of originals that they now knew were literary. Most extreme is the much-mocked dissenting minister, classicist and biblical critic, Edward Harwood (1729–94). His intentions in his 'ridiculous work',[11] *A Liberal Translation of the New Testament* (1768), are

> to exhibit before the candid, the unprejudiced and the intelligent of all parties, the true, original, divine form of Christianity in its beautiful simplicity, divested of all meretricious attire with which it hath been loaded, and solely adorned with its native elegance and charms, which need only be contemplated in order to excite the imagination, transport and love of every ingenuous and virtuous bosom. (p. viii)[12]

Truth matters – and elsewhere (p. iv) Harwood writes of how hard he worked to discover it – but the emphasis is on literary qualities that will affect the reader. This is the furthest an English prose translator has moved from the tradition of literal translation without ceasing to think of himself as a translator. Harwood treats the NT as a Greek classic and aims not only to reproduce the elegance of the original but 'to translate the sacred writers of the NT with the same freedom, impartiality and elegance with which other translations from the Greek classics have lately been executed' (p. iii). So his idea of a faithful translation, which he freely admits is 'liberal and diffusive' and serves as 'explanatory para-phrase' as well as translation (pp. iii–iv), is to 'clothe the genuine ideas and doctrines of the apostles with that propriety and perspicuity in

---

[11] *Boswell: The Ominous Years: 1774–1776*, ed. Charles Ryskamp and Frederick J. Pottle (London: Heinemann, 1963), p. 333.   [12] All quotations are from volume 1.

which they themselves, I apprehend, would have exhibited them had they *now* lived and written in our language' (p. iii). The result of this thoroughly un-Lowthian aim is the greatest loading of the 'meretricious attire' that he claimed to be removing ever seen in an English prose Testament.

This is his conception of how Jesus, following the best contemporary standards, would have spoken in the 1760s:

Survey with attention the lilies of the field, and learn from them how unbecoming it is for rational creatures to cherish a solicitous passion for gaiety and dress – for they sustain no labour, they employ no cares to adorn themselves, and yet are clothed with such inimitable beauty as the richest monarch in the richest dress never equalled. (Matt. 6: 28–9)

If this is how the untalented thought the Bible should sound, it is no wonder that the KJB appeared 'bald and barbarous' (p. v).

Purver and Harwood represent the peak of the reaction against the KJB. They also contain within themselves signs of why the attitudes they represent were soon to pass. Purver noted the growing sense that the KJB's language was the appropriate English for the Bible. Harwood goes further, declaring himself 'conscious that the bald and barbarous language of the old vulgar version hath acquired a venerable sacredness from length of time and custom' (p. v). This pinpoints the clash between the developed standards of the late Augustans and the force of popular feeling which was to do so much to reverse critical attitudes to the KJB's language. Looking to be kings of the earth, the bloated Harwood and the many-toothed Purver stand like dinosaurs at the end of an era, authentic specimens, but grotesque and sterile. They may even have contributed to the demise of the attitudes they represent by showing how unlikely a derivative idea of cultivated taste was to produce acceptable results. Harwood, by reducing taste to absurdity, and Purver, by multiplying examples to excess, helped the literati to revalue the KJB's English along lines that matched both the implications of Lowth's movement towards a positive sense of uncouth and harsh language, and, still more importantly, the growing popular feeling for the KJB.

Certainly there was such a revaluation. It coincides with the change in taste neatly captured by Oliver Goldsmith in *The Vicar of Wakefield* (1766). An actor tells the Vicar, '"Dryden and Rowe's manner, Sir, are quite out of fashion; our taste has gone back a whole century, Fletcher, Ben Jonson, and all the plays of Shakespeare are the only things that go down."' The Vicar's puzzled response articulates the passing age:

"'How", cried I, "is it possible the present age can be pleased with that antiquated dialect, that obsolete humour, those overcharged characters, which abound in the works you mention?'" (ch. 18). The changing tone of reviews of translations suggests how the translators themselves helped to effect this change. In 1764 Richard Wynne (?1718–99) published an NT. His chief concern was to relieve the confusion caused by the chapter and verse divisions, and he intended to copy the KJB verbatim:

but, on comparing that version carefully with the original (though it is a good translation upon the whole), I thought it requisite to deviate from it sometimes, and frequently to alter the language. For some of the words and phrases, familiar to our ancestors, are now grown so obsolete as not to be intelligible to the generality of readers: others are too mean, equivocal or inadequate to the original, which perhaps is owing to the fluctuating state of our language; and some passages are not so exactly rendered by our translators as a work of that kind required. In all these cases I made no scruple of differing from our public translation, endeavouring at the same time to steer in a just medium between a servile literal translation and a paraphrastic loose version; between low, obsolete and obscure language, and a modern enervated style.[13]

There is nothing here that is not found in Purver and Harwood except moderation, and the result is not too far different from the KJB. *The Critical Review* was sympathetic, like Wynne damning the KJB with faint praise, then encouraging further effort to produce 'an accurate and elegant translation':

These divine writings should be translated with accuracy and spirit. Our common version is, indeed, a valuable work, and deserves the highest esteem, but it is by no means free from imperfections. It certainly contains many false interpretations, ambiguous phrases, obsolete words and indelicate expressions which deform the beauty of the sacred pages, perplex the unlearned reader, offend the fastidious ear, confirm the prejudices of the unbeliever and excite the derision of the scorner. An accurate and elegant translation would therefore be of infinite service to religion, would obviate a thousand difficulties and exceptions, prevent a multitude of chimerical tenets and controversial questions, give a proper dignity and lustre to divine revelation, and convince the world that whatever appears confused, coarse or ridiculous in the Holy Scriptures ought to be imputed to the translator. (18 (Sept. 1764), 189)

Clearly Wynne had not gone far enough to satisfy or explode the desire for elegance, so the reviewer looks *for* a new version rather than *to* the old version.

The response in *The Monthly Review* was similar:

---

[13] *The New Testament*, 2 vols. (London, 1764), I: xii–xiii.

We look upon every attempt to improve and render perfect the translation of the New Testament to be of so much importance to the progress of true religion and to the honour of genuine Christianity that we are disposed to receive every work of this kind with the greatest candour: and it is with peculiar satisfaction and pleasure . . . that we see so many of our clergy directing their studies and attention this way. (31 (Dec. 1764), 406)

Reviews of Purver followed within months in each journal, and thereafter the notes of optimism about new versions and lack of interest in the KJB vanish. The nearest the former came to reviving was when *The Monthly Review* looked back to Lowth's *Isaiah* in 1784 and commented that it had removed 'many prejudices which persons of scrupulous minds had conceived against a general revision of the present translation of the Bible' (71 (Sept. 1784), 161). It seems probable that these prejudices were the product not just of popular feeling, which the review discusses candidly, but of failed attempts giving new versions a bad name.

If there is something like a volte-face here, three years later the more outspoken *Critical Review* seems to have undergone a conversion like Saul on the road to Damascus. Reviewing Geddes's *Proposal*, it claims that 'to reform the text of the Bible would have appeared to the ignorant little less than a change of a national religion' (63 (Jan. 1787) 46). What makes this startling is that the reviewer shares the feeling of 'the ignorant'. The literati and the people come together in a passage of unprecedented warmth:

[The KJB's] faults are said to be a defect in the idiom, as English . . . The defect in idiom we cannot allow to be a fault: it raised the language above common use and has almost sanctified it; nor would we lose the noble simplicity, the energetic bravery, for all the idiomatic elegance which a polished age can bestow. Dr Geddes objects to a translation too literal, but we wish not to see the present text changed unless where real errors render it necessary. The venerable tree which we have always regarded with a religious respect cannot be pruned to modern fashions without our feeling the most poignant regret. Our attachment to this venerable relic has involuntarily made our language warm. (p. 48)

Still a contrast is maintained between the standards of the KJB and the elegance of a polished age, but the judgement between the two has shifted decisively. Instead of the achievement of a literary Bible being looked forward to, now the KJB is looked back to as the literary standard. The KJB is not merely a relic but a 'venerable relic' that has beneficially influenced the language. Its age is still recognised but no longer disliked. Critical opinion has followed the people, like Wenceslas's page, treading in warm footsteps.

CHAPTER ELEVEN

The critical rise of the King James Bible

THE INFLUENCE OF POPULAR FEELING

What we have just seen from *The Critical Review* is a reminder of just how important popular feeling was in shaping critical opinion. Ever since Tyndale set out to give the Bible to the ploughboy, there had been an association between the English Bible and the ill-educated: literacy and Bible-reading went hand in hand, as in the stories of William Maldon or of Defoe's Somerset schoolboy (see above, pp. 10 and 214). The kind of simple love and faith such as Bishop Patrick's maid had shown for the singing Psalms (see above, p. 124) were common responses to the Bible. One Josiah Langdale, born in 1673, recalls that 'I had not time for much schooling . . . yet I made a little progress in Latin, but soon forgot it; I endeavoured, however, to keep my English, and could read the Bible and delighted therein.'[1] Such comments have a representative value, as does this recollection of the 'domestic interiors of the husbandmen or farmers' in the Lothians in the 1760s: 'no book was so familiar to them as the Scriptures; they could almost tell the place of any particular passage, where situated in their own family Bible, without referring to either book, chapter or verse; and where any similar one was situated'.[2]

From the 1760s on such intense and widespread feeling and familiarity among the less educated played an important role in the rise of admiration for the KJB among the intelligentsia. In spite of their wider reading and their education in Augustan standards, they were catching up with the people. Though they might maintain a distance from their new opinion by attributing it to the people, which is what the *Critical Review* seems to have been doing in its remarks on Geddes's *Proposal*, they were being genuinely influenced, and reference to popular opinion became a common stepping-stone for their arguments.

[1] Margaret Spufford, *Small Books and Pleasant Histories* (London: Methuen, 1981), p. 30.
[2] George Robertson, *Rural Recollections* (1829), as given in Spufford, p. 47. The same picture is given, more fully and vividly, in Burns's 'The Cotter's Saturday Night' (1785), lines 100–53.

The cleric and critic Vicesimus Knox (1752–1821) shows this in his youthful *Essays, Moral and Literary* (1778). In his essay 'On simplicity of style in prosaic composition', he reports the post-Longinian view that 'the Bible, the Iliad and Shakespeare's works are allowed to be the sublimest books that the world can exhibit. They are also truly simple' (p. 85). At once this suggests that he will be that most useful sort of literary critic, the representative rather than the original. Then, in his essay 'On the best method of exciting literary genius in boys who possess it', he suggests that the Bible is one of the books most suitable for exciting this genius 'if a little care were taken by the superintendents of education, to select those parts which are so beautifully distinguished for simple sublimity and unaffected pathos',[3] and he adds, 'the poetry of the Bible contributed much to the sublimity of Milton' (p. 356). Whether or not he really means these remarks to refer to the KJB, in practice there is no other version they could refer to; it is only when he writes 'On the impropriety of publicly adopting a new translation of the Bible', that he deals explicitly with the KJB. He believes its antiquity is a greater source of strength than any correction of its inaccuracies would be (p. 266), and is thus an early, if not the first, champion of its literary virtues against its scholarly defects: 'I cannot help thinking', he writes, 'that the present translation ought to be retained in our churches for its intrinsic beauty and excellence' (p. 267). This is where popular feeling becomes an important part of the argument. He freely associates himself with 'the middle and lower ranks' in reporting:

We have received the Bible in the very words in which it now stands from our fathers; we have learned many passages of it by heart in our infancy; we find it quoted in sermons from the earliest to the latest times, so that its phrase is become familiar to our ear, and we cease to be startled at apparent difficulties. Let all this be called prejudice, but it is a prejudice which universally prevails in the middle and lower ranks, and we should hardly recognise the Bible were it to be read in our churches in any other words than those which our fathers have heard before us. (p. 267)

---

[3] There were other, more direct attempts to encourage the youth of England to take a literary delight in the Scriptures, most notably by the blue stocking Hannah More (1745–1833), whose *Sacred Dramas, chiefly intended for young persons* (1782) is made up of blank verse playlets on OT subjects and has a verse introduction eulogising the Bible as literature and appealing directly to the taste of the young. Young women were also encouraged to develop their taste from the Bible. Mary Wollstonecraft's anthology, *The Female Reader* (1789), contains a large number of passages from the KJB. Wollstonecraft writes, 'the main object of this work is to imprint some useful lessons on the mind, and cultivate the taste at the same time – to infuse a relish for a pure and simple style, by presenting natural and touching descriptions from the Scriptures, Shakespeare, etc. Simplicity and sincerity generally go hand in hand, as both proceed from the love of truth' (facsimile, intro. Moira Ferguson (Delmar, N.Y.: Scholars' Facsimiles, 1980), p. iv).

Though Knox was still in his twenties when he wrote this, it has an element of conservatism that might remind us of that champion of the old and the popular, William Beveridge.

There is another element here that is perhaps less conservative, for the appeal to popular sentiment goes along with a certain aestheticism: familiarity and beauty seem scarcely distinguishable in Knox's thinking, and he values them more than truth or clarity, an almost novel opinion (it might remind us of Gregory Martin's argument for preserving some of the vocabulary of the Vulgate, given above, p. 45) which has yet maintained its vitality to the present day and which is completely at odds with the minute concern for accuracy so characteristic of biblical translation and criticism even by such aesthetically sensitive men as Lowth. Knox declares roundly:

The poetical passages of Scripture are peculiarly pleasing in the present translation. The language, though it is simple and natural, is rich and expressive. Solomon's Song, difficult as it is to be interpreted, may be read with delight, even if we attend to little else but the brilliancy of the diction; and it is a circumstance which increases its grace that it appears to be quite unstudied. The Psalms, as well as the whole Bible, are literally translated, and yet the translation abounds with passages exquisitely beautiful. Even where the sense is not very clear nor the connection of ideas obvious at first sight, the mind is soothed and the ear ravished with the powerful yet unaffected charms of the style. (p. 268)

This unashamed popular aestheticism leads him to conclude that there is a kind of divine providence in the beauty of the KJB – he is very close to claiming that it is divinely inspired: 'it is our duty to inspect it, and it is graciously so ordered that our duty in this instance may be a pleasure, for the Bible is truly pleasing considered only as a collection of very ancient and curious history and poetry' (p. 269).

Taken at large, Knox is doing no more than restating old ideas of the literary quality of the Bible, but in detail there are two things that are very striking and very expressive of the 1770s. First, the idea of the Bible's literary quality is specifically an idea of the KJB's quality. He may have started off in terms vague enough to allow a scholarly reader to think he was doing the right thing and writing of the quality of the originals, but it rapidly becomes clear that for him the Bible is the KJB. There is a sharp contrast with Temple and his echoers in that they felt similar pleasure in translations but retained a sharp sense of their weaknesses: no 'all the disadvantages of an old prose translation' for Knox, as he seems to forget that the KJB is a translation and is not in the least bothered that it is in prose. Secondly, he reaches his conclusions about the quality of the Bible on a basis Lowth used, his own love for it. The conclusions are much the same as those reached by the argument from divine inspiration to literary perfection, but where Lowth bolstered his views with ample critical demonstration, Knox is content to rest on his and the people's love. This is hardly as persuasive as Lowth. Even so, to argue, or, more accurately, assert from experience is more effective than the hypothetical argument. Popular feeling has helped to reshape the old desire to believe that the Bible is the perfection of eloquence.

LOWTH AND THE ENGLISH BIBLE

It is difficult to imagine the understanding of Hebrew poetry developing as it did without Robert Lowth. He was also a major figure in the progress of English attitudes to the KJB but there is every likelihood these attitudes would have developed in the same way had he not existed. Rather than originating opinion in this area, he picked up things already in the air and gave them the weight of his own authority and prestige. Some of his opinions were more than just in the air. For instance, his judgement that 'the vulgar translation of the Bible . . . is the best standard of our language' (*Short Introduction*, p. 62) simply makes absolute the tendency of Swift's observation that the KJB and the PB 'have proved a kind of standard of language' (see above, p. 211). The effect of such authoritative repetition was to establish the opinion. In 1774 James Burnet, Lord Monboddo, repeated it in his voluminous *Of the Origin and Progress of Language*: 'the translators of our Bible, though . . . they may not have perfectly understood the original, did certainly understand their language very well; and accordingly I hold the English Bible to be the best standard of the English language we have at this day'.[4] Five years later the public could read this from Joseph White, Laudian professor of Arabic etc.:

The English language acquired new dignity by it, and has hardly acquired additional purity since: it is still considered as a standard of our tongue. If a new version should ever be attempted, the same turn of expression will doubtless be employed, for it is a style consecrated not more by custom than by its own native propriety. (*A Revisal*, p. 9)

At the end of the century the reactionary George Burges favoured the public with much the same view:

---

[4] 6 vols. (Edinburgh, 1773–92), II: 141.

The merit of our present received version . . . is sufficiently apparent from the universal and almost enthusiastic respect in which it has long been held by all ranks of people among us. The English Bible . . . may be justly held up, even in these polished times, as the purest standard of the English language and the best criterion of sound and classical composition. (*A Letter*, p. 9)

Only one critic took Lowth to task for this opinion, John Symonds, yet his opening remark confirms how far it had become a commonplace by 1789. 'It will be proper', he notes, 'to inquire into the grounds of an opinion which passes among some persons for an undoubted truth, namely, that the vulgar translation of the Bible is the best standard of the English language' (*Observations*, pp. 6–7). He is willing to accept that it may be a standard for the use of English words 'in preference to those of a foreign growth' (p. 7), but distinguishes between being a standard and being the best standard. He turns Lowth against himself by noting how many corrections he has made of the KJB's grammar in his *Short Introduction*, which is full of examples from the KJB, impartially using it as a model and pointing out some faults, vulgarities and obsolescences. Moreover, even as Lowth makes his observation about the KJB as the best standard, he notes corruptions in its English. Symonds has good reason to question the basis of the 'undoubted truth', but his protest was as ineffectual as the pleas of reason usually are against an idea whose time has come.

Some of Lowth's opinions develop from the less clearly expressed ideas of others. The new criticism of the KJB and the calls for revision had quickly produced defenders. Among the first was the dissenting minister and Hebrew lexicographer, John Taylor (1694–1761). He defends the KJB against criticism of its accuracy on the Beveridgean ground that it is the established translation: one may and should go to the originals for their exact meaning, but the KJB does not need revising:

In above the space of an hundred years, learning may have received considerable improvements, and by that means, some inaccuracies may be found in a translation more than a hundred years old. But you may rest fully satisfied that as our English translation is in itself by far the most excellent book in our language, so it is a pure and plentiful fountain of divine knowledge.[5]

All Taylor is really saying is that, as he puts it, 'whoever studies the Bible, the English Bible, is sure of gaining that knowledge and faith, which, if duly applied to the heart and conversation, will infallibly guide him to

[5] *A Scheme of Scripture-Divinity . . . With a Vindication of the Sacred Writings* (1762); in Watson, ed., *Tracts*, 1: 4–219; p. 188.

eternal life' (p. 188), which is hardly an original position. Nevertheless, his vagueness has led him to imply that, as literature, the Bible is 'the most excellent book in our language'. That there are aesthetic criteria involved is suggested by another vague claim, that 'the language of Nature is most certainly the language of God, the sole author of Nature' (p. 5). He too comes close to the notion of the divine inspiration of the English translation.

Lowth, who seems to have developed his particular attitude to the KJB in the 1760s, clarified the implications of such woolliness, leading the opinion that resulted in the RV being a revision which sought to maintain the style of its predecessor while improving its accuracy. On the one hand as a cleric he believed that more progress had been made in the knowledge of the Scriptures in the 150 years since the publication of the KJB than in the fifteen centuries preceding. He therefore advocated 'an accurate revisal of our vulgar translation by public authority' in order

to confirm and illustrate the Holy Scriptures, to evince their truth, to show their consistency, to explain their meaning, to make them more generally known and studied, more easily and perfectly understood by all; to remove the difficulties that discourage the honest endeavours of the unlearned, and provoke the malicious cavils of the half-learned.[6]

On the other hand, as a literary man he developed Taylor's feeling, combining literary judgement with evidence of, and appeal to, popular taste. Defending the closeness with which he has followed the language of the KJB in his *Isaiah*, he observes that 'the style of [that] translation is not only excellent in itself, but has taken possession of our ear, and of our taste'. A revision is therefore more advisable than a new translation, 'for as to the style and language, it admits but of little improvement; but in respect of the sense and the accuracy of interpretation, the improvements of which it is capable are great and numberless' (pp. lviii–lix). This, by the end of the century, was to be the dominant opinion.

MYTHS ARISE

Suggestions of two myths about the KJB have already been seen, that the translators were divinely inspired, and that it was a literary revision. While the first of these develops little for the time being, a period so

---

[6] Visitation Sermon at Durham, 1758; *Sermons and Other Remains of Robert Lowth*, ed. Peter Hall (London, 1834), p. 85.

concerned with translation was fertile ground for the second myth, and it will be as well to show this before going on. I call the idea that the KJB was a literary revision a myth because, in the form that Pilkington gives it (see above, p. 230), it has little to do with the facts. Yet this is not to say that all versions of the idea are mythical, only those expressions of it which forget just how much the work of the translators was dominated by the demands of scholarship and the care to keep as close as possible to the words and structure of the originals. Now that the KJB was admired as English, it was difficult not to argue backwards from a perception of achievement to a belief in conscious artistry: the translators, it seems, must have engaged in literary rubbing and polishing of the sort that was such a priority with some of the later eighteenth-century translators. Clement Cruttwell, for instance, comments that

More than common care seems to have been taken by Miles Coverdale in the language of his translation: we have some, but they are very few, instances of barbarism, and none which are not authorised by the writers of the times in which he wrote. To him and other translators of the Scriptures, especially of the present Bible by the authority of King James, our language owes perhaps more than to all the authors who have written since . . . they preserve their ancient simplicity pure and undefiled, and in their circumstance and connection perhaps but seldom could be exchanged for the better.[7]

Earlier Hugh Blair had helped to spread such ideas by remarking in his well-known lectures 'that our translators . . . have often been happy in suiting their numbers to the subject'.[8] This envisages deliberate attention to prose rhythm, yet, whatever the KJB translators achieved, there is no explicit evidence that they applied such consideration to their work. Nor, indeed, is there any evidence in the Bible translations that such consciousness produces better prose than the constraints under which the KJB translators worked. So much of beauty lies in the accustomed eye of the beholder.

A third myth sprang up just as easily, that the KJB was an immediate success. Joseph White, one of our echoers of the commonplace about the KJB being the 'standard of our tongue', seems to have been the first to put forward this tenacious notion, observing simply that 'it was a happy consequence of this acknowledged excellence [of the KJB] that the other versions fell immediately into disrepute, are no longer known to the generality of the people, and are only sought after by the curious' (*A Revisal*, p. 9). Now, when the KJB was first offered to the public, the

---

[7] *The Holy Bible . . . with notes by Thomas Wilson*, 3 vols. (Bath, 1785), fol. A1v.
[8] *Lectures in Rhetoric and Belles Lettres*, xiii; intro. Thomas Dale (London, 1853), p. 148.

translators were well aware of the truth that 'he that meddleth with men's religion in any part meddleth with their custom, nay, with their freehold' (preface, p. 2). With prescient pessimism, they anticipated a very different reception from that accorded them by this myth: 'was there ever any thing projected that savoured any way of newness or renewing, but the same endured many a storm of gainsaying and opposition?' (p. 1). If there is irony in this contrast, there is more irony when another expression of the myth comes in context of the same pessimism about the reception of a new version. Geddes laments that

He who undertakes a new translation of the Sacred Scriptures lies under disadvantages, in any country, which no other translator has to encounter, and there are circumstances which make them lie peculiarly heavy on an English translator. The idea that has for almost two centuries prevailed of the superexcellence of our public version is alone an almost insuperable difficulty. Mankind are naturally unwilling to see, and ashamed to acknowledge, not only their own faults but even the faults of those whom, from their earliest years, they have been taught to admire and revere. James's translators have been so long in possession of so high a reputation, and their work has been considered as such a pattern of perfection, that the smallest deviation from their standard is by many deemed a species of literary felony which admits not of benefit of clergy.[9]

The bases for such remarks are palpably simple. First, it is a happy reinforcement of an opinion to believe that it has always been held – here it would detract from either the KJB or the English people if *it* had not been an instant success or if *they* had not recognised it as such. Second, in ignorance of the historical evidence, White and Geddes have generalised backwards from the present dominance of the KJB and ideas of its quality. What has been true for twenty or thirty years can easily be thought to have been true 'for almost two centuries'. So myths arise out of opinion and desire; in due course they influence opinion further and reinforce the desire to attribute perfection to what was once seen as a very human and distinctly imperfect production.

GEORGE CAMPBELL AND THE KJB AS A LITERARY EXAMPLE

As Lowth used the KJB in discussions of the English language, so others used it in literary discussion. The most important of these was a theologian, educator, Bible critic and translator, and a leading figure in what is usually called 'the Scottish enlightenment', George Campbell (1719–96).

---

[9] *General Answer to the Queries, Counsels and Criticisms that have been communicated to him since the publication of his proposals for printing a new translation of the Bible* (London, 1790), pp. 1–2.

From our point of view, it is the frequency, thoroughness and intelligence with which he uses the KJB in *The Philosophy of Rhetoric* (1776) that distinguishes him. He habitually (and, for one part of his argument, exclusively) turns to the KJB for examples. This is in spite of his interest being in 'reputable, national, and present' uses of English (p. 151), which he defines primarily in terms of English Augustan prose writers, and a rather wider range of poets. He is concerned 'that there may be no suspicion that the style is superannuated' (pp. 150–1) in the writers he chooses, but exempts 'the vulgar translation of the Bible' because 'the continuance and universality of its use throughout the British dominions affords an obvious reason for the exception' (p. 151). This takes the KJB as a standard for language (though not as a model of contemporary English) on the sound basis of its achieved popular position, so establishing Campbell as a critic who acted on Lowth's commonplace.

The following is representative of the quality of Campbell's practical criticism:

The third example shall be of an active verb preceded by the accusative and followed by the nominative . . . we are informed by the sacred historian that when Peter and John ordered the cripple who sat begging at the beautiful gate of the temple to look on them, he looked at them very earnestly, expecting to receive something from them. Then Peter said, 'Silver and gold have I none, but such as I have, give I thee; in the name of Jesus Christ of Nazareth, arise and walk' [Acts 3: 6]. Here the wishful look and expectation of the beggar naturally leads to a vivid conception of that which was the object of his thoughts, and this conception as naturally displays itself in the very form of the declaration made by the apostle. But as everything is best judged by comparison, let us contrast with this the same sentence arranged according to the rigid rules of grammar, which render it almost a literal translation of the Italian and French versions quoted in the margin, 'I have no gold and silver; but I give thee that which I have: in the name of –' The import is the same, but the expression is rendered quite exanimate. Yet the sentences differ chiefly in arrangement, the other difference in composition is inconsiderable.

There is another happy transposition in the English version of the passage under view which, though peculiar to our version, deserves our notice, as it contributes not a little to the energy of the whole. I mean not only the separation of the adjective 'none' from its substantives 'silver' and 'gold', but the placing of it in the end of the clause which, as it were, rests upon it. 'Silver and gold have I *none*.' For here, as in several other instances, the next place to the first, in respect of emphasis, is the last. We shall be more sensible of this by making a very small alteration in the composition and structure of the sentence, and saying, 'Silver and gold are not in my possession,' which is manifestly weaker. (pp. 358–9)

Campbell has drawn out the special quality in the order of the words that makes them creators of more than they are saying. This he calls 'the energy of the whole', and it is common in his work for him to illustrate this energy by comparison with other possible renderings. His ability to push beyond his particular point and note also the force of 'have I none' is particularly striking because he presents it as 'a happy transposition peculiar to our version'. Such awareness of a unique literary quality in the KJB, implicitly an improvement on the Greek, could be used as evidence of literary intention and taste on the part of the translators. He characteristically does not draw such a conclusion; nor does he conclude that what he shows proclaims the literary quality of the KJB,[10] but his readers might easily reach both conclusions. Without saying so, he is helping to build the conviction that the KJB was a masterpiece of English literature.

The remarks on the English refer only to the KJB: for all Campbell's knowledge of translations in other languages, he shows no awareness of older English translations. He implies that 'have I none' was the creation of the KJB translators, whereas it is Tyndale's. A knowledge of the other translations could have strengthened his final point, for it would have been more instructive to have Gregory Martin's 'silver and gold I have not' in place of his invented alternative, 'silver and gold are not in my possession'.

Campbell's work is striking in its use of the KJB as a major source of examples for discussion both of literary effects and English literary and grammatical usage, in the quality of the demonstrations of these literary effects and in the treatment of the KJB as a literary text without prejudice against either the NT or the prose parts of the OT. Though *The Philosophy of Rhetoric* is not specifically about the KJB, it contributes importantly to the eighteenth-century literary understanding of the KJB.

THE KJB IN LITERARY DISCUSSIONS OF THE BIBLE

The movement towards increased use and increased accuracy of use of the KJB in general literary discussion is also to be found in literary discussions of the originals. Though the scrupulous and scholarly Lowth leaves his reader in no doubt that his subject is the originals, most other critics use the KJB with a minimal sense that it is a translation. For

---

[10] By no means all of his examples are favourable to the KJB. Like Lowth in *A Short Introduction*, he is as ready to observe faults in it as he is to observe strengths, e.g. pp. 189 and 210.

instance, in the 1750s English readers might have been forgiven for think-ing that Longinus had been reading the KJB, for he brings together a substantial catalogue of beauties from the KJB and PB that have con-vinced him not only of the frequent superiority of the KJB to the Greek classics but also of its divine inspiration. Longinus confesses that he is

greatly astonished at the incomparable elevation of its style and the supreme grandeur of its images, many of which excel the utmost efforts of the most exalted genius of Greece.
   . . . With what majesty and magnificence is the Creator of the world . . . intro-duced making the following sublime inquiry! 'Who hath measured the waters in the hollow of his hand, and meted out heaven with a span, and compre-hended the dust of the earth in a measure, and weighed the mountains in scales, and the hills in a balance?' [Isa. 40: 12]. Produce me, Terentianus, any image or description in Plato himself so truly elevated and divine! Where did these bar-barians learn to speak of God in terms that alone appear worthy of him? How contemptible and vile are the deities of Homer and Hesiod in comparison of this Jehovah of the illiterate Jews! before whom, to use this poet's own words, all other gods are 'as a drop of a bucket, and are counted as the small dust of the balance' [Isa. 40: 15].

Longinus has clearly not just undergone a critical conversion but has learnt the Augustan trick of exclamatory criticism; he has also read the OT closely and found a great deal to admire, not only in the imagery, especially the personification (which 'may be justly esteemed one of the greatest efforts of the creative power of a warm and lively imagination'), but also in the narrative of Joseph's story and in the picture presented in Job.
   This Longinus is the creation of the critic Joseph Warton (1722–1800) in the *Adventurer*, 51 and 53.[11] Warton pretends that a new manuscript of Longinus has been found in which Longinus comes across the Septuagint and then writes in the vein we have seen. Apart from this opening reference, there is nothing to suggest that the subject of 'Longinus's' praise is anything other than the KJB or the PB except that they are not always accurately quoted; so, where the careless reader would take 'Longinus' to be lauding the KJB, the careful reader would think not of the originals – or the Septuagint – but of Warton praising what the English reader can find in the English Bible without absolutely committing himself to the qualities of the translation. In either case attention to the originals has dwindled and there is little to suggest that the literary Bible is not the KJB.

---

[11] May 1 and 22, 1753; in *The British Essayists*, ed. Lionel Thomas Berguer, 45 vols. (London, 1823), XXIV: 50–6, 86–92. The passage given above is from pp. 51–2.

The implication is the same in two other discussions of the Bible as literature from the 1770s, the first of which has special significance less through its intrinsic merits than through being the first American discussion of the subject, 'A dissertation on the history, eloquence and poetry of the Bible' (1772) by the twenty-year-old Timothy Dwight (1752–1817) on the occasion of his taking his master's degree at Yale. Dwight, as others before and since, thought his subject had 'novelty to recommend it', for no one had ever attempted to entertain the Yale audience by 'displaying the excellencies' of the Bible as 'fine writing' (p. 3). In the local context who would wish to deny the youth his claim of originality? Not only was his 'Dissertation' an American first, but, for so young an author, it reveals a considerable confidence and flair in the choice of examples for admiration. For instance, building on Longinus's supposed opinion of Paul's excellence as an orator, he sets Paul against the classical orators and himself against the classicists who hear him 'boldly, unconcernedly prefer St Paul's address to Agrippa [Acts 26: 2–27] for himself before Cicero's to Caesar for Marcellus' (p. 10), and then hear him

trespass still farther in a declaration that [Paul's] farewell to the Ephesians [Acts 20: 18–35] is much more beautiful, tender and pathetic than the celebrated defence of Milo. Never was the power of simplicity in writing so clearly, so finely demonstrated as in this incomparable speech. Not a shadow of art is to be found in it – scarce a metaphor, and not one but the most common, is used – nothing but the natural unstudied language of affection; and yet I flatter myself no person can read it attentively without a profusion of tears. (p. 11)

This is typical Dwight, exclamatory, challenging and personal in his preferences. He does not often quote but when he does he sticks close enough to the KJB to persuade the reader that the numberless beauties he finds are all in that version.

He is too much the enthusiast and too little the scholar to allow himself or his audience to remember that the Scriptures were not originally written in English, except perhaps near the beginning where he accounts for the special perfection of the Bible in terms of the climatic situation of the Hebrews and divine inspiration: 'born in a region which enjoyed this advantage [nearness to the sun] in the happiest degree, and fired with the glorious thoughts and images of inspiration, can we wonder that the divine writers, though many of them illiterate, should so far transcend all others as well in style as in sentiment?' (p. 4). This inspired style, it seems, is fully visible in English, and again we come close to the implication that the KJB is inspired.

It is apt that the American response to the Bible as literature should start with such youthful enthusiasm and with such a close connection with the KJB. Yet it is hardly a declaration of independence, and it may be as well to use Dwight to make a point that might be made about many of the critics of this time. The distinction between Longinian ideas and the old idea of the flowers of rhetoric that had seemed so important at the beginning of the century has all but disappeared. Dwight is at once a thorough admirer of Longinus and the sublime, and a searcher after beauties. In his 'Dissertation' or in Warton's new Longinus we have writings not substantially different from the sixteenth- and seventeenth-century exemplifications of the figures of rhetoric from the Bible. Enthusiasm has replaced method, but the idea of identifiable beauties and figures remains. What were the old and the new have now become the familiar together.

There is one respect in which Dwight points forwards. Others had praised narrative parts of the Bible, but he moves on to something near-allied to this, the Bible's presentation of character. The sacred penmen, he remarks,

have yet inserted an endless variety of incidents and characters . . . Convinced that human manners are the most delightful as well as the most instructive field for readers of the human race, they have exhibited them in every point of view – where are characters so naturally drawn? where so strongly marked? where so infinitely numerous and different? (p. 6)

This is less modern than its generality makes it sound. Dwight continues rhetorically, 'to what can the legislator so advantageously apply for instructions as to the life and laws of Moses? – Whom can the prince propose for examples so properly as Solomon and Jehoshaphat? – In Joshua and Joab the general, the hero are magnificently displayed' (p. 6) – and so on. What he is remarking on is not complexity or depth of characterisation but the wide range of exemplary types visible in the Bible; rather than being the first in what was to become a major line of discussion in the next century, he gives an idea of what might be to come.

Dwight's dissertation reappeared in 1795 as a supplement to a New York edition of the other work of this sort from the 1770s, Samuel Jackson Pratt's *The Sublime and Beautiful of Scripture*. This too is an early work: the young Pratt (1749–1815), eventually to be the author of a large number of miscellaneous works under the pen-name Courtney Melmoth, composed with romantic ardour and enthusiasm a series of essays on literary aspects of the Bible 'in the animated moments of feeling when their author was destined to holy orders, and while the impression made by each passage was yet glowing on the imagination and the heart' (I: vii); he then gave some of them as public lectures in the Edinburgh winter of 1776. Among the more significant aspects of these essays is that Pratt is the first of our critics to use 'literary' in its modern sense: he describes his subject as 'the *literary* excellence of the Holy Bible' (his italics), and links 'literary' with 'entertaining'. Here is the passage at length:

And I am thus particularly earnest to display in this work the *literary* excellence of the Holy Bible because I have reason to apprehend it is too frequently laid by under a notion of its being a dull, dry and unentertaining system, whereas the fact is quite otherwise: it contains all that can be *wished* by the truest intellectual taste, it enters more sagaciously and more deeply into human nature, it develops character, delineates manner, charms the imagination and warms the heart more effectually than any other book extant; and if once a man would take it into his hand without that strange prejudicing idea of flatness, and be willing to be pleased, I am morally certain he would find all his favourite authors dwindle in the comparison, and conclude that he was not only reading the most religious but the most *entertaining* book in the world. (II: 812)

Besides the use of 'literary', and the familiar, indeed perennial, complaint of literary prejudice against the Bible, this is notable for developing Dwight's hint at a modern sense of character. Soon afterwards Pratt writes:

Whoever examines the Scriptures will find the nicest preservation of character, each delicately discriminated, and so admirably contrasted that nothing which marks one is given heterogenously to another. This also has been considered among the first excellencies of composition: its beauty is manifested in Shakespeare much, but in the Bible more. (II: 100)

Besides confirming the new emphasis in criticism, this gives Pratt the honour of another first. We have long seen the Scriptures battling with the classics; recently Knox grouped the Bible, the Iliad and Shakespeare together as the sublimest books (see above, p. 243), and now Pratt awards the Bible the palm over Shakespeare. All that was needed for this to happen was for Shakespeare's reputation to have risen far enough to make him a worthy yardstick and for the Bible to be thought of as a literary work.

This would be peculiarly significant if Pratt had the KJB specifically in mind, for that would make it tantamount to a claim that the KJB is the greatest piece of English literature. He does not make this claim, yet it is implicit in his essays because, as usual, one can hardly believe that he is not writing about the KJB. In this important description of the emotional, personal approach taken to the Bible one may well wonder what Bible Pratt means as, in a ringing phrase, 'the noblest composition in the universe':

The genuine effusions of the author's mind in the progress of perusing the noblest composition in the universe indulging himself now and then in a moral comment upon passages of particular beauty; or, in a tender illustration of some of the most striking and pathetic narratives, are now offered to the reader, in the hope of recommending, and still of *more*, [sic] endearing to him the original. (I: viii–ix)

He has almost used Lowes's phrase for the KJB from a century and a half later, 'the noblest monument of English prose', and the odd thing is that 'the original' is, for the first time, not necessarily used to refer to the Hebrew (Pratt keeps to the OT); rather, Pratt uses it in distinction from his own 'effusions' – *they* will send the reader to the work that originally caused them. That work is of course the KJB, whose language he rarely ever modifies.

Now, his normal method is to base his essays on one or two verses and then to expatiate as the spirit takes him, and there are occasions when the comments depend on the particular language of the version. This is especially evident when he discusses Gen. 1: 3; whereas Boileau's comments on this verse depended on a quality of sense that might be found in any literal version, Pratt's comments do not necessarily survive the transfer to a different form of words (he gives the KJB verbatim but adds his own italics):

'And God said, *let* there be *light*, and there *was* light.' It is altogether *inimitable* and *incomparable*, being infinitely sublime and sacred in itself, and expressed in words exactly suitable. The sentence consists wholly of monosyllables, and those short, smooth and, as it were, insisting upon a rapid pronunciation. The celerity of the words assist in and echo to the command they convey. 'Let there be light' – can anything flow faster or with more facility from the lip? 'And there was light.' If the reader can manage his articulation, the image, the tone and everything else will correspond. Here again we have fresh reason to complain of our great epic poet [Milton], since the five lines he hath employed on this subject contain a great many polysyllables, each demanding a slow, sluggish, reluctant delivery – the sublimest thought may be destroyed by using improper symbols to express it, since every word should . . . resemble the motion it signifies. (I: 9–11)

Pratt does more than imply to the average reader that the KJB is *the* Bible: he not only believes himself that it is but he applies to the KJB the kind of opinions that have frequently been applied to the originals. Often the attribution of perfection to the originals had had a distinctly hypothetical element to it – the version we read has obvious shortcomings but the original, which we cannot read, being inspired, must have been perfect. Pratt is taking the KJB as perfect and supporting his opinion with demonstration; the hypothetical argument comes a little later.

A passage such as the following, which for the most part sounds like an Augustan repetition of the argument from inspiration, becomes remarkable when one realises from the nature of the surrounding discussions that it must refer to the KJB:

the God who created human nature knew intimately the method by which that nature was most forcibly attracted; he knew consequently what mode of address was best adapted and would most readily be admitted into the bosom and work its way into the soul. For this very reason it is obvious he directed a language likely to answer such ends, and this accounts for the remarkable majesty, simplicity, pathos and energy, and indeed all those strokes of eloquence which distinguish the Bible . . . *Religious eloquence* and the rhetoric of the Scriptures are, in the highest degree, favourable to the cause of truth. Nor can they, surely, ever suffer by any critical observations on the splendour, correctness or purity of the diction. (I: 18–19)

Once again there is a strong implication that the KJB is divinely inspired, but adoration of the KJB is not yet full-blown. Where Pratt stops short is in never naming the KJB; he has made one crucial shift by ceasing to distinguish between the KJB and the originals, but he has not made the shift of saying consciously to himself that the Bible is the KJB. If throughout he had used phrases such as 'our authorised version' instead of 'the Scriptures' or 'the Bible' he would not have changed his sense one whit but would have forced himself to recognise more of the implications of his thought.

At the end of the century George Burges takes us closer to a full recognition of these implications. Developing his view of 'the merit of our present received version' (see above, p. 245), he claims that 'every page . . . of the inspired writings is conspicuous for some grace of composition or other' (*A Letter*, p. 9). 'Inspired writings' is a parallel phrase for 'our authoritative version' in the previous sentence. Were it not that he is attempting to preserve some distinction between the original and the translation, this would be a direct claim of inspiration for the translation. Having made such a remark, he 'cannot debar [him]self the pleasure of a few extracts', and presents four of them.[12] However, he has no specific comment to offer that would direct the reader exclusively to the KJB,

12 Ruth 1: 15–17, Job 29: 11–16, Ps. 104: 1–4 and 1 Cor. 15: 51–4.

although he has given its text unaltered. Instead, he reminds his reader that these passages are representations of originals by beginning, 'if a mere English reader . . . may be allowed to form a judgement'. Without this the judgement would be a declaration of the literary perfection of the KJB:

instances of sweeter or sublimer composition, of softened melancholy that fills the mind with sorrow, or of awful grandeur that raises it to adoration are nowhere to be found; and if I did not read my Bible to make me wise unto salvation, I would at least peruse it as the greatest treat to the fervency of imagination and as the best standard for the expression of my thoughts. (p. 11)

Readers did not necessarily have to go outside their Bibles to find such remarks and implications. The well-off or pretentious, for instance, might find them in a handsome folio Bible replete with engravings and annotations, entitled *An Illustration of the Holy Bible* (Birmingham: Boden, 1770). The title of the second edition (1771) goes on significantly: *the notes and comments are selected from the best annotators, whereby the sublime passages are pointed out and some mistranslations rectified.* Never before had readers been able to read annotations of this sort to the KJB text: 'this is as grand a piece of poetry as ever was composed. The descriptions are so lively, the transitions so quick, the ideas so sublime and the apostrophes so noble that it might, exclusive of its being inspired, be considered as the noblest ode that ever world produced.' The subject is Deborah's song and the sentiment is very much Temple's from eighty years earlier, except that any suggestion of the old cliché about the disadvantages of translations and prose is totally missing. In fact this Bible goes almost as far in the opposite direction as Pratt, only stopping short of commentary that would be specific to the language of the KJB. The reader about to embark on Exodus 15 is commanded to admire it, for 'he who can read it without being enraptured must be harder than the rock which gushed out a river and more impenetrable to beauties than the hearts of the Israelites were'.

There is a major novelty here. For all the large amount of literary discussion of the Bible and the increasing frequency of the use of the KJB in such discussion, never before has the Bible of worship contained within itself the invitation to a literary reading. In a narrow sense of the phrase, this is the first Bible as literature. It is thoroughly true to the developments we have been following, and has open debts to commentators such as South, Locke and Lowth,[13] yet one must beware of over-

---

[13] See, for instance, the preface to Lamentations, and the notes to Habakkuk 3 and to 1 Corinthians.

playing its importance: there is not a large amount of annotation, and one can read for long stretches without coming across any sign of literary praise; moreover, this was not a widely-used Bible. It helps to mark the arrival of the sense of the KJB as literature but not the arrival of the Bible presented as literature: that arrival is still over a century away.

REVISION OR 'SUPERSTITIOUS VENERATION'

We have already encountered a few of the century's independent translations and noted how they produced first discussion of the KJB, then a reaction against their arguments that heightened the KJB's reputation. A similar story emerges from the calls for an official revision by the Church.

Of the many rival translators and would-be revisers of the KJB in the latter part of the century we may take the one-armed[14] archbishop of Armagh, William Newcome (1729–1800), as the most representative and influential. He was more successful than anyone, including the livelier and more provocative Geddes, in formulating ultimately acceptable principles of revision. Moreover, he made a major attempt to shape the reputation of the KJB. In perhaps his best work, the Lowthian *Twelve Minor Prophets* (1785) he distils the problem of Bible translation to this: 'whether we shall supply Christian readers and Christian congregations with new means of instruction and pleasure by enabling them to understand their Bible better' (p. xli). Obviously a new version is needed, both for understanding and literary pleasure. Among the reasons for this are 'the mistakes, imperfections and many invincible obscurities of our present version, the accession of many helps since the execution of that work, the advanced state of learning, and our emancipation from slavery to the Masoretic points and to the Hebrew text as absolutely uncorrupt' (pp. xvi–xvii); further, the KJB's qualities are not 'as uniform as the rules of good writing and the refined taste of the present age require' (*Historical View*, p. 238). In short, he is a scholarly and a literary critic, wanting revision in both areas, and unlikely to overpraise the KJB. Yet he cannot avoid the KJB and it has as strong an influence on the rules he draws up for revision as does the time's literary consciousness.

The first rule balances the literal and the literary, for 'the translator should express every word in the original by a literal rendering where the English idiom admits of it, and where not only purity but perspicuity

---

[14] While he was a tutor at Oxford his left arm was crushed in a door because, it is said, of the boisterousness of one of his pupils, Charles James Fox; the arm was amputated (*DNB*).

and dignity of expression can be preserved' (p. xvii).[15] Rule IV revives
the old principle of uniform rendering for the same word in the original
and criticises the KJB translators for varying 'their terms not only unnec-
essarily but so as to mislead the reader' (p. xxvii); here he echoes
Broughton and anticipates the RV.[16] Rule V addresses style:

> The collocation of the words should never be harsh and unsuited to an English
> ear. An inverted structure may often be used in imitation of the original, or
> merely for the sake of rhythm in the sentence, but this should be determined by
> what is easy and harmonious in the English language, and not by the order of
> the words in the original where this produces a forced arrangement or one more
> adapted to the license of poetry than to prose. (pp. xxx–xxxi)

Such a rule is likely to tip the balance from the literal to the literary, but
what is more interesting is that it leads to a particular kind of attention
to the KJB: discussing the rule, Newcome notes that 'our translators . . .
sometimes give a pleasing turn to their clauses by conformity to the
order of the words in the original' (p. xxxi), as in Ezek. 23: 37, 'and with
their idols have they committed adultery'. This is the kind of consciousness of style that attributes stylishness to the KJB. Newcome's other
main stylistic rule is that 'the simple and ancient turn of the present
version should be retained' (p. xxxii). 'This simplicity', he adds, 'arises in
a great measure from the preference of pure English words to foreign
ones'; 'modern terms and phrases, and the pomp and elegance of modernised diction' (p. xxxiii) are to be avoided, as is degeneration 'into
familiar idiom'; Hebraisms that are compatible with English or which
have become familiar should be retained (p. xxxiv). All this means 'that
a translation of the Bible should be a classical book to a foreigner' (p.
xxxiii), a notion which is nowhere repeated but which shows the extent
to which literary consciousness goes in Newcome.

  This is enough of Newcome's rules to show how far he was in tune
with the thinking that eventually produced the RV, enough too to establish a fundamental contrast with the KJB translators and their predecessors. One and three-quarter centuries after the publication of the KJB,
a literary consciousness of the business of translation has added itself to

---

[15] I have used the rules given in *The Twelve Minor Prophets* rather than the later version in chapter 5
of *An Historical View*.

[16] Since this is not as simple a matter as I have made it appear, it may be of interest to give
Newcome's formulation: 'the same original word and its derivatives, according to the leading
different senses, and also the same phrase, should be respectively translated by the same corresponding English word or phrase, except where a distinct representation of a general idea, or
the nature of the English language, or the avoiding of an ambiguity, or harmony of sound,
requires a different mode of expression' (p. xxiv).

the quest for the truth, indeed, has become so significant that at times it seems to be more important than the original quest for truth. This is the consciousness that gave rise to the myth that the KJB was a literary revision.

It would have been surprising if Newcome had not given space to literary praise of the originals carefully distinguished from the KJB – such praise, openly indebted to Lowth, is to be found in the preface to his *Ezekiel* (Dublin, 1788) – but what is of more interest is the way he deals with the KJB. In 1792 he produced a valuable introduction to eighteenth-century opinion, *An Historical View of the English Biblical Translations: the expediency of revising by authority our present translation and the means of executing such a revision.* After a chapter on the history of translation which is a digest of John Lewis's *History of the Several Translations of the Holy Bible,* (London, 1731), he collects 'authorities respecting the received version of the Bible'. These include extracts from many of the figures we have met and are quite sufficient to establish how highly the KJB was thought of in the latter part of the century. Nevertheless, though Newcome claims to have quoted impartially (p. 185), there is a leaning towards authorities that advocate revision. In effect, his tactic is to concede the present high view of the KJB and then to modify it. The reader who knew nothing of the history Newcome partially reveals would first find his established ideas confirmed and then be taught to question them. Many of the later extracts have this qualifying effect, and Newcome then builds on it by considering the objections to an improved version, arguing that such a version is expedient and presenting his rules for its conduct.

As the reputation of the KJB rose there was increasing resistance to change. The danger of unsettling the fragile faith of the people was much canvassed. John Parsons, future Bishop of Peterborough and Master of Balliol, approved Newcome's rules but objected to 'the authoritative substitution of a new version in the room of that which custom has familiarised to the ears and hallowed in the imaginations' because the people 'would lose their veneration for the old version without acquiring sufficient confidence in the new', and so be a prey to doubt and even atheism.[17] Such feelings were compounded by the French revolution and the Napoleonic wars. In face of the horrors across the channel, England turned neophobic, and the revision movement foundered. George Burges (?1764–1853), whom we have already met as

---

[17] *Monthly Review*, vol. 76 (Jan 1787), 46, 44.

a reactionary voice, was the prime spokesman for this feeling as it affected the Bible. France he considered to be 'an awful spectacle to surrounding nations of the dreadful effects which must ever necessarily result from a revolution of government preceding a revolution of mind' (*A Letter*, p. 25). He argues that

if ever an almost superstitious veneration for our excellent version of the Bible required to be inculcated and enforced, it is in a period like the present when the relaxations of society are of such a nature that the wisest men can scarce conjecture upon what basis it will hereafter subsist or by what laws it will be regulated, and when the spirit of revolution, driving rapidly through the world, assimilates in one discordant and heterogeneous mass the sentiments of the philosopher, the Christian and the infidel. (p. 34)

So minor a pamphlet from the little-known Vicar of Halvergate would have had no influence on the public, especially if set against the weight of the Archbishop of Armagh, but the sentiment it reveals took hold on the country, and the 'almost superstitious veneration for our excellent version' continued to grow as the attempt to procure official revision foundered.

The fairest summary of the position the reputation of the KJB had reached is given by an anonymous advocate of revision in 1788:

The present version certainly has to a high degree the qualities of beauty, simplicity and force; and we are taught from our infancy to look upon it with such affection and respect that we not only perhaps give it credit, where it does possess those excellencies, for a greater share of them than it actually has, but frequently persuade ourselves of their existence without any real grounds, and are blind to all but very glaring defects. This opinion of the scripture style, though in part ill-founded, is very conducive to our religious improvement: it may be unfavourable to us as critics, but it tends to make us good Christians.[18]

RANCOROUS REASON AND BROUHAHA

Although I have been careful to point out any tendencies towards the idea that the KJB was an inspired translation, one of the more obvious aspects of later eighteenth-century literary discussion of the Bible is the decline of the idea of inspiration and the growth of the sense that the OT especially is a human product fully open to rational examination. This is not to say that the idea of inspiration disappeared – very few of the general ideas about the Bible do ever disappear, and behind all the developments that so clearly take place there is always a sense of the dur-

---

[18] *Reasons for Revising by Authority Our Present Version* (Cambridge, 1788), pp. 53–4.

ability of basic human opinions. For instance, the 1780s, in spite of the strength of the scientific and aesthetic approach to the Bible, provide one of the baldest statements ever of the argument from inspiration to literary perfection:

When the maker of the world becomes an author, His word must be as perfect as His work: the glory of His wisdom must be declared by the one as evidently as the glory of His power is by the other: and if nature repays the philosopher for his experiments, the Scripture can never disappoint those who are properly exercised in the study of it.[19]

In rampant opposition to this idea came 'a shocking and insulting invective . . . as mischievous and cruel in its probable effects as it is manifestly illegal in its principles' (Erskine, *The Speeches*, pp. 8, 10): *The Age of Reason*[20] by that notorious companion of revolutions, best known for *The Rights of Man*, Thomas Paine (1737–1809). 'My own mind is my own church', he declares (I: 4); 'my endeavours have been directed to bring man to a right use of the reason that God has given him' (III: v). Now, 'the age of reason' might seem to sum up the time and the spirit of a Lowth and a Geddes, yet Paine was ignorant of their work and is using the phrase to proclaim the arrival of reason, represented by his work, in opposition to the inspirationists. Where Lowth and Geddes, particularly, were pioneers moving towards Higher Criticism,[21] Paine, for all that his work is full of a sense of personal discovery, is squarely in the atheist or deist tradition of rationalistic debunking of the Bible that stretches back through figures such as Aikenhead and Rochester to Marlowe. This is to name but three of many: atheism and deism provide a constant background of turbulence to religious discussion in the eighteenth century that varies little in its essentials and so does not need exhaustive coverage here. Paine, the most lively and provocative of them all, writing in France where deism was a stronger force than in England, is the

---

[19] So begins William Jones's *A Course of Lectures on the Figurative Language of the Holy Scripture . . . Delivered in the Parish Church of Nayland in Suffolk in the year 1786* (Oxford and London, 1848), p. 1. The book itself is only of further interest in showing how broadly the sense of the Bible as a literary work was spreading itself.

[20] Part I (Paris, 1793), II (Paris, 1795), III (NY, 1807). I have used the text given in *The Theological Works of Thomas Paine* (London, 1819). This numbers the pages afresh for each part, and includes some minor works in the numbering of part III.

[21] 'Higher Criticism', by contrast with the simple study of textual variations, aims at distinguishing and dating the different sources which have fed into the Bible. Its central element is the assumption that, at least in their composition and transmission, the books of the Bible are human documents subject to rational criticism such as one might apply to other texts. For a historical outline, see *The Cambridge History of the Bible*, 3 vols. (Cambridge University Press, 1963–70), III: 265–89.

culmination of English deism and may, somewhat loosely, be allowed to stand for his predecessors.

There are additional reasons for focussing on Paine. First, he makes a large number of literary judgements; second, because of the extreme yet popular nature of his work, he provoked a considerable number of replies, of which the most interesting, in the short term, is by Richard Watson (1737–1816), Bishop of Llandaff and Regius Professor of Divinity at Cambridge. *An Apology for the Bible* (George III is supposed to have commented that he 'was not aware that any apology was needed for that book')[22] was his most popular work. It circulated widely in both England and America, having the usual effect of publicising what it opposed.[23] The poet William Blake made some significant annotations concerning Watson and Paine, and much later that even more important figure, Samuel Taylor Coleridge developed his subtle and balanced discussion of inspiration in response to both Paine and the inspirationists, observing succinctly that 'this indeed is the peculiar character of the doctrine [of inspiration], that you cannot diminish or qualify it but you reverse it' (*Confessions*, p. 318).

The essence of Paine's deism, which he calls 'the only true religion', is 'the belief of one God, and an imitation of his moral character, or the practice of what are called moral virtues' (II: 74). In this he is as dogmatically pious as Jones has just been in his argument from inspiration to literary perfection. As Paine writes in a pamphlet, 'What! does not the Creator of the Universe . . . know how to write?'[24] but he locates this writing outside the Bible: 'the word of God is the creation we behold: and it is in *this* word, which no human invention can counterfeit or alter, that God speaketh universally to man' (I: 22). Revelation, he argues, cannot consist in writing, principally because it is given to the individual. The individual can report his own experience of revelation, but it is not revelation for any person to whom it is reported; rather, it is hearsay, and that person is entitled freely to decide for himself what is revelation (I: 5). So he regards the theology that is studied in the place of 'natural philosophy' (which is 'the true theology') as 'the study of human opinions, and of human fancies *concerning* God' (I: 26). 'The Christian system of faith' appears to him 'as a species of atheism – a sort of religious

---

[22] *The Cambridge History of the Bible*, III: 251.

[23] See Erskine, *The Speeches*, p. 19. Three quarters of a century earlier Franklin recalls that 'some books against deism fell into my hands . . . It happened that they wrought on me quite contrary to what was intended by them: for the arguments of the deists which were quoted to be refuted appeared to me much stronger than the refutations. In short, I soon became a thorough deist' (pp. 113–4).   [24] 'A letter to . . . Thomas Erskine', in *Complete Writings*, II: 732.

denial of God' (I: 26). Having thus rid the Bible of its claims to be the revealed word of God, Paine examines it in the light of reason, 'the choicest gift of God to man' (I: 21).

Part 1 was written without access to a Bible, so most of the detailed criticism appears in part 2, written after Paine's release from the Bastille, when he had procured a Bible and found its contents 'to be much worse books than I had conceived' (II: vi). He finds it historically uncertain and generally fabulous (e.g. II: 16, 28), and thus to be treated only as a kind of literature. Further, he finds the God portrayed in the OT in particular a hideous travesty of his idea of God, absolutely shocking to humanity:

There are matters in that book, said to be done by the *express command* of God, that are as shocking to humanity and to every idea we have of moral justice, as anything done by Robespierre, by Carrier, by Joseph le Bon, in France, by the English government in the East-Indies, or by any other assassin in modern times . . .

Whenever we read the obscene stories, the voluptuous debaucheries, the cruel and torturous executions, the unrelenting vindictiveness with which more than half the Bible is filled, it would be more consistent that we called it the word of a demon than the word of God. It is a history of wickedness that has served to corrupt and brutalize mankind. (II: 78, I: 13)

This, of course, reverses the view that takes whatever God has written or done as the best, and it also refuses to take the historical perspective that Lowth had begun to develop. Moreover, it is capable of an ironic turn if one takes a Darwinian view of the laws of nature, for Paine's equating of God, nature and moral law is highly optimistic: God's 'work is always perfect, and His means perfect means'.[25]

Of those in the Christian community, only Geddes was able to take Paine's point while rejecting his final position:

we have no intrinsic evidence of inspiration, or anything like inspiration, in the Jewish historians. On the contrary, it is impossible, I think, to read them, devoid of theological prepossessions [and] not to discover in them evident marks of human fallibility and human error . . . As uninspired historians they claim the same indulgence as we grant to other historical writers: we estimate their abilities, genius, style, judgement and veracity by the same rules of comparative criticism . . . Whereas the admission, once, of a perpetual and unerring sufflation not only, in my mind, destroys their credibility throughout, but is, moreover, highly injurious to the Supreme Being, as it makes him the primitive author of all that they relate: so the abettors of this delusive doctrine, so far from

[25] 'Extracts from a Reply to the Bishop of Llandaff', in *Complete Writings*, II: 785.

consulting the honour of God and defending the cause of religion, seem to betray and expose both to contempt and ridicule.[26]

This is to yield the battle and to win the war: Paine's view of the OT as fallible human writings is accepted but its force against Christianity is shattered by the rejection of what Geddes takes to be a quite unnecessary, not to say pernicious element in Christianity, the belief in inspiration. For Geddes as for Paine the OT is 'a poetical history' (II: xii); what is more, he is convinced that if such a view of the Scriptures were generally accepted, they

would be more generally read and studied, even by fashionable scholars, and the many good things which they contain, more fairly estimated. For what chiefly deters the sons of science and philosophy from reading the Bible and profiting of that lecture, but the stumbling block of absolute inspiration, which, they are told, is the only key to open their treasures? Were the same books presented to them as human compositions, written in a rude age, by rude and unpolished writers, in a poor uncultivated language, I am persuaded that they would soon drop many of their prejudices, discover beauties where they had expected nothing but blemishes, and become, in many cases, of scoffers, admirers. (II: xiii)

In one respect this line of arguing is a foretaste of the attitudes of Higher Criticism and an indication of their literary implications. In another respect it repeats an occasionally made argument, that an unprejudiced reading would show the Bible to be an admirable literary work.

Geddes's rationalistic optimism might have appealed to Lowth were he still living, but he was ten years dead and much of his spirit had passed to Germany. Bishop Watson's more simplistic refutation, taking ground that the deistic Voltaire had made his own in *Candide*, was to claim that Paine is inconsistent by not similarly condemning the death of innocents in earthquakes, which is equally death by the command of God (*Apology*, pp. 17–18 etc.). This is to miss the point of Paine's argument even if it is fair comment on the unthinking heart of his deism. Blake would have none of such tangential silliness: 'to me who believe the Bible and profess myself a Christian, a defence of the wickedness of the Israelites in murdering so many thousands under pretence of a command from God is altogether abominable and blasphemous'. He argues that the Jewish scriptures 'are only an example of the wickedness and deceit of the Jews and were written as an example of the possibility of human beastliness in all its branches'.[27]

---

[26] *The Holy Bible . . . faithfully translated*, 2 vols. (London, 1792, 97), II: v.
[27] *Complete Writings*, p. 387. Blake's annotations to Watson were written in 1798, using a 1797 edition of Watson with different pagination from that used here.

Much of Paine's detailed argument consists in close examination of the Bible in order to show inconsistencies which refute its claim to historical truth, and which show that some parts, for instance the early chapters of Genesis, could not have been written by their supposed authors and are therefore, in his simplistic view, forgeries. Some of his arguments, particularly those aimed at dating passages and determining authorship, anticipate later textual scholarship, although the conclusions he comes to about the value of the books are naturally different.

The creation story, the story of Satan and of the Fall, and the story of Jesus' supernatural origins are all, Paine argues, 'sprung out of the tail of the heathen mythology' (I: 6), a point that those familiar with discussions of the relationships between other ancient near-eastern texts such as the epic of Gilgamesh and the early chapters of Genesis would find hard to dismiss absolutely, however distasteful they might find the tone and implications. He ridicules these stories in some of his wittiest writing as absurd and extravagant fables (I: 8). Here is part of his mocking argument:

The Christian mythologists, after having confined Satan in a pit, were obliged to let him out again, to bring on the sequel of the fable. He is then introduced into the Garden of Eden in the shape of a snake or a serpent, and in that shape he enters into familiar conversation with Eve, who is no way surprised to hear a snake talk; and the issue of this tête à tête is, that he persuades her to eat an apple, and the eating of that apple damns all mankind.

After giving Satan this triumph over the whole creation, one would have supposed that the church mythologists would have been kind enough to send him back again to the pit; or, if they had not done this, that they would have put a mountain upon him (for they say that their faith can remove a mountain) or have him put *under* a mountain, as the former mythologists had done, to prevent his getting again among the women and doing more mischief. But instead of this, they leave him at large, without even obliging him to give his parole – the secret of which is, that they could not do without him; and after being at the trouble of making him, they bribed him to stay. They promised him *all* the Jews, *all* the Turks by anticipation, nine-tenths of the world beside, and Mahomet into the bargain. After this, who can doubt the bountifulness of the Christian mythology? (I: 9)

Watson offers only blunt unargued contradiction of this: 'as to the Christian faith being built upon the heathen mythology, there is no ground whatever for the assertion; there would have been some for saying that much of the heathen mythology was built upon the events recorded in the Old Testament' (*Apology*, p. 223). He suggests that if the story of Adam and Eve is not history, it is 'an allegorical representation of death entering into the world through sin, through disobedience to the command of God' (p. 363). Some willingness, characteristic of the defenders of the Bible against deistic objections, to concede that not all the Bible is historically true is evident here. Allegory was the frequent recourse of the defenders, without their showing any desire to go further towards literary interpretation.

Paine's view of Genesis as a whole is in keeping with his opinion of the Fall story, and shows his idea of authenticity:

Take away from Genesis the belief that Moses was the author, on which only the strange belief that it is the word of God has stood, and there remains nothing of Genesis but an anonymous book of stories, fables, and traditionary or invented absurdities, or of downright lies. The story of Eve and the serpent, and of Noah and his ark, drops to a level with the Arabian Tales, without the merit of being entertaining. (II: 18)

Thus the Bible is made bad literature, but again some of the possibilities that modern criticism is now exploring without seeking to diminish the Bible are anticipated. At the end of David Damrosch's *The Narrative Covenant* (1987) there is a stimulating comparison between the Bible and the *Thousand and One Nights*. Paine distinguishes the literature of the OT from, say, the writings of Plato and Homer, in that their poetic merit remains whether the author be known or not; they are works of genius and the Bible is not (II: 9). Though Watson rightly points out that 'anonymous testimony does not destroy the reality of facts' (p. 37), Blake's retort to Watson is still sounder: 'of what consequence is it whether Moses wrote the Pentateuch or no? If Paine trifles in some of his objections it is folly to confute him so seriously in them and leave his more material ones unanswered' (p. 392).

In similar vein Paine dismisses the story in Joshua of the sun standing still as 'a tale only fit to amuse children', but backhandedly concedes that 'as a poetical figure the whole is well enough' (II: 22). Ruth is 'an idle bungling story, foolishly told, nobody knows by whom, about a strolling country girl creeping slyly to bed to her cousin Boaz; pretty stuff, indeed, to be called the word of God'.[28] The Song of Songs he considers 'amorous and foolish enough', but sneers that 'wrinkled fanaticism has called [it] divine'. Isaiah is 'one of the most wild and disorderly compositions ever put together; it has neither beginning, middle nor end', but, with exceptions, 'is one continued incoherent, bombastical rant, full of extravagant metaphor, without application, and destitute of meaning; a school-boy would scarcely have been excusable for writing such stuff'.

---

[28] As given by Watson, *An Apology*, pp. 106–7. (Paine, pp. 25–6 are missing from my edition.)

He adds to this one of his very rare gestures towards the KJB: 'it is (at least in translation) that kind of composition and false taste that is properly called prose run mad' (II: 42). Watson picks this up to observe sniffily that Paine's taste for Hebrew poetry 'would be more correct if you would suffer yourself to be informed on the subject by Bishop Lowth' (p. 167). Of course there was no chance of Paine suffering himself to be so instructed.

Only Job and Psalm 19 escape this malicious onslaught, and the reason is simple: Paine has condemned where he does not believe, but he finds in these some conformity with his deistic views. The most obvious point to come out of all this is the familiar one that literary estimation of the Bible can be thoroughly dependent on preconceived religious attitudes. Paine is a Marlowe or an Aikenhead writ large, and he was lucky that his time, compared with theirs, was an age of reason, but still luckier that he lived out of reach of English justice: the representatives of authority might not be able to attack him personally, but they could attack his printer, Thomas Williams, who was found guilty of publishing a blasphemous work, fined £1,500 and jailed for three years (later, with more mercy than God showed in the flood, so Paine might have sneered, commuted to one); and they could attack his reputation. After Paine's death the story that he had recanted his teaching in *The Age of Reason* was circulated in an effort to further discredit the book, but in fact Paine remained proud of his opinions.[29]

What is most interesting, though, beyond the general point about preconceived ideas, is the tone of the responses: Geddes might successfully meet Paine on his own ground, and others thought they ought to be able to do so, the Bible translator Gilbert Wakefield, for instance, declaring roundly that 'if I should prove unable to vindicate my faith in Christianity upon principles truly rational and unambiguously explicit, I will relinquish it altogether and look for an asylum in the deism of Thomas Paine and the calm philosophy of Hume'.[30] Even Bishop Watson, for all that he is so often content with contradiction, is still arguing with Paine rather than burning his book and, like an Ayatollah, issuing an execution order. At times there is even something approaching concession in his arguments, as in this part of his summary of Paine's arguments against the OT:

In plain language, you have gone through the Old Testament hunting after difficulties, and you have found some real ones; these you have endeavoured to

---

[29] See Audrey Williamson, *Thomas Paine: his Life, Work and Times* (London: Allen and Unwin, 1973), pp. 276 ff. [30] *An Examination of The Age of Reason* (London, 1794), p. 20.

magnify into insurmountable objections to the authority of the whole book. When it is considered that the Old Testament is composed of several books, written by different authors, and at different periods, from Moses to Malachi, comprising an abstracted history of a particular nation for above a thousand years, I think the real difficulties which occur in it are much fewer, and of much less importance, than could reasonably have been expected. (pp. 209–11)

Although argument is again avoided, one feels that Watson might be willing to investigate, or to allow someone else to investigate, some of the problems raised. The proviso would of course be that the investigation be carried out within the reverent overview he sets down. Certainly, he is prepared to read the Bible as a composition having a human element. His overall view of the Bible, given during an exhortation to Paine to become a believer, makes still clearer the concession to the human element:

Receive but the Bible as composed by upright and well-informed, though, in some points, fallible men (for I exclude all fallibility when they profess to deliver the Word of God), and you must receive it as a book revealing to you, in many parts, the express will of God, and in other parts, relating to you the ordinary history of the times. Give but the authors of the Bible that credit which you give to other historians, believe them to deliver the word of God when they tell you that they do so, believe, when they relate other things as of themselves and not of the Lord, that they wrote to the best of their knowledge and capacity, and you will be in your belief something very different from a deist: you may not be allowed to aspire to the character of an orthodox believer, but you will not be an unbeliever in the divine authority of the Bible, though you should admit human mistakes and human opinions to exist in some parts of it. (pp. 110–11)

From Watson's point of view, the concessions and moderation evident here are not the most important element in his work. His prime concern is that Paine's views should be stopped from spreading, and here he speaks with the voice of the establishment:

In accomplishing your purpose you will have unsettled the faith of thousands, rooted from the minds of the unhappy virtuous all their comfortable assurance of a future recompence; have annihilated in the minds of the flagitious all their fears of future punishment; you will have given the reins to the domination of every passion, and have thereby contributed to the introduction of the public insecurity and of the private unhappiness usually and almost necessarily accompanying a state of corrupted morals. (pp. 3–4)

This, of course, is a misrepresentation of Paine's views, but it is a clear reminder of the reactionary spirit of the times. Yet for many, such moderate conservatism was far from sufficient and likely to have the very effect Watson feared. The ordinary inspirationist in the street could not let such heresy pass challenged only by inadequate reason, so one Michael Nash, who had experienced all the doubts of reason but then had been converted back to Christianity and love of the Bible, believed that critics who conceded ground to Paine were no better than Paine himself:

If the foundations be destroyed, what can the righteous do? . . . Take away the Bible from the believer (or make him think it an amphibious fraud, which is all one), and you rob him of more than all that earth can give. And thus languishingly he pines. What! says the true Christian, have I forsaken all the delights of life, its riches, honours, pleasures, and everything the flesh holds dear, in pursuit and expectation of that eternal state of felicity which the Bible unfolds, and that book a fable after all . . . Avaunt, Satan! let my God be true, who is truth itself! Tom Paine and every man that contradicts his word are *liars*.[31]

Such protest, with which one may have some sympathy, suggests that *The Age of Reason*, by producing an inspirationist backlash, may have made it more difficult to think about the Bible with freedom, and so may have hindered the English development of both Higher Criticism and understanding of the Bible as literature.

---

[31] *Paine's Age of Reason . . . Wakefield's Examination of, and a Layman's Answer to The Age of Reason, both weighed in the balance and found wanting* (London, 1794), pp. 82–3.

CHAPTER TWELVE

Writers and the Bible 2: the Romantics

THE FAKER AND THE MADMAN

In 1760 an extraordinary collection of 'poems' appeared purporting to be a translation of much the same sort as the KJB. Part of its preface very nearly describes biblical poems and their translation:

> They are not set to music nor sung. The versification in the original is simple, and to such as understand the language, very smooth and beautiful. Rhyme is seldom used, but the cadence and the length of the line varied so as to suit the sense. The translation is extremely literal. Even the arrangement of the words in the original has been imitated; to which must be imputed some inversions in the style that otherwise would not have been chosen. (pp. vi–vii)

No one reading this with a knowledge of Lowth and an awareness of the KJB's literalness could fail to see the similarities – significantly, the author of the preface was Hugh Blair, later to publicise Lowth's ideas. This is the kind of poetry he is describing:

> My love is a son of the hill. He pursues the flying deer. His grey dogs are panting around him; his bowstring sounds in the wind. Whether by the fount of the rock, or by the stream of the mountain thou liest; when the rushes are nodding with the wind, and the mist is flying over thee, let me approach my love unperceived, and see him from the rock. Lovely I saw thee first by the aged oak; thou wert returning tall from the chase; the fairest among thy friends. (p. 9)

Pratt found this 'not much unlike the scriptural manner of writing', having 'an almost scriptural sublimity' (*Sublime and Beautiful*, I: 155–6). It is the opening of that very successful forgery, *Fragments of Ancient Poetry* (Edinburgh, 1760) by the Scot James Macpherson (1736–96), a work soon to be developed into 'Ossian's' *Fingal*.

The passage is biblical in ways nothing before it had been. It is prose poetry, cadenced but unmetrical; simplicity is at once apparent in the brevity of the sentence structures and the general reliance on unsubordinated statements; there is parallelism and even that oddity of some parts of the Bible, a seemingly illogical switching between second and third person. Though the content is occasionally reminiscent of the Song of Songs, this differs from all previous biblical imitations in being an imitation of style rather than of content. Where paraphrase, like commentary, functions in part as an exposition of meaning, this kind of imitation, like criticism, is an exposition of style, capable of sending the reader back to the KJB with insight into its literary nature. Thus, in the same decade that the critical opinion of the KJB changed from negative to positive, creative writers began to draw on the style of the Bible and, in so doing, to enhance appreciation of the KJB.

Some of the poetry of the much-troubled Christopher Smart (1722–71) also shows a degree of dependence on the style of the KJB. The best known of his biblical works, *A Song to David*, is eloquent of his love for biblical poetry but not otherwise important here, nor is his *A Translation of the Psalms of David*. The posthumously published *Jubilate Agno*, written during his confinement to a madhouse, 1758–63, presents a different and by no means simple picture. If it is a poem at all, it is a poem without rhyme or metre, consisting of a long series of lines beginning with either 'let' or 'for', including one substantial section in which these beginnings alternate. Such a form is inescapably repetitious or parallelistic, and Smart was not only familiar with Lowth's *De Sacra Poesi*, but had publicly characterised it as 'one of the best performances that has been published for a century'.[1]

Here is an example of the poem at its most characteristic:

Let Shimron rejoice with the Kite, who is of more value than many sparrows.
For I this day made over my inheritance to my mother in consideration of her age.

Let Sered rejoice with the Wittal – a silly bird is wise unto his own preservation.
For I this day made over my inheritance to my mother in consideration of her poverty.

(B47–8)

Parallelism is used primarily in the way the pairs of lines echo each other in form, but the latter halves of the 'let' lines add description rather than parallel the first halves, and the 'for' lines are single statements. Just as the subject matter is a mixture of the biblical and the personal that depends to a considerable extent on their incongruity, so is the form, with the result that it is less likely than Macpherson's *Fragments* to send one back to the KJB with insight into its style.

[1] The *Universal Visiter*, Jan. 1756, p. 56; as given in Murray Roston, *Prophet and Poet: The Bible and the Growth of Romanticism* (London: Faber, 1965), p. 148.

Smart's one other biblical work, *The Parables of Our Lord* (1768), had a dismal reception. Smart designed these parables 'for the use and improvement of younger minds' (title) and dedicated them to a three-year-old boy. The *Monthly Review* sneeringly found 'great propriety' in this, and the *Critical Review* damned them by comparing them to Sternhold and Hopkins (Smart, *Poetical Works*, II: 201). Such remarks have an element of justice, but from this distance the *Parables* seem to promise something different from most of the century's paraphrases, and therefore perhaps something better. In them Smart comes closest to the style of the KJB while demonstrating just how difficult it is for regular English verse to be like the KJB. Rather than the audacious experiment of *Jubilate Agno* with a quasi-biblical technique, *The Parables of Our Lord* attempt to use the words of the KJB as far as possible, and to keep necessary alterations to its text within the range of its vocabulary. The results can be peculiarly pleasing, and they often invite comparison with the KJB. Here is the main part of the 38th parable (the word is used loosely), 'The Beam and the Mote':

> Judge not, lest ye be judg'd for pride:
> For with what judgement you decide,
> Ye shall be censur'd like for like;
> And the same measure that ye strike,
> That shall be measured you again.
> And why beholdest thou with pain
> The mote that's in thy brother's eye,
> And thine own beam canst not descry?
> Thy brother, how canst thou reprove,
> 'From thee let me that mote remove,
> 'That I may set thy vision right;'
> When, lo! a beam obstructs thy sight.
> Thou hypocrite with canting tone,
> First cast the beam from out thine own:
> And then shalt thou distinctly note
> Thy brother's eye, and clear the mote.

Preservation decisively outweighs change to the KJB: not only do the key words remain, but several phrases survive as complete lines. Moreover, there is little incongruity of style between the changed and the unchanged. Rather than the Bible neo-classified, this is the KJB lightly tailored to a verse whose rhythm it seems readily adapted to.

In one sense there is a long tradition behind such versification of the Bible, even if few poets of stature had attempted this degree of fidelity, but, coming after a period in which a very different idea of paraphrase held sway, this is significantly new: literature of a sort is not only being found but being shown in the KJB. Moreover, these parables are novel in treating the 'unpoetic' NT in this way. Lowth had been a traditionalist in keeping to the poetic parts of the OT; Smart shows that something like poetry can be found still more widely distributed. In doing so, he helps to create new ways of writing that inevitably attract to themselves those so-common epithets for the style of the Bible, plain and simple.

WILLIAM BLAKE AND 'THE POETIC GENIUS'

Poet, engraver, designer, printer, thinker and prophet, William Blake (1757–1827) is in some ways a natural step from Smart. His best-known collections of poems, *Songs of Innocence* (1789) and *Songs of Experience* (1789–94), have a plainness and simplicity that seem to grow out of the childlike directness of Smart's *Parables*, and they show Blake's perpetual absorption in the Bible. Like Smart, Blake was little known in his own time, and must be taken more as a figure reflecting, however idiosyncratically, the changing sentiments of his time than as one who immediately shaped ideas. Yet, in the longer perspective, he is a shaper of literary attitudes to the Bible: once Alexander Gilchrist's *Life*, published in 1863, began to bring his work the fame it had always deserved, his sense and use of the Bible became public property.

That he knew his Bible intimately almost goes without saying. 'His greatest pleasure was derived from the Bible, – a work ever in his hand, and which he often assiduously consulted in several languages'; he was 'a most fervent admirer of the Bible, and intimately acquainted with all its beauties'.[2] Blake himself writes that he and a friend 'often read the Bible together'. But this friend was an imaginary angel become a devil, and they read the Bible 'in its infernal or diabolical sense'.[3] There is a warning here: however representative he is, in general terms, of turn-of-the-century love for the Bible as literature, he is no orthodox figure.

One of his best-known poems, 'The Tyger' from *Songs of Experience*, shows this quarrelling love of the Bible. It seems to be an addition to the descriptions of the creatures of God's creation in Job 40 and 41, especially the superficially similar questioning description of Leviathan in Job 41: 1–7; moreover, the compressed form of the questioning echoes Job's earlier 'why did the knees prevent me? or why the breasts that I

---

[2] J.T. Smith and William Hayley, as given in G.E. Bentley, Jr, ed., *Blake Records* (Oxford University Press, 1969), pp. 467, 106.
[3] 'A memorable fancy', in 'The Marriage of Heaven and Hell' (c. 1790), *CW*, p. 158.

should suck?' (3: 12). The questions in Job 41 reflect man's impotence against Leviathan, but Blake's questions concern God. Perhaps, disturbingly, they ask whether any creator is powerful enough to dare frame the frightful symmetry of the imagined beast. Such undercurrents run throughout Blake's work.

Biblical allusion pervades the *Songs*, and, particularly in *Songs of Innocence*, there is an un-Augustan simplicity that has, as I have suggested, much in common with Smart's *Parables*. Whereas those were versifications that drew out qualities in the Bible, Blake's simplicity comes in original poems that are less directly connected with the Bible, and so, in their style, make a more muted statement about it. Yet there is nothing muted about Blake's claim in the first poem of *Songs of Experience*, 'Introduction':

> Hear the voice of the Bard!
> Who Present, Past, & Future, sees;
> Whose ears have heard
> The Holy Word
> That walk'd among the ancient trees,
>
> Calling the lapsed Soul,
> And weeping in the evening dew;
> That might controll
> The starry pole,
> And fallen, fallen light renew!

Like a prophet, the poet both sees through all time and has heard God's voice direct, specifically the voice that was heard in Eden after the fall. Blake implies that, like a prophet, the bard will deliver the word of God: his readers are alerted to expect something biblical.[4]

The link between prophecy and poetry pervades Blake. His early statement of principles, 'All religions are one' (c. 1788; *CW*, p. 98), has for epigraph the synoptic Gospels' version of Isa. 40: 3, 'the voice of one crying in the wilderness'. In Mark's version this invokes exactly the point of 'Introduction': 'as it is written in the prophets, Behold, I send my messenger before thy face, which shall prepare thy way before thee. The voice of one crying in the wilderness, Prepare ye the way of the Lord, make his paths straight' (Mark 1: 2–3). Principle five announced under

---

[4] The illuminated version of this poem can be seen as adding to these suggestions. The poem appears celestial, being inscribed on a cloud against a starry background, as if imagined by the naked figure at the foot of the picture. This figure reclines on something that might be a scroll; though sometimes taken as female, it is likely to be the bard, and in some versions Blake underlines the divine aspect by giving it a halo.

this prophetic banner is that 'the religions of all nations are derived from each nation's different reception of the poetic genius, which is everywhere called the spirit of prophecy'. Principle six follows logically: 'the Jewish and Christian Testaments are an original derivation from the poetic genius'.

This is, as it were, from the unknown Blake, but it leads to the most famous of all his poems, known as the hymn 'Jerusalem'.[5] It will be best to consider it first as it commonly appears, removed from its Blakean context:

> And did those feet in ancient time
> Walk upon England's mountains green?
> And was the holy Lamb of God
> On England's pleasant pastures seen?
>
> And did the Countenance Divine
> Shine forth upon our clouded hills?
> And was Jerusalem builded here
> Among these dark Satanic Mills?
>
> Bring me my Bow of burning gold:
> Bring me my Arrows of desire:
> Bring me my Spear: O clouds unfold!
> Bring me my Chariot of fire.
>
> I will not cease from Mental Fight,
> Nor shall my Sword sleep in my hand
> Till we have built Jerusalem
> In England's green & pleasant Land.

It seems to be a magical, barely-understood call to exert one's faith to the uttermost. The language seems to have a biblical simplicity and that impression is reinforced by the obvious references to the lamb of God and to Jerusalem, and by images such as 'chariot of fire' which is directly biblical, and 'arrows of desire' which one feels ought to be biblical since the Bible sometimes uses 'arrows' metaphorically, as in Ezekiel's 'evil arrows of famine' (5: 16). Even the sword might well be the sword of Scripture. As much as any of the *Songs of Innocence and Experience*, it takes one into the world of the Bible and suggests literary power in the Bible. These impressions do not disappear when the poem is read in context, yet a different poem emerges.

Blake wrote the poem as part of the preface to his epic, 'Milton'

---

[5] Sir Hubert Parry's setting was published in 1916, and one can readily imagine how inspirational the hymn would have seemed in wartime.

(1804), a preface in which he takes his idea of the Bible as poetry further than we have so far seen:

The stolen and perverted writings of Homer and Ovid, of Plato and Cicero, which all men ought to contemn, are set up by artifice against the sublime of the Bible, but when the new age is at leisure to pronounce, all will be set right, and those grand works of the more ancient and consciously and professedly inspired men will hold their proper rank, and the daughters of memory shall become the daughters of inspiration. (*CW*, p. 480)

The old ideas that the classics stole from the Scriptures, and that the Bible is sublime and inspired (there is no difference here between religious and literary inspiration) lead to a vision of a new world in which the Scriptures are rightly estimated supreme and there will be a new, inspired poetry. 'Rouse up, O young men of the new age', cries Blake: 'we do not want either Greek or Roman models if we are but just and true to our own imaginations, those worlds of eternity in which we shall live for ever in Jesus our Lord' (p. 480). In part this is a rejection of classical for biblical models, since no difference is made between being true to one's imagination and being true to the Scriptures: they are the books of the imagination. It is here that the song comes, still prefacing the poem proper, and it is followed by the last line of the preface, a slightly adapted quotation from Num. 11: 29: 'would to God that all the Lord's people were prophets'. In this context, the poem is an exhortation to create the new world of the imagination, transforming England into a kingdom of God which is also a kingdom of the imagination, all its people true poets as the poets of the Bible had been in the past. In this way it is a central poem for a literary sense of the Bible and for a religious sense of literature. That this sense should have escaped the public is testimony to the inspiring strength the poem has beyond its specific concern; to return to its Blakean meaning is to underline how far his essential ideas about the Bible, religion and poetry have remained hidden.

Blake's is not the Bible of morality and theology but one of poetry and energy, a Bible that has little to do with common ideas. For him 'the whole Bible is filled with imagination and visions from end to end and not with moral virtues'; it is 'not allegory, but eternal vision or imagination of all that exists'.[6] In the same vein, 'Jesus and his apostles and disciples were all artists', and 'the Old and New Testaments are the great code of art'.[7] This is not, as it might appear, unadulterated aestheticism

---

[6] 'Annotations to Berkeley's "Siris"', '[A Vision of the Last Judgement]', *CW*, pp. 774, 604.
[7] 'The Laocoön', *CW*, p. 777. The latter statement is now a favourite with critics.

but part of what we might call a moral conception of man that values the imagination ahead of reason and abhors the mechanical limitedness of conventional morality. In a relatively early letter that sets out the essence of his views, Blake asks rhetorically, 'why is the Bible more entertaining and instructive than any other book?', and answers at once, 'is it not because [it is] addressed to the imagination, which is spiritual sensation, and but mediately to the understanding or reason?'[8] Perhaps this is no more than the English discovery of the Bible as literature run wild. Yet, as with so much of Blake, it remains a challenge, a challenge aimed at one's response to the Bible in general.

WILLIAM WORDSWORTH AND THE POSSIBILITY OF A NEW LITERARY SENSE OF THE BIBLE

Nature rather than the Bible was the 'great code of art' and true source of inspiration for William Wordsworth (1770–1850), so it is not surprising to find only a little in his work that relates to the Bible. Of course he alludes to the Bible and occasionally uses biblical phrases so naturally that the sense of their source is almost lost, as when he describes how one becomes 'a living soul' (Gen. 2: 7) under the influence of 'that serene and blessed mood' ('Tintern Abbey'). Moreover, he says enough to make it clear that he loved his Bible, but not enough to suggest that this perhaps lukewarm love was of central importance to him: here his silences are more impressive than his utterances. *Ecclesiastical Sonnet* II: XXIX hails the Bible in English as a 'transcendent boon', and in *The Prelude* he mentions vaguely 'the voice / Which roars along the bed of Jewish song' in a passage that characteristically returns to Nature, 'which is the breath of God' (1805 version, V: 202–3; 222).

Wordsworth's most significant piece for the Bible is his preface to *Lyrical Ballads* (1800) and the appendix on poetic diction added in 1802.[9] There he suggests that the best demonstration of what he means by poetic diction would be to put eighteenth-century metrical paraphrases against the KJB. The example he chooses is Johnson's version of Prov. 6: 6–11, after which he remarks with effective simplicity, 'from this hubbub of words pass to the original' (I: 163). Implicitly the KJB shows the affecting and 'genuine language of passion' (I: 160). In context of the argument of the whole preface this brief example is highly suggestive.

---

[8] To Dr Trusler, 23 August 1799, *CW*, p. 794.
[9] *The Prose Works* gives both the 1800 and 1850 texts, with variants; throughout I have used the earliest readings in order to keep the evidence as historical as possible.

The crux of the preface is to justify his decision to focus on 'low and rustic life', and to use the language of common rural men 'purified indeed from what appear to be its real defects' (I: 124). Tyndale's language might also be described as an artful variation of common language, but where Wordsworth varied to avoid 'real defects', Tyndale varied because of the demands of his originals. Wordsworth goes on to argue 'that there neither is nor can be any essential difference' 'between the language of prose and metrical composition' because 'the same human blood circulates through the veins of them both' (I: 134). Indeed, he adds to these observations a footnote on the confusions caused in criticism by treating 'poetry' and 'prose' as antonyms; for him, metre, with or without rhyme, is not the defining characteristic of poetry. This is an often-forgotten rather than a new idea, and it usefully develops Lowth's points that a literal translation of biblical poetry will retain some semblance of versification and that the passions speak irregularly. Though Wordsworth chose to remain a versifier as well as a poet, his preface promotes a recognition that prose can be as powerful as verse. A reader going from this preface to the KJB could take its language, in places at least, as achieved literature without having to see in it a muted appearance of versification. Had he wished, Wordsworth might have written powerfully on the poetry of the KJB. That he did not suggests that, in spite of the affinities between his ideas and ideas of the Bible, the Bible fitted with rather than generated his thought.

One further argument, added in 1802, can be read in a way that is favourable to literary appreciation of the Bible. Just as the Bible is the book of truth, so 'poetry is the breath and finer spirit of all knowledge'; it 'is the first and last' – might one not say, the alpha and omega? – 'of all knowledge'. Wordsworth brings this part of his argument to a climax in religious language that, in Blake's hands, would explicitly invoke *his* supreme poet, Jesus: 'if the time should ever come when what is now called science . . . shall be ready to put on, as it were, a form of flesh and blood, the poet will lend his divine spirit to aid the transfiguration, and will welcome the Being thus produced as a dear and genuine inmate of the household of man' (I: 141). Wordsworth's 'sublime notion of poetry' (I: 141) is plainly religious. Little imagination is needed to reverse the coin and see the Bible as supreme poetry. Yet it is a reversal. Dennis had argued that poetry should become religious (see above, p. 190), and the result, in a sense, had been Blake. The difference lies in the idea of what is religious. For Blake, Christ is the soul of poetry, for Wordsworth poetry is the soul of religion.

In this distinction lies a change that will be important to some ideas of the Bible as literature. Just as Wordsworth takes imagery from religion to describe his aesthetic, so literature adopts characteristics of religion – and higher education takes on some of the characteristics of a church. Where literature was once synonymous with lying, it has become, and remains in many respects, an art of truth. Indeed, though Wordsworth emphasises pleasure equally with knowledge, there are times when literature seems, like religion, to value truth ahead of pleasure. The significance for the Bible of the change Wordsworth suggests is that it helps to make possible reverence for it as literature rather than as religion. By virtue of the pleasure it gives, particularly in its poetic insight into man and his passions, but also in the felt beauty of its language, it changes from being the canon of Christian writing to being part of the canon of literature. The Bible may now be religion because it is literature. Wordsworth, of course, does not make such a claim, but it will be the basis of Shelley's view of the Bible. What he does, quite incidentally to his own purposes, is to suggest the possibility of such a change in a way that is more obvious than in any previous writer.

SAMUEL TAYLOR COLERIDGE AND 'THE LIVING EDUCTS OF THE IMAGINATION'

Both Wordsworth and Samuel Taylor Coleridge (1772–1834) are reported to have

> thought the bad taste in writing which now prevails, is owing to works of two celebrated authors, Pope's translation of Homer and the Odyssey, and Johnson's *Lives of the Poets*. These models of art and an inflated style have been imitated to the destroying of all simplicity. – The Old Testament, they say, is the true model of simplicity of style.[10]

Almost all of this fits Wordsworth's argument in the preface to *Lyrical Ballads* and its appendix, but it has one peculiarly Coleridgean aspect, the restriction to the OT. Late in his life, Coleridge declared,

> I think there is a perceptible difference in the elegance and correctness of the English in the versions of the Old and New Testament. I cannot yield to the authority of many examples of usages which may be alleged from the New Testament version. St Paul is very often most inadequately rendered, and there are slovenly and vulgar phrases which would never have come from Ben Jonson or any good writer of the times.[11]

[10] Joseph Farington, *Diary*, ed. James Greig (8 vols., 1922–8), V: 132 (28 March 1809). As given in Coleridge, *Biographia Literaria*, *CW* 7, I: 39n.   [11] *Table Talk*, 17 August 1833, *CW* 14, I: 430.

This makes it probable that the remark was principally Coleridge's, and it immediately shows that he had a qualified respect for the KJB.

His few other remarks on the KJB's English fit with the idea of it as 'the true model of simplicity'. He once observed that 'intense study of the Bible will keep any writer from being vulgar in style'. Moreover, he viewed the KJB not just as a model but as a beneficial influence on the language, remarking that 'our version of the Bible [is] most valuable in having preserved a purity of meaning to many of the plain terms of natural things; without this our vitiated imaginations would refine away the language to mere abstractions'.[12] He went so far as to suggest that its English affected the passionate expressions of the people: 'if a mother had lost her child she was full of the wildest fancies, the words themselves assuming a tone of dignity for the constant hearing of the Bible and Liturgy clothed them not only in the most natural but most beautiful forms of language'.[13]

There is much that is familiar in these remarks: they have a lineage that goes back through Lowth proclaiming the KJB to be 'the best standard of our language' (see above, p. 245) to Swift's observation that the KJB and PB 'have proved a kind of standard for language, especially to the common people' (above, p. 211). Nevertheless, there is a sense of freshness and discovery that distinguishes them from mere repetitions of received ideas, and, in Coleridge's last observation particularly, there is a larger aesthetic dimension. Swift's concern was for the stability of English, Coleridge's (and Wordsworth's) is with quality of language, for he sees the KJB as an influence towards beauty.

A somewhat similar observation is reported from the next lecture, but this time Coleridge seems to be thinking directly of poetic quality in the KJB and a new, peculiarly Coleridgean idea begins to emerge:

When Coleridge read the song of Deborah he never supposed that she was a poet, although he thought the song itself a sublime poem. It was [as] simple [a] dithyrambic poem as exists but it was the proper effusion of a woman, highly elevated by triumph . . . When she commenced, 'I Deborah the mother of Israel', it was poetry in the highest sense. (I: 310)

Here he may be following Wordsworth, who described the song as a 'tumultuous and wonderful poem', and had cited it to show that 'repetition and apparent tautology are frequently beauties of the highest kind'.[14] The idea fits Wordsworth's willingness to find poetry in prose

---

[12] *Table Talk*, 7 June 1830, I: 165 and 24 June 1827, I: 75.

[13] *Lectures 1808–1819 on Literature*, *CW* 5, I: 292.

[14] Note on *The Thorn*, *The Poetical Works of William Wordsworth*, ed. E. De Selincourt, 5 vols. (Oxford University Press, [1944] 1952), II: 513.

more easily than it does Coleridge, for the two part company on the question of poetry and prose. Coleridge did not agree that there was no essential difference between poetry and prose (*Biographia Literaria*, II: 55), believing rather that, 'wherever passion was, the language became a sort of metre'.[15] He demonstrated the point at some length in the same lecture in his most detailed commentary on the KJB as literature. The report of the lecture goes on:

> So closely connected . . . was metre with passion that many of the finest passages we read in prose are in themselves, in point of metre, poetry – only they are forms of metre which we have not been familiarised to and not brought forwards to us and other English readers in the shape of metre – Coleridge had paid particular attention to the language of the Bible and had found that all persons had been affected with a sense of their high poetic character – not merely from the thoughts conveyed in them, but from the language enclosing those thoughts – from the stately march of the words, which had affected them in a degree and kind altogether different from that of common writing, and different from the narrative and preceptive parts of the same books. It had been his business to discover the cause, and he found that in almost every passage brought before him as having produced a particular effect there was metre and very often poetry – not indeed regular – not such as could be scanned on the fingers – but in some cases fragments of hexameter verses, . . . of dactyls and spondees, forming sometimes a complete hexameter verse . . . [here he gave two examples from the Psalms].
>
> Thus taking the first chapter of Isaiah, without more than four or five transpositions and no alteration of words, he had reduced it to complete hexameters. (*CW* 5, I: 222–3)

Unfortunately, most of the evidence of Coleridge's sense of metre in the KJB is unsatisfactory because the quotations are substantially different from the KJB.[16] The best example (taken from the same passage) is what Coleridge claims to be 'a rare instance of a *perfect* hexameter . . . in the English language':

God came | up with a | shout: our | Lord with the | sound of a | trumpet.

This is close to the KJB's 'God is gone up with a shout, the Lord with the sound of a trumpet' (Ps. 47: 5), but much less impressive than Milton using 'he gave me of the tree and I did eat' verbatim in *Paradise Lost* (see above, p. 182): that was a true demonstration of metre in the KJB.

The relationship between Coleridge the literary critic, Coleridge the textual critic and Coleridge the religious thinker is complex. His

---

[15] *Lectures 1808–1819*, I: 223.

[16] See *Letters*, I: 532, paraphrase of Psalm 46 as 'Hexameters' in *Poems*, and note prefixed to 'Hymn to the Earth', *Poems*, p. 327.

marginal annotations to his KJBs, for instance, sometimes show a literary response, sometimes a text-critical response, sometimes a religious response, sometimes two or even all of these responses mixed.[17] In works such as *Aids to Reflection, Confessions of an Inquiring Spirit, The Statesman's Manual* and his lectures on religious subjects, he appears as a religious rather than a literary thinker about the Bible, and he frequently describes the Bible in terms many an unliterary divine would use. So *The Statesman's Manual* is subtitled 'the Bible the best guide to political skill and foresight', and he presumes that his reader 'will indeed have directed your *main* attention to the promises and the information conveyed in the records of the evangelists and apostles . . . Yet not the less on this account will you have looked back with a proportionate interest on the *temporal* destinies of men and nations, sorted up for our instruction in the archives of the Old Testament.'[18] There is no hint of aesthetic interest here. Yet the links between his literary and his religious thought constantly assert themselves: they were bound to, for he believed poetry to be 'the blossom and the fragrancy of all human knowledge, human thoughts, human passions, emotions, language' (*Biographia Literaria*, II: 26). This is exactly Wordsworth's idea that 'poetry is the breath and finer spirit of all knowledge', but Coleridge pushes well beyond Wordsworth into the religious implications. Trying to read the Scriptures as he would any other work (*Confessions, CW* 11, II: 1120), he finds he cannot because they 'are distinguishable from all other books pretending to inspiration . . . in their strong and frequent recommendations of truth. I do not here mean veracity, which cannot but be enforced in every code which appeals to the religious principle of man, but knowledge.'[19] The essence of this knowledge – common to his idea of poetry and his idea of the Bible – lies not in the reason but in the feelings. He writes in *Aids to Reflection*, 'in wonder all philosophy began: in wonder it ends: and admiration fills up the interspace. But the first wonder is the offspring of ignorance: the last is the parent of adoration. The first is the birth-throe of our knowledge: the last is its euthanasy and apotheosis' (*CW* 9, 286). This is largely secular language for the mystic experience of insight, at once a religious and an aesthetic experience. It is far removed from the previous century's emphasis on reason, yet close in temper to that century's rediscovery of sublimity, for one may say that wonder is the

---

[17] See *Marginalia, CW* 12, I: 426 ff.

[18] *Lay Sermons, CW* 6, p. 8. A similar passage comes in *Confessions of an Inquiring Spirit, Shorter Works and Fragments, CW* 77, II: 1152.

[19] Both *The Friend, CW* 6, I: 104, and *The Statesman's Manual, Lay Sermons*, pp. 47–8.

response aroused by the sublime, and we have already seen that 'sublime' was an essential critical term in Coleridge's vocabulary, and that he believed sublimity to be Hebrew by birth. It is this wondering response that he describes, almost as if it is so obvious as to go without saying, in *Confessions*:

And need I add that I met everywhere [in the Bible] more or less copious sources of truth and power and purifying impulses {& that I found} words for my inmost thoughts, songs for my joy, utterances for my hidden griefs, pleadings for my shame and my feebleness? In short *whatever finds me* bears witness for itself that it had proceeded from a Holy Spirit, even from the same Spirit 'which remaining in itself yet regenerateth all other powers, and *in all ages* entering into holy souls maketh them friends of God and prophets'.[20]

The wondering experience of being *found* by the Bible is precisely what he describes in the opening aphorism of *Aids to Reflection*: 'in philosophy equally as in poetry it is the highest and most useful prerogative of genius to produce the strongest impressions of novelty, while it rescues admitted truths from the neglect caused by the very circumstance of their universal admission' (p. 11). In this essential respect, philosophy – and, of course, religion – and poetry are united. The effect produced by the Bible is not different in kind from that produced by other writing or, in Coleridge's case as in Wordsworth's, by nature, only different in extent, as he underlines at the beginning of the next letter in *Confessions*: 'more . . . than I have experienced in all other books put together . . . the words of the Bible *find me* at greater depths of my being' (II: 1123).

The Bible is inseparably bound up with Coleridge's complex ideas of the imagination. When, in a memorable phrase, he described scripture histories as 'the living educts of the imagination',[21] he was making an early statement of the idea that they find him: they bring out the essential imagination within him. But that imagination must be present in the individual to begin with. So he looks for a quality of the imagination in the individual to match the original creative imagination, and exclaims later in *The Statesman's Manual* (p. 50):

O what a mine of undiscovered treasures, what a new world of power and truth would the Bible promise to our future meditation, if in some gracious moment one solitary text of all its inspired contents should but dawn upon us in the pure untroubled brightness of an IDEA, that most glorious birth of the God-like within us which, even as the light, its material symbol, reflects itself from a thousand surfaces and flies homeward to its parent mind enriched with

[20] Wisd. 7: 27, paraphrased. *CW* 11, II: 1121–2.
[21] *The Statesman's Manual, Lay Sermons*, p. 29.

a thousand forms, itself above form and still remaining in its own simplicity and identity!

This is a reworking of part of one of his finest poems, 'Dejection: an Ode':

> O Lady! we receive but what we give,
> And in our life alone does Nature live:
> Ours is her wedding garment, ours her shroud!
>   And would we aught behold, of higher worth,
> Than that inanimate cold world allowed
> To the poor loveless ever-anxious crowd,
>   Ah! from the soul itself must issue forth
> A light, a glory, a fair luminous cloud
>   Enveloping the Earth –
> And from the soul itself must there be sent
>   A sweet and potent voice, of its own birth,
> Of all sweet sounds the life and element!

The joy that he laments the loss of in this poem is essentially the same as the wonder he writes of in *Aids to Reflection*. In the poem he can no longer feel that joy in the world of nature; if there is a hint of a similar dejection in the passage from *The Statesman's Manual*, it is nevertheless clear from most of his declarations of his response to the Bible that he did recover something of the joy and wonder in that world, if not in the world of nature. 'The primary imagination' that he held 'to be the living power and prime agent of all human perception, and as a repetition in the finite mind of the eternal act of creation in the infinite I AM' (*Biographia Literaria*, I: 304), remained active and responsive in his study of the Bible.

There is a further link here, between God the creator and the artist as creator. So, on the one hand, he can image the supreme human artist as the Creator: 'in Shakespeare one sentence begets the next naturally; the meaning is all inwoven. He goes on kindling like a meteor through the dark atmosphere – yet when the creation in its outlines is once perfect, then he seems to rest from his labour and to smile upon his work and tell himself it is very good' (*Table Talk*, 5 April 1833, I: 356–7). On the other hand, he can hint at the familiar idea of the Bible being a perfect work of art because it has the supreme author: 'the content of every work must correspond to the character and designs of the workmaster; and the inference in the present case is too obvious to be overlooked' (*The Statesman's Manual*, p. 5). He saw the same quality of literary genius in the Bible that he saw in Shakespeare. A key element in Shakespeare is that 'in all his various characters we still feel ourselves communing with the same human nature . . . that just proportion, that union and interpenetration of the universal and the particular which must ever pervade all works of decided genius and true science' (*The Friend*, I: 457), and he found the identical quality in the Bible, where 'every agent appears and acts as a self-subsisting individual: each has a life of its own, and yet all are one life' (*The Statesman's Manual*, p. 31).

In spite of this fundamental identity in his religious and aesthetic ideas, Coleridge did make some separation of kind between the Bible and literature. He asks explicitly at the beginning of essay II of 'The Landing-Place' whether it is 'most important to the best interests of mankind . . . that [the Bible] . . . should be distinguished from all other works not in degree only but even in *kind*?', and noted in one copy that he was, with reservations, 'on the affirmative side'.[22] His observation in *Biographia Literaria* that 'the first chapter of Isaiah . . . is poetry in the most emphatic sense' comes almost immediately after his almost hedonistic definition of a poem as 'that species of composition which is opposed to works of science by proposing for its *immediate* object pleasure, not truth' (II: 13), so he adds, 'yet it would be not less irrational than strange to assert that pleasure, and not truth, was the immediate object of the Prophet' (II: 15). The apparently pure aestheticism of his definition of a poem must be qualified by the poetry of the book of truth: there pleasure is the signature of truth, but truth is the key. Coleridge's sense of the unsurpassed beauty of the Bible is, at the last, grounded not on aesthetics but belief. Yet if that truth did not arouse pleasure, it would not be truth. The Bible, particularly the NT, is the yardstick of truth by which to measure the quality of other books. Like a Tyndale expounding the necessity of reading the Bible with a baptismal predisposition to believe in the heart, he would advise 'a nephew or son about to enter into Holy Orders' to read the NT 'with a prepared heart', which is as much as to say, with the primary imagination active. He adds, 'did you ever meet any book that went to your heart so often and so deeply – are not other books . . . wonderfully efficacious in proportion as they resemble the New Testament. . . ?' (*Notebooks*, III: 3440).

PERCY BYSSHE SHELLEY AND 'SCRIPTURE AS A COMPOSITION'

Hellenist, probably atheist, perhaps deist, but definitely not Christian, Percy Bysshe Shelley (1799–1822) pursues the implications of

---

[22] *The Friend*, I: 135. His reservations came principally from his reading of Chillingworth, for he recognised the importance of church authority and tradition (see *Table Talk*, I: 231).

Wordsworth's sense that poetry is the soul of religion. For him, reversing Coleridge almost mirror-like, the Bible is literature, and this is what makes it religious. This may seem strange for one who was so notoriously anti-Christian – surely the position of a Paine would have been more natural, rejection of the Bible at once as religion and as good literature? But Shelley, admirer as he was of Paine, distinguished sharply between the practise of Christianity and Christianity 'in its abstract purity',[23] between the teaching of Jesus and its interpretation or corruption: he could abstract Jesus from the institutional religion he so reviled. He knew his Bible as well as most of the orthodox and he read it to the end of his life, even if he had Keats's poems in his pocket rather than a Bible when he drowned. Evidently there had been a rumour to this effect: Byron set the record straight, adding significantly, 'however, it would not have been strange, for he was a great admirer of Scripture as a composition'.[24] The importance for us of the comment is that it is almost the first use of a phrase analogous to 'the Bible as literature'. That it should come in connection with a literary man who was not a Christian anticipates a major aspect of ideas about the Bible as literature, that very often they come either from unbelievers or are directed towards them.

Shelley never wrote at length on the Bible, but his scattered remarks on parts of the OT and his more connected discussions of Jesus confirm that he was indeed 'a great admirer of Scripture as a composition'. The essence of this admiration is summarised in 'A Defence of Poetry': 'it is probable that the astonishing poetry of Moses, Job, David, Solomon and Isaiah had produced a great effect upon the mind of Jesus and his disciples. The scattered fragments preserved to us by the biographers of this extraordinary person are all instinct with the most vivid poetry' (*CW*, VII: 126). In a similar passage he supposes that

The sublime dramatic poem entitled Job had familiarised [Jesus's] imagination with the boldest imagery afforded by the human mind and the material world. Ecclesiastes had diffused a seriousness and solemnity over the frame of his spirit glowing with youthful hope, and made audible to his listening heart

> The still, sad music of humanity
> Not harsh or grating but of ample power
> To chasten and subdue.
> ('Essay on Christianity', VI: 229)

Finally, in a letter he refers to Job and the Song of Songs as 'models of poetical sublimity and pathos'.[25]

---

[23] 'A Defence of Poetry', *Complete Works*, VII: 127.
[24] Letter to Thomas Moore, 27 August 1822, *Letters and Journals*, IX: 198.
[25] To Leigh Hunt, 3 November 1819, X: 110.

Like and unlike Blake, he views Jesus as a poet, indeed, he seems to make him the supreme poet of the Bible, but he does this partly on the basis of his morality. Again 'A Defence of Poetry' makes the essential point:

Plato, following the doctrines of Timaeus and Pythagoras, taught . . . a moral and intellectual system of doctrine comprehending at once the past, the present and the future condition of man. Jesus Christ divulged the sacred and eternal truths contained in these views to mankind, and Christianity, in its abstract purity, became the exoteric expression of the esoteric doctrines of the poetry and wisdom of antiquity. (VII: 127)

Central to these ideas of the Bible as poetry and Jesus as poet is Shelley's idea of poetry. The climactic passage of 'A Defence of Poetry' begins in this way:

Poetry is indeed something divine. It is at once the centre and circumference of knowledge; it is that which comprehends all science, and that to which all science must be referred. It is at the same time the root and blossom of all other systems of thought; it is that from which all spring, and that which adorns all; and that which, if blighted, denies the fruit and the seed, and withholds from the barren world the nourishment and the succession of the scions of the tree of life. It is the perfect and consummate surface and bloom of things; it is as the odour and the colour of the rose to the texture of the elements which compose it, as the form and the splendour of unfaded beauty to the secrets of anatomy and corruption. (VII: 135)

The equation with divinity is essential, and it is perhaps not surprising that the passage as a whole reminds one of Paul on charity: charity, the vital essence of meaning, is a supreme quality for Paul, as poetry is the supreme element for Shelley. There is another familiar quality in this passage: it echoes Wordsworth's claim that 'poetry is the breath and finer spirit of all knowledge', and Coleridge's that poetry is 'the blossom and the fragrancy of all human knowledge'. Shelley is playing a cadenza on his predecessors' ideas and images. The difference from them comes not in his sense of poetry or in his literary sense of the Bible, but in his sense of religion. He remains apart from Christianity but poetry is religion and the Bible is, in parts, poetry. So linking poetry and belief in the 'Defence', he declares that

it exceeds all imagination to conceive what would have been the moral condition of the world if neither Dante, Petrarch, Boccaccio, Chaucer, Shakespeare, Calderon, Lord Bacon nor Milton had ever existed; if Raphael and Michaelangelo had never been born; if the Hebrew poetry had never been translated; if a revival of the study of Greek literature had never taken place; if no monuments of ancient sculpture had been handed down to us; and if the poetry of the religion of the ancient world had been extinguished together with its belief. (VII: 133–4)

In the same vein, he included the Bible in his catalogue of the 'few well-chosen titles' that might make up a good library. The list starts with Greek drama and Plato, and finishes 'last, yet first, the Bible'.[26] What was suggested by Wordsworth's ideas has indeed happened: the Bible has become part of the canon of literature.

AN INFIDEL AND THE BIBLE: LORD BYRON

Lord Byron (1788–1824), for all his notoriety, was neither an enemy of the Bible nor especially interested in religious truth. Lacking the intellectual urgency and subtlety of Coleridge or Shelley, he is more like a representative figure. He was brought up – as who was not before the twentieth century? – with the Bible before him. Though he lapsed as a Christian he remained a literary admirer of the Bible. In 1821 he asked his publisher, John Murray, to send him 'a common Bible of good legible print . . . – Don't forget this – for I am a great reader and admirer of those books – and had read them through and through before I was eight years old – that is to say the *Old* Testament – for the New struck me as a task – but the other as a pleasure.'[27] This surely describes the experience of many. More specifically, he noted, 'of the Scriptures themselves I have ever been a reader and admirer as compositions, particularly the Arab-Job – and parts of Isaiah – and the song of Deborah'.[28] This, from 1821, is the first appearance of the phrase, 'as compositions'. He passed the occasional favourable literary comment on the Bible in his conversation, observing once,

Since we have spoken of witches, what think you of the witch of Endor? I have always thought this the finest and most finished witch-scene that ever was written or conceived; and you will be of my opinion if you consider all the circumstances and the actors in the case, together with the gravity, simplicity and dignity of the language. It beats all the ghost scenes I ever read.[29]

Byron composed two works that connect with the Bible, *Hebrew Melodies* (1815) and the drama *Cain* (1821), but the connection is too slight

---

[26] Thomas Medwin, *Revised Life of Shelley* (London, 1913), p. 255, as given in Newman Ivey White, *Shelley*, 2 vols. (New York: Knopf, 1940), II: 234.

[27] Letter of 9 October 1821, *Letters and Journals*, VIII: 238.

[28] Letter to Annabella Milbanke, 15 February 1814; as given in Thomas L. Ashton, *Byron's Hebrew Melodies* (London: Routledge, 1972), p. 67.

[29] From James Kennedy's *Conversations on Religion with Lord Byron* (1830, p. 154), as given by Ashton, p. 174n.

to make them genuine contributions to a literary sense of the Bible. They are a further reflection of the growing literary rather than religious feeling for the Bible, and of the taste for poetic antiquities that had been slowly developing from the time of Husbands' work through that of Macpherson and Bishop Percy. This is what he made of Job 4: 13–21:

> A spirit passed before me: I beheld
> The face of Immortality unveiled –
> Deep sleep came down on ev'ry eye save mine –
> And there it stood, – all formless – but divine:
> Along my bones the creeping flesh did quake;
> And as my damp hair stiffened, thus it spake:
>
> 'Is man more just than God? Is man more pure
> Than he who deems even Seraphs insecure?
> Creatures of clay – vain dwellers in the dust!
> The moth survives you, and are ye more just?
> Things of a day! you wither ere the night,
> Heedless and blind to Wisdom's wasted light!'

However kindly or unkindly one may judge this, it does not take one with renewed appreciation to the language of the KJB; rather, it functions like the multitude of exclamations at gems in the Bible, as an identification of an excellence. The taste that produces it may be more romantic (and in keeping with the liking for the witch of Endor) than the taste which produced the eighteenth-century paraphrases, but the result, though less expansive, is hardly more biblical.

Hebrew Melodies scooped a project Byron's friend the Irishman Thomas Moore (1779–1852) had been working on, *Sacred Songs* (1816); many of these are paraphrases of the Bible, and sometimes they show a greater fidelity to the KJB, as in his version of Isaiah 60, which begins:

> Awake, arise, thy light is come;
>   The nations, that before outshone thee
> Now at thy feet lie dark and dumb –
>   The glory of the Lord is on thee!
>
> Arise – the Gentiles to thy ray,
>   From ev'ry nook of earth shall cluster;
> And kings and princes haste to pay
>   Their homage to thy rising lustre.

As so often in versifications, the pursuit of regular metre removes the felicity, and there are other typical signs of the pressure of verse form in additions that smack of poetic diction such as 'thy rising lustre', and in the omissions. In particular, the parallelism that is so striking in the prose version is diminished: one has to perceive it across the interruption of two lines in the first verse, and between pairs of lines in the second. A couple of phrases survive more or less intact, so one is reminded of the KJB, but, by comparison with the prose parallelism of Macpherson sixty years earlier, and the slightly more recent work of Smart and Blake, this sounds less biblical. The cause is the fundamental incompatibility between regular lyric versification and the almost free verse form of the parallelistic prose. The movement towards a more biblical style that was occasionally evident in pre-romantic and early romantic poetry has faded out.

There is, then, plenty of evidence from Wordsworth through to Byron (with the exception of Keats) that the major romantic poets admired the Bible as literature, indeed, that some of them regarded it as literature rather than as religion, but, with the possible exception of Wordsworth, little evidence that it affected their writing. This is not just because they rarely turned to the Bible for subjects but also because their styles, both in verse and prose, are fundamentally un-biblical. Coleridge, of them all the most devoted to the Bible, was also the one who wrote least like it, not only in his verse but in his extraordinarily erudite and convoluted prose. In the long perspective, perhaps the most striking thing to emerge is the beginning of the idea of the Bible as literature in the way Shelley and Byron take pleasure in the Bible without accepting the framework of institutional religion that usually surrounds it.

A BIBLE FOR THE ROMANTIC READER

Here is part of a report of a conversation that perhaps took place about 1829:

Something was observed about Byron and Tom Paine as to their attacks upon religion; and I said that sceptics and philosophical unbelievers appeared to me to have just as little liberality or enlargement of view as the most bigoted fanatic. They could not bear to make the least concession to the opposite side. They denied the argument that because the Scriptures were fine they were therefore of divine origin, and yet they virtually admitted it; for, not believing the truth, they thought themselves bound to maintain that they were good for nothing. I had once, I said, given great offence to a knot of persons of this description by contending that Jacob's dream was finer than anything in Shakespeare, and that Hamlet would bear no comparison with, at least, one character in the New Testament. A young poet had said on this occasion, he did not like the Bible because there was nothing about flowers in it; and I asked him if he had forgot the passage, 'Behold the lilies of the field', etc? 'Yes,' said Northcote, 'and in the Psalms and in the book of Job there are passages of unrivalled beauty. In the latter there is the description of the warhorse that has been so often referred to, and of the days of Job's prosperity; and in the Psalms I think there is that passage, "He openeth his hands, and the earth is filled with plenteousness; he turneth away his face, and we are troubled; he hideth himself, and we are left in darkness;" [cf. Ps. 104: 28–9] or, again, how fine is that expression, "All the beasts of the forests are mine, and so are the cattle upon a thousand hills!" [Ps. 50: 11, PB]. What an expanse, and what a grasp of the subject! Everything is done upon so large a scale, and yet with such ease, as if seen from the highest point of view. It has mightily a look of inspiration or of being dictated by a superior intelligence. They say mere English readers cannot understand Homer because it is a translation; but why will it not bear a translation as well as the book of Job, if it is as fine?'

The author is the voluminous essayist and critic, William Hazlitt (1778–1830).[30] He does not guarantee the accuracy of his reports but hopes they have a verisimilitude, and this one, especially in the haziness of the quotations, certainly does. The literary virtues of the Bible were a subject of conversation among the intelligentsia, and the mixture of standard and personal examples of excellence is characteristic of what we have seen; so is the rivalry with Shakespeare and with the classics. As would have been so in the two preceding centuries, most of the comments seem to be vaguely referred to the originals, but the superiority of the KJB as a translation to translations of all other literary works is also taken for granted. One aspect of the conversation, however, distinctly belongs to this late romantic time. The explicit statement 'that because the Scriptures were fine they were therefore of divine origin' is a striking culmination of some of the ideas we have been following. The literary superiority bespeaks inspiration, and who should inspire if not God? Literary and divine inspiration seem to have become indistinguishable, though they are not coupled quite as Blake had coupled them; for Blake divine inspiration was literary inspiration, but here literary inspiration is divine inspiration.

It makes no difference whether this was really Northcote's idea or whether Hazlitt was using him as a stalking-horse. Thought about the Bible as literature was clearly developing in this direction from Wordsworth on, and Hazlitt was helping that development, here going beyond the praise he had accorded the Bible in his *Lectures on the English Poets*[31] or his *Lectures on the Dramatic Literature of the Age of Elizabeth*. In these

---

[30] *Conversations with James Northcote*, *Complete Works*, XI: 245–6. For the comments on accuracy referred to in the next sentence, see p. 350.   [31] 'On poetry in general', *Complete Works*, V: 16–17.

latter comes a phrase that epitomises the movement towards reading the Bible as literature rather than religion, 'leaving religious faith quite out of the question'.[32] This is part of what is, as always in Hazlitt, a long passage. Description of the Bible's impact in Elizabethan times becomes an account of its literary excellence, and herein lie two ideas that were gradually to become important, first, that the English Bible was a literary influence, and, second, an idea closely akin to the myth that the KJB was an instant success, that it had had this kind of influence almost from the time it first appeared:

But the Bible was thrown open to all ranks and conditions 'to run and read,' with its wonderful table of contents from Genesis to the Revelations . . . I cannot think that all this variety and weight of knowledge could be thrown in all at once upon the mind of a people and not make some impressions upon it, the traces of which might be discerned in the manners and literature of the age. For to leave more disputable points and take only the historical parts of the Old Testament, or the moral sentiments of the New, there is nothing like them in the power of exciting awe and admiration, or of rivetting sympathy. We see what Milton has made of the account of the Creation from the manner in which he has treated it, imbued and impregnated with the spirit of the time of which we speak. Or what is there equal (in that romantic interest and patriarchal simplicity which goes to the heart of a country and rouses it, as it were, from its lair in wastes and wildernesses) equal to the story of Joseph and his brethren, of Rachel and Laban, of Jacob's dream, of Ruth and Boaz, the descriptions in the book of Job, the deliverance of the Jews out of Egypt, or the account of their captivity and return from Babylon? There is in all these parts of the Scripture, and numberless more of the same kind, to pass over the Orphic hymns of David, the prophetic denunciations of Isaiah or the gorgeous visions of Ezekiel, an originality, a vastness of conception, a depth and tenderness of feeling, and a touching simplicity in the mode of narration which he who does not feel need be made of no 'penetrable stuff.' There is something in the character of Christ too (leaving religious faith quite out of the question) of more sweetness and majesty, and more likely to work a change in the mind of man by the contemplation of its idea alone, than any to be found in history, whether actual or feigned. This character is that of a sublime humanity. (VI: 182–3)

What is of most significance here is the way that the idea is formed: the Bible is so excellent a creation that it must have exercised a literary influence, and this is to be proved not by showing that influence but by exclaiming at the beauty of the Bible in terms that are redolent of romantic sensibility. The passage is rhetoric rather than literary criticism or history: it is a powerful persuasion to a literary opinion, but it neither

---

[32] 'General view of the subject', *Complete Works*, VI: 183.

proves that opinion to be right nor draws out a true history. Nevertheless, it is important. If Coleridge (with Swift behind him) was the first to argue that the KJB had influenced the English language (and influenced it for the better), Hazlitt is the first to argue that the English Bible has been a literary influence.

The terms and the items Hazlitt selects suggest one more thing, the gradual replacement of poetry by the novel as the predominant literary mode. If the highest English literary achievements between 1790 and 1820 belong to the poetry, still it is a close-run thing; in Victorian times they belong to the novel. Where, say, Lowth had unhesitatingly confined himself to the poetry of the OT, Hazlitt, without in any way denying the power of the poetry, passes over it, as if the securest demonstration of quality can now be made from examples which take, by and large, the territory of the novel: moving histories, moral sentiments, and character. He is creating a Bible for the readers of Sir Walter Scott's novels.[33]

CHARLOTTE BRONTË AND THE INFLUENCE OF THE KJB

In spite of what we have seen from Say and from Lowth among the critics, and Smart, Macpherson and Blake among the poets, there are good grounds for thinking that signs of the influence of the KJB's language are more likely to be found in prose than in verse – at least until the establishment of free verse – and one novel shows that influence in a particularly useful way, Charlotte Brontë's *Jane Eyre* (1848). It not only shows the obvious distinction between use of and influence by the KJB, but it suggests distinctions between kinds of influence, distinctions which will allow us to cut through the difficulties that would arise if we took the whole field of the influence of the Bible (itself a subject to generate at least one large book) as part of the present subject.

In *Jane Eyre*, romanticism, religion and the KJB come together to create important artistic effects, and the result is sometimes insight into the KJB. It contains many examples of quotation or allusion (the line is a fine one). When Rochester, analysing Jane's character, says, "'strong wind, earthquakeshock, and fire may pass by: but I shall follow the guiding of that still small voice which interprets the dictates of conscience'" (II: 4), the biblical echo would have been obvious enough: he

---

[33] In passing, Scott's well-known love for the Bible is worth recording. As he lay dying he asked his future biographer, John Gibson Lockhart, to read to him, 'and when I asked from what book, he said, "Need you ask? There is but one." I chose the 14th chapter of St. John's Gospel' (*Memoirs of Sir Walter Scott* [1837–8], 5 vols. (London: Macmillan, 1900), V: 423).

is both alluding to and quoting 1 Kgs 19: 11–12. What makes this different from most biblical allusions in works that pre-date the literary rise of the KJB is the inescapable presence of its language in 'still small voice'. Such quotation needs no quotation marks or typographical distinction because it is fully integrated with the language of the novel. Familiarity with both content and language of the KJB is used in a straightforward but unostentatious manner to enrich the text.

But Charlotte Brontë does not just use the KJB, her language is in a number of respects shaped by it: it is an influence on her as well as a source for her to draw on. This mixture of use and influence in her language is clearest at the end of volume II as the desolation following the broken wedding overwhelms Jane:

My eyes were covered and closed: eddying darkness seemed to swim round me, and reflection came in as black and confused a flow. Self-abandoned, relaxed and effortless, I seemed to have laid me down in the dried-up bed of a great river; I heard a flood loosened in remote mountains, and felt the torrent come: to rise I had no will, to flee I had no strength. I lay faint; longing to be dead. One idea only still throbbed life-like within me – a remembrance of God: it begot an unuttered prayer: these words went wandering up and down in my rayless mind, as something that should be whispered; but no energy was found to express them: –

'Be not far from me, for trouble is near: there is none to help.'

It was near: and as I had lifted no petition to heaven to avert it – as I had neither joined my hands, nor bent my knees, nor moved my lips – it came: in full, heavy swing the torrent poured over me. The whole consciousness of my life lorn, my love lost, my hope quenched, my faith death-struck, swayed full and mighty above me in one sullen mass. That bitter hour cannot be described: in truth, 'the waters came into my soul; I sank in deep mire: I felt no standing; I came into deep waters; the floods overflowed me.'

In important ways this is similar to Bunyan's description of Christian and Hopeful wading into the river of death (see above, p. 184): both are climactic passages, both quote or adapt the Psalms, including, in both cases, Ps. 69: 2. Moreover, neither passage is written in a purely biblical style: just as one could distinguish Bunyan from the Bible, so one can distinguish Brontë. The crucial difference between the two passages becomes apparent when one recognises that, by contrast with the Bunyan, the Brontë is typical of the style of the whole novel. Where the Bunyan uses the Bible for a local effect, and so suggests little in the way of a literary sense of the language of the KJB, the Brontë rings with admiration for the KJB.

The quotations (Ps. 22: 11 and Ps. 69: 1–2) adapt the originals in two ways, to the grammatical demands of the local context and for rhythmic effect. The latter is the significant change: Brontë has eliminated linking words to heighten the drumbeat parallelism of clause against clause. This is how the second quotation reads in the KJB, with Brontë's omissions italicised:

Save me, O God; for the waters are come in unto my soul. I sink in deep mire, *where* there is no standing: I am come into deep waters, *where* the floods overflow me.

Yet the effect is not of a departure from the style of the KJB, for the rhythm is still biblical, as the next verse of Psalm 69 shows:

I am weary of my crying: my throat is dried: mine eyes fail while I wait for my God.

The first three clauses, balancing on colons, have the same drumbeat. Brontë's quotations, in their adapted but still biblical rhythm, are at one with the dominant rhythm of her prose, which is based on parallel phrases and, a development beyond the Bible, parallel words. The rhythm of the quotations is matched by the rhythm of 'my life lorn, my love lost, my hope quenched, my faith death-struck', or 'to rise I had no will, to flee I had no strength'. That there are other effects and influences in the language besides the biblical, or that there are other biblical turns of phrase, need not bother us here: the crucial point is that a major element in the style proclaims its origin in the KJB, and the language of the KJB is shown to be like the artful language of the novel. This demonstrates literary quality in the KJB as surely as good practical criticism: *Jane Eyre* creates literary appreciation of the Bible in a way that Bunyan's work does not.

One last example may make the distinction between allusion and influence still clearer. Brontë's idea of love is intensely religious and constantly expressed in religious language. When Rochester first proposes (II: 8) in an 'Eden-like' setting, it is a call 'to the paradise of union'. Jane describes their relationship as 'communion'; to have it broken would be 'to have my morsel of bread snatched from my lips, and my drop of living water dashed from my cup'. So far the biblical references are obvious. Moving towards the avowal of love, Jane develops her sense of communion: '"I have talked, face to face, with what I reverence; with what I delight in, – with an original, a vigorous, an expanded mind. I have known you, Mr Rochester"'. Only 'reverence' here explicitly sustains the religious idea of love. 'Face to face' is too ordinary a phrase to invite us to treat it as an allusion, but, if we do, the result is surprising.

Twice the KJB uses the phrase in an everyday way, but six of the seven OT uses of it describe man and God together (the seventh, Judg. 6: 22, concerns Gideon and the angel of the Lord), and the novel several times presents the love relationship as a relationship with God, or with a god. The most striking use of 'face to face' comes in Paul:

For now we see through a glass, darkly; but then face to face: now I know in part; but then shall I know even as also I am known. And now abideth faith, hope, charity, these three; but the greatest of these is charity. (1 Cor. 13: 12–13)

Brontë's 'face to face' links with knowledge just as this passage does, and the aptness of the passage becomes still greater if one substitutes 'love' for 'charity', for love is what matters most to Brontë. This is enough to show that 'face to face' might be an allusion, but not to prove that it is or to demonstrate that she herself was aware of the connection. Indeed, the probability is otherwise: if she seeks an effect, she seeks it openly. Nevertheless, the aptness of the connection shows just how far her idea of love was created by her religious upbringing: the Bible has influenced her even more than she is aware, and more than any ordinary reader could realise. Now, influence of this sort shows a writer's absorption in the Bible and religion, but it neither tells of the writer's attitude to the Bible nor does it help to create an attitude to the Bible in the reader. For both reasons, such influence lies outside the scope of this book.

CHAPTER THIRTEEN

Literary discussion to mid-Victorian times

THE PIOUS CHORUS

If to adore an image be idolatry,
To deify a book is bibliolatry.

This *bon mot*, the *OED*'s first example of 'bibliolatry', comes from John Byrom (d. 1763) in the course of an argument against the idea that the Holy Spirit is present in the Bible, for 'Books are but books; th'illuminating part / Depends on God's good spirit, in the heart'.[1] Nearly a century later the English opiumeater, Thomas De Quincey (1785–1859) defined 'bibliolatry' as 'a superstitious allegiance – an idolatrous homage – to the words, to the syllables and to the very punctuation of the Bible'.[2] The invention of the word, though overdue, was particularly appropriate for the latter part of the eighteenth century and the nineteenth century, but what is most striking about De Quincey's engaging and witty discussion of bibliolatry is that none of it concerns literary attitudes. A new word is needed to denote not just literary bibliolatry but its English form, already so thoroughly evident, reverence for the KJB. 'AVolatry' (in preference to 'KJBolatry') has been rife since the 1760s. Typically it emerges in a pious chorus of adoration that is more often an exercise in rhetoric than criticism. Commentators seem to vie to produce the most resounding and memorable praise of the KJB.

The greatest spur to the chorus was the pressure of rival versions, and the chorus increasingly takes on a polemic aspect as argument for an official revision made it more and more possible that the revered old treasure would be left to moulder in the vault of antiquities. Yet it would be wrong to view the chorus as mere political agitation spurred by

---

[1] 'A stricture on the Bishop of Glocester's doctrine of grace', in Samuel Johnson, ed., *The Works of the English Poets*, 21 vols. (London, 1810), XV: 267.

[2] 'Protestantism' (1847), *The Collected Writings of Thomas De Quincey*, ed. David Masson (London, 1897), VIII: 263.

reactionary nostalgia. There may be an element of unthinking over-statement but there is no hypocrisy in stating what, in common with most of your peers, you believe, nor is rational examination necessary to make that belief sincere. Indeed, though a De Quincey might debunk bibliolatry, the first half of the nineteenth century was a time when it was difficult to question AVolatry, so fashionable had it become. The literary historian Henry Hallam (1777–1859), recognised the difficulty and raised mild but ineffectual protest:

The style of this translation is in general so enthusiastically praised that no one is permitted either to qualify or even explain the grounds of his approbation. It is held to be the perfection of our English language. I shall not dispute this proposition; but one remark as to a matter of fact cannot reasonably be censured, that, in consequence of the principle of adherence to the original versions which had been kept up ever since the time of Henry VIII, it is not the language of the reign of James I. It may, in the eyes of many, be a better English, but it is not the English of Daniel, or Raleigh, or Bacon, as any one may easily perceive. It abounds, in fact, especially in the Old Testament, with obsolete phraseology, and with single words long since abandoned, or retained only in provincial use. On the more important question, whether this translation is entirely, or with very trifling exceptions, conformable to the original text, it seems unfit to enter. It is one which is seldom discussed with all the temper and freedom from oblique views which the subject demands, and upon which, for this reason, it is not safe for those who have not had leisure or means to examine it for themselves, to take upon trust the testimony of the learned.[3]

This fairly accounts for the unsatisfactoriness that one may find in the declarations of AVolatry and is sufficient warning of political motivation in some of the arguments.

The typical – and not unfamiliar – sound of the chorus can be heard in three remarks from the first twenty years of the century. Citing Swift and Monboddo, Thomas Rennell, Dean of Winchester, later Master of the Temple, declared 'that the grandeur, dignity and simplicity of [the KJB] is confessed even by those who wish eagerly to promote a revision, and by the most eminent critics, and masters of style it is allowed to exhibit a more perfect specimen of the *integrity* of the English language, than any other writing which that language can boast'.[4] Reverence for the translators and the belief that their work was an instant success are natural corollaries of this judgement. Both were voiced in response to another new version, John Bellamy's (1818). The *Quarterly Review* declared,

---

[3] *Introduction to the Literature of Europe in the Fifteenth, Sixteenth, and Seventeenth Centuries*, 4 vols. (1837–9; sixth edn, London, 1860), II: 464. [4] *Discourses on Various Subjects* (London, 1801), p. 240.

He has no relish or perception of the exquisite simplicity of the original, no touch of that fine feeling, that pious awe which led his venerable predecessors to infuse into their version as much of the Hebrew idiom as was consistent with the perfect purity of our own; a taste and feeling which have given perennial beauty and majesty to the English tongue.[5]

Creation implies a creator, art an artist. It is a kind of atheism to deny that beauty was created deliberately. Evidently the good taste of the translators led them to adopt aesthetic criteria, criteria which perfected their language and made it either a monument of the 'perennial beauty and majesty of English', or an influence for beauty and majesty in English. Moreover, it is a confirmation of beauty to believe that it has always been appreciated. So another critic responding to Bellamy, John William Whittaker, was full of confidence:

it may safely be asserted, without fear of contradiction, that the nation at large has always paid our translators the tribute of veneration and gratitude which they so justly merit . . . Their version has been used ever since its first appearance, not only by the Church, but by all the sects which have forsaken her, and has justly been esteemed by all for its general faithfulness and the severe beauty of its language.[6]

The ease with which this is tossed off confirms that recognition of the linguistic merits (at least) of the KJB was thoroughly well established.

Nationalism is implicit in Whittaker's reference to 'the nation at large'. In the following year a chauvinistic nationalism, far outstripping any previous comparisons with the Bibles of other nations, was added to the chorus in the conclusion of a work defending the textual basis and scholarly accuracy of the KJB:

The language of our present version has the full tide of popular opinion strongly in its favour; it exhibits a style appropriately biblical, and is distinguished by a general simplicity of expression, which the most uncultivated mind may comprehend, and the most cultivated admire. It is a translation in possession of characteristical merits, which might be extinguished, but cannot be augmented, by principles of transitory taste and ephemeral criticism; a translation which, with all its imperfections in whatsoever part of Scripture the comparison be made, is superior to every other in our own, and inferior to none in any foreign language.[7]

---

[5] *Quarterly Review* 38: 455; as given in Henry John Todd, *A Vindication of our Authorised Translation* (London, 1819), p. 80.   [6] *An Historical and Critical Inquiry* (Cambridge, 1819), pp. 92–3.

[7] Anon. [Archbishop Richard Lawrence], *Remarks upon the Critical Principles, and the practical application of those principles, adopted by writers, who have at various periods recommended a new translation of the Bible as expedient and necessary* (Oxford, 1820), pp. 161–2.

The meaningless concession to imperfections in no way disguises the fact that this is AVolatry rampant: the KJB is supreme. Of special interest is the circularity of one part of the comment, that 'it exhibits a style appropriately biblical'. The translators, as I argued in chapter 1, had no special biblical English available to them. Time has made their language appear the only possible English for the Bible.

The best-known pre-Victorian nugget of AVolatry comes from the enormously popular historian, critic and poet Thomas Babington Macaulay (1800–59). He proclaimed of 'the English Bible' that it was 'a book which, if everything else in our language should perish, would alone suffice to show the whole extent of its beauty and power'.[8] For its pithiness and excess of a truth many would like to believe (is the beauty and power of English confined to a vocabulary of some 6,000 words? is Shakespeare's English to be confined within the range of the Bible? is the beauty and power of subordinated sentence structures to be lost?), this has often been quoted. What was it that prompted the magnificent and incisive Macaulay to such a remark? It was not just his 'talent for saying what is ordinary and familiar in impressive language'.[9] The remark comes as an aside in an elaborate argument that the imaginative and the critical faculties cannot flourish together; he has extolled Shakespeare to the skies (like so many, he is a bardolater before he is an AVolater) when Shakespeare is, as it were, writing naturally, but scorned him when he attempts to write to the critical standards of his time, especially the standards for prose. Herein lie two important factors beyond his personal response to the KJB. He has argued that times are more important than capacities to the productions of genius or the making of discoveries, and the English Bible belongs to the most fertile time in English literary history: did not that time produce Shakespeare? Secondly, he sees a key factor in the quality of the Bible as its independence from the critical tastes of the time, a quality it shares with Shakespeare. He observes in the next sentence that 'the respect which the translators felt for the original prevented them from adding any of the hideous decorations then in fashion'. Though this stops short of AVolatrous acclaim for the genius of the translators, the logic is still not compelling. Moreover, it is instructive to see bardolatry and AVolatry coming together in what we may call an imaginative truth. The KJB's reputation probably did little for Shakespeare's, but his certainly helped

[8] 'John Dryden', *The Edinburgh Review*, January 1828; *The Life and Works of Lord Macaulay Complete*, 10 vols. (London: Longman, 1903), V: 101.
[9] Margaret Cruickshank, *Thomas Babington Macaulay* (Boston: Twayne, 1978), p. 20.

the KJB's; together they are the key to seeing the late Elizabethan and early Jacobean period as the greatest in English literature.

Macaulay never elaborated on his literary sense of the Bible, but he did tell his beloved sister Hannah Macaulay that 'a person who professed to be a critic in the delicacies of the English language ought to have the Bible at his finger's ends'.[10] Had this been a public pronouncement it would have commanded instant assent not just from AVolaters but from the critical public at large.

An echo of Macaulay's brand of AVolatry appeared shortly afterwards at the end of Hartley Coleridge's brief and sympathetic account of Anthony Parver (as he calls Purver); observing that his Bible has received less attention than it merited, he adds presciently,

We doubt, indeed, whether any new translation, however learned, exact or truly orthodox, will ever appear to English Christians to be the real Bible. The language of the Authorised Version is the perfection of English, and it can never be written again, for the language of prose is one of the few things in which the English have really degenerated. Our tongue has lost its holiness.[11]

This expresses so exactly how many people now think that it is easy to forget what a massive change it represents from Augustan attitudes, easy to forget, too, just how many magnificent writers of prose were yet to delight the world. Swift's idea that the KJB should be a standard for language has reached its apotheosis: the KJB is more than the standard, it is perfection. The rise of AVolatry is part of that idealisation of the past and contempt for the present that is so typical of our own age.

The sweetest voice of all this chorus, frequently elevated to solo by later writers, belonged to a man Calvinistically reared who became an Anglican priest and consummated his rise to the heights by converting to Catholicism, Father Frederick William Faber (1814–63):

If the Aryan heresy was propagated and rooted by means of beautiful vernacular hymns, so who will say that the uncommon beauty and marvellous English of the Protestant Bible is not one of the great strongholds of heresy in this country? It lives on in the ear like a music that never can be forgotten, like the sound of church bells which the convert hardly knows how he can forego. Its felicities seem often to be things rather than mere words. It is part of the national mind and the anchor of the national seriousness. Nay, it is worshipped with a positive idolatry, in extenuation of whose grotesque fanaticism its intrinsic beauty pleads availingly with the man of letters and the scholar. The

---

[10] Letter to Hannah Macaulay, 30 May 1831, *The Letters of Thomas Babington Macaulay*, ed. Thomas Pinney, 6 vols. (Cambridge University Press, 1974–81), II: 22.
[11] *Biographia Borealis* (London, 1833), p. 718.

memory of the dead passes into it. The potent traditions of childhood are stereotyped in its verses. The power of all the griefs and trials of a man is hidden beneath its words. It is the representative of his best moments, and all that there has been about him of soft, and gentle, and pure, and penitent, and good, speaks to him forever out of his English Bible. It is his sacred thing which doubt never dimmed and controversy never soiled. It has been to him all along as the silent, but O how intelligible voice, of his guardian angel; and in the length and breadth of the land there is not a Protestant, with one spark of religiousness about him, whose spiritual biography is not in his Saxon Bible. And all this is an unhallowed power! The extinction of the Establishment would be a less step towards the conquest of the national mind, than, if it were possible (but we are speaking humanly and in our ignorance), to adopt that Bible, and correct it by the Vulgate. As it is, there is no blessing of the Church along with it, and who would dream that beauty was better than a blessing?[12]

Perhaps the argument that the aesthetic qualities of the KJB have been basic to the hold Protestantism has on England could only have been made by one who knew from experience the power of the KJB but now had to explain why his adopted Church was not dominant in England. In a sense, Faber gives the other side of the much-repeated idea that pleasure in the Scriptures will lead to religious enlightenment: seeing this enlightenment as heresy frees him from the obligation to regard the KJB's aesthetic qualities as subservient to its qualities as religious truth. The same freedom could only begin to be possible for English Protestants when a new version of the Bible, the Revised Version (RV), became available as a more authoritative representative of religious truth.

Faber's passage was pounced on: it was not only powerful, it was the enemy admitting much that the AVolaters believed. Among the pouncers was the then Dean of Westminster, later to be Archbishop of Dublin, a man of wide scholarly accomplishment who originated the scheme for the *OED* and was one of the translators of the RV, Richard Chenevix Trench (1807–86). Discussing the relationship between the Latin and the Saxon elements in English, he refers to the KJB since he can find no 'happier example of the preservation of the golden mean in this matter'.[13] The translators, he declares, steered a middle course with 'happy wisdom' and 'instinctive tact'; instantly wisdom and tact become inspiration as he turns to Faber:

There is a remarkable confession to this effect, to the wisdom, in fact, which guided them from above, to the providence that overruled their work, an hon-

---

[12] 'An essay on the interest and characteristics of the Lives of the Saints', in F.W. Faber, *The Life of S. Francis of Assisi* (London, 1853), pp. 116–7.
[13] *English, Past and Present* (1855; 4th edn, London, 1859), p. 32.

ourable acknowledgement of the immense superiority in this respect of our English version over the Romish, made by one now unhappily familiar with the latter, as once he was with our own. (p. 33)

And so he cites Faber, diplomatically omitting the sentence beginning, 'nay, it is worshipped with a positive idolatry', and the last three sentences.

Trench develops the argument into a new point: in his view, though the language of the KJB is 'the chief among the minor and secondary blessings which that version has conferred' (p. 32), it has an important religious significance. If the KJB had used the Latin-English of the Rheims-Douai Bible, he suggests, 'our loss would have been great and enduring, one which would have searched into the whole religious life of our people, and been felt in the very depths of the national mind' (p. 35).

In a later work Trench uses a phrase that was to become the essence of AVolatry, 'the first English classic'. The context is plainly literary. Looking to revision and arguing the importance of being able to read the Bible 'with pleasure', he declares that 'the sense of pleasure in it, I mean merely as the first English classic, would be greatly impaired by any alterations which seriously affect the homogeneousness of its style' (*On the Authorised Version*, p. 24). The ease with which the phrase rolls off his pen suggests it was not new, and indeed it had already been used several times in America (see below, p. 360). It seems unlikely that Trench knew this, but he may have known a less close antecedent in George Gilfillan's declaration that the Scriptures are 'the classics of the heart' (see below, p. 326). The phrase was picked up by the American scholar, George P. Marsh, in the 28th of his influential *Lectures on the English Language*: the KJB 'has now for more than two centuries maintained its position as an oracular expression of religious truth, and at the same time as the first classic of our literature – the highest exemplar of purity and beauty of language existing in our speech'.[14] Later Talbot W. Chambers, one of the members of the American Revision Committee, wrote an essay entitled 'the English Bible as a classic' (1879), but the phrase's most significant use came in the preface to the RV OT (1885): there the revisers, riding roughshod over history, describe the KJB as a translation 'which for more than two centuries and a half had held the position of an English classic' (pp. v–vi). This was enough to make the phrase a cliché and to prompt the celebrated author of *The Golden Bough*, Sir James George Frazer, to begin the preface to his *Passages of the Bible*

---

[14] William Smith, ed. (London, 1862), p. 441.

Chosen for their Literary Beauty and Interest (1895) thus: 'that our English version of the Bible is one of the greatest classics in the language is admitted by all in theory, but few people appear to treat it as such in practice'. As so often in religious and quasi-religious matters, practice falls short of dogma. Viewed with a rigour few of us would survive, that falling-short is an index of hypocrisy. One of the fascinations of ideas of the Bible as literature is the spectacle of attempts to correct that hypocrisy.

For all his caution and learning, Trench leans towards AVolatry. It is, therefore, thoroughly understandable that he should have omitted from Faber's remarks the charge of AVolatry ('it is worshipped with a positive idolatry'), and yet Faber's charge is only a little removed from a comment Trench himself was to make, that the English of the KJB 'has been very often, and very justly, the subject of highest commendation; and if I do not reiterate in words of my own or of others these commendations, it is only because they have been uttered so often and so fully, that it has become a sort of commonplace to repeat them' (*On the Authorised Version*, p. 9). Trench implies the lack of thought needed to iterate such praise. Hallam had previously hinted that critical thought about the KJB was becoming difficult, and now Faber has made the accusation explicit. Such suggestions and accusations were as drops of water on a forest fire.

The chorus still sounds its song, but only one more of its notes needs recording at this point. Spenser had described Chaucer as a 'well of English undefiled' (*The Faerie Queen* 4: 2, 32), and the phrase was too good to ignore. Johnson, for instance, writes in the preface to his dictionary of 'the writers before the Restoration, whose works I regard as "the wells of English undefiled"' (fol. C1r). Prompted by either Spenser or Johnson, the Unitarian advocate of revision, John R. Beard, attempting to diminish AVolatry and magnify Tyndale, argues that the KJB translators attenuated the force and injured the expressiveness and unity of the Bible by their use of Latinisms. So, 'whenever a proper revision of our English Bible is undertaken, reference for improvements should be made to the learned and cultured yet thoroughly English William Tyndale, from whose "well of English undefiled" may be drawn many words and phrases of the true old English flavour'.[15] The argument for Tyndale as 'the first and, it may be added, the best translator of the Bible into English' (p. 17) perhaps had some effect, but the mixture of sensible and prejudiced criticism of the KJB did not. Possibly spurred by

---

[15] *A Revised English Bible the Want of the Church and the Demand of the Age* (London and Manchester, 1857), pp. 53–4.

Beard,[16] three of the makers of the RV picked up Spenser's phrase. Joseph Barber Lightfoot almost uses it in describing the KJB as 'not only the storehouse of the highest truth, but also the purest well of their native English' (*Fresh Revision*, p. 191), and the Americans Philip Schaff and Chambers both call the KJB '"the pure well of English undefiled"'.[17] Just as the phrase 'an English classic' sealed the KJB's literary status, this phrase sealed its linguistic status.

Inevitably what might, in the present context, be called chorus-books began to appear.[18] The American Methodist George P. Eckman's Mendenhall Lectures at DePauw University, published as *The Literary Primacy of the Bible* (1915), have substantially this character: in them is to be found a very wide range of authorities assembled as the primary building blocks to prove the assertion in his title. It is useful to take one of his examples, for it shows the same kind of editorial manipulation that Trench applied to Faber. T.H. Huxley, redoubtable champion of Darwin and inventor of the word 'agnostic', was, to popular perception, as unlikely a champion of the Bible as Faber was of the KJB. Yet he did advocate the use of the Bible in schools, and Eckman, like several others such as Newton and Chambers, enlists part of what he wrote in the ranks of bibliolatry. Eckman twice quotes part of Huxley's passage, the second time introducing it with the remark that 'Huxley will not be regarded as a prejudiced witness for the Bible, yet he could say' (p. 162). Huxley appears first as an AVolater, second as a bibliolater. So, in a paragraph that goes on to quote Macaulay and Green, we read: 'it is almost impossible to exaggerate the influence of the English Bible upon our language. Of the Authorised Version Huxley says: "it is written in the noblest and purest English, and abounds in exquisite beauties of a merely literary form"' (p. 39). Later a longer quotation is given as one of four testimonies that 'the Bible is the supreme guide for conduct' (p. 162).

In context, Huxley is more reserved. William Forster's Education Bill

---

[16] I have already noted the apparently independent and contemporaneous use of the phrase 'as a classic' in England and America. Halsey probably had not read Beard (their books appeared a year and an ocean apart). He writes that the KJB, 'this grand old English Bible . . . has come down to us with every quality and attribute that could make any book a "well of English undefiled"' (p. 36). When the time is right more than one man can invent or discover the same thing, as Darwin and Alfred Wallace found.

[17] Philip Schaff, *The Revision of the English Versions of the Holy Scriptures* (New York, 1873), p. xx; Chambers, 'The English Bible as a classic', in *Anglo-American Bible Revision* (New York and London, 1879), p. 40. Chambers opens the quotation at 'well'.

[18] Perhaps the best of these are Jane T. Stoddart's two volumes, *The Old Testament in Life and Literature*, and *The New Testament in Life and Literature* (London: Hodder, 1913, 1914). Each is an anthology some 500 pages long of passages relating to individual books of the Bible.

of 1870 attempted to establish state schools free of sectarian teaching. Huxley, who was standing for the Metropolitan School Board, gave the issue careful and often witty consideration in 'The School Boards: what they can do, and what they may do' (1870). The question of the Bible's place in primary education was central to the issue, and we will see later that it prompted Matthew Arnold to work of major significance for this history. Huxley defined his own position, beginning thus:

I have always been strongly in favour of secular education, in the sense of education without theology; but I must confess I have been no less seriously perplexed to know by what practical measures the religious feeling, which is the essential basis of conduct, was to be kept up, in the present utterly chaotic state of opinion on these matters, without the use of the Bible. The pagan moralists lack life and colour, and even the noble Stoic, Marcus [Aurelius] Antonius, is too high and refined for an ordinary child. (p. 397)

Clearly he would rather not recommend the Bible if that were possible, for it is too closely associated with theology (Huxley it was who declared that he would rather be descended from a humble monkey than a man such as Bishop Wilberforce). But religious feeling, by which he means neither sectarian belief nor Christianity at large but 'love of some ethical ideal' (p. 396), and the responsive ability of an ordinary child are key points for Huxley. It is after these points that Eckman begins to quote:

Take the Bible as a whole; make the severest deductions which fair criticism can dictate for shortcomings and positive errors; eliminate, as a sensible lay-teacher would do, if left to himself, all that it is not desirable for children to occupy themselves with; and there still remains in this old literature a vast residuum of moral beauty and grandeur. And then consider the great historical fact that, for three centuries, this book has been woven into the life of all that is best and noblest in English history;[19] that it has become the national epic of Britain, and is as familiar to noble and simple, from John-o'Groat's House to Land's End, as Dante and Tasso once were to the Italians; that it is written in the noblest and purest English, and abounds in exquisite beauties of mere literary form; and, finally, that it forbids the veriest hind who never left his village to be ignorant of the existence of other countries and other civilisations, and of a great past, stretching back to the furthest limits of the oldest nations in the world. By the study of what other book could children be so much humanised and made to feel that each figure in that vast historical procession fills, like themselves, but a momentary space in the interval between two eternities; and earns the blessings or the curses of all time, according to its effort to do good and hate evil, even as they also are earning their payment for their work?

[19] Eckman omits the rest of this sentence.

Here the quotation ends. Huxley, however, had more to say, and he takes care to remind his reader that his view is carefully qualified: 'on the whole, then, I am in favour of reading the Bible, with such grammatical, geographical, and historical explanations by a lay-teacher as may be needful, with rigid exclusion of any further theological teaching than that contained in the Bible itself' (pp. 397–8). Shortly afterwards he remarks that 'if Bible-reading is not accompanied by constraint and solemnity, as if it were a sacramental operation, I do not believe there is anything in which children take more pleasure'. He adds a personal testimony that might have been included in chorus-books but for its scorn of religious teaching:

At least I know that some of the pleasantest recollections of my childhood are connected with the voluntary study of an ancient Bible which belonged to my grandmother . . . What comes vividly back on my mind are remembrances of my delight in the histories of Joseph and of David; and of my keen appreciation of the chivalrous kindness of Abraham in his dealing with Lot. Like a sudden flash there returns back upon me my utter scorn of the pettifogging meanness of Jacob, and my sympathetic grief over the heartbreaking lamentation of the cheated Esau, 'Hast thou not a blessing for me also, O my father?' And I see, as in a cloud, pictures of the grand phantasmagoria of the book of Revelation.

I enumerate, as they issue, the childish impressions which come crowding out of the pigeon-holes in my brain, in which they have lain almost undisturbed for forty years. I prize them as an evidence that a child of five or six years old, left to his own devices, may be deeply interested in the Bible, and draw sound moral sustenance from it. And I rejoice that I was left to deal with the Bible alone; for if I had had some theological 'explainer' at my side, he might have tried, as such do, to lessen my indignation against Jacob, and thereby have warped my moral sense for ever. (pp. 401–2)

We may take these last remarks as further testimony to the prevalence of youthful pleasure in the Bible at this time. But the larger point is this: the passage and the way it has been used show that there was a real desire both to enlist as many voices as possible in the choir and to ensure that they sang in harmony.

AN INSPIRED TRANSLATION

In 1832 an advocate of translation, James Scholefield, described the translators as 'those venerable men who were raised up by the providence of God and endowed by his Spirit to achieve for England her greatest blessing in the authorised translation of the Scriptures'.[20] The

---

[20] *Hints for an Improved Version of the New Testament* (Cambridge, 1832), pp. vi–vii.

idea of inspiration naturally attaches itself to the established version of Scripture in the minds of the faithful. Explicit statements that, in the words of an anonymous critic writing in 1857, the KJB was regarded as having 'a sort of inspiration belonging to it'[21] began to appear. The strongest comes in *The Translators Revived; a biographical memoir of the authors of the English version of the Holy Bible* (New York, 1853) by a prominent American evangelist associated with the Presbyterian, Congregational and Dutch Reformed Churches, Alexander Wilson McClure (1808–65). The subject of the work is significant, for it is one that is rarely tackled,[22] and yet it is natural that a reverence for the KJB should lead to a curiosity about its creators. McClure notes that his curiosity about 'the personal qualifications for their work possessed by King James's translators' (p. iii) was aroused more than twenty years before the book was published. By offering the fruits of his curiosity 'to all who are interested to know in regard to the general sufficiency and reliableness of the Common Version' (p. iv), he makes clear the sequence from reverence for the version to reverence for the translators. He continues with a declaration of assurance that

these biographical sketches of its authors . . . will afford historical demonstration of a fact which much astonished him when it began to dawn upon his convictions, – that the first half of the seventeenth century, when the translation was completed, was the *Golden Age* of biblical and oriental learning in England. Never before, nor since, have these studies been pursued by scholars whose vernacular tongue is the English with such zeal and industry and success. This remarkable fact is a token of God's providential care of his word as deserves most devout acknowledgement.

Such an assertion goes against the long-repeated argument that the KJB needed revising because of the great advances in scholarship, and in this McClure is a rare voice. Yet, from a different point of view, this is but another aspect of the kind of period-worship exhibited by Macaulay (see above, p. 302).

From period-worship and AVolatry, the idea of 'God's providential care of his word' is a short move that has been made with considerable dogmatism by some twentieth-century fundamentalists (see below, pp. 397 ff.). The line between 'providential care' and plenary inspiration is a thin one. This is how McClure crosses it:

---

[21] Anon., *Will the Version by the Five Clergymen Help Dr. Biber?* (London, 1857), p. 5.
[22] The other two works devoted to the subject are both recent, Gustavus S. Paine's *The Men Behind the King James Version*, and Olga S. Opfell's *The King James Bible Translators* (Jefferson and London: McFarland, 1982).

Taking into account the many marked events in divine providence which led on
to this version and aided its accomplishment and necessitated its diffusion . . .
we are constrained to claim for the good men who made it the highest measure
of divine aid short of plenary inspiration itself . . .

But we hold that the translators enjoyed the highest degree of that special
guidance which is ever granted to God's true servants in exigencies of deep con-
cernment to his kingdom on earth. Such special succours and spiritual assistances are always vouchsafed where there is a like union of piety, of prayers and
of pains to effect an object of such incalculable importance to the church of the
living God. The necessity of a supernatural revelation to man of the divine will
has often been argued in favour of the extreme probability that such a revelation has been made. A like necessity, and one nearly as pressing, might be
argued in favour of the belief that this most important of all the versions of
God's revealed will must have been made under His peculiar guidance, and His
provident eye. And the manner in which that version has met the wants of the
most free and intelligent nations in the old world and the new may well confirm
us in the persuasion that the same illuminating Spirit which indited the original
Scriptures was imparted in rich grace to aid and guard the preparation of the
English version. (pp. 247–9)

As so often, the hedging with which an extreme point is made is
ineffectual. McClure's readers would have been in no doubt that the
KJB was as inspired as the originals – which is the view taken by the later
exponents of this line of argument.

McClure's interest in the KJB is religious rather than literary, but
nothing in his argument excludes the literary point of view. He is openly
arguing backwards from the present perception of achievement to an
inspiration inherent in both translators and the period. Though going
further than most would, especially in England, he expresses the tendency of both literary and religious AVolatry.

Yet this is not quite as far as the idea of the inspiration of the KJB can
go. Some people thought it more inspired than the originals. Benjamin
Jowett, Regius Professor of Greek at Oxford, seems to have been one of
these. His response to the RV NT was to observe that the Revisers 'seem
to have forgotten that, in a certain sense, the Authorised Version is more
inspired than the original'.[23] If he did indeed say this as reported (on the
face of it, it seems unlikely from the controversial author of 'The interpretation of Scripture' in *Essays and Reviews*), then others must have held
the view at the time, for it is treated as a truth that has been forgotten.
At all events, it has been picked up at least once and accepted as

---

[23] As reported in Evelyn Abbott and Lewis Campbell, *The Life and Letters of Benjamin Jowett*, 2 vols.
(London, 1897), I: 406.

reasonable. Eckman cites the remark and explains it with what we may call a cumulative theory of inspiration:

this startling statement is not the rash thing that some would suppose. It is to be presumed that the translators in 1611, being very devout men, constantly invoked the blessing of God upon their work, and that infinite wisdom was pleased to grant their request, so that upon the inspiration originally given to the Bible writers there was added the inspiration which God gave to the revered translators of the ancient tongues into the English vernacular. (*Literary Primacy*, p. 197)

In short, the KJB is the most inspired Bible ever given to humanity.

THE KJB AS A LITERARY INFLUENCE

In the 1830s there was sufficient interest in the question of the Bible as a literary influence for discussion to begin to appear on both sides of the Atlantic. Earlier Hazlitt had broached the subject in England, and in a sense it derives from Addison's comment that 'our language has received innumerable elegancies and improvements from that infusion of Hebraisms which are derived to it out of the poetical passages in Holy Writ' (see above, p. 207). By 1819 this comment was beginning to turn into an explicitly literary idea, as a passing remark by John William Whittaker shows: 'the great number of Hebraisms in the English Bible have had a powerful effect upon our language, more particularly observable in our national poetry' (*Historical Inquiry*, pp. 113–14).

A more general background to American interest in the subject may be glimpsed in an 1839 work by the prominent Pastor of the Brick Presbyterian Church, New York, Gardiner Spring (1785–1873), *The Obligations of the World to the Bible*. The title itself indicates an interest in the Bible as the foundation of all things, an interest that must have been natural in a country so highly conscious of its biblical foundations. Included are lectures on the Bible's influence on 'oral and written language – upon history and literature – upon laws and government' (p. 16), and on 'social institutions', 'slavery', 'the extent and certainty of moral science' and 'moral happiness' (table of contents).

Among all these large questions of influence, the proposition that 'English literature is no common debtor to the Bible' (pp. 61–2) perhaps gets no more attention than it deserves, two pages. In them Spring includes a passage from 'an anonymous writer' supporting the point, and notes that

At the suggestion of a valued friend, I have turned my thoughts to the parallel between Macbeth and Ahab – between Lady Macbeth and Jezebel – between the announcement to Macduff of the murder of his family, and that to David of the death of Absolom by Joab – to the parallel between the opening of the Lamentations of Jeremiah and Byron's apostrophe to Rome as the Niobe of nations – to the parallel between his ode to Napoleon and Isaiah's ode on the fall of Sennacherib – and also to the resemblance between Southey's chariot of Carmala in *The Curse of Kehama* and Ezekiel's vision of the wheels; and have been forcibly impressed with the obligation of this class of writers to the sacred Scriptures. (p. 63)

This bespeaks both the desire to discover the Bible as a prime source of English literary excellence, and a literary sense of the Bible. It is a fair hint for others to work on. More important, though, is the sense it gives of interest in the Bible as a literary influence being in the air by the 1830s.

The first sustained discussion of the subject seems also to come out of a background of interest, for this is the likeliest cause of the fellows of Trinity College, Cambridge, setting it, as I presume they did, as a subject for their annual prize. It is the only work of William Thomas Petty (later FitzMaurice), Earl of Kerry, *An Essay upon the Influence of the Translation of the Bible upon English Literature, which obtained the annual prize at Trinity College* (1830). Considering the Bible 'only as a literary work' (p. 2n), Petty sets up camp immediately with the AVolaters by exclaiming, 'what beauties are not united in its pages! beauties almost incompatible with one another' (p. 2). He intends

to examine the influence which the translation of this truly great work into our language has produced upon English literature; a subject than which none could have been selected of more importance, or of greater difficulty; which embraces the consideration of the effects which the most interesting work ever committed to the hands of mankind has produced upon that language. (pp. 2–3)

In spite of this, he has little to say about influence on language, and nowhere does his discussion become specific enough for it to matter what version he is writing about: he is a bibliolater masquerading as an AVolater.

One of his major positions is 'that from the very nature of these compositions, which are adorned with all the flowery style and dazzling imagery of the East, it was to be expected (and it will be found upon examination to be true) that they should exercise a far greater influence upon poetry than upon prose' (p. 19). The extent of the logic is to associate imagery with poetry, but all logic disappears when he later declares that 'the very nature of the Book of Holy Writ' is poetical, and this prevents it from being an influence on prose; he immediately adds a qualification that seems all-embracing, 'except as far as it has contributed to the general purity of the language, by having served as a standard of style' (p. 74). These assertions combine the position that runs back through Lowth to Swift with the even older tendency to think of poetry as the highest literature and the present tendency to think of the whole Bible as great literature.

Not without repetition, he spells out his view of the KJB's influence:

We may . . . justly infer that the vulgar translation has probably exercised a beneficial influence upon our literature: first, as being a standard of the purity of our language; secondly, as having naturalised in our country foreign idioms and words, and having thereby enriched our tongue; thirdly, as having thrown open the gate of the Holy Scriptures to all persons, and having thereby conferred on every one the power of profiting by the beauties which they contain. (p. 22)

The opening statement is of historical importance as being the first clear *published* expression of this idea, yet we can only credit it with limited originality. Only in the explicitness of its generalisation is it new. What follows already sounds familiar, and when he moves to detail the result is disappointing. His method is 'to quote from the most distinguished authors of this age a few of those passages which appear to have been most indebted to the English translation of the Holy Bible' (pp. 52–3). Milton is particularly used, but the proof of influence rests on no more than the discovery of sources for allusions, phrases and figures. The KJB is treated as a sourcebook rather than as an influence, and there is no demonstration of how it has operated as 'a standard of the purity of our language'.

In spite of such failings, Petty's conclusion picks up his main points in a strong and original claim for the KJB's literary importance: it is

that the translation of the Bible into our language is a most remarkable event in the history of English literature: that the influence it has exerted upon our writers has been more fully developed in our poetical than our prose authors; but that it has, in general, been great and beneficial, whether the translation be considered as a book of reference, or a standard of style. (p. 81)

That he had only shown the Bible functioning as 'a book of reference' matters little. This claim for the publication of the KJB as a major event in English literary history is important, and was only slowly picked up.

As a historical first – but on no other grounds – Petty's work does not deserve the total oblivion into which it fell. The one other British work on literary aspects of the Bible to appear before 1850, John Murray McCulloch's *Literary Characteristics of the Holy Scriptures* (1845), was a little more successful. It too touches on the question of influence. The first of the supplementary notes in the second edition, 'obligations of English poetry to the Scriptures', contains this:

some intimate connexion there must be between the Bible and English poetry – otherwise the fact of their contemporaneous prosperity and contemporane-ous decline would not meet us so frequently in the course of our literary annals. The Bible is doubtless far from being the only influence to which English poetry owes its peculiar mould; but it may be confidently affirmed to be one of the chief influences. At all events the two have hitherto invariably flourished and faded together. Our English eolian-harp, it would seem, yields its peculiar music freely and abundantly only when the wind that sweeps over its strings is the breath of the Lord. (pp. 129–30)

McCulloch here develops Petty's sense of the Bible's importance to English literature by adding to it a vague suggestion that divine inspira-tion then operated at large. Though this is rather like the idea of the importance of their time as a major factor in Shakespeare's and the KJB's greatness, the claim that poetry and the Bible have flourished and faded together requires some ingenuity to make sense of. Does he simply mean that the best English poetry comes from the most pious times? Or is he casting aspersions on the eighteenth century? He does not say, perhaps because he could not: such statements are cosmic dust.

   McCulloch's work as a whole reflects the progress of the idea of the KJB as literature and as a literary force, but contributes little in the way of new understanding. It is an attempt 'simply to present such a sample of the beauty and fruitfulness of "the good land" as may induce the student to "go up" and explore it for himself' (p. 5), and has two main parts. The first deals with characteristics of subject-matter: originality – which, illogically for one who claims the Bible as the first and best work of literature, he says 'displays itself either in throwing out new thoughts, or in re-casting old thoughts into new and striking forms' (p. 14 – here he is applying accepted criteria of literary quality thoughtlessly) –, depth of thought, sublimity, spirituality, 'a singular reserve on all subjects of mere curiosity', the 'miscellaneous and unsystematic manner in which [the Scriptures] convey religious instruction', and 'harmony with itself'. The second section deals with characteristics of style, and McCulloch, in keeping with Tyndale and Addison, comments that 'the disadvantage of estimating an author's style from a translation [he means the KJB], is happily much less in the case of the Bible than of any other book' because of its '*translatableness* . . . with little loss of its original colour and energy' (p. 56). This allows that the originals are best while suggesting that the KJB loses nothing significant of their quality.

McCulloch's work is suggestive of his time rather than either a contribution to scholarship or a moulder of opinion. Perhaps its single most interesting declaration is an echo of Petty's determination to consider the Bible 'only as a literary work': 'irrespective of its peculiar claims and character as the record of divine truth, the Bible stands, *as a mere book*, apart and aloft from all others'. That he should italicise 'as a mere book' shows just how acceptable it was becoming to think of the Bible as literature, but the complete statement is blatantly a literary judgement arrived at for religious reasons. The Bible is 'apart and aloft' because it is God's book, 'the earliest and the brightest star in the literary heavens' (p. 12). This was now the dominant view of the Bible, and its natural corollary was the claim that the KJB is 'the first English classic'.

George Gilfillan's *The Bards of the Bible* touched on the subject of the Bible's literary influence in 1851 but will need separate discussion; the last work signalling the arrival of interest in the subject is largely an exercise in panegyric by the Reverend J.A. Seiss of Baltimore, 'The influence of the Bible on literature' (1853). It begins with seven pages of bibliolatry acclaiming the Bible as 'the oldest of all books' (p. 1), 'the most *original* of books' (p. 3), 'the Daguerrotype of the universe', the '*sublimest and most beautiful* of books' (p. 5), and as 'a literary *aereolite*, with characteristics kindred to nothing earthly; and whose own superior attributes demonstrate that it has come down from some high and holy place' (p. 3). Then he makes a turn which shows just how closely interest in the Bible's literary influence is linked with bibliolatry: 'since the Bible is the most ancient, original and sublime of books . . . it must needs have made its deep broad marks upon the entire world of letters' (p. 8). This opens up a vast range – anything written about the Bible, all theology and most works of science, archaeological, geological or natural, all are influenced by the Bible – so vast a range that at last he stands back and asks, 'what is modern learning and the march of intellect and the reading million but one great monument of the quickening power of sacred truth upon the human mind?' (p. 15). This is influence so broadly conceived as to be meaningless.

In between these last two remarks, Seiss surveys a wide range of literature and, given the confines of an article, the result is better than such a setting would lead us to expect. For instance, he invites his reader to:

look at the unbelieving Shakespeare. Hear that admired and much quoted passage in his *Tempest*:

> The cloud-capp'd towers, the gorgeous palaces,
> The solemn temples, the great globe itself,
> Yea, all which it inherit, shall dissolve
> And, like this insubstantial pageant faded,
> Leave not a wrack behind. We are such stuff
> As dreams are made on, and our little life
> Is rounded with a sleep.

This certainly is but another edition of the scripture sentiments, 'the heavens shall pass away; the elements shall melt; the earth also, and all the works that are therein shall be burned up; these things shall be dissolved' [2 Pet. 3: 10–11, adapted]. 'For what is your life? It is even a vapour that appeareth for a little time, and then vanisheth away' [Jas. 4: 14]. (pp. 13–14)

The sentiments and a little of the imagery are close enough for the connections to be enlightening, but not close enough to account for the quality of Shakespeare's passage or to demonstrate antecedent excellence in the Bible; nevertheless, Seiss's fundamental point, that there are parallels, holds good, and the Bible may have helped shape the passage. He goes on to show more substantial parallels in Portia's speech on 'the quality of mercy'; within the scope of a short paper this is impressive.

Minor and little-known as it must have been, Seiss's article takes us beyond Petty and McCulloch: *they* signal the arrival of an awareness, *it* shows ways the awareness might be explored. Exploration was not long in coming. The first of many books on individual authors and the Bible was T.R. Eaton's *Shakespeare and the Bible* (London, 1858). Eaton declares his purpose to be 'to show, by new evidence, the vastness of Shakespeare's Bible lore' (p. 2), but the real effect of the book is to bring bardolatry and religion together. He sketches the Bible's dramatic mode of teaching, remarks that this 'must have had an irresistible charm to one of Shakespeare's peculiar bent' (p. 3), and finds it 'pleasant to fancy the delight with which young Shakespeare must have feasted upon these and like divine lessons, unconscious the while that he was strengthening his pinions for loftier flights than had ever been attained by uninspired man' (p. 4). His drift is clear, that Shakespeare's quality comes from the Bible even before it comes from God's creation or inspiration: 'in storing his mind, Shakespeare went first to the word and then to the works of God. In shaping the truths derived from these sources, he obeyed the instinct implanted by Him who had formed him *Shakespeare*' (p. 4). With the addition of a touch of AVolatry, he pictures Shakespeare and the KJB as having the same fundamental qualities:

Shakespeare perpetually reminds us of the Bible, not by direct quotation, indirect allusion, borrowed idioms, or palpable imitation of phrase and style, but by an elevation of thought and simplicity of diction which are not to be found elsewhere. A passage, for instance, rises in our thoughts, unaccompanied by a clear recollection of its origin. Our first impression is that it *must* belong *either* to the *Bible* or to *Shakespeare*. (pp. 4–5)

This is as much general argument as Eaton offers but it is sufficient to show how Shakespeare and the KJB's reputations have come together. For the rest of the book he pursues his aim of demonstrating the wealth of Shakespeare's knowledge of the Bible by accumulating sometimes sharp examples of passages in Shakespeare which refer or allude to the Bible, and by suggesting some more general similarities.

Six years later appeared Bishop Charles Wordsworth's *On Shakespeare's Knowledge and Use of the Bible* (London, 1864). Wordsworth thought himself the first to undertake this subject, which suggests that bardolatry, AVolatry and literary studies had come together sufficiently by this time for such works to be inevitable. Though this is a better book than Eaton's, Wordsworth's purpose is the same and he adds only one point of real significance here, the passing suggestion 'that our translators of 1611 owed as much, or more, to Shakespeare than he owed to them' (p. 9). Later he notes that the KJB has 'well stricken in years' (Luke 1: 7) where Tyndale and the Great Bible had 'well stricken in age', and asks,

Is it possible that our translator of St Luke altered the expression out of deference to the following passage of Shakespeare?

> We speak no treason, man; we say the King
> Is wise and virtuous: and his noble Queen
> Well struck in years. (*Richard III*, 1: 1) (p. 42)

Such an argument, though in this instance unsustainable,[24] if developed, would complement the idea that the Bible is central to Shakespeare's strength: did Shakespeare's mastery of language contribute to the literary strength of the KJB? Bardolatry and AVolatry have almost merged into one: Shakespeare is biblical, and the Bible is Shakespearean.

---

[24] 'Well stricken in years' is used by Tyndale and most subsequent translators later in the chapter (v. 18). Moreover, the KJB uses 'stricken in age' almost as often as it uses 'stricken in years'. The reason is a matter of accuracy, not aesthetics: 'age' and 'years' represent different Hebrew words. Occasionally, where the context demands, 'years' is used for the word generally translated 'age', but not the other way round.

PARALLELISM REVISITED

With the pious chorus singing so loud and long, it may seem odd that there was little substantial literary discussion of the Bible in general and even less of the KJB through much of the nineteenth century. Absolute praise succeeds best uncluttered by particulars, but there were other factors, the most important of which will be the subject of the next chapter, the pre-occupation with the question of revision. Two books in particular merit consideration before the story of revision is taken up.

Lowth's work on the poetry of the Old Testament remained magisterial for many years. Only one English work before mid-century sought to extend it and, gently, to criticise it, John Jebb's *Sacred Literature; comprising a review of the principles of composition laid down by the late Robert Lowth . . .: and an application of the principles so reviewed to the illustration of the New Testament; in a series of critical observations on the style and structure of that sacred volume* (1820). Jebb's purpose is 'to prove by examples that the structure of clauses, sentences and periods in the New Testament is frequently regulated after the model afforded in the poetical parts of the Old' (p. 1). He anticipates the usual advantages from such a proof, including correction of the text, resolution of grammatical difficulties, general clarification, and a sharpened awareness of some of the proprieties and beauties of conception and style. Behind the undertaking lies a belief in the unified inspiration of the whole Bible, for

design pervades the whole matter of both Testaments; and unity is the soul of that design; but the matter and manner of Scripture are, beyond the matter and manner of any other body of writings, most intimately connected; so intimately connected that unity of matter demands and implies, in this divine book, a correspondent unity of manner. And, on this ground alone, we may reasonably conclude that a manner largely prevalent in the Old Testament cannot be relinquished in the New. (p. 77)

He has other reasons for this belief, notably that most of the writers of the NT were steeped in the OT and so would naturally have followed its manner of writing. Such thinking set him to searching the NT for passages 'which bear evident marks of intentional conformity to the Hebrew parallelism' (p. 79).

Before embarking on these passages he outlines Lowth's theories and proposes a modification to them. He dislikes the idea of synonymous parallelism because it implies 'gross tautology' (p. 39), and so he proposes an alternative, 'progressive parallelism' (p. 38), observing that 'in the parallelisms commonly termed synonymous, the second or responsive clause invariably diversifies the preceding clause; and generally so as to rise above it, forming a sort of climax in the sense' (p. 35). Some of his examples are persuasive, but the general argument is flawed by a confusion between grammar and effect: synonymity describes the grammatical relationship, progression its common effect. Repetition, even of the identical words, commonly produces an effect of intensification or progression. Consequently the result of his argument is not a correction of Lowth but a change of emphasis that points to a quality in most parallelisms, whether synonymous or not. The new emphasis is on a sense of the mind and imagination moving forward.

Jebb has one other development of Lowth's ideas to offer, a development that became well known through John Kitto's admiring summary in his popular *Daily Bible Illustrations*.[25] A close attention to parallelism, he argues, will reveal in some places a stanza form for which he suggests the term 'introverted parallelism'; in this form, 'whatever be the number of lines, the first line shall be parallel with the last, the second with the penultimate, and so throughout' (p. 53). Here is one of his more complex examples, Isa. 27: 12–13, using the words of Lowth's translation:

> And it shall come to pass in that day;
>   Jehovah shall make a gathering of his fruit:
>   From the flood of the river;
>   To the stream of Egypt:
>   And ye shall be gleaned up, one by one;
> O ye sons of Israel.
>
> And it shall come to pass in that day;
>   The great trumpet shall be sounded:
>   And those shall come, who were perishing in the land of Assyria;
>   And who were dispersed in the land of Egypt;
>   And they shall bow themselves down before Jehovah;
> In the holy mountain, in Jerusalem.

He argues that this shows not only the stanzaic form he has suggested but also an 'utmost precision of mutual correspondence, clause harmonising with clause, and line respectively with line' as the second stanza repeats in literal terms what is figured in the first (pp. 54–5). He has changed Lowth's presentation, adding indentations and dividing some lines into two, but the result is not the complete success that would justify his affectation of surprise at Lowth's failure to see this pattern. Some of the correspondences he elicits, as between the second and fifth lines of

---

[25] 1850–54; 1901 edn, reprinted as *Kitto's Daily Bible Illustrations*, 2 vols. (Grand Rapids, Mich.: Kregel, 1981), II: 136–43,

the first stanza ('Jehovah shall make a gathering of his fruit / And ye shall be gleaned up, one by one'), and between the opening lines of the two stanzas, appear quite persuasive, but there is as much appearance of parallelism in 'And it shall come to pass in that day / The great trumpet shall be sounded', as there is in the parallelism Jebb substitutes, 'And it shall come to pass in that day / In the holy mountain, in Jerusalem'. Moreover, if we retreat a verse in Lowth it becomes obvious that Jebb could not be proposing stanza form as a regular organising principle:

> When her boughs are withered, they shall be broken:
> Women shall come, and set them on a blaze.
> Surely it is a people void of understanding;
> Wherefore he, that made him, shall not have pity on him;
> And he, that formed him, shall show him no favour.

Here two obvious pairs of lines straddle a line that has no parallel, a quite different structure from that just identified. The idea of stanzas, with its implication of regularity, is therefore problematic. What Jebb has really shown is that there are patterns of parallelism that can form into larger structures: we should not confine ourselves to thinking just of pairs of lines.

The latter part of the book is devoted to showing how parallelism, as Jebb understands it, is to be found in the NT. First he argues that the NT writers preserve the parallel form as well as the meaning of their quotations from OT poetry ('no trifling evidence that they were skilled in Hebrew poetry' (p. 97)), and he demonstrates that original parallelisms, such as 'my soul doth magnify the Lord; / And my spirit hath rejoiced in God my saviour' (Luke 1: 46–7; p. 143), are to be found in the NT. He is at his most interesting with longer passages, as with the following 'tremendous apostrophe to the unbelieving Jews [which] is in the grandest style of Hebrew poetry' (p. 258; as with all his NT passages, he gives the Greek first):

> Come now, ye rich men, weep, howl,
> For the stunning afflictions which are coming upon you;
> Your riches are putrefied;
> And your robes are moth-eaten:
> Your gold and silver are cankered with rust;
> And their rust shall be a witness against you;
> And shall eat your flesh as fire:
> Ye have laid up treasures for the last days!
>
> Behold! the hire of the labourers who have reaped your fields
> Fraudfully kept back by you, crieth:

And the outcries of those who have gathered in your harvest,
Have entered into the ears of the Lord of Hosts:
Ye have lived delicately upon the earth; ye have been luxurious;
Ye have pampered your hearts, as for a day of slaughter:
Ye have condemned, ye have slain the Just One;
He is not arrayed against you!   (Jas. 5: 1–6)

What attracts Jebb's particular attention is the passage's use of climax, first in the ascending scale of 'weep, howl . . . stunning afflictions', then in the poetic amplification of the three kinds of wealth, '1. stores of corn, wine, oil, etc., liable to putrefaction; 2. wardrobes of rich garments . . . proverbially the prey of the moth . . . and 3. treasures of gold and silver, liable to rust or, at least, to change of colour' (pp. 259–60). Only one parallelism is specifically mentioned, 'Your riches are putrefied; / And your robes are motheaten', but the attention to climax in this example is, in his view, at one with his sense of progressive parallelism.

There are three more general ways, each connected with the other, in which Jebb's work is significant. He is the first to use 'literature', in its modern sense, for the Bible in the title of a work. This striking variation from Lowth's 'Sacred Poetry' was probably prompted by the focus on the prose of the NT as well as the need for a different but related title, but it shows almost as conclusively as the changing titles of the early translations of Longinus (see above, p. 191) a change in values. Just as 'sublime' replaced 'eloquence' as the key word for literary quality, so 'literature' replaces 'poetry' as the key word for itself. Criticism is beginning to recognise that the highest achievements of writing are not necessarily to be found in poetry. Secondly, the distinction between poetry and prose becomes redundant in Jebb's discussion: now the essential qualities of OT poetry are matched by the prose of the NT, which Jebb does not hesitate on occasions to call poetry. Matching the substitution of 'literature' for 'poetry' is the application of 'poetry' to prose. The prose is literature if you are looking forward, poetry if you are looking back; either way, the old position of poetry and its association with verse is broken down. Lastly, matching the extension of 'poetry' to the point where 'literature' is the better word, Jebb has taken a large step towards seeing literary excellence in the whole Bible. In this as much as in his ideas of parallelism he is a successor to Lowth. What Lowth did for the Prophets in relation to the Psalms and other songs of the OT, Jebb does for the NT in relation to the OT. Yet *Sacred Literature* is not the major work *Sacred Poetry* was: it shows movements happening but is not their cause.

GEORGE GILFILLAN AND 'THE LESSON OF INFINITE BEAUTY'

George Gilfillan's (1813–78) *The Bards of the Bible* (1851) is a fine example of extended bibliolatry. Gilfillan, a Scots Presbyterian minister and noted literary critic and editor, thought of the book as repaying 'in a certain measure, our debt to that divine volume which, from early childhood, has hardly ceased for a day to be our companion – which has coloured our imagination, commanded our belief, impressed our thought and steeped our language' (p. 11). Many people evidently shared this sense of indebtedness, for, though it has been ignored by subsequent writers on the Bible as literature, *Bards* was a popular book, going through at least seven British editions by 1888, as well as several American editions. It not only reflects its time, but, by its popularity, helped to form and confirm attitudes.

Though familiar with some of his scholarly predecessors, Gilfillan did not aim to make his work scholarly. Rather, he intended that it should be 'a prose poem or hymn in honour of the poetry and poets of the inspired volume' (p. iii), because 'every criticism on a true poem should be itself a poem'. He goes on:

We propose, therefore, to take up this neglected theme – the bards of the Bible, and in seeking to develop their matchless spirit as masters of the lyre, to develop, at the same time, indirectly, a subordinate though strong evidence that they are something more – the rightful rulers of the belief and the heart of man. Perhaps this subject may not be found altogether unsuited to the wants of the age. If properly treated, it may induce some to pause before they seek any longer to pull in vain at the roots of a thing so beautiful. It may teach others to prize that Book somewhat more for its literature which they have all along loved for its truth, its holiness and its adaptation to their nature. It may strengthen some faltering convictions, and tend to withdraw enthusiasts from the exclusive study of imperfect, modern and morbid models, to those great ancient masters. It may, possibly, through the lesson of infinite beauty, successfully insinuate that of eternal truth into some souls hitherto shut against one or both; and as thousands have been led to regard the Bible as a book of genius, from having first thought it a book of God, so in thousands may the process be inverted. (pp. 10–11)

This bibliolatrous linking of 'infinite beauty' and 'eternal truth' is familiar enough. His intention is to praise the beauty, leading those who believe to a wider appreciation of the Bible, and leading those who do not to the beauty, and thence the truth. These too are familiar desires.

Less familiar is the extent to which Gilfillan sees the Bible as literature. His chapter headings indicate that he will touch on the whole Bible, not just the obviously poetic parts of the Old Testament. This is a natural consequence of the growing enthusiasm for the Bible and of his close linking of beauty and truth, for he sees poetic beauty in the quality of thought. So:

'God is a spirit,' or 'God is love,' contains, each sentence, a world of poetic beauty, as well as divine meaning. Indeed, certain prose sentences constitute the essence of all the poetry in the Scriptures . . . Truly the songs of Scripture are magnificent, but its statements are 'words unutterable', which it is not possible for the tongue of man to utter! (p. 58)

In other words, the statements are such as only God could make. The argument moves from divine authorship through divine meaning to poetic beauty. Where it differs from Dennis's position that religion produces poetry (see above, pp. 190 ff.), is that Dennis believes the ideas which come from religion have to be expressed 'with passion equal to their greatness', whereas Gilfillan believes that the quality of the idea alone is the essence of poetry: the highest poetry can be embodied in the plainest statement. In keeping with this, he uses (or, perhaps, invents) the term 'prose-poetry', noting that this 'abounds in the historical books, and constitutes the staple of the entire volume' (p. 56). He also calls this 'seed poetry' (p. 57), perhaps meaning statement that is capable of growing into poetry, having the essence but yet to take the form. If this is indeed what he means, he has put his finger on a major element in appreciation of the Bible as literature: it has the potential for growing within the minds of believers into great literature.

On the basis of this idea of seed poetry, Gilfillan 'would arrange Hebrew poetry under the two general heads of song and poetic statement' (pp. 56–7). Song he divides into exulting, insulting, mourning, worshipping, loving, reflecting, interchanging, wildly-luxuriating, narrating (this includes 'the simple epic – Psalm 78, Exodus, etc.'), and predicting. His four kinds of statement are:

1st, Of poetic facts (creation, etc.).
2nd, Of poetic doctrines (God's spirituality).
3rd, Of poetic sentiments, with or without figurative language (golden rule, etc.).
4th, Of poetic symbols (in Zechariah, Revelation, etc.). (p. 57)

This is nearly all-embracing, as he realises:

Song and statement appear to include the Bible between them, and the statement is sometimes more poetical than the song. If aught evade this generalisation, it is the *argument*, which is charily sprinkled throughout the Epistles of Paul. Even that is logic defining the boundaries of the loftiest poetical thought. All else, from the simple narrations of Ezra and Nehemiah up to the most ornate and oratorical appeals of the Prophets, is genuinely poetic, and ought by no means to be excluded from the range of our critical explication and panegyric. (p. 57)

The circularity of this consists in finding 'literary' categories to cover all parts of the Bible, and then saying all of the Bible is literature, whilst the importance is that it brings into the open the inclusive tendency of bibliolatry. The size of the move makes Jebb's extension of parallelism to the NT look modest indeed.

It is difficult for someone who defines poetry so broadly and who sees the whole Bible as expressive of divine meaning to make any critical judgement other than that, while some parts are higher than others, all are beyond mortal literature, and therefore open only to explication and panegyric. This is naked bibliolatry, but Gilfillan himself would reject the charge: he comments that 'there is, or was till lately, extant, a vulgar bibliolatry, which would hardly admit of any preference being given to one scripture writer over another, or of any comparison being instituted between its various authors' (p. 292), but the point is only that he has favourites among the bards of the Bible.

The emphasis on meaning leads away from discussion of any particular version of the Bible, which is why I have referred to bibliolatry rather than AVolatry. His quotations are often inaccurate, and his comments are never specific to the KJB. Consequently, *The Bards of the Bible*, like many of its eighteenth-century predecessors, appears to be about the originals. Gilfillan's philosophical basis for this is the same extreme version of the idea of the 'translatableness' of the Bible that Jebb subscribed to. Rather than observing a compatibility between Hebrew and English, he sees the Bible as written in a kind of universal language, what he calls 'the oldest speech', which is independent of any particular form of words:

This beauty, too, is free of the world. It passes, unshorn and unmingled, into every language and every land. Wherever the Bible goes, 'beauty,' in the words of the poet, 'pitches her tents before it.' Appealing, as its poetry does, to the primitive principles, elements and 'all that must eternal be' of the human mind – using the oldest speech, older than Hebrew, that of metaphors and symbols – telling few, but life-like stories – and describing scenes which paint themselves easily and forever on the heart – it needs little more introduction than does a gleam of sunshine. It soon domesticates itself among the Caffres, or the Negroes, or the Hindoos, or the Hottentots, or the Chinese, who all feel it to be intensely human before they feel it to be divine. What heart but must palpitate at the sight of this virgin daughter of the Most High, going forth from land to land, with no dower but innocence, and with no garment but beauty; yet powerful in her loveliness as light, and in her innocence safe as her Father who is in heaven? (p. 356)

The image of the Bible as 'this virgin daughter of the Most High' helps to link this idea of a universal language with the voice of God. Gilfillan's view of the Bible, then, is essentially this: it is the voice of God, anterior to all languages and so speaking through all languages direct to the human heart; it is felt as poetry, and, coming from truth, it is beautiful. The books of the Bible are 'the *classics* of the *heart*' (p. 42).

The last three chapters move beyond 'the bards of the Bible'. They deal with 'the poetical characters in Scripture', 'comparative estimate, influences, and effects of Scripture poetry', and the 'future destiny of the Bible'. He begins the first of these chapters: 'beside the authors and poets of the Old and New Testaments, there are, in the course of both, a number of characters depicted teeming with peculiar and romantic interest, and who are abundantly entitled to the epithet poetical' (p. 309). 'Poetical' here means that they live in his imagination, again as if independent of the text. In this chapter his method is at its clearest. For instance, he correctly notes of Cain that 'we can hardly judge accurately or distinctly, apart from the many poetic shapes which, since the account of Moses, he has assumed' (p. 312). This he follows with a key statement for understanding his method: 'yet our idea of him may be uttered'. And so he imagines the life behind the text:

Born amid great expectations, called by his mother 'the man, the lord,' he grew up, disappointing every fond hope and becoming a somewhat sullen drudge, 'a tiller of the ground.' Meanwhile, his younger brother is exhibiting the finer traits of the pastoral character. The 'elder is made to serve the younger.' Fiercely does the once-spoiled child kick against the pricks, till at last the fury of conscious inferiority breaks out in blood – the blood of Abel. Conscience-struck, hearing in every wind the voice of his brother's gore – nay, carrying it in his ear, as the shell carries inland the sound of ocean's waters – he flees from his native region, and a curse clings to him, and the whole story seems to prove – first, the evil of over-excited and disappointed hopes; secondly, the misery of the murderer; and, thirdly, how God can deduce good from evil, and mingle mercy with judgment. (pp. 312–3)

This readiness of critics to find the life behind the text is crucial to the growth of literary admiration for the Bible. Yet Gilfillan does not pause to ask what creates the life. Is it (narrowing the possibilities to two) the text, or is it the reader's imagination, left to its own devices by a text that is both skeletal and totally familiar?

CHAPTER FOURTEEN

The Revised Version

RULES FOR THE REVISION

By far the most important new English version of the Bible to appear in the 350 years between 1611 and 1961, when the New English Bible was published, was the Revised Version (NT 1881, OT 1885, Apocrypha 1895), yet its significance here lies not so much in its achievement as in the insight it gives into the business of translation, its effects on opinions of the KJB and, to a minor extent, its role in generating the multitude of twentieth-century versions. This is not to belittle its achievements nor to gloss over its weaknesses, but to recognise that, even though a literary welcome was given to its work on some of the OT books, it has not become a significant work of English literature. In spite of – and even because of – the RV, the KJB's general reputation continued to grow.

As a revision, the RV has much in common with the KJB. If the decision to make the RV was taken tardily as against the almost indecent haste of the decision to make the KJB, if political and sectarian motives had their role in generating the KJB while the RV was the result of scholarly agitation, nevertheless each revision proceeded with exemplary care and thoroughness. Both were made by committees of the leading churchmen and scholars of the day; moreover, in terms of their scholarship and their own literary achievements outside of their translation, there is nothing to choose between the two groups (unless one were to argue for the preface to the KJB or for Lancelot Andrewes's sermons). The later revisers were as well qualified for the work as their predecessors.

The essentials of the background to the RV have all, with one exception, been seen. There is no need to follow here the long sequence of nineteenth-century criticism of the KJB's scholarly accuracy since it adds nothing to the story of literary attitudes and is a continuation of the kind of discussion that had received a temporary setback through the conservative temper induced by the Napoleonic wars. The one exception – and it is a major one – is the renewed criticism of the language of the KJB, but it will be more convenient to examine this in connection with the RV's linguistic revisions. In the meantime it will be best to look at the kind of evidence which parallels that available for the KJB, and then to move on to other kinds of evidence. In this way it is possible to see whether similar evidence leads to similar conclusions, and then whether other evidence modifies those conclusions.

The similar evidence is, of course, the instructions to the revisers and the revisers' prefaces to their work. Going beyond this, there is a wealth of discussion by the revisers of their work: for a historian, one of the major differences between the two translations is that there are so many such commentaries, to say nothing of a similar abundance of reviews, whereas almost nothing survives from the earlier version.

The task undertaken by the Jacobeans and the Victorians was substantially the same, to revise the previous official version in the light of the best scholarship of the day. Here are the instructions issued to the makers of the RV:

1. To introduce as few alterations as possible into the text of the Authorised Version consistently with faithfulness.
2. To limit, as far as possible, the expression of such alterations to the language of the Authorised and earlier English versions.
3. Each company to go twice over the portion to be revised, once provisionally, the second time finally, and on principles of voting as hereinafter is provided.
4. That the text to be adopted be that for which the evidence is decidedly preponderating; and that when the text so adopted differs from that from which the Authorised Version was made, the alteration be indicated in the margin.
5. To make or retain no change in the text on the second final revision by each company, except *two thirds* of those present approve of the same, but on the first revision to decide by simple majorities.
6. In every case of proposed alteration that may have given rise to discussion, to defer the voting thereupon till the next meeting, whensoever the same shall be required by one third of those present at the meeting, such intended vote to be announced in the notice for the next meeting.
7. To revise the headings of chapters and pages, paragraphs, italics and punctuation.
8. To refer, on the part of each company, when considered desirable, to divines, scholars and literary men, whether at home or abroad, for their opinions. (RV NT preface, p. viii)

The first and chief of these is identical to the first rule for the KJB, 'the ordinary Bible read in the Church, commonly called the *Bishops' Bible*, to be followed, and as little altered as the truth of the original will permit'. Most of the remaining instructions concern the method of working and they have the same aim as the KJB rules, to ensure that the revision is as carefully made as possible. It would be hard to say which is the better set of instructions. Those for the KJB envisage consultation between the different companies, whereas the RV was made by two companies, one for each Testament (the Apocrypha was undertaken later). As the work developed, each company consulted with an equivalent American company. Only in one area of practice did the two revisions differ to a significant extent: the RV as a whole was not given a final revision by a small group of revisers. If that final revision had made a significant difference to the literary quality of the KJB, the method adopted for the RV might be judged significantly inferior. On the other hand, the revisers saw one distinct advantage in their method, the use of only one committee for the whole of the NT (implicitly the same advantage existed for the OT). The KJB's division of the NT between two companies is seen by the writer of the preface to the RV NT as being 'beyond all doubt the cause of many inconsistencies' (p. vii).

In large part, then, the task set the Victorian revisers was the same as that set their Jacobean predecessors, and their way of working was not significantly different. Since there is nothing to choose between the two groups of men as far as their qualifications for the work is concerned, we might expect a version of broadly similar quality to result. But we have seen that the perception of the quality of the KJB depended principally on historical circumstances, and the circumstances of the Victorian revision were quite different from that of its predecessor. The chief of these differences is pointed to in the second rule for the RV, to keep to the language of the KJB and earlier English versions. Nothing in the rules for the KJB corresponds to this. The KJB translators (I call them translators to distinguish them from their Victorian successors, not to make a distinction between the two versions) worked with a nearly established biblical English, sometimes altering the largely Anglo-Saxon tone of the Tyndale tradition by bringing in Gregory Martin's Latinate vocabulary, and they worked with an English that was not too far removed from their own. The RV revisers had before them not only an absolutely established biblical English, but one which they revered and which was substantially different from their own language. If they wished to make changes they had often to write pastiche. Further, although the KJB translators worked with a largely established language, they still worked in a situation in which the English text of the Bible was not generally felt to be fixed: not only were there competing versions but the habit of verbal fidelity to the English text had not yet become ingrained. By the 1870s the KJB had had no significant rivals for generations and its precise phraseology was not only thoroughly well known but had acquired an aura of holiness. In effect the KJB was to the Victorians what the Vulgate was to the pre-Reformation Church. Far more than their predecessors, the RV revisers were 'meddling with men's religion' (KJB preface, p. 2). Rather than standing at the end of an era of textual instability, they stood at the beginning of a new era of instability. The KJB finished a process and this was a key to its eventual success. The RV began a new process, and this put it in a position where it was unlikely to gain the monopoly that a version needs to conquer the hearts of the people.

One more major difference shows up in rule 8: this reproduces rule 11 for the KJB, to consult with 'any learned man in the land' on obscure places, but, where the KJB rule envisages only scholarly consultation, that for the RV adds 'literary men' to divines and scholars. Although the rule was only once acted on,[1] its spirit is crucial. The revisers were charged with more than preserving the language of 'the first English classic': they had to remember that they were translating a great work of literature and that the result of their labour should be a stylistic achievement as well as the most faithful rendering of the book of truth yet achieved. Was this rule a hint that they should rub and polish – to give those words now a fully literary turn – the language of the KJB, not only removing archaisms and purging grammatical faults, but improving its cadences and diction wherever improvements, consistent with faithfulness, might be made? At least one advocate of revision, taking a swipe at AVolatry, had argued this very point, claiming that the KJB 'is impaired by manifold literary blemishes which any one moderately acquainted with English literature may easily detect', and so, 'even in its character *as* an English composition . . . is capable of extensive improvement'.[2] In short, it seems they were to work with the kind of literary consciousness that their time commonly imputed to their predecessors but for which almost no evidence can be found apart from one's sense of the fineness of the KJB. Here the tasks set before the two groups of translators and their sense of their work really diverge. It will be a crucial matter to see whether such a task and consciousness did affect the work.

---

[1] The NT company consulted with the First Sea Lord as to the correctness of the nautical terms used in Acts 27 (Ellicott, *Addresses on the Revised Version*, pp. 31–2).

[2] David Johnston, *Plea for a New English Version* (London, 1864), p. 190.

AVolatry (inseparably linked with a mumpsimus conservatism) and the conviction that the Bible was literature were the forces behind the rule for the style of the RV. Had AVolatry been the only force there would of course have been no revision: by itself the idea that the KJB could be improved as a literary version would never have been sufficient motivation for an official revision. The RV was a compromise between the irresistible need to revise and the immovable monument of the KJB.

The remaining rules all reflect the fundamental reason for making the RV, the certainty among most scholars stretching back to Hugh Broughton that the KJB did not perfectly represent the truth of the originals. The key word is 'faithfulness' in the first rule. Moving beyond the kind of evidence available for the KJB, we can be absolutely certain how the revisers understood 'faithfulness'. Charles John Ellicott (1819–1905), Bishop of Gloucester and Bristol, and chairman of the NT committee, recalls

a very full discussion on the true meaning of the word at one of the early meetings of the [NT] Company. Some alteration had been proposed in the rendering of the Greek to which objection was made that it did not come under the rule and principle of faithfulness. This led to a general and, as it proved, a final discussion. Bishop Lightfoot, I remember, took an earnest part in it. He contended that our revision must be a true and thorough one; that such a meeting as ours could not be assembled for many years to come, and that if the rendering was plainly more accurate and more true to the original, it ought not to be put aside as incompatible with some supposed aspect of the rule of faithfulness. (*Addresses on the RV*, pp. 98–9)

The highly scholarly Joseph Barber Lightfoot had been more specific:

the most important changes in which a revision may result will be due to the variations of reading in the Greek text. It was not the fault, it was the misfortune of the scholars from Tyndale downward, to whom we owe our English Bible, that the only text accessible to them was faulty and corrupt . . . the permanent value of the new revision will depend in a great degree on the courage and fidelity with which it deals with the questions of readings [of the Greek]. (*On a Fresh Revision*, pp. 19, 32)

The result was a clear understanding on the NT committee that, in Ellicott's words, 'faithfulness' meant fidelity 'to the original in its plain grammatical meaning as elicited by accurate interpretation' (p. 98). This is precisely what the KJB translators aimed at.

THE PREFACE TO THE NEW TESTAMENT

Because the RV NT and OT were made and published separately, the RV has two prefaces. In the words of the NT preface, the task was to produce 'a version that shall be alike literal and idiomatic, faithful to each thought of the original, and yet, in the expression of it, harmonious and free' (p. xv); the OT preface states more simply that the 'leading principle [was] the sincere desire to give to modern readers a faithful representation of the meaning of the original documents' (p. x). Faithfulness to the meaning, or, more ambiguously, thought, of the original, is indeed fundamental. Deliberately echoing the KJB preface, the NT preface says earlier, 'to render a work that had reached this high standard of excellence still more excellent, to increase its fidelity without destroying its charm, was the task committed to us' (p. vii).

Discussing the KJB and taking matters in order of importance, the NT preface deals first with the Greek text the translators used. Quietly it makes the point that the scholarship of the translators was as good as it could have been at that time but that advances in scholarship and the discovery of 'nearly all the more ancient of the documentary authorities' mean that 'it is but recently that materials have been acquired for executing [a revision] with even approximate completeness' (pp. v–vi).

Next the general character of the KJB is outlined through a commentary on the major rules for its conduct and the degree to which they were followed. One major criticism is made, that the 'studiously adopted . . . variety of expression . . . would now be deemed hardly consistent with the requirements of faithful translation' (p. vi). This would have brought a grim smile of satisfaction to the face of Hugh Broughton, but that worthy would have been less amused by this very important statement:

We have had to study this great version carefully and minutely, line by line; and the longer we have been engaged upon it the more we have learned to admire its simplicity, its dignity, its power, its happy turns of expression, its general accuracy and, we must not fail to add, the music of its cadences and the felicities of its rhythm. (p. vii)

As so often, the order matters. This is critical AVolatry wherein the KJB's general qualities of language are admired ahead of its accuracy, and yet cadence and rhythm come last. The definition of the task as increasing fidelity without destroying charm follows. Literary admiration for the KJB is balanced against scholarly reservation. There is no sign that the revisers felt that they could or should improve the language.

The real interest of the preface lies in the explanation of the changes. The revisers found themselves 'constrained by faithfulness to introduce changes which might not at first sight appear to be included under the rule' of introducing as few alterations as possible. Five classes of scholarly change are specified in the following order: changes required by a changed reading of the Greek, changes where the KJB is wrong or chooses 'the less probable of two possible renderings', clarification of obscure or ambiguous renderings, corrections of inconsistencies and, finally, subsequent alterations necessitated by these changes (p. x). On the face of it, none of these classes involves literary alteration – indeed, the shunning of ambiguity may well result in placing doctrinal considerations ahead of literary ones – but the preface allows that the consequential alterations may be literary, for sometimes they are made 'to avoid tautology, sometimes to obviate an unpleasing alliteration or some other infelicity of sound, sometimes, in the case of smaller words, to preserve the familiar rhythm' (p. xi).

Language is discussed separately. The revisers 'have faithfully adhered' to rule 2 prescribing the language of the KJB and its predecessors:

We have habitually consulted the earlier versions; and in our sparing introduction of words not found in them or in the Authorised Version we have usually satisfied ourselves that such words were employed by standard writers of nearly the same date, and had also that general hue which justified their introduction into a Version which has held the highest place in the classical literature of our language. We have never removed any archaisms, whether in structure or in words, except where we were persuaded either that the meaning of the words was not generally understood, or that the nature of the expression led to some misconception of the true sense of the passage. The frequent inversions of the strict order of the words, which add much to the strength and variety of the Authorised Version and give an archaic colour to many felicities of diction, have been seldom modified. Indeed, we have often adopted the same arrangement in our own alterations; and in this as in other particulars we have sought to assimilate the new work to the old.

In a few exceptional cases we have failed to find any word in the older stratum of our language that appeared to convey the precise meaning of the original. There, and there only, we have used words of a later date; but not without having first assured ourselves that they are to be found in the writings of the best authors of the period to which they belong. (pp. xii–xiii)

Nothing could be more explicit. Revision of language, except where dictated by the classes of scholarly change, is only made where there is a question of either 'the meaning of the words', or 'the true sense of the passage', or 'the precise meaning of the original' (these are the key phrases) being misunderstood or misconceived. Modernisation for its own sake is not even contemplated; archaism is tolerated and even cultivated. By one count, the RV NT is more archaic than the KJB in at least 549 places (Hemphill, *A History of the RV*, p. 85). Moreover, the introduction of new words is fenced in by pedantry rather than subject to taste.

One more thing is important. Quotations from OT poetry and the poems in Luke 1 and 2 are printed as verse lines: 'such an arrangement', the preface declares, 'will be found helpful to the reader, not only as directing his attention to the poetical character of the quotation, but as also tending to make its force and pertinence more fully felt' (p. xiv). In other words, it is to 'ensure a clear and intelligent setting forth of the true meaning of the words' (p. xv), which is the way the revision of the punctuation is described. The visual representation of parallelism, then, is regarded by the NT revisers as a scholarly rather than a literary device. Oddly, the OT preface is less detailed, simply remarking that 'in the poetical portions . . . [the revisers] have adopted an arrangement in lines so as to exhibit the parallelism which is characteristic of Hebrew poetry', and adding that 'they have not extended this arrangement to the prophetical books, the language of which, although frequently marked by parallelism, is, except in purely lyrical passages, rather of the nature of lofty and impassioned prose' (p. viii). This is a retreat from Lowth and his followers, and one can only presume that it stems from the revisers' caution, since Lowth's argument that the prophetic books were poetical had nowhere been refuted. One of the American revisers, Talbot W. Chambers, is more explicit, arguing that the old uniform printing of verse and prose is unfortunate 'not only in that many readers fail to see that the Scriptures are in part poetical, but also in that the parallelisms, which are so important a part of Hebrew verse and which often do so much to facilitate the understanding of difficult passages, are greatly obscured'. He makes no claim that the division is perfect but thinks even an incorrect division is better than none at all because it draws the reader's attention to the form and allows him, if he wishes, to make corrections.[3] The appearance of verse form, then, is no more than an appearance, designed to remind the reader of the literary nature of the text and to help him to perceive the meaning. It is an aid to what Chambers so often calls 'perspicuity'. The implication of the NT

---

[3] *A Companion to the Revised Old Testament* (New York and London, 1885), pp. 23–4.

preface that this apparently literary device is really employed as a rather approximate scholarly aid is confirmed.

The NT preface as a whole produces an effect entirely in keeping with the presentation of the work. At every point the sober scholarship of 'a company of earnest and competent men'[4] predominates. Literary awareness is there, but it operates as a restraining rather than as a constructive principle except where change has to be made. The degree of explicit literary awareness goes well beyond that found in the KJB preface, yet it is everywhere subordinated to the scholarly purpose.

EVIDENCE FROM THE NEW TESTAMENT REVISERS

The recollections of the revisers reinforce this conclusion. Ellicott makes the key statement of their position. Of rule eight, to consult with 'divines, scholars and literary men', he observes:

> It has sometimes been said that it would have been better, especially in reference to the New Testament, if this rule had been more frequently acted on, and if matters connected with English and alterations of rhythm had been brought before a few of our more distinguished literary men. It may be so; though I much doubt whether in matters of English the Greek would not always have proved the dominant arbiter. (*Addresses on the RV*, p. 32)

This is exactly what we have been taught to expect by the English translators from Tyndale to the KJB, and it is exactly in keeping with the RV NT preface. The two Cambridge professors, Brooke Foss Westcott and Fenton John Anthony Hort, formidable scholars and joint editors of the Greek NT, were chief influences in the committee; with Lightfoot, they vigorously promoted 'linguistic accuracy' over 'literary picturesqueness'.[5] Westcott puts the matter thus: 'faithfulness, the most candid and the most scrupulous, was the central aim of the revisers . . . And the claim which they confidently make – the claim which alone could justify their labours – is that they have placed the English reader far more nearly than before in the position of the Greek scholar' (*Some Lessons*, pp. 18, 4). In the end, the RV NT accommodates but does not cater for the aesthetic reader. Scholarship – the truth of fact, not the truth of beauty – is the essence of truth.

This is not to say that the truth of beauty did not find a voice in the committee. Hort recalls Dean Arthur Stanley 'fighting for every antique

---

[4] So described by one of the company, Charles J. Vaughan, *Authorised or Revised?* (London, 1882), p. ix.   [5] *DNB* account of William F. Moulton.

phrase which can be defended', and Ellicott says of Stanley that 'the Revised Version bore many marks of the culture and good taste of the Dean, and graceful diction and harmonious numbers found in him a constant friend. The Dean, too, defended the retention of some innocent archaisms which had become honoured in the minds of the people, and they were spared accordingly'.[6]

There is more direct evidence still of the NT revisers preserving KJB readings. Copies of proofs of the 'First and Provisional Revision' are preserved in the Cambridge University Library. One of these contains annotations by that leading proponent of heavy revision, Hort. Not all his annotations correspond to the final text but it is significant that some of them are restorations of KJB readings which the final text did indeed retain. Mark 2: 23 in the KJB reads, 'and it came to pass, that he went through the corn fields on the Sabbath day, and his disciples began as they went, to pluck the ears of corn'. The first revision changed the latter part of this to 'and his disciples began to make their way plucking the ears of corn'. Hort crosses out 'to make their way plucking', restores 'as they went, to pluck', and relegates the revision to the margin, 'Gr: *to make* their *way plucking*'. Whether this represents his considered judgement in preparation for the appropriate meeting or his record of the committee's discussion does not matter: it confirms that the familiar was sometimes retained at the expense of what was considered a more correct reading. Such testimony and examples make it clear that the NT revision was not as heavy as it might have been: faithfulness was tempered with respect for the KJB's language, but it is no more than a tempering.

AN ENGLISH ACCOUNT OF CHANGES IN THE NEW TESTAMENT

Westcott's is by far the best account of changes made in the NT, and, as a corollary, is also the best detailed account of the scholarly weaknesses of the KJB translators. Yet, for all the authority of tone that Westcott characteristically adopts, it represents throughout a personal view of the changes, and that view is from one of the extremes of the committee. Westcott was probably the chief proponent of what he himself calls 'heaviness of rendering' (*Some Lessons*, p. 25), and he frequently comments on renderings in the RV which he considers did not go far enough. At the furthest remove from Dean Stanley, whom Ellicott regarded so benevolently, he reserves his last and sharpest barb for the advocates of

---

[6] Hort, letter of July 7, 1870; Ellicott, *The Times*, July 20, 1881; both as given in Hemphill, *A History of the RV*, p. 78.

aesthetic translation, claiming that the experience of the student who has 'learnt to interrogate [the text] with intelligent patience . . . will teach him to look with something more than suspicion upon the criticisms of scholars who appear to find nothing better than solemn music in the English version of words of life, and to admit no hope of riper knowledge from the discipline of two centuries and a half' (p. 222).

Westcott assumes that his 'readers are anxious to use to the best purpose the fresh materials which the Revised Version offers for the understanding of the apostolic writings', and so gives 'typical illustrations . . . of the purpose and nature of the changes which the revisers have introduced' (p. 1). The book is therefore a guide for the English reader wanting to approach as nearly as possible the position of the Greek scholar; particularly, it is an aid 'for him to trace out innumerable subtleties of harmonious correspondence between different parts of the New Testament which were hitherto obscured' (p. 4). Consequently Westcott, who again and again stresses faithfulness, gives this telling description of a translator's duty: he

is bound to place all the facts in evidence, as far as it is possible for him to do so. He must feel that in such a case he has no right to obscure the least shade of expression which can be rendered; or to allow any prepossessions as to likelihood or fitness to outweigh direct evidence, and still less any attractiveness of a graceful phrase to hinder him from applying most strictly the ordinary laws of criticism to the determination and to the rendering of the original text. (pp. 5–6)

Going on, he raises the question that is so important here, what are 'the relative claims of faithfulness and elegance of idiom when they come into conflict'? We already know his answer, but it is an important piece of evidence for the view of the work of the KJB translators that has been offered here that this leader in the new effort at revision should appeal to the KJB as a precedent for his own adhesion to faithfulness:

the example of the Authorised Version seems to show that it is better to incur the charge of harshness than to sacrifice a peculiarity of language which, if it does nothing else, arrests attention and reminds the reader that there is something in the words which is held to be more precious than the music of a familiar rhythm. (pp. 6–7)

This to take the KJB as a literal version which places faithfulness ahead of beauty.

The essential nature of Westcott's book is best illustrated by a discussion that turns on the precise rendering of two prepositions and leads directly to a theological truth:

Two alterations . . . each of a single syllable, are sufficient to illuminate our whole conception of the Christian faith. How few readers of the Authorised Version could enter into the meaning of the baptismal formula, the charter of our life; but now, when we reflect on the words, 'make disciples of all the nations, baptising them into (*not* in) the name of the Father and of the Son and of the Holy Ghost' (Matt 28: 19), we come to know what is the mystery of our incorporation into the body of Christ. And as we learn this we enter into St Paul's words, 'the free gift of God is eternal life in (*not* through) Christ Jesus our Lord' (Rom 6: 23). It is indeed most true that the Son of God won life for us, but it is not anything apart from Himself. We live, as He has made it possible for us to realise life, only in Him . . . Am I then wrong in saying that he who has mastered the meaning of these two prepositions now truly rendered – '*into* the Name', '*in* Christ' – has found the central truth of Christianity? Certainly I would gladly have given the ten years of my life spent on the revision to bring only these two phrases of the New Testament to the heart of Englishmen. (pp. 62–3)

Precision in even the smallest details, the result the closest possible apprehension of the truth of the Bible – the one is Westcott's method, the other his aim: in such a passage he encapsulates the school of trans-lation that includes not only the RV, but the KJB, and behind that the work of Gregory Martin (to some extent), the Bishops, the Geneva trans-lators, Coverdale, Tyndale and the Wyclif translators; and, still further back, the Vulgate and the Septuagint.

In this context, Westcott's evidence on matters of vocabulary, English construction and rhythm is particularly interesting. He gives, as one would expect, many examples of places where familiar rhythms are sacrificed or new roughnesses tolerated in the interest of faithfulness. Attention to the Greek article changes 'the seats of them that sold doves' to 'the seats of them that sold the doves' (Matt. 21: 12), and he remarks, 'if at first hearing [this] sounds harsh, the pointed reference to the common offering of the poor is more than a compensation' (p. 59). This is not just a gain in accuracy for the sake of accuracy: it is also a gain in meaningfulness. Westcott often brings out such gains of literary vivid-ness (here, as opposed to literary rhythm): many of the examples in chapter 4, 'vivid details: local and temporal colouring', show how the English reader is 'able to catch the fresh vigour of the original language' (p. 147). In such examples he often implies a literary artistry in the orig-inal. Showing the RV's fidelity to the Greek tenses, he notes how the KJB failed to mark the force of the imperfect in some parts of John's Gospel where the verb 'to stand' is used. He gives seven examples of the RV's amendment of the KJB's 'stood' to 'was standing', and concludes: 'in all these places the Authorised Version has "stood", for which the Revised Version has substituted the strict rendering, except in 7: 37, where the combination "was standing, and he cried" seemed unhappily (I think) to many too harsh. The detail is perhaps a small one; but still is it not just the master-touch which kindles each scene with life?' (pp. 46–7). Impatient readers who dismiss such changes as trivial or pedantic will 'lose a lesson on the vivid power of the Gospel narrative' (p. 43).

It seems that aesthetic matters hardly entered Westcott's mind while he worked at the Greek text and the English revision. He was happy to recognise gains in this area if they chanced to occur but is quite unapologetic for losses. Only in discussing changes he would have preferred but which were not made does he show aesthetic judgement entering into the business of the revision; in such cases it was the collective judgement of the committee that the proposed change was too harsh or that 'the power of association was too strong to allow the disturbance of a familiar phrase' (p. 57n).

Taking Westcott's evidence with the slightly more liberal evidence from the rest of the committee and from the preface, we have found no more than might have been expected, that scholarship ruled, but that the literary consciousness of the time and AVolatry affected the committee, even if it often did so only after scholarship had produced its verdict. This is of major importance for it allows two possible ways of viewing the evidence from the KJB. We may speculate that if that evidence had been fuller it would have shown something like the literary consciousness that affected the RV. Alternatively, we may refuse to speculate and conclude that no more literary consciousness went into the KJB than the absolute minimum that we have seen from Bois's notes. Either way, the result is the same: scholarship – or faithfulness – was bound to be the decisive force, as it was with the RV NT.

THE NEW TESTAMENT REVISERS AT WORK

Taking us even closer to the actual discussions are unofficial minutes of some parts of the work kept by Samuel Newth, variously Professor of Classics, Principal and Lee Professor of Divinity, New College, London.[7]

---

[7] 'New Testament Company, Notes of Proceedings, Taken and Transcribed by Samuel Newth', British Library MSs Add 36,284–6. These notes are a fair copy begun by Newth in 1893 of his original pencil notes, British Library MSs Add 13,279 etc. Official minutes of the meetings of the RV British NT committee were kept and presumably survive somewhere. I also draw here on Newth's *Lectures on Bible Revision* (London, 1881), pp. 105–27.

For the most part these notes record, on the recto of the leaves, suggested readings and how the voting went on them. Three things came to a vote in John 1: 5, which reads in the KJB, 'And the light shineth in darkness; and the darkness comprehended it not'. There was general agreement for 'the darkness'. Westcott's suggestion, 'overcame it not', was carried 8 to 7, and the marginal annotation, 'Or apprehended it not', found general agreement (II: 39r). On the verso of the leaves Newth added other notes, occasionally bringing out the reasoning behind the suggested readings and translations. He did so on this occasion:

There was considerable discussion of οὐ κατέλαβεν. Sc[ott] proposed 'overcame it not' referring to ch XII.35, & contending that while καταλαμβ in mid[dle voice] = comprehend, it never did in act[ive voice]. He quoted also I K.18.44. W[estcott] concurred but suggested 'intercepted it not', & pointed out that the verb is used in Plut[arch] in connexion with eclipses. Ho[rt] objected this meaning does not suit the context as the figure is not of the darkness overtaking or coming suddenly upon the light since the light is described as shining in the darkness.

Mem. Sc[ott]'s view is that taken by Chrysostom. (II: 38v, 39v)

This is probably no more than a glimpse of 'considerable discussion'; other unrecorded suggestions may well have been made without finding enough support to go to a vote. Newth records only the part of the discussion that contributed directly to the decision. Robert Scott, Master of Balliol, still famous as co-author of the Liddell and Scott *Greek–English Lexicon*, used his lexicographical knowledge in relation to the KJB's 'comprehended it not' to show that that reading is without support elsewhere in Greek literature.[8] Presumably he was arguing against a general inclination to keep the KJB reading, and this led him to multiply examples. So next he brought up a connected verse, John 12: 35, where the same Greek verb is rendered in the RV, 'that darkness overtake you not', and then, impressively, moved on to the Septuagint, which has another active use of the verb at 1 Kgs 18: 44. Westcott remembered a passage from Plutarch, and took up the argument, making an unsuccessful attempt to bring out a figurative sense. This was duly refuted by his fellow editor of the Greek text, Hort, who brought the committee's attention back to the figurative meaning of the whole verse. We may guess from the contradiction between the basic note and the record of the discussion that Westcott now took over Scott's reading and formally

---

[8] Nevertheless, though nineteenth-century editions did not, Liddell and Scott now gives this verse (with several other citations) for the sense, 'seize with the mind, comprehend'.

proposed it for a vote. And we may further guess from the closeness of the vote that there was substantially more argument, very likely against Scott and Westcott's position and for the KJB reading. This is implicit in the general agreement to put 'or apprehended it not' in the margin. 'Apprehended' would seem to be an intelligent compromise between Scott's argument and the desire to keep 'comprehended', intelligent because, in keeping with the verb's basic meaning, to lay hold or seize, it retains the more physical sense of arrest. Finally, Newth's last comment, that Scott's view is Chrysostom's, may be a later note of his own, a product of further research into the verse.

There was still the second revision to come. The annotated proofs show that the proposed reading, 'overcame it not', was reconsidered, and changed places with the marginal reading, 'apprehended it not'. That some of the same ground was traversed is evident from the addition at this point of the main reference Scott used, John 12: 35 in the Greek.

So much work, in the end, then, produced no more than a change of one syllable, 'apprehended' for 'comprehended', and a marginal alternative complete with a cross-reference. Translation and revision are hard and earnest tasks.

THE RECEPTION OF THE NEW TESTAMENT

In absolute contrast to the dearth of evidence for the reception of the KJB, the RV NT may well have been the most discussed English translation of them all. This is because it occupies a unique position in the history of English translations by being both the first ecclesiastical revision in two and a half centuries and the first made in a time when there was an ample structure for public discussion. Moreover, it was greeted with an unsurpassed eagerness. If the English were keen for it, the Americans were keener still, and its reception outdid even the famous occasion when the episode of *The Old Curiosity Shop* containing Little Nell's death was awaited by crowds on the dockside calling to the ship's passengers, 'is Little Nell dead?' More than 300,000 copies of the NT were sold on the first day, daily newspapers (having had the text wired to them) serialised it, and reprints sprang up everywhere.

Unprecedented interest did not guarantee success. Favourable response largely ignored questions of the English literary quality of the revision, and came from scholarly churchmen who shared Westcott's desire to know the truth of the Greek as closely as possible. Some of the negative criticism also confined itself to scholarly grounds: the revisers' mastery of Greek was questioned, and the principles on which the Greek text had been constructed were the subject of more serious objections. But it is the literary response that concerns us, particularly because its central element is a rooted dislike of the new such as we have seen on many occasions and which will continue to appear to the present day. Its archetypal anecdote is the mumpsimus story (see above, p. 24) and its archetypal figure William Beveridge declaring that 'it is a great prejudice to the new that it is new, wholly new; for whatsoever is new in religion at the best is unnecessary' (see above, p. 121). This is not to pass judgement on the rightness or otherwise of the response but to keep clearly in mind the close link between familiarity and literary preference.

The *Edinburgh Review* may be allowed to stand for the generality of responses. Back in 1855 it had advocated a revision on several grounds, scholarship, presentation and archaism, and concluded that 'neither the researches of the clergy nor the intelligence of the laity have remained stationary. We have become desirous of knowing more, and they have acquired more to teach us.'[9] Whether or not the review of the RV NT is by the same author, by referring to this article, it begins from a position of sympathy perhaps representative of the expectations and hopes of many serious Christians. Nevertheless, a confession of disappointment comes quickly. The first effect of comparing the new with the old 'has been to enhance in no small degree the high estimate which we had previously formed of the merits of a work which . . . may well be regarded as unsurpassed in the entire range of literature, whether sacred or profane'.[10] Disappointment with the RV and reinforced AVolatry lead to this very important distinction:

we cannot read a chapter of the Gospels without perceiving the diametrically opposite principles which govern the procedure of the revisers of 1611 and of 1881. The former coveted earnestly, as the best gifts of translators, forcible English. They determined to make their version flexible and rhythmical; they cared but little for precision and minute accuracy; and literal reproduction of their original they utterly ignored, even to the verge of the limits prescribed to faithful rendering from one language to another. Our revisers strive, with undoubted learning and almost incredible industry, to reproduce the very order and turn of the words, the literal force of each tense and mood, and the rendering of each Greek term by the same English equivalent as far as practicable. They have obtained their ends, but at too great a price . . . Every phase of New Testament scholarship was represented in the New Testament Company, but the niceties of idiomatic English appear to have found no champion, and no

---

[9] Review of paragraph Bibles, vol. 102, no. 208 (Oct. 1855), 418–35; p. 429.
[10] Vol. 154, no. 315 (July 1881), 157–88; p. 158.

voice was raised to warn these eminent scholars of the dangers that threatened their work from over-refinement. (p. 173)

What a turnaround is here: the RV is exactly the same kind of literal translation that Selden in particular had characterised the KJB as being. Selden, whose comments had been noted in the *Review*'s 1855 article, had complained that 'the Bible is translated into English words rather than into English phrase', and added that this was 'well enough so long as scholars have to do with it, but when it comes among the common people, Lord what gear do they make of it' (see above, p. 107). The people's reaction may have changed, but what a defence of their work could the revisers have found here. The *Edinburgh Review* shows both how far the response to the KJB's language had changed and how far percep-tion of literary quality can mould the perception of intentions. The KJB translators, creators of the familiar and loved, were supreme artists; the revisers, creators of the new and destroyers of the loved, were supreme pedants. The pedantry has its value, yet 'we are left with another critical commentary on the New Testament, but not with a new version which will mould our thoughts and afford a dignified vehicle for the great truths of revelation' (p. 188). So, in sorrow, the article concludes.

Cutting as all this is, it comes from a moderate critic predisposed to be friendly to the revision. There is no need to survey the enemies of the revision except to note that the most outspoken of them all, John William Burgon, Dean of Chichester, leaves no doubt that he is at least as much a Beveridge reborn as the Broughton he was so often dismissed as (see Hemphill, *History of the RV*, p. 101): 'we never spend half an hour over the unfortunate production before us without exclaiming with one in the Gospel, "the old is better" [Luke 5: 39]. Changes of *any* sort are unwelcome in such a book as the Bible, but the discovery that changes have been made *for the worse*, offends greatly.'[11]

The strength of the hostile criticism may have affected the OT revis-ers, and it is worth noting that some of the reservations were expressed by revisers currently working on the OT. To take the earliest example, the future Bishop, John Perowne, found many of the new renderings praiseworthy, but objected to the practice of uniform rendering of single words as 'mere pedantry . . . the surest way to destroy all freedom and all dignity of language', to that 'uncouth literalism' as a perpetual remin-der to the reader 'that he is reading a translation', and to the 'inversion of the natural order of words in English' as 'construing rather than

---

[11] *The Revision Revised* (London, 1883), p. 145.

translating'.[12] Such views would have made themselves heard in the OT committee, and the vehemence with which they were expressed would have been all the stronger for the distaste caused by the NT. Despite the facts that the NT revisers were also critical, and that the negative criticisms were all made within the committee while it was at work – facts which might be taken as negating the points just made – it seems probable that the NT's often extreme adherence to its sense of faithfulness helped to make the OT a somewhat different kind of translation. At all events, another of the OT revisers, Frederick Field, proposed an alternative understanding of faithfulness while discussing the NT, 'faithfulness to the sense and spirit of the original', not to its 'grammatical and etymological proprieties'.[13]

THE PREFACE TO THE OLD TESTAMENT

Nothing in the preface to the Old Testament contradicts that to the New, yet it leaves a different impression and, without saying so directly, leads one to expect a lighter revision. One basic reason for this is that the OT revisers did not have to establish a new text of the original; rather, they 'have thought it most prudent to adopt the Massoretic Text as the basis of their work, and to depart from it, as the Authorised translators had done, only in exceptional cases' (p. v). Consequently, there was less scholarly pressure to revise the OT. There is another reason why the pressure was less, though the preface does not imply it: the NT is the theological heart of the Bible and there was less sense of significant errors in the KJB OT. The OT (and the Apocrypha) was revised because the NT was being revised rather than because there was an overwhelming need for it. So, referring to rules one and two, the preface makes its already-quoted reference to the KJB as 'an English classic' and, rather than stressing faithfulness, says simply that 'the revisers have borne in mind that it was their duty not to make a new translation but to revise one already existing' (p. v). The preface goes on to describe what looks like light revision: the revisers

have therefore departed from [the KJB] only in cases where they disagreed with the translators of 1611 as to the meaning or construction of a word or sentence; or where it was necessary for the sake of uniformity to render such parallel passages as were identical in Hebrew by the same English words, so that an English reader might know at once by comparison that a difference in the translation

---

[12] *Contemporary Review*, July 1881; adapted from Hemphill, pp. 93–4.
[13] *Otium Norvicense*, as given in Hemphill, p. 99.

corresponded to a difference in the original; or where the language of the Authorised Version was liable to be misunderstood by reason of its being archaic or obscure; or, finally, where the rendering of an earlier English version seemed preferable, or where by an apparently slight change it was possible to bring out more fully the meaning of a passage of which the translation was already substantially accurate. (p. vi)

What is not said here is truly eloquent. Not only has 'faithfulness' – as a word though not as a general idea – disappeared, but so has the NT preface's criticism of the KJB's 'variety of expression'. The very next paragraph explains that the revisers have generally followed the KJB's use of 'Jehovah' rather than inserting it uniformly, and then, two paragraphs later, attention is drawn to one distinction that has 'been introduced with as much uniformity as appeared practicable or desirable'. The distinction is between 'tabernacle' and 'tent' 'as the renderings of two different Hebrew words', and is given as an example of the treatment of 'some words of very frequent occurrence'. This seems like an exception to prove the rule, and the explanation given for it confirms the difference of principle: it is not to promote scholarly perception of uniformities in the original (a tricky if not impossible task in the OT), but to avoid the confusion caused by the KJB's inconsistency.

A paragraph remarkable for its vagueness comes at the end of the general discussion: 'in making minor changes, whether in translation or language, the revisers have followed the example of the translators of the Authorised Version, who allowed themselves in this respect a reasonable freedom, without permitting their liberty to degenerate into license' (p. viii). The vagueness is surely there to avoid making it too obvious that the OT revisers dissented from their NT brethren. There is only one thing, with respect to language, that they can mean by following the example of the KJB, that 'reasonable freedom' is 'the studied avoidance of uniformity' which the NT preface declared to be 'one of the blemishes' of the KJB, and it is clear that the OT preface dissents from the practice of the NT revisers. Part of this dissent emerges as a stress on the example of the KJB rather than the truth of the original. This is not to say that accuracy was not the OT revisers' first principle – it clearly was – but that, in modern political slang, they were wet to Westcott's dry: consideration of English weighed more strongly against – but did not outweigh – consideration of the original. The OT preface announces, as softly as possible, a revision such as the majority of critics had wanted.

It is no surprise, then, that most of this preface is concerned with questions of language. A nice example of the desire to conform to the KJB

is given in the discussion of the need to be consistent and to avoid misleading language:

In consequence of the changes which have taken place in the English language,
the term 'meat offering' has become inappropriate to describe an offering of
which flesh was no part; and by the alteration to 'meal offering' a sufficiently
accurate representation of the original has been obtained with the least possible
change of form. (p. vi)

However, what is most interesting from the present point of view is the
general discussion of archaism:

In regard to the language of the Authorised Version, the revisers have thought
it no part of their duty to reduce it to conformity with modern usage, and have
therefore left untouched all archaisms, whether of language or construction,
which though not in familiar use cause a reader no embarrassment and lead to
no misunderstanding. They are aware that in so doing they will disappoint the
large English-speaking race on the other side of the Atlantic, and it is a question upon which they are prepared to agree to a friendly difference of opinion.
(p. vii)

Following an outline of principles similar to those of the NT preface,
'two typical examples' are given:

The verb 'to ear' in the sense of 'to plough' and the substantive 'earing' for
'ploughing' were very reluctantly abandoned, and only because it was ascer-
tained that their meaning was unknown to many persons of good intelligence
and education. But it was easy to put in their place equivalents which had a ped-
igree of almost equal antiquity, and it would have been an excess of conservatism to refuse to substitute for an unintelligible archaism an expression to which
no ambiguity could be attached. On the other hand the word 'bolled' (Exod. 9:
31), which signifies 'podded for seed' and is known in provincial dialects, has no
synonym in literary English. To have discarded it in favour of a less accurate or
more paraphrastic expression would have been to impoverish the language; and
it was therefore left, because it exactly expresses one view which is taken of the
meaning of the original. (p. viii)

This is eloquent of care for the language: accuracy is consulted, ambiguity removed wherever possible, but changes are only made in the most
pressing cases, and then both dialect and literary English are consulted.
Evidently the American revisers desired a fuller revision of the language,
and the preface returns to this near the end, observing that many of the
changes in the American appendix are 'changes of language which are
involved in the essentially different circumstances of American and
English readers' (p. x).

In a sense this revision of language, though it had an aesthetic purpose, was not an aesthetic matter. The revisers were not guided by taste in making their decisions; rather, they had a standard prescribed to them and they followed it scrupulously. Only when 'the final review, which was in reality the completion of the second revision', is described does it appear that taste played a part: 'the company employed themselves in making a general survey of what they had done, deciding finally upon reserved points, harmonising inconsistencies, smoothing down roughnesses, removing unnecessary changes and generally giving finish and completeness to their work' (p. x). Smoothing roughnesses and giving finish, which sounds like the rubbing and polishing of the KJB preface, is here certainly a matter of style. And again there is the care that no unnecessary changes should be allowed to remain.

The OT preface points us towards language, and again there is an account of the work and a set of notes which, though less full than Newth's, is illuminating.

AN AMERICAN ACCOUNT OF CHANGES IN THE OLD TESTAMENT

The OT's equivalent of Westcott's book is *A Companion to the Revised Old Testament* by Talbot W. Chambers (1819–96), minister of the Collegiate Dutch Church of New York. His purpose is 'to furnish a tolerably fair conception of the revisers' work, both in amount and character'. He is careful to point out that he is working from memory, but thinks it unlikely that errors have crept in for the curious reason that 'the revision never contemplated novelties, but only a summing up of the results of criticism during the last two centuries' (p. 80). Since the English revisers did not communicate the reasons for their decisions to the Americans, Chambers' account cannot be taken as speaking for the British revisers. Nor, given that it is based on memory and 'the results of criticism', can it be taken as a properly authoritative account of the Americans' reasons. Even so, it is uniquely informed, as indispensible for any student of translation as Westcott's account of the NT revisions, and as biassed: Chambers constantly stresses the aesthetic side of translation.

Many of the changes Chambers discusses combine scholarly and stylistic considerations. In Gen. 49: 5 the KJB's margin (slightly altered, though Chambers does not mention this) is used 'as being both more literal and more expressive' (p. 82). Lev. 17: 11 is changed from 'for it is the blood that maketh an atonement for the soul' to 'for it is the blood that maketh atonement by reason of the life' because this 'is at once more faithful and expressive than the Authorised Version' (p. 86). 'The

voice of one speaking' (Num. 7: 89) becomes 'the Voice speaking', 'which
is more literal and more vivid' (p. 87).

So far, though the changes are examined with less scholarly thoroughness and without method, there is nothing out of keeping with the
changes Westcott details. However, Chambers does not hesitate to give
reasons that are principally aesthetic. The change to Num. 24: 2–3 and
15–16, 'representing the seer [Balaam] in the first instance with eyes
closed and in the second with eyes opened, is quite agreeable to the original, and at the same time much more poetic and striking than the
Authorised Version, since it conveys the conception of one whose bodily
vision is closed against all outward things, while his inner sense, on the
contrary, is divinely illumined' (p. 89). This is a change for felicity of
meaning that is neither justified nor forbidden by the original, but rather
'quite agreeable' to it. Many similar examples contain no reference to
the originals, but rest on an assertion of some kind of superiority to the
KJB, with faithfulness to an ambiguous original being taken for granted.

In most cases the literary aspect of the changes is a matter of poetic
force and clarity. Only in one instance does sound come close to playing
a part, the change from 'be merciful, O Lord, unto thy people Israel,
whom thou hast redeemed, and lay not innocent blood unto thy people
of Israel's charge, and the blood shall be forgiven them' (Deut. 21: 8) to
'forgive, O Lord, thy people Israel, whom thou hast redeemed, and
suffer not innocent blood *to remain* in the midst of thy people Israel. And
the blood shall be forgiven them'. Taking the tone of a reviewer rather
than a reporter, Chambers says this is more accurate and smooth (p. 93).

Chambers makes no attempt to arrange his comments according to
type; rather, he works steadily through the Bible. Job, by common
consent, was the most successfully revised of the OT books. Here, complete and characteristic, is what Chambers reports on Job 30 and 31:

In ch. 30 many obscurities are removed. In v. 20 'thou regardest me *not*' is properly changed to 'thou lookest at me' – i.e., in silent indifference, as the sense
requires. In 31: 31 an obvious error that disturbs the sense and the connection
is amended; and in 35, instead of the prosaic and incorrect, 'Oh that one would
hear me! Behold, my desire is that the Almighty would answer me', the revision
reproduces the vigour of the original,

> Oh that I had one to hear me!
> (Lo, here is my signature, let the Almighty answer me;)
> And that *I had* the indictment which my adversary hath written!

Job offers to affix his sign manual to the protestations of innocence already
made, and prays to see the charge against him, which is very different from the

KJB's absurd rendering, 'Oh that mine adversary had written a book!' (pp. 116–7)

Particularly significant is the sense of the literary quality of the original and the pleasure in having been able to reproduce some of it.

Such examples are sufficient to confirm that the OT revisers worked with a literary awareness and to suggest that sometimes it was their primary motive. This is not to say that questions of scholarship do not predominate but that Chambers is particularly keen to show changes where an increase in accuracy – and often in literalness – has literary benefits. In part he can do this because he makes, at best, a blurred distinction between scholarly and stylistic matters, constantly seeing gains in clarity, that is, improvements in the faithful rendering of the original, as literary gains. Nevertheless, the emphasis he repeatedly gives to these literary gains and the emphasis the OT preface gives to questions of language show that the character of the OT revision was somewhat different from that of the NT revision. This is confirmed by the surviving notes from the work.

NOTES FROM THE FIRST REVISION OF GENESIS

William Aldis Wright, secretary of the OT committee, scrupulously recorded all the changes proposed to the first six chapters of Genesis during the initial consideration of these chapters. The notes are headed 'proposed alterations in the Authorised Version'. Against every verse where alterations were proposed Wright records the original reading, the proposed change or changes and a number or numbers which correspond to 'the members of the Company in the order in which they stand in the printed list'. What is missing from the notes is any record of the reasons for the suggested changes, but they show enough to give a good sense of the way these revisers worked and thought.

In the KJB, Gen. 3: 6 reads:

And when the woman saw, that the tree *was* good for food, and that it *was* pleasant to the eyes, and a tree to be desired to make one wise, she took of the fruit thereof, and did eat, and gave also unto her husband with her, and he did eat.

The RV changes the verse to:

And when the woman saw that the tree was good for food, and that it was a delight to the eyes, and that the tree was to be desired to make one wise, she took of the fruit thereof, and did eat; and she gave also unto her husband with her, and he did eat.

All the changes appear in Wright's notes (he uses a square bracket to denote the end of the KJB's phrases, and *m* to note when a suggestion is made for the margin; for convenience, I have divided the note into separate paragraphs for each phrase):

And when the . . . she took] and the . . . and she took 4. 16.

pleasant to] a lust of (1 John 2. 16) 5. desirable to 27. a delight (or, desire) to 7. 27*m*.

and a tree . . . wise] yea, delightsome was the tree to contemplate 19.

and a tree] and that the tree was 11. 16. 21. 22. 27.

to be desired to make one wise] to be desired to make one sagacious 11. desirable to look upon 4*m*. to be desired to look upon 2*m*. 13*m*. to be desired to make wise (& in marg. many of the versions have *desirable to behold*) 6. pleasant to regard (or, contemplate) 7. 27. desirable to behold 8.

the fruit thereof] its fruit 19.

and gave] and she gave 16. (pp. 5–6)

Some of the considerations are scholarly – the suggested link with 1 John's 'the lust of the flesh' and the suggested marginal note to 'many of the versions' – but more are literary in a way that was not evident in the NT work. To change 'wise' to 'sagacious', or 'look upon' to 'behold', would be to raise the literary tone of the passage. 'Yea, delightsome was the tree to contemplate' shows both the desire to increase the archaic flavour and the desire for elegance. In the end only one of the changes adopted is clearly made for the sake of the language, the substitution of 'and that the tree was' for the more awkward 'and a tree to be desired'. Other phrases that appear awkward by modern standards such as 'her husband with her' are left unaltered. This one verse, then, shows that literary considerations did enter into the work and affect the result, but also that the revisers resisted the temptation some of them felt to make substantial 'improvements'.

Even so small a sample of the notes shows both diligence and eventual restraint. Every jot and tittle of the text was considered, and it is worth bearing in mind that the notes from the first revision only represent those occasions when, after consideration, at least one of the revisers contemplated a change. Yet, even having worked so carefully, the revisers remained open to further thoughts, and they often rejected change when, at the last, they felt it was insufficiently justified.

The relative infrequency of pressing matters of scholarship made the OT a comparatively light revision wherein necessity was more often a deciding factor than faithfulness: the bulk of the suggestions recorded by Wright were rejected, and many of those suggestions were stylistic.

Where the NT revisers found themselves considering questions of the Greek ahead of questions of English, the OT revisers, though just as attentive to their original, found that their decisions much more often depended on questions of English. Accordingly there is a larger, though still subordinate, aesthetic dimension to their work.

CONCLUSION

Many people have imagined that the KJB was a stylistic revision made to capture the English language at its best and to give an appropriate aura of beauty to the English Bible. The revised OT is the closest an official translation has come to giving direct evidence of something like these concerns, so we must speculate as to whether we would have found the same aesthetic dimension if notes such as Wright's had been preserved and if a Chambers had been found among the KJB translators. The first point has to be negative. Although Wright and Chambers take us further than the OT preface, they are consistent with its discussion of questions of language and its implications that stylistic matters were considered. These aspects are missing from the KJB preface, so we have no basis for supposing that a record of the initial discussions of the first Westminster company would have shown the interest in style exhibited by the OT revisers. Rather, if we have to make a supposition, it would go the other way, since the only bases for it are the implications of the preface and the example of Bois's notes.

However, this is not to close the matter. The revised OT does show that a group of scholarly translators making an official revision under a primary rule of faithfulness could still bring an aesthetic dimension to their work, at least in circumstances where style was a real issue and where the truth of the original was not an overwhelming issue. Did these circumstances exist for some or all of the companies that made the KJB? We can give a reasonably firm negative to the first on several grounds. First, literary translation of the Bible until, at the earliest, the end of the eighteenth century, produced very different results from the KJB. It is only when one comes to a reviser such as Noah Webster in the nineteenth century that something not too far from a literary revision produces a result similar to that produced by the great sequence of translations, and that result is of course a product of admiration for the KJB as a masterpiece of language and literature. Second, literature and religion were quite separate through the time of the great translations, whereas for the Victorians and their counterparts in America the separation hardly existed. Not one of the KJB translators could have elided literary and scholarly considerations as Chambers did. Third, there is no evidence that the KJB translators thought highly of the style of their work, and substantial evidence in their preface that their sense of good style was very different from the language in which the demands of the original and the ideal of being understood even by the very vulgar forced them to translate.

It is difficult to be as clear about the second circumstance, especially as 'the truth of the original' is a complex matter. Much of the literalism of the RV NT comes from a belief that every single detail of the Greek is ascertainable and significant, and ought to be rendered if at all possible. Mostly the truth can be determined; where it is uncertain, the doubt can and should be recorded. Here truth seems to be an almost scientific matter, attainable by exact scholarship. But the OT revisers seem to have had a more poetic conception of the truth of the original, perhaps because it was more often uncertain, perhaps also because it was often less theologically urgent. We simply do not know how difficult a matter all the groups of KJB translators found this question. Bois and his fellow workers certainly laboured just as hard as Westcott at the truth of the Greek, but at other stages and in other parts of the work the translators may have felt differently, though in just what way is uncertain. It seems that the greater a translator's sense of the theological importance and precision of the original, the less freedom he has to consider the quality of the translation as language. The probabilities, therefore, are against our hypothetical lost evidence proving that something like the literary consciousness that went into the making of the revised OT did indeed go into the making of parts, at least, of the KJB.

AN ASIDE: DIALECT VERSIONS

Much of the history of Bible translation is a history of attempts to open the Bible to the people in their own language. All such translations in a sense are dialect versions and many of them were made into languages that had no established register into which to cast the Bible. The effort to make such versions continued and continues, from the making of the Welsh Bible (1567) and the attempts to make Gaelic Bibles (an Irish Gaelic NT was published in 1602) through the multitudinous efforts of the Bible Societies to contemporary efforts such as the present work on a new Maori Bible. The purpose of almost all these versions is evangelistic.

Another purpose began to appear in some mid-nineteenth century dialect versions, the preservation of language. The projected new Maori version of the Bible, though it is essentially evangelical, points in this direction, for it is intended in part as a 'book for students studying the language'.[14] Bible translation could be used as a way of preserving endangered languages or dialects, or as a way of demonstrating linguistic variation. This latter philological interest seems to have been the motivation for a series of versions of the Song of Songs, many of which were made especially for Prince Louis Lucien Bonaparte, who paid for their publication in editions of 250 between 1858 and 1860. One set formed the *Celtic Hexapla, being the Song of Solomon in all the living dialects of the Gaelic and Cambrian languages* (London, 1858), but of greater interest is the dialect series: it contains, for instance, four different Yorkshire versions, North, West, Craven and Sheffield. Here is part of Henry Scott Riddell's version in Lowland Scotch (1858):

Pu' me, we wull rin efter thee: the King hes brung me intil his chammers; we wull be gladsome an' rejoyce in thee; we wull mind thy loefe mair nor wyne: the leal an aefauld loe thee. I am blak but bonnie, O ye douchters o' Jerusalem, as the sheilins o' Kedar, as the coortins o' Solomon. Glowerna at me becaus I am blak, becaus the sun hes shaine on me: my mither's childer wer angrie wi' me; thaye maede me keepir o' the vyneyairds, but mine ain vyneyaird I haena keepet. Acquant me, O thou wham my saul loeist, wi' whare thou feedist, wi' whare thou mak'st thy hirsel til rest at nuun: for wharefor shud I be als ane that gangs danderin' agley efter the hirsels o' thy cumrades? (I: 4–7)

A Sassenach is under almost as much difficulty in commenting on this as a Pakeha on a Maori version, yet it seems hardly likely to commend itself as a felicitous version with its triple uncertainty of tone – the Hebraic elements seem more alien in such a setting, and the idiom of the KJB jars against the occasional energetic colloquialism such as 'gangs danderin' agley'. But such commentary probably misses the point: what Riddell has produced is the mirror image of Rolle's Psalter or the early Wycliffite version, a version that is the equivalent of an interlinear gloss, but as a guide to the Lowland Scotch rather than a guide to the meaning of the translated version, the KJB. Now, knowing the meaning of the passage, one can go to Riddell's version and discover that the Lowland Scotch for 'flock' is 'hirsel'. If there is a lesson for translators, it is essentially that of versions like Rolle's: the energy of a new language is vitiated by adherence to the form of another language – until, that is, that

---

[14] *The Evening Post* (Wellington, New Zealand), 15 April 1985.

form becomes sufficiently familiar to be accepted as a special form of the new language.

These versions not only take the KJB as a perennial standard against which to reflect their dialect but they also show the Bible becoming a book of linguistic as well as literary interest. Descended from them are versions of less purely philological interest and, often, greater literary success. A twentieth-century version has illustrative value here. It is the work of a pioneer of interracial farming in Georgia, USA, who held a doctorate in NT Greek from Southern Baptist Theological Seminary, Clarence L. Jordan (1912–69). His *Cotton Patch Version of Matthew and John* was intended

to help the modern reader have the same sense of participation in [the Scriptures] which the early Christians must have had . . . By stripping away the fancy language, the artificial piety and the barriers of time and distance, this version puts Jesus and his people in the midst of our modern world, living where we live, talking as we talk, working, hurting, praying, bleeding, dying, conquering, alongside the rest of us. It seeks to restore the original feeling and excitement of the fast-breaking *news* – good news – rather than musty history. (pp. 9–10)

The following is characteristic, in its weaknesses as well as its strengths, of Jordan's work.

When Jesus came into the region of Augusta, he asked his students, 'Who do people think the son of man is?'

They said, 'Some say John the Baptizer, others say Elijah, and still others, Jeremiah or one of the famous preachers.'

'But you, who do you think I am?' he asked.

Simon the Rock spoke right up and said, 'You are the Leader, the Living God's Man.'

'You are beautiful, Simon Johnson!' exclaimed Jesus. 'This isn't human reasoning, but divine revelation. And I want to tell you, you are Rock, and on this rock I will build my fellowship, and the doors of death will not hold out against it. I will give you the keys of the God Movement, and whatever you bind in the physical realm shall have been bound in the spiritual realm, and whatever you loose in the physical realm shall have been loosed in the spiritual realm.' Then he strongly warned them to tell no one that he was the Leader.

From then on Leader Jesus began to make clear to his students that he had to go to Atlanta and to go through terrible things at the hands of the leading church people – to be killed, and three days later to be raised! But Rock collared him and began to take him to task. 'Not on your life, sir,' he said, 'Be dadblamed if this will ever happen to you.' Jesus whirled on Rock and said, 'Get away from here, you devil; you are gumming up the works for me, because you're not following God's ideas but human reasoning!' Jesus then said to his students, 'If a

man wants to walk my way, he must abandon self, accept his lynching, and share
my life. For the person who aims to save his life will lose it, and the one who loses
his life for my cause will find it. What's a man's advantage if in getting the whole
world he loses his life? Indeed, what shall a man trade in his life for?' (Matt. 16:
13–26)

To some extent it is as if Uncle Remus or Huck Finn had set out to tell
the Bible story: Jordan is in their tradition of semi-literate slang story-
telling. The accent is closer to Uncle Remus than to Huck, but Joel
Chandler Harris framed Uncle Remus with standard English narrative;
like Twain, Jordan uses a colloquial narrator. However, he does not
exploit varying levels of language as, say, Scott and James Hogg did in
their portrayals of a variety of Scottish religious characters. Jordan's
idiom is, as far as he can make it, homogeneous. Like the geography of
his translation, his narrator, his Jesus and the disciples, his Jews, gentiles,
publicans and pharisees are all Georgian; all speak a language spiced
with slang. The result is, by and large, a real sense of homely humanity.
It is even a sense of universal humanity. As Scott, exploiting varieties of
Scottish English, or Twain exploiting Huck's Mississippi idiom, or
Lawrence exploiting Nottinghamshire working-class language – so one
could go on –, Jordan is writing in a language all English speakers can
read. William Laughton Lorimer's *The New Testament in Scots* (Edinburgh:
Southside, 1983) confirms the point. Only a Scots reader can understand, 'syne he stricklie chairged the disciples no tae mouband a wurd til
onie-ane at he wis the Christ' (Matt 16: 20), most particularly because of
'mouband'. Lorimer has crossed the line between accessible slang and a
partly separate and therefore exclusive language.

For all Jordan's efforts, his is not a pure slang: the tug of standard
English is often felt, as in 'then he strongly warned them to tell no one
that he was the Leader', but such phrases emerge as flatness in the prose
rather than an inconsistency as in Riddell's version. The flavour is weakened rather than destroyed. Occasionally too there are failures of imagination in the rendering of images, as in the retention of the image of
binding and loosing. But such failures are rare and serve rather to underline just how successful Jordan usually is in his adaptations. He comments on one of the bolder changes, the use of 'lynching', in the
introduction:

there just isn't any word in our vocabulary which adequately translates the
Greek word for 'crucifixion'. *Our* crosses are so shined, so polished, so respect-
able that to be impaled on one of them would seem to be a blessed experience.
We have thus emptied the term 'crucifixion' of its original content of terrific

emotion, of violence, of indignity and stigma, of defeat. I have translated it as 'lynching', well aware that this is not technically correct. Jesus was officially tried and legally condemned, elements generally lacking in a lynching. But having observed the operation of Southern 'justice', and at times having been its victim, I can testify that more people have been lynched 'by judicial action' than by unofficial ropes. Pilate at least had the courage and the honesty publicly to wash his hands and disavow all legal responsibility. 'See to it yourselves,' he told the mob. And they did. They crucified him in Judea and they strung him up in Georgia, with a noose tied to a pine tree. (pp. 10–11)

This is a powerful statement of method and purpose. As Jordan concludes his introduction, Jesus 'may come alive. And we too'. The effect is neither to produce a version that sounds appropriately biblical nor a banal everyday version, but to show that it is possible to translate the Bible so as to give it the energetic immediacy normally associated with some kinds of fiction, and to make one feel that the original had something of this quality.

In a sense this is literary translation, but it could hardly be further removed from such 'literary' efforts as Harwood's. In that work a conception of literary supremacy led to a disastrous elaborative paraphrase, but here a conviction of the text's imaginative presence, a conviction that is both religious and literary, produces a translation of genuine literary quality. One might ordinarily think of Jordan's work as paraphrase, yet, by comparison with most literary paraphrases, it is a translation, not just carrying the words across to a new language but carrying the people, the places and the frame of reference across to the new environment. The passage shows Jerusalem translated as Atlanta, and this literal transference (the verbal root is the same) is applied throughout. Moreover, for all that the language seems so casual, there lies behind it a sharp awareness of the Greek. The passage from Matthew has one of Jordan's rare footnotes after 'on this rock':

A literal translation of the Greek goes like this: 'You are *petros* [rock, masculine gender] and on this *petra* [rock, feminine gender] I will build . . .'. Obviously the masculine form refers to the disciple. The feminine cannot refer to Rock himself, but possibly to his 'revelation' (feminine gender in the Greek) that Jesus is the Living God's Man. (p. 58)

Jordan's willingness to translate names has produced here a translation that preserves the pun of the original in a way that few English versions manage. It is the kind of small triumph that so boldly imaginative a translation deserves to meet with now and then.

The effect of *The Cotton Patch Version* may, in some respects, be similar to the effect Tyndale's version had on some of his early readers. Though, as I have suggested, Tyndale's work would have seemed to his earliest readers to have a difficult, inkhorn element, it also had the effect of putting the Bible in plain clothes, and only a version such as Jordan's can reproduce that kind of effect for a modern reader. The Vulgate was more occult than the KJB, Jordan is more colloquial than Tyndale, but Jordan in relation to the KJB is not too far removed from Tyndale in relation to the Vulgate. As a result, *The Cotton Patch Version* helps point a larger lesson about translation than just an insight into the effect of Tyndale. By the nineteenth century the KJB had taken on a major characteristic of the Vulgate: it had become the revered biblical standard of language. To attempt a version in its language was not to attempt Tyndale's kind of translation nor even to attempt the KJB's kind of translation. The RV might preserve much of the linguistic character of the older version but it could not have the same kind of effect on its readers and hearers. Jordan (who is but one example from several that might have been taken) shows that a genuine vitality can be achieved by ignoring the biblical English of the fixed version and avoiding both standard and high literary English.

CHAPTER FIFTEEN

'The Bible as literature'

THE BIBLE 'AS A CLASSIC': LE ROY HALSEY

Byron noted that Shelley 'was a great admirer of the Scripture as a composition', and he described himself in the same terms; earlier Knox had used a similar phrase (see above, pp. 288, 290 and 244). The phrase is an almost exact equivalent of 'the Bible as literature', which I have used for any seemingly literary response to the Bible, even where that response is no more than a fleeting aspect of quite different concerns. Such a broad usage is the inevitable fate of an easy phrase. But strictly it designates a narrowed approach to the Bible: the most obvious approach, the Bible as religion, is set aside. Moreover, it signals an awareness of this narrowed focus that is rarely to be found in discussions prior to the middle of the nineteenth century. To some extent it is a new phrase for a new phase. Though the new phase easily runs into AVolatry, it needs to be treated separately for two reasons: it often takes little notice of the KJB, and it often involves a non-religious approach to the Bible. These are the very things implied by the phrase: the *Bible*, not the KJB, as *literature*, not as religion.

The idea of the Bible as literature is closely associated with school Bible reading, a common enough practice but by no means universal in the British Isles: attempts to promote wider reading of the Bible in schools occurred periodically in the nineteenth century (to look no further). There was, for instance, an ecumenical effort to improve Irish education, *Extracts from the Old and New Testaments, for the use of schools in Ireland, according to the respective translations of the Church of England and the Church of Rome* (Dublin, 1814). This, as the preface explains, took its starting point from 'the Fourteenth Report of the Commissioners of Education in Ireland'. The Report disclosed that the books adopted in most of the 4,600 schools 'for the instruction of children of the lower orders . . . too often, "instead of improving, corrupt the mind, being calculated to incite to lawless and profligate adventure, to cherish superstition and to lead to dissension and disloyalty'" (p. iii). Consequently it recommended

for the use of schools, the selection of 'extracts from the Sacred Scriptures, an early acquaintance with which we deem of the utmost importance, and indeed indispensable in forming the mind to just notions of duty and sound principles of conduct. The study of such a volume would, in our opinion, form the best preparation for . . . more particular religious instruction'. (p. iv)

There is no trace of literary purpose here: the Bible is to be the antidote to depravity caused by secular literature. Nevertheless, the anonymous editor of the volume allows something like literary response as a contributing factor in the Bible's ability to improve. He concludes his preface with a paternalistic, not to say patronising, reference to 'the vacant minds and mental leisure of our peasantry'; the well-educated, he declares, are unaware 'of the manner in which the first disclosure of the histories of the Old and New Testament have been found to captivate their imaginations and to excite the best passions of their nature' (p. v). Rudimentarily, this is an argument for the utility of the literary pleasure the Bible gives, but the moral point is paramount. In such basic form, no special value is given to *literary* pleasure: churches commonly lure potential converts to the truth through the provision of pleasurable activities such as singing or sport.

The choice of extracts allows narrative portions of the OT to predominate, but 'passages from the Psalms, the Proverbs and Ecclesiastes are added to convey juster ideas of the Supreme God and useful directions for the moral conduct of mankind' (p. iv); the selections from the NT give the Gospel story, Paul preaching before Agrippa, and the doctrine of the Resurrection. In this bias towards narrative there is a more even balance between literary and religious considerations, but the presentation of the extracts, though free of editorial material other than titles, is unsurprisingly biblical, being in single-column numbered verses. The one real peculiarity of the book is that it presents the KJB and the Rheims-Douai versions on facing pages. This, 'a mere experiment of the editor's' (p. v), is a far cry from Fulke's 1601 adoption of the same presentation for controversial purposes. In this ecumenical context nothing can be said of the relative merits of either version, so the question of the merits of the language of the KJB for forming style does not arise.

The real use for present purposes of this pious and laudable (but, one judges from the lack of further editions if not from the continued sectarian divisions of Ireland, unsuccessful) book is its similarity to, yet difference from, the books that usher in the phrase 'the Bible as literature'. A literary consideration is allowed to creep in for its pedagogical usefulness in leading to moral improvement, but there is no question of literary enjoyment for its own sake.

With the phrase 'the Bible as a classic' we come closer to 'the Bible as literature'. We also cross the Atlantic. The statement that 'the Bible [is] the best of the classics' goes back at least as early as 1837, to an article by a North Carolina lawyer, Thomas Grimkee, in a school reader.[1] It was picked up by a Presbyterian American doctor of divinity, Le Roy J. Halsey (1812–96), first for an 1855 discourse at Louisville, Kentucky, 'Thoughts for the time: or the Bible as a classic', then for a work that shows the next stage of the movement towards the Bible as literature, *The Literary Attractions of the Bible; or, a plea for the Word of God considered as a classic* (1858). Though it is unfair to write it of him and of none of the other figures in this history, Halsey is a windbag, and much of his book is an exercise in rhetoric and assertion, with the word 'belief' constantly substituting for demonstrated argument. In short, his book is second-rate (to distinguish no more finely). Yet it is one of those marvellously revealing bad books: leaning heavily and openly on Johann Gottfried von Herder's *The Spirit of Hebrew Poetry* (a work better known in the States than in England) and on Gilfillan, it mixes their ideas with dogmatism in a way that leads to something that looks like originality. It shows how diligent exploitation of a few current ideas can give those ideas new turns that anticipate developments still to come from far more substantial figures.

In spite of his title, Halsey's purposes are as religious as those of the anonymous editor of *Extracts*, and he is even more hostile towards popular literature than the Irish commissioners of education. Just as *Extracts* attempted to bring Irish children to the Bible through its narrative appeal, so Halsey is trying to sell the Bible through advocation of its literary merits set against the horrors of fiction. He explains that

The object of these pages is to tell, at least in part, what [the Bible] contains; to gain the eye of those who, under an impression that there is nothing in the Bible but religion, really do not know how much there is in it; to bring out to their view some of its many treasures; and to present them in such a way that they shall desire to see more, and so be attracted to the book itself. (p. vi)

[1] McGuffey's *Eclectic Fourth Reader* (Cincinnatti, 1837); cited in John H. Westerhoff, 'The struggle for a common culture: biblical images in nineteenth-century schoolbooks', in David L. Barr and Nicholas Piediscalzi, eds., *The Bible in American Education* (Philadelphia: Fortress; Chico: Scholars, 1982), pp. 25–40; p. 30.

Implicit in this object is a sense that the Bible has two aspects. Halsey wants to bring his readers to the Bible 'as a book of religion' by setting forth 'what may be called [its] incidental attractions, or, in other words . . . its claims both as a classic and as a book of general education' (p. 13). It is an inevitable consequence of this division that he should use the word 'as', and clearly 'the Bible as literature' lurks round the corner, especially with the use of 'literary' in the title. But his opposition to contemporary literature dictates his preference for the Bible 'as a classic': he would rather see the Bible in relation to the Greek and Latin classics. Moreover, by treating the Bible also 'as a book of general education', he is keeping his view wider than 'the Bible as literature' would allow.

Here is part of the way he develops his sales pitch:

> But whilst it is chiefly as a book of religion, and especially of religious education, that the Bible has spread civilisation among the nations, still, it is true that, regarded simply as a book of learning, of taste and genius, of history and eloquence, it has exerted an influence which cannot be too highly estimated. As such, it has claims which commend themselves to every cultivated understanding. Independently of all its higher glories – the knowledge which it gives us of the way to heaven and the hope with which it inspires us of a blessed immortality – there are attractions which may be felt and appreciated even by the irreligious and the worldly-minded. (p. 14)

These people as well as the youth of the country may be led to 'peruse [the Bible] with growing interest until, advancing from the less to the greater, and from the outer to the inner sanctuary, they find for themselves that other attraction which is its chief glory – even a Saviour who is God over all blessed forever' (pp. 16–17). Blatant in this is one of the main aspects of presentations of the Bible as literature: they involve unbelievers. Halsey, presenting the Bible as a classic in order to bring unbelievers to its truth, shows the commonest but not the only form of this involvement.

One section of Halsey's first chapter is devoted to the topic of the Bible 'as a classic'. This is how it begins:

> It is greatly to be desired that our children and youth should grow up with the conviction firmly fixed in their minds that the Bible is a classic of the very highest authority in all matters of education, taste and genius; that it holds the same place of pre-eminence in the republic of letters which it holds in the church of God. It is exceedingly important that the public mind should be made to understand what the most eminent scholars of all ages and all lands have always understood and confessed – that there is no book in the world which can stand before the Bible as a classic. Such an impression, early implanted and generally received, would do much to save our young people from the evils of that

flimsy, superficial literature which, in the form of the wild, extravagant romance, the lovesick novel and the run-mad poem, is coming in upon us like a flood. It would do much to rescue the rising generation from that deluge of fiction which now threatens to overlay the learning of this boasted nineteenth century with a deeper detritus of trash than that of all the geological epochs. (pp. 18–19)

This is *Extracts* writ large, and writing large is Halsey's forte. The whole section is so full a collection of assertions that it reads rather like parts of the index to this book: the Bible is 'at once the most ancient, the most substantial, the most wonderful of all the classics'; it 'is as truly a classic as Homer or Virgil, Xenophon or Cicero, Milton or Addison' (p. 19); 'it stands without a rival at the head of all human literature' (p. 20), and is 'classical and indigenous on every soil, in every era'; 'it bears its own credentials; it carries a self-evidencing power, not only of religious truth but of classic beauty. It is true to nature and true to man' (p. 21); it 'is the truest cosmos. And of all students, the Bible student is the most thorough cosmopolite' (p. 23). At the back of all these grandiosities lies the idea of inspiration, divine or human, whichever one cares to believe in. Halsey concludes:

Call it what you will, a divine revelation or a human production – an inspiration from God or an inspiration of genius; still it must be admitted to be the most remarkable book in the world, and to exhibit the most remarkable achievement that has ever been made by man, or for man, in his advance towards perfection . . . We hold it to be the greatest of classics because it is inspired of God – the most perfect work of the human mind because a mind more than human is everywhere at work in it. 'Thy testimonies are wonderful' [Ps. 119: 129]. (pp. 24–5)

The quotation at the end is the only evidence given: it is the Bible evidencing itself. The blatant circularity of this is the essence of Halsey's position.

This is as far as we need to go to show the way bibliolatry, as soon as it admits divine *and* human attractions in the Bible, opens up phrases that begin, 'the Bible as. . .'. It is also as far as we need go in showing that such thinking connects easily and naturally with thought about the Bible's role in education. The ground for 'the Bible as literature' is thoroughly prepared. But it is useful to follow Halsey one step further. So far he has been writing about the Bible either in the originals or as transcending any particular language, and he does maintain both these positions, declaring on the one hand that 'it ought to be studied in its original tongues just as our youth study the Greek and Latin authors' (pp. 32–3), and on the other that it is 'designed to be translated into all the languages of the earth' (p. 83). It is the perfect book, most perfect in the originals, but still perfect in any language and any translation: 'translate it, however badly', he declares, 'dilute it, however much with paraphrases, still it is almost impossible to hide the native beauty of its imagery or the original lustre of its thoughts' (pp. 20–1). The reader can readily guess the way in which Halsey writes about the KJB. Having turned to this version, he makes another significant use of 'as': 'it is chiefly as an English classic, the best and most important in our language, that we advocate its claims' (p. 33). 'Its' refers to the Bible in general though the sentence as a whole refers to the KJB, 'a translation . . . which, simply as an English book, is as classical to our language as it is faithful and true to the original' (p. 36).

THE AMERICAN CONSTITUTION AND SCHOOL BIBLE READING

There are some particularly American forces behind Halsey's work, and they lead directly to some contemporary aspects of the Bible as literature. America's especially intense biblical heritage does not need rehearsing here. Its early schools centered on Bible reading and Protestant belief. A lawyer in an 1869 case could 'not refrain from saying that the common schools of this country owe their existence to [the] Bible – that they were organised and are principally maintained by men who adhere to its teachings'.[2] By this time, however, the American conception of the role of the Bible, and of religious education generally, in public schools was changing. The reasons were both Constitutional and demographic. In the 1840s, the arrival of large numbers of Roman Catholics, mostly of Irish or German background, challenged Protestant dominance and spurred debate about the value of Bible reading.[3]

The lawyer I have just quoted was arguing in a Cincinnati Superior Court case that has representative value. The Cincinnati Board of Education had resolved 'that religious instruction, and the reading of

---

[2] *The Bible in the Public Schools* (Cincinnati, 1870), p. 57. In addition to the use of the Bible in schools, it is worth remembering that between the American Revolution and the Civil War, Bible societies made vast efforts to make sure everyone had a Bible. For example, the Monroe County (New York) Bible Society gave a Bible to the 1,200 households in the county that an 1824 census had shown to be without it (Mark A. Noll, 'The image of the United States as a biblical nation, 1776–1865', in Hatch and Noll, *The Bible in America*, pp. 39–58; p. 40).

[3] See, for example, Donald E. Boles, *The Bible, Religion, and the Public Schools* (1961; new, revised edn, New York: Collier, 1963), pp. 32–8.

religious books, including the Holy Bible, are prohibited in the common schools of Cincinnati, it being the true object and intent of this rule to allow the children of the parents of all sects and opinions, in matters of faith and worship, to enjoy alike the benefit of the Common School fund' (pp. 6–7). A group of Cincinnati citizens sought to have this rule nullified. Behind the Board's rule lay the First Amendment to the Constitution, adopted in 1791; it states that 'Congress shall make no law respecting an establishment of religion, or prohibiting the free exercise thereof'. Eventually this was taken to mean that, in the words of a crucial 1963 Supreme Court judgement, 'in the relationship between man and religion the State is firmly committed to a position of neutrality'.[4] Consequently religious practice or teaching, including reading of the Bible, in State schools came to be seen as unconstitutional. In 1870 the Cincinnati Superior Court judged otherwise, but it is not so much the judgement as some of the arguments that are of real interest here.

Among the exhibits at the trial was the series of readers that contained the first use of the idea of the Bible as 'the best of classics', *McGuffey's Eclectic Readers*. Little remembered now in the United States, and never known in the United Kingdom, they sold in numbers which must be the envy of all commercial authors. By the time their use declined in the 1920s, some 122 million had been published, and most of these had gone through several sets of hands. Their influence was enormous. In the *Eclectic First Reader* young children were given plentiful references to biblical teaching as well as stories such as that of Mr Post who finds a baby on his doorstep. He raises her. She loves him. The tale, with some words divided for ease of reading, concludes: 'Mr. Post taught her to read, and at night Ma-ry would read the Bi-ble to her fa-ther; and when Mr. Post got so old that he could not work, Ma-ry took care of him.'[5] The fifth and sixth readers contained a substantial number of biblical passages, usually given without the source being specified. William Holmes McGuffey, the chief but not the sole compiler, included this note about his use of the Bible in most of the early editions:

From no source has the author drawn more copiously in his selections than from the Sacred Scriptures. For this he certainly apprehends no censure. In a Christian country that man is to be pitied who, at this day, can honestly object to imbuing the minds of youth with the language and spirit of the Word of God.

The student of the Bible will, it is believed, be pleased to find a specimen of

---

[4] 'Abington School District v. Schempp', *United States Supreme Court Reports*, Lawyers' edition, second series, 10: 844–914; p. 861.
[5] Stanley W. Lindberg, ed., *The Annotated McGuffey* (NY: Van Nostrand Reinhold, 1976), p. 11.

the elegant labors of Bishop Jebb, and some specimens of sacred poetry, as arranged by Dr. Coit, in which the exact words of our authorised translation are prescribed, while the poetic order of the original is happily restored.[6]

In later editions, however, the KJB was not always followed verbatim. Even so, to find a lesson headed 'Song of Moses at the Red Sea', given as verse lightly revised from the KJB, followed by an extremely enthusiastic article by Gardiner Spring on 'the poetry of the Bible' would have been a strong spur to appreciation of the KJB.[7] From such lessons many millions of Americans must, over the years, have become familiar with the idea that biblical passages could be presented in a literary way and keep equal company with passages from Shakespeare.

Now, McGuffey's *Readers* had been used in the schools of Cincinnati for upwards of twenty years 'as the regular and only authorised text books for lessons in reading' (*The Bible in the Public Schools*, p. 19). Stanley Matthews, a Presbyterian elder, argued for the rule banning Bible reading. He sought to distinguish different ways in which passages from the Bible might be read:

When the Bible is read in the morning as a part of the opening exercises of the school, when singing accompanies it, that is instruction in religion because it is an act of worship, because the exercises are devotional, because the necessary implication is that you are listening to the inspired and revealed will of God. But when the class takes up the Fifth Reader and reads the fifth chapter of Matthew – and I don't think any better reading could be found – it is done . . . not as the words that fell from the second person in the Godhead, when incarnate on earth, but as a beautiful specimen of English composition – fit to be the subject of the reading of a class – and stands, as far as that exercise is concerned, on the same footing precisely as a soliloquy from Hamlet, or the address of Macbeth to the air drawn dagger. (p. 211)

Devotional use of the Bible is unacceptable (because it constitutes State support of religion and because it is sectarian), but the Bible's literary qualities exist separately, so it can be used elsewhere in the curriculum.

The reply to this was twofold. First, McGuffey's *Readers* consist 'not merely of extracts from the Bible, but some of the most beautiful lessons of religion and morality . . . compiled, arranged and adorned . . . for laying the foundation of religious character, virtue and morality broad and deep throughout the country' (p. 294; see also p. 323). Second, the

---

[6] P. 316. Lindberg gives only one example of a biblical passage, Psalm 37, set as verse, with some omissions and rearrangements (pp. 315–16).
[7] *McGuffey's Newly Revised Rhetorical Guide; or Fifth Reader, Revised and Improved* (New York: Clark, Austin and Smith, 1853), pp. 294–8.

Bible is inescapably a religious book, so 'if the Bible is not thus read as an act of worship, it must be by way of religious instruction' (p. 129).

Matthews' point is the nearest approach to AVolatry in the trial, but it is worth noting that he does not rest his argument on the qualities, literary or scholarly, of the KJB. Neither side, especially that advocating Bible reading, emphasised versions, for there the sectarian issue comes in. So, in the opinion of one of the judges, 'we do not suppose there is any very essential difference between the versions' (p. 383). In general, the parties (often including Roman Catholics) who wished Bible reading to continue were willing, like the Irish editor of *Extracts*, to admit the Rheims-Douai Bible (or other versions), as desired by the individual readers.[8] At heart what they wanted was the Bible behind the versions.

Arguments of this sort were heard in and out of court rooms in nineteenth and twentieth-century America. The Constitutional separation between the state and religion made Americans especially used to seeing a distinction between sacred and secular. It is a spur to the central element implied in phrases beginning, 'the Bible as . . .', seeing the Bible in different aspects. For an American Christian there might therefore be real advantages in demonstrating qualities of secular importance in the Bible since the Bible considered only as a religious book might be removed from public schools.

The 1963 Supreme Court ruling on the matter took the position the Cincinnati School Board had unsuccessfully anticipated: public school reading from the Bible, associated with prayers at the beginning of the school day, was found to be unconstitutional. Nevertheless, all parties in the case, and the Court itself, agreed that 'the Bible was of great moral, historical and literary value' (p. 851), and the Court did not accept the contention that to ban such readings was to institute a 'religion of secularism'. Part of its decision reads as follows:

It is insisted that unless these religious exercises are permitted a 'religion of secularism' is established in the schools. We agree of course that the State may not establish a 'religion of secularism' in the sense of affirmatively opposing or showing hostility to religion, thus 'preferring those who believe in no religion over those who do believe' . . . We do not agree, however, that this decision in any sense has that effect. In addition, it might well be said that one's education is not complete without a study of comparative religion or the history of relig-

---

[8] Such a picture of inter-denominational harmony is necessarily a simplification. An 1842 Roman Catholic attempt to have the Rheims-Douai Bible read by children of their faith in Philadelphia schools led to the formation of anti-Catholic organisations, the burning of two Catholic churches and a number of deaths (Gerald P. Fogarty, 'The quest for a Catholic vernacular Bible in America', in Hatch and Noll, *The Bible in America*, pp. 163–80; pp. 165–6).

ion and its relationship to the advancement of civilisation. It certainly may be said that the Bible is worthy of study for its literary and historic qualities. Nothing we have said here indicates that such study of the Bible or of religion, when presented objectively as part of a secular programme of education, may not be effected consistently with the First Amendment. (p. 860)

This was what Matthews had tried to argue, only to be let down by McGuffey's *Readers*. And the failure of those readers is of course significant. As the Court acknowledged, 'the line which separates the secular from the sectarian in American life is elusive' (p. 863). The long history of Bible reading in schools is consistently an attempt to take pupils across this line; books such as Halsey's attempt to win their readers to the religious qualities of the Bible through advocation of its literary qualities. In effect, the Supreme Court decision told religious communities that if they wanted to have the Bible in schools at all, it must be the Bible as something other than religion: consequently the Court gave religious educators a major encouragement to present the Bible as literature.

In a sense this was encouragement to camouflage. Not all books on the Bible as literature are genuinely literary studies. John B. Gabel and Charles B. Wheeler's *The Bible as Literature: an Introduction* (1986) starts from a position that appears to be dictated by the Constitutional situation. It is addressed to 'college undergraduates enrolled in a Bible course offered by a department of literature', and the authors hasten to define what they are not doing:

It is not a commentary on the Bible . . . Nor is the book an attempt to impose an interpretive scheme or point of view on the Bible, for that would usurp the function of religion. Nor, finally, does it advocate or presume the value of the Bible as a vehicle of moral instruction or as a provider of religious insights or as a source of inspiration for the conduct of daily life. We do not deny these values, but we shall not take them into account either. It is sufficient for our purposes that the Bible be – as it were – a fascinating human document of enormous importance to the culture and history of the modern world, a document that can speak volumes to humans about their own humanity . . . everything beyond [this view] is in the area of personal beliefs and is subject to sectarian controversy. (pp. xi–xii)

Such tiptoeing neutrality appears throughout, as in the sectless conclusion to the last chapter, 'the religious use and interpretation of the Bible':

In a sense the Bible has no religious meaning until we see it through religious eyes. Our religious eyesight has been developed through the lenses of our catechism and creed; we have learned how to see at Sunday School, Hebrew

School, Daily Vacation Bible School, parochial school, youth group, Bible conference, synagogue, church. Not surprisingly, what we see when we look at the Bible through our religious eyes is what we expect to see – the customary, the familiar. This is not the least of the miracles associated with this remarkable book. (p. 267)

The point is thoughtful but tinged with bibliolatry: what is most significant is the use of 'we': the reader is assumed to be religious. This assumption, coupled with the need to be non-sectarian and non-religious, shapes the book, which contains almost nothing of what ought to be basic to a literary discussion of the Bible, reading of the text. The chapter on the Pentateuch, for instance, deals with questions of its composition and makes no attempt to give its college student reader insight into the nature or quality of any of the narratives contained therein. A further indicator of the nature of this introduction to 'the Bible as literature' is that only once do the suggestions for further reading at the ends of the chapters contain a reference to a work specifically on literary aspects of the Bible, and then it is to Kermode's article on the canon in *The Literary Guide to the Bible* (1987). In short, this book is not what it appears to be: it provides a commendable unbiassed background for study of the Bible (of whatever kind), but it is not a 'systematic general introduction to the study of the Bible as literature' (p. xi). The idea of the Bible as literature it embodies need not trouble us again.

MATTHEW ARNOLD

The phrase, 'the Bible as literature' was first used by one of Lowth's successors as both Oxford Professor of Poetry and as a reviser of Isaiah, the poet turned literary, social, educational and religious critic, Matthew Arnold (1822–88). It was a logical outcome not only of his time and the British educational context but also of his own work. In *Culture and Anarchy* (1869) and in *Literature and Dogma* (1873), he had argued at length for the importance of culture, associating it particularly with poetry and religion. He also argued that the language of the Bible was literary rather than scientific, 'that is, it is the language of poetry and emotion, approximate language thrown out, as it were, at certain great objects which the human mind augurs and feels after, and thrown out by men very liable, many of them, to delusion and error' (*Complete Prose*, VII: 155). Developing these views in *God and the Bible*, he declared 'that no one

---

[9] 2nd edn (New York: Oxford University Press, 1990), pp. xi–xii.

knows the truth about the Bible who does not know how to enjoy the Bible' (*Complete Prose*, VII: 148). This is not aestheticism for its own sake; rather, it is a deeply held view of the role the feelings and the imagination, along with the intellect, have in religion.

Arnold was a school inspector. He feared that the Education Bill of 1870 might remove the Bible from state schools altogether, so he prepared a revision of Isaiah 40–66 for school use. The original introduction to this is crucial.[10] The argument as he mounts it does not start from either the religious question or from the Bible, but from Arnold's 'conviction of the immense importance in education of what is called *letters*; of the side which engages our feelings and imagination' (VII: 499). By 'letters' he means 'poetry, philosophy, eloquence' (VII: 500); these are 'a beneficent wonder-working power in education' (VII: 503), and they make themselves felt by 'the apprehension . . . of a single great literary work as a connected whole' (VII: 501). A work from the Bible is the most appropriate choice because there is only 'one great literature for which the people have had a preparation – the literature of the Bible' (VII: 503). He then quotes his own 1868 report on the Wesleyan Training College at Westminster:

Chords of power are touched by this instruction which no other part of the instruction in a popular school reaches, and chords various, not the single religious chord only. The Bible is for the child in an elementary school almost his only contact with poetry and philosophy. What a course of eloquence and poetry (to call it by that name alone) is the Bible in a school which has and can have but little eloquence and poetry! and how much do our elementary schools lose by not having any such course as part of their school-programme. All who value the Bible may rest assured that thus to know and possess the Bible is the most certain way to extend the power and efficacy of the Bible. (VII: 503–4)

Thus he is advocating the Bible as a school literary text without feeling any of the pressure there was in America to set aside the Bible's religious role. Indeed, the opposite pressure may have been at work. Whereas in America the Bible as literature became a disguise for the Bible as religion, in Arnold there is a sense that the Bible as religion is a disguise for the Bible as literature, for his recommendation of the Bible as a school reader is not as evangelical as would appear from what has just been quoted. The stress of his argument is on literature: in itself the discovery 'of a single great literary work as a connected whole' is a sufficient

---

[10] *A Bible-Reading for Schools. The great prophecy of Israel's restoration (Isaiah, chapters 40–66) arranged and edited for young learners* (1872). The work was revised for general readers. Some of the passages to which I refer were omitted, but may be found in the textual notes to *Complete Prose*, VII: 499 ff.

aim; it is a religious aim only in so far as his literary ideas are part of his religious ideas. So the last twenty-seven chapters of Isaiah are argued for not because they are part of the Bible but because they are a great and accessible literary work.

Two problems make the phrase, 'the Bible as literature', inevitable. First, 'the Bible stands before the learner as an immense whole' which is too much to grasp: 'this is one reason why the fruitful use of the Bible, as literature, in our schools for the people, is at present almost impossible'. Second, there are 'defects of our translation, noble as it is; defects which abound most in those very parts of the Bible which, considered merely as literature, might have most power' (VII: 504). Specifically, the KJB often does not make sense (it later becomes clear that the same may be said of the originals). Out of these difficulties comes his version, presenting the last part of Isaiah as a coherent whole, which means isolating it, arranging it and correcting some of the translation.

To put a comma in the phrase – 'the Bible, as literature' – is to suggest a restricted aspect of something larger, and that suggestion is emphasised in 'considered merely as literature'. This is careful writing. Arnold is aware of potential difficulties, so he goes to the heart of the matter, whether it is legitimate to treat the Bible in this way. 'We must make a distinction', he argues:

There is a substratum of history and literature in the Bible which belongs to science and schools; there is an application of the Bible and an edification by the Bible which belongs to religion and churches. Some people say the Bible altogether belongs to the Church, not the school. This is an error; the Bible's application and edification belong to the Church, its literary and historical substance to the school. Other people say that the Bible does indeed belong to school as well as Church, but that its application and edification are inseparable from its literature and history. This is an error, they *are* separable. (VII: 510)

He goes on to distinguish between the beliefs that are built on texts and the historical or literary sense: the texts' 'application and edification are what matter to a man far most' (VII: 510–11), but they are a source of religious differences, whereas there can be little dissent about the other, less important, sense. Arnold, then, would admit that the Bible can be read without being read as religion. On the one hand, this is pragmatic: the Bible has various aspects; on the other, it is an insignificant distinction because of the ethical and religious weight he gives to 'culture' and 'literature'. Such views are by no means universally held: this first full use of the idea of the Bible as literature mounts a solid case for the concept, but much of the solidity rests on Arnold's idea of the literary nature of the Bible and of the religious nature of literature. Other ideas of religion and literature give different meanings, favourable and unfavourable, to the idea of the Bible as literature.

RICHARD MOULTON AND LITERARY MORPHOLOGY

Though Arnold invented 'the Bible as literature', its subsequent use may not depend on his work, especially since, as we have seen, he used it in a school rather than a general edition of his Isaiah. The phrase came naturally from his way of thinking, much of which can be parallelled in other writers on the Bible, and it owed a good deal to his contemporary situation. In short, 'the Bible as literature' was a phrase waiting to be invented. Yet it did not begin to establish itself until the final year of the century when a book of that title was published. This was one of a succession of works by the most energetic populariser of a literary approach to the Bible there has ever been, Richard Green Moulton (1849–1924). Son of a Wesleyan Methodist minister, he became one of Cambridge's first and most successful University Extension lecturers; in 1892 he was appointed Professor of Literature in English at the University of Chicago; nine years later, doubtless at his instigation, his title was changed to Professor of Literary Theory and Interpretation. As well as work on Shakespeare and classical drama, he produced a school syllabus entitled *The Literary Study of the Bible*, and in 1895 used the same title for a substantial 'account of the leading forms of literature represented in the sacred writings; intended for English readers' (subtitle). Also in 1895 he began publishing *The Modern Reader's Bible* in twenty-one volumes; this was to be collected into a single, densely printed volume, and to be published in a school edition and in selections, and it remained in print until at least 1952. Then, in 1899, with various collaborators, he published a collection of essays, *The Bible as Literature*, and in 1901, aiming at a more general readership, *A Short Introduction to the Literature of the Bible*. Such industry (the list I have given is incomplete), applied to both presentation and appreciation of the text, would give him a fair claim to be considered the father of modern literary study of the Bible, if such study needed a father.

The Literary Study of the Bible, popular enough to be reprinted until 1935, is representative of his work.[11] Moulton was a structuralist before his

---

[11] I have used the revised and partly rewritten second edition, 1899. This was the form in which the book was best known, and Moulton gives more developed expression to his ideas of literature in it.

time, and this leads to some peculiarities. First, he is not interested in
style, remarking that 'questions of style seem to me to belong to the study
of language rather than to the study of literature' (p. 263), and so, bibliolater that he manifestly is, he is no AVolater. He bases his study, as he
based his *Modern Reader's Bible*, on the RV. This does not represent a
judgement on the usual grounds of magnificence of style versus accuracy. Discussion of stylistic merits, he argues, has

been conducted on a wrong footing. The critics will take single verses or expressions and, as it were, test them with their mental palate to see whether the literary flavour of the old or the new be superior. But comparisons of this kind are
a sheer impossibility. No one, least of all a cultured critic, can separate in his
mind between the sense of beauty which comes from association, and the
beauty which is intrinsic; the softening effect of time and familiarity is needed
before any translation can in word and phrase assume the even harmony of a
classic. (pp. 91–2)

Others had suggested that the RV needed time before a fair judgement
could be made, but nobody else had seriously suggested that comparative stylistic judgement was an impossibility. In Moulton's view, the right
basis for discussion is the question of the coherence of the text. Only the
RV, he argues, is reliable if one wishes to attend 'to the connection
between verse and verse, to the drift of an argument and the general
unity of a whole poem' (p. 85). The medieval attention to verses in iso-
lation, he goes on, is thoroughly evident in Coverdale and stands behind
the KJB, so that the difference between the KJB and the RV is 'a
difference of kind and not of degree, and one which is as wide as the distinction between the words "text" and "context"' (p. 91). The argument
leads him to a resounding challenge: 'speaking from the literary point of
view, I make bold to say that the reader who confines himself to the
Authorised Version excludes himself from half the beauty of the Bible'
(p. 92).

It would be reasonable to assume from this kind of argument that
Moulton's literary treatment of the Bible will be, in effect, a treatment
of the originals, taking the RV as their best representative. The opposite
turns out to be true. The subtitle concluded, 'intended for English
readers', and throughout he treats the RV, as he has edited it, as an
autonomous anthology of literature: his criticism is always directed
towards the text the reader reads rather than the text behind it. This is
implicit in his declaration that, 'whoever may be responsible for the
Sacred Scriptures as they stand, these are worthy of examination for
their own sake; and the literary study of the Bible brings to bear on these

writings the light that comes from ascertaining the exact form they are found to present' (p. vi). Few literary discussions of the Bible do this and yet it is an essential position if the Bible is to be appreciated as English literature. The value of this approach, however, is vitiated by his choice of the RV, since this is not the text that has, historically speaking, been the Bible in and of English literature. Much but not all of Moulton's discussion illuminates the KJB, but that is only because the two versions have so much in common. Moreover, his refusal to deal with style means that the discussion is, at best, partial. Idiosyncrasy has its strengths and weaknesses.

Moulton's idiosyncrasies come in large part from his view of himself as a pioneer. He argues that what he means by the literary study of the Bible is something new and that its newness is connected with the fact 'that the study of literature, properly so called, is only just beginning' (p. iv). It is based on recognising that literature is an entity on its own, with its own unity and its own special focus, the study of form: it is the science, as he more than once calls it (e.g. p. 74), of literary morphology (pp. iv–v). As we have seen, this science (how Arnold would have deprecated the term!) is distinguished from the study of language, which includes the study of style. It is evident from his practice that it is also distinguished from the study of character and of morality (here Arnold would have been more than deprecatory). It is distinguished from older literary studies, which were essentially studies of literatures and stressed the historical side of things; it is also distinguished from textual criticism, and therefore from biblical Higher Criticism, for those are also historic and linguistic studies: 'literary investigation stops short at the question *what* we have in the text of the Bible, without examining *how* it has come to us' (p. vi). Finally, it is not interested in authors: he argues that the study of authors is 'quite a distinct thing', and 'that the study of literature will never reach its proper level until it is realised that literature is an entity in itself, as well as a function of the individuals who contributed to it' (p. 96). This is all quite remarkable in a turn-of-the-century critic and entitles Moulton to a significant place in the history of modern criticism.

Moulton's sense of the principal difficulty in the way of literary response to the Bible, that it 'is the worst-printed book in the world' (p. 45), led him to work at the elucidation of form, and this in turn became the cornerstone of his idea of literature. 'Nowhere', he argues,

has literary morphology so important a place as in application to the Sacred Scriptures . . . it comes to most people as a novelty to hear that the Bible is made up of epics, lyrics, dramas, essays, sonnets, philosophical works, histories and the like. More than this, centuries of unliterary tradition have so affected the outer surface of Scripture that the successive literary works appear joined together without distinction, until it becomes the hardest of tasks to determine, in the Bible, exactly where one work of literature ends and another begins. The morphological analysis of Scripture thus urgently required is precisely the purpose to which I have applied myself in the present work . . . its underlying principle is that a clear grasp of the outer literary form is an essential guide to the inner matter and spirit. (pp. v–vi)

His interest in form extends from the minutiae of verse form through to but not beyond the overall structure of the individual books: he shows no desire to treat the Bible as a single book. His treatment of verse form is characteristic. With a brief glimpse at Lowth, he neatly demonstrates the basis of parallelism by taking Psalm 105 and showing that it makes 'excellent historic prose' if the second half of each couplet is omitted, and then how it becomes 'verse full of the rhythm and lilt of a march' if given in full and set out as verse with every second line indented (p. 47). He then proceeds to an extraordinary description of the variety of biblical verse form, and extends things still further in an appendix, 'A metrical system of biblical verse'. Parallelism may work through couplets or triplets, and through larger units such as quatrains or octets. It may be antistrophic or strophic, and these forms may be inverted or reversed. Refrains are sometimes used, and there may be two other kinds of structure, 'the envelope figure, by which a series of parallel lines running to any length are enclosed between an identical (or equivalent) opening and close' (p. 56), and 'the pendulum figure', which is 'a swaying to and fro between two thoughts' (p. 58).

Moulton's scheme, like Jebb's before him, develops Lowth's suggestions that there are larger patterns to be discovered (see above, esp. p. 227), but it is more successful than Jebb's in that it is supported by a larger range of persuasive examples. Yet it is too complex to be properly useful as a scheme: its benefits lie in persuading the reader not that there is a coherent range of interrelated patterns to be discovered, but that it is frequently profitable to attend closely to the progression of thought and language in a poem, because often (Moulton would say *always*) there is a coherent structure to be discovered.

Though the belief that there is always an admirable form to be drawn out is a shaping premise that rules out of court negative criticism and so disables discrimination, much of Moulton's discussion has in common with Lowth the willingness to attend open-mindedly to what the text is doing. Central to his method is his comment, near the end of his analysis of Job, that 'he would be a very perverse reader who should cry out against these characteristics of Job as literary faults: on the contrary, they are evidence that the character of the work is insufficiently described by the terms drama and discussion' (p. 40). In other words, Job is *sui generis*, and the task is to understand just what kind of thing Job is through faithful attention. Such attention leads to one of his most valuable insights, introduced in this way:

We saw that Hebrew rests its verse system not upon metre or rhyme but upon parallelism of clauses. But, as a matter of universal literature, parallelism is one of the devices of prose: the rhetoric of all nations includes it. If then a particular language bases its verse upon something which is also a property of prose, it is an inevitable consequence that in that language prose and verse will overlap: and such is the case with biblical literature. I do not of course mean that the verse literature of the Bible taken as a whole could be confused with the biblical literature of prose . . . But while in their extremes they are totally different, yet there is a middle region of biblical style in which verse and prose meet: a high parallelism in which transition can rapidly be made from the one to the other, or even the effects of the two can be combined. It is this overlapping of verse and prose that I call the most important distinguishing feature of Hebrew literature. (pp. 113–14)

The first four verses of Amos 1: 3–15, in his presentation, show just how close the overlapping can be:

1

    Thus saith the Lord:
      For three transgressions of Damascus,
      Yea, for four,
    I will not turn away the punishment thereof;

because they have threshed Gilead with threshing instruments of iron:

      But I will send a fire into the house of Hazael,
      And it shall devour the palaces of Ben-hadad.

And I will break the bar of Damascus, and cut off the inhabitant from the valley of Aven, and him that holdeth the sceptre from the house of Eden: and the people of Syria shall go into captivity unto Kir, saith the Lord.

2

    Thus saith the Lord:
      For three transgressions of Gaza,
      Yea, for four,
    I will not turn away the punishment thereof . . . (p. 115)

He admits that the prose passages could be divided into verses, but offers instead an analysis which depends on the logic of the whole passage, which he designates 'higher parallelism':

this prophecy against seven peoples is made up of common formulae expressing ideal transgressions and ideal dooms, together with particular descriptions of actual sins and actual sufferings. It is surely in keeping with such a general plan that the formulae and ideal portions should be found to be in verse, and the particular descriptions in prose. Moreover, when we examine the denunciation of Israel, the final climax up to which all the rest leads, we find that it is just here that the description is most difficult to compel into the form of verse: if this goes best as prose then the parts correlated with it should be prose also. Finally, if we look at the whole for a moment simply as a work of art, we must be struck with the superb elasticity of utterance which Hebrew obtains from the power of combining the two styles: the speaker can at any moment suspend rhythm in order to penetrate with unfettered simplicity of prose into every detail of realism, sure of being able to recover when he pleases the rhythmic march and the strong tone of idealisation. (pp. 118–19)

Whether or not this is truly the form of the original, the arrangement and explanation illuminate. Where a reader would have struggled to see the whole as a succession of parallel lines, suddenly it has become a marvellously effective pattern. Lowth's analysis of parallelism had been a liberating insight. Moulton has now similarly liberated the reader from some of the limitations of parallelism.

Taken as a whole, *The Literary Study of the Bible* is a strong contribution to one part of literary appreciation of the Bible. And it is made stronger by its unusual willingness to treat an English version as an autonomous work. Since it has no successors as a bold attempt to bring out the forms latent in the English text, it remains a book to be returned to. At times, as when one reads the argument on overlapping prose and verse, even such praise seems lukewarm.

ANTHOLOGISTS

For Arnold and Moulton, as for Lowth before them, re-presentation of the text was a major part of their work. This is characteristic of the Bible as literature: a good deal of this movement is taken up with either biblical anthologies or whole new editions, all designed to encourage literary appreciation of the text.

In 1895 appeared *Passages of the Bible Chosen for their Literary Beauty and Interest*, edited by the redoubtable folklorist and anthropologist, Sir James George Frazer. Though not the first of a number of such anthologies, it had sufficient popularity to be issued in an enlarged second edition in 1909 and to be reprinted at least until 1932. The following is fully a third of the preface to the first edition:

That our English version of the Bible is one of the greatest classics in the language is admitted by all in theory, but few people appear to treat it as such in practice. The common man reads it for guidance and comfort in daily life and in sorrow; the scholar analyses it into its component parts and discusses their authorship and date; and the historian, the antiquary and the anthropologist have recourse to it as a storehouse of facts illustrative of their special subjects. But how many read it, not for its religious, its linguistic, its historical and antiquarian interest, but simply for the sake of the enjoyment which as pure literature it is fitted to afford? It may be conjectured that the number of such readers is very small. The reason, or, at all events, a chief reason, of this is not far to seek. The passages of greatest literary beauty and interest – those on which the fame of the book as a classic chiefly rests – are scattered up and down it, imbedded, often at rare intervals, in a great mass of other matter which, however interesting and important as theology or history, possesses only subordinate value as literature. It seemed to me, therefore, that a service might be rendered to lovers of good literature by disengaging these gems from their setting and presenting them in a continuous series . . . it is noble literature; and like all noble literature it is fitted to delight, to elevate and to console. (pp. v–vi, viii)

On the surface, brevity apart, this seems much like Arnold, especially in the insistence on the delight of literature. Nevertheless, there are some significant differences. 'As pure literature' rather than 'as literature' is the most telling. The gems of the Bible may be read as nothing more than literature, that is, in a spirit of pure aestheticism. There is no sign of Arnold's philosophical and religious sense of literature, nor of his sense of the religious importance of the Bible, and the preface to the second edition makes clear Frazer's dissociation from devout attitudes (he was later to write privately that he rejected 'the Christian religion utterly as false').[12] He observes with gratification

that the example which I set of treating the Bible as pure literature has since been followed by others who have similarly edited the Old and New Testaments or portions of them in a form divested, as far as possible, of all purely theological import. The publication of such books may be welcomed as a sign that the love of the Bible is not confined to those who accept its dogmas. Though many of us can no longer, like our fathers, find in its pages the solution of the dark, the inscrutable riddle of human existence, yet the volume must still be held sacred by all who reverence the high aspirations to which it gives utterance, and

---

[12] Letter, 18 April 1904; as given in Robert Ackerman, *J.G. Frazer: His Life and Work* (Cambridge University Press, 1987), pp. 188–9.

the pathetic associations with which the faith and piety of so many generations have invested the familiar words. (pp. ix–x)

Frazer here is driving the very wedge between the Bible as religion and the Bible as literature that 'the Bible as literature' implies. Arnold's *Isaiah* was for potential Christians, Frazer's anthology is for lapsed Christians. As such, it is the obverse of works such as Halsey's that present the Bible as a classic or as literature in order to bring unbelievers to its religion. It is the Bible without religion, that is, the Bible for unbelievers.

Yet to read the anthology itself gives a different impression: it is full of passages of belief, as any liberal sampling of both testaments cannot help being. Moreover, as a presentation of passages from the KJB, it is exemplary (though, by Moulton's extraordinary standards, conservative). All the passages are titled and referenced. There are no introductory comments or references to the notes, which are tucked away at the end of the volume for readers to take or leave as they wish. Thus the passages are left to make their own impression, religious, literary or other. They appear either as paragraphed prose or, in the poetic parts, as free but not stanzaic verse. Frazer does not intrude on the text, and the result is as good a Bible reader as any of its scale.

A third of a century later, William Ralph Inge, Dean of St Paul's, published an anthology that is an instructive counterpart to Frazer's, *Every Man's Bible: An Anthology Arranged with an Introduction* (London: Longmans, 1934). The scale is the same, the presentation almost as admirable, and over a third of the passages chosen are identical. Yet the intention is opposite to Frazer's. The introduction, as long as Frazer's is brief, begins:

The object of this anthology is to help those who wish to use the Bible as their chief devotional book. For many generations the regular reading of the sacred volume, chapter by chapter, without explanation and without commentary, brought comfort and edification to many pious souls. This practice has now so far declined that many Christians have almost ceased to read their Bibles at all. This is a grievous loss to our national Christianity. (p. ix)

Frazer's contrasting starting point was the fewness of those who read it 'simply for the sake of the enjoyment which as pure literature it is fitted to afford'. The similarity of the two anthologies, setting aside the introductions and notes and Inge's one real piece of shaping within the anthology, his arrangement of the passages by religious theme, shows how close in practice the Bible as devotion and the Bible as literature can be. The surrounding beliefs differ but the texts themselves stay substantially the same.

The differences between the anthologists' attitudes to the Bible turn out to be less absolute than their difference of belief might lead us to expect. Frazer is more than reserved about Christianity, but Inge has few reservations about the Bible as literature. Inge may seem to be attacking that approach by observing that 'we are on holy ground, and we cannot read the Bible "like any other book". We read it because for us it is not like any other book' (p. x). But he has no wish to exclude literary appreciation, and notes two sentences later that 'the literary beauty of many passages can be appreciated only when they are given entire'. So, with an ambiguity that was not present in the preface to the KJB, he writes of helping 'some readers to rediscover for themselves the inexhaustible treasures which are hidden in the most widely read and incomparably the most important collection of writings in the literature of the world' (p. x), and he even uses one of Frazer's formulations, 'the gems of the Bible' (p. xxxv). For many in the twentieth century the literary quality of the Bible was less contentious than its truth. This was not just because it was less important: with exceptions, the stigma attached to literature had long since disappeared, and most people with literary opinions, whether or not they were practising Christians, had been brought up with the language of the KJB as a foundation of their consciousness and with acclaim for the KJB's literary greatness as an unassailed truth. In some hands, the Bible as literature, especially the Bible as pure literature, might exclude the Bible as devotion, but believers, loving the Bible and also desiring to have it read by everyone, were unlikely to challenge what they took to be both their literary pleasure in the text and a means of converting the unfaithful. The problem exposed in Inge's declaration that 'we cannot read the Bible "like any other book"' greatly exercised critics such as C.S. Lewis, but for many readers it mattered not a jot.

So far we have been starting from the Bible and seeing how it is shaped as literature. But if all the declarations about the Bible being a classic of English prose were truly believed by literary men, should it not be possible to find literature reaching out to the Bible – would one not expect to find passages from the KJB in anthologies of English prose in the same way that one routinely finds some discussion of the English Bible in histories of English literature? Kenneth Muir, introducing an anthology of English prose, suggests one reason why one should not: 'the Authorised Version is not represented here as it will be accessible to all readers'.[13] If this is only an excuse, it is an excuse for the practice of a

[13] Kenneth Muir, ed., *The Pelican Book of English Prose*, vol. I: *Elizabethan and Jacobean Prose: 1550–1620* (Harmondsworth: Penguin, 1956), p. xx.

good many anthologists. Nevertheless, some do give a taste of the KJB. Herbert Read and Bonamy Dobrée, for instance, include four passages in *The London Book of English Prose* (1931). Two of the passages (Song of Songs 7 and Job 3) are generally thought of as poetry, and all four look rather like verse because the verse divisions are preserved as paragraphing. This may suggest some unease on the editors' parts: 'the noblest monument of English prose' is often poetry, so could it somehow belong in an anthology of English verse?

Only one compiler that I know of thought so, a literary man of miscellaneous accomplishments, William Ernest Henley (1849–1903). His *English Lyrics*[14] is a magnificent exception among anthologies, giving 42 passages over 53 pages (Shakespeare is given 11 pages for 22 lyrics). The passages range from Exodus 15 through ten Psalms, ten chapters from Job and almost all of the Song of Songs to Habakkuk 3. The opening words of the passages in the Vulgate are used as titles, then the KJB text is given, lineated as free verse. The effect is to remove the biblical appearance of the texts and to allow the poetry of the KJB to stand as the most substantial achievement of English lyric. The poet Francis Thompson's response to this treatment of the Bible is worth recording. He thanked 'Mr Henley for his tremendous gift of lyrical passages from the Old Testament . . . they appear in this book so unexpectedly as almost to constitute a fresh body of poetry'. Of Henley's arrangement of Psalm 137 he exclaims, 'does it not gain – is not its beauty emphasised – by the new arrangement?', and he thinks the quantity of the selection gives the volume 'exceptional interest'.[15]

Henley's rationale for including the Bible is almost as brief as Muir's was for excluding it. First, 'verse in English is, *ipso facto*, English verse'. Second, 'the Authorised Version is a monument of English prose. But the inspiration and effect of many parts of it are absolutely lyrical'. He adds what amounts to a claim that the KJB presents the highest achievement of English lyric: 'on those parts I have drawn for such a series of achievement in lyrism as will be found, I trust, neither the least interesting nor the least persuasive group in an anthology which pretends to set forth none but the choicest among English lyrics' (p. vii). He later writes of 'the noble numbers – passionate, affecting, essentially lyrical – from one of the two greatest books in English', and describes the KJB as an 'achievement in art' and as 'an English book' (p. xiii). This is indeed the kind of conclusion one would expect from sincere AVolaters in the liter-

---

[14] *English Lyrics: Chaucer to Poe, 1340–1809* (1897; 2nd ed., London, 1905).
[15] 'Mr Henley's anthology' (1897); *Literary Criticisms*, pp. 497–9.

ary world. Yet Henley, as an anthologist, seems to have been alone in taking this line.

PRESENTING THE TEXT AS LITERATURE

Moulton went further than anybody else before or since in presenting the whole text, rather than its gems, in literary form in *The Modern Reader's Bible*, and this long-lived work is one of the three modern literary presentations of the Bible most worth hunting for in second-hand book shops. Nevertheless, much of its character may be inferred from the earlier discussion, and, noting that it includes some 358 densely printed pages of introductions and notes tactfully placed at the end of the volume, we may move on to the two other presentations most worth hunting for. One stands between Moulton and the anthologies in that it misses out some parts. It is Ernest Sutherland Bates's *The Bible Designed to be Read as Living Literature* (1936; in England known as *The Bible Designed to be Read as Literature* (1937)). Bates argues that, from a literary point of view, the Bible is full of 'redundancy and irrelevance' that may ruin the finest aesthetic qualities (p. x). The way he describes the difficulties confronting a reader of the OT bears repetition, though the overlap with Moulton will be obvious:

In following the epic history of the Jews through the first sixteen books of the Old Testament, the reader is hopelessly thrown off his course by the legal codes, the census reports and genealogies, the beautiful but totally out-of-place fiction of Ruth, the double narrative of the same events in Kings and Chronicles. He then comes upon another piece of prose-fiction in Esther, the poetic drama of Job, the lyrical anthology of the Psalms, the collection of folk Proverbs, the philosophical treatise of Ecclesiastes, and the secular love poetry of the Song of Songs – nearly all of this section being the product of a late highly self-conscious period; after which, without warning, he is whirled back four hundred years to the early group of the Prophets who made their appearance once before in the book of Kings. Then, if he can indeed recognise without difficulty the greatness and appreciate the special quality of the pre-exilic Amos, Hosea and Isaiah, and could even, if he had a fair chance, detect the poignant difference in the post-exilic work of the mighty Unknown Poet at the end of Isaiah, as he goes on from these, Jeremiah and Ezekiel to the later imitative school of minor Prophets, his ears are dinned with endless ever weaker repetitions (always excepting Micah, who belongs among the earlier writers). Also, misplaced amid the prophetical books, he encounters the prose fiction of Daniel and Jonah, similar in type to Ruth and Esther – propagandist fiction all of it, four antithetical works, Ruth and Jonah generous appeals for international tolerance, Esther and Daniel impassioned pleas for patriotism. (pp. x–xi)

The argument for reorganisation and selection is powerful. Bates 'is emboldened to proclaim the final heresy – that the part is greater than the whole, and that, for literary appreciation, one wants not all the Bible but the best of it' (p. xi).

Yet, persuasive as the argument is and good as the result is, it is still something like a heresy, even from a literary point of view. This becomes apparent when, in the same spirit, he observes that 'the reader finds his sense of the events in the life of Jesus confused both by the repetitions and the divergences of the four Gospels' (p. xi). We might class this with the incomprehending objections to the repetitions in biblical poetry, or, in another sphere, with the rewritings of Shakespeare by worthies such as Nahum Tate. The effect of the Gospel story is inescapably fourfold, and 'to give the basic biography of Jesus found in . . . Mark, the earliest and most authoritative, supplemented by those incidents and teachings not found in Mark but in the other Gospels' (p. xii), is to falsify in the name of improvement. The repetitions and confusions not only between but within the Gospels drive the reader from the texts to a composite truth behind them in a way that rarely happens in other literature. Yet this is a literary effect, and any selective presentation that eliminates it makes the Gospels into something they are not. Reordering the books of the Bible seems unobjectionable, so does the identification of the different parts of Isaiah, because there one is making editorial changes to editorial matters. But to edit and select among individual books can be to interfere at a different level: it can be to change the text. In literary terms this is a heresy.

Some of the Bible's warts come from the authors, some from editors. The latter are fair game, but there is no clear line between the two. Are we rescuing a truer version of Job by omitting Elihu? Or giving a truer version of Ruth by omitting the last five verses? We are certainly making the books read better by our standards of literature and we may be eliminating later additions to those works. But we are also falsifying the whole experience of the individual works as they have come down to us. The issues cannot be argued to a resolution, and it is not my purpose to impeach Bates. In the end, however much one appreciates what he has done, one has also to read the books in a complete Bible and to reach one's own judgement as to what constitutes each book, what its literary quality is, and what the historical experience of it has been. And, behind these problems, there is of course the question of whether the Bible is a single whole or not. Not everyone would agree that it has become a single whole *only* as the result of a long editorial progress, and some would argue that it can only be read truly (a phrase that might mean many things) as a whole. Bates's 'heresy' is provocative.

One other aspect of Bates's work might be regarded as heretical. Mostly he gives the KJB's text re-presented, but for Job, Ecclesiastes, Proverbs and the Song of Songs he uses the RV because it 'is admittedly far superior' (p. xii). Moulton had used the RV throughout for the same reason. There is another question involved here besides the irresolvable one of relative quality, a historical question. Allowing for the sake of argument that the KJB is sometimes bettered by other translations both older and newer, do readers want the 'best' version of the individual texts or the version that in literary and linguistic terms has been central for the English-speaking world? Readers, after all, are likely to be readers of both the Bible and literature in English: in the latter capacity they cannot escape a historical and cultural awareness that dictates the use of the KJB. For them, it, but no other version, is the English classic.

Bates's heresies are indeed provocative. One may suggest that there is no such thing as the ideal Bible as English literature, either in theory or practice. A strictly historical view might promote Pollard's facsimile of the KJB as the ideal. This magnificent volume gives exactly and completely what became the Bible of most English literature through the last three centuries. But against this choice there lie at least four sets of arguments, those against standard presentation of the text, those against an archaic presentation which few people, relatively speaking, experienced, those for selection and those for the superiority of other versions.

A looser historical view would still insist on the text of the KJB as of paramount importance as the English wording of the text. In this looser view, what is needed is still a complete KJB, but one in which the editorial interference with reading caused especially by verse and chapter divisions and by annotation was eliminated. One editorial rearrangement might be added, namely the presentation of parts generally agreed to be poetic as free verse. In other words, the form of presentation might return to something very like the presentation of Tyndale's 1526 NT. Only his insertion of numbered chapter divisions might be deleted in favour of Bates's natural divisions with titles such as 'the creation of the world', 'the fall of man', 'the first murder', etc. Yet there are dangers in this general reversion to 1526: not everyone will agree as to what is poetry and what not, and the line divisions will always be contentious even if one does not go as far as Moulton and others, and argue that stanzaic arrangement is also necessary.

An illustration of some of the difficulties is readily given. Even if one can determine which is right, which is the better of these two presentations of the beginning of Isaiah 40 as poetry?

> 1
> 'Comfort ye, comfort ye my people,'
> Saith your God.
> 'Speak ye comfortably to Jerusalem,
> And cry unto her,
> That her warfare is accomplished,
> That her iniquity is pardoned:
> For she hath received of the Lord's hand
> Double for all her sins.'

> 2
> 'Comfort ye, comfort ye my people,' saith your God.
> 'Speak ye comfortably to Jerusalem, and cry unto her,
> That her warfare is accomplished,
> That her iniquity is pardoned:
> For she hath received of the Lord's hand double for
> all her sins.'

There is an obvious lack of agreement as to what the length of the poetic line is. The first version opts for consistently short lines with the result that attention is drawn to details of parallelism that are apparent more subtly in the longer lines of the second version. A strong analytical awareness is achieved at the expense of making the text staccatto. Moreover, the desire for consistency in line length produces breaks in the text that do nothing more than interfere with the flow of the sense, as in 'For she hath received of the Lord's hand / Double for all her sins'. In a short passage such differences may appear to be of minimal importance, but in the long run they are likely to have a real effect on readers' sense of the pace and rhythm of the writing.

In spite of these difficulties, let us assume that the advantages of signalling to the reader that some parts of the Bible are poetic outweigh the disadvantages of leaving too much to the fancy of an individual editor and of leaving these parts unmarked, that is, leaving them as prose. The first version is from Bates, the second from an edition that is exactly (save that it uses chapter divisions) what I have been describing, *The Reader's Bible* (London: Cambridge University Press, Oxford University Press, Eyre and Spottiswood, 1951). It is the third of the modern literary presentations most worth hunting for. Its presentation of the beginning of Luke is, from an editorial point of view, almost exactly Tyndale's. The chapter divisions are marked with centered titles, but there are no verse numbers or annotations. Paragraphs and poetic lines are used, and the only differences from Tyndale are that 'and Mary said' is not high-lighted, and the line division in the poetry is not always the same.

The Reader's Bible is the nearest there has been to an ideal complete KJB for the two kinds of readers mentioned earlier, readers of English literature and literary readers of the KJB. If the KJB is an acceptable Bible for religion, then one might also call this an ideal Bible for a third group of readers (not necessarily to be distinguished from the other two), religious readers, because it throws them back to the contextual reading which so many people, along with Tyndale, would see as a necessity for true understanding. Now, it is an obvious indicator of the way the Bible is normally used that *The Reader's Bible* is long since out of print while the full variety of standard religious editions of the KJB continues to be printed. A complete reading version of the KJB is an aberration on the market because the Bible is still read – or used – as the book of religion. Distinctively religious presentation remains far more marketable than literary presentation, and the utility of verse division seems to be inesca-pable.

The disadvantages of complete Bibles are well rehearsed by Bates, and the practice of selecting from an author has an ancient lineage. Comprehensive reading may be a necessity if one is to aim at a complete understanding, but for most readers selection is a normal, unobjection-able fact of life. It is better to read *Hamlet* twice than *Hamlet* and *The Merry Wives of Windsor* once each, better to know the best of Keats than to half-know all of Keats. The function of selection is to open what is best opened and to invite to the rest. Ideal presentations of the complete KJB are for readers who have already come to the Bible. For readers seeking to discover the pleasures of reading the Bible, selection is an ideal. And from this point of view, Bates's *The Bible Designed to be Read as Living Literature* is still the best edition.

Following his introduction, Bates gives two pages to quotations 'in praise of the Bible'. Rather than pursuing a survey of modern reading editions too far, it will be better to take Bates's opening two quotations as a way in to a final point. First comes Goethe: 'the greater the intellec-tual progress of the ages, the more fully will it be possible to employ the Bible not only as the foundation but as the instrument of education'; next is Robert Louis Stevenson: 'I believe it would startle and move any one if they could make a certain effort of imagination and read it freshly like a book, not droningly and chillily like a portion of the Bible' (p. xiii). These indicate two central aspects of *The Bible Designed to be Read as Living*

Literature, its connection with education and its attempt to freshen the Bible by making it like any other book in appearance. Literary presentations of the Bible descend directly from editions such as the Irish *Extracts from the Old and New Testaments* and from the work of critics such as Halsey and Arnold. A further connection is visible if we place Stevenson's remark in context. It comes from an article entitled 'Books which have influenced me':

The next book, in order of time, to influence me was the New Testament, and in particular the Gospel according to St. Matthew. I believe it would startle and move any one if they could make a certain effort of imagination and read it freshly like a book, not droningly and chillily like a portion of the Bible. Any one would then be able to see in it those truths which we are all courteously supposed to know and all modestly refrain from applying'.[16]

Literary presentation of the Bible may be more than an attempt to bring fresh readers to the Bible – it may also be an attempt to revive the freshness of response that was so common a childhood experience in the nineteenth century. It is no accident that so many of these presentations come from men who grew up in a time when the Bible was an inescapable and widely remarked childhood experience, but who then lived their adult life in a time of declining faith.

[16] *The Works of Robert Louis Stevenson*, Swanston edn, 25 vols. (London: Chatto, Heinemann and Longmans, 1912), XVI: 274.

CHAPTER SIXTEEN

The later reputation of the King James Bible

TESTIMONIES FROM WRITERS

In considering the reputation of the KJB over the century since the RV, it may be best to start with a somewhat amorphous collection of testimonies from writers to their experience of the KJB and, sometimes, its influence on their work, *The History of the English Bible* (1894) by the American Baptist minister and professor, author of *The Religious Influence of Wordsworth*, T. Harwood Pattison (1838–1904). It begins ordinarily enough but goes on to chapters on 'the Bible in English literature', and 'the Bible and the nation'. An observation Pattison attributes to the American Prebyterian minister Charles Henry Parkhurst sums up the motivation for this development: '"I am interested in the people who made the Bible, but I am more interested in the people whom the Bible makes, for they show me the fibre and genius of Scripture as no mental studiousness or verbal exegesis can do"' (p. 222). So in these chapters Pattison moves beyond opinions of the literary excellence of the Bible to testimonies from writers that their work was shaped by the Bible. His aim is to show that, 'from John Bunyan to John Ruskin . . . we owe more than we can ever tell to our early training in the English of the Bible. The character of our national tongue has been tempered by it; and to it our great writers are largely indebted for the sobriety, the strength and the sweetness which distinguish their best efforts' (p. 185). He by no means confines himself to style, but the question of where a writer gets his style recurs. The following passage is characteristic of what he wants to know and the kind of answer he wants, even if the answer does not come directly from the author of *Through the Dark Continent*:

[The Bible's] influence upon a style originally deficient in the essentials of distinction has been illustrated within a few years in the experience of Mr Stanley, the African explorer. Of him a competent writer asks: 'Where did he get his present style?' and then proceeded to answer his own question, thus: 'A clue may be found in his own story of the Bible which Sir William Mackinnon gave him at starting. He read it through, he tells us, three times . . . He has read, I will venture to guess, the greater Prophets of the Old Testament and the Epistles in the New Testament till his mind has become saturated with them. There is no imitation of any of these writers, or no conscious imitation . . . But they have modified his habits of thought and his methods of expression. He has brooded over them in the recesses of his awful forest till they have become part of his spiritual and part of his intellectual life.'[1]

Not every writer discusses his or her formative reading and only a few of those who do discuss their reading think to remark on the Bible. Moreover, it is only after Petty, McCulloch and Seiss had begun to establish the subject that people would ask writers where they got their style, hoping that they would say as Charles Dickens is supposed to have done, 'Why, from the New Testament, to be sure'.[2] Such answers, even when obtained, may not be genuinely informative. If Dickens did indeed make such a statement, we might well ask what spirit it was said in, what he might have had in mind and whether a New Testament quality can be seen in his style. It may be that the same spirit prompts the answers as prompts Pattison's interest, a spirit of automatic reverence for the KJB as a model of language: few of the testimonies which might be gathered from authors are anything more than harmonious contributions to the pious chorus.

Like the passage on Stanley, a good many of Pattison's examples are indirect, not really testimony at all. He cites, for instance, a fairly well-known story about Thomas Carlyle: in the course of conducting family worship, he began to read Job and continued through all forty chapters because he thought there was 'nothing written . . . in the Bible or out of it, of equal literary merit'.[3] Similar pieces of loose evidence are easily found. Pattison might have cited, say, Walt Whitman, who wrote with extreme enthusiasm of 'the Bible as poetry',[4] or Herman Melville, whose long poem *Clarel* (1876) is dense with biblical allusion. However, the examples that really make the Stanleyesque kind of statement that Pattison is looking for tend to postdate his book. George Bernard Shaw (1856–1950), for example, declared, 'that I can write as I do without having to think about my style is due to my having been as a child steeped in the Bible, *The Pilgrim's Progress* and *Cassell's Illustrated Shakespeare*'.[5]

---

[1] Pp. 200–1. Pattison refers to the *New York Tribune*, 28 May 1890.

[2] Pattison (p. 191) cites this as the answer to Walter Savage Landor's question, but I have been unable to authenticate Pattison's report.

[3] P. 204; *On Heroes, Hero Worship and the Heroic in History* (1841), lecture 2; ed. Israel Gollancz (London: Dent, 1901), p. 60.   [4] *The Critic* 3 (3 February 1883), 39–40.

[5] *Everybody's Political What's What* (London: Constable, 1944), p. 181.

A third of a century after Pattison, another American, Robert T. Oliver, set out to test the truth of what he took to be commonplace remarks, that 'the Bible, as a force to be reckoned with in writing, is dead', and that 'the old conception that the King James translation of the Bible is the best monument to English prose style is hopelessly out of date' (p. 350). Rather than relying on published material, Oliver wrote to 'a group of prominent American writers, frankly asking them their impressions of the situation' ('The Bible and style', p. 351), and gathered a selection from the replies into a unique and neat little article. As he observes, the responses are individualistic and not subject to easy generalisation beyond the observation that there were then still 'many contemporary writers who find the King James Bible as powerfully moving as it has been in any age' (p. 355). Few of the 'prominent' respondents are now household names, but some of their responses have a familar ring, while others come as a much-needed splash of fresh water on the face. Hendrick Willem van Loon noted that 'the King James version means very little in my life because it was not until my twentieth year that I discovered that God had not written the Bible originally in the vernacular of the delegates to the Synod of Dordrecht' (p. 351). He added, 'why waste your time on this sort of thing? You know that everyone will tell you that they loved their King James version'. Indeed a good many did just that, giving simplistic answers which are vulnerable to the kind of contempt Carl van Doren gave voice to: 'most prose writers who say they have studied the Bible and modelled their style on it are, I believe, liars' (p. 352). Simple statements deserve such simple contradictions.

The remarks become interesting and begin to escape from van Doren's condemnation when they give reasons for the love, and comment on both use and influence. Edwin Markham seems to have gone to school with Stanley. He studied biblical style, especially that of the Prophets, and was certain that 'the remarkable simplicity and directness of those masters of speech helped greatly to fashion my style in both prose and verse' (p. 355), but, if he knew how it had fashioned his style, he does not say. Lew Sarett, a poet, also studied the KJB for its literary beauty, yet, unlike Markham, 'never tried to use the elements of its style. But I respond so deeply . . . that perhaps unconsciously I have been influenced' (p. 352). Hamlin Garland's grandparents knew the KJB almost by heart; he himself not only knew it well but 'as I grew toward manhood I heard much talk of its noble simplicity'. From this background he makes a suggestion a shade more precise than Sarett's: 'I doubt if it influenced me directly, but indirectly it undoubtedly served as a corrective to the vernacular of my neighbours and the slovenly English of the press' (p. 353).

Only one of Oliver's respondents, Bess Streeter Aldrich, goes much beyond this, and she is best seen in company with some other more detailed accounts. The most interesting writer from this point of view is the British novelist, poet and miscellaneous writer, D.H. Lawrence (1885–1930), not just because of the detail he gives and the insight he shows, but because he is similar to Charlotte Brontë in the way he both uses and is shaped by the KJB. He is arguably the most biblical major writer of the twentieth century, and one might devote a book to showing ways in which this is true. At the simple level of direct use of the Bible, his work includes commentary on the Bible (*Apocalypse*), an adaptation of part of David's story for the stage that retains much of the language of the KJB (*David*), a rewriting of the last part of Jesus's life (*The Man Who Died* or *The Escaped Cock*), and novels which make substantial use of biblical imagery and language such as *The Rainbow*. More complex is the question of his language, which is often, though not always, strikingly parallelistic. How much and how deliberately this is biblical cannot be solved here. One might attribute this parallelism in part to the tendency of a spontaneous speaking voice to move forward by amplifying repetition. Nevertheless, it is difficult to imagine that Lawrence's use of parallelism would have developed in the way it did had he not been intimate with the KJB. He once defended his use of 'continual, slightly modified repetition' with the remark that 'it is natural to the author . . . every natural crisis in emotion or passion or understanding comes from this pulsing, frictional to-and-fro, which works up to culmination'.[6] This is very like an early description of parallelism: 'so soon as the heart gives way to its emotions, wave follows upon wave, and that is parallelism'.[7] The *prima facie* case these observations establish that Lawrence was influenced unconsciously as well as consciously by the KJB gives his comments on it a special interest.

He characterises Jack, the hero of his co-authored novel *The Boy in Bush*, as knowing

the Bible pretty well, as a well-brought-up nephew of his aunts. He had no objection to the Bible. On the contrary, it supplied his imagination with a chief stock of images, his ear with the greatest solemn pleasure of words, and his soul

---

[6] 'Foreword to *Women in Love*', *Phoenix II*, ed. Warren Roberts and Harry T. Moore (London: Heinemann, 1968), p. 276.
[7] Johann Gottfried von Herder, trans. James Marsh, *The Spirit of Hebrew Poetry*, 2 vols. (Burlington, Vt., 1833), I: 41.

with a queer heterogeneous ethic. He never really connected the Bible with Christianity proper, the Christianity of aunts and clergymen. He had no use for Christianity proper: just dismissed it. But the Bible was perhaps the foundation of his consciousness.[8]

This biblical foundation of consciousness is so strong that in one place Jack responds like Bunyan in *Grace Abounding* (see above, p. 186): 'Jack was always afraid of those times when the mysterious sayings of the Bible invaded him. He seemed to have no power against them' (ch. 12).

Jack represents Lawrence's sense of the Bible in a nutshell. Lawrence himself turns straightforwardly autobiographical in his final work, *Apocalypse*:

From earliest years right into manhood, like any other nonconformist child I had the Bible poured every day into my helpless consciousness, till there came almost a saturation point. Long before one could think or even vaguely understand, this Bible language, these 'portions' of the Bible were *douched* over the mind and consciousness, till they became soaked in, they became an influence which affected all the processes of emotion and thought. So that today, although I have 'forgotten' my Bible, I need only begin to read a chapter to realise that I 'know' it with an almost nauseating fixity. And I must confess, my first reaction is one of dislike, repulsion, and even resentment. My very instincts *resent* the Bible.

The reason is now fairly plain to me. Not only was the Bible, in portions, poured into the childish consciousness day in, day out, year in, year out, willy nilly, whether the consciousness could assimilate it or not, but also it was day in, day out, year in, year out expounded, dogmatically, and always morally expounded, whether it was in day-school or Sunday School, at home or in Band of Hope or Christian Endeavour. The interpretation was always the same, whether it was a Doctor of Divinity in the pulpit or the big blacksmith who was my Sunday School teacher. Not only was the Bible verbally trodden into the consciousness, like innumerable footprints treading a surface hard, but the footprints were always mechanically alike, the interpretation was fixed, so that all real interest was lost.

The process defeats its own ends. While the Jewish poetry penetrates the emotions and the imagination, and the Jewish morality penetrates the instincts, the mind becomes stubborn, resistant, and at last repudiates the whole Bible authority, and turns with a kind of repugnance away from the Bible altogether. And this is the condition of many men of my generation.[9]

The depth of influence is persuasively shown. The claim that 'this is the condition of many men of my generation' is large but perhaps not excessive: a divided response, and the consequent need to see the Bible in

---

[8] D.H. Lawrence and M.L. Skinner, *The Boy in the Bush* (1924), ch. 10.
[9] 1931; ed. Mara Kalnins (Cambridge University Press, 1980), pp. 59–60.

different aspects is a common feature of ideas of the Bible as literature. Lawrence writes from a non-conformist – specifically, a Congregationalist – background and from the generation that suffered the First World War. It may well be that the Congregationalism he grew up in was especially vigorous, certainly the war was a crucial destroyer of faith. As George Orwell (1903–50) remarks in his 1939 state-of-England novel, *Coming up for Air*, 'it would be an exaggeration to say that the war turned people into highbrows, but it did turn them into nihilists for the time being' (2: 8).

Though Orwell was almost a generation younger than Lawrence and from a background of India and Eton, he gives a similar sketch of response to the Bible, also in *Coming up for Air*. George Bowling, the lower-middle-class middle-aged narrator whose typicality Orwell stresses, recollects the church of his youth:

You took it for granted, just as you took the Bible, which you got in big doses in those days. There were texts on every wall and you knew whole chapters of the OT by heart. Even now my head's stuffed full of bits out of the Bible. And the children of Israel did evil again in the sight of the Lord [Judg. 3: 12, etc.]. And Asher abode in his breaches [Judg. 5: 17] . . . And all mixed up with the sweet graveyard smell and the serge dresses and the wheeze of the organ.

That was the world I went back to . . . For a moment I didn't merely remember it, I was *in* it. (I: 4)

Bowling concludes the first part of his story with a summary of this lost world of 1900 (Bowling is his creator's senior by a decade; I omit the preceding sentence, 'the drunks are puking in the yard behind the George', to get rid of Orwell's pervasive note of disenchantment, and so, like other collectors of testimonies, to produce the desired effect):

Vicky's at Windsor, God's in heaven, Christ's on the cross, Jonah's in the whale, Shadrach, Meshach, and Abednego are in the fiery furnace, and Sihon king of the Amorites and Og the king of Bashan are sitting on their thrones looking at one another . . .

Is it gone for ever? I'm not certain. But I tell you it was a good world to live in. I belong to it. So do you. (I: 4)

In a sense it does not matter if we take this as autobiographical (as I suspect it is) or as Orwell's idea of the typical experience of the generation that fought in the trenches, for both have a validity, and the final, characteristic, challenge, 'I belong to it. So do you', if it does not define an intellectual history, helps to create one.

Orwell thought that 'within the last generation the Bible reading which used to be traditional in England has lapsed. It is quite common to meet with young people who do not know the Bible stories even as *stories.*'[10] In general terms this may be true, but there are too many exceptions for it to be useful. Lawrence and Orwell were, I suggest, writing of an experience of the Bible that continues to occur, even if not to so many as it used to. Two generations after Lawrence, a continent away, and brought up in a different faith, the Canadian Jewish novelist Mordecai Richler (b. 1931) tells engagingly of much the same experience:

Torah was literally banged into me and seven other recalcitrant boys in a musty back room of the Young Israel Synagogue, our *cheder*, by a teacher I'll call Mr Feinberg. If I got anything wrong, or if I was caught with an Ellery Queen paperback or, say, a copy of the Montreal *Herald* on my lap open at the sports pages, Mr Feinberg would rap my knuckles with the sharp end of his ruler or twist my ear. However, what all of us feared even more than his blows was his bad breath. Grudgingly we attended Mr Feinberg's classes after regular school was out – while other boys, who weren't lucky enough to come from such good homes, were playing street hockey or snooker or just hanging out, smoking Turret cigarettes, five cents for a pack of five.[11]

It is quickly apparent that the tone is different – reminiscent comedy as against Lawrence's metaphorical description of the sensibility being formed – but the nature of the experience is similar, from the link between a 'good home' and religious education to the child's resistance and inattention. Canadian or English, Christian or Jewish (to say nothing of more local sectarian differences), 1890s or 1930s – none of these differences seem to weigh much set in the scales against an intensity of biblical education. Moreover, for all the generalisations about the present being a secular age, with not only God but religion having died, churches and families that insist on biblical learning are far from extinct.

To return now to Oliver. The most interesting response to his questioning came from a contemporary of Lawrence, the popular and sentimental novelist of mid-west pioneer days, Bess Streeter Aldrich (1881–1954). It is something of a companion piece to the Lawrence, the Orwell and the Richler:

Born of a pioneer mother who was deeply religious, I have no earlier recollection than her deep-throated voice intoning the majestic lines of the Psalms . . . The lilting words meant more to me as poetry than as any statement of religious fervour.

She seemed to half sing the verses – they accompanied my whole childhood

---

[10] 'The English people' (written 1944); in Sonia Orwell and Ian Angus, eds., *The Collected Essays, Journalism and Letters of George Orwell*, 4 vols. (Harmondsworth: Penguin, 1970), III: 22.

[11] 'Deuteronomy', in Rosenberg, ed., *Congregation*, p. 51.

as a deep-toned organ accompanies a service. This – more than any study of the Bible on my own part – has had its influence on my writing. Sometimes as I work, if perchance there comes a musically turned sentence, it seems in some queer way to be connected with that long-silenced intonation of the Psalms. One hesitates to set down in cold and often cruel black and white the experiences of the heart. But something about my mother's sincere religious nature, the rhythm of the verses she recited from memory, the majesty of the biblical language as she repeated it, has never left me. Does this early influence help me write? I do not know. All I know is that when I have agonised over a clumsy sentence and have finally turned it into something satisfying, for the brief fraction of a moment I have a feeling of oneness with the deep-throated singing of the Psalms.

This, more than any study of the stylistic qualities of the Bible, has influenced me. (p. 354)

There is no resistance here because the literary experience, of which the Psalms are a part, is part of the dearly-loved mother–daughter relationship. It may be that the experience recorded here is entirely a product of the way the mother read and the way the child felt, and so has little to do with actual qualities in the KJB. So, when Aldrich turns to Oliver's question about the effect of the Bible on her, it is to identify a quality of satisfaction in the process of writing: turning a clumsy sentence into something satisfying seems to be a pleasure of the same sort as listening to the mother, which in turn is of the same sort as being held in the mother's arms. The depth and genuineness of emotion associated with the Psalms is not in doubt. What is in doubt is whether it is possible to say anything more than '*associated with* the Psalms', in other words, to say that specific qualities of the Psalms produce the emotion. Aldrich herself thinks it is the 'feeling of oneness' rather than 'the stylistic qualities of the Bible' that counted.[12]

A second recent Jewish account of response to the Bible, like Richler's solicited for Rosenberg's *Congregation*, suggests how the Bible might have a similar effect on narrative. The account is of special interest because it comes from one of the great masters of the art of the short story, Isaac Bashevis Singer (1904–91). And, as one would expect from Singer, it is a delight in itself. He tells of his childhood study of Genesis, of his 'enlightened' brother Joshua's rational attitude to it and his own consequent scepticism about the science Joshua espoused:

[12] George Eliot, writing a decade before Aldrich was born and setting her writing still earlier in the century, describes a similar kind of response in one of her characters, Caleb Garth: 'whenever he had a feeling of awe he was haunted by a sense of Biblical phraseology, though he could hardly have given a strict quotation' (*Middlemarch* (1871–2), ch. 40).

While I became as skeptical about science and scientists as I was about God and His miracles, I acquired a great love and admiration for the stories told in the Book of Genesis. They were more believable and made more sense than many of the books my brother gave me to read. The description of Noah's ark and the way he rescued all the animals and kept them alive in the time of the Flood was a story I never got tired of reading. It kindled my imagination . . .

I could see before my eyes the people who in later generations had built the Tower of Babel . . . I was wandering with Abraham . . . I walked with Jacob . . . I was there when the brothers sold Joseph . . . I lived these tales. (Rosenberg, ed., *Congregation*, pp. 6–7)

This is Orwell's 'I was *in* it' writ beautifully large. But Singer has one more thing to add about this sense of the present aliveness of biblical narrative:

Whenever I take the Bible down from my bookcase and I begin to read it, I cannot put it down. I always find new aspects, new facts, new tensions, new information in it. I sometimes imagine that, while I sleep or walk, some hidden scribe invades my house and puts new passages, new names, new events into this wonderful book. It is the good luck of the Jewish people, and also of all people, that they were given a book like this.[13] It is God's greatest gift to humanity. (pp. 7–8)

This has taken us beyond youthful response, but what Singer is describing is the prime quality he associates with biblical narrative. Just as Aldrich tried to create the kind of feeling she associated with the Psalms in her writing, so Singer took the Genesis narratives as an ideal: 'there is perfection in these stories written by a single genius, from whom all writers can and should learn . . . I am still learning the art of writing from the book of Genesis and from the Bible generally' (p. 7).

Such accounts suggest ways the Bible may have influenced language and narrative, but testimonies to the influence of the Bible on writers would not be complete without a reminder of something so obvious that it is likely to be forgotten, that the Bible may influence a writer through its effect on his beliefs or perceptions. The Roman Catholic poet Francis Thompson (1859–1907), best known for 'The Hound of Heaven', responded late in life to what he thought of as 'the whole content and soul' of the Bible. So he thinks he was influenced in a different way from most writers:

My style being already formed could receive no evident impress from it: its vocabulary had come to me through the great writers of our language. In the first place its influence was mystical. It revealed to me a whole scheme of

---

[13] The KJB – and the PB – had already been described in these terms (see below, p. 455).

existence and lit up life like a lantern. Next to this, naturally, I was attracted by the poetry of the Bible, especially the prophetic books.

But beyond even its poetry, I was impressed by it as a treasury of *gnomic* wisdom. I mean its richness in utterances of which one could, as it were, chew the cud. This, of course, has long been recognised, and biblical sentences have passed into the proverbial wisdom of our country. But the very finest, as too deep for popular perception, have remained unappropriated. Such is that beautiful saying in Proverbs: 'As in water face answereth to face, so the heart of man to man' [27: 19] . . . None of the eastern and other heathen 'sacred volumes' sometimes brought into comparison with it have anything like the same grave dignity of form or richness of significance in their maxims. Upon this single quality, I think, I finally would elect to take my stand in regard to the Bible; and by this it has firmest hold of me.[14]

In the end this tells nothing about the working of influence, and it could be set down as a better than average piece of appreciation. Nevertheless, it does suggest that the Bible can affect a writer in non-technical areas, and that one may be influenced at any time of life.

The influence of the KJB on literature – and on language – becomes the subject for books in its own right. Here we can go little further than noting both the personal variety of response and the way the KJB has gone on being felt as a significant presence. Making due allowance for the particularly developed literary sensibility of writers, the experiences these passages record suggest something of the general impact of, usually, the KJB on young minds who could not avoid it even if they wished to. The passages also form a background to the occasional discussions of the literary influence of the KJB.

For a final example of a writer's sense of his childhood encounters with the Bible, we may turn back to the nineteenth century, to the very writer Pattison named as his latest example of a writer who owed much to the KJB, John Ruskin (1819–1900). The Bible was inescapably present in his childhood, as he recalls in his autobiographical *Praeterita* (1885–9):

After our chapters (from two to three a day, according to their length, the first thing after breakfast . . .), I had to learn a few verses by heart, or repeat, to make sure I had not lost, something of what was already known; and, with the chapters thus gradually possessed from the first word to the last, I had to learn the whole body of the fine old Scottish paraphrases, which are good, melodious and forceful verse; and to which, together with the Bible itself, I owe the first cultivation of my ear in sound.

It is strange that of all the pieces of the Bible which my mother thus taught me, that which cost me most to learn, and which was, to my child's mind, chiefly

---

[14] 'Books that have influenced me' (1900); *Literary Criticisms* pp. 542–4.

repulsive – the 119th Psalm – has now become of all the most precious to me, in its overflowing and glorious passion of love for the law of God.[15]

The punctiliousness of this learning extended as far as a three-day struggle over the stressing of a particular phrase (p. 32), and, though the intention was not in the least literary, the general result was:

From Walter Scott's novels I might easily, as I grew older, have fallen to other people's novels; and Pope might, perhaps, have led me to take Johnson's English, or Gibbon's, as types of language; but, once knowing the 32nd of Deuteronomy, the 119th Psalm, the 15th of 1st Corinthians, the sermon on the mount and most of the Apocalypse, every syllable by heart, and having always a way of thinking with myself what words meant, it was not possible for me, even in the foolishest times of youth, to write entirely superficial or formal English; and the affectation of trying to write like Hooker and George Herbert was the most innocent I could have fallen into. (p. 6)

Though Ruskin has no doubt that the KJB was the chief influence on his writing, he does not claim that he wrote like it; rather, he sees it as a restraining influence and a basis for his taste. Such an influence must often be impossible to demonstrate: one can see the positive effect of an influence – this writing or this element in it is the way it is because of an influence – but how can one show that something would have been written differently had the influence not existed? This makes Ruskin's testimony peculiarly useful, for the kind of moderating influence he describes must have been common and not only undemonstrable but also something of which many authors would not have been conscious.

FUNDAMENTALISTS AND THE GOD-GIVEN TRANSLATION

The appearance of the RV spurred rather than checked AVolatry. It helped to drive apart literary and scholarly approaches to the Bible, forcing many critics to choose between the beauty and the truth of holiness, and challenging future translators to the apparently impossible task of producing a generally acceptable new reconciliation of the two. This is not to say that there was an absolute separation between the literary and the scholarly, or between the Bible as literature and the Bible as religion. As we have seen, so-called literary approaches are often thinly disguised and diluted presentations of the results of theological and textual scholarship. While for some the appearance of the RV (and the subsequent destabilisation of the Biblical text through the accumulation

---

[15] Ed. Kenneth Clark (London: Hart-Davis, 1949), p. 31.

of quasi-authoritative versions) changed the KJB from being the book of truth to being a literary monument, for others it cemented the KJB's position as the only book of truth.

This latter movement may be dealt with immediately. It is the last manifestation of what, for most Christians, has ceased to be an issue at all, the question of the KJB's accuracy. Though this is not a literary movement, it tells much about that central force in changing literary attitudes, love for the established. Some of the more fundamental Protestant sects refused, in Myles Smith's phrase, to have their religion meddled with and so developed arguments to justify their continued use of the KJB. The Textus Receptus, essentially Estienne's Greek NT of 1551, is defended against all later textual criticism. Because none of the more modern Bibles return to this, but instead use the discredited fruits of 'naturalistic criticism',[16] the KJB is consequently defended: it is the truest and latest representative of the true original text. One caricature presentation of this view – I take it from a comic magazine[17] – has the original Greek (every word of which is direct from God) preserved first by John of Patmos, then by the true Christians in Antioch, then by the Waldensians. When 'the greatest scholars the world had ever seen' (p. 28), the KJB translators, gathered together NT manuscripts, 98 per cent of the evidence came from Antioch. Meantime, Satan, through the Roman Catholic Church (a form of Baal worship disguised as Christianity), made every effort to corrupt the true Bible, and eventually succeeded through Westcott and Hort, 'who secretly supported the Roman Catholic Church' (p. 29). The result has been a total undermining of confidence in the Bible and destruction of true religion. One must return to the true Word, as given in the KJB. That this picture is accompanied by violent anti-Catholicism and anti-Ecumenism goes without saying, nor does it need saying that many of the proponents of the KJB and the Textus Receptus would be far from happy with so simplistic a picture.

The desire – the need, even – for absolute certainty underlies these attitudes. But the arguments that support them are circular: they begin from the premise of the infallible inspiration of the Scriptures (are we not saved by faith?), and this premise becomes their conclusion. Two further premises support the argument, those of the eternal origin of the Scriptures and of their providential preservation – an idea we have

---

[16] See, e.g., Edward F. Hills, *The King James Version Defended!* chapter 4. The alternative is 'consistently Christian, Bible-believing' textual criticism.

[17] Jack T. Chick, *Sabotage* (Chino, Ca: Chick, 1979).

already seen in Scholefield's claim that the KJB translators 'were raised up by the providence of God' (see above, p. 309). The God who inspired the original Scriptures would not have allowed them to be corrupted. Implicitly (more often than explicitly), this means the KJB is the inspired translation. For Chick it is 'the God honoured text'. Hills is fuller but just as simple:

the King James Version is the historic Bible of English-speaking Protestants. Upon it God, working providentially, has placed the stamp of His approval through the usage of many generations of Bible-believing Christians. Hence, if we believe in God's providential preservation of the Scriptures, we will retain the King James Version, for in so doing we will be following the clear leading of the Almighty. (p. 214)

In short, because the KJB has been generally used, it should go on being used.

Tradition is God-given truth, hence the slogan for the KJB, 'the Bible God uses and Satan hates'. An earlier proponent of this way of thinking, Benjamin G. Wilkinson, though he does not claim direct inspiration for a translation, nevertheless makes the essentially inspirationist claim for the KJB that 'when the Bible was translated in 1611, God foresaw the wide extended use of the English language; and therefore, in our Authorised Bible, gave the best translation that has ever been made, not only in the English language, but as many scholars say, *ever made in any language*'.[18] This differs from the familiar attribution of artistry to the KJB translators only in that the artistry and the foresight that produced perfection are now God's, but the crucial point is that literary AVolatry and conservative fundamentalism share ways of thinking. There is no difference between the traditional (which is the word one would use in a religious context) and the familiar (the word I have used in a literary context) except in the shade of temperamental response made to them.

The fundamentalist, of course, is not much concerned about beauty. His or her world is a desperate battleground between God and Satan, and belief is the most precious thing. The language of the KJB matters only for reasons that are felt to be religious. Just as the language of the Greek NT 'was biblical rather than contemporary', so 'the language of the Bible should be venerable as well as intelligible, and the King James Bible fulfils these two requirements better than any other Bible in English' (Hills, *King James Version Defended!*, pp. 208, 212). Moreover, the KJB's English encourages memorisation, especially by children, and

---

[18] *Our Authorized Bible Vindicated* (Washington, D.C.: the author, 1930), p. 256.

memorisation places the word of God in the heart (p. 213), whereas the unstable text produced by the surfeit of modern-language versions discourages memorisation.

One cannot admire or even respect argument built on a rigid position in order to prove that position (the 'proof' is there only to make the believer more comfortable). This is especially so when one of the consequences is intolerance of other positions, another the failure to realise that sincerity and a conviction of truth are not confined to a single group of people, and a third the rejection of rational argument. Yet the desire for stability and certainty is very real, and veneration of the familiar lies at the heart of many critics' love for the KJB as literature. Such simplism on the religious side of AVolatry may make us more sceptical of literary AVolatry, and it certainly helps to show AVolatry's major negative aspect, its tendency to produce condemnation of the new. The rampant traditionalism of a Hills or a Chick condemns all modern Bibles as the work of Satan. Similarly, though less dangerously, literary AVolatry condemns modern Bibles as lacking literary quality because they are not the KJB. Time has made it the beautiful Bible, and time might possibly do the same for another version – if one could imagine any Bible in the future obtaining the monopoly on consciousness that the KJB had for so long. Such a development is at best unlikely. Christianity is no longer an inescapable national institution, and within Christianity the single verbal form of the Scriptures in translation has been so broken down that it is never likely to be restored.[19]

MODERN AVolatry

AVolatry reached its peak in the first half of the twentieth century. Thereafter, with major variations from community to community, the plethora of competing versions and the declining force of institutional Christianity have weakened its hold. Nevertheless, they have not changed its essential nature much beyond giving it something of the deadness that is the usual fate of clichés: we are the inheritors of AVolatry even if we are not true believers.

Grandiose claims that often fly in the face of historical evidence or scholarly attention to the subject, and repetition of received opinions are two of the foremost characteristics of modern AVolatry. In the sort of

[19] Chick would see this as the final triumph of Satan, while Hills would deny the triumph by reasserting the principle of the providential preservation of Scripture, for that principle guarantees that God's truth will never be lost.

book that gives a bad smell to the phrase, 'the Bible as literature', by twaddle such as characterising 'Tyndale's peculiar contribution to the English Bible [as] that indefinable something we call charm', Charles Allen Dinsmore declared that the KJB 'is a finer and nobler literature than the Scriptures in their original tongues'.[20] In an openly secondhand but, for all that, much better book, Wilbur Owen Sypherd was of the same opinion. The context he puts it in is thoroughly familiar: 'a towering monument marks the highest point of perfection to which English-speaking people have yet attained in the expression of their deepest thoughts and noblest emotions. The King James version has a rare distinction. As a translation from two great languages of antiquity . . . it has given to the world a literature greater than that of the original tongues.'[21] If we think of such remarks in the context of the widespread belief in the perfection of the original Scriptures, it is indeed a monumental claim. That original perfection came from God, and we have seen that the common tendency to attribute artistry to the translators sometimes went as far as attributing divine inspiration to the translation. Another expression of the idea of the KJB's literary superiority unashamedly links providence and the time of the KJB:

It is true that the Greek of the New Testament is common Greek and in many of the books destitute of literary embellishment. But why should we not rejoice in the fact that the Bible in our mother tongue excels the original as literature? If the New Testament was written in the silver age of Greek and the King James in the golden age of English, is it not all Providence? The apostolic Christians worshipped in crypts and sand pits. Should we then tear down our cathedrals and seal up our organs?[22]

A good deal of the general sense of the KJB's reputation comes from John Livingston Lowes's 'The noblest monument of English prose' (1930). This is quintessential AVolatry. The title phrase itself is much repeated, yet it was not new to Lowes. It was anticipated by, among others, Pratt's phrase, 'the noblest composition in the universe' (see above, p. 256), Arnold had used part of it in calling the KJB 'a great national monument' (*Complete Prose*, VII: 66), and Henley had it almost pat in 'a monument of English prose' (above, p. 380). The essay is packed with declarations such as this, 'the English Bible has a pithiness and raciness, a homely tang, a terse sententiousness, an idiomatic flavour which

---

[20] *The English Bible as Literature* (London, 1931), pp. 83, 78.
[21] *The Literature of the English Bible* (New York: Oxford University Press, 1938), p. 40.
[22] Paul K. Jewett, 'Majestic music of the King James', *Christianity Today* 1: 4 (26 November 1956), 13–15; p. 13.

comes home to men's business and bosoms', or this, 'utter simplicity, limpid clearness, the vividness of direct, authentic vision – these are the salient qualities of the diction of the men who wrote the Bible' (pp. 48, 54). Nothing more than rhetoric, such claims are just as derivative as the title. 'Business and bosoms', for instance, comes from Robert Louis Stevenson by way of Eckman (*Literary Primacy*, p. 43). Surely that arch-student of literary sources, Lowes, knew he was borrowing his title just as surely as he must have known that many of the generalisations he filled his essay with were diluted from the work of one of his predecessors at Harvard, John Hays Gardiner.

In some respects Gardiner's *The Bible as English Literature* (1906) is the closest there is to a substantial good study of the KJB as a work of English literature. Yet, for all that it does have some stimulating insights and, *faute de mieux*, is still worth reading, it is not a good book. The mixture of vagueness and repetition is lamentable, and AVolatry, as usual, blinkers the critical faculty. In a general way the book is interesting because it is the first to come out of a university course on the Bible offered within a department of English, and it is hardly surprising that it comes from an American University. Interest in the Bible as literature has always been stronger in America than England, and many of the major figures in developing the subject have been American.

Gardiner begins from this position:

In all my discussion I have assumed the fact of inspiration, but without attempting to define it or to distinguish between religious and literary inspiration. The two come together in a broad region where everyone who cares for a delimitation must run his line for himself. It is obvious, however, that no literary criticism of the Bible could hope for success which was not reverent in tone. A critic who should approach it superciliously or arrogantly would miss all that has given the book its power as literature and its lasting and universal appeal. (pp. vi–vii)

The vagueness is characteristic, and the dangers of assuming inspiration hardly need rehearsing. The explicitness of the identification of 'religious and literary inspiration' is new, but the result is the old one: just as the Bible is the supreme book of religion, so it is the supreme literary work. This is Gardiner's fundamental point, that the Bible – as far as English is concerned, in the form of the KJB – is supreme as literature. This leads at last to the seemingly odd yet inevitable position of setting the KJB up in opposition to all other literature. The real emphasis is less on the Bible *as* literature than on the Bible *against* literature. At bottom, the reasoning is again straightforward and familiar: the Bible is the best literature; all other literature must be measured by its standard, and, so measured, is found wanting. 'Much reading in the Bible', Gardiner writes, 'will soon bring one to an understanding of the mood in which all art seems a juggling with trifles and an attempt to catch the unessential when the everlasting verities are slipping by' (pp. 382–3). After many repetitions, he develops the cliché that the KJB is a standard of the language just this far: 'one can say that if any writing departs very far in any way from the characteristics of the English Bible, it is not good English writing' (p. 388), and he concludes that 'it remains true, therefore, in a broad way with the substance of English literature as with the style, that the English Bible stands as the norm about which all the rest can be arranged and as the standard by which it is not unreasonable to estimate it' (pp. 394–5).

He frequently lapses into the weakest of generalisations, such as naming the general qualities of English prose style, as measured by the KJB, 'simplicity and earnestness' (p. 389). Nevertheless, there is a larger idea in the background. In part it grows out of his sense of the characteristics of Hebrew, principally that Hebraic thought 'knew only the objective and solid facts of which man has direct sensation, and the simple and primitive emotions which are his reaction to them' (p. 86). By contrast, almost all other literature, and modern literature in particular, is essentially abstract and never free from 'the restless egotism that is the curse of the artistic temperament' (p. 384). It may have a greater subtlety and ability to develop thought, but with these gains there are greater losses, namely, of the power to move directly and of the trust in intuition which arrives 'at glimpses of the verities which lie behind the mask of experience' (p. 170). 'It is only', he preaches, 'by virtue of the deep infusion of feeling which always goes with knowledge attained by intuition that the human mind can soar to the eternal and the infinite' (p. 207). 'Abstract and therefore pale' (p. 120) sums up his judgement on the weakness of modern literature against the strength of the Bible.

With these general arguments goes an essentially familiar view of 'the crowning monument of English literature' (p. 357). The 'large and noble qualities' of the originals 'not only survived the process of translation, but in our English Bible almost gained new power' (p. 278; here he is a touch more cautious than his successors, Dinsmore and Sypherd, yet one suspects the 'almost' is modest rather than meaningful). The KJB has 'unequalled vitality and freshness of expression . . . it not only gives us the denotation of the books which it translates, but it clothes its own language with the rich connotation of the original and with the less definable but no less potent expressive power of sound' (p. 283). The strength comes in part from the period, but Gardiner does not resort to the simple argument of the KJB's contemporaneity with Shakespeare. He draws out with often good detail the contributions of the various translators from Tyndale – 'one of the great heroes of the English race' (pp. 315–16) – to the King James translators, and adds to this the most persuasive aspect of his argument against modern abstraction: he notes how Tyndale had written (in his prologue to Genesis) of 'sucking out the sweet pith of the Scriptures', and comments that

we today should probably have written 'extract the essence', and thereby with what is to us the quaintness we should have lost also the eagerness and delight which colour Tyndale's words with their halo of feeling. The language of this sixteenth century was lacking in many of our commonest general words, and as a result men used figures of speech more naturally . . . all the men who worked on our English Bible . . . must sometimes have adopted figurative forms of expression for the reason that the abstract word had not yet been assimilated in the language. (pp. 358–9)

This is but part of a more detailed argument, but it is sufficient to show that Gardiner's vagueness and anti-literary AVolatry do at times cohere into detail that gives a cogency to what in other hands had been the easy cliché of putting AVolatry with bardolatry. One-eyed as it is, his denigration of modern literature has some real insight to it. If Gardiner's excesses and weaknesses contribute to the bad odour of AVolatry, his strengths remind us that AVolatry has some truth to it. The history of AVolatry may be largely a history of human critical weakness, but that in itself is illuminating, and it has never been proof that a view is wrong because it is widely held or stupidly repeated.

THE SHAKESPEAREAN TOUCH

AVolatry made the question of the source of the KJB's perfection very real. One product of that question needs following here. Among the respectable contributors to AVolatry was the magisterial egoist, George Saintsbury (1845–1933), Professor of Rhetoric and English Literature at Edinburgh University. An out-and-out aesthete, he presents parts of the KJB as among 'the highest points of English prose', as triumphs of 'ornateness', of which 'rhythm is the chief and the most difficult form or constituent' (*A History of English Prose Rhythm*, p. 142). He rests his case primarily on Isaiah 60, secondarily on 1 Corinthians 13, 'perhaps the finest passage, rhythmically, of the New Testament, as "Arise, shine" is not far from being the finest of the Old' (p. 152). With no hesitation or embarrassment he raises the ensign of aestheticism, declaring that to compare Isaiah 60 in the KJB 'with the same passage in other languages is a liberal education in despising and discarding the idle predominance of "the subject"' (p. 142). The subject and the imagery are common to all versions, 'but "oh! the difference to *us*" of the expression!' (p. 150). And, having declared his competence to judge rhetorical value in a sufficient range of languages (barring Hebrew), he asserts in the vein that Dinsmore and Sypherd were to mine: 'that any one of the modern languages (even Luther's German) can vie with ours I can hardly imagine anyone who can appreciate both the sound and the meaning of the English maintaining for a moment' (p. 143), and then proceeds to scan several verses – as prose, using Latinate quantitative scansion – from the KJB, the Septuagint and the Vulgate. This leads to a virtuoso comparative discussion of the three and then an equally detailed discussion of the development of the English through the versions from Coverdale onwards that curious readers may well wish to read for themselves, for there is no comparative discussion of qualities of sound and rhythm like it to be found anywhere else, and brief quotation cannot properly represent it. Out of it emerges a picture of the process of translation as a matter of achieving not a perfect presentation of meaning – the meaning is in all the versions – but a perfect sound. 'The noblest stuff is worthy of the noblest fashion' (p. 157), Saintsbury declares (but we know what happens when translators try to make this their principle), and to read him is to see the successive translators acting not at all as scholars but as artists, with the KJB translators collectively the greatest artists.

Out of this vision of the translators as artists comes the discussion's one real lameness. Given the lack of 'very distinguished men of letters as such' (p. 158) among the translators, where did the artistry come from? All Saintsbury can offer is the old idea of the period, 'the literary tact shown must have been due to an extraordinary diffusion of it among the men of the time': he reminds his reader of some of the great prose artists of the time, including Shakespeare and Bacon, and wonders in a parenthetical return to his best sarcastic mode, 'why has no one contended that Andrewes and the rest were merely "Rosicrucian masks"' for Bacon? The allusion of course is to the long-running attempt to prove that Shakespeare could not possibly have written the plays attributed to him and that the true author was Bacon. It seems, though, that a quasi-Baconian attempt was made to prove that Shakespeare was the real genius behind the KJB. Shakespeare was 46 in 1610, and the KJB was receiving its final rubbing and polishing. The 46th word of the 46th Psalm is 'shake', and the 46th word from the end of the same Psalm is 'spear'. It was on just such ingenious observations within Shakespeare's plays that their Baconian authorship was 'proved'. The key thing about Baconianism for us, though, is that it reflects a preoccupation with the artist that did indeed affect thought about the KJB as literature in this period of high AVolatry.

The rhythms and assonances of the KJB were a likely source of conversation among literary men, and in one such conversation the novelist and future governor general of Canada, John Buchan, made Saintsbury's point, saying 'it was strange that such splendour had been produced by a body of men learned, no doubt, in theology and in languages, but including among them no writer. Could it be, he wondered, that they had privately consulted the great writers of the age, Shakespeare, perhaps and Jonson and others?'[23] Hearing this, Rudyard Kipling remarked, '"that's an idea" and away he went to turn it over'. The result was his fine short story, '"Proofs of Holy Writ"' (1934). In it Shakespeare, reclining in a Stratford orchard in the company of Ben Jonson, receives from Myles Smith some proofs of Isaiah 'for a tricking-out of his words or the turn of some figure' (pp. 345–6). Glancing at Smith's proofs and the earlier versions, Shakespeare, with help from the erudite but not entirely sober Jonson, follows his genius and revises the very verses that Saintsbury had scanned and discussed. The result is a beautifully suggestive imagining of the process of artistic revision and creation that also captures the essence of this side of AVolatry.

Kipling, who knew Saintsbury well, acknowledged that worthy's help in the writing of the story,[24] and many of the comments are Saintsbury dramatised. But near the end of the story, Shakespeare boasts:

'But, Ben, ye should have heard my Ezekiel making mock of fallen Tyrus in his twenty-seventh chapter. Miles sent me the whole, for, he said, some small touches. I took it to the Bank – four o'clock of a summer morn; stretched out in one of our wherries – and watched London, Port and Town, up and down the river, waking all arrayed to heap more upon evident excess. Ay! "A merchant for the peoples of many isles" . . . "The ships of Tarshish did sing of thee in thy markets"? Yes! I saw all Tyre before me neighing her pride against lifted heaven . . . But what will they let stand of all mine at long last? Which? I'll never know.' (p. 354)

[23] Hilton Brown, prefatory note to the *Strand Magazine* (1947) reprint of Rudyard Kipling's '"Proofs of Holy Writ"'. As given in Philip Mason, '"Proofs of Holy Writ"': an introduction', *Kipling Journal* 62 (March 1988), p. 33.   [24] *Something of Myself* (London: Macmillan, 1937), p. 86.

Read carefully, this is more than a suggestion of another passage where a reader may care to find Shakespearean quality in the KJB. It is also a question mark placed against the unremitting admiration of the AVolaters, for the first of the two phrases Shakespeare claims as his own is not the KJB's more awkward 'a merchant of the people for many isles'. His final questions, especially the 'which?', have real point: the KJB did not always produce results the imagined perfect artist would have done. The same point is implicit but less obvious in some of the suggestions Shakespeare makes for the verses from Isaiah. This gives the story a quiet undercurrent of criticism of AVolatry. It at once wittily imagines the nature of artistic revision and suggests that AVolatry can go too far.

DISSENTING VOICES

There were much more explicit attacks on AVolatry and related ideas. On April 30th, 1918, Thomas Hardy, aged 77, made this note:

By the will of God some men are born poetical. Of these some make themselves practical poets, others are made poets by lapse of time who were hardly recognised as such. Particularly has this been the case with the translators of the Bible. They translated into the language of their age; then the years began to corrupt that language as spoken and to add grey lichen to the translation; until the moderns who use the corrupted tongue marvel at the poetry of the old words. When new they were not more than half so poetical. So that Coverdale, Tyndale and the rest of them are as ghosts what they never were in the flesh.[25]

In a sense this belongs with Buchan's search for an alternative explanation of the KJB's quality, but it has a quality of scepticism to it that suggests a reaction against one part of AVolatry, the attribution of supreme artistry to the translators.

The note probably never became well known – it was not published until 1930, and only one book on the KJB mentions it, and then it is in order to refute it[26] – so its significance is not as an influence but as an indicator of a small, or at least, rarely expressed, undercurrent of reaction. The critic John Middleton Murry was thinking along similar lines at the same time in his *The Problem of Style* (1922). He raises some crucial issues, for a moment even tackling AVolatry head-on. To him it is 'the dogma of the infallibility of the style of the English Bible', and should not be allowed to go unchallenged (p. 120). So he says (the work was originally a series of lectures):

---

[25] *The Life and Work of Thomas Hardy*, ed. Michael Millgate (London: Macmillan, 1984), p. 416.
[26] Gustavus S. Paine, *The Men Behind the King James Version*, p. 171.

It is difficult to object when we are told – as we very frequently are told – that there are two supereminent works of literature in English – the Bible and Shakespeare; but I always feel uneasy when I hear it. I suspect that the man who says so does not appreciate Shakespeare as he ought; and that he is not being quite honest about the Bible. The reason why it is difficult to object is that there is a sense in which it is true that the style of the Bible is splendid. (p. 121)

But his sense of what is splendid about it is a complex one, and he refuses to allow that the style of the whole Bible is splendid: indeed, 'it seems to me scarcely an exaggeration to say that the style of one half of the English Bible is atrocious' (p. 121). This, he knows, may be thought heresy, but he has gone out of his way to say it because 'the superstitious reverence for the style of the Authorised Version really stands in the way of a frank approach to the problem of style' (p. 122).

These frank heresies emerge from a consideration of the way the 'emotional susceptibility' (p. 114) of an audience affects its judgement of style. The point is important, so it will be worthwhile to quote it at length, especially as it will take us back to Sir Thomas Browne's comments on the Bible and the Koran (see above, p. 169):

But there are certain realms of experience in which the level of emotional susceptibility of the audience is much higher than in others. There is, for instance, the realm of religion. Any deeply religious man is habituated to thoughts and feelings of a kind utterly remote from those which are the accompaniment of his practical life. A man who really believes in a just and omnipotent, a merciful and omniscient God has for his familiar companion a conception and an emotion which are truly tremendous. No suggestion of the poet or the prose-writer can possibly surpass them in force or vehemence. When an old Hebrew Prophet wrote: 'and the Lord said', he had done everything. The phrase is overwhelming. Nothing in *Paradise Lost* can compare with it.

> When the most High
> Eternal Father from his secret cloud
> Amidst, in thunder uttered thus his voice

is almost trivial by its side. 'And they heard the voice of the Lord God walking in the garden in the cool of the day.' Two thousand years of Christian civilisation bend our minds to these words; we cannot resist them. Nor can we refuse to them the title of great style. All that we have, as critics of literature, to remember is that style of this kind is possible only when the appeal is to a habit of feeling and thought peculiar to religion. Possibly that very phrase 'and the Lord said' might seem even ridiculous to one brought up in one of the transcendental religions of the East, just as some of the poignant verses of the New Testament are said to be grotesque to an educated Mohammedan. (pp. 114–5)

Seemingly by accident, Murry slides from this by way of comments on the variety of underlying styles in the KJB to something that becomes a major point. He observes 'two masterly effects – I hardly know whether to call them effects of style' in Matthew 26: 'then all the disciples forsook him, and fled', and, of Peter after his denials, 'and he went out and wept bitterly'. Initially he links these with 'and the Lord said', 'in the sense that the emotional suggestion is not in the words themselves', but then makes the crucial distinction: 'the reserves of emotion which Matthew's simple statements liberate in us have been accumulated during the reading of the narrative . . . The situation given, the force of the words is elemental' (pp. 115–16). As he says of his next example, Matt. 11: 28–30, 'in whatever language that sentence was spoken to you, your depths would be stirred' (p. 116). What Murry is developing is essentially the distinction between content and style. The effect is in the KJB but not of it. The literary quality of the Bible is not necessarily a matter of style. He could not be further removed from Saintsbury's scorn for 'the idle predominance of "the subject"'. Yet Saintsbury was able to show literary quality, and Murry is just as convincing.

Murry prefers to develop the point through a contrast between language which creates its own meaning, and statements whose effect is created by the context. The force of these latter

is supplied by the previous narrative; we have formed in our mind a picture of the circumstances; we know from his own words the nature of the man who has been denied. If we were to adopt, as one critic has done, the distinction between 'kinetic' and 'potential' language, we might say that the half-dozen words describing Peter are merely 'potential'.

'And the Lord said' is an example of potential speech where the charge comes wholly from the mind of the audience. 'Come unto me all ye that labour' is partly kinetic – the actual beauty of the words has a positive effect – partly potential: the longing to which the appeal is made is universal in mankind. (p. 120)

The distinction is helpful, and may, in its idea of 'potential' language, remind one of Gilfillan's idea of seed poetry (see above, p. 324). Murry has one further thought to add to it as part of his attack on 'the superstitious reverence for the style of the Authorised Version'. He suggests that in the Gospels there are

only two elements that can possibly lay claim to be considered creative literature; the actual words of Christ reported, such as 'come unto me . . .' and 'my God, my God . . .', and the dramatic effects, such as, 'then all the disciples forsook him and fled'. The first do not belong to the Gospels, but to their author, and the second are not really effects of style at all. It is not the authors of the Gospels who have given us the imaginative realisation of the character of Jesus on which these dramatic effects depend. Take away the words of Jesus which they reproduce and nothing of that character remains. The written evidence of an honest police-constable would give us as much. The most elementary conditions of the presence of style are lacking. (p. 122)

Here Murry has gone too far without going far enough. To deny stylistic effect wholesale to the narratives is to dismiss much in the words of Jesus – to look no further – that is clearly indebted to the style of the individual Gospel-writers, for the words are not reported identically in each Gospel. It is quite possible to place together, say, the two versions of the houses built on rock and sand or earth (Matt. 7: 24–7 and Luke 6: 47–9), and show not only that they have what he calls a 'kinetic' effect but that the effect is different in kind and quality between the two versions, even though the basic meaning remains unchanged. Moreover, it is possible to distinguish effects of style which belong to the original reporter (Murry's identification of Christ as 'the author' will not do: we only know how his words were reported or recreated, not what, verbatim, he said), and also effects which belong specifically to the translation. Matthew's 'sand' is more evocative than Luke's 'earth', for one is blatantly a fool to build a house on sand whereas houses are commonly built on the earth; moreover, the exact verbal repetition between the two parts of the image in Matthew draws sharper attention to the differences between the two (which is the point of the image) than Luke's less patterned rendering. These contrasts belong to the original Greek. And one quality in Matthew belongs in part to the original and in part to the KJB, which is not quite identical with any of its predecessors or successors. Rhythm and image unite in the description of the storm in a way that is marvellously kinetic if hardly surprising since cadence of course invokes falling: 'and the rain descended, and the floods came, and the winds blew, and beat upon that house; and it fell: and great was the fall of it'. The quick, emphatic rhythm of 'and beat upon that house' detaches the previous phrase, 'and the winds blew', from the first two phrases, dividing the four phrases into pairs both in terms of meaning and rhythm, evoking the force of the storm. Then the two cadences do their work, especially because the stress in the last phrase falls on 'great'. By contrast, the NEB has, 'down it fell with a great crash', with equal stresses on the final words: the meaning of the words is left to work unaided. Though much of the KJB's effect in this passage is clearly the result of literal translation, the final cadence marks a departure from the word order of the Greek, so we may set it down as an artistic effect created by Tyndale and preserved by the KJB in spite of alternative suggestions from Geneva and Rheims.

Such discussion undermines much of Murry's point: there very obviously are effects of style of the sort he denies both in the originals and in the translation. But his 'honest police-constable' is not entirely to be dismissed: much of what we read in the Gospels does appear as incompetent narrative and, paradoxically, may be the more effective for so appearing, since the reader is often driven through the text to the thing-in-the-text. To attribute this effect to 'potential language' is at once to break the bonds of received ideas and to start an insight.

With greater vehemence and less insight, an entirely forgotten critic, E.E. Kellett, also took up the cudgels against AVolatry. Like Murry he too protests against the idea of the perfection of the whole of the KJB: 'a little leaven leaveneth the whole lump; and the beauty of some parts of the Version has made many people imagine that the whole is beautiful'.[27] Most importantly, he develops the hint found in Hardy and uses the idea of familiarity to account for the beauty of the KJB, suggesting that 'there is in fact every reason to believe that the "beauty" of the Authorised Version is, to a greater extent than we imagine, the creation of our intimacy with it' (p. 97); tellingly, he cites Selden's evidence (see above, p. 107). This is his counter to the prevailing admiration for the rhythms of the KJB:

Often the 'rhythm' is merely another word for 'familiarity'. . . . the 'rhythms' of the Prayer Book version of the Psalms are usually preferred by churchmen; those of the Authorised Version by nonconformists of equal taste and culture: and the difference is due solely to the fact that churchmen are familiar from their childhood with the one, and nonconformists with the other. (p. 96)

This is fair enough, but it does not make that rhythm any the less real and valuable to those Churchmen and non-conformists. Kellett opens up but does not explore the questions of time and subjectivity, and simply to raise the questions is not, as the whole tenor of his article suggests, to prove that the KJB is bad.

Much of the scepticism about prevailing attitudes that runs through these remarks and discussions comes to a head in what is still the best of the dissenting articles, 'The literary impact of the Authorised Version'

---

[27] 'The translation of the New Testament', *Reconsiderations: Literary Essays* (Cambridge University Press, 1928), pp. 77–104; p. 98.

(1950), by C.S. Lewis (1898–1963). The primary target of Lewis's scepticism is the idea that the KJB has been a great influence on English literature, but he allows himself to range more widely than this. Beginning somewhat in Murry's spirit, he directs attention away from the KJB and towards 'the Bible in general' as represented in 'any good translation'. So his opening proposition is that 'the literary effect of any good translation must be more indebted to the original than to anything else. This is especially true of narrative and of moral instruction.' And he quickly adds to this an interest in the subject of the present book, 'the literary fortunes of our English Bible'. Appropriately, he warns against 'our dangerous though natural assumption that a book which has always been praised' – here he suggests an ignorance that some of his evidence contradicts – 'has always been read in the same way or valued for the same reasons' (p. 26). After surveying a few of the early literary comments on the Bible, he turns to the English translations and offers the view of translation that has been argued for in this book:

when we come to compare the versions we shall find only a very small percentage of variants are made for stylistic or even doctrinal reasons. When men depart from their predecessors it is usually because they claim to be better Hebraists or better Grecians . . .

It is not, of course, to be supposed that aesthetic considerations were uppermost in Tyndale's mind when he translated Scripture. The matter was much too serious for that; souls were at stake. The same holds for all the translators. (pp. 32, 34)

The desire to correct AVolatry is clear here, and it also informs his next topic, the question of the KJB's influence as an English book. With very English understatement, he remarks of this that 'there has been misunderstanding . . . and even a little exaggeration' (p. 35), and he sets about trying to correct the picture.

Distinguishing between a source and an influence – 'a source gives us things to write about, an influence prompts us to write in a certain way' (p. 35) – he admits that the KJB has been a source 'of immense importance' but argues that this has little to do with the particular qualities of the KJB and has 'no place in an account of the influence of the Authorised Version considered as an English book' (p. 36). He will not even allow embedded quotations to be taken as signs of influence because they depend for their effect on their difference from their context:

our embedded quotations from the Authorised Version are nearly always in exactly this position. They are nearly always either solemn or facetious. Only because the surrounding prose is different – in other words, only in so far as our English is not influenced by the Authorised Version – do they achieve the effect the authors intended. (p. 38)

As a generalisation, this is fair enough, but it will not sufficiently account for passages such as the one from *Jane Eyre* (above, p. 296) where embedded and open quotations mix with signs of influence, nor will it account for those biblical phrases which have become so much a part of the language as to be generally unrecognisable as quotations. What Lewis does allow – and it bears a close relation to the unrecognised quotations – is the influence of the KJB on vocabulary. He has in mind words such as 'beautiful', 'longsuffering', 'peacemaker' and 'scapegoat', as distinguished from words kept alive by the KJB but only available for poetic or archaic use. These latter he would class as very short embedded quotations. The brevity of his remarks here betrays a desire to diminish the idea of the KJB's influence: AVolatry has produced an excessive reaction.

A similar excess is visible in his remarks on the influence of the rhythm of the KJB, for he treats rhythm as nothing more than stress pattern. Of course his reader will agree that 'at the regatta Madge avoided the river and the crowd' has the same stress pattern as 'in the beginning God created the heaven and the earth', but to leave the point at that is cheap and destructive. We might agree that 'the influence of rhythm, isolated from imagery and style, is perhaps an abstraction' (p. 39), but this is to leave out of account not only the effect of the rhythm but also the fact that the Bible has rhythms of meaning – we have seen how parallelism affected *Jane Eyre* – and structural rhythms, most notably rhythms of repetition. A corrective to AVolatry was certainly needed, but not one that tries to dismiss the question of influence. A similar dismissiveness is present even when Lewis admits influence, as he does when he supposes that imagery has had a great effect but confesses that he has been unable to invent a method of checking it.

Lewis gives most attention to whether the KJB has influenced 'the actual build of our sentences' (p. 40), and here he is more persuasive. Consistently diminishing AVolatry, he proposes that the influence is not what it is generally thought to be, and takes two telling examples. One is Ruskin's passage claiming that the Bible influenced him (see above, p. 397), the other is Bunyan. With the Ruskin, Lewis prefers to go the opposite way from mine and emphasise that it is indeed Johnsonian and ultimately indebted to Latin:

A structure descending from Cicero through the prose of Hooker, Milton and Taylor, and then enriched with romantic colouring for which Homer and the Bible are laid under contribution – that seems to me the formula for Ruskin's style. If you could take away what comes from the Bible it would be impaired. It would hardly, I think, be crippled. It would certainly not be annihilated. This is real influence, but limited influence. (pp. 41–2)

The little that he does allow as influence is visible in embedded quotations and imagery. I would not dissent from this: Ruskin's style does belong to the essentially Latin tradition in English prose, but this does not answer the question that Ruskin himself raises, what would his prose have been like if he had not been steeped in the KJB?

Murry makes a point that is useful here. For all its purity ('a very arbitrary conception when applied to language'), the vocabulary of the KJB is far less useful as an instrument than Shakespeare's: 'I can conceive no modern emotion or thought – except perhaps some of the more Hegelian metaphysics – that could not be adequately and superabundantly expressed in Shakespeare's vocabulary: there are very few that would not be mutilated out of all recognition if they had to pass through the language of the Bible' (p. 121). As far as the Bible is concerned – and in spite of Macaulay's grand assertion to the contrary (above, p. 302) – this is obviously true, and, following Gardiner, we may make the same point about sentence structures: the Bible's largely unsubordinated range of structures would not be adequate for the modern awareness of complex interrelationships. The Latin heritage of structure and vocabulary has added more to the expressive power of the native language than any other single source. In relation to it, the Bible has contributed little and acts as a conservative and moderating force, as Ruskin suggested in a part of his passage that Lewis chooses to omit. This suggests that the Bible remains an influence in a way that Latin (and its Romance descendants) are not: they have created the standard form of the language, but the Bible may continue to influence by tempering that form.

In the case of Bunyan, Lewis argues that much of the apparent similarity to the style of the Bible is superficial, the result of both seeming now rather archaic and simple in syntax. After giving a passage he suggests that the appropriate 'question is not how much of this might occur in the Authorised Version, but how much might be expected to occur in Bunyan if he had not read it' (p. 42). This dodges the real question, how much of the style could only have been as it is because Bunyan had read the KJB, but the dodge has its uses. It allows Lewis to suggest that 'his prose comes to him not from the Authorised Version but from the fireside, the shop and the lane', and so 'might have been much the same without the Authorised Version' (pp. 43, 44). This knocks down the idea that Bunyan's prose is essentially biblical, but it does not actually confront the question of influence.

Such discussion is salutary but less than satisfactory. Excess has been corrected, but replaced only with tangential insights. Rather than developing an account of how the influence has worked, Lewis attempts to explain why the KJB's 'strictly literary influence has mattered less than we have often supposed'. He suggests two reasons, changing taste and, recognising that it will sound paradoxical, familiarity. Citing Harwood, 'no doubt . . . by our standards, an ass', he suggests that the ancient perception of the Bible's lack of elegance persisted longer than generally recognised and that the change in attitude to it is to be associated with the romantic 'taste for the primitive and the passionate which can be seen growing through nearly the whole of the eighteenth century' (p. 44). It was the development of this taste that made the Bible an attractive model and which changed the way it was heard. Rather than being inelegant, to this taste the Bible was sublime if it was admired, or florid or inflated if it was disliked. Given that much of the admiration of the Bible is admiration for its once-despised simplicity, whatever the admirer understands by that, this may seem strange, but it picks up the admiration for the oriental aspect of the Bible. A rather different dissenting voice, Somerset Maugham, confirms Lewis's point:

To my mind King James's Bible has been a very harmful influence on English prose. I am not so stupid as to deny its great beauty. It is majestical. But the Bible is an oriental book. Its alien imagery has nothing to do with us. Those hyperboles, those luscious metaphors, are foreign to our genius . . . Those rhythms, that powerful vocabulary, that grandiloquence, became part and parcel of the national sensibility. The plain, honest English speech was overwhelmed with ornament. Blunt Englishmen twisted their tongues to speak like Hebrew Prophets . . . English prose has had to struggle against the tendency to luxuriance.[28]

Familiarity Lewis treats in a teasingly different way from the way I have treated it. The Bible was so familiar, he suggests, that it could only be echoed 'with conscious reverence or with conscious irreverence, either religiously or facetiously', and he concludes that 'an influence which cannot evade our consciousness will not go very deep' (p. 46). The illogic is transparent: conscious use producing instant response does not

---

[28] *The Summing Up* (London: Heinemann, 1938), p. 36.

prove that the language of the Bible does not also live in one's subconscious.

If the Bible is not an influence when it is so well known, Lewis wonders if it will become more of a literary influence 'now, when only a minority of Englishmen regard the Bible as a sacred book' (p. 46), and this leads him to perhaps the most stimulating part of the lecture. At the beginning, he had warned that 'there is a certain sense in which "the Bible as literature" does not exist' because of the heterogeneous nature of the originals and the non-literary reasons for gathering them together; but where Kellett makes this a ground for condemning the KJB, Lewis points the paradox that, 'for good or ill', 'when we turn from the originals to any version made by one man, or at least bearing the stamp of one age, a certain appearance of unity creeps in', and so the Bible is read as a single book. Nevertheless, it is still a single book 'read for almost every purpose more diligently than for literary pleasure' (p. 27).

This will become his final point, a challenge to the whole idea of the Bible as literature in the sense that that idea seems to ignore the fact that the Bible is religion. Some fifteen years earlier one of the century's foremost poets and critics, T.S. Eliot (like Lewis, an eminent Christian), had vented his spleen on this idea:

I could fulminate against the men of letters who have gone into ecstasies over 'the Bible as literature', the Bible as 'the noblest monument of English prose'. Those who talk of the Bible as a 'monument of English prose' are merely admiring it as a monument over the grave of Christianity . . . the Bible has had a *literary* influence upon English literature *not* because it has been considered as literature, but because it has been considered as the report of the Word of God. And the fact that men of letters now discuss it as 'literature' probably indicates the *end* of its 'literary' influence.[29]

Lewis, more temperately, makes the same insistence on the religious character of the Bible:

Unless the religious claims of the Bible are again acknowledged, its literary claims will, I think, be given only 'mouth honour' and that decreasingly. For it is, through and through, a sacred book . . . It is, if you like to put it that way, not merely a sacred book but a book so remorselessly and continuously sacred that it does not invite, it excludes or repels, the merely aesthetic approach. You can read it as literature only by a *tour de force* . . . It demands incessantly to be taken on its own terms: it will not continue to give literary delight very long except to

---

[29] 'Religion and literature' (1935); *Selected Prose*, ed. John Hayward (Harmondsworth: Penguin, 1953), pp. 31–42; pp. 32–3.

those who go to it for something quite different. I predict that it will in the future be read as it always has been read, almost exclusively by Christians. (pp. 48–9)

The importance of this argument can hardly be overestimated even if it is not a final truth. Familiarity is a basic reason for the love of the Bible, and that familiarity is founded on its religious position. But still more important are the twin perceptions of a tendency to falsity in attempts to see the Bible as something which may be read as literature alone, and of elements in the text which repel such reading. These elements have never, I think, been properly analysed, and the lack of such analysis is part of a greater lack that supports Lewis's views. The idea that the KJB is a classic of English literature has been oftener proclaimed than acted on. In spite of calls to do so, the KJB has never really been studied as if it was a classic like the other classics of English literature. The fullest studies of it are those which take it as a translation and seek to illuminate its qualities as such. It is still often used as the form of the text to illustrate discussions that are really discussions of the originals or of what is common to most versions, for it is difficult to take what is really a fictional step, and treat it as if it is an autonomous work of English literature. In England it has never become an integral part of the curriculum of English literature. In America, where courses on the Bible as literature are more common, they occupy an uneasy ground between literary and theological studies, and they do not necessarily use the KJB. Until now the Bible's critical heritage has not received more than the most glancing attention, whereas the critical heritages of all the major authors and a vast number of the minor authors of English and American literature have received detailed attention. In brief, the profession of literature has never properly acted on the idea of the KJB as an English classic. This supports Lewis's contentions that there is either an insincerity in the idea of the Bible as literature or that there are elements in the Bible that refuse to become part of literature because they are too inescapably something else.

A quite different kind of dissenting voice has been heard recently. Until 1994, when Tyndale's quincentenary was celebrated, hardly a doubt had been raised that the KJB, as a literary achievement, was the supreme English Bible. But with the quincentenary came claims for Tyndale's work as the greatest English translation, at least as far as language was concerned. The argument was mounted with greatest thoroughness and insight by David Daniell in *William Tyndale: a Biography*. He sets out his stall at once: 'William Tyndale gave us our

English Bible. The sages assembled by King James to prepare the Authorised Version of 1611, so often praised for unlikely corporate inspiration, took over Tyndale's work. Nine-tenths of the Authorised Version's New Testament is Tyndale's. The same is true of the first half of the Old Testament' (p. 1). 'Unlikely corporate inspiration' takes us back to Kipling's story and the search for a genius behind the KJB: there was indeed a genius behind the KJB, not Shakespeare tricking-out some phrases, but Tyndale creating nine-tenths of much of the text. So a major aspect of Daniell's work is to right the historical injustice done to Tyndale both as theologian and as writer: 'Tyndale as conscious craftsman has been not just neglected but denied: yet the evidence of the book that follows makes it beyond challenge that he used, as a master, the skill in the selection and arrangement of words which he partly learned at school and university, and partly developed from pioneering work by Erasmus' (p. 2).

Daniell moves immediately to defining Tyndale's priorities as a translator, and the nature of his dissent from AVolatry begins to show itself:

> For him, an English translation of the Bible had to be as accurate to the original languages, Greek and Hebrew, as scholarship could make it; and it had to make sense. There are times when the original Greek, and for good reason even more the Hebrew, are baffling. A weak translator goes for paraphrase, or worse, for philological purity, and hang the sense (as the Authorised Version did often with the Prophets, for example, in those books lacking Tyndale as a base). Tyndale is clear. (p. 2)

Making clarity a prime virtue – clarity rather than accuracy – Daniell characterises the KJB translators as weak philological purists when not guided to better things by Tyndale. The polemic drift is unmistakable: when the KJB follows Tyndale it is good, when it does not have him for model it is weaker, and when it changes his work it is usually for the worse (he does allow 'one moment where the Authorised Version improves on Tyndale', Exod. 11: 5 (p. 314)).

As an attitude to the KJB, this is far removed from AVolatry. Rather than being the culmination of the English translations, making, in the words of its preface, 'of many good ones, one principal good one, not justly to be excepted against' (p. 9), the KJB is not only over-philological, but also over-literal to the point of incomprehensibility (e.g. p. 302), Latinate and artificially holy (p. 139); consequently it feels less modern than Tyndale (p. 135). Moreover, it is less sensitive to rhythm, sometimes undoing what was well done in Tyndale. An example of this last point must stand for the abundance of examples Daniell offers, and also for the pleasure to be found in, especially, Tyndale's OT work. As part of an extended discussion of 1 Kings 17–19, Daniell notes:

From the beginning, Tyndale's ear for English rhythms is keen – compare his 'there shall be neither dew nor rain these years, save as I appoint it' with the Authorised Version's 'there shall not be . . . but according to my word' [17: 1]: Tyndale's dactyl stresses 'save as/I app/oint it' have an authority in English which the Authorised Version's phrase, though it chimes with the ancient versions, does not have . . .

Again, though Geneva and the Authorised Version take over 'what have I to do with thee, O thou man of God?' Tyndale's rhythm is later lost in both. Tyndale, alone unlike the ancient versions, puts the verbs 'thought on' and 'slain' last, making her cry come to a climax on 'slain'. Geneva and the Authorised Version's 'to call my sin to remembrance and to slay my son' is cluttered after Tyndale's 'that my sin should be thought on and my son slain' [17: 18]. (p. 352)

We might be reading Saintsbury. Command of English rhythm, with clarity, is the highest virtue, even if it is at the expense of literal accuracy, as the comparisons with 'the ancient versions' show. On this basis, Daniell's examples are persuasive: Tyndale very often betters his successors.

Daniell must debunk AVolatry if he is to succeed in giving Tyndale his rightful historical place. Yet his work is in some important ways similar to AVolatry, as in this summary of Tyndale's literary achievement and its historical significance:

In his Bible translations, Tyndale's conscious use of everyday words, without inversions, in a neutral word-order, and his wonderful ear for rhythmic patterns, gave to English not only a Bible language, but a new prose. England was blessed as a nation in that the language of its principal book, as the Bible in English rapidly became, was the fountain from which flowed the lucidity, suppleness and expressive range of the greatest prose thereafter. (p. 116)

Only change the subject of this from Tyndale to the KJB, and it becomes thoroughly familiar. Yet the change in subject creates a freshness and energy that is very welcome. The KJB remains the central Bible of English cultural history from the eighteenth century to the present, but its claim to be the best English Bible as literature is inescapably challenged. It is ironic that, in a century that has produced more translations of the Bible than any other, most of them made with some explicit consciousness of style, the real challenge should come from the oldest printed version.

THE HEBREW INHERITANCE AND THE VIRTUES OF LITERALISM

The best modern insights into the KJB come from discussions of its relationship with the original Hebrew. Gardiner, ignorant of Hebrew, relied on the French scholar, Ernest Renan, but I focus on him rather than Renan because he develops Renan's points and directs them, in the end, towards the KJB. Renan identifies the essential difference in structure between Hebrew and modern languages as Hebrew's lack of 'one of the degrees of combination which we hold necessary for the complete expression of the thought. To join the words in a proposition is as far as they go; they made no effort to apply the same operation to the propositions' (p. 21; as given in Gardiner, *The Bible as English Literature*, p. 68). Gardiner elaborates:

In consequence of this poverty in connectives the Hebrew language could not express swiftly and compactly the relations of facts and ideas to each other; and it was wholly incapable of expressing most of the subtle modulations which give variety and flexibility to modern writings. It was a language in which solid fact followed solid fact in hardly changing sequence. (pp. 68–9)

Moreover, since Hebrew has only two tenses, one signifying an uncompleted or imperfect act, the other a completed act, each of them past, present or future, Renan observes that

Perspective is almost entirely lacking in the Semitic style . . . One must even allow that the idea of style as we understand it was wholly lacking among the Semitic people. Their period is very short; the extent of discourse which they embrace at a time never passes one or two lines. Wholly preoccupied with the present thought, they do not construct in advance the mechanism of the phrase and take no thought of what has gone before or of what is coming.[30]

Gardiner adds that 'down to the end of the third Gospel there is no narrative in the Bible which departs from' the unpremeditated simplicity described by Renan (p. 70). He demonstrates the point first by contrasting an OT with an NT narrative (1 Sam. 17: 38–43 and Acts 28: 1–6), and then by making a contrast with Bunyan's description of Christian resting in the arbor half way up the hill Difficulty, and losing his roll in his sleep (*Pilgrim's Progress*, p. 173). The latter contrast sounds a real warning to all over-simple claims for influence:

In this passage the clauses run to three and four and even five lines; and instead of all the clauses being co-ordinate and of equal value, every sentence shows subordination of one idea to another . . . Such writing as this is of another kind

---

[30] Renan, *Langues sémitiques*, p. 20; Gardiner, *Bible as English Literature*, pp. 69–70.

from that of the Bible narrative. Like the speeches ascribed to St Paul in Acts, Bunyan's writing belongs to a mode of thought and of style which are unknown in the Old Testament. (p. 76)

Still following Renan's characterisation of Hebrew, Gardiner moves to his own explanation of 'the permanent expressive power of the Bible narratives' (p. 86). It comes out of a simplicity made universal by direct contact with the world and the self. So Hebraic thought 'was essentially simple. It knew only the objective and solid facts of which man has direct sensation, and the simple primitive emotions which are his reaction to them' (p. 86). This limitation is fundamental strength, for the narratives 'are an unbroken stream of objective realities. Their whole texture is composed of the things which men can feel and see and hear' (pp. 86–7). In the same vein, he describes 'the distinguishing characteristic of the poetry [as] its absolute objectivity: it knew only facts which are concrete and which mean always the same to all men' (p. 88), and so 'gives the impression of being born in the very heat of joy or grief or triumph' (p. 96). The opening of Psalm 69, used so powerfully by Bunyan and Brontë, makes the point:

Save me, O God; for the waters are come in unto my soul. I sink in deep mire, where there is no standing: I am come into deep waters, where the floods overflow me. I am weary of my crying: my throat is dried: mine eyes fail while I wait for my God.

There is neither characterisation nor abstraction here. Gardiner invites us to 'notice the number of sensations which are named' (p. 116); physical sensations and the elaborated natural metaphor of flooding do indeed create a universal image of the abstract idea, despair.

Behind this lies Renan's point that all Hebrew words 'went back immediately[31] to things of sense, and in consequence even their everyday language was figurative in a way which we can hardly imagine. The verb "to be jealous" was a regular form of the verb "to glow", the noun "truth" was derived from the verb meaning "to prop", "to build" or "to make firm". The word for "self" was also the word for "bone"' (pp. 113–14; cf. Renan, *Langues sémitiques*, p. 23). Now, thus far there is nothing

---

[31] 'Immediately' is the most debatable word here, for what Gardiner and Renan are touching on is a commonly made point about language. They suggest that in Hebrew there was a special intensity to the figurative link. No one, to my knowledge, has considered this idea about Hebrew in relation to the general idea that abstract language has a metaphorical origin. Useful starting points might be Owen Barfield's essay, 'The meaning of "literal"', in *The Rediscovery of Meaning and other essays* (Middletown, Conn.: Wesleyan University Press, 1977), pp. 32–43, and Prickett's discussion of Barfield and others in *Words and the Word* (Cambridge University Press, 1986), pp. 86 ff.

that is specific to the KJB, but it will be obvious that the drift of the discussion is to give substance to the familiar idea of the translatability of the Bible: content, it seems, is unusually present in the Bible, form unusually absent. Part of the discussion's effect is to alert the reader to characteristics of the KJB.

An earlier work, evidently unknown to Gardiner, takes the subject further, William Rosenau's *Hebraisms in the Authorized Version of the Bible* (1902). Rosenau has that rare qualification among writers on the KJB, a good knowledge of Hebrew, and he uses this to assemble very detailed listings of words, phrases and constructions in the KJB that are literal reproductions of the Hebrew rather than what was natural English. Not all the examples are convincing, sometimes because they can be shown to antedate the English translations, sometimes (and these are inescapable difficulties) because one's sense of English is different or because one may feel that the Hebraism is not the necessary source of the English phrase.[32] A larger difficulty lies in the limitations of scope. A Saintsbury might well retort that we know the KJB contains Hebraisms: what of the rhythmic superiority of the KJB to its predecessors, which were also literal translations to the degree that Rosenau shows the KJB to be literal? At the least we must put this minor qualification on Rosenau's evidence, that it applies to the tradition of translation as embodied in the KJB. It does not in itself negate the aesthetic view of the translation: rather, it provides a wealth of material for further study of how the KJB came to be and how it influenced English.

Rosenau divides Hebraisms into two classes, lexicographical and syntactical. Syntactical Hebraisms preserve Hebrew forms that are alien to English. Here are some of them (selected from chapter 8, with some additional comments of my own). The plural may be used where a singular is expected, for instance 'heavens' or 'rivers' (as in 'by the rivers of Babylon'). The Hebrew use of apposition sometimes produces phrases such as 'Nathan the Prophet' where the natural English order would be 'the Prophet Nathan' (yet such constructions have become so familiar as often to pass unnoticed). Hebrew cognate accusatives produce phrases such as 'to dream a dream'. Similarly, the superlative form, 'king of kings' or 'song of songs' is alien to English yet has become sufficiently

---

[32] For example, one may take one's choice whether 'went down to buy corn in Egypt' (Gen. 42: 3) has led to 'go down town' and 'go down to Washington' as used in Baltimore (p. 103), or whether such phrases, including 'go up to town', are not the natural result of topography or the imagining of north on a map as up. Rosenau classes 'down' as a superfluous preposition, and his general point is that Hebrew sometimes uses prepositions that are unnecessary in English.

familiar to produce phrases not found in the Bible, such as 'heart of hearts'. Genitives are often used differently, as in 'altar of stone' for 'stone altar' or 'men of truth' for 'honest men'. Again, some of these genitives have become so familiar a part of English that they pass unnoticed, such as 'man of war'. Prepositions with nouns are often used instead of adverbs, as in 'eat in haste' for 'eat hastily'. Pronouns are sometimes used redundantly as in 'the Lord your God, he shall fight for you'. Verbs are often co-ordinated where English would subordinate one, as in the familiar but still obviously biblical 'answered and said'. And so we may go on, noting that the pervasive use of 'and' in the KJB is Hebraic rather than normal written English.

Such itemising of grammatical points is not easy to read: it is no different from starting to learn a new language, but even so abbreviated a list is sufficient to suggest that the extent of Hebraic elements surviving in the KJB because of literal translation is large, and that this is not generally realised for two reasons, one minor, one major: ignorance of Hebrew and acquired familiarity with the idioms. As observed before, what was so harsh and strange to the translators and their early readers is now substantially familiar. The same is true with lexicographical Hebraisms, that is, literal English renderings of words or phrases which give the English an abnormal sense, as in 'heard the voice of your words'. Some very familiar words have an unusual range of meaning as they appear in the KJB, a range that English would normally distinguish by a variety of words. So 'flesh' may signify muscles, meat, body, kinsman, creatures, mankind or pudenda; 'blood', blood, murder, blood-guilt, innocent person, bloodstains, relative or juice; 'hand', hand, power, leadership, supervision, possession, blow, violence, external influence, or it may be used for a personal pronoun; and 'heart' may signify breast, wish, judgement, motive, mind, spirit, desire, courage, excitement, affections or middle, or may be used instead of personal or reflexive pronouns. Though these are not standard synonym-lists, it is clear that the relatively limited vocabulary of Hebrew has contributed to the range of meaning of some English words.

Such insight is of real importance for an understanding of the history of English vocabulary and constructions, and for the real rather than the apparent meaning of some of the KJB's language. Rosenau makes but does not stress the point that his examples also help to show how far Hebraisms have become naturalised in English. Such evidence goes along with that from the lists of obsolete words given in the previous two centuries. From them it was apparent that KJB rescued some words from obsolescence, and this said much about the KJB's power over English as the most familiar book in the language. Rather than confining ourselves to Rosenau's Hebraisms, it is worth extending the point here. A substantial number of phrases and images have become so naturalised that we are often unaware that they are biblical in origin. Other staples of English literature have made such contributions – we might recognise 'groves of academe' as going back to Milton, but not 'all hell broke loose' – but none so substantial as the Bible and related works. By related works I mean, say, Handel's *Messiah*, or Bunyan's *The Pilgrim's Progress*, or *Paradise Lost*, or the PB, or even earlier translations, or the Sternhold and Hopkins Psalter. This last, for instance, is the now unrecognised origin of the phrase, 'for ever and a day',[33] while 'take him at his word' goes back to Coverdale (1 Kgs 20: 33), but is not found in the KJB. Here are some naturalised Hebraisms: 'a drop in a bucket' (making sense of Isa. 40: 15, 'a drop of a bucket'), 'the last gasp' (2 Macc. 7: 9), 'the skin of my teeth' (also making sense of a Hebraism, 'with the skin of my teeth', Job 19: 20), 'lick the dust' (Ps. 72: 9), 'fell flat on his face' (Num. 22: 31), 'to set one's face against' (Lev. 20: 3), 'a man after his own heart' (1 Sam. 13: 14), 'heart-searching' (from Judg. 5: 16), 'pour out one's heart' (Lam. 2: 19), 'heap coals of fire upon his head' (Prov. 25: 22), 'die the death' (Num. 23: 10), 'far be it from me' (1 Sam. 20: 9), 'from time to time' (but meaning 'at set times', Ezek. 4: 10), 'gird one's loins' (2 Kgs 4: 29), 'the land of the living' (Ps. 27: 13), 'put words in his mouth' (Exod. 4: 15), 'sick to death' (from 'sick unto death' meaning 'almost dead', 2 Kgs 20: 1), 'rise and shine' (from 'arise, shine', Isa. 60: 1, but also Handel's *Messiah*), 'go from strength to strength' (Ps. 84: 7), 'sour grapes' (Ezek. 18: 2), 'a lamb to the slaughter' (Isa. 53: 7), and 'stand in awe' (Ps. 4: 4). From the NT: 'a thorn in the flesh' (2 Cor. 12: 7), 'kick against the pricks' (Acts 9: 5), 'a house divided' (Mark 3: 25), 'den of thieves' (Mark 11: 17), 'labour of love' (1 Thess. 1: 3), and 'no respecter of persons' (Acts 10: 34).

This is not a complete listing, and perhaps no such listing is possible, but to extend it much further would be to begin to give examples where a phrase is only based on the Bible, as 'a fly in the ointment' ('dead flies cause the ointment of the apothecary to send forth a stinking savour', Eccles. 10: 1) or 'the [hand]writing on the wall' (based on Dan. 5: 5 and sometimes used as a page heading in later editions of the KJB), or examples that are more likely to be recognised as biblical, such as 'pride goeth before a fall' (Prov. 16: 18) or 'babes and sucklings' (Ps. 8: 2) or 'cast thy

---

[33] 'What is his goodness clean decayed / for ever and a day' (Ps. 77: 8, trans. John Hopkins). This may be a variation on the older 'for ever and ay'.

bread upon the waters' (Eccles. 11: 1), or examples where one cannot be sure that the phrase really comes from the Bible: 'the twinkling of an eye' comes in 1 Cor. 15: 52 but had been used as early as 1303; was it a native idiom or a translation of the Vulgate's 'in ictu oculi'? Given the size of the Bible, the list may seem brief, but the familiarity of the examples and the fact that they come from all parts of the Bible including the Apocrypha gives an undeniable impression of depth of influence. Naturalisation of this sort is the most striking evidence of the familiarity with the KJB that is so essential to the turnaround in its literary fortunes. It tells us more of the penetrative power of the Bible's language and imagery than do all the assertions of familiarity (true as they may be), or the multitudinous demonstrations of individual writers' and speakers' deliberate use of quotation and allusion.

The third book to explore such connections is a recent one, Gerald Hammond's *The Making of the English Bible* (1982). Hammond writes from the unique position of an intimate knowledge of both Hebrew and the English translations. Though his book is essentially about translation rather than the English Bible as literature, it develops independently the kinds of insights that have been gleaned from Rosenau, Renan and Gardiner in ways not to be found in any of the multitudinous histories of translation. It is a detailed study of the practice of translation, illuminating 'the stylistic relationships between the original and its translation' (p. 14). The KJB, in part because 'its word order is for many verses at a time the word order of the original and [because] it translates the great majority of Hebrew idioms literally' (p. 3), emerges as the most powerful of the English translations. Hammond unashamedly connects literalness and power, and the discussions of the Hebraic qualities of the original OT that we have been following provide an immediate reason for accepting that the connection is valid. But it is not literalism alone which produces the power: in Hammond's view 'the Renaissance Bible translator saw half of his task as reshaping English so that it could adapt itself to Hebraic idiom' (p. 2). In making this point he draws telling contrasts with the practice of modern translators as exemplified in the New English Bible. In effect, there is artistry in the literalism, and much of the discussion brings out ways this faithful artistry worked. This is not to say that Hammond takes a blinkered view of the KJB or its predecessors: he judges for himself where strength and weakness lie, and is candid that there is weakness in the KJB. He resists synthesising his observations into a reductive overview of the stylistic qualities of the KJB, observing that 'no label will properly describe the variety of biblical English'. This is a slap in the eye for the AVolaters and their grandiosely repetitive label-lings. Hammond continues: 'I do not want to end up with a demonstra-tion that the style can be categorised and understood in certain highly specific ways: less ambitious than that, I aim to analyse the kinds of deci-sions which we might judge the translators to have made, and the kinds of principles they might be considered to have held' (p. 14).

After discussion of the earlier translators, Hammond looks in his last two chapters at how the KJB handles words and sentences. Here is an instance of how he takes us beyond Rosenau and Gardiner through illus-trating the translators' practice:

The number of verbs in biblical Hebrew is severely limited. This fact encour-aged the English translators to use common English verbs in figurative senses. The Hebrew verb *'āchaz* gives us examples. Its meaning is 'to grasp, take hold of, take possession', and it is often used with an abstract subject such as pain or fear. In this usage the Geneva Bible prefers to render it as 'come upon', while the Authorised Version has the more vivid – and more literal – 'take hold of'. Two places in the Psalms show the contrasting effects. In 48: [6] Geneva's 'fear came there upon them' becomes, in the Authorised Version, 'fear took hold upon them there'; and in 119: 53, Geneva's 'fear is come upon me' becomes 'horror hath taken hold upon me'. (pp. 202–3)

Hammond takes five more examples, comparing the KJB's treatment of this verb in figurative uses with two other Latin and two other English Bibles, showing that where the other translations 'vary their renderings in their attempts to find the exact shade of meaning', the KJB 'uses a verb form containing the word "hold"' (pp. 203–4). There can be no doubt of the strength produced here by greater literalism, nor that the strength is inseparable from the highly physical nature of the Hebrew verb.

Hammond is similarly illuminating on sentences. He shows that it was one of the translators' 'great priorities . . . to keep as close as possible to the original's word order' (p. 228), and he analyses some of the results. His discussion of the treatment of the Hebrew infinitive brings out what he calls the KJB's 'neatnesses of rendering' (p. 218):

The infinitive is often used in tandem with a finite verb, so that its sense is essen-tially adverbial. The Authorised Version's treatment of it shows a greater care than in any of its predecessors to give it a grammatical status different from the finite verb – usually by means of a participle or gerund . . . where [the exam-ples] become important is when we consider their accumulative effect upon English biblical style as it came to be set in 1611. Put simply, it means that the participle becomes a typical part of this style. (p. 218)

He instances Isa. 31: 5 which ends, in his literal translation, 'to-defend he-will-deliver to-pass-over he-will-save'. Coverdale, and the Bishops after him, use four equal finite verbs, 'keep, save, defend, and deliver', while Geneva uses participles divided into pairs, 'by defending and delivering, by passing through and preserving it'. It is the KJB that reflects the Hebrew most closely by using a participle before a finite verb, and we recognise that this is peculiar English, the Hebraic English of the Bible:

As birds flying, so will the Lord of hosts defend Jerusalem: defending also he will deliver it, and passing over he will preserve it.

In the sense that this reflects the Hebrew without wasting words, it is indeed a neat rendering; whether it is also felicitous is a different matter. Most important, though, is that it is a characteristic rendering: Hammond goes on to show some other uses of participial forms to render infinitives and observes that the KJB uses them to a greater extent than previous English versions. A particular quality of the KJB's language is thus identified.

Hammond concludes his study with an examination of the way the KJB deals with two more Hebraic constructions, the *casus obliquus* and the *casus pendens*. In the latter the subject or object is separated from the main body of the sentence and then repeated in some pronominal form, producing either emphasis or something like a cadence (p. 225). So we get structures such as this in the KJB's rendering, 'and the Levite that is within thy gates, thou shalt not forsake him' (Deut. 14: 27). But the KJB's most characteristic way of dealing with this structure is to use 'as for', for example, 'as for his judgements, they have not known them' (Ps. 147: 20). The *casus obliquus* is more complex. It is a form of repetition in which a pronoun implicit in the verb form is also given separately. Hammond instances Gen. 27: 34 which, in his literal rendering, reads 'bless-me also-I my-father' (p. 229). The KJB, following Geneva, renders this, 'bless me, even me also, my father', and Hammond argues that '"even" turns out to be the best weapon in the Authorised Version's armoury for reproducing Hebraic repetition' (p. 232). Other methods are also used, and, as so often, Hammond notes that the KJB does not always reproduce the construction literally, 'probably reflecting the triumph of the aesthetic over the accurate'. On the other hand, sometimes accuracy triumphs only to produce 'a stubborn, pedantic fidelity to the Hebrew idiom', as in, 'is it time for you, O ye, to dwell in your ceiled houses' (Hag. 1: 4; p. 232). But what is perhaps most interesting is the number of instances he gives of the KJB replacing a natural form of English in its predecessors with a Hebraic form. So the Geneva Bible uses a natural English word order for Isa. 1: 7, 'your land is waste, your cities are burnt with fire; strangers devour your land in your presence'. The KJB, however, marks the *casus pendens* in the second part, so reproducing the Hebraic word order: 'your country is desolate, your cities are burned with fire: your land, strangers devour it in your presence' (pp. 228–9). In such examples Hammond not only alerts us to peculiarities of the KJB but shows that it did indeed give a higher priority to fidelity than to the requirements of natural or artful English. Without denying that aesthetic considerations affected the translation, he, like Rosenau, shows just how misleading the AVolatrous ideas of the KJB's English are. He concludes that the ways the KJB treats the three grammatical forms he has discussed

give us accessible paradigms for understanding the essentially formulaic tendency of the translation. Individual examples mean little until their cumulative effect is registered. Match them to the practices of the earlier translators which the Authorised Version happily inherited, like the reproduction of a consecutive narrative syntax and the use of the noun plus 'of' plus noun form to translate the Hebrew construct form, and we can grasp the integrity and consistency of English biblical style – and understand why it kept so powerful a hold over English minds for the next three hundred and fifty years. (p. 233)

Strictly, Hammond's is no more a book about the KJB as English literature than Rosenau's: both are books about translation that show the range of Hebraic qualities in the KJB's English. Especially for readers with no Hebrew, the insight is invaluable. Yet it is strange that these two books, so widely separated in time, should represent the bulk of what the twentieth century has contributed to an understanding of the KJB as literature. Much has been and still is being written about the KJB, but if one takes away the histories of translation and the effusions of AVolatry one is left with three things: occasional internal examinations of translation, books about the Bible as literature that use the KJB for quotations but which are not really books about the KJB, and dissenting essays such as Lewis's. In other words, given the claims for the KJB as a great, or even as the greatest, work of English literature, there is a void where one would expect plenitude: there are no substantial, good studies of the KJB as a work of English literature. Books like Hammond's and Rosenau's are on one edge of the void, the studies of the Bible as literature on the other edge. The simplest explanation lies in the fact that the KJB is a translation. Good discussions of it as a translation must illuminate its literary qualities, but they go no further than examining the way the original is represented. And discussions of the Bible as literature, for good reason, tend to concentrate on qualities that are general to the originals and all reasonably close representations of them. A second and somewhat less simple explanation is that the claim for the KJB as great English literature is really a quite narrow claim, that its language is great English, and that scholars are not willing to treat the KJB as a whole, because that would mean pretending that it is an autonomous work of English literature whereas it is obviously but one representation of a body of foreign literature. There may well also be a more complex explanation that lies in the often peculiar relationship of the Bible's language to its content. To a degree that is highly unusual for the great works of English literature, there is a separation between the Bible's content and its words. The KJB translators' image, inherited from Tyndale, of translation as a process 'that breaketh the shell, that we may eat the kernel' is helpful here, for the Bible text itself constantly implies that it too is a shell and so invites its reader to create or discover the kernel as something separate. To give but one obvious example, the multiple narrative of the Gospel story (even without accumulated tradition that makes much of it familiar apart from any text) invites the reader to synthesise an independent version. The Bible text, then, is often a text which, peculiar as it may seem, drives the reader beyond itself. It tends to evade the traditional, text-centred method of literary discussion. Discussion that separates language and content is encouraged.

Whatever the explanation, there is a void, and it remains a challenge to literary criticism to fill it. Close discussion of the range of the KJB's literary qualities in all their aspects is needed not just because such discussion does not exist, but, much more importantly, because it will illuminate our understanding of the most important book in the English cultural heritage, both for what it still offers its readers and for what it has contributed to that heritage.

CHAPTER SEVENTEEN

The New English Bible

AIMS

Whatever differences there may be between the faiths of the Reformation and the present, as far as the history of the Bible is concerned the two periods are alike in that an old standard has ceased to command allegiance from a large range of sects, but has yet to be replaced by a new standard. The Vulgate was archaic to the point of being arcane, and Christianity was a mystery religion. Moreover, the Vulgate was thought by its defenders to be truer than the Greek and Hebrew originals, and by its opponents to be inferior to them. The parallels with the KJB are obvious. The main difference, that the KJB is in a form of the still current language, is a matter of degree. In relation to contemporary Bibles, the KJB stands as the Vulgate stood in relation to the vernacular translations of the sixteenth century.

From Tyndale onwards (with minor exceptions) the Protestants translated from the Hebrew and the Greek, and they tended to avoid language that sounded too much like the Vulgate. The Catholics translated from the Vulgate and did their best to preserve its vocabulary. All the modern versions pretend to represent some form of the Hebrew and Greek originals, but they divide into two groups according to whether or not they show an allegiance to the modern equivalent of the Vulgate, that is, to the KJB. The majority make a deliberate effort to avoid the language of the KJB and to translate or paraphrase into some form of contemporary English.

The most interesting of these anti-KJB translations for the purposes of this study is *The New English Bible* (NEB; NT 1961, OT 1970). As a pioneering translation it shows certain problems at their most acute, and so aroused more controversy than any of the subsequent versions. What made the NEB unique as an ecclesiastical committee translation was its linguistic aim: part of its origin lay in the feeling that the language of the KJB had become a barrier to the communication of the Bible to the people. Archbishop Donald Coggan's preface notes that, prior to World War Two, Oxford and Cambridge University Presses had contemplated a revision in the KJB tradition, but that a new, independent suggestion was made as the war drew to a close:

In May 1946 the General Assembly of the Church of Scotland received an over-ture from the Presbytery of Stirling and Dunblane . . . recommending that a translation of the Bible be made in the language of the present day, inasmuch as the language of the Authorised Version, already archaic when it was made, had now become even more definitely archaic and less generally understood. (p. v)

A large number of churches recommended 'that a completely new translation should be made . . . and that the translators should be free to employ a contemporary idiom rather than reproduce the traditional "biblical" English'. Geoffrey Hunt gives some further explanation of these decisions:

The experience of many British pastors, chaplains, teachers and youth leaders in the War of 1939–45, when they were trying under difficult conditions to expound and convey the message of the Bible, was that very frequently the lan-guage of the Authorised Version was not a help but a hindrance. It was beau-tiful and solemn, but it put a veil of unreality between the scriptural writers and the people of the mid-twentieth century who needed something that would speak to them immediately. 'Whenever we have a certain time to teach a par-ticular Bible passage', was the complaint, 'we have to spend half that time giving an English lesson, "translating" the Bible English into the current lan-guage of today. We need a Bible translation in which this is already done for us; then we can start from where people actually are and give them the Bible message in language they understand'. (*About the NEB*, pp. 9–10)

The growth of AVolatry had made the language of an English trans-lation a major issue. Up to this point it had also settled the issue: Bibles should be in Bible English. As long as this was to be the outcome, the work of revision could concentrate on matters of scholarship. The NEB's change of language shifted the balance, with the result that it belongs with the large group of maverick translations, including Harwood's and Jordan's, in which a linguistic purpose shapes the work. This at first sight is odd company, especially when Harwood's name is invoked. Most of these translations were made with the intention of achieving some sort of appropriate beauty of translation. They put beauty ahead of literal faithfulness. But now that beauty had become so associated with the KJB, to choose to translate into a new idiom could be an anti-aesthetic move.

A good many reviewers thought that the translators had deliberately set out to destroy the beauty of the Bible. Certainly they set out as far as possible to avoid the English of the KJB, but ideas of the literary beauty of the Bible were inescapable. This is clearest in C.H. Dodd's memorandum, written at an early stage of the work in his capacity as General Director, entitled 'Purpose and intention of the project'. Dodd first distinguishes three kinds of reader, those outside the church who are put off by the language of the KJB, the young 'for whom the Bible, if it is to make any impact, must be "contemporary"', and those for whom it is too familiar to engage their minds (Hunt, pp. 22–3). The language appropriate for reaching such an audience is clearly of more importance than scholarly faithfulness. This is how Dodd goes on to describe it:

With this tripartite public in view, we aim at a version which shall be as intelligible to contemporary readers as the original was to its first readers – or as nearly so as possible. It is to be genuinely English in idiom . . . avoiding equally both archaisms and transient modernisms. The version should be plain enough to convey its meaning to any reasonably intelligent person (as far as verbal expression goes), yet not bald or pedestrian. It should *not* aim at preserving 'hallowed associations'; it *should* be without pedantry. It is to be hoped that, at least occasionally, it may produce arresting and memorable renderings. It should have sufficient dignity to be read aloud. Although it is not intended primarily to be read in church, we should like to think that it may prove worthy to be read occasionally, even at public worship . . . We should like to produce . . . a translation which may in some measure succeed in removing a real barrier between a large proportion of our fellow-countrymen and the truth of the Holy Scriptures.

The closest the prefaces come to implying aesthetic ambitions is Coggan's phrase in the general preface, 'a delicate sense of English style' (p. v). This comes in connection with a major innovation in the method of translation. There was a Joint Committee and three panels, one for each part of the Bible, and a literary panel. Coggan explains: 'apprehending, however, that sound scholarship does not necessarily carry with it a delicate sense of English style, the [joint] committee appointed a fourth panel, of trusted literary advisers, to whom all the work of the translating panels was to be submitted for scrutiny'. Taking the words of the KJB preface as they appear to a contemporary reader rather than as they were intended, this panel was to rub and polish the translation. They were to do what Kipling envisaged Shakespeare doing for the KJB. Rule 8 for the making of the RV, that literary men among others should be referred to for their opinions, is elevated into a major part of the whole process. Thus the long growth of literary ideas of the Bible is formalised in the making of a new translation. Moreover, for good or ill, the separation between form and content which is to be found in the Bible and which makes translation possible, is, for the first time, reflected in the formal process of translation. One committee dealt with the content, one with the form, and one with the combined result.

The literary panel was an integral part of the project and every bit of the translation had to receive not only its consideration but its approval. The members of the panel

> could say, in effect: 'this may be what the Greek means, but it is not good current English; we suggest such and such amendments.' To which the panel of translators was free to reply: 'the amended version may be good English but it is not what the Greek means' – and so the dialogue between the two panels would go on until a version was reached which satisfied the members of both. At this stage a book was ready for the comments of the joint committee and if passed by them, was filed to await the process of final revision when all the books had passed both panels and could be reviewed together. (Nineham, *The NEB Reviewed*, p. xi)

The one moderately detailed account of the working of the literary panel only corrects this in one minor respect. The author, Basil Willey, a much respected English don, was a member of the literary panel through the full period of the work. Much of the dialogue between the translators and the literary panel took place within the meetings of the literary panel. The convener of the appropriate translation panel attended the literary panel's meetings to ensure, as Willey recalls, 'that, in our zeal for English style, we did not depart from the true meaning of the text' ('On translating the Bible', p. 12).

Willey's article divides in two. Much of it is an exceptionally perceptive and lucid account of the KJB and some of the issues involved in the making of the NEB. He notes, for instance, that 'the old translators achieved literary distinction largely because they were not self-consciously aiming at it . . . Like all good style, theirs was a by-product; aiming at truth, they achieved beauty without effort or contrivance' (p. 2). It is a neat formulation. He goes on to remark 'how fortunate it was that the accepted English translation was made when it was, and not (for instance) in the eighteenth century' (p. 3), as he shows by some judicious specimens from Harwood. What he does not note is that Harwood aimed at literary distinction through effort and contrivance. Indeed, Harwood's aims sound in part like those of the NEB, to 'clothe the genuine ideas and doctrines of the apostles with that propriety and perspicuity in which they themselves . . . would have exhibited them had they *now* lived and written in our language' (above, p. 238). Nevertheless, Willey recognises that the NEB might be an effort of the same sort: 'should we perhaps be producing something which, *mutatis mutandis*, might appear later as absurd as Dr Harwood's version now appears to ourselves?' (p. 4). Some critics would answer in the affirmative: for better or worse, everyday English for the man in the street, that is, proper, per-spicuous English, is as much the fetish of the present day as neo-classi-cal elegance was to the Augustans.

Having so praised the KJB, Willey tackles the question of the need for a new translation. This leads him to dispraise. He is one of the few modern critics before Daniell to produce examples of bad English in the KJB. He sees the main reason for such failures as the KJB's tendency, especially in obscure passages, to rely on word-for-word translation. After examples such as 'the noise thereof sheweth concerning it, the cattle also concerning the vapour' (Job 36: 33),[1] he comments:

Those who exalt Bible English as the grandest and noblest in our literature ignore this kind of thing. And there is something else they overlook, namely the constant failure of the old translators to translate, i.e. to render Hebrew or Greek idioms, constructions and modes of speech by English counterparts. Too often they simply transliterate and give us mongrel English which we tolerate only because we are accustomed to hearing it in church. (pp. 6–7)

'Mongrel English': this is intended as a condemnation, yet it identifies one of the sources of the KJB's strength. One begins to suspect that Willey's brief, to care for the English of the translation as good modern English, has blinded him to strengths in the originals, strengths which the KJB has reflected. Indeed, it seems that the panel felt that, as well as avoiding the language of the KJB, they should avoid reflecting any char-acteristics of the originals that were not also characteristics of contem-porary English. So Willey's most curious revelation is that the literary panel at first tried, like Blackmore (see above, p. 219) and many another paraphraser before them, to get rid of parallelism:

This method of poetic utterance is foreign to the English mind and language, and the NEB translators at first struggled hard, whenever they could, to make one statement out of the two without losing whatever was significant in either. In the end, however, they were forced to give up and admit defeat; there was far

---

[1] Ronald Knox, the Roman Catholic translator, chooses Mark 7: 3 as an example of bad English: 'For the Pharisees, and all the Jews, except they wash their hands oft, eat not, holding the tradi-tion of the elders' (*On Englishing the Bible*, p. 4). Nineham cites 2 Cor. 6: 1113: 'O ye Corinthians, our mouth is open unto you, our heart is enlarged. Ye are not straitened in us, but ye are strait-ened in your own bowels. Now for a recompense in the same, (I speak as unto my children,) be ye also enlarged' (*The NEB Reviewed*, p. xiin).

too much of this kind of thing for even their patience and ingenuity to cope with – it was like trying to change the colour of the Ethiopian's skin. (p. 8)

The last image, biblical of course, slips in too easily. Throughout, Willey writes (as did Harwood) in terms that separate form from content: it is clear that the panel would, if possible, have changed the Ethiopian's skin and the leopard's spots in order to do good. But there have to be limits, and translators in the end have not the freedom of the paraphrasers to make an absolute separation between meaning and expression.

Willey's remarks on parallelism may suggest some naivety about translation that a judicious reading of Lowth might have cured – though naivety, as I observed in connection with Tyndale, is often a valuable aid in the accomplishment of a major task. But eighteen years of active involvement in translation must eventually have left the literary panel with a highly practical sense of the possibilities of their task.

The latter part of Willey's article is a fascinating glimpse of the panel at work. He calls it 'a few dramatised passages from a typical Old Testament session' (p. 12). It seems to belong somewhere between Kipling's '"Proofs of Holy Writ"' and Bois's notes on the KJB or Wright's notes on the RV, though in the key matter of authenticity it belongs with Bois and Wright. In the absence of other such evidence, Willey's account is most useful if taken in the way he suggests, 'as representative rather than actual' (p. 13). Not being free to mention names, he identifies the speakers by letters. Only one of them, 'R' for Rabbi, the representative of the OT panel, is identifiable, Godfrey Driver. 'As in all human discussions of whatever kind,' Willey notes, 'we had a right-wing and a left; the radicals, who wanted down-to-earth "contemporary" language, and the conservatives who stood out for dignity, and often preferred closeness to the AV. A good many of the discussions centred upon the questions: "What *is* 'contemporary' English?" and "What *is* obsolete?"' (p. 13). The notations in square brackets are Willey's, the passage is from 1 Samuel 19:

The Rabbi reads aloud:

R. 'Saul spoke to Jonathan his son and all his servants about killing David. But Saul's son Jonathan was (much attached to (very fond of)) David, and said to him, "My father Saul is seeking to kill you. Be careful tomorrow morning, and stay quietly in hiding. Then I will come out and join my father . . . and if I find anything amiss I will tell you." Jonathan spoke well of David to his father Saul, and said to him, "Sir, do not sin against your servant David, for he has not sinned against you; his conduct towards you has been exemplary. He risked his life and slew the

Philistine . . . why should you sin against an innocent man and put David to death for no reason?'"

Pause

A.   What about 'servants'? Is that the right shade of meaning?

R.   No, not really; it means his entourage, his personal attendants at court. 'Retinue'? No, that suggests a procession.

A.   'Household'? [*Agreed*]

B.   In the next sentence, do we need to say 'Saul's son' again?

R.   Well, it's in the Hebrew, but I agree: let's leave it out.

C.   I don't like either of the alternatives 'much attached to' and 'very fond of'; the first suggests offhand and the second commonplace. I suggest 'devoted to'. [*Agreed*] And 'be careful' is so colourless.

R.   Yes, and the Hebrew means 'look after yourself'. Why not 'be on your guard'? [*Agreed*]

D.   I'm not happy about 'sin against'. 'Sin' isn't a contemporary idea anyway, but quite apart from that the phrase is archaic. 'Do not wrong your servant David'? [*Agreed*]

C.   'His conduct . . . has been exemplary' – I feel that this phrase is out of a different sort of book, or perhaps a school report. 'Blameless' would be better, I think. [*Agreed*][2]

B.   I'm not sure about 'for no reason'. The question begins with 'why', which means 'for what reason', so you're really saying 'for what reason should you . . . put David to death for no reason?' 'Without cause' would perhaps still be open to the same objection, but less so, I think.

C.   Oh dear, aren't we getting rather hyper-subtle? Still, 'without cause' is all right, and rhythmically a much nicer concluding phrase than 'for no reason'. [*Agreed*]

Chairman.   Shall we go on?

C.   Just one little point, my lord. I think we're in danger all the time of becoming flat and prosy. So much that was picturesque and vigorous in the AV has to be sacrificed that we should neglect no chance of putting a bit of life into our version. Here, for instance: 'He risked his life and slew the Philistine' – if we put this in the form of a rhetorical question it would at once enliven the passage: 'Did he not take his life in his hands and slay the Philistine?'

R.   Oh yes, that's all right. It's not a question in the Hebrew, but I'm sure the OT panel will accept that. (pp. 13–14)

A discussion of whether 'slay' is archaic follows. To *C*'s sorrow, the committee decides that it is and adopts 'kill' instead. His rhetorical question, born out of a desire to enliven the text, became 'Did he not take his life in his hands when he killed the Philistine?'

So far Willey has shown the translators leaving the literary panel a choice of phrases – 'much attached to' or 'very fond of' – and the panel working in a variety of ways. They scrutinise shades of meaning, and it

---

[2] NEB reads 'beyond reproach'.

quickly becomes apparent that the translators were not necessarily precise in the choice of phrases offered to the literary panel: 'be careful' is not only colourless but a weak representation of the Hebrew. Archaism, register and rhythm are all considered, and then comes the revelation in the acceptance of *C*'s rhetorical question, that the translators, collectively, felt themselves free to rewrite the original. If grammar can be altered even when a correct representation of the original grammar makes satisfactory English, the line between translation and improvement would seem to have been crossed. Literary considerations override faithfulness, and, for a moment, the translators are placed in Harwood's camp.

Soon afterwards Willey gives an example that most readers would probably agree stays on the translation side of the line. The translators proposed the following verses 9–10:

An evil spirit from the Lord came upon Saul; he was sitting in the house holding his spear and David was playing the harp. Saul tried to pin David to the wall, but he broke away from Saul's presence so that Saul drove the spear into the wall. (pp. 14–15)

Among the comments were these by *E*:

'Sitting in the house holding his spear' – I don't like two '-ings' so close together; and besides, doesn't this suggest that 'holding his spear' was (so to speak) Saul's whole-time occupation just then? I suggest 'with his spear in his hand'. And aren't there too many 'Saul's' in this passage? Why not say 'he broke away from the King's presence and Saul drove . . .', etc. (p. 15)

The objection to the 'ings' starts as a perhaps pedantic matter of style but suddenly transforms itself into a sharp perception of the implications of the phrasing. 'With his spear in his hand' changes the grammar, and so avoids potentially risible implications while giving an appropriate sense of the importance of the observation. However, the substitution of pronoun for noun that follows is a matter of changing the Ethiopian's skin exactly as Purver had done (see above, p. 233).

Willey reports that the panel agreed to both these suggestions. But what finally appeared was this (the changes from the draft are italicised):

An evil spirit from the Lord came upon Saul *as* he was sitting in the house *with his spear in his hand*; and David was playing the harp. Saul tried to pin David to the wall *with the spear*, but he *avoided the king's thrust* so that Saul drove the spear into the wall.

Not all the suggestions agreed to in the literary panel were adopted, which is no more than one would expect. 'Avoided the king's thrust' is a change of sense made by the translators at a later stage.

The next part of the discussion again concerns archaism. *C*, the real conservative on the panel, suggests that the translation may preserve fine words that are on the verge of obsolescence. *A* suggests this is 'rather a dangerous argument', and Willey notes, 'prolonged wrangle sets in' (p. 16). The conservative line loses, and the implication is that the NEB rejected the idea that it had a duty to preserve language.

The last part of Willey's dramatisation concerns poetry, part of David's lament over Jonathan and Saul (2 Sam. 1: 19–20). Again *C*, playing the part Dean Stanley played in the RV (see above, p. 335), is the central figure:

The Rabbi reads from David's lament over Jonathan and Saul

R. The flower of the nation lies slain upon your
        heights, O Israel!
    Fallen are the warriors.
    Do not tell it in Gath,
    Do not proclaim it in the streets of Ashkelon!

C. (*warming to a congenial opportunity*) Now of course this is *poetry*, and different canons of translation must be applied. We're allowed a more elevated diction and various rhetorical devices; and this makes an appeal to everyday modern usage irrelevant. So let's begin:

> O flower of the nation lying slain!
> The men of war are fallen;
> Fallen they lie upon your heights, O Israel!
> [*General approval*]

Well then, if we're allowed so much – if we're allowed such a departure from prose order as the inversion 'Fallen they lie', why not go on:

> Tell it not in Gath,
> Publish it not in the streets of Ashkelon?

G. B-b-but this is pure AV! Just the sort of thing we've been directed to avoid!

C. I know, I know; but what is the alternative? 'Do not tell it in Gath' – could anything be more utterly banal and hopeless? It's terrible how much the English language has lost in ceasing to use 'not' after an imperative, and putting in 'do'. How much finer is 'Fear not', or 'Judge not', than 'Do not fear', 'Do not judge'! I think in this poetic context 'Tell it not' is permissible. And as for its being an AV phrase, 'Tell it not in Gath' is so familiar as to have become an English saying; and any re-wording will appear as just what it is – a mere attempt *not* to use an AV phrase.

G. Hm. It's arguable. Very well, I'll agree – but not without misgiving. (pp. 16–17)

C's trap is neatly laid. He does not try to preserve 'how are the mighty fallen' but sets a style that leads to direct quotation from the KJB. He has proved this to be *the* style for poetic translation. And in this instance he almost wins the day: 'publish' was later changed to 'proclaim'. The normal deliberate avoidance of KJB language is set aside. Willey concludes as any one of this group of translators might, making a clear separation between medium and message and reminding his reader of a point he has made several times, that for many the KJB is no more than a 'numinous rumble' (p. 5):

Those who talk of 'loss' – loss of mystery, awesomeness, ceremony and so on – should make very certain that they themselves, in responding to the AV, have not mistaken a sort of liturgical trance for true understanding and spiritual discernment. Much of the Bible has an enduring message and admonition for every age; and it is hoped that readers, seeing clearly at last what it is saying, may find their consciences disturbed at points formerly protected by the comfortable sonorities of the old version. The translation was made in the belief that the Bible's message had for too long been embalmed in beautiful or familiar archaism, and that it was high time to let it speak home to our condition. (p. 17)

RECEPTION

In Bois's notes there was every indication of concern for correctness of understanding and accuracy of rendering, but minimal concern for aesthetic qualities. Willey's dramatisation, though representing only part of the process, takes us almost as far in the other direction. Like the very existence of the literary panel whose activity it recreates, it is eloquent testimony to the change in attitude to the nature of the Bible that has taken place. Even if the intention is as narrow as to make the Bible's message 'speak home to our condition', a literary awareness of the Bible pervades the business of translation. The NEB may be the first ecclesiastical translation in modern dress, but it is as much dominated by the literary success of the KJB as the RV and its successors. *They* reflect that domination by preservation; the NEB reflects it by reaction.

The NEB's reception similarly reflects the changed spirit. All there was of contemporary reaction to the KJB was Broughton's disconsolate anathematising. Dennis Nineham was able to fill a book with responses to the NEB, and yet leave much unrecorded. From the point of view of this history the most interesting responses are the hostile ones, for they are the ones most concerned with literary questions. Nevertheless, two examples of the favourable responses to the NT, taken from Nineham's collection, will be useful, not least because it is a new sight to see a major version received with substantial applause.

With a generosity and sympathy uncommon among rivals and literary scholars, the popular translator J.B. Phillips declared the NEB NT 'a magnificent and memorable accomplishment'. For him this was the word of God reborn in English. He continues:

There is an evenness of texture which runs through the whole volume – not, of course, the evenness of style which is so evident in the version of 1611, but a kind of common spiritual authority which binds the various authors together. They obviously have access to the same living God. If they speak in different ways they speak with one voice, and that voice speaks unerringly to the innermost heart of man.

All in all I see no loss of spiritual potency in this rendering of the New Testament into the English of today; indeed, I see great gain. Striking and priceless truths, which have lain dormant for years in the deep-freeze of traditional beauty, spring to life with fresh challenge and quite alarming relevance to the men of the jet age. There is no need to argue about inspiration, for the word of God is out of its jewelled scabbard and is as sharp, as powerful and as discerning as ever. (*The NEB Reviewed*, p. 135)

In short, the NEB NT is all the translators hoped it might be, and more. Already the suggestion of inspiration hovers close to the translators. And one notes a novel turning of the idea of language as the dress of thought in the idea of the KJB as scabbard for the sword of truth.

From the other side of the Atlantic, Frederick W. Danker observed: 'because it communicates in timely idiom and yet with timeless phrase it merits classification with the choicest products of *English* literary art' (p. 40). Although writing in a theological journal, Danker suggests that 'the first test of a work which claims to be a new translation is whether it communicates in contemporary terms without erasing to the point of illegibility the historical gap' (p. 41). Accuracy seems so much to be taken for granted that it is forgotten about. Danker appears to think in the very way the translators themselves are accused of thinking by another American, Ernest C. Colwell: 'in this new translation, style is king, and whenever accuracy or clarity interfere with style, they are sacrificed' (p. 37). But, if style is indeed king, Danker finds it magnificent:

Felicitous expressions meet one everywhere in astounding prodigality. There is the rasp of desert sand in words like these, 'No bullying; no blackmail; make do with your pay!' (Luke 3: 14), that captures the man who dared to take the path to greatness through the obscure way. The social game of petty character sniping comes to a halt at words like these:

Why do you look at the speck of sawdust in your brother's eye, with never a thought for the great plank in your own? How can you say to your brother, 'My dear brother, let me take the speck out of your eye', when you are blind to the plank in your own? You hypocrite! First take the plank out of your own eye, and then you will see clearly to take the speck out of your brother's [Luke 6: 41–2] . . .

The watchful and sensitive ears of a special committee of experts on the English language have insured this version against the banal and pedestrian . . . Many of its cadenced phrases will become a part of tomorrow's literary expression. 'Do not feed your pearls to pigs' (Matt. 7: 6) . . . All one-syllable words, cleanly hewn. Here is modern speech, tomorrow's idiom and liturgical rhythm in rare combination . . . In this 350th anniversary year of the publication of the [KJB] we can pay our British cousins no higher tribute than to say: You have done it again! (pp. 41, 57, 59)

The praise could not be higher, and the examples give one some opportunity to form one's own opinion. This is just as well, since the identical examples are given by the elder statesman of poetry, T.S. Eliot. Citing Matthew's version of the saying about the plank (7: 4), 'Or how can you say to your brother, "Let me take the speck out of your eye", when all the time there is that plank in your own?', he suggests it 'may be literally accurate but will certainly, if it is read in church, raise a giggle among the choirboys' (pp. 97–8). It may indeed, but only because the meaning has become inescapable. The KJB escapes risibility by chance misunderstanding: common sense knows that one cannot have a roof-beam in one's eye, but 'beam' sounds like 'gleam', which is something one can have in one's eye. Eliot's objection looks like fear of the real meaning of the Bible, Danker's praise like welcome for the meaning.

Eliot gives more detailed attention to 'do not feed your pearls to pigs', chosen as a version of a familiar phrase. He tries it against the KJB:

We notice, first, the substitution of 'pigs' for 'swine'. The Complete Oxford Dictionary says that 'swine' is now 'literary' but does not say that it is 'obsolete'. I presume, therefore, that in substituting 'pigs' for 'swine' the translators were trying to choose a word nearer to common speech, even if at the sacrifice of dignity.

I should have thought, however, that the word 'swine' would be understood, not only by countryfolk who may have heard of 'swine fever', but even by the urban public, since it is still applied, I believe, to human beings as a term of abuse.

Next, I should have thought that the sentence would be more in accordance with English usage if the direct and indirect objects were transposed, thus: 'Do not feed pigs upon your pearls' . . .

The most unfortunate result, however, is that the substitution of 'feed' for 'cast' makes the figure of speech ludicrous. There is all the difference in the world between saying that pigs do not *appreciate* the value of pearls, and saying, what the youngest and most illiterate among us know, that they cannot be *nourished* on pearls. (p. 97)

For three paragraphs this looks like nit-picking, but the last paragraph convicts the translators, and Danker for admiring the phrase. Later editions of the NEB revert to the sense of the KJB, 'do not throw your pearls to the pigs'. It looks as if some critics admired the NEB because it was not the KJB, and others for the same reason reviled it. Certainly the same thing may produce opposite responses, and the dispassionate judge is likely sometimes to sympathise with one side, sometimes with the other.

Some of the hostile responses were as intemperate as Broughton's. But there is a telling difference. Broughton despaired because the KJB appeared to him a compendium of scholarly errors. The modern reviewers, like Eliot, despaired because of the language of the NEB.

Worthy Bishop Beveridge spoke for millions when he declared that 'it is a great prejudice to the new that it is new, wholly new; for whatsoever is new in religion at the best is unnecessary' (above, p. 121). Moreover, the KJB translators knew well that 'he that meddleth with men's religion in any part meddleth with their custom, nay, with their freehold' (preface, p. 2). Were the hostile moderns mere new-born Beveridgeans? Were they protesting because their religion had been meddled with? And, since some of the protesters were not churchmen, were they protesting because their religion was, not Christianity but AVolatry? All these questions might be answered in the affirmative, and conclusions reached about mankind's ineradicable fidelity to the familiar.

Since it was published in two parts, the NEB was subject to two sets of reviews. It also became involved in the controversy that surrounded the Church of England's revisions of the Liturgy. This controversy came to a head with the presentation of three petitions for the preservation of the old to the General Synod of the Church of England on November 5, 1979. These petitions were published in the *PN Review*, and there was substantial correspondence in the British press.

Beveridge was a Bishop, and one might well expect his spirit to live on in his modern successors, members of that General Synod that approved so much change, and a more adventurous, forward-looking spirit to be found in leading intellectuals of the day. The Reverend Michael Saward, Vicar of Ealing, member of the General Synod and Church Commissioner, makes a key point about the Synod in a letter to *The Times* (17 November 1979):

Why is it that the present Synod and its predecessor, both relatively conservative bodies, have pursued liturgical change together with the authorisation of
modern Bible translations for liturgical use with such dedication?

Anyone who knows the Synod with real intimacy will recognise that it cannot
possibly be because of a love for change for its own sake. No, the issue is far
more fundamental than that. What is at stake is the whole future of Anglican
Christianity in this country. Put at its starkest, the choice in the next 30 years lies
between a jewelled corpse or a living pilgrim . . . What is at stake is the *truth* of
Christianity and its capacity to save and transform men and women. If that be
not true and demonstrable, then all the cultural and literary beauty of Tudor
English is nothing more than the cosmetic mask of a Hollywood cadaver.

Just what this last rhetorical flourish means I am uncertain, but the main
point is important and also familiar. The revisions were being made not
for the sake of change but because, as in the Reformation, souls (and
institutions) were at stake. Not much of the protest at the revisions comes
from the clergy because the point made at the inception of the NEB
holds good, that the KJB had ceased to speak to large numbers of the
people the Church wanted to speak to.

It may also be true – here again there is a parallel with the
Reformation – that the KJB had ceased to speak with sufficient meaning
to some of the clergy. S.G. Hall, reverend professor of Ecclesiastical
History, suggests this in another letter to *The Times* (29 November 1979).
He castigates a group of the protesters 'as outsiders meddling irrele-
vantly and irreverently in matters of no concern to them', and declares
that 'the ordinary earnest clergyman is deeply concerned to generate
warm, spontaneous, directly expressed and intelligent worship from a
congregation which knows what it is saying and doing'. The KJB and
the PB often get in the way of this, and Hall goes on to look at the clergy's
preference for a version about which he is scathing, the Good News
Bible. 'They favour it', he suggests, 'because they themselves can understand it, and so can the lay people who are invited to participate by
reading parts of the service. Many of the clergy themselves do not read
the Authorised Version intelligibly, perhaps because they do not understand it enough to give the words the right emphasis and punctuation.'
In other words, the clergy's literacy has been weakened to the point
where they are in danger of saying 'mumpsimus' rather than 'sumpsimus'. Hall does not blame the clergy for this; rather, it is – he does say
'in part' – the fault of 'the leaders of the national and educational establishment who by their indifference or contempt have forced the confession of God in Christ out of national and university life into the
sectarian backwater of private belief, personal taste and gathered congregations'. The fault, then, lies largely with the very people who signed

the petitions to the Synod, though Hall decently refrains from sending the shaft that far home. And, as Peter Mason, Vicar of Writtle, simplistically observes, 'it is difficult to find any suggestion in the New Testament that the Church's task includes that of preserving a cultural and literary heritage' (letter to *The Times*, 21 November 1979).

One other shaft is worth recording. It comes from the Reverend Douglas Bean, Vicar of St Pancras. He suggests that the clamour for the old forms is 'purely academic':

Two per cent of the population of Great Britain attend Holy Communion on Sundays. The percentage who attend the divine offices of Mattins and Evensong is even less. How the linguistic heritage of the Authorised Version of the Bible and the Book of Common Prayer can be influential on the people of this country when the great majority of them are not present at the services of the Church is a question I would like to be answered. (Letter to *The Times*, 21 November 1979)

This is fair enough, but his final point is truly barbed: 'This church is a hundred yards or so from the centre of London University and there are several halls of residence within the parish. I have not noticed professors of English or students attending in any numbers to appreciate the beauties of the Liturgy, nor, as a matter of fact, at any other of the main churches of the country.' The academy and the church, it seems, have nothing to do with each other.

Yet the academy has taken upon itself to be the defender of traditional religion because the language of the NEB and the new liturgy is abhorrent to it. This is the main petition that was presented to the General Synod:

We, the undersigned, are deeply concerned by the policies and tendencies which decree the loss of both the Authorised Version of the English Bible and the Book of Common Prayer. This great act of forgetting, now under way, is a tragic loss to our historic memory and an impoverishment of present awareness. For centuries these texts have carried forward the freshness and simplicity of our language in its early modern splendour. Without them the resources of expression are reduced, the stock of shared words depleted, and we ourselves diminished. Moreover, they contain nothing which cannot be easily and profitably explained.

We ask for their continued and loving use in churches as part of the mainstream of worship and not as vestiges indulged intermittently. We welcome innovation and experiment, but hope that changes will take place alongside the achievements of the past. The younger generation in particular should be acquainted as far as possible with their inheritance.

Clearly this is not an issue confined only to the churches or communities of faith. Some of us do not claim religious belief. Yet we hope that steps are taken to ensure a lively pleasure in the Authorised Version of the Bible in the nation at large. If humane education means anything it includes access to the great renderings of epic and wisdom, prophecy and poetry, epistle and gospel. (*PN Review*, p. 51)

The 600-odd signatories to this are an awe-inspiring gathering, so much so that it would be invidious to single out anyone: it is as representative as could be of the intellectual and cultural leaders of the time. Concern for the cultural heritage embodied in the KJB and the PB was general among the literati. And it is essentially a concern for the Bible as literature.

Some of the signatories, like C.H. Sisson, were quite candid that 'familiarity and continuity are what are at stake' (*PN Review*, p. 8). Now, one readily admits the value of familiarity and continuity – only a rampant anarchist would not. Humanity has made itself what it is through its ability to combine memory of the past with innovation. Without continuity we would still be reinventing the wheel. But without innovation, the wheel would never have been invented in the first place. Sitting back and surveying the literary ruckus over the appearance of the NEB, one sees it as an expression of the fear that all continuity will be lost in the face of innovation: so innovation is attacked. Yet, in the field of biblical translations it seems that all innovations (apart from the legendary Septuagint) have needed decades if not centuries to gain acceptance. No generation has made the same judgement on its own work as subsequent generations.

Familiarity and continuity were not all that were at stake. There is also the question of the appropriate language for religion – and here it is perhaps a pity that revision of the liturgy became mixed up with revision of the Bible as an issue. Liturgy, being sacramental and ceremonial, would seem naturally to demand a liturgical quality of language. But is it so obvious that a Bible should be in biblical style? To some extent the argument against the NEB rode on the back of the argument against the revision of the liturgy, and most of the arguers seemed to believe that the Bible had to be in what they recognised as biblical style. The educationalist and philosopher, Mary (later Baroness) Warnock put the matter most carefully. There is, she argues, another ground besides the cultural for retaining the KJB and the PB. It is that their particular language, and the particular contexts in which it is used, has a particular suggestiveness to which the imagination responds. 'It is not only the clarities of language', she reminds her readers, 'that are significant, but the obscurities, the ambiguities, the suggestions. And these may suggest to us things which we cannot, indeed could never, fully grasp or express more clearly, though we may try' (*PN Review*, p. 16). Religious truth is not religious truth without this imaginative quality:

Religious truths cannot be adequately or precisely stated. There must in the nature of the case be something ambiguous, parodoxical, even mysterious in their proper expression. No religious writer, no philosopher of religion has ever denied this. Thus the effort to clean up the language of the Bible and the prayer book, to sanitise it, to render it exact, up-to-date and unambiguous is itself an anti-religious effort. The ideas of religion . . . are for ever just beyond the scope of language. (p. 17)

In a letter to *The Times*, she and some other notable Oxford figures put the matter even more simply: 'the full meaning of the Bible cannot be conveyed in a strictly non-poetic language' (14 November 1979). This is a reasoned challenge to the linguistic rationale of the NEB. Though it sounds rather like John Dennis 275 years earlier (see above, p. 190), one only begins to suspect this when one observes the company it keeps and sees how it comes out from less diplomatic pens. Then it begins to be subject to the reservation the editor of the *Daily Telegraph* voiced about the whole *PN Review* collection, that 'here is the spectacle of a collection of outsiders making points about language which are aesthetic rather than religious' (6 November 1979, p. 18).

Here is one example of the AVolatrous company these careful arguments keep:

I find it difficult to describe in temperate language my feelings regarding the current tendency to reject the Jacobean translation of the Scriptures to say nothing of the Book of Common Prayer in favour of recent versions of these masterpieces.

Whether one is a believer or not, it is surely not open to question that, with Shakespeare, these works are the main background of our literary heritage. To substitute for their marvellous cadences and deep spiritual and poetic appeal, these supreme examples of literary insensibility . . . seems to me an outrage which, if it were not a real danger, one would never believe to be possible . . . What would [the young] – or we – say of an attempt to rewrite one of Hamlet's soliloquies in modern English? All eyes would be dry. How much more so to be condemned is this forcing the adoption of such parodies of the greatest literary manifestations of one of the great religions of the world. (*PN Review*, p. 17)

Missing the point that the NEB is not a revision of the KJB but a new translation of the originals, this implies that 'marvellous cadences and deep spiritual and poetic appeal' are what matter most. It is as if cadences were the key to religion (and the old the key to culture and education). Moreover, the implication that the KJB, rather than the unconsidered originals, is the true word of God hovers in the background. Passages such as this undermine the credibility of the petition, and one suspects that it was only included because of the prestige of the author, Lord Robbins, economist and chairman of the English Committee on Higher Education that produced the *Higher Education Report* to parliament (1963) commonly known by his name.

The fullest and most vehement development of Mary Warnock's arguments came from a lecturer in English language at the University College of Swansea, Ian Robinson, in a piece that, for all that it has important things to say, is marked by outspoken criticism, a total lack of sympathy for the NEB's aims and a scorn for the judgements of others; Broughtonian is a suitably ugly adjective for it. Robinson asks, for instance, 'why the translators can't write English at all (and why so glaringly obvious a fact was generally missed by the literary critics who reviewed the version)' (*The Survival of English*, p. 24). His case against the NEB is based on the idea that the division between content and form which has persisted in asserting itself throughout this history is false. 'The way "things" are said affects the "things"' (p. 46). This should be obvious if it were not so absolutely stated: if 'can affect' were substituted for 'affects' the statement would be so true as to be hardly worth making. But Robinson's belief is that meaning only exists in form. It is a belief that stretches common sense into absurdity. Yet the absurdity is rarely apparent because it is so close to common sense and because the belief is fairly generally held within the academic community.

Robinson's sense of the inextricability of language and meaning is closely linked to something highly prized in literary discussion, the ability to show what is good in a piece of writing. A comparison between the KJB's and the NEB's renderings of the first four verses of Genesis leads him to this:

The 1611 version is so good here because its translators command the style for the subject. The slow, measured rhythmic sentences, one for each step in creation, convince one in a poetic way as well as being, I am told, closer to the procedure of the Hebrew . . . Look at the different use of 'and' – the difference made to the rhythm of the passage, its pace, phrasing and stressing. That was, at least, done by people who were masters of the craft of writing English. (p. 26)

Though this is not in the same class as Boileau's observation on verse three (above, p. 193), it is a reasonable suggestion that the repeated 'and's help to bring home to the reader a ritualistic sense of the stage-by-stage quality of the action, and that therefore the form of the passage contributes to the perception of the meaning. Robinson, however, would not accept such a formulation. When he returns to the passage it is to use it as a dogmatic demonstration of the Saintsburyan point that the rhythm of the passage is its meaning:

To say that the Bible's mastery of language is primarily a question of rhythm, the careful and strong rhythms of the individual phrase controlled by the tempo of a whole passage, is not to reduce it to 'orotundity' or 'resonant opacity', but to discuss the meaning and credibility of what is said. That is why it was insufficient, though true, to say that the 1611 opening of Genesis was done by masters of the craft of writing. The old translators were religious artists, the truth of whose utterance depended on their grasp of their language. (p. 58)

A contributing element has been made into the whole. We might well accept that the meaning is not so well created in the NEB, even that the meaning is not quite the same, but it is nonsense to imply that the whole meaning disappears if the phrasing is changed. If that were true then 'the meaning and credibility of what is said' would not be there in the original Hebrew, nor in any other language, nor in any other English version. All that is true is that the precise character of phrasing that produces a particular character of response in a particular individual would be missing. The particular character of the response may be very important, it may be shared by a large number of people, but there is a dogmatism about the way Robinson has moved from commentary to assertion. We have reached literary fundamentalism rather than insight.

Robinson goes almost as far as proclaiming outright what I have just suggested is self-evident nonsense, that the meaning and credibility are not there in the original language. The preface to the NEB OT observes that the Greek of the NT 'is indeed more flexible and easy-going than the revisers were ready to allow, and invites the translator to use a larger freedom'. To this he retorts: 'Only if [the translator] is radically confused about the purpose of his translation, which is in this case to produce a New English Bible, not a modern replica of an easy-going first-century text. The intended fidelity is *not* to whatever it is that allowed the text to become the Bible' (p. 44). The stress is not mine but his. Apparently the original Greek was not the Bible. And it was not the Bible because a key characteristic of a Bible is that it should be in religious language and have a sense of tradition behind it. He sums up this part of his ideas thus:

Religious English is the style of our common language that makes religion possible (or not, as the case may be). Religious English can only make religious seriousness possible to the individual, in whom any religion is not restricted or standardised but perpetually new, unique and his own; it could not do so, however, without the many generations whose lives have expressed themselves in our language, in the context of the many Christian languages, in *their* context of history and human nature. (pp. 55–6)

All this flows from the dogma that meaning and expression are inseparable. It might as well be a belief in the divine inspiration of the KJB, for the end result, reached by a different route but with equal vehemence, is no different from the position held by fundamentalists such as Hills and Chick.

One other aspect of Robinson's argument reaches, challengingly, something like this position. He characterises the style of the NEB as journalism, and incompetent journalism at that (pp. 22, 39). 'Its one consistent effect', he adds, 'is that it cheapens' (p. 22). Consequently 'the NEB miracles all seem gross impostures, superstitions as reported by the modern journalist' (p. 37). It will be useful to follow some of the development of this point in detail, not least because it will correct the impression that Robinson is not worth attending to:

In the NEB the story of the resurrection, the central miracle of Christianity, is simply nonsense.

> The angel then addressed the woman: 'You,' he said, 'have nothing to fear. I know you are looking for Jesus who was crucified. He is not here; he has been raised again, as he said he would be. Come and see the place where he was laid, and then go quickly and tell his disciples: "He has been raised from the dead and is going on before you into Galilee; there you will see him." That is what I had to tell you.' [Matt. 28: 5–7]

The angel is obviously an imposter: he speaks far too much like a usually reliable source, flustered by an impossible brief. To take a miracle so much as a matter of course ('He has been raised from the dead and is going . . .') is a sign either of extraordinary stupidity or a wide credibility gap. So it is hardly surprising that Matthew's continuation of the story would convince no dispassionate reader.

> After meeting with the elders and conferring together, the chief priests offered the soldiers a substantial bribe and told them to say, 'His disciples came by night and stole the body while we were asleep.' They added, 'If this should reach the Governor's ears, we will put matters right with him and see that you do not suffer' [28: 12–14].

A likely tale! Roman soldiers expected to put out the story that they had been asleep on duty but yet knew what happened. Even so, in this version some sort of body-snatching seems the most likely solution to a question which almost puts the book into the genre of detective novel.

The Jerusalem Bible's angel is similarly unangelic and even chatty. The 1885 version is . . . the only one of the three I could in any sense believe in:

> And the angel answered and said unto the women, Fear not ye: for I know that ye seek Jesus, which hath been crucified. He is not here; for he is risen, even as he said. Come, see the place where the Lord lay. And go quickly and tell his disciples, He is risen from the dead; and lo, he goeth before you into Galilee. (p. 38)

This is not quite as persuasive as it appears at first sight, for Robinson resorts to assertion just when close discussion is most needed. Declaring the RV the only one of the three fairly modern versions he 'could in any sense believe in', he probably expects his reader to agree that it positively escapes his Paine-like condemnation of NEB and Jerusalem.

If one takes the whole of what he quoted from the NEB in the RV, or, better still, in the KJB with the few differences from his quotation italicised, the comparison can begin to be fairly made:

And the angel answered and said unto the women, Fear not ye: for I know that ye seek Jesus, which *was* crucified. He is not here: for he is risen, *[. . .]* as he said. Come, see the place where the Lord lay. And go quickly, and tell his disciples *that* he is risen from the dead; and, *behold*, he goeth before you into Galilee; there shall ye see him: lo, I have told you . . . And when they were assembled with the elders, and had taken counsel, they gave large money unto the soldiers, Saying, Say ye, His disciples came by night, and stole him away while we slept. And if this come to the governor's ears, we will persuade him, and secure you. So they took the money, and did as they were taught: and this saying is commonly reported among the Jews until this day. (Matt. 28: 5–7, 12–15, KJB)

Is this angel also an imposter? The answer depends most on 'lo, I have told you'. Does this have the impressiveness of an annunciation, created by a combination of the archaic trumpet-call[3] of 'lo' and a stress on 'I', implying, 'I, an angel'? Or does it have something of the worldly Rosamond Vincy confessing to Dorothea that everything had been her own fault and that Will Ladislaw had been telling her he loved Dorothea: she adds, beginning to return to her characteristic self-righteousness, 'But now I have told you, and he cannot reproach me any more' (*Middlemarch*, ch. 81)? Both readings are possible. Nevertheless, if the

---

[3] Doubtless I am less sensitive than Saintsbury, who wrote of the 'clarion sound' of the 'i's in 'Arise, shine'. One should imagine what Saintsbury might have written of this passage.

annunciatory quality is something of what convinces Robinson, then we must agree with him that it is not possible in the NEB's version. But it is also true that the quality in the KJB is created by a combination of archaism, sound, and the reader's collusion, that is, the reader's willingness to find the appropriate stress in 'I'.

Does the KJB's angel 'take a miracle as a matter of course'? He says, 'he is risen from the dead; and, behold, he goeth . . .'. It is the pause, followed by 'behold' (or 'lo' in the RV), that makes the difference: statement is turned into exclamation, so the miracle is indeed wondered at. With the evidence to be seen if they will go and look, the angel convinces his hearers of the miraculous, as if saying, 'look, there He is! Believe!'

Robinson dismisses verses 12–15 in the NEB as 'a likely tale', but does not show how any other version might appear more likely. The information in the KJB is the same and there is nothing in the manner of telling that makes much difference except for a vagueness that comes from an odd use of familiar words in 'we will persuade him, and secure you'. Here I think Robinson shows what dangerous ground he is treading on: the denial of credibility to the NEB can in a moment slip into rationalistic denial of the story told. He almost joins company with Paine. But he differs from him in that his grounds for criticism, the convincingness of the style, is not only subjective but passes over a range of questions. Is he asserting that the versions are convincing or otherwise as truth or as fiction? If the former, does he accept the miraculous and the existence of angels?

Such questions matter. They leave one uneasy over what appears initially as a reasonable but not fully persuasive piece of comparative discussion. The unease suddenly becomes a major worry as Robinson gives his version of Mary Warnock's claim that making the Bible's language 'exact, up-to-date and unambiguous is itself an anti-religious effort':

The failure of style here *is* a failure of belief. How can the new translators have felt right, in those words? How can they have felt they have said what the Bible says? By satisfying themselves with incompetent journalism they have branded their own religion as shallow and chaotic. In that sense they have published work that is not sincere. (pp. 38–9)

This is a drastic charge, distasteful to read and, one hopes, distasteful to make. Yet surely it stems from an excessive equating of style and meaning. We are being asked to accept that sincerity will produce writing that is good or convincing, and that poor writing is a sign of insincerity and shallowness.

Robinson sees the NEB as a sign of the times (p. 22). Others too take it as a sign, usually of the decline of the present age in both moral and linguistic terms. The very thing Swift feared, that English will 'at length infallibly change for the worse' (above, p. 211), has happened. T.S. Eliot, finding the NEB far below the level of dignified mediocrity, asked in alarm, 'what is happening to the English language?' (Nineham, *The NEB Reviewed*, p. 96). Henry Gifford, in a review which Robinson applauds (p. 27), claims that 'over the past hundred years literature has been steadily losing ground' (Nineham, p. 107), and, pithily, that 'the English language is becoming a dustbowl, the deposits of centuries blown away, and a thin temporary soil remaining' (p. 108). He shows the version's tendency to cliché, and comments that 'translators are perhaps bound to mediate the world of their own time. Here we can recognise the grey, anonymous, oatmeal-paper forms, the ill-phrased regulations, the barren communiqués and reassuring statements from which there is no escape' (p. 109). A tellingly chosen collage of phrases from the NEB follows. The case is powerfully suggested, but what is perhaps most significant is that it is the exact reflex of reverence for the time of Shakespeare and the KJB. A great time produced a great Bible – or did a great Bible bespeak a great time? Now a shallow, faithless time produces a Bible that is both its symptom and its image.

A PRINCELY EPILOGUE

A scholar king gave the nod to the work of revision that became the KJB. A scholar prince may be allowed the last word. Charles, Prince of Wales, revived the debate about the merits of the PB, the KJB and their modern revisions with a speech on the occasion of the 500th anniversary of the birth of Archbishop Cranmer, 19 December 1989.[4] He was presenting a prize commemorating the occasion and designed to encourage familiarity with the PB among secondary-school pupils. The sentiments are authentic Prince Charles, but one witty reference to speech-writers might lead us to a Baconian heresy. It is certainly a good speech. Yet we may also see it as a series of echoes.

Beginning with a reflection on the dangers of speaking out about the importance of the British heritage, the Prince places himself firmly in the company of Bishop Beveridge:

The fear of being considered old-fashioned seems to be so all-powerful that the more eternal values and principles which run like a thread through the whole

---

[4] The full text may be found in *The Daily Telegraph*, 20 December 1989, p. 14.

tapestry of human existence are abandoned under the false assumption that they restrict progress. Well, I'm *not* afraid of being considered old-fashioned, which is why I am standing here at this lectern wearing a double-breasted suit and turn-ups to my trousers, ready to declaim the fact that I believe the Prayer Book is a glorious part of every English-speaker's heritage and, as such, ought to be a grade I listed edifice!

This is essentially the view of all the signatories to the petition to the General Synod. Like Sisson, the Prince believes in 'the profound human need for continuity and permanence'. Like Robinson, he believes that 'the words *are* the thoughts'. Not yet titular head of the Church of England, he can take the unclerical, academic view 'that for solemn occasions we need exceptional and solemn language: something which transcends our everyday speech. We commend the "beauty of holiness", yet we forget the holiness of beauty. If we encourage the use of mean, trite, ordinary language we encourage a mean, trite and ordinary view of the world.' So he comments that he 'would have liked to begin with a ringing phrase from the King James's Version of the Bible: "hearken to my words"'. However, the NEB 'translates the phrase in less commanding terms: "give me a hearing". It might seem more humble but it also sounds less poetic.' As Robinson or Saintsbury would tell us, there is indeed an authority to the rhythm of 'hearken to my words' that comes from opening and closing the phrase with stresses. But what is most important is the clear identification between beauty, poetry and religious feeling. So, if we lose the liturgy and the Bible as literature, we lose religion.

This leads the Prince to reflect on the issue that concerned Eliot, Gifford and Robinson, the decline of 'the world's most successful language'. It 'has become so impoverished, so sloppy and so limited – that we have arrived at such a dismal wasteland of banality, cliché and casual obscenity'. As if inspired by Lord Robbins's reflection on what the young would make of a Hamlet soliloquy in modern English, the Prince gives a version of 'to be or not to be': 'Well, frankly, the problem as I see it at this moment in time is whether I should just lie down under all this hassle and let them walk over me, or whether I should just say OK, I get the message, and do myself in.' This is light relief, but it shows a danger. Hamlet saying, 'well, frankly . . .', is no prince but one of the groundlings Hamlet himself is so scornful of, 'the groundlings, who for the most part are capable of nothing but inexplicable dumb-shows and noise' (3: 2). The modern prince condemns the present by the groundlings and reveres the past through the old prince. It is the age of Shakespeare against the age of Nick Cotton in *EastEnders*.

Prince Charles makes an earnest plea 'to uphold standards amid the general spread of mediocrity', and concludes:

Ours is the age of miraculous writing machines but not of miraculous writing. Our banalities are no improvement on the past; merely an insult to it and a source of confusion in the present. In the case of our cherished religious writings, we should leave well alone, especially when it is better than well: when it is great. Otherwise we leave ourselves open to the terrible accusation once levelled by that true master of the banal, Samuel Goldwyn: 'You've improved it worse.'

Not surprisingly, there were ruffled feathers among the clergy, for the Prince had brought together most of the arguments being used against the clergy's innovations without consideration of any religious matters except the relation between poetry and religion:

Astonishment was not confined to the Church of England. Roman Catholics, for example, are unlikely to be amused by the Prince's choice of a passage to illustrate the 'crassness' of the [Alternative Service Book]. Exactly the same words occur in the modern Roman missal.

For the Church of England, of course, the future Defender of the Faith's distaste for the ASB is embarrassing. Even the stoutly traditionalist Bishop of London uses the new prayer book; some observers thought he looked distinctly uncomfortable sitting next to the Prince yesterday.

At least one supporter of the ASB has already resolved to try to change the Prince's mind. Canon Donald Gray of Westminster Abbey, one of the volume's authors, told me: 'I'd like to talk it over with him and put the other side. Knowing him, I think he might give us the chance.' ('Peterborough', *Daily Telegraph*, 20 December 1989)

If the Prince is on the side of the academy, the other side is of course the church. The two have remained as closely linked as form and meaning. The academy has taken on much of the form of the church, and much of the meaning of the church is now to be found in the academy. To speak plainly, culture, in the form of higher education, has taken on many of the characteristics of religion. Moreover, religion has been so long a part of the culture of everyman that it is still difficult to admit it could lose that place.

A history of the Bible as literature turns out to be an examination of the shifting interrelationships between religion and culture. It does not reach a conclusion because the interrelationships continue to shift and because one becomes convinced that ways of thinking are perennial. The commonest way of thinking seems to be what so often issues as fundamentalism, an adherence to the past and a dread of the new. Bishop

Beveridge is the representative figure, easily made into a figure of fun because we none of us like to be behind the times, but yet a figure whom we should all see something of ourselves in. His most recent incarnation is Prince Charles, complete with double-breasted suit and turn-ups to his trousers. One of his earlier incarnations was the old Catholic priest who chanted 'quod in ore mumpsimus'. They represent the desire for religious feeling and the inability to distinguish that feeling from a love of the past and a sense of beauty. It is they, as well as the great line of translators from Tyndale to Myles Smith, who created the beauty of the English Bible. And it is because they are creators as well as representative of something deep within ourselves that I choose to end with them.

But a consequence of ending with such conservative figures is that condemnation of the NEB, representative of the new effort at translation, is left ringing in our ears. We have seen enough of contemporaries' judgements of new translations to be thoroughly sceptical of our own judgements. Too many factors independent of the intrinsic qualities of a translation are involved in its eventual fate and reputation. However, it seems to me likely that no translation will ever become what the KJB has been to the English-speaking world. I do not suggest this as a judgement on either the quality or the quantity of modern translations, but as a reflection on the decline of Christianity to effective non-existence for the majority of English-speaking people. No Bible can become a classic if it is not perpetually and inescapably encountered by all of us. It was the KJB's good fortune to be inescapable for centuries; many would add that it was the good fortune of the English-speaking peoples that they had such a Bible to live with. Iris Murdoch, novelist, philosopher and signatory to the petition to the Synod, may speak for them (*PN Review*, p. 5): 'the Bible and the Prayer Book were great pieces of literary good fortune, when language and spirit conjoined to produce a high unique religious eloquence. These books have been *loved* because of their inspired linguistic perfection. Treasured words encourage, console and save.'

Bibliography

Bibliographical information for works cited in one place only is given at that place.

Allen, Ward, trans. and ed. *Translating for King James: Being* a True Copy *of the Only Notes made by a Translator of King James's Bible*. Nashville, Tenn.: Vanderbilt University Press, 1969.

Arnold, Matthew. *The Complete Prose Works of Matthew Arnold*. Ed. R.H. Super. 11 vols. Ann Arbor: University of Michigan Press, 1960 etc.

Bates, Ernest Sutherland, ed. *The Bible Designed to be Read as Living Literature*. New York: Simon and Schuster, 1936. *The Bible Designed to be Read as Literature*. London: Heinemann, 1937.

Baxter, Richard. *The Practical Works of the Late Reverend and Pious Mr Richard Baxter*. 4 vols. London, 1707.

The Bay Psalm Book. Facsimile of *The Whole Book of Psalms Faithfully Translated into English Metre* (Cambridge, Mass., 1640). University of Chicago Press, 1956.

Becon, Thomas. *The Works of Thomas Becon*. 3 vols. London, 1560–4.

Beveridge, William. *A Defence of the Book of Psalms*. London, 1710.

The Bible in the Public Schools. Arguments in the case of John D. Minor et al. versus the Board of Education of the City of Cincinnati et al. Cincinnati, 1870.

Blackmore, Richard. *A Paraphrase on the Book of Job* (1700). Second edn: London, 1716.

Blackwall, Anthony. *An Introduction to the Classics*. London, 1718.
  The Sacred Classics Defended and Illustrated. 2 vols. London, 1725, 1731.

Blake, William. *The Complete Writings of William Blake*. Ed. Geoffrey Keynes. London: Oxford University Press, 1966.

Boileau-Despréaux, Nicolas. *Oeuvres complètes de Boileau*. Ed. A.C. Gidel. 4 vols. Paris, 1872–3.

Boyle, Robert. *Some Considerations Touching the Style of the Holy Scriptures*. London, 1661.

Brontë, Charlotte. *Jane Eyre* (1847). Oxford University Press, 1973.

Broughton, Hugh. *Epistle to the Learned Nobility of England Touching Translating the Bible*. Middleburgh, 1597.

The Works of the Great Albinonean Divine . . . Mr Hugh Broughton. London, 1662.

Bunyan, John. *Grace Abounding to the Chief of Sinners* and *The Pilgrim's Progress*. Ed. Roger Sharrock. London: Oxford University Press, 1966.

Burges, George. *A Letter to . . . the Lord Bishop of Ely on the subject of a new and authoritative translation of the Holy Scriptures*. Peterborough, 1796.

Byron, George Gordon. *Byron's Letters and Journals*. Ed. Leslie A. Marchand. 12 vols. London: John Murray, 1973 etc.

Campbell, George. *The Philosophy of Rhetoric* (1776). Ed. Lloyd F. Bitzer. Carbondale: Southern Illinois University Press, 1963.

Cartwright, Thomas. *The Answer to the Preface of the Rhemish Testament*. Edinburgh, 1602.

A Confutation of the Rhemists' Translation. Leiden, 1618.

Cawdray, Robert. *A Treasury or Storehouse of Similes*. London, 1600.

A Table Alphabetical (1604). Facsimile, intro. Robert A. Peters. Gainesville: Scholars' Facsimiles & Reprints, 1966.

Coleridge, Samuel Taylor. *The Poems of Samuel Taylor Coleridge*. Ed. Ernest Hartley Coleridge. Oxford University Press, 1912.

Collected Letters of Samuel Taylor Coleridge. Ed. Earl Leslie Griggs. 6 vols. Oxford University Press, 1956–71.

The Notebooks of Samuel Taylor Coleridge. Ed. Kathleen Coburn. 3 vols. London: Routledge, 1957–73.

The Collected Works of Samuel Taylor Coleridge. Princeton University Press; London: Routledge, 1971 etc.

Coverdale, Myles. *Biblia: the Bible*. Reprinted as *The Holy Scriptures, Faithfully and Truly Translated by Myles Coverdale*. London, 1838.

Writings and Translations of Myles Coverdale. Ed. George Pearson. Cambridge, 1844.

Remains of Myles Coverdale. Ed. George Pearson. Cambridge, 1846.

Cowley, Abraham. *Abraham Cowley, Poems*. Ed. A.R. Waller. Cambridge University Press, 1905.

Daniell, David. *William Tyndale: A Biography*. New Haven and London: Yale University Press, 1994.

De Laune, Thomas, and Keach, Benjamin. *Tropologia: A Key to Open Scripture-Metaphors*. London, 1682.

Deanesly, Margaret. *The Lollard Bible and Other Medieval Biblical Versions*. Cambridge University Press (1920), 1966.

Dennis, John. 'The Grounds of Criticism in Poetry' (1704). In Elledge, ed., *Eighteenth-Century Critical Essays*, I: 102–42.

Donne, John. *The Sermons of John Donne*. Ed. George R. Potter and Evelyn M. Simpson. 10 vols. University of California Press: Berkeley and Los Angeles, 1953–62.

Dwight, Timothy. 'A dissertation on the history, eloquence and poetry of the Bible' (1772). Facsimile in *The Major Poems of Timothy Dwight*. Intro. William J. McTaggart and William K. Bottorff. Gainesville: Scholars' Facsimiles & Reprints, 1969. Pp. 545–58.

Eckman, George P. *The Literary Primacy of the Bible*. New York: Methodist Book Concern, 1915.

Elledge, Scott, ed. *Eighteenth-Century Critical Essays*. 2 vols. Ithaca: Cornell University Press, 1961.

Ellicott, Charles John. *Addresses on the Revised Version of Holy Scripture*. London: SPCK, 1901.

Erskine, Thomas. 'The speeches of the Hon. Thomas Erskine . . . on the trial of the King versus Thomas Williams for publishing *The Age of Reason*'. 2nd edn: London, 1797. Facsimile in *The Prosecution of Thomas Paine: Seven Tracts*. New York and London: Garland, 1974.

Felton, Henry. *A Dissertation on Reading the Classics*. London, 1713.

Ferguson, Robert. *The Interest of Reason in Religion*. London, 1675.

Foxe, John. *The Acts and Monuments of John Foxe* (1563). 4th edn: revised Josiah Pratt. 8 vols. London: Religious Tract Society, ?1877.

Frazer, James George. *Passages of the Bible Chosen for their Literary Beauty and Interest* (1895). 2nd edn: London: Macmillan, 1909.

Fulke, William. *A Defence of the Sincere and True Translations of the Holy Scriptures into the English Tongue*. Ed. Charles Henry Hartshorne. Cambridge, 1843.

Gardiner, John Hays. *The Bible as English Literature*. London: Fisher and Unwin, 1906.

Gell, Robert. *An Essay toward the Amendment of the Last English Translation of the Bible*. London, 1659.

Gildon, Charles. *The Complete Art of Poetry*. 2 vols. London, 1718.
The Laws of Poetry Explained and Illustrated. London, 1721.

Gilfillan, George. *The Bards of the Bible* (1851). 4th edn: Edinburgh, 1856.

Guardian, The. Ed. John Calhoun Stephens. Lexington: University Press of Kentucky, 1982.

Halsey, Le Roy J. *The Literary Attractions of the Bible; or, a plea for the word of God considered as a classic* (1858). 3rd edn: New York, 1860.

Hammond, Gerald. *The Making of the English Bible*. Manchester: Carcanet, 1982.

Harwood, Edward. *A Liberal Translation of the New Testament*. 2 vols. London, 1768.

Hatch, Nathan O., and Mark A. Noll, eds. *The Bible in America*. New York and Oxford: Oxford University Press, 1982.

Hazlitt, William. *The Complete Works of William Hazlitt*. Ed. P.P. Howe. 21 vols. London: Dent, 1931–4.

Head, Richard, and Kirkman, Francis. *The English Rogue* (1665). London: Routledge, 1928.

Hemphill, Samuel. *A History of the Revised Version of the New Testament*. London: Elliot Stock, 1906.

Herbert, A.S. *Historical Catalogue of Printed Editions of the English Bible, 1525–1961*. Revised and expanded from the edition of T.H. Darlow and H.F. Moule, 1903. London: The British and Foreign Bible Society; New York: The American Bible Society, 1968.

Hills, Edward F. *The King James Version Defended!* (1956). Des Moines: Christian Research, 1973.

Hudson, Anne, ed. *Selections from English Wycliffite Writings*. Cambridge University Press, 1978.

Hunt, Geoffrey. *About the New English Bible*. Cambridge: Oxford University Press and Cambridge University Press, 1970.

Husbands, John. *A Miscellany of Poems by Several Hands*. Oxford, 1731.

Huxley, Thomas Henry. 'The School Boards: what they can do, and what they may do' (1870). In *Collected Essays* (1893). London: Macmillan, 1910. III: 374–403.

Jebb, John. *Sacred Literature*. London, 1820.

Johnson, Antony. *An Historical Account of the Several English Translations of the Bible* (London, 1730). In Richard Watson, ed., *A Collection of Theological Tracts*. 6 vols. Cambridge, 1785. III: 60–100.

Johnson, Samuel. *A Dictionary of the English Language*. 2 vols. London, 1755.

Jordan, Clarence. *The Cotton Patch Version of Matthew and John*. Piscataway: New Century, ?1970.

Kipling, Rudyard. '"Proofs of Holy Writ"'. In *The Sussex Edition of Kipling's works*. London: Macmillan, 1937–9. XXX: 339–56.

Knox, Vicesimus. *Essays, Moral and Literary* (1778). Vol. I of *The Works*. 7 vols. London, 1824.

Laud, William. *The Works*. 7 vols. Oxford, 1847–57.

Lewis, C.S. 'The literary impact of the Authorised Version' (1950). In *They Asked for a Paper*. London: Bles, 1962. Pp. 26–50.

Lightfoot, Joseph Barber. *On a Fresh Revision of the English New Testament*. London and New York, 1871.

Lloyd, John. *A Good Help for Weak Memories*. London, 1671.

Locke, John. *A Paraphrase and Notes on the Epistles of St Paul*. London, 1707.

Longinus. *Dionysius Longinus of the Height of Eloquence*. Trans. John Hall. London, 1652.

  A Treatise of the Loftiness or Elegancy of Speech. Trans., from the French, J. Pulteney. London, 1680.

  Dionysius Longinus on the Sublime. Trans. William Smith. London, 1739.

  On the Sublime. Trans. T.S. Dorsch. *Classical Literary Criticism*. Harmondsworth: Penguin, 1965.

Lowes, John Livingston. 'The noblest monument of English prose'. In *Of Reading Books*. London: Constable, 1930. Pp. 47–77.

Lowth, Robert. *De Sacra Poesi Hebraeorum Praelectiones*. London, 1753.

  Lectures on the Sacred Poetry of the Hebrews. Trans. George Gregory. 2 vols. London, 1787.

  Isaiah: a New Translation (1778). 10th edn: London, 1833.

  A Short Introduction to English Grammar (1762). Facsimile of Philadelphia, 1775 edn. Intro. Charlotte Downey. Delmar: Scholars' Facsimiles & Reprints, 1979.

Luther, Martin. *Selected Writings of Martin Luther*. Ed. Theodore G. Tappert. 4 vols. Philadelphia: Fortress, 1967.

McCulloch, John Murray. *Literary Characteristics of the Holy Scriptures* (1845). 2nd edn, with additions and supplementary notes: Edinburgh, 1847.

Macpherson, James. *Fragments of Ancient Poetry*. Edinburgh, 1760.

Marten, Anthony. *The Commonplaces of . . . Peter Martyr*. London, 1583.

Martin, Gregory. *A Discovery of the Manifold Corruptions of the Holy Scriptures by the Heretics of our Days*. Rheims, 1582. Reprinted in Fulke, *A Defence*.

Milton, John. *The Works of John Milton*. Ed. Frank Patterson et al. 18 vols. New York: Columbia University Press, 1931–38.

    Complete Prose Works of John Milton. Ed. Don. M. Wolfe et al. 8 vols. New Haven: Yale University Press, 1953–82.

Mombert, J.I. *English Versions of the Bible*. London, 1883.

More, Thomas. *The Complete Works of St. Thomas More*. New Haven and London: Yale University Press, 1963 etc.

Moulton, Richard Green. *The Literary Study of the Bible* (Boston, 1895). 2nd edn: Boston, 1899.

    The Modern Reader's Bible (1895 etc.). New York: Macmillan, 1907.

Mozley, J.F. *William Tyndale*. London: SPCK, 1937.

    Coverdale and his Bibles. London: Lutterworth, 1953.

Murry, John Middleton. *The Problem of Style*. London: Oxford University Press, 1922.

Newcome, William. *An Attempt towards an Improved Version . . . of the Twelve Minor Prophets*. London, 1785.

    An Historical View of the English Biblical Translations. Dublin, 1792.

Newton, A. Edward. *The Greatest Book in the World*. London: Lane, 1926.

Nineham, Dennis, ed. *The New English Bible Reviewed*. London: Epworth, 1965.

Oliver, Robert T. 'The Bible and style'. *Sewanee Review* 42 (July 1934), 350–5.

Orwell, George. *Coming up for Air*. (1939). London: Secker & Warburg, 1986.

Paine, Gustavus S. *The Men Behind the King James Version*. Grand Rapids: Baker Book House, 1977. Originally *The Learned Men* (1959).

Paine, Thomas. *The Theological Works of Thomas Paine*. London, 1819.

    The Complete Writings of Thomas Paine. Ed. Philip S. Foner. 2 vols. New York: Citadel Press, 1945.

Parker, Matthew. *The Whole Psalter Translated into English Metre*. London, ?1567.

Pattison, T. Harwood. *The History of the English Bible*. London, 1894.

Petty, William Thomas (later FitzMaurice), Earl of Kerry. *An Essay upon the Influence of the Translation of the Bible upon English Literature*. Cambridge, 1830.

Pilkington, Matthew. *Remarks upon Several Passages of Scripture*. Cambridge, 1759.

PN Review 13: Crisis for Cranmer and King James. Ed. David Martin. 6: 5 (1979).

Pollard, A.W. *The Holy Bible. A Facsimile in a Reduced Size of the Authorized Version Published in the Year 1611*. Oxford University Press, 1911.

Pope, Alexander. *The Twickenham Edition of the Poems of Alexander Pope*. General ed., John Butt. 11 vols. London: Methuen; New Haven: Yale University Press, 1961–9.

Pratt, Samuel Jackson. *The Sublime and Beautiful of Scripture*. 2 vols. London, 1777.

Prynne, William. *Canterbury's Doom*. London, 1646.

Purver, Anthony. *A New and Literal Translation of all the Books of the Old and New Testament*. 2 vols. London, 1764.

Renan, Ernest. *Histoire générale et système comparé des langues sémitiques* (1855). 7th edn: Paris, n.d.

Robinson, Ian. *The Survival of English*. Cambridge University Press, 1973.

Rosenau, William. *Hebraisms in the Authorized Version of the Bible* (1902). Baltimore: Friedenwald, 1903.

Rosenberg, David, ed. *Congregation*. San Diego: Harcourt Brace Jovanovich, 1987.

Saintsbury, George. *A History of English Prose Rhythm*. London: Macmillan, 1912.

Seiss, J.A. 'The influence of the Bible on literature'. *The Evangelical Review* 27 (July 1853), 1–17.

Shelley, Percy Bysshe. *The Complete Works of Shelley*. Ed. Roger Ingpen and Walter E. Peck. 10 vols. New York: Gordian, 1965.

Sidney, Philip. *An Apology for Poetry* (1580). London, 1595.

Sidney, Philip, and Pembroke, Mary. *The Psalms of Sir Philip Sidney and the Countess of Pembroke*. Ed. J.C.A. Rathmell. New York University Press, 1963.

Smart, Christopher. *The Poetical Works of Christopher Smart*. Ed. Karina Williamson. 4 vols. Oxford University Press, 1980–7.

South, Robert. *Sermons Preached upon Several Occasions*. New edition. 7 vols. Oxford, 1823.

Sprat, Thomas. *The History of the Royal Society* (London, 1667). Facsimile. Ed. Jackson I. Cope and Harold Whitmore Jones. St Louis: Washington University Studies, 1958.

Spring, Gardiner. *The Obligations of the World to the Bible*. New York, 1839.

Symonds, John. *Observations on the Expediency of Revising the Present English Version of the Four Gospels and of the Acts of the Apostles*. Cambridge, 1789.

Tate, Nahum. *An Essay for Promoting Psalmody*. London, 1710.

Thompson, Francis. *Literary Criticisms*. Ed. Terence L. Connolly. New York: Dutton, 1948.

Trench, Richard Chenevix. *On the Authorised Version of the New Testament*. London, 1858.

Tyndale, William. *Doctrinal Treatises*. Ed. Henry Walter. Cambridge, 1848.
   Expositions of Scripture and Practice of Prelates. Ed. Henry Walter. Cambridge, 1849.
   Answer to Sir Thomas More's Dialogue (1531). Ed. Henry Walter. Cambridge, 1850.
   The New Testament [1526 text]. Ed. John Wesley Sawyer. Milford, Ohio: John the Baptist Printing Ministry, 1989.
   Tyndale's New Testament. [1534 text]. Ed. David Daniell. New Haven and London: Yale University Press, 1989.
   Tyndale's Old Testament. Ed. David Daniell. New Haven and London: Yale University Press, 1992.

Ussher, Ambrose. Epistle dedicatory and first chapter of Genesis from his unfinished translation. In *Fourth Report of the Royal Commission on Historical Manuscripts*. London, 1874. Pp. 589, 598–9.

Watson, Richard, ed. *An Apology for the Bible* (1796). 3rd edn: London, 1796.

A Collection of Theological Tracts. 6 vols. Cambridge, 1785.

Westcott, Brooke Foss. *Some Lessons of the Revised Version of the New Testament.* London, 1897.

W[histon], E. *The Life and Death of Mr Henry Jessey.* London, 1671.

White, Joseph. *A Revisal of the English Translation of the Old Testament Recommended.* Oxford, 1779.

Whittaker, John William. *An Historical and Critical Inquiry into the Interpretation of the Hebrew Scriptures, with remarks on Mr Bellamy's new translation.* Cambridge, 1819.

Willey, Basil. 'On translating the Bible into modern English'. *Essays and Studies,* new series 23 (1970), 1–17.

Wilson, Thomas. *A Christian Dictionary* (1612). 2nd edn: London, 1616. 8th edn: *A Complete Christian Dictionary.* Cont. John Bagwell, enlarged Andrew Simson. London, 1628.

Wither, George (Archdeacon of Colchester). *A View of the Marginal Notes of the Popish Testament.* London, 1588.

Wither, George (poet). *A Preparation to the Psalter.* London, 1619.
   The Scholar's Purgatory. London, 1624.
   The Psalms of David. The Netherlands, 1632.

Woodford, Samuel. *A Paraphrase upon the Psalms of David.* London, 1667.

Wordsworth, William. *The Prose Works of William Wordsworth.* 3 vols. Ed. W.J.B. Owen and Jane Worthington Smyser. Oxford University Press, 1974.

Wright, William Aldis. 'Proposed alterations in the Authorised Version'. Hectographic reproduction of manuscript notes. Cambridge University Library, Adv C 100 17[1].

Wyclif, John. *The Holy Bible . . . in the Earliest English Versions . . . by John Wyclif and his Followers.* Ed. Josiah Forshall and Frederic Madden. 4 vols. Oxford, 1850.

General Index

Abbott, George, 92
Addison, Joseph, 189, 207, 208, 312, 315, 362
  'Best writer of our language', 233
Aeneas, 175
Aesop, 169
Aikenhead, Thomas, **168–71**, 173, 263, 269
Ainsworth, Henry, 93
Alcaeus, 143
Aldrich, Bess Streeter, 390, **393–4**, 395
Alehouses, 165–7, 172
Allegory, 42, 80, 184, 268, 278
American Constitution
  First Amendment, 364
  School Bible reading, 363–8
Ancients versus moderns, 194–5
Andrewes, Lancelot, 327, 405
Apollo, 144
Arabian tales, 268
Aristotle, 50, 148, 203
  Inferior to Paul, 154
Arnold, Matthew, 308, **368–71**, 373, 376, 377, 386, 401
Articles, The Thirty-nine, 140
Atheism, 110, 133, 165, **168–73**, 261, **263–71**
Augustine, 42, 44, 64, 67, 134, 146, 151, 217

Bacon, Francis, 289, 300, 405
Baines, Richard, 167–8
Bancroft, Richard, 61, 75
Bankes, Thomas, 216
Barker, Robert, 83, 85–6, 91
Bates, Ernest Sutherland, 381–6
Baxter, Richard, 148–9
Bean, Douglas, 444
Beard, John R., 306–7
Becke, Edmund, 81
Becon, Thomas, 55, 115, **140–4**, 146, 153
Bellamy, John, 300–1
Bernard, Richard, 54
Berners, John, 146

Beveridge, William, **121–3**, 124, 212, 244, 246, 342, 343, 442, 452, 455
Bevis of Hampton, 2, 169
Beza, Theodore, 44, 115, 154
Bibliander, Theodor, 155
Bilney, Thomas, 12–13
Birch, Thomas, 109–10
Blackmore, Richard, 188, **194–6**, 197, 198, 204, 205, 219, 434
Blackwall, Anthony, 88, 206, **207–10**, 220
Blair, Hugh, 248, 272
Blake, William, 264, 266, 268, **275–9**, 280, 289, 292, 293, 295
Boccaccio, 289
Boileau-Despréaux, Nicolas, **192–3**, 199, 200, 205, 206, 212, 256, 447
Bois, John, **71–2**, 339, 351, 352, 435, 439
Bonaparte, Prince Louis Lucien, 353
Boswell, James, 238
Boyle, Robert, 99n, 107, **110–14**
Bray, Thomas, 124
Brontë, Charlotte, **295–8**, 390, 413, 421
Broughton, Hugh, **56–60**, 63, 67n, 68, **73–5**, 94, 96, 101, 133, 142, 208, 260, 331, 332, 343, 439, 442, 447
  Attack on the KJB, 74–5
  Idea of divine inspiration, 56–7
  Theories of translation, 58–60
Brown, Joseph, 216
Browne, Thomas, **169–70**, 172, 408
Buchan, John, 406, 407
Bunyan, John, **183–7**, 296, 297, 387, 388, 391, 413, 414–15, 420–1, 424
Burges, George, 245–6, 257–8, 261–2
Burgon, John William, 343
Burke, Edmund, 222
Burnet, Gilbert, 172–3
Burnet, James, Lord Monboddo, 245, 300
Burns, Robert, 242n
Butler, Samuel ('Hudibras' Butler), 108

Biblical Index

Books of the Bible are listed in alphabetical order of their name: hence 1 Corinthians is to be found under 'C'. All references to the original Scriptures or to the Bible in general are listed under 'Scripture'.

Psalms, 74, 76, 80, **115–24**, 126, **128–39**, 224,
359, 380, 393–4
1–8: versified by Milton, 179–80
1: 1: difficulties with the Sternhold and
Hopkins rendering, 123; KJB's language
versified by Milton, 180
4: 4, 424
6: 10, 150
8: translated by Sidney, 129–30; translated
by Sternhold, 117–18
8: 2, 237, 424; KJB's language versified by
Milton, 180
18, 198–9
18: 4: adapted by Bunyan, 184–5
19, 269
19: 1, 153
19: 10, 13
22: 11, 296
23: expanded by Woodford, 164; translated
by Wither, 136–8
23: 1: *Bay Psalm Book*, 120; translated by
Whittingham, 117
23: 1–2: translated by Rolle, 6; Wycliffite
versions, 7
27: 13, 424
29: 2 and 4, 25
34: 14, 236
37, 365n
42: 7: adapted by Bunyan, 184–5
45: 3, 66n
46, 283n; 'shake' and 'spear', 406
47: 5, 283
48: 6, 426
50: 10: praised, 293
51: 8, 13
64: 10, 106
69: 1–2, 296–7; adapted by Bunyan, 184–5
69: 1–3, 421
69: 3, 297
72: 9, 424
75: 2–3, 104
77: 8, 424n
78, 324
78: 1–2, 200–1
80–88: versified by Milton, 179
84: 7, 424
95: 11, 102
104: 1–4, 257n
104: 28–9, 293
105: effect of omitting second halves of the
couplets, 374
105: 28: Coverdale's reading objected to,
61n
106: 30: Great Bible reading objected to,
61n

114: paraphrased by Milton, 179
116: praised by Becon, 143–4
117: middle and shortest chapter of the
Bible, 216n
118: charming repetitions, 218
118: 8: middle verse of the Bible, 216n
119: 'overflowing and glorious passion', 397
119: 34, 42
119: 53, 426
119: 129, 362
127, 198
127: 3, 236
135: 11, 392
136: paraphrased by Milton, 179
137, 380
137: 1, 422
137: 1–2: Coverdale's prose version, 34;
versified by Coverdale, 33–4
147: 20, 427
148: adapted by Milton, 180
'As many elegancies as the most renowned
authors', 133
'Heavenly poesy', 127
'Incomparable hymns' poorly esteemed by
the people, 131
'Jesus Christ's Psalms', 124
'Lyrical anthology', 381
'Passages of unrivalled beauty', 293
'Perfect and pleasant hexameter verses', 126
'Simple and foolish', 'homely writings', 131
'So difficult and harsh to our ears, even in
prose', 163
'Treasure house of the Holy Scripture', 115
Art 'so excellent that it is an excellence even
to translate them', 127
Can seem distracted, unnecessary and
ridiculous, 133
Contain rhetoric for souls, not for ears, 133
Coverdale's metrical version, 33–4
Divine poetry expressing passions 'much
otherwise than they ought to be in plain
and familiar speech', 164
KJB: 'abounds with passages exquisitely
beautiful', 244; preferred by non-
conformists, PB by Anglicans, 411
Latin: 'perfection of divine writing', 5
Loved by Luther, 17
More eloquent than Cicero, 17
Must not be versified or set to tunes, 149
Praised by Milton, 177

Quakers' Bible, 232

Rachel and Laban: story admired, 294
Reader's Bible, 384–5